# A Practical Guide to Medicare Appeals

Daniel A. Cody and
Kathleen Scully-Hayes

AMERICAN BAR ASSOCIATION

HEALTH LAW SECTION

# The
# **Practical Guide**
# Series

HIPAA: A Practical Guide to the Privacy and Security of Health Data

Defending Liberty
Pursuing Justice

Practical Guide Series

# A Practical Guide to Medicare Appeals

Daniel A. Cody and
Kathleen Scully-Hayes



CAN BAR ASSOCIATION
ending Liberty
rsuing Justice

AMERICAN BAR ASSOCIATION
HEALTH LAW SECTION

Cover design by ABA Publishing



Printed in the United States of America.

11 10 09 08 07

Library of Congress Cataloging-in-Publication Data

Scully-Hayes, Kathleen.
A practical guide to Medicare appeals / Kathleen Scully-Hayes, Daniel A. Cody.
p. cm. — (Practical guide series)
Includes bibliographical references and index.
ISBN 978-1-59031-827-0 (alk. paper)
1. Medicare—Law and legislation. 2. Administrative remedies—United States. 3. Medicare—Claims administration. I. Cody, Daniel A. II. American Bar Association. Health Law Section. III. Title.

KF3608.A4S38 2007
344.7302′26—dc22

2007008296

Discounts are available for books ordered in bulk. Special consideration is given to state bars, CLE programs, and other bar-related organizations. Inquire at ABA Publishing, Book Publishing, American Bar Association, 321 N. Clark Street, Chicago, IL 60610.

www.ababooks.org

# Table of Contents

**Foreword** xiii
**Acknowledgments** xv
**Introduction** xvii

*CHAPTER 1*
**Overview of the Medicare Program** 1
Medicare "Parts" 1
Medicare Part A 1
Medicare Part B 2
Medicare Part C 3
Medicare Part D 4
Medicare Program Administration 6
Federal Agencies and Private Contractors 6
Payment 6
Survey and Certification 7

*CHAPTER 2*
**Beneficiary Appeals** 9
Medicare Part A and B "Fee-for-Service" Appeals (42 C.F.R. Part 405 (Subparts G, H, and I)) 9
General 9
History of Medicare "Fee-for-Service" Appeals Reform 9
Medicare Part A and Part B "Fee-for-Service" Appeals 10
*Overview* 10
*What May Be Appealed? (42 C.F.R. §§ 405.900, .904; 478.10–.14)* 10
*Who May Appeal? (42 C.F.R. §§ 405.906–.912; 478.15)* 11
Appeals Process 12
*Initial Determinations (42 C.F.R. §§ 405.920–.928)* 12
*Redeterminations (42 C.F.R. §§ 405.940–.958)* 12
*Reconsiderations (42 C.F.R. §§ 405.960–.978)* 13
*ALJ Hearings (42 C.F.R. §§ 405.1000–.1054)* 15
*MAC Reviews (42 C.F.R. §§ 405.1100–.1134)* 16
*Judicial Review (42 C.F.R. §§ 405.1136–.1140) and Expedited Judicial Review (42 C.F.R. § 405.990)* 17

*Additional Issues Regarding Medicare Fee-for-Service Appeals* 17
Reopenings (42 C.F.R. §§ 405.980–.986) 17
Transfer of Appeals from SSA to HHS 18
Medicare Part A Appeals of Provider Service Terminations (42 C.F.R. Part 405 (Subpart J)) 19
Overview 19
What May Be Appealed and Who May Appeal? 19
*Notifying Beneficiaries of Provider Service Terminations (42 C.F.R. § 405.1200)* 19
Appeal Process 20
*Expedited Determination Procedures (42 C.F.R. § 405.1202)* 20
*Expedited Determinations for Inpatient Hospital Discharges (42 C.F.R. § 405.1206)* 23
*Hospital Requests for Expedited QIO Review (42 C.F.R. § 405.1208)* 26
*Expedited Reconsiderations (42 C.F.R. § 405.1204) (applies to all settings)* 26
Ambulatory Surgical Center Appeals (42 C.F.R. § 416.150) 28
What May Be Appealed and Who May Appeal? 28
Medicare Part B Coverage Appeals (42 C.F.R. Part 408 (Subpart F)) 29
Overview 29
What May Be Appealed and Who May Appeal? (42 C.F.R. § 408.100) 29
Appeals Process (42 C.F.R. § 408.100–.104) 29
Medicare LCD/NCD Appeals (42 C.F.R. Part 426) 30
Overview 30
What May Be Appealed? (42 C.F.R. § 426.325) 30
Who May Appeal? (42 C.F.R. §§ 426.110, .320) 31
LCD Appeal Process 31
*The Complaint (42 C.F.R. § 426.400)* 31
*ALJ Review (42 C.F.R. §§ 426.405, .410, .417, .425, .431, .447, .450)* 31
*DAB Review (42 C.F.R. §§ 426.460, .465, .470, .476, .482, .488)* 33
*Judicial Review (42 C.F.R. § 426.490)* 34
NCD Appeals Process (42 C.F.R. § 426.500–.587) 34

*CHAPTER 3*
**Provider Appeals** 35
Medicare Part A Appeals before the Provider Reimbursement Review Board (42 C.F.R. Part 405 (Subpart R)) 35
Overview 35
What May Be Appealed? (42 C.F.R. §§ 405.1801, .1804) 35
Who May Appeal? (42 C.F.R. § 405.1835) 36
Appeals Process (42 C.F.R. § 405.1835–.1877) 36
*Filing an Appeal (42 C.F.R. § 405.1835)* 36
*Expedited Judicial Review (42 C.F.R. § 405.1842)* 37
*PRRB Hearing and Decision (42 C.F.R. § 405.1845, .1869, .1871)* 37
*Administrator's Review (42 C.F.R. § 405.1875)* 38
*Judicial Review (42 C.F.R. § 405.1877)* 38
Medicare Geographic Classification Appeals (42 C.F.R. 412.230–.280) 39
Overview 39
What May Be Appealed? 40
Who May Appeal? (42 C.F.R. § 412.258) 40
Appeal Process (42 C.F.R. §§ 412.256–.273) 40
*Administrator's Review (42 C.F.R. § 412.278)* 42
HMO and CMP Contract Appeals (42 C.F.R. §§ 417.640–.694) 43
Overview 43
What May Be Appealed? (42 C.F.R. § 416.640) 43
Who May Appeal? (42 C.F.R. § 417.660) 44
Appeals Process 44
*Initial Determination (42 C.F.R. § 417.644)* 44
*Reconsideration (42 C.F.R. § 417.650)* 44
*Hearing Officer Review (42 C.F.R. §§ 417.660–.690)* 44
*Reopening of Initial or Reconsidered Determination or Decision by a Hearing Officer (42 C.F.R. § 417.692)* 45
Hospice Care Payment Appeals (42 C.F.R. § 418.311) 46
Overview 46
Provider Agreement Termination Appeals (42 C.F.R. § 489.52, .53, .54) 46
Overview 46
What May Be Appealed and Who May Appeal? (42 C.F.R. § 489.53(c)(3), (4)) 48
Appeals Process (42 C.F.R. § 489.53(d)) 48
Provider and Supplier Enrollment Denial Appeals (42 C.F.R. Part 498) 48
Overview 48

*CHAPTER 4*

**Part C Appeals** **51**

Medicare Advantage (Part C) Appeals (42 C.F.R. Part 422 (Subpart M)) 51

Overview 51

What May Be Appealed and Who May Appeal? 51

*Grievances (42 C.F.R. § 422.564)* 51

*Organization Determinations (42 C.F.R. §§ 422.566–.568)* 52

*Expediting Certain Organization Determinations (42 C.F.R. § 422.570–.572)* 54

Appeals (42 C.F.R. § 422.578–.612) 55

*Reconsideration Procedures (42 C.F.R. § 422.578–.590)* 55

*Reconsideration by an Independent Review Entity (42 C.F.R. § 422.592–.596)* 55

*ALJ Review (42 C.F.R. § 422.600–.602)* 56

*Medicare Appeals Council (MAC) Review (42 C.F.R. § 422.608)* 56

*Judicial Review (42 C.F.R. § 422.612)* 56

*Appeals Procedures for Inpatient Hospital Settings (42 C.F.R. § 422.620–.622)* 57

*Requesting Immediate QIO Review of Noncoverage of Inpatient Hospital Care (42 C.F.R. § 422.622)* 58

*Appeals Procedures for Skilled Nursing Facilities (SNFs), Comprehensive Outpatient Rehabilitation Facilities (CORFs), and Home Health Agencies (HHAs) (42 C.F.R. § 422.624–.626)* 59

Notifying Enrollees of Termination of Provider Services (42 C.F.R. § 422.624) 59

Fast-Track Appeals of Service Terminations to QIOs (42 C.F.R. § 422.626) 60

Medicare Advantage Contract Denial and/or Termination Appeals (42 C.F.R. § 422.641) 62

Overview 62

What May Be Appealed? (42 C.F.R. § 422.641) 62

Who May Appeal? (42 C.F.R. §§ 422.650(c), .660) 63

Appeals Process (42 C.F.R. § 422.648–.692) 63

*Reconsideration (42 C.F.R § 422.650–.658)* 63

*Hearing Officer Review (42 C.F.R. § 422.660–.690)* 63

*Administrator's Review (42 C.F.R. § 422.692)* 64

*CHAPTER 5*
**Part D Grievances, Coverage Determinations, and Appeals** 67
Medicare Part D Grievances, Coverage Determinations, and Appeals (42 C.F.R. Part 423 (Subpart M)) 67
Overview 67
What May Be Appealed? (42 C.F.R. § 423.560) 67
Who May Appeal? (42 C.F.R. § 423.568) 67
Appeals Process 68
*Grievances (42 C.F.R. § 423.564)* 68
*Expedited Grievances* 68
*Coverage Determinations (42 C.F.R. § 423.566)* 68
*Standard Coverage Determinations (42 C.F.R. § 423.568)* 69
*Expediting Certain Coverage Determinations (42 C.F.R. § 423.570)* 69
*Exceptions Process (42 C.F.R. § 423.578)* 69
*Appeals* 70
*Right to a Redetermination by a Plan Sponsor (42 C.F.R. § 423.580)* 71
*Standard Redeterminations (42 C.F.R. § 423.582)* 71
*Expedited Redeterminations (42 C.F.R. § 423.584)* 71
*Reconsideration by the Independent Review Entity (42 C.F.R. § 423.600)* 71
*Review by an ALJ (42 C.F.R. § 423.610)* 72
*Review by the Medicare Appeals Council (42 C.F.R. § 423.620)* 72
*Judicial Review (42 C.F.R. § 423.630)* 73
Part D Plan Sponsor Contract Termination Appeals (42 C.F.R. § 423.500) 73
Overview 73
What May Be Appealed? (42 C.F.R. § 423.641) 74
Who May Appeal? (42 C.F.R. § 423.645) 74
Appeals Process 75
*Reconsideration (42 C.F.R. § 423.645–.649)* 75
*Hearing Officer Review (42 C.F.R. § 423.650–.663)* 75
*Administrator's Review (42 C.F.R. § 423.666)* 76
Retiree Prescription Drug Plan Sponsor Appeals (42 C.F.R. § 423.890) 77
Overview 77
What May Be Appealed? (42 C.F.R. § 423.890(a)) 77
Who May Appeal? 77

Appeals Process 77
*Informal Written Reconsideration (42 C.F.R. § 423.890(a))* 77
*Informal Hearing (42 C.F.R. § 423.890(b))* 78
*Administrator's Review (42 C.F.R. § 423.890(c))* 78
*Reopening (42 C.F.R. § 423.890(d))* 78

*CHAPTER 6*
**Miscellaneous Appeals** **81**
Long-Term Care Facilities—Action on Complaints of Neglect and Abuse, Misappropriation of Property (42 C.F.R. § 488.335) 81
Overview 81
What May Be Appealed and Who May Appeal? 81
Appeals Process 81
Intermediary Termination Appeals (42 C.F.R. § 421.100) and Carrier Termination Appeals (42 C.F.R. § 421.200) 82
Overview 82
Group Health Plan Nonconformance Appeals (42 C.F.R. § 411.120) 83
Overview 83
What May Be Appealed? 84
Who May Appeal? (42 C.F.R. § 411.120) 84
Appeals Process 84
*On-the-Record Review (42 C.F.R. § 411.121(a)(4))* 84
*Oral Hearing (42 C.F.R. § 411.121(a)(5))* 84
*Decision (42 C.F.R. § 411.122)* 85
*Administrator's Review (42 C.F.R. § 411.124)* 85
*Internal Review Service Referral (42 C.F.R. § 411.130)* 85
Drugs and Biologicals Payment Appeals (42 C.F.R. § 414.916) 85
Overview 85
What May Be Appealed and Who May Appeal? 86
Appeals Process 86
Medicare Supplemental Policies—Policy Certification Appeals (42 C.F.R. § 403.200) 89
Overview 89
What May Be Appealed? 89
Who May Appeal? 90
Appeals Process (42 C.F.R. § 403.248) 90
Provider Termination and Exclusion Appeals (42 C.F.R. Part 498) 90
Overview 90

What May Be Appealed? (42 C.F.R. §§ 498.3, .20) 90
Who May Appeal? (42 C.F.R. § 498.5, .10) 91
Appeals Process 91
*Reconsideration (42 C.F.R. §§ 498.22, .24, .25)* 91
*Reopening of Initial or Reconsidered Determinations (42 C.F.R. § 498.30)* 91
*Administrative Law Judge (ALJ) Hearing (42 C.F.R. §§ 498.40, .44, .47, .50, .52, .58, .61, .74)* 92
*DAB Review (42 C.F.R. § 498.80, .82-.88)* 92
*Judicial Review (42 C.F.R. § 498.95)* 93
*Reopening of ALJ and DAB Decisions (42 C.F.R. §§ 498.100–.103)* 93

**Appendix A**
**Comparison of Former and Current Fee-for-Service Appeals Processes** **95**
**Appendix B**
**List of Abbreviations and Acronyms** **97**
**Appendix C**
**Contact Information for Administrative Entities Processing Appeals** **99**
**Not-for-Profit Advocacy Group Contact Information** **100**
**Appendix D**
**U.S. Department of Health and Human Services Medicare Appeals Processes: Selected Sections of Regulation Text (Unofficial Version)** **101**
**Index** **403**
**About the Authors** **411**

# Foreword

The Health Law Section of the ABA is excited to publish ***A Practical Guide to Medicare Appeals,*** the second in a series of practical guides aimed at providing focused economic resources for the health lawyer. The first practical guide in the series, ***HIPAA: A Practical Guide to the Privacy and Security of Health Data,*** soon became an ABA Publishing best seller.

As the authors indicate in the Acknowledgments, many people have volunteered their time and expertise to help bring this valuable work to fruition. The Health Law Section relies upon the continued willingness of volunteers who appreciate the value of contributing to the common good. The Section's leadership has strongly supported the efforts of the Publications Committee to develop valuable products for its members and for others who are interested in the many fascinating areas subsumed by the broad field of health law. The Section is also blessed to have such a wonderful and supportive professional staff.

Finally, and most importantly, we thank authors Kathleen Scully-Hayes and Daniel A. Cody for recognizing the need for a practical guide to assist others with understanding the nuances of the Medicare appeals processes, and then devoting the countless hours of time and effort to accomplish their goal. Their hard work and willingness to share their expertise reflect the very best of the Health Law Section.

Paul R. DeMuro
Chair (2006–2007)

Michael E. Clark
Publications Chair

Health Law Section
American Bar Association

# Acknowledgments

The authors express their heartfelt thanks for the valuable assistance they received from colleagues and editors in preparation of this book. The authors are particularly indebted to a host of employees from the Centers for Medicare & Medicaid Services (CMS) who willingly read through various sections of the manuscript and provided thoughtful, clarifying comments and constructive criticism. Special thanks go to Steve Kirsh, Director of the Jurisdiction and Case Management Division, and Paul Crofton, Director of the Hearings and Decisions Division at the CMS Office of Hearings, as well as the following members of their staffs—Maureen Sacratini, Martin Grimm, Michael Baier, Melanie Marolf-Fetchik, and Benjamin Cohen—for their review of the Provider Reimbursement Review Board, Medicare Geographic Classification Review Board, and CMS Hearing Officer sections of the manuscript.

The authors also extend their appreciation to Anthony Culotta, Director of the CMS Medicare Enrollment and Appeals Group, and his staff, particularly Arrah Tabe-Bedward, Director of the Division of Appeals Policy, as well as Dave Dabek, Chris Gayhead, Tim Roe, John Scott, Stephanie Simons, and Eileen Zerhusen whose review of the new beneficiary appeals processes was invaluable. Special thanks to Oliver Potts, Chief Civil Remedies Division, Departmental Appeals Board, for review of the provider termination and exclusion appeals section. The authors also wish to thank Andrew Wachler of Wachler & Associates, P.C. for his previously prepared materials regarding Medicare fee-for-service appeals. Thank you also to Helaine Fingold, Center for Beneficiary Choices, Sandra Bastinelli, Director, Division of Medical Review, Program Integrity Group, Office of Financial Management, and Cassandra Black, Deputy Director, Division of Ambulatory Services, Center for Medicare Management, for their constructive comments on the Medicare Advantage organization appeals, the local coverage decision/national coverage decision appeals, and the Part B Drugs and Biologicals Competitive Acquisition Plan program sections.

Last, but not least, the authors wish to thank the Health Law Section of the American Bar Association for endorsing this manuscript and Kathryn Watson of Reed Smith LLP for editorial assistance.

# Introduction

This book will set forth the practical aspects of appeals under Title XVIII of the Social Security Act (the Act), commonly known as the Medicare program. Medicare involves not only those who are beneficiaries of the health care services made available through the program, but also health care providers and suppliers, as well as the government agencies and contractors responsible for administering the program. Practically every aspect of Medicare includes a right to an appeal for individuals and entities dissatisfied with either the coverage or payment provided by Medicare.

***A Practical Guide to Medicare Appeals*** consolidates into one resource, a concise overview of the numerous appeal avenues available under Parts A, B, C, and D of the Medicare program. The Guide includes a brief historical overview of the four "parts" of Medicare, as well as citations to and an appendix of controlling regulations for each appeal process. The Guide also includes a detailed chart of the recently revised Part A and Part B "fee-for-service" appeals process for beneficiaries. Additionally, Web sites have been provided for each appeal venue, as well as information regarding several not-for-profit groups that may offer further guidance or assistance to Medicare beneficiaries. Finally, the Guide includes practical tips to assist the reader attempting to navigate through a particular appeal process.

CHAPTER 1

# Overview of the Medicare Program

In July 1965, the Compromise Social Security Amendments of 1965 were enacted adding Title XVIII (42 U.S.C. § 1395 *et seq.*) (Medicare) and Title XIX (42 U.S.C. § 1396 *et seq.*) (Medicaid) to the Act, creating what is now known as the Medicare program. The federal Medicare program is a social health insurance program for eligible elderly and disabled individuals whereby physicians, hospitals, and other providers and suppliers are reimbursed directly for both covered services, and certain supplies and equipment provided to program beneficiaries. Congress significantly revised the Medicare program in the Balanced Budget Act of 1997 (BBA) (Pub. L. No. 105-33) and with subsequent reform legislation, including the Balanced Budget Refinement Act of 1999 (BBRA) (Pub. L. No. 106-113), the Medicare, Medicaid, and SCHIP Benefits Improvement and Protection Act of 2000 (BIPA) (Pub. L. No. 106-554), and most recently, the Medicare Prescription Drug, Improvement, and Modernization Act of 2003 (MMA) (Pub. L. No. 108-173).

## MEDICARE "PARTS"

The Medicare program is comprised of separate and distinct components or "parts." Part A and Part B each are financed by different trust funds that pay for beneficiary coverage. The BBA added Part C and the MMA established a new Part D prescription drug benefit.

### Medicare Part A

Medicare Part A is financed through the Hospital Insurance (HI) Trust Fund and by contributions from employees, employers, and the self-employed. The interest income that accumulates in the Hospital Insurance (HI) Trust Fund also is utilized to defray program costs. Due to rapidly rising health care costs, among other factors, the solvency of the HI Trust Fund has occasionally been threatened.

The Medicare program provides Part A coverage to persons who qualify for Social Security retirement or survivor benefits and are sixty-five years or older. Individuals who are sixty-five and are otherwise not entitled to Medicare may voluntarily enroll in the Part A program by paying a monthly premium. Additionally, certain disabled individuals, regardless of age, who are entitled to disability benefits under Social Security or Railroad Retirement for twenty-five consecutive months and individuals with end-stage renal disease (ESRD) also may apply for Medicare Part A coverage. Medicare Part A covers inpatient hospital care, skilled nursing facility (SNF) services, home health services, and hospice care.

### Medicare Part B

Medicare Part B, a voluntary program, is financed through the Supplemental Medical Insurance (SMI) Trust Fund. Medicare Part A beneficiaries may elect to maintain Part B coverage for a monthly premium that also finances the SMI Trust Fund.

As discussed above, an individual is entitled to Medicare Part A benefits by entitlement to Social Security retirement or disability benefits, Medicare-qualified government employment, or ESRD benefits. Any individual entitled to Part A benefits is automatically enrolled in Medicare Part B, unless the beneficiary declines coverage. Medicare Part B coverage also extends to individuals who are sixty-five or over and are residents of the United States, citizens of the United States, or aliens lawfully admitted for permanent residence who have resided in the United States continuously during the five years immediately prior to enrollment.

Medicare Part B generally covers medical and other health care services not covered by Part A, subject to specific coverage exclusions and conditions of coverage. Generally, services rendered under Medicare Part B must be *medically necessary*. This phrase is defined as reasonable and necessary to the diagnosis or treatment of illness or injury, or to improve the functioning of a malformed body member.[1] Additionally, the medical or other health care service must be safe and effective. Health care screening tests, routine physical exams, and cosmetic surgery generally are not covered. Unless specifically made eligible for coverage, experimental or investigational drugs and devices (as well as the services associated with their use) are not covered.

A variety of providers and suppliers furnish services covered under Medicare Part B, including physicians. *Physicians' services* means the professional services performed by a physician for a patient, including diagnosis, therapy, surgery, consultation, and care plan oversight. Covered physician services include services performed by certain limited license practitioners, including dentists and oral and maxillofacial surgeons, optometrists, podiatrists, and chiropractors. Services of nonphysician practitioners are generally covered *under arrangement* with hospitals or *incident to* physician services.[2] Nonphysician practitioners include: (1) physical therapists; (2) speech pathologists; (3) occupational therapists; (4) clinical psychologists; (5) certified registered nurse anesthetists; (6) clinical social workers; (7) nurse-midwives; (8) nurse practitioners; (9) clinical nurse specialists; (10) physician assistants; and (11) registered dieticians and nutrition professionals. Outpatient providers and freestanding supplier entities include: (1) hospital outpatient departments; (2) ambulatory surgical centers; (3) comprehensive outpatient rehabilitation facilities (CORFs); (4) providers of outpatient physical therapy, occupational therapy, and speech pathology services; (5) ESRD facilities; (6) federally qualified health centers; (7) rural health clinics; (8) clinical laboratories; (9) suppliers of portable X-ray services; (10) durable medical equipment suppliers; (11) physician-directed clinics; (12) independent diagnostic testing facilities; (13) freestanding radiation therapy centers; (14) ambulance services; (15) home health services, when Part A home health benefits are exhausted; and (16) inpatient hospital ancillary services, when Part A inpatient benefits are exhausted.

## Medicare Part C

Medicare Part C is a program of private health coverage for Medicare beneficiaries created by the BBA. Historically referred to as "Medicare+ Choice" or "M+C," this program offers beneficiaries a full range of Medicare coverage options. Specifically, Medicare Part C provides choice between the traditional fee-for-service programs (Medicare Parts A and B) or enrollment in a health maintenance organization (HMO), preferred provider organization, point-of-service plan, provider-sponsored organization, or an insurance plan operated in conjunction with a medical savings account.

With enactment of the MMA, Medicare+Choice has been replaced with a new Medicare Advantage (MA) program. In addition to the types of plans historically available under M+C, MA offers additional health plan options at the regional and local level. The new program also changes the way that participating health plans are reimbursed for the services provided under Medicare.

All individuals entitled to Medicare Part A and enrolled under Medicare Part B (except for individuals with ESRD) may elect to receive benefits through either traditional Medicare or a MA plan. The beneficiary must reside in a plan's service area in order to elect that plan. The beneficiary must complete and sign an election form and agree to abide by the rules of the MA organization. Every MA organization must accept, without restriction, all eligible individuals who elect the plan during initial coverage election periods, annual election periods, and special election periods.

Plans must provide enrollees with coverage of the basic benefits of traditional Medicare, plus supplemental benefits. The MA plan must offer its benefits packages to all Medicare beneficiaries residing in the service area for the plan at a uniform premium and with a uniform level of cost sharing. Regardless of any other restrictions, MA plans must make timely and reasonable payments to a provider, even one that does not contract with the MA organization, for the following services: emergency services, urgently needed services, renal dialysis services provided while the enrollee is out of the program service area, and post-stabilization care services.

## Medicare Part D

Pursuant to the MMA, a new Medicare Part D prescription drug outpatient benefit became effective January 1, 2006. All beneficiaries enrolled in basic coverage under Part D receive the same core prescription drug coverage. The Part D benefit covers insulin, vaccines, certain biological products, and any other medically necessary drugs not currently covered under Medicare Part B that are: (1) dispensed according to a prescription; (2) administered on an outpatient basis; and (3) currently covered by the Medicaid program.

Any individual entitled to coverage under Medicare Part A or enrolled in Medicare Part B will be eligible to purchase coverage for outpatient prescription drugs under Medicare Part D. Medicare beneficiaries are not required to elect coverage under Part D, but if they so elect, beneficiaries must enroll in either: (1) a qualified prescription drug plan (PDP)—a stand-alone insurance benefit offered by a private entity licensed to offer health insurance under state law; (2) a MA plan (formerly Medicare+ Choice) that includes prescription drug coverage (MA-PDP); or (3) a "fall-back prescription drug plan" in any area where there are not at least two plans offering Part D coverage (at least one of which is a PDP) with the United States bearing the cost of paying claims made under such plan (collectively, the Plans).

At a minimum, Plans are required to offer either "standard coverage" or its actuarial equivalent that has an out-of-pocket threshold and deductible amounts that do not exceed those of standard coverage ("basic coverage"). Beneficiary premiums for basic coverage vary from Plan to Plan depending, at least in part, upon the geographic region where the beneficiary is located. For basic coverage, the Congressional Budget Office estimates that premiums will be $35 per month on average in the first year, increasing to $58 per month in 2013.

The specific premium amount for each Plan is determined utilizing a formula that calculates a base beneficiary premium and adjusts the base premium to reflect the difference between the base and a geographically adjusted national average monthly bid amount. The premium amount must be uniform for all persons enrolled in a particular Plan, with the exception of those persons receiving low-income subsidies or who are subject to a late enrollment penalty. Beneficiary premium payments may be made either directly to the Plan by the beneficiary, through withholding from the beneficiary's Social Security payment, or by electronic funds transfer.

In 2007, the annual deductible for standard coverage will be $265. Subsequently, the deductible will be indexed to increase annually by the growth in per capita Part D drug spending per Medicare beneficiary.

Once a beneficiary meets the annual deductible, the Plan will cover seventy-five percent of drug costs incurred between $265 to $2,400. Once the $2,400 limit is reached, the beneficiary will be solely responsible for paying drug costs until out-of-pocket costs[3] reach $3,850—this gap period represents the so-called "doughnut hole" in coverage. Out-of-pocket costs exceeding $3,850 will be covered by the Plan, except for a nominal beneficiary cost-sharing amount equal to the greater of: (1) $2 for a generic drug or preferred multiple source drug and $5 for any other drug; or (2) 5 percent coinsurance.

In order to supply covered Part D prescription drugs to enrolled beneficiaries, Plans are required to develop a network of community, storefront pharmacies (i.e., not solely mail-order entities) sufficient to ensure convenient patient access to at least one pharmacy. Plans must allow beneficiaries the option of receiving benefits through a community pharmacy rather than through mail order if the beneficiary so chooses. Plans may, however, require a beneficiary to pay any differential in costs between obtaining prescription drugs at the community pharmacy versus utilizing a mail-order service.

When developing a network, Plans must accept any pharmacy into the network meeting the terms and conditions for participation.

Additionally, pharmacies joining a Plan's network must be willing to accept payment from the Plan according to the contractual rates negotiated between the Plan and the pharmacy, rather than the fixed, national formula-based rates they presently receive for drugs covered under Medicare Part B. Although Plans are free to negotiate payment rates with pharmacies, Plans may not condition participation in the network upon a pharmacy agreeing to accept risk or share risk with the Plan.

Plans also will be required, at all times, to provide beneficiaries with access to negotiated prices for covered outpatient prescription drugs, even if the beneficiary directly pays for the drugs due to the application of the deductible or during the doughnut hole gap. This includes access to all discounts, direct or indirect subsidies, rebates, price concessions, or other direct or indirect remuneration the Plan receives from pharmaceutical manufacturers or suppliers. In accordance with national standards to be developed by the Secretary, Plans must issue a card or other method by which beneficiaries can access the negotiated prices.

## MEDICARE PROGRAM ADMINISTRATION

### Federal Agencies and Private Contractors

Medicare is administered by the United States Department of Health and Human Services (HHS), CMS (formerly known as the Health Care Financing Administration (HCFA)) and certain private contractors known as *Fiscal Intermediaries* (FIs) (Part A) and *Carriers* (Part B). In addition to publishing and implementing regulations, CMS issues various Medicare health insurance manuals including, among others, the: (a) Provider Reimbursement Manual (CMS-Pub. 15); (b) Coverage Issues Manual (CMS-Pub. 6); (c) Hospital Manual (CMS-Pub. 10); (d) Medicare Intermediary Manual (CMS-Pub. 13); and (e) Medicare Carriers Manual (CMS-Pub. 14).

### Payment

For the first seventeen years of the Medicare program, hospitals and other providers were reimbursed for inpatient services provided to Medicare beneficiaries on the basis of a retrospective, cost-based reimbursement system. In more recent years, a variety of prospective payment systems have been implemented in an effort to curtail health care costs.

Medicare does not pay for services when Medicare is not the "primary" payor. Consequently, Medicare payment for any items or services that may be covered under other health insurance plans or policies such as workers' compensation, liability insurance, or employer health benefit plans is prohibited. In these instances, Medicare's liability for payment is deemed "secondary" to that of other health insurance plans.[4]

## Survey and Certification

The Secretary of HHS (the Secretary) utilizes conditions of participation (CoPs) to establish a health care provider's eligibility for participation in the Medicare program.[5] The CoPs are facility standards and requirements that providers must adhere to for receipt of Medicare reimbursement. Compliance with the CoPs is determined by the state department of health or similar agency that surveys, inspects, and certifies providers for Medicare participation under an agreement with HHS.

Providers also must enter into a written agreement with the Secretary and agree to comply with all of the Medicare program's requirements.[6] This provider agreement is automatically renewed each year and may be terminated by the Secretary based upon substantial noncompliance. The Secretary also has the authority to completely exclude providers from Medicare for certain offenses, including patient abuse and neglect, submission of false claims, program fraud, and financial misconduct.

## NOTES

1. *See* 42 U.S.C. § 1395y(a)(1)(A) (2006).
2. *See id.* §§ 1395x(w)(1), 1395cc(a)(1)(H); 42 C.F.R. §§ 410.26, 414.34 (2006).
3. "Out-of-pocket" or incurred drug costs are payments made by the beneficiary, made on behalf of the beneficiary by Medicaid or a state pharmaceutical assistance program, or made through the low-income cost-sharing subsidy provisions of the MMA, for deductible, cost-sharing amounts, or costs not paid because of the initial coverage limit. Out-of-pocket costs do not include amounts for which no benefits were provided because of the application of a formulary. Additionally, out-of-pocket costs do not include costs for which the beneficiary is reimbursed by insurance.
4. *See* 42 U.S.C. § 1395y(b)(2); 42 C.F.R. §§ 411.32–.33.
5. *See* 42 U.S.C. § 1395x(f); 42 C.F.R. pts. 482–498.
6. *See* 42 U.S.C. § 1395cc; 42 C.F.R. §§ 489.10, .12, .53.

# CHAPTER 2

# Beneficiary Appeals

## MEDICARE PART A AND PART B "FEE-FOR-SERVICE" APPEALS (42 C.F.R. PART 405 (SUBPARTS G, H, AND I))

### General

In March 2005, Centers for Medicare & Medicaid Services (CMS) published an interim final rule (the Rule) concerning broad changes to the Medicare Part A and Part B appeals process.[1] The Rule implements provisions of both the Medicare, Medicaid and SCHIP Benefits Improvement and Protection Act of 2000 (BIPA) and the Medicare Prescription Drug, Improvement, and Modernization Act of 2003 (MMA). Additionally, the Rule addresses industry comments to CMS's November 2002 proposed rule.[2] The Rule was effective May 1, 2005, but included a staggered implementation schedule due to the numerous changes impacting the appeals process and the complexity of employing those changes. Effective January 1, 2006, however, the Rule has been fully implemented.

### History of Medicare "Fee-for-Service" Appeals Reform

In 2000, § 521 of BIPA amended the Act to require revisions to the Medicare fee-for-service appeals process. Specifically, BIPA required certain substantive and procedural changes to the Medicare appeals process as follows:

- establishment of an uniform appeals process for Part A and Part B appeals;
- revised time frames for filing appeals;
- implementation of fixed time frames for issuing decisions;
- creation of a new Qualified Independent Contractor (QIC) to conduct reconsiderations; and
- utilization of de novo review by the Medicare Appeals Council (MAC) of an Administrative Law Judge (ALJ) decision made following a hearing.

In November 2002, CMS published a proposed rule to implement BIPA's changes.

The enactment of the MMA required further revisions to the Medicare claims appeals process. The MMA:

- required presentation of evidence early in the appeals process;
- imposed specific content requirements for appeal notices;
- established specific eligibility requirements for QICs, and reduced the number of QICs from twelve to a minimum of four;
- revised appeal time frames and amount in controversy requirements;
- created an expedited judicial review process; and
- transferred the ALJ function from the Social Security Administration (SSA) to the Department of Health and Human Services (HHS).

## Medicare Part A and Part B "Fee-for-Service" Appeals

### *Overview*

With promulgation of the Rule, CMS is implementing the provisions of both BIPA and the MMA. The new regulations govern the Medicare Part A and Part B appeals process and are contained in new subpart I of 42 C.F.R. Part 405. The regulations previously contained in subpart G (Part A) and H (Part B) will continue to exist until all appeals filed under those subparts of have been resolved.

In sum, the new, uniform five-step appeals process for Medicare fee-for-service claims is as follows. First, following an *initial determination*, a party to the initial determination (a beneficiary, provider, or supplier) has 120 days to file a *redetermination* with the fiscal intermediary (FI) or carrier (collectively, "Medicare contractors"), as appropriate. Following the Medicare contractor's redetermination decision and within 180 days of receipt, a party to the redetermination may file for *reconsideration* by a QIC.

Following the QIC's reconsideration decision (and assuming the amount in controversy requirement is satisfied), a party to the reconsideration may then file a request for an ALJ hearing. The ALJ hearing request must be made within sixty days from receipt of the QIC's decision. The fourth level of appeal is with the MAC. Any such appeal also must be filed within sixty days from receipt of the ALJ's hearing decision and the party must identify the aspects of the ALJ decision with which the party disagrees. The final level of appeal is at the federal district court.

### *What May Be Appealed? (42 C.F.R. §§ 405.900, .904; 478.10–.14)*

Generally, there are two types of Medicare initial determinations that may be appealed—*entitlement appeals* and *claim appeals*. Entitlement appeals concern initial determinations related to whether an individual is entitled to benefits under Medicare Part A or Part B. For example, an individual can appeal an adverse initial determination by the SSA regarding the individual's application for Medicare benefits or entitlement to Medicare benefits. Entitlement determinations and redeterminations are handled by the SSA.

Claim appeals concern initial determinations related to the amount of benefits available to a beneficiary under Medicare Part A or Part B. For example, a Medicare beneficiary may appeal an initial determination by a Medicare contractor regarding the coverage of items or services under Part A or Part B.

Any other initial determination relating to a claim for benefits under Medicare Part A or Part B also may be appealed. For example, certain initial determinations made by a quality improvement organization (QIO) may be appealed. A QIO makes initial determinations regarding whether services that are furnished (or proposed to be furnished) are reasonable and necessary. Additionally, with respect to inpatient services, QIOs also make initial determinations whether such services are delivered in the most appropriate setting. Lastly, QIOs may change the diagnostic or procedural coding information related to a Medicare inpatient claim as part of payment review.

### *Who May Appeal? (42 C.F.R. §§ 405.906–.912; 478.15)*

As a general matter, individuals seeking Medicare benefits, Medicare beneficiaries, providers, and suppliers may appeal Medicare initial determinations. With respect to QIO diagnostic or procedural coding changes discussed above, providers or practitioners may appeal if the change causes an assignment to a different diagnostic-related group (DRG) or if the change results in lower payment. A beneficiary may seek review if the change results in noncoverage of a furnished service.

Prior to the Rule, providers and suppliers could appeal initial determinations only in limited situations. For example, Part A providers could not directly appeal claims when services failed to meet the requirements of a covered benefit. In these instances, Part A providers typically sought to act as the beneficiary's representative by obtaining and submitting an Appointment of Representative form signed by the beneficiary. Pursuant to the Rule, however, providers, participating suppliers, nonparticipating suppliers who have accepted assignment for the items or services at issue in the claim, and providers and suppliers who are not parties, but have accepted assignment of the beneficiary's appeal rights, may file appeals to the same extent as beneficiaries. In other words, all these parties now have direct appeal rights with respect to all Medicare initial determinations.

Additional changes and clarifications were made in the Rule with respect to party status. Medicaid state agencies may file redetermination requests directly on claims for items or services furnished to dually eligible beneficiaries when the state agency has made payment for, or may be liable for, the cost of such items or services. The state agency retains party status after becoming a party at the redetermination level. Further, at the ALJ level, CMS or its contractors may choose to participate in the hearing or elect to become a party to the hearing.

## Appeals Process

### *Initial Determinations (42 C.F.R. §§ 405.920–.928)*

The Rule requires that parties be notified of initial determinations in writing. For initial determination notices sent to beneficiaries, the notice must be written in a manner that can be understood by the beneficiary and contain (among other items): (1) the reasons for the determination; (2) the procedures for obtaining additional information concerning the Medicare contractor's determination; and (3) information regarding the right to a redetermination if dissatisfied with the initial determination. For initial determination notices sent to providers and suppliers, the notice must contain (among other items): (1) the basis for any full or partial denial; (2) information regarding the right to a redetermination if dissatisfied with the initial determination; (3) all applicable claim adjustment reason and remark codes explaining the initial determination; (4) the source of the remittance advice and who may be contacted for further information; and (5) all content requirements of the standard adopted for use by covered entities under the Health Insurance Portability and Accountability Act (HIPAA) of 1996.

Medicare contractors must issue initial determinations concerning "clean claims" within thirty days—otherwise interest will accrue on the claim. There is a forty-five-day statutory time frame for issuing initial determinations on non-clean claims. Interest does not accrue on non-clean claims when contractors fail to timely process the claim.

### *Redeterminations (42 C.F.R. §§ 405.940–.958)*

As under the previous system, providers, suppliers, and beneficiaries continue to be able to appeal an initial determination to the FI or carrier. This first level of appeal is now known as the redetermination stage. Absent good cause, redetermination requests are required to be filed within 120 days from receipt of the notice of initial determination. There is no amount in controversy requirement at this level of appeal.

All redetermination requests must be submitted in writing and must be signed by the appellant. The request must include an explanation of the basis for disagreement with the contractor's determination and should include any applicable evidence. The requirement of a written submission promotes early submission of evidence which may lead to resolving appeals at lower levels of review.[3]

Any redetermination affirming an initial determination, in whole or in part, must be written in a manner that can be understood by a beneficiary and contain (among other items): (1) a clear statement indicating whether the reconsideration is favorable or unfavorable; (2) a summary of the facts; (3) an explanation of how applicable law, regulations, and policies apply to the facts; (4) a summary of the rationale for the redetermination; (5) notification of the right to a reconsideration and any specific missing documentation that must be submitted along with a request for reconsideration (discussed below); and (6) a statement that all the evidence that the appealing party desires to introduce during the remainder of the appeal process must be submitted with the request for reconsideration (discussed below). For decisions that are a full reversal of the initial determination, the redetermination also must be in writing and provide a clear statement indicating that the decision is wholly favorable to the appellant.

Medicare contractors are required to mail their decision within sixty days of receiving a request for determination. This sixty-day limit may be extended up to an additional fourteen days each time additional evidence is submitted after the filing of a redetermination request. While the regulations provide no penalties for contractor failure to adhere to these deadlines, these time frames may be enforced through corrective action plans and other tools to ensure that contractors adhere to their responsibilities.

### *Reconsiderations (42 C.F.R. §§ 405.960–.978)*

One of the Rule's most striking changes is the addition of an uniform second-level appeal stage conducted by QICs. A QIC is a contractor independent of FIs and carriers that conducts reconsiderations. Prior to the Rule, Part B suppliers were afforded a "carrier hearing" as their second-level appeal. Part A providers, however, were not afforded this level of review. As such, the Rule effectively adds another step in the appeals process for these entities.

Absent good cause, a request for reconsideration must be filed in writing within 180 days from receipt of a redetermination decision. Unlike the prior rules, there is no amount in controversy requirement.[4]

Consistent with § 933(a) of the MMA, the Rule includes a requirement at the reconsideration appeal level of "full and early presentation of evidence." As such and as discussed above, when filing a reconsideration request, providers and suppliers must present all evidence relevant to the issues in dispute and explain their disagreement with the initial determination and redetermination. Absent good cause, failure to submit evidence prior to the issuance of the notice of reconsideration precludes consideration of the evidence at subsequent levels of the appeals process. In other words, evidence not introduced at the reconsideration stage may be determined ineligible for utilization at further appeal stages. Importantly, however, there is an exception to this full and early presentation of evidence requirement for appealing beneficiaries who are not represented by providers or suppliers.

The QIC reconsideration is an "on-the-record" review (as opposed to an in-person hearing) consisting of review of the initial determination, the redetermination decision, and all issues related to the payment of the claim at issue. The QIC reviews evidence and findings in the record, any additional evidence submitted by the parties, and any evidence the QIC obtains on its own.

The Rule requires that if the initial determination at issue involves a finding on whether an item or service was reasonable and necessary, the QIC's reconsideration must involve evaluation by a panel of physicians or other appropriate health care professionals, and be based upon clinical experience, the patient's medical records, and medical, technical, and scientific evidence. If the claim involves physician services, the reviewing professional must be a physician. All QIC panel members must have sufficient medical, legal, and other expertise, including knowledge of the Medicare program.

In making their review, QICs are bound by National Coverage Decisions (NCDs), CMS rulings, and applicable laws and regulations, but are not bound by Local Coverage Decisions (LCDs), Local Medical Review Policies (LMRPs), or CMS program guidance such as manual instructions. Importantly, while not bound by these latter authorities, the QIC gives substantial deference to such authorities unless the particular instruction or policy is determined to be inapplicable to the facts of the case.

The reconsideration must be written in a manner that can be understood by a beneficiary and contain (among other items): (1) a clear statement indicating whether the reconsideration is favorable or unfavorable; (2) a summary of the facts; (3) an explanation of how applicable law, regulations, and policies apply to the facts; (4) in cases concerning whether an item or service is reasonable and necessary, an explanation of the medical and scientific rationale for the decision; (5) a summary of the rationale for the reconsideration; (6) notification of the right to an ALJ hearing and the applicable amount in controversy requirement; and (7) if appropriate, the requirements for expedited access to judicial review.

Generally, QICs are required to issue a decision within sixty days of receipt of a request for reconsideration. Similar to redeterminations, however, this sixty-day mandatory period can be extended up to fourteen days each time a party submits additional evidence after filing the request for reconsideration.

At the end of the sixty-day period (or the applicable fourteen-day extension period), the QIC must either: (1) notify all parties of its reconsideration decision; (2) dismiss the reconsideration request; or (3) notify the appealing party that it cannot complete the reconsideration by the deadline and allow the appellant an opportunity to "escalate" the appeal to the next level—to an ALJ. If the appellant exercises its escalation right in writing then, within five days, the QIC must either complete the reconsideration or acknowledge the escalation and forward the appeal to the ALJ. Unless the QIC receives a written request for escalation, the QIC is required to continue the reconsideration process even if the sixty-day (or applicable fourteen-day) period is exceeded.

### *ALJ Hearings (42 C.F.R. §§ 405.1000–.1054)*

The third level of appeal is an ALJ hearing. Absent good cause, a request for an ALJ hearing must be filed in writing within sixty days following receipt of notice of the QIC decision. Additionally, the request must meet the amount in controversy requirement.

While the Rule states that ALJ hearings can be conducted in person, by video teleconference (VTC), or by telephone, the Rule requires that hearings be conducted by VTC if such technology is available. Additionally, a telephone hearing also may be conducted if it would be more convenient for one or more of the parties. Upon a showing of good cause, parties may object to a VTC or telephone hearing, and request an in-person hearing. This request for an in-person hearing must be in writing, detail the reason(s) for the objection, and suggest the time and place for the in-person hearing. An example of good cause might include a showing that the case presents complex issues necessitating an in-person hearing. Should the request be granted, the party requesting the in-person hearing would waive the ninety-day time frame for holding a hearing and rendering a decision (discussed below).

The Rule formally grants ALJs the authority to request CMS (and/or its contractors) to participate in ALJ hearings, permits CMS to participate or act as a party to an ALJ hearing, and allows CMS to seek MAC review (discussed below) of an ALJ decision. Discovery is permitted in an ALJ hearing only when CMS is participating in the hearing as a party. In these instances, the ALJ may permit certain limited discovery.

The Rule provides that ALJs are bound by NCDs, CMS rulings, and applicable laws and regulations, but not LCDs, LMRPs, or CMS program guidance. While not bound by these latter authorities, ALJs give substantial deference to such authorities unless the particular instruction or policy is determined to be inapplicable to the facts of the case. In cases involving statistical sampling, ALJs are required to base their decision on a review of all claims in the sample and not just a portion of the claims.

In most cases, an ALJ is required to issue a decision, enter a dismissal order, or remand to the QIC within ninety days from the date the request for ALJ hearing is received. The time frame may be extended if the appellant requests and in-person hearing, the case is escalated form the QIC, or a party seeks to submit new evidence. Similar to the escalation provisions in the QIC reconsideration context, the appellant may request escalation to the next level of review–the MAC–if a decision is not issued within the applicable time frame. As discussed above, if the appellant exercises its escalation right in writing, within five days, then the ALJ must issue a decision or a dismissal, remand the case, or acknowledge the escalation and forward the appeal to the MAC.

### *MAC Reviews (42 C.F.R. §§ 405.1100–.1134)*

The fourth level of review is before the MAC. The MAC is part of the Departmental Appeals Board (DAB) of HHS. Absent good cause, a party to the ALJ hearing must file a request for MAC review within sixty days after receipt of the ALJ's decision or dismissal. The appellant must specify the portions of the ALJ action with which the party disagrees and explain the reason for the dispute. The MAC limits its review to the exceptions raised by the party. There is no MAC review available for an ALJ's remand to the QIC or an ALJ's affirmation of a QIC's dismissal of a request for reconsideration. The MAC standard of review is *de novo*.

Additionally, on its own motion, the MAC may review a decision or dismissal by an ALJ. Moreover, CMS or its contractors may refer cases to the MAC to consider whether its own motion review is appropriate. The MAC may take its own motion review of a case if the ALJ decision or dismissal contains an error of law material to the outcome of the appeal, or presents a broad policy or procedural issue that may affect the public interest. Lastly, the MAC may take its own motion review in cases where CMS or its contractor participated in the ALJ hearing, and the ALJ's decision or dismissal is not supported by the preponderance of evidence in the record or the ALJ abused his or her discretion.

Upon request, the MAC will grant parties a reasonable opportunity to file briefs or other written statements. Additionally, parties may request to appear before the MAC to present oral argument. Such request may be granted if the MAC determines that the case involves an important question of law, policy, or fact that cannot be readily decided based upon the written submissions.

Following review of all the evidence in the administrative record, the MAC makes a decision or remands that case to the ALJ. In general, the MAC issues decisions within sixty days of receipt of a request for review unless extended as provided for in the regulations.

Similar to the previous stages of review, appealing parties have the right to request escalation to the next level of review—federal district court. As discussed above, if the appealing party exercises its escalation right in writing, within five days, then the MAC must either act or acknowledge the escalation and send a notice to the appealing party.

### *Judicial Review (42 C.F.R. §§ 405.1136–.1140) and Expedited Judicial Review (42 C.F.R. § 405.990)*

The final stage in the appeals process is judicial review in federal court. Appealing parties must file an action in federal district court within sixty days after receipt of the MAC notice of decision and must meet the amount in controversy requirement ($1,090 in 2006). In a federal court action, the findings of fact by the Secretary are deemed conclusive if supported by substantial evidence.

Appellants may request expedited access to judicial review (EAJR) in place of an ALJ hearing or MAC review if certain requirements are met. First, a review entity (comprised of an entity of up to three reviewers who are ALJs or members of the DAB) must certify that the MAC does not have the authority to decide the question of law or regulation, and that no material facts are in dispute. Second, each party in the appeal must agree in writing with the request for EAJR. The review entity has sixty days to issue a certification for EAJR or to deny the request. If the review entity fails to act within sixty days, the requester may bring an action in federal district court within sixty days of the end of the time period.

### *Additional Issues Regarding Medicare Fee-for-Service Appeals*

#### Reopenings (42 C.F.R. §§ 405.980–.986)

Although reopening is not an appeal, the Rule allows for a reopening process concerning initial determinations, redeterminations, reconsiderations, ALJ hearings, and MAC reviews. A reopening is a remedial action to change a final determination or decision that resulted in either overpayment or underpayment, even though the determination or decision was correct based on the evidence in the record at the time the determination or decision was made. Contractors are required to process as reopenings (rather than redeterminations) minor errors such as clerical errors, denials of claims as duplicates, inaccurate date entry, and similar errors. Importantly, the reopening and appeals processes may not be employed simultaneously.

Parties can request that a contractor reopen an initial determination or a redetermination within one year for any reason or within four years upon a showing of good cause. Good cause may be established based upon new and material evidence which was not previously available or known, and may result in a different decision, or where obvious error was made. The Rule states that a change of legal interpretation, CMS guidance, or CMS policy is not a basis for reopening. The decision to reopen or not reopen a determination or decision is discretionary and is not subject to appeal.

### Transfer of Appeals from SSA to HHS

Although not addressed in detail in the Rule, the MMA mandates that the responsibility for ALJ appeals be transferred from SSA to HHS. In March 2004, SSA and HHS jointly developed the required plan.[5] As of July 1, 2005, all Medicare appeals that would otherwise have been sent to SSA now are sent to HHS for adjudication.

The plan seeks to ensure independence of the ALJs by creating a new central administrative office located in Arlington, Virginia, that is organizationally and functionally separate from CMS. Moreover, the ALJs report to and are subject to the general supervision of the Secretary. Currently, there are four HHS hearing offices located in Arlington, Virginia; Miami, Florida; Cleveland, Ohio; and Irvine, California.

## Practical Tips

**Adhere to the appeal time frames.** The amended "fee-for-service" appeals process requires that evidence be presented in the appeals process. While this requirement is relaxed for beneficiaries representing themselves, providers, suppliers, and represented beneficiaries should be sure to adhere to the applicable time frame in the appeals process. Failure to do so could result in key evidence being excluded from the appeal.

**Take advantage of on-the-record review.** While the removal of in-person hearings at the reconsideration stage arguably impacts certain types of appeals (e.g., large post-payment audit cases), other appellants may find that on-the-record reviews expedite resolution of their appeal. This also may be beneficial to the extent that appeals are subject to recoupment prior to exhaustion of the appeals process.

**Obtain affidavits from experts early.** Given the reduction in the availability of in-person hearings and the early presentation of evidence requirement, appellants should not rely upon the ability to offer expert testimony at a hearing. Instead, appellants should, to the extent practicable, obtain affidavits from experts early in the appeals process and include as evidence.

## MEDICARE PART A APPEALS OF PROVIDER SERVICE TERMINATIONS (42 C.F.R. PART 405 (SUBPART J))

### Overview

Medicare beneficiaries have the right to an expedited determination of a provider's decision to terminate services when that provider determines that the beneficiary no longer meets Medicare coverage requirements. Providers are required to issue expedited determination notices to beneficiaries informing them that their health care services will be terminated and explaining their right to appeal to a QIO for an expedited determination. Regulations regarding expedited determinations in outpatient residential settings (skilled nursing facilities (SNFs), hospices, and swing beds) and nonresidential settings (HHAs), and comprehensive outpatient rehabilitation facilities (CORFs) can be found at §§ 405.1200 and 405.1202. Regulations for expedited determinations in the inpatient hospital settings are found at § 405.1206.

### What May Be Appealed and Who May Appeal?

#### *Notifying Beneficiaries of Provider Service Terminations (42 C.F.R. § 405.1200)*

A beneficiary may appeal his or her termination from a SNF, swing bed, hospice, CORF, or HHA. A termination is defined as a complete cessation of coverage at the end of a course of treatment prescribed in a discrete increment, regardless of whether the beneficiary agrees that the services should end. A termination does not include a reduction in services or the termination of one type of service by the provider if the beneficiary continues to receive other Medicare-covered services from the provider. In the HHA and CORF settings, a physician must certify that failure to continue services will place the beneficiary's health at significant risk. Before any termination of services, the provider of the service must deliver valid written notice to the beneficiary of its decision to terminate services.

The provider must use a standardized notice (as specified by CMS) and the following procedures:

- *Timing.* The provider must notify the beneficiary of its decision to terminate the covered services no later than two days before the proposed end of the services. If the services are expected to be fewer than two days in duration, the provider must notify the beneficiary at the time of admission to the provider. If the services are provided in a nonresidential setting and the span of time between services exceeds two days, the beneficiary must be given notice no later than the next to last time services are furnished.
- *Content of the notice.* The standardized termination notice must include the date that coverage of services ends, the date the beneficiary's financial liability for continued services begins, a description of the beneficiary's right to an expedited determination by a QIO, how to request it, and an explanation of the beneficiary's right to submit evidence showing that services must continue.
- *Valid delivery.* Delivery of the termination notice is valid if the beneficiary or authorized representative has signed and dated the notice indicating that he or she has received the notice and comprehends its contents, and the notice is delivered and contains all of the elements required above. If the beneficiary refuses to sign the notice, the provider may annotate the notice to indicate that the beneficiary refused to accept it, and the date of refusal is considered to be the date of receipt of the notice.

A provider of services is financially liable for continued services until two days after the beneficiary receives valid notice, or until the service termination date specified on the notice, whichever is later. A beneficiary may waive continuation of services if he or she agrees with being discharged sooner than the planned service termination date.

## Appeals Process

### *Expedited Determination Procedures (42 C.F.R. § 405.1202)*

The Medicare beneficiary has a right to an expedited determination by the QIO under the following circumstances: (1) for services furnished by a nonresidential provider, the beneficiary disagrees with the provider's determination that services should be terminated, and a physician certifies that failure to continue the provision of the services may place the beneficiary's health at significant risk; and (2) for services furnished by a residential provider or a hospice, the beneficiary disagrees with the provider's decision to discharge the beneficiary.

A beneficiary who wishes to appeal a provider service termination must submit a request for an expedited determination to the QIO no later than noon of the next calendar day following receipt of the notice. A beneficiary or his or her authorized representative must be available to answer questions or to supply information that the QIO may request as it conducts its review. The beneficiary may, but is not required to, submit evidence to be considered by the QIO in making its decision. If the beneficiary makes an untimely request for QIO review, the QIO will accept the request and make a determination as soon as possible, but the financial liability protection and the seventy-two-hour time frame (see below) do not apply.

*Coverage of provider services.* Coverage of provider services continues until the date and time designated on the termination notice, unless the QIO reverses the provider's service termination decision. If the QIO's decision is delayed because the provider did not timely supply necessary information or records, the provider may be liable for the costs of any additional coverage, as determined by the QIO. If the QIO determines that the beneficiary did not receive valid notice, coverage of the provider services continues until at least two days after valid notice has been received. Continuation of coverage is not required if the QIO determines that coverage could pose a threat to the beneficiary's health and safety.

*Burden of proof.* When a beneficiary requests an expedited determination by a QIO, the burden of proof rests with the provider to demonstrate that termination of coverage is the correct decision, either on the basis of medical necessity, or based upon other Medicare coverage policies. In order for the QIO to determine whether the provider has met the burden of proof, the provider should supply any and all information required by the QIO to sustain the provider's termination decision.

*Procedures the QIO must follow.* On the day the QIO receives the request for an expedited determination, it must immediately notify the provider of those services that such a request has been made, and must determine whether the provider delivered a valid notice of termination to the beneficiary or to the authorized representative. The QIO examines the medical and other records pertaining to the services in dispute. If applicable, the QIO determines whether a physician has certified that failure to continue the provision of services may place the beneficiary's health at significant risk. The QIO must also solicit the views of the beneficiary who requested the expedited determination or his or her authorized representative, and must provide an opportunity for the provider/practitioner to explain why the termination or discharge is appropriate.

No later than seventy-two hours after receipt of the request for an expedited determination, the QIO must notify the beneficiary, the beneficiary's physician, and the provider of services of its determination whether termination of Medicare coverage is the correct decision—either on the basis of medical necessity or based upon other Medicare coverage policies. If the QIO does not receive the information needed to sustain a provider's decision to terminate services, it may make its determination based upon the evidence at hand or may defer a decision until it receives the necessary information. If the delay results in extended Medicare coverage of those services to the beneficiary, the provider may be held financially liable as determined by the QIO. The QIO's initial notification may be by telephone, followed by a written notice including the following information: (1) the rationale for the determination; (2) an explanation of the Medicare payment consequences of the determination and the date a beneficiary becomes fully liable for the services; and (3) information about the beneficiary's right to a reconsideration of the QIO's determination, including how to request a reconsideration and the time period for doing so.

*Responsibilities of providers.* When a QIO notifies a provider that a beneficiary has requested an expedited determination, the provider must send a detailed notice to the beneficiary by close of business of the day of the QIO's notification. The detailed termination notice must include the following information: (1) a specific and detailed explanation of why services are either no longer reasonable and necessary or no longer covered; (2) a description of any applicable Medicare coverage rule, instruction, or other Medicare policy, including citations to the applicable Medicare policy rules or information about how the beneficiary may obtain a copy of the Medicare policy; (3) facts specific to the beneficiary and relevant to the coverage determination that are sufficient to advise the beneficiary of the applicability of the coverage rule or policy to the beneficiary's case; and (4) any other information required by CMS.

Upon notification by the QIO of the request for an expedited determination, the provider must supply all information that the QIO needs to make its expedited determination, including a copy of the notices required by 42 C.F.R. § 405.1200(b) and (f)(1). The provider must furnish this information as soon as possible, but no later than by close of business of the day the QIO notifies the provider of the request for an expedited determination. At the discretion of the QIO, the provider may make the information available by telephone or in writing (with a written record of any information not transmitted initially in writing).

At a beneficiary's request, the provider also must furnish the beneficiary with a copy of, or access to, any documentation that it sends to the QIO including records of any information provided by telephone. The provider may charge the beneficiary a reasonable amount to cover the costs of duplicating the documentation and/or delivering it to the beneficiary. The provider must accommodate such a request by no later than close of business of the first day after the material is requested.

*Coverage during QIO review.* When a beneficiary requests an expedited determination meeting the regulatory requirements, the provider may not bill the beneficiary for any disputed services until the expedited determination process and reconsideration process, if applicable, has been completed.

### *Expedited Determinations for Inpatient Hospital Discharges (42 C.F.R. § 405.1206)*[6]

A beneficiary who has received a notice of noncoverage under § 1154(e)(1) of the Act and 42 C.F.R. § 412.42(c)(3)[7] may request an expedited determination by the QIO when a hospital (acting directly or through its utilization review committee and with physician concurrence) determines that inpatient care is no longer necessary. A beneficiary who timely requests an expedited review and who meets the conditions of § 1879(a)(2) of the Act (that is, the individual did not know and could not reasonably have been expected to know that payment would not be made for such items or services under Part A or Part B) may remain in the hospital with no additional financial liability until the QIO makes its determination.

Valid delivery of the notice of noncoverage requires that the beneficiary or the beneficiary's authorized representative has signed and dated the notice to indicate that he or she has received the notice and can comprehend its contents. If the beneficiary refuses to sign the notice, the provider may annotate its notice to indicate the refusal and the date of refusal is considered the date of receipt of the notice.

A beneficiary who fails to timely request an expedited determination and remains in the hospital, may request an expedited review at any time during the course of his or her inpatient stay. The QIO will issue a decision, but the escalation procedures and financial liability rules of §§ 405.1204(c)(5) and 405.1206(f)(2) do not apply. A beneficiary who fails to request an expedited determination and who is no longer an inpatient of the hospital, may request QIO review within thirty calendar days after receipt of the notice of noncoverage, as provided by § 1154(e)(1) of the

Act or at any time for good cause. The QIO will issue a decision, but the escalation procedures and the financial liability rules described in § 405.1204(c)(5) and 405.1206(f)(2) do not apply.

*Procedures the beneficiary must follow.* For the expedited appeals process, the beneficiary must submit the request for an expedited determination to the QIO that has an agreement with the hospital (under 42 C.F.R. Part 475). The request must be in writing or by telephone, and must be made by noon of the first working day after the beneficiary receives written notice that the hospital has determined that the hospital stay is no longer necessary. The beneficiary or authorized representative upon request by the QIO must be prepared to discuss the case with the QIO.

*Procedures the QIO must follow.* On the date that the QIO receives the beneficiary's request, the QIO must notify the hospital that the beneficiary has filed a request for immediate review. The hospital must supply the QIO with any information, including medical records that the QIO requires to conduct its review. The hospital must make such information available by telephone or in writing by the close of the first full working day after the day the beneficiary receives notice of the planned discharge.

The QIO must examine the pertinent records pertaining to the services and it must solicit the views of the beneficiary who requested the expedited determination (or the beneficiary's authorized representative). For timely requests, the QIO must make a determination and notify the beneficiary, the hospital, and the physician of its determination by close of business of the first working day after it receives all requested pertinent information.

When the beneficiary does not make a timely request for an expedited determination, but instead requests an expedited review and remains an inpatient in the hospital, the QIO will make a determination and notify the beneficiary, the hospital, and physician of its determination within two working days following receipt of the request and pertinent information. When the beneficiary does not make a timely request for an expedited determination and is no longer an inpatient in the hospital, the QIO will make a determination and notify the beneficiary, the hospital, and the physician of its determination within thirty calendar days after receipt of the request and pertinent information.

*Coverage during QIO expedited review.* In general, if the beneficiary remains in the hospital after receiving the hospital-issued notice of noncoverage, and the hospital, the physician who concurred in the hospital's termination determination, or the QIO subsequently finds that the beneficiary requires an acute level of inpatient care, the beneficiary is not financially responsible for continued care until the hospital once again determines that the beneficiary no longer requires inpatient care, secures concurrence from the physician responsible for the beneficiary's care or the QIO, and notifies the beneficiary again.

*Timely filing and limitation on liability.* If the beneficiary files a request for an expedited determination in accordance with the regulations and meets the conditions of § 1879(a)(2) of the Act (the individual did not know and could not reasonably have been expected to know that payment would not be made for such items or services under Part A or Part B), the beneficiary is not financially responsible for inpatient hospital services furnished before noon of the calendar day after the date the beneficiary or designated representative receives notification, either orally or in writing, of the expedited determination by the QIO.

*Untimely filing.* If the beneficiary does not file a request for expedited determination by the QIO in accordance with the regulations, the beneficiary may be responsible for charges that extend beyond the date specified on the hospital's advance written notice of termination or as otherwise stated by the QIO.

*QIO notification of an expedited determination.* When a QIO issues an expedited determination, the QIO must notify the beneficiary, physician, and the hospital of its decision by telephone and subsequently in writing. The written notice of the expedited determination must contain the following: the basis for the determination, including a detailed rationale for the determination; a statement explaining the Medicare payment consequences of the expedited determination and date of liability, if any; a statement explaining the Medicare payment consequences of the expedited determination and the date of liability, if any; a statement informing the beneficiary of his or her subsequent appeal rights; and the time frame for requesting a reconsideration by the QIC.

*Effect of an expedited QIO determination.* The QIO determination is binding on the beneficiary, physician, and hospital except in the following circumstances:

- when a beneficiary who made a timely request remains in the hospital and is dissatisfied with the determination, he or she may request a reconsideration according to the procedures described in § 405.1204 (see below); and
- when a beneficiary does not make a timely request for an expedited QIO determination and remains in the hospital, the time frames described in § 405.1204(c)(3), the escalation procedures described in § 405.1204(c)(5), and the coverage rule described in § 405.1204(f) will not apply.

If a beneficiary is no longer an inpatient in the hospital and is dissatisfied with the QIO's determination, the determination is subject to the general claims appeal process.

### *Hospital Requests for Expedited QIO Review (42 C.F.R. § 405.1208)*

If the hospital (acting directly or through its utilization review committee) believes that the beneficiary does not require further inpatient hospital care but is unable to obtain the agreement of the physician, it may request an expedited determination by the QIO.

*Procedures the hospital must follow.* The hospital must notify the beneficiary that it has requested the review. The hospital also must supply any pertinent information the QIO requires to conduct its review and must make such information available by telephone or in writing by close of business of the first full working day immediately following the day the hospital submits its review request.

*Procedures the QIO must follow.* The QIO must notify the hospital that it has received the request for review and must notify the hospital if it has not received all pertinent records. The QIO must examine the records pertaining to the services and must solicit the views of the beneficiary in question. The QIO then makes a determination and notifies the beneficiary, the hospital, and the physician within two working days of the hospital's request and receipt of any pertinent information submitted by the hospital. Notification of the QIO's determination must be done by telephone and subsequently in writing. The determination must contain the following: (1) the basis for the determination; (2) a detailed rationale for the determination; (3) a statement explaining the Medicare payment consequences of the expedited determination and the date of liability, if any; and (4) a statement informing the beneficiary of his or her appeal rights and the time frame for requesting an appeal.

*Effect of an expedited determination.* The expedited determination is binding on the beneficiary, the physician, and the hospital except in the following circumstances: (1) if the beneficiary is still in the hospital and is dissatisfied with the determination, he or she may request a reconsideration according to the procedures in 42 C.F.R. § 405.1204; or (2) if the beneficiary is no longer in the hospital and is dissatisfied with the determination, the determination is subject to the general claims appeal process.

### *Expedited Reconsiderations (42 C.F.R. § 405.1204) (applies to all settings)*

A beneficiary dissatisfied with a QIO's expedited determination for either inpatient hospital services or SNF/CORF/home health/hospice services, may request an expedited reconsideration by the appropriate QIC. The request must be submitted to the appropriate QIC, in writing or by telephone, by no later than noon of the calendar day following initial notification receipt of the QIO's determination. If the QIC is unable to accept the beneficiary's request, the beneficiary must submit the request by noon of the next day the QIC is available to accept a request.

The beneficiary or authorized representative must be available to answer questions or supply information that the QIC may request to conduct its reconsideration. The beneficiary may, but is not required to, submit evidence to be considered by a QIC in making its decision. A beneficiary who does not file a timely request for an expedited QIC reconsideration may subsequently request reconsideration through the standard claims appeal process, but the coverage protection, time frames, and the escalation process described in the regulations at §§ 405.1204(c)(3) and (c)(5) would not apply.

*Procedures the QIC must follow.* On the day the QIC receives the request for an expedited reconsideration, the QIC must immediately provide notification of the request for an expedited reconsideration to the QIO that made the expedited determination being reconsidered and the provider of services. The QIC must offer the beneficiary and the provider an opportunity to provide further information. Unless a request for an extension of time is made by the beneficiary (*see* 42 C.F.R. § 405.1204(c)(6)) no later than seventy-two hours after receipt of the request for expedited reconsideration and any medical or other records needed, the QIC must notify the QIO, the beneficiary, the beneficiary's physician, and the provider of services of its decision on the reconsideration request.

The OIC's initial notification may be done by telephone, followed by a written notice which includes: the rationale for the reconsideration decision; an explanation of the Medicare payment consequences of the determination and the beneficiary's date of liability; and information about the beneficiary's right to appeal the QIC's reconsideration decision to an ALJ, including how to request an appeal and the time period for doing so. If the QIC does not issue a decision within seventy-two hours of receipt of the request, the QIC must notify the beneficiary of his or her right to have the case escalated to the ALJ hearing level if the amount in controversy after the QIO determination satisfies the applicable threshold.

*Extension of time.* A beneficiary requesting an expedited reconsideration may request that the QIC grant an extension of time, not to exceed fourteen days, for the reconsideration. The QIO must supply the QIC with all the information the QIC needs to make an expedited reconsideration. At the beneficiary's request, the QIO must furnish the beneficiary with a copy of, or access to, any documentation sent to the QIC. The QIO must accommodate the request by no later than close of business of the first day after the material is requested, and may charge the beneficiary a reasonable amount to cover the cost of duplicating and/or delivering the documentation to the beneficiary.

*Responsibilities of the provider.* A provider may but is not required to submit evidence to be considered by a QIC in making its decision. If a provider fails to comply with a QIC's request for additional information beyond that furnished to the QIO, the QIC makes its reconsideration decision based on the information available.

*Coverage during the QIC reconsideration process.* When a beneficiary timely requests an expedited reconsideration, the provider may not bill the beneficiary for any disputed services until the QIC makes its determination.

### Practical Tips

**Beneficiaries (or authorized beneficiary representatives) should be careful in waiving continuation of services.** In connection with provider service terminations, providers are generally financially liable for continued services until two days after the beneficiary receives notice or until the services termination date on the notice. Beneficiaries (or authorized beneficiary representatives) may waive continuation of services, but should do so only when he or she agrees with being discharged sooner than the planned service termination date.

**Beneficiaries (or authorized beneficiary representatives) should assemble relevant information before contacting the QIO.** Beneficiaries (or authorized beneficiary representatives) may initiate requests for expedited determination of provider services terminations with the QIO in their state. Prior to initiating the request, the beneficiary (or authorized representative) should assemble all relevant information in order to be able to respond to questions from the QIO or to supply relevant information or documentation.

## AMBULATORY SURGICAL CENTER APPEALS (42 C.F.R. § 416.150)

### What May Be Appealed and Who May Appeal?

Utilizing the appeals process discussed above for "Medicare Part A and B 'Fee-for-Service' Appeals," a beneficiary or ambulatory surgical center (ASC) may request a hearing if the beneficiary or ASC: (1) is dissatisfied with a carrier's denial of a request for payment made on a beneficiary's behalf by an ASC; (2) is dissatisfied with the amount of payment; or

(3) believes the request for payment is not being acted on with reasonable promptness.

## MEDICARE PART B COVERAGE APPEALS (42 C.F.R. PART 408 (SUBPART F))

### Overview

As discussed in Chapter One, participation in Medicare Part B is voluntary and subject to payment of a monthly premium. When a beneficiary's enrollment in Part B is terminated based upon failure to pay the required premiums, the beneficiary may appeal the termination determination. In certain instances, Medicare Part B coverage may be reinstated without interruption of benefits.

### What May Be Appealed and Who May Appeal? (42 C.F.R. § 408.100)

A determination by the SSA to terminate a beneficiary's Medicare Part B coverage for nonpayment of premiums may be appealed by the beneficiary. A grace period has been established which ends with the last day of the third month after the billing month (e.g., if January is the billing month, the grace period expires on April 30). Termination determinations are not effective until fifteen days after the end of the grace period.

### Appeals Process (42 C.F.R. § 408.100–.104)

Between fifteen and thirty days after the end of the grace period, the SSA sends the beneficiary a notice of termination. This notice of termination must include information regarding the beneficiary's right to appeal. During the period, CMS also will notify any Medicare contractors of the termination determination.

A beneficiary's coverage may be reinstated without interruption if the beneficiary satisfies the following conditions: (1) appeals the termination by the end of the month following the month in which the SSA sent the notice of termination; (2) alleges and it is found that the beneficiary did not receive timely and adequate notice that the Medicare Part B premiums were due; and (3) pays, within thirty days after SSA's subsequent request for payment, all premiums due through the month in which the termination was appealed. Examples of untimely and inadequate billing notices include instances where the bill was lost in the mail or where, based upon information from the SSA, the beneficiary believed that premiums were being paid by some other means. A beneficiary's Medicare Part B coverage may not be reinstated if the beneficiary: (1) received timely and adequate notice that premiums were due, but failed to pay within the grace period; or (2) appealed the determination more than one month after the month in which the SSA sent the termination notice.

### Practical Tip

**Beneficiaries (or authorized beneficiary representatives) should adhere to appeal time frames.** Beneficiaries (or authorized beneficiary representatives) appealing termination of Medicare Part B coverage based on failure to pay premiums should be sure to adhere to applicable time frames for filing an appeal. A grace period has been established ending the last day of the third month after the billing month. Between fifteen and thirty days after the end of the grace period, notice of termination is sent. To be valid, an appeal must be filed by the end of the month following the month in which the notice of termination was sent.

## MEDICARE LCD/NCD APPEALS (42 C.F.R. PART 426)

### Overview

Sections 1869(f)(1) and (f)(2) of the Act (42 U.S.C. § 1395ff) provide for the review of LCDs and NCDs, and certain determinations that are deemed to be NCDs. A NCD is defined by statute as a determination by the Secretary with respect to whether or not a particular item or services are covered nationally. Similarly, the statute defines a LCD as a determination by a FI or carrier under Medicare Part A or Part B as to whether or not a particular item or service is covered on an intermediary or carrier-wide basis. Generally, ALJs conduct reviews of challenged LCDs and the DAB conducts reviews of NCDs (or deemed NCDs). LCDs, however, can be appealed to the DAB. Reviews of LCDs and NCDs are distinct from the claims appeals processes set forth elsewhere in this Guide.

### What May Be Appealed? (42 C.F.R. § 426.325)

Only LCDs, NCDs, and deemed NCDs that are in effect may be challenged. Deemed NCDs include determinations made by the Secretary in response to certain requests for a NCD under the Act, that no national coverage or NCD is appropriate, or the Secretary's failure to meet applicable NCD deadlines. Certain items are not reviewable including, among others: (1) pre-decisional material (e.g., drafts, templates); (2) retired LCDs or withdrawn NCDs; (3) LCD or NCD provisions that are no longer in effect due to revisions or reconsiderations; (4) interpretive policies that are not LCDs or NCDs; (5) payment amounts or methodologies; (6) procedure coding issues; (7) Medicare contractor bulletin articles, educational materials, or Web site frequently asked questions; or (8) individual claim determinations.

### Who May Appeal? (42 C.F.R. §§ 426.110, .320)

Only *aggrieved* parties may initiate a review of a LCD or NCD (or provisions of a LCD or NCD) by filing an acceptable complaint. An aggrieved party is a Medicare beneficiary (or the estate of a Medicare beneficiary) who: (1) is entitled to benefits under Medicare Part A, enrolled in Part B, or both (including an individual enrolled in fee-for-service Medicare, in a Medicare+Choice plan, or in another Medicare managed care plan); (2) is in need of coverage for a service that is denied based upon an applicable LCD or NCD; and (3) has obtained documentation of the need by the beneficiary's treating physician.

### LCD Appeal Process

#### *The Complaint (42 C.F.R. § 426.400)*

An aggrieved party may initiate a review of a LCD by filing a written complaint with CMS. The complaint must be filed within (1) six months of the issuance of documentation from the beneficiary's treating physician of the need for the service (if the beneficiary's challenge is made before receiving the service), or (2) 120 days of the initial denial notice. The complaint must include beneficiary-identifying information, representative information, a statement from the treating physician or the treating physician's order, LCD-identifying information, and a statement from the aggrieved party explaining what service is needed and why the provision(s) of the LCD is not valid under a reasonableness standard. Further, the complaint must include copies of clinical or scientific evidence supporting the complaint.

#### *ALJ Review (42 C.F.R. §§ 426.405, .410, .417, .425, .431, .447, .450)*

An ALJ conducts a hearing and defers only to reasonable findings of fact, interpretations of law, and applications of law to fact. In applying the reasonableness standard to a provision of a LCD, the ALJ must follow all applicable laws, regulations, rulings, and NCDs. The ALJ has the authority to hold conferences, consult with scientific and clinical experts, examine witnesses, issue subpoenas, and rule on motions and other procedural matters (among other powers).

The ALJ assigned to the LCD review determines if the complaint is acceptable. If the complaint is unacceptable, aggrieved parties are afforded one opportunity to amend the complaint. If the complaint is acceptable, the ALJ: (1) sends a letter to the aggrieved party acknowledging the complaint and the deadline for the contractor to produce the LCD record; (2) forwards a copy of the complaint and supporting documentation to the contractor and CMS; and (3) requires CMS or the contractor to send a copy of the LCD record to the ALJ and all parties within thirty days. In providing the LCD record to the aggrieved party, the contractor need not include proprietary data, privileged information, or new evidence.

Upon receipt of the contractor's LCD record, the aggrieved party must file a statement detailing why the contractor's LCD record is not complete or not adequate to support the validity of the LCD under a reasonableness standard. This statement must be submitted to the ALJ and contractor (or CMS as appropriate) within thirty days of receipt of the contractor's LCD record. The contractor then has thirty days to submit a response to the ALJ in defense of the LCD.

The ALJ reviews the aggrieved party statement and contractor's response, utilizing a reasonableness standard, to determine whether the LCD record is complete and adequate to support the validity of the LCD. If the ALJ determines that the record is complete and adequate, ALJ review is complete and a decision is issued (discussed below). If the ALJ determines that the record is not complete and adequate, the ALJ will permit discovery and taking of evidence. Within ninety days of closing the record to the taking of evidence, the ALJ must either (1) issue a written decision, including a description of appeal rights, or (2) provide written notification that a decision is pending, including an approximate date of issuance of the decision.

An ALJ's decision must include one of the following: (1) a determination that the provision of the LCD is valid or is not valid under the reasonable standard; (2) a statement dismissing the complaint, including a rationale for the dismissal; or (3) a determination that the LCD record is complete and adequate to support the validity of the LCD provision under the reasonableness standard. The ALJ's decision also must include a basis for his or her conclusion, a summary of the evidence reviewed, and a statement of appeal rights.

If the ALJ finds that the provisions of the LCD discussed in the complaint are not valid under the reasonableness standard, and no appeal is filed by the contractor or CMS, the contractor must (1) provide for individual claim review whereby the claim of the aggrieved party is reopened and adjudicated without utilizing the invalid LCD, or (2) provide for coverage determination relief by implementing the ALJ's decision.

### *DAB Review (42 C.F.R. §§ 426.460, .465, .470, .476, .482, .488)*

If the ALJ finds that the provisions of the LCD discussed in the complaint are valid under the reasonableness standard, the aggrieved party may appeal to the DAB. Absent good cause, the appeal must be filed with the DAB within thirty days of the date of issuance of the ALJ's decision. An appeal to the DAB must include: (1) the names and addresses of the parties, including the name of the LCD; (2) the date of issuance of the ALJ's decision; (3) the docket number of the ALJ's decision; (4) a statement identifying the parts of the ALJ's decision being appealed; and (5) a statement why the ALJ's decision should be reversed.

The DAB reviews the appeal to determine if it is acceptable. If the complaint is unacceptable, *the DAB must dismiss the appeal.* If the complaint is acceptable, the DAB: (1) sends a letter to the appellant acknowledging the appeal; (2) forwards a copy of the appeal and supporting documentation to all parties in the appeal; and (3) requires the ALJ to send a copy of the LCD review record to the DAB.

The DAB then: (1) permits the non-appealing party to file a response to the appeal; (2) hears oral argument if the DAB determines it helpful; (3) reviews the LCD review record and the parties' arguments; and (4) issues a written decision either upholding, modifying, or reversing the ALJ decision, or remanding the case to the ALJ for further proceedings. In making its review, the DAB determines whether the ALJ decision contains any failure to properly apply the reasonableness standard or the ALJ erred in determining that the contractor's record was complete and adequate. Like the ALJ, the DAB is bound by applicable laws, regulations, and NCDs. The DAB's written decision must include a summary of the ALJ decision, a rationale for the DAB's decision, and a description of appeal rights.

If the DAB upholds the ALJ's decision that a LCD is valid or reverses an ALJ decision that a LCD is invalid, the contractor or CMS is not required to take any action. If the DAB upholds an ALJ determination that the LCD is invalid, then the individual claim review or coverage determination relief procedures discussed above must be performed.

### *Judicial Review (42 C.F.R. § 426.490)*

A decision by the DAB (other than a remand) constitutes final agency action which is subject to judicial review. Neither the contractor nor CMS may appeal the DAB's decision.

## NCD Appeals Process (42 C.F.R. § 426.500–.587)

The NCD appeals process is procedurally and substantively similar to a LCD appeal except that the complaint is filed directly with the DAB (not an ALJ) and a decision by the DAB constitutes final agency action subject to judicial review.

## Practical Tips

**Be sure that the appealing party is *aggrieved*.** Only aggrieved parties may initiate review of a LCD or NCD. An aggrieved party is expressly defined as a Medicare beneficiary who is in need of coverage for a service that has been denied *and* has obtained documentation of the need by the beneficiary's treating physician.

**Be sure to obtain and include clinical or scientific evidence supporting the complaint.** Aggrieved parties may initiate reviews of LCDs and NCDs by filing a written complaint with CMS. Among other requirements, the complaint must include copies of clinical or scientific evidence supporting the complaint. This information is vital to a successful appeal and should be carefully prepared and referenced in the complaint.

**Request for DAB must be complete.** Unlike other appeals processes allowing for amendment to requests for appeal, an appeal to the DAB of an ALJ decision regarding LCDs and NCDs must be complete. If the appeal request is unacceptable, the DAB must dismiss the appeal.

## NOTES

1. *See* 70 Fed. Reg. 11,420 (Mar. 8, 2005).
2. *See* 67 Fed. Reg. 69,312 (Nov. 15, 2002).
3. *See* 42 C.F.R. § 405.944(b).
4. *Id.*
5. *See* HHS and SSA, Report to Congress, *Plan for the Transfer of Responsibility for Medicare Appeals* (Mar. 2004).
6. New regulations at §§ 405.1205, 405.1206 for Inpatient Hospital Expedited Determinations were published on November 27, 2006, and will be implemented July 1, 2007. They will replace these regulations at § 405.1206.
7. Revised regulations at § 412.42(c) were published on November 27, 2006, and will be implemented July 1, 2007.

# CHAPTER 3

# Provider Appeals

## MEDICARE PART A APPEALS BEFORE THE PROVIDER REIMBURSEMENT REVIEW BOARD (42 C.F.R. PART 405 (SUBPART R))

### Overview

A provider of services dissatisfied with the amount of reimbursement received from the Medicare program may appeal Part A and Part B payment issues to the Provider Reimbursement Review Board (PRRB or the Board). Congress created the PRRB in 1972 and the statutory authority for the Board is found at 42 U.S.C. § 1395oo. The Board was created to give Medicare providers an independent forum for resolving payment disputes arising from final determinations made by fiscal intermediaries (FI).

These disputes are generally challenges by a provider alleging that the FI improperly applied certain regulations or manual provisions in determining the amount of reimbursement to which the provider is entitled. The Board is composed of five members who are appointed by the Secretary to serve three-year terms which are renewable once for an additional three years. The statute requires that the Board members be knowledgeable about provider reimbursement and that one member must be a certified public accountant.[1] The Board is administratively staffed by the CMS Office of Hearings.

### What May Be Appealed? (42 C.F.R. §§ 405.1801, .1804)

A Medicare provider of services annually files a cost report with its Medicare FI. A provider of services[2] is defined by statute to include a hospital, rural primary care hospital, a skilled nursing facility (SNF), a comprehensive outpatient rehabilitation facility (CORF), a home health agency (HHA), or a hospice program. In the cost report, the provider identifies all of the items and services provided to Medicare beneficiaries for which the provider believes it is entitled to be reimbursed by the Medicare program.

The FI audits the provider's cost report. Upon completion of the audit, the FI issues to the provider a notice of program reimbursement (NPR). If the provider is dissatisfied with the total amount of reimbursement determined by the FI and meets certain jurisdictional requirements, the provider may appeal to the PRRB. The threshold jurisdictional requirements for a Board appeal are: (1) the appeal must be from a FI determination; (2) the appeal must be filed within 180 days of the date of the final determination; and (3) there must be at least $10,000[3] in dispute.[4] Additionally, the PRRB will hear appeals from final determinations on end-stage renal disease (ESRD) exception requests issued by CMS, as well as final determinations on requests for Tax Equity and Fiscal Responsibility Act of 1982 (TEFRA) exceptions and adjustments to rate-of-increase ceiling, also issued by CMS.[5]

## Who May Appeal? (42 C.F.R. § 405.1835)

A provider of services dissatisfied with a final determination issued by either the FI, Centers for Medicare & Medicaid Services (CMS), or the Secretary may file an appeal with the PRRB. No other individual, entity, or party has a right to a hearing before the Board. Issues may be appealed in one of three ways: (1) individual provider appeal—see jurisdiction requirements set forth above; (2) optional group appeal—a group of providers may bring an appeal before the PRRB provided that each provider in the group would be entitled to such a PRRB hearing, but for the amount in controversy, the matters at issue involve a common question of fact or interpretation of law, regulations or CMS Rulings, and the aggregate amount in controversy must equal $50,000; or (3) mandatory group appeal—providers that are under common ownership or control appealing an issue that is common to more than one provider, and meeting the $50,000 amount in controversy requirement for a group appeal, must form group appeals for the issues they have in common.[6] In addition to the providers, the FI responsible for the final determination under appeal is a party to the dispute. Neither the Secretary nor CMS may be made a party to the proceedings.[7]

## Appeals Process (42 C.F.R. § 405.1835–.1877)[8]

### *Filing an Appeal (42 C.F.R. § 405.1835)*

A provider of services dissatisfied with a final determination from a FI must file a request for a hearing before the PRRB. The provider's request for a Board hearing must be submitted in writing to the Board and the request must include: (1) a demonstration that the provider satisfies the requirements for a Board hearing, including a specific identification of the

FI or Secretary determination under appeal; (2) for each specific item at issue, an explanation of the provider's dissatisfaction with the FI or Secretary determination under appeal, including an explanation of why the provider believes Medicare payment is incorrect for each disputed item; how and why the provider believes Medicare payment must be determined differently for each disputed item; and (3) a copy of the FI or Secretary determination under appeal and any other documentary evidence the provider considers necessary. A provider may identify additional aspects of the FI's determination with which it is dissatisfied and add those to its hearing request up to the time of the hearing.[9]

Upon receipt of a provider's written appeal request, the PRRB will notify the provider in writing of its case number, position paper due dates, and tentative hearing date. The PRRB instructions are available online and contain detailed information about its hearing procedures. The instructions can be found at http://www.cms.hhs.gov/providers/prrb/prrb.asp.

Prior to the hearing, parties may engage in discovery.[10] Often the parties are able to resolve their disputes without going to a hearing. The PRRB encourages the parties to administratively resolve issues prior to a hearing wherever possible and provides mediators for those parties interested in alternative dispute resolution.[11]

### *Expedited Judicial Review (42 C.F.R. § 405.1842)*

A provider may seek expedited judicial review (EJR) of a legal question relevant to a specific matter at issue in a PRRB appeal if there is Board jurisdiction to conduct a hearing on the matter and the Board determines that it lacks the authority to decide the legal question.[12] Specifically, the Board does not have the authority to invalidate any provisions of Title XVIII of the Act or regulations issued to implement the Act. The Board also must comply with all CMS Rulings and must give great weight to interpretive rules, general statements of policy, and rules of agency organization, procedure, and practice established by CMS.

### *PRRB Hearing and Decision (42 C.F.R. § 405.1845, .1869, .1871)*

For those parties that are unable to administratively resolve their disputes, the PRRB will conduct a formal administrative hearing. The hearings are adversarial. Witnesses are examined and evidence is presented by both parties to the appeal. A transcript is made of the proceedings. After a hearing, the PRRB will issue a written decision deciding the merits of the specific matter at issue.

### *Administrator's Review (42 C.F.R. § 405.1875)*

The CMS Administrator, at his or her discretion, may immediately review any final decision of the PRRB. Non-final decisions or actions of the Board are generally not immediately reviewable. The Administrator may exercise this discretionary review authority on his or her own motion, or in response to a request from a party to the appeal, CMS, or in some instances another affected non-party to the Board appeal. All requests for Administrator review must be sent to the CMS Office of the Attorney Advisor. If the Administrator decides to review the PRRB decision, he or she must do so no later than sixty days after the date of receipt by the provider of the reviewable decision.

### *Judicial Review (42 C.F.R. § 405.1877)*

A provider has a right to obtain judicial review of a final decision of the Board, or of a timely reversal, affirmation, or modification by the Administrator of a final PRRB decision. Providers seeking judicial review must file a civil action in a federal district court with venue, no later than sixty days after the date of receipt by the provider of a final Board or Administrator decision. The Secretary, not the CMS Administrator or CMS, is the proper defendant in such a civil action.

## Practical Tips

**Do not miss your filing deadline.** Providers and/or their counsel miss the filing deadline for a variety of reasons, including change of personnel, mergers, etc. Although the regulations give the PRRB the authority to extend a filing deadline for good cause, the PRRB rarely considers anything other than an extraordinary event (a fire, a hurricane, an earthquake) as a basis for an extension.

Additionally, the courts have generally supported the PRRB when it has dismissed cases for a missed deadline.[13] So do not miss the filing deadline to begin with! For other filings, if you miss a due date, ask for an extension as soon as you realize you missed the due date and file the missing document at the same time. Again, while the Board is loath to grant extensions of time and/or reinstate cases dismissed for missed due dates, if your case has not already been dismissed, the Board may grant your request and accept the missing document.

**Request that your case be mediated.** The PRRB has a staff of trained mediators who will meet with the parties to an appeal and attempt to work out a mutually acceptable resolution. The average case takes at least three years to work through the PRRB process, and usually at least four years to get to district court should the provider not prevail before the CMS Administrator. Most cases have issues that do not need to be decided by the PRRB, but can instead be resolved through discussions between the parties.

Mediation not only speeds up the process (cases that are mediated can be resolved in as little as one year) but, subsequent to the initial appeal filing, mediation also allows the parties to defer the filing requirements until the mediation process has finished. Therefore, if you have a case with six issues and are able to resolve five through mediation, your position papers and other Board filings will cover only the remaining issue and not the five previously settled. This shortens the time it takes to resolve the appeal and saves both parties valuable resources.

**Keep an open dialog with your FI.** A provider that receives a NPR it is dissatisfied with from its FI should immediately contact the intermediary to determine what is needed to resolve the outstanding issues. Fiscal intermediaries are under tight time constraints to complete audit work and issue NPRs. It may be that the FI is missing a particular document that the provider can readily provide. (This is often the case when, during the year, there has been a change of ownership or management.) Rather than going through the formal appeals process, see if you can resolve some of the issues before it is time to file your appeal with the Board, or between filing the request for hearing and the hearing. Again, this will conserve both time and resources in getting the appeal resolved.

## MEDICARE GEOGRAPHIC CLASSIFICATION APPEALS (42 C.F.R. 412.230–.280)

### Overview

Effective for fiscal year 2005 and subsequent fiscal years, an individual hospital may be redesignated[14] from a rural area to an urban area, from a rural area to another rural area, or from an urban area to another urban area for the purpose of using the other area's wage index value. To be redesignated to another rural area or an urban area, a hospital must demonstrate a close proximity to the area to which it seeks redesignation by meeting certain criteria. Certain limitations apply including that a hospital may not be redesignated to more than one area.[15] Wage index reclassification only applies to payment made under the inpatient prospective payment system (IPPS). To use another area's wage index for IPPS, hospitals may apply to the Medicare Geographic Classification Review Board (MGCRB). This does not apply to outpatient services.

The regulations outline specific criteria that must be met in order to apply for redesignation.[16] Hospitals must submit applications for redesignation to the MGCRB. The MGCRB consists of five members, including a Chairman, all of whom are appointed by the Secretary. Members are appointed for three-year terms and may be reappointed. The MGCRB must include two members who are representative of prospective payment system hospitals located in rural areas and at least one individual who is knowledgeable in analyzing the costs of inpatient services.

### What May Be Appealed?

An IPPS hospital seeking redesignation to a different rural or urban area has the right to submit an application to the MGCRB. A hospital may apply for redesignation individually, as a member of a group of hospitals, or as a member of an application for a Statewide Wage Index area including all Medicare IPPS hospitals in that state.[17] Additionally, a group of hospitals has the right to submit an application to the MGCRB requesting redesignation of all prospective payment hospitals in a county if all prospective payment hospitals located in that county agree to the request. The MGCRB will make a determination on the application and will issue a decision. Unless reviewed by the CMS Administrator, that decision is final and binding.

### Who May Appeal? (42 C.F.R. § 412.258)

The parties to the MGCRB proceeding are the hospital or group of hospitals requesting a change in geographic designation.

### Appeals Process (42 C.F.R. §§ 412.256–.273)

In order to start the reclassification process, a prospective payment hospital must complete and submit an application to the MGCRB with a copy to CMS. Hospitals must apply to the MGCRB to reclassify by September 1 of the year preceding the year during which reclassification is sought. For example, an application for reclassification effective for FY 2008–FY 2010 would need to be submitted by September 1, 2006. Note that September 1 is the filing deadline unless it falls on a federal holiday or a non-work day. Then, the filing due date is the next business day. The application must be submitted by mail and facsimiles or other electronic filings will not be accepted. The criteria for such applications are set forth at 42 C.F.R. § 412.256.

The MGCRB will review the application within fifteen days of receipt to determine whether the application is complete. If the MGCRB determines that the application is incomplete, it will notify the hospital with a copy to CMS, within the fifteen-day period that the MGCRB has determined that the application is incomplete and it may dismiss the application if a complete application is not filed by September 1.

If the MGCRB dismisses the case, the hospital may appeal the MGCRB dismissal to the Administrator within fifteen days of the date of the notice of dismissal. The Administrator has twenty days to affirm or reverse the dismissal. If the Administrator reverses the dismissal, the case will be remanded to the MGCRB to determine whether reclassification is appropriate.

As noted above, a complete application must be received by the MGCRB no later than the first day of the thirteen-month period preceding the federal fiscal year for which reclassification is requested (September 1). Once the MGCRB determines that a hospital's application is complete, it notifies the hospital in writing with a copy to CMS that the application is complete and the case may proceed to hearing. CMS has thirty days from the date the agency receives notice of the completed application to submit written comments and recommendations to the MGCRB (with a copy to the hospital). The hospital then has fifteen days from the date it receives CMS's comments to submit responsive comments to the MGCRB (with a copy to CMS).

If the MGCRB decides that an oral hearing is necessary, it will set the time and place for the hearing and will notify the parties in writing, with a copy to CMS. Before a decision is issued and during an oral hearing, the parties may present evidence or comments to the MGCRB concerning the case. The MGCRB will rule on the admissibility of evidence and comments and will exclude irrelevant, immaterial, or unduly repetitious evidence and comments. A complete record of the proceedings before the MGCRB is made in all cases. The record will not be closed until a decision has been issued by the MGCRB. A transcript of an oral hearing will be made at a party's request and at the expense of the requesting party. The MGCRB rarely grants a hospital an oral hearing because of the statutory time constraints on the Board's decision-making process requiring decisions to be issued within 180 days of the September 1 filing deadline.

The MGCRB may affirm or change a hospital's geographic designation. The MGCRB's decision is based on evidence in the record including the hospital's application and any other evidence obtained or received by the MGCRB. A wage index classification change is effective for three years beginning with discharges occurring on the first day (October 1) of the second federal fiscal year in which the complete application is filed. The MGCRB notifies the parties in writing, with a copy to CMS, and issues a decision within 180 days (March 1) after the first day of the thirteen-month period preceding the federal fiscal year for which a hospital has filed a complete application. The hospital has fifteen days from the date of the decision to request Administrator review.

### *Administrator's Review (42 C.F.R. § 412.278)*

A hospital or a group of hospitals dissatisfied with the MGCRB's decision regarding geographic designation may ask the CMS Administrator to review the decision. The request for review must be in writing and must be received by the Administrator within fifteen days after the date the MGCRB issues the decision. CMS has fifteen days thereafter to submit to the Administrator any comments (with copies to the hospital). Within ten days of receipt of CMS's submission, the hospital may submit in writing a response to the Administrator, again with a copy to CMS.

The Administrator may, at his or her discretion, review any final MGCRB decision. If the Administrator decides to do so, he or she will promptly notify the hospital that the decision will be reviewed. The notice of review will indicate which issues are being reviewed and also will include copies of any CMS comments received concerning the decision.

The hospital then has fifteen days to submit a response in writing to the Administrator with a copy to CMS. The regulations spell out the criteria for such discretionary review (*see* 42 C.F.R. § 412.278(d)). The regulations require that the Administrator may not receive or consider any new evidence and must issue a decision based only on the record as it appeared before the MGCRB. In cases where the hospital has requested review, the Administrator must issue a decision within ninety days, though at his or her discretion for good cause shown, the Administrator may toll the ninety-day requirement. In cases where the review was at the discretion of the Administrator, a decision must be issued within 105 days of the MGCRB decision. The Administrator's decision is the final Departmental decision *and is not subject to judicial review*.

## Practical Tips

**File your reclassification application on time.** The regulations make no provisions for a good cause exception for filing a late application. Failure to timely file an application with the MGCRB means that the applicant must wait until the next year to file, thereby delaying any chance of reclassification until three years later.

**Use the official application form or an exact copy; sign and date the affidavit—it is part of the application.** Because of the annual changes CMS makes to the IPPS regulations, the MGCRB application also changes every year. Contact the CMS Office of Hearings in order to ensure you are using the correct application. Failure to sign and date the affidavit means the application is not complete and may be rejected.

**Submit an application for reclassification to the area or areas for which you want consideration.** If you want to be considered for more than one area, you must submit an application for each area. Mark your applications primary, secondary, etc., to indicate order of preference.

**After the filing deadline, do not amend your requested area of reclassification.** The MGCRB considers amended applications to be new applications. Such an application would be dismissed for late filing.

## HMO AND CMP CONTRACT APPEALS (42 C.F.R. §§ 417.640–.694)

### Overview

Section 1876 of the Act (42 U.S.C. § 1395mm) provides for Medicare payments to health maintenance organizations (HMOs) and Competitive Medical Plans (CMPs) that contract with CMS to enroll Medicare beneficiaries and furnish Medicare-covered health care services. Section 234 of the Medicare Prescription Drug, Improvement, and Modernization Act of 2003 (MMA) requires § 1876 contractors to operate under the same provisions as Medicare Advantage (MA) plans where two plans of the same type enter the cost plan contract's service area. Effective January 1, 2006, the rights, procedures, and requirements relating to beneficiary appeals and grievances set forth in subpart M of part 422 also apply where Medicare enrollees are dissatisfied with a determination made by a HMO or CMP.[18]

The regulations found at part 417, subpart R, provide an appeal process for review of CMS determinations concerning HMO and CMP contracts.

### What May Be Appealed? (42 C.F.R. § 416.640)

The following initial determinations may be reviewed: (1) a determination by CMS that a HMO or CMP is not qualified to enter into a contract with CMS; (2) a determination that a HMO or CMP is qualified only for a reasonable cost contract; and (3) a determination to terminate or a refusal to renew such a contract because the HMO or CMP has failed to substantially carry out the terms of the contract, no longer meets the applicable conditions, is carrying out the contract in a manner inconsistent with the efficient and effective administration of the statute, or the HMO or CMP has failed to comply with the composition of enrollment requirements.

## Who May Appeal? (42 C.F.R. § 417.660)

A HMO or CMP that has been determined to be qualified only for a reasonable cost contract or whose contract with CMS has been terminated or has not been renewed may appeal.

## Appeals Process

### *Initial Determination (42 C.F.R. § 417.644)*

CMS makes an initial determination and notifies the HMO or CMP in writing. The notice specifies the reasons for the determination and the HMO's or CMP's right to request reconsideration. CMS must mail the notice of termination to the HMO or CMP at least ninety days before the end of the contract period, or in the case of a termination, at least ninety days before the effective date of the termination. The initial determination is final and binding unless a request is made for a reconsideration or it is revised pursuant to a reopening.

### *Reconsideration (42 C.F.R. § 417.650)*

Reconsideration is the first step for appealing a determination by CMS to terminate the HMO or CMP contract. A request for reconsideration must be made in writing and filed with any CMS office within sixty days from the date of the notice of initial determination. CMS may, in response to a party's written petition showing good cause, accept a request for reconsideration after the expiration of the sixty-day period.

The parties to the reconsideration have the opportunity to present as evidence any documents or written statements that are relevant and material to the matters at issue. CMS issues a reconsideration affirming, reversing, or modifying the initial determination. The decision is based on a review of the initial determination, the evidence and findings on which it was based, and any other written evidence submitted before notice of the reconsidered determination is mailed, including facts relating to the status of the HMO or CMP subsequent to the initial determination. CMS gives the parties written notice of the reconsidered determination, including the specific reasons for the determination, and informs the HMO or CMP of its right to a hearing if dissatisfied with the decision.

### *Hearing Officer Review (42 C.F.R. §§ 417.660–.690)*

A request for a hearing must be made in writing and filed by an authorized official of the entity, HMO, or CMP that was a party to the determination under appeal. The request may be filed with any CMS office and must be filed within sixty days after the date of receipt of the notice of the initial or reconsidered determination. The regulations allow CMS to grant an extension of time for filing a request for hearing for good cause shown. CMS will designate a hearing officer to conduct the hearing. The hearing officer does not have to be an ALJ. The regulations allow for disqualification of a hearing officer.[19] If the hearing officer is disqualified, CMS will appoint another hearing officer to conduct the hearing.

A party may appoint its own representative to the hearing. Anyone not disqualified or suspended from acting as a representative before CMS or otherwise prohibited by law may represent the HMO or CMP. The representative is responsible for giving or accepting any notice or request relevant to the proceedings, may present evidence and allegations as to the facts and law, and may obtain information to the same extent as the party. Prehearing discovery is permitted if timely requested by a party. The hearing officer's order on all discovery matters is final.

The hearing is open to the parties and to the public. The hearing officer will inquire into all the matters at issue and will receive in evidence the testimony of the witnesses and any relevant and material documents. The hearing officer may examine the witnesses, and each party is permitted to examine their witnesses and to cross-examine witnesses of other parties. A complete record of the proceedings at the hearing is made and transcribed and made available to all parties upon request. The record may not be closed until a hearing decision has been issued. In exercising his or her authority, the hearing officer is bound by the provisions of Title XVIII, as well as the regulations and general instructions issued by CMS.

The regulations do not set a specific time frame for issuance of the hearing officer's decision, stating only that the decision should be issued "as soon as practical after the close of the hearing." The hearing officer must issue a written decision that is based on the record, and contains separately numbered findings of fact and conclusions of law. The hearing officer provides a copy of the decision to each party, and the decision is final and binding unless it is reopened and revised.

### *Reopening of Initial or Reconsidered Determination or Decision by a Hearing Officer (42 C.F.R. § 417.692)*

An initial or reconsidered determination may be reopened and revised by CMS upon its own motion within one year of the date of the notice of the determination. A final decision of the hearing officer may be reopened and revised by the hearing officer upon the hearing officer's own motion within one year of the notice of the hearing decision.

## HOSPICE CARE PAYMENT APPEALS (42 C.F.R. § 418.311)

### Overview

Medicare beneficiaries entitled to Part A who have terminal illnesses, and a life expectancy of six months or less, may opt for hospice benefits instead of standard Medicare coverage.[20] Pursuant to the Act, CMS establishes payment amounts for specific categories of covered hospice care.[21] These categories include: routine home care day; continuous home care day; inpatient respite care day; and general inpatient care day. The payment amounts for the categories of hospice care are fixed payment rates established by CMS.

The FI reimburses the hospice a payment amount for each day for which an eligible Medicare beneficiary is under the hospice's care. Regulations found at 42 C.F.R. §§ 418.302–.309 set forth the methodology for determining the proper payment rate. A hospice that believes its payments have not been properly determined may request a review from the FI or the PRRB if the amount in controversy is at least $1,000 or $10,000, respectively. The procedures for appeals before the PRRB are discussed at 35–39, and the regulations are found at 42 C.F.R. Part 405, Subpart R. The methods and standards for the calculation of payment rates by CMS are not subject to appeal.

## PROVIDER AGREEMENT TERMINATION APPEALS (42 C.F.R. § 489.52, .53, .54)

### Overview

Pursuant to § 1866 (42 U.S.C. § 1395cc) of the Act, providers seeking payment for services provided to Medicare beneficiaries must first enter into an agreement with the Secretary of the Department of Health and Human Services (HHS). Before entering into such an agreement, the prospective provider must meet a variety of requirements, undergo a survey process, and file the required forms for a provider agreement. Once a provider has met the applicable conditions of participation and conditions of coverage, its provider agreement is effective.

A provider may voluntarily terminate its provider agreement by filing a written notice with CMS. CMS may accept the termination date proposed by the provider if one is offered, or it may set a different date not to exceed six months from the date on the provider's notice of intent to terminate.[22] The provider must give notice to the public at least fifteen days before the effective date of termination.

CMS may terminate a provider agreement with a provider if CMS finds that the provider has failed to meet certain requirements.[23] Examples of reasons for termination by CMS include among other things: (1) the provider no longer meets the appropriate conditions of participation; (2) the provider fails to supply information necessary to determine whether payments are due or were due and the amounts of such payments; (3) the provider refuses to permit examination of its fiscal records, including medical records; or (4) the provider fails to comply with civil rights requirements. CMS gives the provider notice of termination at least fifteen days before the effective date of the termination of the provider agreement.

There are two exceptions to this requirement, both concerning situations where CMS has identified deficiencies in care that pose immediate jeopardy to patient safety.[24] For hospitals with emergency departments, if CMS finds the provider to be in violation of 42 C.F.R. § 489.24(a)–(e), and further determines that the violation poses immediate jeopardy to the health and safety of individuals who present themselves to the hospital for emergency services, CMS will notify the hospital that its provider agreement will be terminated within twenty-three days if it does not correct the deficiencies or refute the finding. If the deficiencies are not corrected, CMS will give the hospital a final notice of termination and concurrent notice to the public at least two, but not more than four, days before the effective date of termination of the provider agreement. For SNFs with deficiencies identified by CMS as posing immediate jeopardy to the health or safety of residents, CMS gives notice at least two days before the effective date of the termination of the provider agreement.

Finally, the HHS, Office of Inspector General (OIG) may terminate a provider agreement of any provider: (1) having knowingly and willfully made false statements or representations of material facts for use in an application or request for Medicare payment; (2) submitting or causing to be submitted requests for Medicare payment of amounts that substantially exceed the costs incurred in furnishing the services for which payment is requested; or (3) furnishing services that the OIG has determined to be substantially in excess of the needs of the individual or are of a quality that fails to meet professionally recognized standards of health care.[25]

The OIG will give the provider notice of termination at least fifteen days before the effective date of the termination of the agreement and will concurrently give notice of the termination to the public. A provider may appeal a termination of its agreement by the OIG in accordance with 42 C.F.R. § 1001.2007.

### What May Be Appealed and Who May Appeal? (42 C.F.R. § 489.53(c)(3), (4))

The notice of termination of the provider agreement, issued by CMS, may be appealed by the provider. The notice states the reasons for the termination, provides the effective date, and explains the extent to which services may continue to be provided after that date. CMS will concurrently give notice of the termination to the public. This is typically done through a notice published in the provider's local public newspaper.

### Appeals Process (42 C.F.R. § 489.53(d))

A provider may appeal the termination of its provider agreement by CMS in accordance with the provisions set forth at 42 C.F.R. Part 498.[26]

## PROVIDER AND SUPPLIER ENROLLMENT DENIAL APPEALS (42 C.F.R. PART 498)

### Overview

Certain practitioners and suppliers, including Durable Medical Equipment, Prosthetics, Orthotics, and Supplies (DMEPOS) suppliers, must enroll in the Medicare program by completing the CMS-855 enrollment form. When the application is approved, a supplier billing number is issued to the practitioner or supplier, and must be used in order to receive payment for Medicare services furnished. Prior to the enactment of MMA, the Act did not include appeal rights for suppliers and practitioners whose applications for enrollment were denied.

Although there was no specific statutory requirement to create an appeals process, CMS established three separate mechanisms by which suppliers and practitioners could seek to appeal adverse enrollment decisions. Certain suppliers and practitioners had appeal rights pursuant to Part 498 of the regulations.[27] Specific types of suppliers (as identified at 42 C.F.R. § 498.2) dissatisfied with an initial determination that its services no longer met the conditions of coverage were entitled to a hearing before an Administrative Law Judge (ALJ). If dissatisfied with the ALJ's decision, the supplier could request review of the decision by the Departmental Appeals Board (DAB). Those suppliers generally did not have the right to seek judicial review of the decision of the DAB.

CMS also established by regulation an appeal process for DMEPOS suppliers seeking to contest a denial of an application for a billing number. That process included a hearing before a CMS hearing officer who was required to issue a written decision within two weeks of the hearing. No further right of administrative or judicial review was available.[28]

Additionally, in December 1998, CMS issued Ruling 98-1 establishing an appeals process for physicians and nonphysician practitioners whose application for an enrollment number had been denied. That process was similar to the process for DMEPOS suppliers and also did not include any further right of administrative or judicial review.

Section 936(a) of the MMA eliminated the various provider and supplier appeals processes developed over the years by CMS and established a uniform appeals process for all DMEPOS suppliers, and physician and nonphysician practitioners.[29] The MMA provisions required the Secretary to establish a process for providers and suppliers to appeal adverse enrollment decisions, extending to all practitioners and suppliers the right to a hearing before an ALJ and ultimately judicial review of an enrollment denial. While the MMA did not specifically direct that such appeals would be processed by the DAB's ALJs, the MMA did direct that all such appeals were to be afforded a hearing and judicial review no later than December 2004. At that time, the only ALJs in HHS were at the DAB. As such, all practitioner and supplier enrollment denial appeals were transferred as of December 2004 and are now processed by the DAB's ALJs pursuant to the regulations at 42 C.F.R. § 498, the same regulations and process in use for provider termination and exclusion appeals.[30]

## NOTES

1. *See* 42 C.F.R. §§ 405.1845, .1847.
2. *See* 42 U.S.C. § 1395x(u).
3. Cases involving less than $10,000 in dispute are appealed to the Intermediary Hearing Officer. *See* 42 C.F.R. §§ 405.1809–.1833.
4. *See* 42 C.F.R. §§ 405.1835, .1873.
5. *See* 42 C.F.R. § 413.194, 413.40(e).
6. *See* 42 U.S.C. § 1395oo(b); 42 C.F.R. § 405.1837.
7. *See* 42 C.F.R. § 405.1843.
8. On June 25, 2004, CMS published a proposed rule to update, clarify, and revise various provisions of the regulations governing provider reimbursement determinations and appeals, as set forth in 42 C.F.R. Part 405. *See* 69 Fed. Reg. 35,716 (June 25, 2004). Publication of the final rule is expected in early 2007.
9. *See* 42 C.F.R. § 405.1841. The proposed rule limits the ability of a provider to add issues to a pending appeal to sixty days after the expiration of the initial 180-day appeal period. *See* 69 Fed. Regs. 35,716, 35,750 (June 25, 2004).
10. *See* 42 C.F.R. § 405.1853.
11. *See* PRRB Instructions at http://www.cms.hhs.gov/providers/prrb/prrb.asp.

12. *See* 42 C.F.R. § 405.1867 (outlining the Board's scope of authority).

13. *See* Michael Reese Hosp. and Medical Ctr. v. Thompson, 427 F.3d 436 (7th Cir. 2005); High Country Home Health v. Thompson, 359 F.3d 1307 (10th Cir. 2004); UHI v. Thompson, 250 F.3d 993 (6th Cir. 2001); Inova Alexandria Hosp. v. Shalala, 244 F.3d 342 (4th Cir. 2001).

14. "Redesignation" and "reclassification" are used interchangeably throughout the MGCRB regulations.

15. *See* 42 C.F.R. § 412.230(a)(5).

16. *See* 42 C.F.R. §§ 412.232-.235.

17. The MGCRB has only received one Statewide Wage Index application which was withdrawn before a decision was issued. An appropriate statewide entity (e.g., a state's department of health or a state hospital association) must file the application.

18. *See* 70 Fed. Reg. 4,713 (Sept. 12, 2005).

19. *See* 42 C.F.R. § 417.668.

20. *See* 42 U.S.C. § 1395x(dd)(1) (defining hospice care and the Medicare hospice program).

21. *See* 42 U.S.C. § 1395f(i)(1)(A).

22. *See* 42 C.F.R. § 489.52(a).

23. *See* 42 C.F.R. § 489.53(a)(1)-(14).

24. *See* 42 C.F.R. § 489.53(c)(2).

25. *See* 42 C.F.R. § 489.54; 42 C.F.R. § 1001, Subparts B and C.

26. For the Part 498 appeals process, see 42 C.F.R. § Part 498 at 90-93.

27. *See* 42 C.F.R. § 498.2.

28. *See* 42 C.F.R. § 405.874.

29. *See* 42 U.S.C. § 1395cc(j).

30. For provider termination and exclusion appeals process, see 42 C.F.R. Part 498, at 90-93.

# CHAPTER 4

# Part C Appeals

## MEDICARE ADVANTAGE (PART C) APPEALS (42 C.F.R. PART 422 (SUBPART M))

### Overview

Enrollees in a Medicare Advantage (MA) organization are entitled to have their complaints about any part of their care as a plan member addressed by their plan. A complaint under the Part C program may be handled as a grievance, a coverage determination, or an appeal, depending on the subject of the complaint. Subpart M of Part 422 establishes the procedures that MA organizations must follow for processing Part C grievances, coverage determinations, and appeals.

### What May Be Appealed and Who May Appeal?

Section 1852(f) (42 U.S.C. § 1395w-22(f)) of the Act provides that a MA organization must establish meaningful grievance procedures. Section 1852(g) (42 U.S.C. § 1395w-22(g)) of the Act establishes requirements that a MA organization must meet concerning organization determinations and appeals. This subpart of the regulations addresses both grievance procedures and appeals of organization determinations.[1]

#### *Grievances (42 C.F.R. § 422.564)*

A *grievance* is defined as any complaint or dispute (other than one that constitutes an organization determination) expressing dissatisfaction with any aspect of a MA organization's or provider's operations, activities, or behavior, regardless of whether remedial action is requested.[2] The regulations require that each MA organization must have established: (1) grievance procedures for addressing issues that do not involve organization determinations; (2) procedures for making timely organization determinations; and (3) appeal procedures for issues that involve organization determinations.

When a MA organization receives a complaint, it must promptly determine and inform the enrollee whether the complaint is subject to its grievance procedures or appeal procedures. Grievances may be filed by enrollees or their representative.[3] An enrollee may file a grievance with its MA organization either orally or in writing, and must do so no later than sixty days after the event or incident that precipitates the grievance. The MA organization must notify the enrollee of its decision as expeditiously as the case requires, based upon the enrollee's health status, but no later than thirty days after the date the MA organization receives the grievance. The MA organization may extend the thirty-day time frame up to fourteen days if the enrollee requests the extension, or the organization can justify the need for additional information and document how the delay is in the interest of the enrollee.

The MA organization must inform the enrollee of the disposition of the grievance using the following procedures: (1) all grievances submitted in writing must be responded to in writing; (2) grievances submitted orally may be responded to either orally or in writing, unless the enrollee requests a written response; and (3) all grievances related to quality of care, regardless of filing format, must be responded to in writing and must include a description of the enrollee's right to file a written complaint with the quality improvement organization (QIO).

*Expedited grievances.* A MA organization must respond to an enrollee's grievance within twenty-four hours (1) if the complaint involves a MA organization's decision to invoke an extension relating to an organization determination or reconsideration, or (2) if the complaint involves a MA organization's refusal to grant the enrollee's request for an expedited organization determination or reconsideration.

### *Organization Determinations (42 C.F.R. §§ 422.566–.568)*

*Organization determinations* are defined as actions that include any determination made by a MA organization with respect to: (1) payment for temporarily out of the area renal dialysis services, emergency services, post-stabilization care, or urgently needed services; (2) payment for any other health services furnished by a provider other than the MA organization that the enrollee believes are covered under Medicare, or if not covered under Medicare should have been furnished, arranged for, or reimbursed by the MA organization; (3) the MA organization's refusal to provide or pay for services, in whole or in part, for services the enrollee believes should be furnished or arranged for by the MA organization;

(4) discontinuation or reduction of a service if the enrollee believes that continuation of the services is medically necessary; and (5) failure of the MA organization to approve, furnish, arrange for, or provide payment for health care services in a timely manner, or to provide the enrollee with timely notice of an adverse determination, such that a delay would adversely affect the health of the enrollee.[4]

A MA organization must have a standard procedure for making determinations and must also have an expedited procedure for situations in which applying the standard procedure could seriously jeopardize the enrollee's life, health, or ability to regain maximum function.

*Who can request an organization determination.* The enrollee or their representative, an assignee of the enrollee (that is a physician or other provider who has furnished a service to the enrollee and formally agrees to waive any right to payment from the enrollee for that service), or the legal representative of a deceased enrollee's estate may request an organization determination.[5]

*Time frame for request for service.* When a party has made a request for service, the MA organization must notify the enrollee of its determination as expeditiously as the enrollee's condition requires, but no later than fourteen calendar days after the date the MA organization receives the request. The MA organization may extend the time frame if it is requested by the enrollee, or if the organization justifies a need for additional information and explains how the delay is in the interest of the enrollee.

*Time frame for requests for payment.* The MA organization must process requests for payment according to the prompt payment provisions at 42 C.F.R. § 422.520.

If the MA organization decides to deny service or payment in whole or in part, or if the enrollee disagrees with the MA organization's decision to discontinue or reduce the level of care for an ongoing course of treatment, or if an enrollee requests a MA to provide an explanation of a practitioner's denial of an item or service in whole or in part, the MA organization must give the enrollee written notice of the determination.

*Form and content of the MA organization notice.* The notice of any denial must: (1) use approved notice language in a readable and understandable form; (2) state the specific reasons for the denial; and (3) inform the enrollee of his or her right to a reconsideration. If the MA organization fails to provide the enrollee with timely notice of an organization determination, the failure itself constitutes an adverse organization determination and may be appealed.

### *Expediting Certain Organization Determinations (42 C.F.R. § 422.570–.572)*

An enrollee or a physician (regardless of whether the physician is affiliated with the MA organization) may request that a MA organization expedite an organization determination involving issues related to the MA organization's refusal to pay for services in whole or in part that the enrollee believes should be furnished or arranged for by the MA organization, or issues related to the discontinuation or reduction of a service if the enrollee believes the service is medically necessary.

To request an expedited determination, an enrollee or a physician must submit an oral or written request directly to the MA organization or, if applicable, the entity responsible for making the determination. A physician may provide written or oral support for an expedited determination.

*How the MA organization must process expedited requests.* The regulations require that the MA organization must establish and maintain procedures for processing requests for expedited determinations. The MA organization must establish an efficient and convenient means for individuals to submit oral or written requests, and it must document all oral requests in writing and maintain documentation in the case file. The MA organization must promptly decide whether to expedite a determination based on the following criteria: (1) for a request made by an enrollee, the MA organization must provide an expedited determination if the organization determines that applying the standard time frame for making a determination could seriously jeopardize the life or health of the enrollee or the enrollee's ability to regain maximum function; or (2) for a request made or supported by a physician, the MA organization must provide an expedited determination if the physician indicates that applying the standard time frame for making a determination could seriously jeopardize the life or health of the enrollee or the enrollee's ability to regain maximum function.

If the MA organization denies a request for expedited determination, the organization must automatically transfer a request to the standard time frame and make a determination within fourteen days. The MA organization must also promptly orally notify the enrollee of the denial and subsequently deliver, within three calendar days, a written explanation.[6] If a MA organization grants a request for an expedited determination, it must make its determination and notify the enrollee and the physician involved as expeditiously as the enrollee's health condition requires, but no later than seventy-two hours after receiving the request.[7]

## Appeals (42 C.F.R. § 422.578–.612)

An appeal is defined as the procedure for addressing the review of adverse organization determinations of the health care services the enrollee believes he or she is entitled to receive. This includes delay in providing, arranging for, or approving the health care services, or on any amounts the enrollee must pay for services.

### *Reconsideration Procedures (42 C.F.R. § 422.578–.590)*

A party to a MA organization determination may request that the determination be reconsidered. An enrollee or physician acting on the enrollee's behalf may request an expedited reconsideration.[8] A reconsideration consists of a review of an adverse organization determination, the evidence and findings on which it was based, and any other evidence the parties submit or the MA organization or Centers for Medicare and Medicaid Services (CMS) obtains.

A party to a MA organization determination must ask for a reconsideration of the determination by making a written request to the MA organization that made the original determination. The request must be filed with the MA organization within sixty calendar days from the date of the notice of the organization determination. A person or persons who were not involved in making the organization determination must conduct the reconsideration.

If the MA organization makes a reconsidered determination that is completely favorable to the enrollee, the MA organization must issue and effectuate the determination as expeditiously as the enrollee's health condition requires, but no later than thirty calendar days from the date it receives the request for a standard reconsideration. There are provisions for extensions of time.[9] If the MA organization makes a reconsidered determination that affirms, in whole or in part, its adverse organization determination, the organization must prepare a written explanation and send the case file to the independent entity contracted by CMS as expeditiously as the enrollee's health condition requires, but no later than thirty calendar days from the date the MA organization received the request.

### *Reconsideration by an Independent Review Entity (42 C.F.R. § 422.592–.596)*

When the MA organization affirms, in whole or in part, its adverse organization determination, the issues that remain in dispute must be reviewed and resolved by an independent review entity (IRE) contracted with CMS. The IRE must conduct the review as expeditiously as the enrollee's health condition requires, but must not exceed the deadlines specified in the contract the entity has with CMS. The parties to the IRE reconsideration include all of the parties involved in the MA organization's reconsideration, with the addition of the MA organization.

When the IRE makes a reconsidered determination, it is responsible for mailing a notice of its reconsidered determination to the parties and for notifying CMS. The notice must state the specific reasons for the IRE's decisions in understandable language and, if the reconsidered determination is adverse, it must inform the parties of their right to an Administrative Law Judge (ALJ) hearing if the amount in controversy is $100 or more and describe the procedures a party must follow to obtain an ALJ hearing.[10]

### *ALJ Review (42 C.F.R. § 422.600–.602)*

If the amount remaining in dispute after reconsideration by an IRE meets the threshold requirements, any party to the reconsideration (except the MA organization) who is dissatisfied with the IRE's determination has a right to a hearing before an ALJ. A party must file a written request for an ALJ hearing. Absent an extension of time granted by the ALJ, a party must file its hearing request within sixty days of the date of the IRE's determination. The time and place for the hearing will be set in accordance with 42 C.F.R. § 405.1020.

The parties to the ALJ hearing are the parties to the reconsideration, the MA organization, and any other person or entity whose rights with respect to the reconsideration may be affected by the hearing, as determined by the ALJ. If at any time the ALJ determines that the amount in controversy does not meet the requirements of 42 C.F.R. § 422.600, the ALJ will discontinue the proceedings and dismiss the case.

### *Medicare Appeals Council (MAC) Review (42 C.F.R. § 422.608)*

Any party to the hearing, including the MA organization, who is dissatisfied with the ALJ hearing decision may request that the MAC review the ALJ's decision or dismissal. The regulations found at 42 C.F.R. §§ 405.1100–.1134 establish the requirements and procedures for MAC review.

### *Judicial Review (42 C.F.R. § 422.612)*

Any party, including the MA organization, may request judicial review upon notifying the other parties of an ALJ's decision if the MAC denied the party's request for review and the amount in controversy meets the threshold requirement established annual by the Secretary. A party also may request judicial review, after notification of the other parties, of the MAC decision if it is a final decision of CMS and the amount in controversy requirement has been satisfied.

In order to request judicial review, a party must file a civil action in a district court of the United States in accordance with § 205(g) of the Act. Regulations at 42 C.F.R. § 405.1136–.1140 describe the procedures to follow when requesting judicial review.

### *Appeals Procedures for Inpatient Hospital Settings (42 C.F.R. § 422.620–.622)*[11]

*How enrollees of MA organizations must be notified of noncovered inpatient hospital care (42 C.F.R. § 422.620).* Where a MA organization plan has authorized coverage of the inpatient hospital admission of an enrollee, either directly or by delegation (or the admission constitutes emergency or urgently needed care), the MA organization is required to issue the enrollee under the circumstances described below a written notice of noncoverage—the Notice of Discharge and Medicare Appeals Rights (NODMAR).

*Notice of discharge and Medicare appeal rights.* The model NODMAR is a written notice that is designed to inform Medicare enrollees that their covered inpatient hospital care is ending. The NODMAR must include the following: (1) the specific reason why inpatient hospital care is no longer needed or covered; (2) the effective date and time of the enrollee's liability for continued inpatient care; (3) the enrollee's appeal rights; (4) if applicable, the new lower level of care being covered in the hospital setting; and (5) any additional information specified by CMS.

The model NODMAR meets the notice requirements set forth in 42 C.F.R. § 422.620.[12] CMS encourages MA organizations to use the model form, but they are allowed to develop their own NODMAR. All NODMARs must be approved by the MA organization's Regional Office Plan Manager until such time that CMS issues a standardized form. Before the MA organization can issue a NODMAR to an enrollee, the physician who is responsible for the enrollee's inpatient hospital care must concur with the decision to discharge or lower the enrollee's level of care within the same hospital facility.

*When to issue a NODMAR.* Consistent with 42 C.F.R. § 422.620, MA organizations (and hospitals that have been delegated responsibility by a MA organization to make the discharge/noncoverage decision) will distribute the NODMAR when:

- The enrollee expresses dissatisfaction with his or her impending discharge; or
- The MA organization (or the hospital that has been delegated the responsibility) is not discharging the individual but no longer

intends to continue coverage of the inpatient hospital stay. In other words, the MA organization intends to lower the enrollee's level of care from inpatient acute to, for example, skilled nursing, within the same hospital facility (a change that could be transparent to the enrollee if no notice were provided). The MA organization should deliver the NODMAR as soon as possible after learning of the enrollee's dissatisfaction with the discharge decision, but no later than 6:00 p.m. of the day before discharge. If the enrollee is incompetent or otherwise incapable of receiving notice, the notice must be delivered to the enrollee's representative.

*Requesting Immediate QIO Review of Noncoverage of Inpatient Hospital Care (42 C.F.R. § 422.622)*

An enrollee remaining in the hospital who wishes to appeal the MA organization's discharge decision must request immediate QIO review of the determination in accordance with this section's requirements. An enrollee will not incur any additional financial liability if:

- the enrollee remains in the hospital as an inpatient;
- the enrollee submits the request for immediate review to the QIO that has an agreement with the hospital;
- the request is made in writing, by telephone, or fax; and
- the request is received by noon of the first working day after the enrollee receives written notice of the MA organization's determination that the hospital stay is no longer necessary.

The following rules apply to the immediate QIO process:

- On the date that the QIO receives the enrollee's request, the QIO must notify the MA organization that the enrollee has filed a request for immediate review;
- The MA organization and/or hospital must supply any information that the QIO requires to conduct its review. This must be made available by phone, by fax, or in writing, by the close of business of the first full working day immediately following the day the enrollee submits the request for review;
- In response to a request from the MA organization, the hospital must submit medical records and other pertinent information to the QIO by close of business of the first full working day immediately following the day the MA organization makes its request;

- The QIO must solicit the views of the enrollee who requested the immediate QIO review; and
- The QIO must make an official determination of whether continued hospitalization is medically necessary, and notify the enrollee, the hospital, and the MA organization by close of business of the first working day after it receives all necessary information from the hospital, the MA organization, or both.

An enrollee failing to request immediate QIO review in accordance with these requirements may file a request for an expedited reconsideration with the MA organization. The MA organization should expedite the request for a reconsideration. Likewise, if the QIO receives a request for immediate QIO review beyond the noon filing deadline and forwards that request to the MA organization, the MA organization should expedite that request. Thus, the MA organization would generally make another decision about the services within seventy-two hours. The financial liability rules governing immediate QIO review, however, do not apply in an expedited review situation.

*Liability for hospital costs.* A timely filed appeal for an immediate QIO review entitles the enrollee to automatic financial protection by the MA organization. This means that if the MA organization authorizes coverage of the inpatient hospital admission directly or by delegation, or this admission constitutes emergency or urgently needed care, the MA organization continues to be financially responsible for the costs of the hospital stay until noon of the calendar day following the day the QIO notifies the enrollee of its review determination.

### *Appeals Procedures for Skilled Nursing Facilities (SNFs), Comprehensive Outpatient Rehabilitation Facilities (CORFs), and Home Health Agencies (HHAs) (42 C.F.R. § 422.624–.626)*[13]

#### Notifying Enrollees of Termination of Provider Services (42 C.F.R. § 422.624)

*A termination of service* is defined as the discharge of an enrollee from covered provider services or discontinuation of covered provider services, when the enrollee has been authorized by the MA organization, either directly or by delegation, to receive an ongoing course of treatment from that provider. Termination includes cessation of coverage at the end of a course of treatment preauthorized in a discrete increment, regardless of whether the enrollee agrees that such services should end.

*Advance written notification of termination.* Prior to any termination of service, the provider of the service must deliver valid written notice to the enrollee of the MA organization's decision to terminate services. The provider must use a standardized notice, required by the Secretary, in accordance with the following procedures:

- *Timing of notice.* The provider must notify the enrollee of the MA organization's decision to terminate covered services no later than two days before the proposed end of the services. If the enrollee's services are expected to be fewer than two days in duration, the provider should notify the enrollee at the time of admission to the provider. If, in a non-institutional setting, the span of time between services exceeds two days, the notice should be given no later than the next to last time services are furnished.
- *Content of the notice.* The standardized termination notice must include the date that coverage of services ends, the date that the enrollee's financial liability for continued services begins, a description of the enrollee's right to a fast-track appeal including information about how to contact the QIO, an enrollee's right to submit evidence showing that services should continue, and the availability of other MA appeal procedures if the enrollee fails to meet the deadline for a fast-track QIO appeal.
- *Delivery of the notice.* Delivery of the termination notice generally is not valid unless the notice contains the required elements listed above and the enrollee (or the enrollee's representative) has signed and dated the notice to indicate that he or she has received the notice and can comprehend its contents.
- *Financial liability for failure to deliver valid notice.* A MA organization is financially liable for continued services until two days after the enrollee receives valid notice.

### Fast-Track Appeals of Service Terminations to QIOs (42 C.F.R. § 422.626)

An enrollee of a MA organization has a right to a fast-track appeal of a MA organization's decision to terminate provider services. An enrollee who desires a fast-track appeal must submit a request for an appeal to the QIO, in writing or by telephone, by noon of the first day after the day of delivery of the termination notice. If, due to an emergency, the QIO is closed and unable to accept the enrollee's request for a fast-track appeal, the enrollee must file a request by noon of the next business day that the QIO is open for business. If an enrollee fails to make a timely request to the QIO, he or she may request an expedited reconsideration by the MA organization, as described in 42 C.F.R. § 422.584.

Coverage of provider services continues until the date and time designated on the termination notice, unless the enrollee appeals and the QIO reverses the MA organization's decision. If the QIO's decision is delayed because the MA organization did not timely supply necessary information or records, the MA organization is liable for the costs of any additional coverage required by the delayed QIO decision. If the QIO finds the enrollee did not receive valid notice, coverage of provider services by the MA organization continues until at least two days after valid notice has been received. The burden of proof rests with the MA organization to demonstrate that termination of coverage is the correct decision either on the basis of medical necessity, or based on other Medicare coverage policies.

On the date the QIO receives the enrollee's request for a fast-track appeal, the QIO must immediately notify the MA organization and the provider that the enrollee has requested a fast-track appeal, and must notify the MA organization of its responsibility to submit required documentation. Before making its decision, the QIO also must solicit the enrollee's views regarding the reason for termination of services. The QIO must make a decision on an appeal, notify the enrollee, the MA organization, and the provider of services by close of business of the day after it receives the information necessary to make the decision.

*MA organization responsibilities.* When the QIO notifies a MA organization that an enrollee has requested a fast-track appeal, the MA organization must send a detailed notice to the enrollee by close of business of the day of the QIO's notification. The detailed termination notice must include a specific and detailed explanation why services are no longer covered, any applicable Medicare coverage rule including citations, and any applicable MA organization policy or rationale. Upon an enrollee's request, the MA organization must provide the enrollee a copy of, or access to, any documentation sent to the QIO by the MA organization.

Upon notification by the QIO of a fast-track appeal, the MA organization must supply any and all information including a copy of the notice sent to the enrollee that the QIO needs to make a decision on the appeal. The MA organization must supply this information as soon as possible, but no later than by close of business of the day the QIO notifies the MA organization that an appeal has been received from the enrollee. A MA organization is financially responsible for coverage of services regardless of whether it has delegated responsibility for authorizing coverage or termination decisions to its providers.

If a QIO reverses a MA organization's termination decision, the MA organization must provide the enrollee with a new notice. If the QIO upholds the MA organization's termination decision in whole or in part, the enrollee may request, no later than sixty days after notification, that the QIO reconsider its original decision. The QIO must issue its reconsidered determination as expeditiously as the enrollee's health condition requires, but no later than within fourteen days of receipt of the enrollee's request for reconsideration.

If the QIO reaffirms its decision in whole or in part, the enrollee may appeal the QIO's reconsidered determination to an ALJ, the MAC, or a federal court. If on reconsideration, the QIO determines that coverage of provider services should terminate on a given date, the enrollee is liable for the costs of continued services after that date unless the QIO's decision is reversed on appeal. If the QIO's determination is reversed on appeal, the MA organization must reimburse the enrollee, consistent with the appealed decision, for the costs of any covered services for which the enrollee has already paid the MA organization.

### Practical Tips

**Adequately document an enrollee's medical condition**. With respect to organization determinations, the MA organization and entities performing subsequent reviews must act as expeditiously as the enrollee's condition requires (but no later than certain timelines). As such, the enrollee's medical condition should be adequately and thoroughly documented so that determinations throughout the appeals process are timely provided.

## MEDICARE ADVANTAGE CONTRACT DENIAL AND/OR TERMINATION APPEALS (42 C.F.R. § 422.641)

### Overview

Entities seeking to contract with CMS as MA organizations must meet certain requirements. Those requirements are found at 42 C.F.R. § 422.500 *et seq*. Both a determination by CMS that an entity does not meet the qualifications to hold a contract as a MA organization and a decision by CMS to terminate an entity's existing contract have appeal rights.[14]

### What May Be Appealed? (42 C.F.R. § 422.641)

A determination by CMS that an entity is not qualified to enter into a contract with CMS under Part C to serve as a MA organization and a determination by CMS to terminate a contract with a MA organization are appealable determinations.

## Who May Appeal? (42 C.F.R. §§ 422.650(c), .660)

An authorized official of the contract applicant or MA organization that was the subject of a contract termination may file a request for reconsideration. A contract applicant that has been determined in a reconsidered determination to be unqualified to enter into such a contract with CMS under Part C or a MA organization whose contract with CMS has been terminated or has not been renewed is entitled to a hearing before a CMS hearing officer.

## Appeals Process (42 C.F.R. § 422.648–.692)

### *Reconsideration (42 C.F.R § 422.650–.658)*

The regulations require that CMS issue written notice to a MA organization when it makes a contract determination. The notice must specify the reasons for the determination and set forth the MA organization's right to request reconsideration. The request must be filed in writing with any CMS office and must be filed within fifteen days from the date of the notice of the initial determination.

CMS will permit the MA organization, or the contract applicant and the CMS official who made the determination, to submit any documents or written statements in support. CMS will notify the MA organization or the contract applicant of its reconsidered determination in writing. The redetermination is based upon a review of the contract determination, the evidence and findings that it was based on, and any other written evidence submitted before the notice of the reconsidered determination is mailed. The reconsidered determination must affirm, reverse, or modify the initial determination.

### *Hearing Officer Review (42 C.F.R. § 422.660–.690)*

If dissatisfied with the reconsidered determination, the MA organization and/or the contract applicant has the right to request a hearing. A request for a hearing must be made in writing, and filed by an authorized official of the contract applicant or MA organization that was the party to the determination under appeal. The request may be filed with any CMS office and must be filed within fifteen days after the date of the reconsidered determination. CMS will designate a hearing officer to conduct the hearing. The hearing officer need not be an ALJ. Once the request has been filed, the hearing officer will establish a time and place for the hearing, not to exceed thirty days from the receipt of the request for the hearing, and will notify the parties to the hearing in writing.

A party to the hearing may appoint as its representative at the hearing anyone not disqualified or suspended from acting as a representative before the Secretary or otherwise prohibited by law. The hearing is open to the parties and the public. The parties may present evidence by either witnesses or documentary submissions. A complete record of the proceedings at the hearing is transcribed and made available to the parties upon request. The hearing officer must issue a written decision "as soon as practical" after the close of the hearing. The hearing decision is final and binding unless it is reversed or modified by the Administrator following review.

### *Administrator's Review (42 C.F.R. § 422.692)*

A MA organization that has received a hearing decision upholding a contract termination determination may request review by the CMS Administrator within fifteen days of receiving the hearing officer's decision. The Administrator will review the hearing officer's decision and determine, based upon the decision, the record from the hearing and any other submissions made by the MA organization, whether the termination decision should be upheld, reversed, or modified. The Administrator will issue a written decision to the MA organization. The regulations do not set a deadline for issuance of the Administrator's decision.

The regulations also do not allow for Administrator's review of a hearing officer decision upholding a determination that an entity is not qualified to enter into a contract with CMS to be a MA organization. *The regulations contain no provisions for judicial review.*

## Practical Tips

**Apply for state licenses early.** In order to qualify as a MA organization, an entity must meet the multiple requirements of 42 C.F.R. § 422.503. Included in the list is the requirement that a MA organization be licensed by the state as a risk-bearing entity in each state in which it seeks to offer a MA plan. If a MA organization has not obtained the necessary state licensure, CMS has no recourse but to deny the application. States have differing requirements and time frames for issuing such licensure, and the MA organization should start the process as early as possible.

**If the denial is because of a missing license, go through the reconsideration/appeals process.** The regulations require that CMS notify the MA organization by May 1 of its determination to not authorize a contract. All favorable reconsideration determinations, including those resulting from a hearing or Administrator's review, must be issued by

July 15 for the contract to be effective on January 1 the following year. If the MA organization has not received the necessary state licensure by May 1, going through the appeals process gives an additional seventy-five days in which to secure the missing license.

## NOTES

1. The rights, procedures, and requirements relating to beneficiary appeals and grievances described in this section (42 C.F.R. § 422.560 *et seq.*), now also apply to Medicare contracts with Health Maintenance Organizations (HMOs) and Competitive Medical Plans (CMPs) under § 1876 of the Act. *See* 70 Fed. Reg. 4713 (Jan. 28, 2005).
2. *See* 42 C.F.R. § 422.561.
3. *See* 42 C.F.R. § 422.564.
4. *See* 42 C.F.R. § 422.566.
5. *See* 42 C.F.R. § 422.574.
6. *See* 42 C.F.R. § 422.570(d)(2).
7. *See* 42 C.F.R. § 422.572.
8. *See* 42 C.F.R. § 422.584.
9. See 42 C.F.R. § 422.590.
10. *See* 42 C.F.R. § 422.594.
11. HCPPs are not regulated by the rules contained in 42 C.F.R. § 422.620–.622. Therefore, enrollees who are in health care prepayment plans (HCPPs) follow the original Medicare immediate review process contained in 42 C.F.R. Part 405.
12. CMS is in the process of implementing a revised notice of noncoverage form through the Office of Management and Budget's paperwork Reduction Act process.
13. HCPPs are not regulated by the rules contained in 42 C.F.R. 422.624–.626. Therefore, enrollees in HCPPs follow the original Medicare expedited review process contained in 42 C.F.R. Part 405.
14. *See* 42 C.F.R. §§ 422.641–.698.

# CHAPTER 5

# Part D Grievances, Coverage Determinations, and Appeals

## MEDICARE PART D GRIEVANCES, COVERAGE DETERMINATIONS, AND APPEALS (42 C.F.R. PART 423 (SUBPART M))

### Overview

Enrollees in Medicare Part D prescription drug plans are entitled to have their complaints about any part of their care as a plan member resolved by their plan sponsors. A complaint under the Part D program may be handled as a grievance, a coverage determination, or an appeal depending on the subject of the complaint. Subpart M of Part 423 establishes the procedures that Plan D sponsors must follow for processing Part D grievances, coverage determinations, and appeals.

### What May Be Appealed? (42 C.F.R. § 423.560)

An enrollee in Medicare Part D may appeal adverse coverage determinations made by the Part D plan sponsor on the benefits under a Part D plan the enrollee believes he or she is entitled to receive, including delay in providing or approving the drug coverage (when a delay would adversely affect the health of the enrollee), or on any amounts the enrollee must pay for the drug coverage.

### Who May Appeal? (42 C.F.R. § 423.568)

The Part D plan enrollee or his or her appointed representative, and the prescribing physician, on behalf of the enrollee, may request a coverage determination and may appeal from adverse coverage determinations.

## Appeals Process

### *Grievances (42 C.F.R. § 423.564)*

Each Part D plan sponsor must provide meaningful procedures for timely hearing and resolving grievances between an enrollee and the Part D plan sponsor or any other entity through which the Part D plan sponsor provides covered Part D benefits. Upon receiving a complaint, the Part D plan sponsor must promptly determine if the complaint is a grievance or an appeal, and notify the enrollee about how the complaint is being processed. For quality of care issues, an enrollee may file a grievance with the Part D plan sponsor, the Quality Improvement Organization (QIO), or both.

A grievance may be filed orally or in writing, and must be filed with the plan sponsor no later than sixty days after the event or incident that precipitates the grievance. The Part D plan sponsor must notify the enrollee of its decision as expeditiously as the case requires, based upon the enrollee's health status, but no later than thirty days after the date the Plan D plan sponsor receives the grievance.[1] All grievances related to the quality of care must be responded to in writing, whether received in writing or orally, and must include a description of the enrollee's right to file a written complaint with the QIO.

### *Expedited Grievances*

A Part D plan sponsor must respond to an enrollee's grievance within twenty-four hours if the complaint involves a refusal by the Part D plan sponsor to grant an enrollee's request for an expedited coverage determination or redetermination and the enrollee has not yet purchased or received the drug that is in dispute.

### *Coverage Determinations (42 C.F.R. § 423.566)*

Each Part D plan sponsor must establish procedures for making timely coverage determinations regarding the prescription drug benefits an enrollee is entitled to receive under the plan, including basic prescription drug coverage and supplemental benefits, as well as the amount (including any cost sharing) that an enrollee is required to pay for a drug. Actions that are coverage determinations include: (1) a decision to not provide or pay for a Part D drug that the enrollee believes may be covered by the plan (including a decision to not pay because the drug is not on the plan sponsor's formulary,[2] the drug is determined not to be medically necessary, the drug is furnished by an out-of-network pharmacy, or because the Part D plan sponsor determines that the drug is excluded); (2) failure to provide a coverage determination in a timely manner when a delay would adversely affect the health of the enrollee; (3) a decision concerning certain exception requests; or (4) a decision on the amount of cost sharing for a drug.

*Standard Coverage Determinations (42 C.F.R. § 423.568)*

When a party makes a standard request for a drug benefit, the Part D plan sponsor must notify the enrollee of its determination as expeditiously as the enrollee's health condition requires, but no later than seventy-two hours after receipt of the request. The notice of any denial must be in writing, state the specific reasons for the denial, and inform the enrollee of his or her right to a redetermination.[3] For drug coverage denials, the notice must describe the procedures for the standard and the expedited redetermination processes, as well as the rest of the appeals process. For payment denials, the notice must describe the procedures for the standard redetermination process and the rest of the appeals process.

*Expediting Certain Coverage Determinations (42 C.F.R. § 423.570)*

An enrollee or an enrollee's prescribing physician may request that a Part D plan sponsor expedite certain coverage determinations. A request for an expedited determination may be made either orally or in writing. The request must be submitted directly to the Part D plan sponsor or, if applicable, to the entity responsible for making the determination as directed by the Part D plan sponsor. An enrollee's prescribing physician may provide oral or written support for an enrollee's request for an expedited determination. The plan sponsor must expedite a request when it is made or supported by a prescribing physician and the physician indicates, either orally or in writing, that applying the standard time may seriously jeopardize the enrollee's life, health, or ability to regain maximum function.

If a Part D plan sponsor denies a request to expedite a coverage determination, the plan sponsor must treat the request as a standard request for a determination and must issue its determination within the standard time frame. If a Part D plan sponsor expedites a request for a coverage determination, it must notify the enrollee of its decision as quickly as the enrollee's health condition requires, but no later than twenty-four hours after receiving the request.[4]

*Exceptions Process (42 C.F.R. § 423.578)*

Coverage determinations include a plan sponsor's decision on an exception request. An enrollee, an enrollee's appointed representative, or an enrollee's prescribing physician may request either an exception to a plan sponsor's tiered cost-sharing structure, or an exception to a plan sponsor's formulary. When an exception is requested, the enrollee's prescribing physician must also submit a statement supporting the request.

Each Part D plan sponsor that manages its Part D benefit through the use of a tiered formulary must establish and maintain reasonable and complete procedures for processing and resolving tiered cost-sharing structure exception requests. A Part D plan sponsor must grant a tiering exception whenever it determines that the preferred drug for treatment of the enrollee's condition would not be as effective as the requested drug or would have adverse effects for the enrollee, consistent with the physician's supporting statement.

The plan sponsor also must establish and maintain reasonable and complete procedures for processing and resolving exceptions that involve non-formulary Part D drugs. A plan sponsor must grant a formulary exception whenever it determines that: (1) a non-formulary drug is medically necessary for treating an enrollee's condition because all covered Part D drugs on the formulary for treating the same condition would not be as effective or would have adverse effects for the enrollee; (2) the number of doses under a dose restriction has been or is likely to be ineffective for the enrollee; or (3) the prescription drug alternative(s) listed on the formulary or required to be used in accordance with step therapy has been or is likely to be ineffective for the enrollee. A plan sponsor's exception procedures also must address situations where the formulary changes during the year and an enrollee is using a drug affected by the change.

If an exception is granted, the plan sponsor is prohibited from requiring the enrollee to request approval for a refill or new prescription to continue using the Part D prescription drug approved under the exceptions process for the remainder of the plan year so long as (1) the enrollee remains enrolled in the plan, (2) the physician continues to prescribe the drug for the enrollee, and (3) the drug continues to be safe for treating the enrollee's condition. Although not required, a plan sponsor may extend approval for an exception into the subsequent plan year for a renewing member.

### *Appeals*

Enrollees in Medicare Part D prescription drug plans receiving adverse coverage determinations from Part D plan sponsors have the right to appeal such determinations. The appeal rights under Part D are similar to the appeal rights established for beneficiaries in Medicare Advantage plans. A Part D plan enrollee must initially pursue his or her appeal through the Part D plan sponsor's redetermination process. If the enrollee remains dissatisfied, he or she may seek review from the independent review entity (IRE), an Administrative Law Judge (ALJ), the Medicare Appeals Council (MAC), and a federal district court.

### *Right to a Redetermination by a Plan Sponsor (42 C.F.R. § 423.580)*

An enrollee who has received an adverse coverage determination may request a redetermination. An enrollee may ask for a redetermination by making a request to the Part D plan sponsor that made the coverage determination. The request must be filed within sixty calendar days from the date of the notice of the coverage determination.[5] When the issue is the denial of coverage based on a lack of medical necessity, the redetermination must be conducted by a physician with expertise in the field of medicine that is appropriate for the services at issue.[6]

### *Standard Redeterminations (42 C.F.R. § 423.582)*

An enrollee or an enrollee's appointed representative may request a standard redetermination by filing a written request with the Part D plan sponsor.[7] The Part D plan sponsor must notify the enrollee of its determination in writing as quickly as the enrollee's health condition requires, but no later than seven calendar days from the date it receives the request.[8]

### *Expedited Redeterminations (42 C.F.R. § 423.584)*

An enrollee, an enrollee's appointed representative, or an enrollee's prescribing physician may request an expedited redetermination. The request may be made orally or in writing and must be submitted directly to the Part D plan sponsor. An enrollee's prescribing physician may provide oral or written support for a request to expedite a redetermination. The plan sponsor must expedite a request when it is made or supported by a prescribing physician and the physician indicates, either orally or in writing, that applying the standard time may seriously jeopardize the enrollee's life, health, or ability to regain maximum function.

If a Part D plan sponsor denies a request to expedite a redetermination, the plan sponsor must treat the request as a standard request and issue its determination within the standard time frame. If a Part D plan sponsor expedites a request for a redetermination, it must notify the enrollee of its determination as quickly as the enrollee's health condition requires, but no later than seventy-two hours after receiving the request.[9]

### *Reconsideration by the Independent Review Entity (42 C.F.R. § 423.600)*

An enrollee who is dissatisfied with the redetermination of a Part D plan sponsor has the right to a reconsideration by an IRE that contracts with Centers for Medicare & Medicaid Services (CMS). If an enrollee or an enrollee's appointed representative wishes to request a reconsideration, he or she must file a written request for reconsideration with the IRE within sixty days of the date of the redetermination by the Part D plan sponsor.[10] The IRE is required to solicit the views of the prescribing physician, and a written account of the prescribing physician's views must be contained in the IRE's record.

The IRE must conduct the reconsideration as expeditiously as the enrollee's health condition requires, but must not exceed the deadlines for making standard or expedited redeterminations. When the issue is the denial of coverage based on the lack of medical necessity, the reconsideration must be conducted by a physician with expertise in the field of medicine that is appropriate for the services at issue.[11]

When the IRE makes a reconsidered determination, it is responsible for mailing or otherwise transmitting notice of the decision to the enrollee, the Part D plan sponsor, and CMS. The notice must state the specific reasons for the decision in understandable language. If the decision is adverse, it must inform the enrollee of his or her right to an ALJ hearing if the amount remaining in controversy requirement is satisfied and describe the procedures for obtaining an ALJ hearing.[12]

### *Review by an ALJ (42 C.F.R. § 423.610)*

If an enrollee is not satisfied with the IRE's reconsideration determination and the amount remaining in controversy meets the threshold requirement, the enrollee has a right to a hearing before an ALJ. If an enrollee or an enrollee's appointed representative wishes to appeal to an ALJ, he or she must file a written request with the entity specified in the IRE's decision within sixty days of the date of the IRE's determination.[13] The time and place for the ALJ hearing will be set in accordance with 42 C.F.R. § 405.1020. If at any time the ALJ determines that the amount in controversy does not meet the requirements of 42 C.F.R. § 422.610, the ALJ will discontinue the proceedings and dismiss the case.

### *Review by the Medicare Appeals Council (42 C.F.R. § 423.620)*

An enrollee or an enrollee's appointed representative who is dissatisfied with an ALJ's hearing decision may request the MAC to review the ALJ's decision. The ALJ's decision will provide instructions about how to request a review by the MAC. The request must be filed in writing with the MAC within sixty days of the date of receipt of the ALJ's hearing decision or dismissal. The MAC may grant an extension of the filing deadline if the enrollee can show good cause for missing the deadline.

### *Judicial Review (42 C.F.R. § 423.630)*

An enrollee or an enrollee's appointed representative who is dissatisfied with a decision made by the MAC may request judicial review of the MAC's decision if the amount remaining in controversy meets the applicable threshold requirement. An enrollee or an enrollee's appointed representative also may request judicial review of an ALJ's decision if a request for review was filed with the MAC, the MAC denied the request for review, and the amount remaining in controversy meets the applicable threshold requirement. A request for judicial review must be filed in a district court of the United States in accordance with § 205 of the Act.[14] The decisions by the ALJ and MAC will provide instructions about how to request a review by a federal district court.

### Practical Tips

**Get the prescribing physician on-board early**. Throughout the appeals process for Part D coverage determinations, the enrollee's prescribing physician plays a key role. For example, the prescribing physician may provide support for an enrollee's request for an expedited determination or note when a formulary drug would not be as effective as the requested drug or would have adverse effects. It is vital that the enrollee or the enrollee's representative work closely right away with the prescribing physician to ensure that detailed support is provided for the requested drug.

## PART D PLAN SPONSOR CONTRACT TERMINATION APPEALS (42 C.F.R. § 423.500)[15]

### Overview

A Part D drug plan sponsor must enter into a contract with CMS before it can enroll beneficiaries and be paid on behalf of eligible Part D enrollees. A contract may cover more than one Part D plan. The conditions for entering into such a contract are found at 42 C.F.R. §§ 423.504–.506. Provisions for nonrenewal of a Part D plan sponsor contract, by either the Plan sponsor or by CMS, are set forth at 42 C.F.R. § 423.507. Additionally, such a contract may be modified or terminated by mutual consent.[16]

CMS may terminate a Part D Plan sponsor contract if it determines, among other things, that the Part D sponsor: (1) failed to substantially carry out the terms of the contract; (2) is carrying out the contract in a manner inconsistent with the effective and efficient implementation of Part D;

(3) no longer meets the requirements for being a contracting organization; or (4) there is credible evidence that the Part D sponsor committed or participated in false, fraudulent, or abusive activities affecting the Medicare program, including the submission of false or fraudulent data.[17]

If CMS decides to terminate a contract, the agency must notify the Part D plan in writing ninety days before the intended date of termination. The Part D plan sponsor must notify its enrollees by mail at least thirty days before the effective date of the termination. The sponsor also must notify the general public at least thirty days before the effective date of the termination by publishing a notice in one or more newspapers of general circulation in each community or county located in the Part D plan sponsor's service area. The regulations also allow a Part D plan sponsor to terminate its contract if CMS fails to substantially carry out the terms of the contract. Similar notice requirements also must be met.[18]

Before terminating a contract for reasons other than fraud or financial difficulties so severe that the plan's ability to provide necessary prescription drug coverage is impaired to the point of posing an imminent and serious risk to the health of its enrollees, the regulations allow for Part D plan sponsors to implement a corrective action plan. CMS must provide the Part D plan sponsor with a reasonable opportunity to develop and receive approval of a corrective action plan to address the deficiencies identified as the basis for the termination.

If CMS decides to terminate a contract, it sends written notice to the Part D plan sponsor. The notice must inform the Part D plan sponsor of its termination appeals rights which are set forth at 42 C.F.R. § 423.642. The contract determination is final and binding unless the determination is reconsidered in accordance with 42 C.F.R. § 423.644-.649, or a timely request for hearing is filed.

## What May Be Appealed? (42 C.F.R. § 423.641)

Several determinations may be appealed including a determination that an entity is: (1) not qualified to enter into a contract with CMS under Part D; (2) not to authorize a renewal of a contract with a Part D program sponsor; or (3) to terminate a contract with a Part D program sponsor.

## Who May Appeal? (42 C.F.R. § 423.645)

Only an authorized official of the contract applicant or Part D plan sponsor that was the subject of a contract determination may file a request for reconsideration.

## Appeals Process

### *Reconsideration (42 C.F.R. § 423.645–.649)*

Reconsideration is the first step for appealing a contract termination. CMS will reconsider the initial contract determination, if the Part D plan sponsor timely files a written request with any CMS office. The reconsideration request must be filed within fifteen days from the date of the notice of the initial determination.

CMS provides the Part D plan sponsor and the CMS officials who made the contract determination a reasonable opportunity to present evidence, including any relevant documents or written statements material to the contract determination. CMS must then issue a reconsidered determination which is based on a review of the contract determination, the evidence and findings on which that was based, and any other written evidence submitted before notice of the reconsidered determination is mailed, including facts related to the status of the Part D plan sponsor subsequent to the contract determination.

Unlike other reconsideration regulations, this particular one does not identify who within CMS is to serve as a reconsideration official. A reconsidered determination affirms, reverses, or modifies the initial determination. Any favorable redetermination, including those resulting from a hearing or Administrator review, must be made by July 15 for the contract to be effective on January 1 of the following year. The reconsidered determination is final and binding unless a request for a hearing is filed.

### *Hearing Officer Review (42 C.F.R. § 423.650–.663)*

A Part D plan sponsor whose contract with CMS is terminated or is not renewed as a result of a contract determination is entitled to a hearing before a CMS Hearing Officer. A request for a hearing must be made in writing and filed by an authorized official of the Part D plan sponsor that was a party to the determination under appeal. The request for hearing must be filed with any CMS office within fifteen days after the date of the reconsidered determination. The parties to the hearing include the Part D plan sponsor, CMS, and, at the discretion of the hearing officer, any interested parties who make a showing that their rights may be prejudiced by the decision.

CMS will postpone the proposed effective date of the contract determination to terminate a contract with a Part D plan sponsor until a hearing decision is reached and affirmed by the Administrator in instances where a Part D plan sponsor requests review by the Administrator.[19] There will be no postponement of the effective date for terminations resulting from fraud or financial difficulties so severe that the plan's ability to provide necessary prescription drug coverage is impaired to the point of posing an imminent and serious risk to the health of its enrollees.

The CMS-appointed hearing officer will set a date for a hearing which must be within thirty days of receipt of the request for a hearing. The parties to the hearing will be notified in writing of the time and place of the hearing. A party may appoint, as its representative at the hearing, anyone not disqualified or suspended from acting as a representative before the Secretary or otherwise prohibited by law. The representative gives and/or accepts any notice or request with respect to the proceedings, presents evidence and allegations of fact and law, and obtains information to the same extent as the party.

The hearing is open to the public. The hearing officer will inquire fully into all matters at issue and receives in evidence the testimony of witnesses and any documents that are relevant and material. A complete record of the hearing is transcribed and made available to all parties upon request. In exercising his or her authority, the hearing officer is required to comply with the provisions of the Act, the regulations issued by the Secretary, and general instructions issued by CMS in implementing the Act. As soon as practical after the close of the hearing, the hearing officer issues a written decision based on the evidence in the record. The decision must contain separately numbered findings of fact and conclusions of law. The Hearing Officer provides a copy of the decision to each party which is final and binding unless it is reversed or modified by the Administrator.

*Administrator's Review (42 C.F.R. § 423.666)*

A Part D plan sponsor that receives a hearing decision upholding a contract termination may request review by the Administrator within fifteen days of receiving the hearing decision. The Administrator reviews the hearing officer's decision, the hearing record, and any written arguments submitted by the Part D plan sponsor to determine whether the termination decision must be upheld, reversed, or modified.

The Administrator will issue a written decision which it provides to the Part D plan sponsor that requested the review. The regulations do not set a deadline for issuance of the Administrator's decision. Once issued, that decision is final and binding unless it is reopened and revised by the Administrator within one year of the notice of the Administrator's decision. *The regulations contain no provisions for judicial review.*

### Practical Tips

As the Medicare Part D benefits program has only recently begun, there have been few, if any, contract termination appeals. Thus, the authors have no practical tips to offer, but hope to do so in future editions of this Guide.

## RETIREE PRESCRIPTION DRUG PLAN SPONSOR APPEALS (42 C.F.R. § 423.890)

### Overview

Section 1860D-22 (42 U.S.C. § 1395w-132) of the Act provides for subsidy payments to sponsors of qualified retiree prescription drug plans. Sponsors of qualified plans can receive an annual subsidy equal to 28 percent of specified retiree drug costs. CMS has published regulations establishing the process sponsors must go through to qualify for the subsidies.[20] The regulations allow for an appeal by a sponsor dissatisfied with the subsidy received.

### What May Be Appealed? (42 C.F.R. § 423.890(a))

The regulations identify certain determinations with respect to the subsidy payments that may be appealed. Those include the amount of the subsidy payment, the actuarial equivalence of the sponsor's retiree prescription drug plan, whether an enrollee in a retiree prescription drug plan is a qualifying covered retiree, or any other similar determination that affects eligibility for or the amount of a subsidy payment.

### Who May Appeal?

A sponsor dissatisfied with a CMS determination may request a reconsideration of the decision. If still dissatisfied, a sponsor may request an informal hearing.

### Appeals Process

#### *Informal Written Reconsideration (42 C.F.R. § 423.890(a))*

A sponsor is entitled to an informal written reconsideration of an adverse initial determination. A request for reconsideration must be made in writing and filed with CMS within fifteen days of the date on the notice of adverse determination, and must specify the findings or issues with which the sponsor disagrees and the reasons for those disagreements. The request for reconsideration may include additional documentation for CMS to consider.

In conducting the reconsideration, CMS will review the original subsidy determination and any other written evidence submitted by the sponsor. Once the reconsideration is completed, CMS will inform the sponsor of the decision either orally or through electronic mail. At the sponsor's request, CMS will send a written decision.

### *Informal Hearing (42 C.F.R. § 423.890(b))*

If dissatisfied with the reconsidered determination, the sponsor is entitled to an informal hearing before a CMS hearing officer. A request for hearing must be made in writing and filed with CMS within fifteen days of the date the sponsor receives the CMS reconsideration decision. The request must include a copy of the reconsideration decision and must identify the issues in the decision with which the sponsor disagrees.

CMS will provide written notice to the sponsor of the time and place of the informal hearing at least ten days before the scheduled date. The CMS hearing officer is limited to the review of the record that was before CMS when CMS made both the initial and reconsideration determinations. If CMS did not issue a written reconsideration decision, the hearing officer may request a written statement from CMS or its contractors explaining the basis for its determination. Once the CMS hearing officer decides the case, he or she must issue a written decision to the sponsor, explaining the basis for the decision. The regulations do not set a time frame for hearing officer review.

### *Administrator's Reviews (42 C.F.R. § 423.890(c))*

A sponsor that has received a hearing officer decision upholding a CMS initial or reconsidered determination may request Administrators review within fifteen days of receipt of the decision. The Administrator may review the decision, any written documents submitted to CMS or the hearing officer, as well as any other information included in the hearing officer's decision. The Administrator has the authority to uphold, reverse, or modify the hearing officer's decision. The Administrator's determination is final and binding, and *the regulations do not provide for any further right of review*.

### *Reopening (42 C.F.R. § 423.890(d))*

CMS may reopen and revise an initial or reconsidered determination upon its own motion or at the request of a sponsor within one year of the date of the determination for any reason, within four years for good cause, or at any time when the underlying decision was obtained through fraud or similar fault. The regulations state that a decision by CMS not to reopen an initial or reconsidered determination is final and binding and may not be appealed.

### Practical Tips

As this program has only recently begun, there have been no Retiree Prescription Drug Plan Sponsor appeals filed yet. Thus, the Authors have no practical tips to offer, but hope to do so in future editions of this Guide.

## NOTES

1. In certain circumstances, a plan sponsor may extend the time frame by up to fourteen days for good cause. *See* 42 C.F.R. § 423.564(e)(2).

2. Formulary decisions include decisions about whether a prior authorization or other utilization management requirement has been satisfied.

3. Initial notice of an adverse decision may be provided orally, so long as written notice is sent to the enrollee within three calendar days after oral notice is provided.

4. An enrollee's request for payment of a Part D drug already received cannot be expedited.

5. A plan sponsor may grant an extension of the filing deadline if the enrollee demonstrates good cause for missing the deadline.

6. The physician making the redetermination need not, in all cases, be of the same specialty or subspecialty as the prescribing physician.

7. A Part D plan sponsor may adopt a policy for accepting oral requests.

8. *See* 42 C.F.R. § 423.590.

9. Initial notice of an adverse decision may be provided orally, so long as written notice is sent to the enrollee within three calendar days after oral notice is provided.

10. The IRE may grant an extension of the filing deadline if the enrollee demonstrates good cause for missing the deadline.

11. The physician making the reconsideration need not, in all cases, be of the same specialty or subspecialty as the prescribing physician.

12. *See* 42 C.F.R. § 422.594.

13. An ALJ may grant an extension of the filing deadline if the enrollee demonstrates good cause for missing the deadline. *See* 42 C.F.R. § 423.612(b).

14. *See* 42 C.F.R. §§ 405.1136 through 450.1140 for a description of the procedures for requesting judicial review.

15. *See* 42 C.F.R. § 423.642 for contract termination appeal rights.

16. *See* 42 C.F.R. § 423.508.

17. *See* 42 C.F.R. § 423.509 (listing eleven different bases for termination).

18. *See* 42 C.F.R. § 423.510.

19. *See* 42 C.F.R. § 423.666.

20. *See* 42 C.F.R. § 423.880 *et seq.*

# CHAPTER 6

# Miscellaneous Appeals

## LONG-TERM CARE FACILITIES—ACTION ON COMPLAINTS OF NEGLECT AND ABUSE, MISAPPROPRIATION OF PROPERTY (42 C.F.R. § 488.335)

### Overview

Pursuant to the Act, states are required to review all allegations of resident neglect and abuse, and misappropriation of resident property. States are required to have written procedures for the timely review and investigation of such allegations and must review all allegations regardless of their source. Individuals having been preliminarily found to have neglected, abused, or misappropriated resident property have certain hearing rights.

### What May Be Appealed and Who May Appeal?

A preliminary determination by a state, based upon oral or written evidence and investigation, may be appealed by implicated individuals.

### Appeals Process

Upon making its preliminary determination, the state must notify both the individual implicated in the investigation and the current administrator of the facility in which the incident occurred. The written notice must be made within ten working days of the state's investigation and include the: (1) nature of the allegation(s); (2) date and time of the occurrence; (3) right to a hearing; and (4) intent to report the substantiated findings in writing to the nurse aide registry or appropriate licensure authority once the individual has had the opportunity for a hearing; (5) the fact that the individual's failure to request a hearing in writing within 30 days from the date of the notice will result in reporting the substantiated findings to the nurse aide registry or appropriate licensure authority; (6) the consequences of waiving the right to a hearing;

(7) the consequences of a finding through the hearing process that the alleged resident abuse or neglect, or misappropriation of resident property, did occur; and (8) the fact that the individual has the right to be represented by an attorney at the individual's own expense.

The state must complete the hearing within 120 days from the date of receipt of the hearing request and must hold the hearing at a reasonable place and time convenient for the implicated individual. Importantly, a substantiated finding may not be made if the individual demonstrates that alleged neglect was caused by factors beyond the individual's control. If the finding is that the individual has neglected or abused a resident or misappropriated resident property or if the individual waives the right to a hearing, the state must report the finding in writing within ten days to the: (1) individual; (2) current administrator of the facility where the incident occurred; (3) administrator of the facility currently employing the individual (if different than where the incident occurred); (4) licensing authority for individuals used by the facility other than nurse aides, if applicable; and (5) nurse aide registry for nurse aides.

Only the state survey agency may report the findings to the nurse aide registry, and this must be done within 10 working days of the findings, in accordance with 42 C.F.R. § 483.156(c). The state survey agency may not delegate this responsibility. The survey agency must also retain the information as required by 42 C.F.R. § 483.156(c). The survey agency must promptly review the results of all complaint investigations and determine whether the facility has violated Medicare requirements, and take appropriate actions.

## INTERMEDIARY TERMINATION APPEALS (42 C.F.R. § 421.100) AND CARRIER TERMINATION APPEALS (42 C.F.R. § 421.200)

### Overview

CMS contracts with private insurance companies to process claims, perform audits, make payments, enroll providers and suppliers, and process appeals. These functions have been performed by various fiscal intermediaries (FIs), Medicare carriers, the National Supplier Clearinghouse (NSC), and four Durable Medical Equipment Regional Carriers (DMERCs) generally assigned according to geographic location. Pursuant to the Medicare Contracting Reform provisions of the Medicare Prescription Drug, Improvement, and Modernization Act of 2003 (MMA) administration of the Medicare program is to be streamlined and simplified.

Beginning in 2006, all of the functions previously performed by FIs, carriers, the NSC, and the DMERCs will be taken over by Medicare Administrative Contractors (MACs) which will service both Part A and Part B. The country has been divided into fifteen MAC jurisdictions.[1] The first MAC contract was awarded in the summer of 2006, with the remaining contracts to be awarded and responsibilities to be transitioned over a five-year period. The MMA requires that all MAC contracts be awarded by 2011; however, Centers for Medicare & Medicaid Services (CMS) expects implementation to be completed before then. The MMA also requires that each MAC contract be re-competed every five years.

Until MACs completely assume their administrative responsibilities, many providers and suppliers will continue to rely on FIs and carriers for claims processing and payment. Failure of a FI or a carrier to meet or demonstrate the capacity to meet proscribed standards and criteria may be grounds for an adverse action by the Secretary or CMS, such as reassignment of providers, offer of a short-term agreement, termination of a contract, or nonrenewal of a contract.

A Medicare carrier's contract many be terminated at any time if the Secretary determines that the carrier has failed substantially to carry out any material terms of the contract or has performed its function "in a manner inconsistent with the effective and efficient administration of the Medicare Part B program." Similarly, the Secretary may terminate a FI agreement if the Secretary finds the intermediary has failed to comply with the regulatory requirements, criteria, or standards. If the Secretary or CMS decides to terminate a FI agreement or carrier contract, the regulations provide for a hearing before a hearing officer designated by the Secretary and, subsequently, judicial review in accordance with 5 U.S.C. Chapter 7.

## GROUP HEALTH PLAN NONCONFORMANCE APPEALS (42 C.F.R. § 411.120)

### Overview

Section 1862(b) (42 U.S.C. § 1395y) of the Act provides that Medicare is a secondary payer under specified conditions for services covered under certain types of group health plans. The regulations at 42 C.F.R. § 411.100–.106 set the general provisions for limitations on payment for services covered under such plans. CMS may require a group health plan (GHP) or a large group health plan (LGHP) to demonstrate that it has complied with the Medicare secondary payer (MSP) provisions and to submit supporting documentation by an official authorized to act on behalf of the entity, under penalty of perjury. If a GHP or a LGHP fails to provide acceptable evidence or documentation that it has complied with the MSP prohibitions and requirements, CMS may make a determination of nonconformance for both the year in which the services were furnished and the year in which the request for information was made.[2]

## What May Be Appealed?

The CMS determination that the GHP or the LGHP is nonconforming may be appealed. CMS will issue a notice detailing the determination, its basis, the right of the parties to request a hearing, and an explanation of the hearing procedures.

## Who May Appeal? (42 C.F.R. § 411.120)

The parties to the appeal are CMS, the GHP, or LGHP which was found in nonconformance, and any employers or employee organization that contributed to the plan during the calendar year for which CMS determined nonconformance.

## Appeals Process

A party's request for hearing must be filed in writing within sixty-five days from the date on the notice. The request may include rationale showing why the parties believe the determination is incorrect as well as supporting documentation. CMS will appoint a hearing officer to hear the case.

### *On-the-Record Review (42 C.F.R. § 411.121(a)(4))*

Ordinarily, the CMS hearing officer will make a decision based upon review of the data and documents on which CMS based its determination of nonconformance and any other documentation submitted within sixty-five days from the date of the notice.

### *Oral Hearing (42 C.F.R. § 411.121(a)(5))*

The hearing officer may provide for an oral hearing, on either his or her own motion, or at the request of the parties if the hearing officer determines that such an oral hearing is necessary. Within thirty days of receipt of the oral hearing request, the hearing officer notifies the parties in writing of the request and whether it will be granted. If granted, the hearing officer will set a time and place for the hearing. Notice must be issued at least thirty days before the scheduled date. The hearing officer has the discretion to grant or deny discovery requests.

The hearing officer determines the conduct of the hearing, and may receive both documentary and other evidence that is material to the appeal. Witness testimony also is allowed, and a record of the proceedings at the oral hearing is made and transcribed in all cases. The record does not close until the decision is issued.[3]

*Decision (42 C.F.R. § 411.122)*

If the decision is based on the review of the record, the hearing officer mails the decision to all parties within 120 days from the date of the request for hearing. If the decision is based on an oral hearing, the hearing officer mails the decision to all known parties within 120 days from the conclusion of the hearing. The hearing officer's decision is the final HHS decision and is binding on all parties unless the Administrator chooses to review the decision or it is reopened by the hearing officer.

*Administrator's Review (42 C.F.R. § 411.124)*

A party must request review of a hearing officer's decision in writing within twenty-five days of the date of the decision. Review by the Administrator is discretionary. The Administrator must notify the parties in writing of his or her decision to review or not to review. The Administrator has 120 days from the date of the hearing officer decision to issue a review decision. The Administrator's review decision may affirm, reverse, or modify the hearing officer decision, or may remand the case to the hearing officer for further proceedings. The hearing officer takes action in accordance with the Administrator's instructions in the case of remand and again issues a decision. The Administrator may review or decline to review that decision as well. The Administrator's review decision, or the hearing officer's decision following the remand, is the final Department of Health and Human Services (HHS) decision and is binding on all parties.

*Internal Review Service Referral (42 C.F.R. § 411.130)*

After CMS determines that a plan has been a nonconforming GHP in a particular year, the agency refers that determination to the Internal Revenue Service (IRS) after all parties have exhausted all appeal rights.

## DRUGS AND BIOLOGICALS PAYMENT APPEALS (42 C.F.R. § 414.916)

### Overview

Pursuant to § 1847B (42 U.S.C. § 1395w-3b) of the Act, CMS implemented a competitive acquisition program (CAP) for physicians who administer drugs to patients in their offices. The CAP applies to Medicare Part B physician-injectable drugs and biologicals usually provided incident to the physician's service. Importantly, CAP does not apply to Medicare Part D drugs.

CAP drugs are supplied to the physician by an approved CAP vendor. The claim for the prescribed drug is submitted by the approved CAP vendor that supplied the drug to the physician, and payment is made only to that vendor. The approved CAP vendor is also responsible for collecting applicable deductible and coinsurance for the drug furnished under the CAP, but may do so only after the drug is administered by the physician to the beneficiary.

## What May Be Appealed and Who May Appeal?

The regulations provide for two types of appeal. The first concerns cases where an approved CAP vendor is dissatisfied with denied drug claims.[4] These appeals are resolved by a voluntary alternative dispute resolution process delivered by the designated carrier and a reconsideration process provided by CMS.

The second type of appeal concerns cases where a participating CAP physician finds an approved CAP service or the quality of a CAP drug supplied by the approved vendor to be unsatisfactory. The physician may address the issue first through the approved CAP vendor grievance process,[5] and second through an alternative dispute resolution process administered by the designated carrier and CMS. If CMS suspends an approved CAP vendor's CAP contract for noncompliance or terminates the CAP contract, the approved CAP vendor may request reconsideration.[6]

## Appeals Process

*Dispute resolution for vendors and beneficiaries.* When a CAP vendor is not paid for claims submitted to the designated carrier, the vendor may appeal to the carrier to counsel the responsible participating CAP physician to file a clean claim and pursue an administrative appeal.[7] If problems persist, the CAP vendor may ask the designated carrier to review the participating CAP physician's performance and potentially recommend that CMS suspend the participating CAP physician's election agreement.

The designated carrier must gather information from the local carrier, the participating CAP physician, the beneficiary, and the CAP vendor, and make a recommendation to CMS as to whether the participating CAP physician has been filing his or her CAP drug claims in accordance with the requirements.

CMS will review the recommendation, gather additional relevant information from the physician, and decide whether to suspend the participating CAP physician's election agreement. A suspension beginning before October 1 will conclude on December 31 of the same year. A suspension beginning on or after October 1 will conclude on December 31 of the next year.

The participating CAP physician may appeal the suspension by requesting reconsideration by CMS. The reconsideration request must be filed by the physician within thirty days of receipt of the CMS decision to suspend the physician's election agreement. The contents of a request for reconsideration are set forth at 42 C.F.R. § 414.916(c)(4).

CMS may, at its discretion, provide the participating CAP physician the opportunity for an informal hearing. The hearing will be conducted by a CMS hearing officer appointed by the director of the CMS Center for Medicare Management. The hearing may be conducted in person or by telephone. While not open to the public, it is open to CMS, the participating CAP physician, authorized representatives, technical advisors, representatives from the local carrier and the approved CAP vendor, as well as legal counsel. The hearing officer will receive relevant testimony, and the parties may call and examine witnesses. The hearing officer does not have the authority to compel by subpoena the production of witnesses or other evidence.

Within thirty days of the hearing officer's receipt of the hearing request, the hearing officer must present his or her findings and recommendations to the participating physician in writing. If a hearing is requested, the hearing officer has ten days to issue a hearing notice. Thirty days after the conclusion of the hearing, the hearing officer must present his or her findings and recommendations to the participating physician in writing.

The hearing officer's decision is final unless the director of the CMS Center for Medicare Management, or his or her designee (CMS official), chooses to review that decision within thirty days. If the decision is favorable, the physician may resume his or her participation in CAP. The hearing officer and the CMS official may review decisions that are favorable or unfavorable. The CMS official may accept, reject, or modify the hearing officer's findings. If the CMS official reviews the hearing officer's decision, the CMS official issues a final, written reconsideration determination. If the final decision is unfavorable to the physician, his or her election agreement is terminated.

*Dispute resolution for suspension and termination of a CAP contract.* If CMS suspends an approved CAP vendor's CAP contract for noncompliance or terminates the CAP contract, the approved CAP vendor may request reconsideration. When a participating CAP physician is dissatisfied with an approved CAP vendor's service or the quality of a CAP drug supplied by the CAP vendor, the physician may use the CAP vendor's grievance process. If the service or quality issues are not resolved, the participating CAP physician may request that the designated carrier review the CAP vendor's performance and potentially recommend termination of the vendor's CAP contract.

The designated carrier must gather information from the local carrier, the participating CAP physician, the beneficiary, and the CAP vendor, and make a recommendation to CMS as to whether the participating CAP vendor has been meeting the service and quality obligations of its CAP contract. CMS will review the recommendation and gather additional relevant information from the CAP vendor, the participating CAP physician, the local carrier, and the beneficiary before deciding whether to terminate the approved CAP vendor's CAP contract.

An approved CAP vendor dissatisfied with a determination that its CAP contract has been suspended or terminated by CMS may request reconsideration. The reconsideration request must be filed in writing by the CAP vendor within thirty days of receipt of the CMS decision to suspend or terminate its CAP contract. The contents of a request for reconsideration are set forth at 42 C.F.R. § 414.917(c)(4).

CMS may, in response to a request for reconsideration and at its discretion, provide the CAP vendor the opportunity for an informal hearing. The hearing will be conducted by a CMS hearing officer appointed by the director of the CMS Center for Medicare Management. The hearing may be conducted in person or by telephone. CMS will provide written notice of the time and location of the hearing at least ten days prior to the hearing. While not open to the public, it is open to CMS, the CAP vendor, authorized representatives, technical advisors, representatives from the local carrier and the designated carrier, the participating CAP physician who requested the suspension, as well as legal counsel. The hearing officer will receive relevant testimony, and the parties may call and examine witnesses. The hearing officer does not have the authority to compel by subpoena the production of witnesses or other evidence.

Within thirty days of the hearing officer's receipt of the hearing request, the hearing officer must present his or her findings and recommendations in writing to the CAP vendor. If a hearing is requested, the hearing officer has ten days to issue a hearing notice. Thirty days after the conclusion of the hearing, the hearing officer must present his or her written findings and recommendations to the CAP vendor.

The hearing officer's decision is final unless the director of the CMS Center for Medicare Management, or his or her designee (CMS official), chooses to review that decision within thirty days. If the decision is favorable, the CAP vendor may resume his or her participation in CAP. The hearing officer and the CMS official may review decisions that are favorable or unfavorable. The CMS official may accept, reject, or modify the hearing officer's findings. If the CMS official reviews the hearing officer's decision, the CMS official issues a final, written reconsideration determination to the CAP vendor.

## MEDICARE SUPPLEMENTAL POLICIES—POLICY CERTIFICATION APPEALS (42 C.F.R. § 403.200)

### Overview

Section 1882 (42 U.S.C. § 1395ss) of the Act establishes standards to enable Medicare beneficiaries to identify Medicare supplemental policies that do not duplicate Medicare and that provide adequate, fairly priced protection against expenses not covered by Medicare. There are two methods used for informing beneficiaries of which policies meet those standards. Policies may be approved through a state approved program. A Supplemental Health Insurance Panel determines whether a policy meets the minimum requirements for the regulation of Medicare supplemental policies. In states without an approved program, the Secretary will certify policies voluntarily submitted by insuring organizations for review against the standards.[8]

Policies must be re-certified annually. If CMS decides not to certify a policy or determines that a policy no longer meets the standards for certification, CMS will notify both the insuring organization and all State Commissioners and Superintendents of Insurance that the policy is no longer certified. The CMS determination will go into effect thirty days from the date of the notice unless the insuring organization requests an administrative review. If the insuring organization requests administrative review, the policy retains its certification until CMS makes a final determination.

### What May Be Appealed?

A CMS determination that a Medicare supplemental policy does not meet the standards for certification may be appealed.

### Who May Appeal?

The insuring organization may request administrative review of the determination that the policy does not meet the standards for certification.

### Appeals Process (42 C.F.R. § 403.248)

If the insuring organization requests an administrative review, a CMS official not involved in the initial CMS determination will initiate and complete an administrative review within ninety days of the date of the notice. The reviewing official will consider the original material submitted for review and any additional information the insuring organization submits to CMS. Within fifteen days after the administrative review is completed, CMS will inform the insuring organization in writing of the final decision, with an explanation. If the final decision is that a policy loses its certification, the loss will go into effect fifteen days after the date of the CMS notice informing the insuring organization of the final decision.

## PROVIDER TERMINATION AND EXCLUSION APPEALS (42 C.F.R. PART 498)

### Overview

The Act provides for a hearing and judicial review for any institution or agency dissatisfied with a determination that it is not a provider, or certain determinations that serve as the basis for termination of a provider agreement. The Act also provides appeals procedures for certain determinations made by the Office of Inspector General (OIG), including exclusion from Medicare and imposition of civil money penalties (CMPs).

### What May Be Appealed? (42 C.F.R. §§ 498.3, .20)

Certain initial determinations by CMS and OIG may be appealed. CMS makes initial determinations with respect to (among other initial determinations): (1) whether a prospective provider qualifies as a provider; (2) whether a prospective department of a provider, a remote location of a hospital, or satellite facility qualifies for provider-based status; (3) whether an institution is a hospital eligible to claim and continue to claim payment for emergency hospital services; (4) termination of certain provider agreements; (5) a finding of noncompliance for a skilled nursing facility (SNF) that results in certain remedies; and (6) the level of noncompliance found in a SNF (but only if a successful challenge implicates the range of CMPs or approval of its nurse aide training program). Initial determinations by the OIG includes (among other initial determinations): (1) the OIG's termination of a provider agreement; (2) suspension or exclusion based on fraud or abuse, or conviction of crimes related to Medicare participation; and (3) the imposition of certain sanctions. Such initial determinations must be mailed to the affected party and detail the basis for the determination, the effect of the determination, and the party's right to reconsideration or hearing.

## Who May Appeal? (42 C.F.R. § 498.5, .10)

Affected prospective providers and suppliers, enrolled providers and suppliers, and certain practitioners, nonparticipating hospitals that furnish emergency services, and suspended or excluded practitioners, providers, or suppliers have appeal rights. Affected parties may appoint as their representative anyone not disqualified or suspended from acting as a representative before the Secretary or otherwise prohibited by law.

## Appeals Process

### *Reconsideration (42 C.F.R. §§ 498.22, .24, .25)*

CMS initial determinations affecting a prospective provider or supplier or a hospital seeking to qualify to claim payment for emergency hospital services, but not OIG initial determinations, are subject to reconsideration. A dissatisfied affected party must file the reconsideration request with CMS or the state survey agency within sixty days from receipt of the notice of initial determination. The request must state the issues or the findings of fact with which the affected party disagrees, along with the reason(s) for disagreement. CMS then receives written evidence and statements, and considers: (1) the initial determination; (2) the findings on which the initial determination was based; (3) the evidence considered in making the initial determination; and (4) any submitted written evidence and statements.

The reconsideration decision made by CMS will either affirm or modify the initial determination. CMS must mail notice of the reconsideration decision to the affected party and give the reasons for the decision. If the decision is adverse, the notice must specify the conditions or requirements of law that the affected party failed to meet and informs the party of its right to a hearing.

### *Reopening of Initial or Reconsidered Determinations (42 C.F.R. § 498.30)*

CMS or OIG may, on its own initiative, reopen certain initial or reconsidered determinations within twelve months after the date of notice of the initial determination. Initial or reconsidered determinations concerning whether a prospective provider is a provider or that a hospital qualifies to elect to claim payment for emergency services may not be reopened.

### *Administrative Law Judge (ALJ) Hearing (42 C.F.R. §§ 498.40, .44, .47, .50, .52, .58, .61, .74)*

An affected party entitled to a hearing under 42 C.F.R. § 498.5 may file a request for hearing with CMS or the OIG, as appropriate, or with the Office of Hearing and Appeals (OHA). The written request must be filed within sixty days from receipt of the notice of initial, reconsidered, or revised determination, as appropriate. The request also must identify the specific issues, findings of fact, or conclusions of law that the affected party disagrees with and specify the basis for challenging the findings and conclusions.

An ALJ of the Department of Appeals Board (DAB) will be designated to hear and decide the case. At any time prior to the hearing, the ALJ may call a prehearing conference for purposes of delineating the issues in controversy, identifying evidence and witnesses, and obtaining stipulations. The agreements and stipulations entered into at the prehearing conference are binding on all parties, unless a party presents facts that, in the opinion of the ALJ, would make an agreement unreasonable or inequitable. The ALJ issues an order setting forth the results of the prehearing conference. Parties have 10 days to file objections.

The ALJ sets the time and place for the hearing and provides the parties with at least ten days written notice prior to the scheduled hearing date. The ALJ also may issue subpoenas if they are reasonably necessary for the full presentation of the case. Subpoenas will be issued only if a party specifies the pertinent facts the party expects to establish and indicates why those facts could not be established without use of a subpoena. Parties have 20 days to submit rebuttal to briefs or motions of the opposing party. Evidence may be received at the hearing even though it may be inadmissible under the Federal Rules of Evidence.

As soon as practical after the close of the hearing, the ALJ issues a written decision in the case based on the evidence in the record. The ALJ must mail a copy of the decision to the parties.

### *DAB Review (42 C.F.R. § 498.80, .82-.88)*

Either party has the right to request DAB review of the ALJ decision. Any dissatisfied party must file a written request for review with the OHA within sixty days from receipt of the ALJ's decision. The request for review must specify the issues, the findings of fact or conclusions of law with which the party disagrees, and the basis for contending the findings and conclusions are incorrect.

The DAB may dismiss, deny, or grant a request made by CMS or the OIG for review. The DAB will grant an affected party's request for review unless it determines that the affected party did not file timely (or show good cause for late filing), does not have a right to review, or a previous decision based on the same facts and law, and regarding the same issue, has become final through judicial affirmance. Upon granting a request for review, the parties are given, upon request, a reasonable opportunity to file briefs or other written statements, and to appear before the DAB to present evidence or oral arguments. The DAB may admit evidence into the record in addition to evidence admitted by the ALJ.

The DAB may issue a decision, remand the case to an ALJ for hearing and decision, or make a recommended decision to the ALJ. The DAB's decision must be in writing, contain findings of fact and conclusions of law, and may modify, affirm, or reverse the ALJ's decision.

### *Judicial Review (42 C.F.R. § 498.95)*

Any affected party that is dissatisfied with a DAB decision and is entitled to judicial review must commence a civil action within sixty days from receipt of the DAB's decision. For good cause, the DAB may extend the time for seeking judicial review.

### *Reopening of ALJ and DAB Decisions (42 C.F.R. §§ 498.100–.103)*

An ALJ decision may be reopened within sixty days from the date of the decision upon the motion of the ALJ or DAB, or upon the petition of either party to the hearing. A decision of the DAB only may be reopened by the DAB. A reopened decision may be revised based on new evidence. Notice of any revised decision is mailed to the parties states the basis or reason for the revised decision and informs them of their right to DAB or judicial review, as appropriate.

## NOTES

1. A CMS map of the fifteen MAC jurisdictions can be found at http://www.cms.hhs.gov/MedicareContractingReform/Downloads/Primary_AB_MAC_Jurisdictions_MAP.pdf.

2. *See* 42 C.F.R. § 411.110–.114 (outlining both conformance and non-conformance).

3. *See* 42 C.F.R. § 411.121

4. *See* 42 C.F.R. § 414.916.

5. *See* 42 C.F.R. § 414.908.

6. *See* 42 C.F.R. § 414.917.

7. *See* 42 C.F.R. § 405, Subpart H; for Part B claims appeals process, *see also* 42 C.F.R. Part 408, at 29.

8. *See* 42 C.F.R. § 403.232 (detailing the requirements and procedures for obtaining certification.

# APPENDIX A

# Comparison of Former and Current Fee-for-Service Appeals Processes

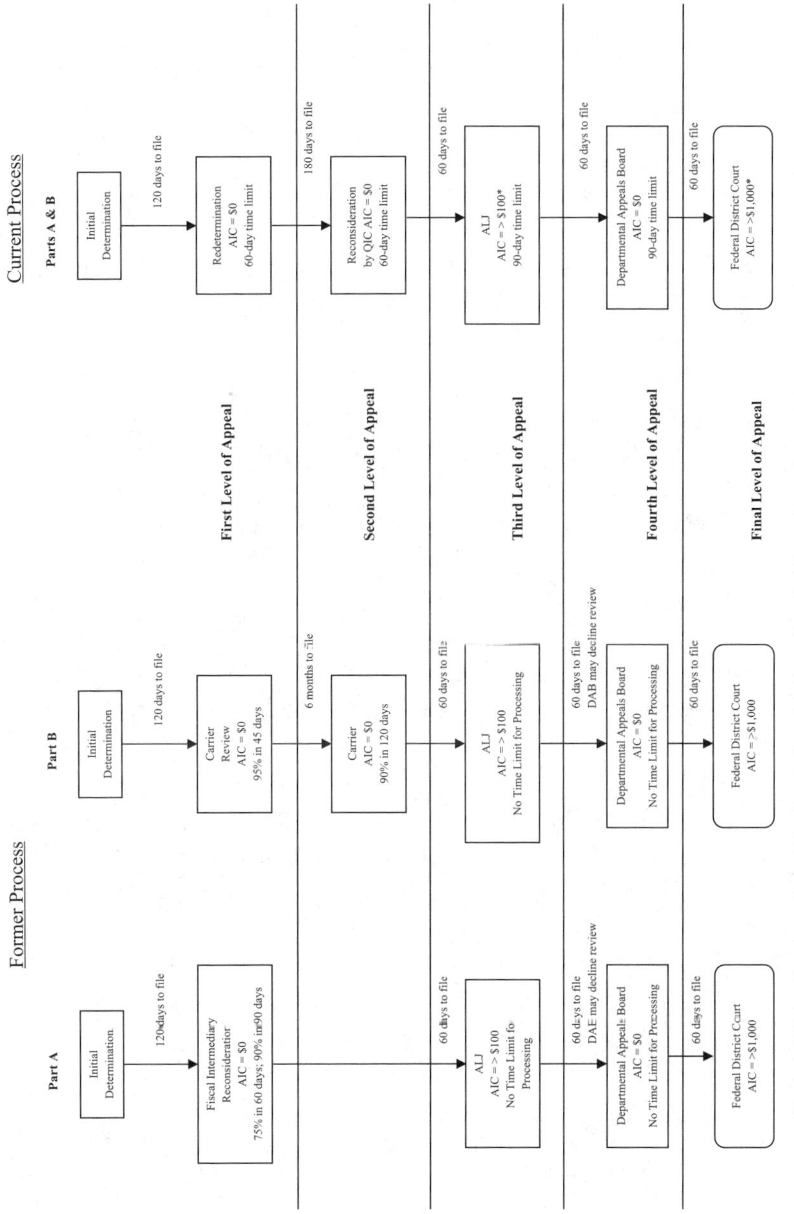


* Starting in 2005, the AIC requirement for an ALJ hearing and Federal District Court will be adjusted in accordance with the medical care component of the consumer price index.
AIC, Amont in controversy.

# APPENDIX B

## List of Abbreviations and Acronyms

| | |
|---|---|
| AIC | Amount in Controversy |
| ALJ | Administrative Law Judge |
| ASC | Ambulatory Surgical Center |
| BBA | Balanced Budget Act of 1997 |
| BBRA | Balanced Budget Refinement Act of 1999 |
| BIPA | Medicare, Medicaid and SCHIP Benefits Improvement and Protection Act of 2000 |
| CAP | Competitive Acquisition Plan |
| CMP | Competitive Medical Plan |
| CMPs | Civil Money Penalties |
| CMS | Centers for Medicare & Medicaid Services |
| CoPs | Conditions of Participation |
| CORF | Comprehensive Outpatient Rehabilitation Facility |
| DAB | Departmental Appeals Board |
| DMEPOS | Durable Medical Equipment, Prosthetics, Orthotics, and Supplies |
| DMERCs | Durable Medical Equipment Regional Carriers |
| DRG | Diagnosis-related Group |
| EAJR | Expedited Access to Judicial Review |
| EJR | Expedited Judicial Review |
| ESRD | End-Stage Renal Disease |
| FI | Fiscal Intermediary |
| GHP | Group Health Plan |
| HCFA | Health Care Financing Administration |
| HCPP | Health Care Prepayment Plan |
| HHA | Home Health Agency |
| HHS | United States Department of Health and Human Services |
| HI | Hospital Insurance |

| | |
|---|---|
| HIPAA | Health Insurance Portability and Accountability Act of 1996 |
| HMO | Health Maintenance Organization |
| IPPS | Inpatient Prospective Payment System |
| IRC | Internal Revenue Code |
| IRE | Independent Review Entity |
| IRS | Internal Revenue Service |
| LCD | Local Coverage Decision |
| LGHP | Large Group Health Plan |
| LMRP | Local Medical Review Policy |
| MA | Medicare Advantage |
| MAC | Medicare Appeals Council, or Medicare Administrative Contractor |
| MA-PDP | Medicare Advantage Prescription Drug Plan |
| MGCRB | Medicare Geographic Classification Review Board |
| MMA | Medicare Prescription Drug, Improvement, and Modernization Act of 2003 |
| MSP | Medicare Secondary Payer |
| NCD | National Coverage Decision |
| NPR | Notice of Program Reimbursement |
| NSC | National Supplier Clearinghouse |
| OHA | Office of Hearing and Appeals |
| OIG | Office of Inspector General |
| PDP | Prescription Drug Plan |
| PRRB | Provider Reimbursement Review Board |
| QIC | Qualified Independent Contractor |
| QIO | Quality Improvement Organization |
| SMI | Supplemental Medical Insurance |
| SNF | Skilled Nursing Facility |
| SSA | Social Security Administration |
| TEFRA | Tax Equity and Fiscal Responsibility Act of 1982 |
| VTC | Video Teleconference |

# APPENDIX C

# Contact Information for Administrative Entities Processing Appeals

In most cases, the address an appellant should use when filing an appeal is included in the document from which a person wants to appeal. Most appeal entities, however, have Web sites with contact information and/or further appeal information that may be helpful.

- **HHS Administrative Law Judge appeals**
  www.hhs.gov/OMHA

- **HHS Departmental Appeals Board**
  www.hhs.gov/DAB

- **Medicare Appeals Council appeals**
  www.hhs.gov/DAB

- **DAB Administrative Law Judge appeals**
  www.hhs.gov/DAB

- **LCD/NCD appeals**
  www.medicare.gov/coverage/static/appeals.asp

- **Provider Reimbursement Review Board appeals**
  www.cms.hhs.gov/PRRBReview/

  The instructions for PRRB appeals can be found at:
  http://www.cms.hhs.gov/providers/prrb/prrb.asp

- **Medicare Geographic Classification Review Board appeals**
  www.cms.hhs.gov/MGCRB/

- **CMS Hearing Officer appeals**
  CMS Hearing Officer
  2520 Lord Baltimore Drive, Suite L
  Baltimore, MD 21244-2670

## NOT-FOR-PROFIT ADVOCACY GROUP CONTACT INFORMATION

**Center for Health Care Rights**
520 South Lafayette Park Place, Suite 214
Los Angeles, CA 90057
(213) 383-4519 (phone)
(213) 383-4598 (facsimile)
www.healthcarerights.org

**Families USA**
1201 New York Avenue, NW, Suite 1100
Washington, D.C. 20005
(202) 628-3030 (phone)
(202) 347-2417 (facsimile)
www.familiesusa.org

**National Health Law Program**
2639 South La Cienega Boulevard
Los Angeles, CA 90034-2675
(310) 204-6010 (phone)
(310) 204-0891 (facsimile)

1101 14th Street, NW, Suite 405
Washington, D.C. 20005
(202) 289-7661 (phone)
(202) 289-7724 (facsimile)
www.healthlaw.org

**Center for Medicare Advocacy, Inc.**
1101 Vermont Avenue, Suite 1001
Washington, D.C. 20005
(202) 216-0028 (phone)
(202) 216-0119 (facsimile)
www.medicareadvocacy.org

**Medicare Rights Center**
1460 Broadway, 17th Floor
New York, NY 10036
(212) 869-3850 (phone)
(212) 869-3532 (facsimile)

1030 15th Street, NW, Suite 250
Washington, D.C. 20005
(202) 589-1316 (phone)
(202) 589-1310 (facsimile)
www.medicarerights.org

**National Senior Citizens Law Center**
1101 14th Street, NW, Suite 400
Washington, D.C. 20005
(202) 289-6976 (phone)
(202) 289-7224 (facsimile)
www.nsclc.org

# APPENDIX D

# U.S. Department of Health and Human Services Medicare Appeals Processes: Selected Sections of Regulation Text

**(Unofficial Version)**

**Title 42: Public Health**

**PART 403—SPECIAL PROGRAMS AND PROJECTS**

**Subpart B—Medicare Supplemental Policies**

**Source:** 47 FR 32400, July 26, 1982, unless otherwise noted.

**§ 403.200 Basis and scope.**

(a) *Provisions of the legislation.* This subpart implements, in part, section 1882 of the Social Security Act. The intent of that section is to enable Medicare beneficiaries to identify Medicare supplemental policies that do not duplicate Medicare, and that provide adequate, fairly priced protection against expenses not covered by Medicare. The legislation establishes certain standards for Medicare supplemental policies and provides two methods for informing Medicare beneficiaries which policies meet those standards:

(1) Through a State approved program, that is, a program that a Supplemental Health Insurance Panel determines to meet certain minimum requirements for the regulation of Medicare supplemental policies; and

(2) In a State without an approved program, through certification by the Secretary of policies voluntarily submitted by insuring organizations for review against the standards.

(b) *Scope of subpart.* This subpart sets forth the standards and procedures CMS will use to implement the voluntary certification program.

**§ 403.245 Loss of certification.**

(a) A policy loses certification if—

(1) The insuring organization withdraws the policy from the voluntary certification program; or

(2) CMS determines that—

(i) The policy fails to meet the requirements specified in § 403.232(a); or

(ii) The insuring organization has failed to meet the requirements for submittal of material specified in § 403.239.

(b) If a policy loses its certification, CMS will inform all State Commissioners and Superintendents of Insurance of that fact.

(c) If a policy that displays the emblem, or that has been marketed as a certified policy without the emblem, loses certification, the insuring organization must notify each holder of the policy, or of a certificate issued under the policy, of that fact. The notice must be in writing and sent by the earlier of—

(1) The date of the first regular premium notice after the date the policy loses its certification; or

(2) 60 days after the date the policy loses its certification.

**§ 403.248 Administrative review of CMS determinations.**

(a) This section provides for administrative review if CMS determines—

(1) Not to certify a policy; or

(2) That a policy no longer meets the standards for certification.

(b) If CMS makes a determination specified in paragraph (a) of this section, it will send a notice to the insuring organization containing the following information:

(1) That CMS has made such a determination.

(2) The reasons for the determination.

(3) That the insuring organization has 30 days from the date of the notice to—

(i) Request, in writing, an administrative review of the CMS determination; and

(ii) Submit additional information to CMS for review.

(4) That, if the insuring organization requests an administrative review, CMS will conduct the review, as provided for in paragraph (c) of this section.

(5) That, in a case involving loss of certification, the CMS determination will go into effect 30 days from the date of the notice, unless the insuring organization requests an administrative review. If the insuring organization requests an administrative review, the policy retains its certification until CMS makes a final determination.

(c) If the insuring organization requests an administrative review, CMS will conduct the review as follows—

(1) A CMS official, not involved in the initial CMS determination, will initiate and complete an administrative review within 90 days of the date of the notice provided for in paragraph (b) of this section.

(2) The official will consider—

(i) The original material submitted to CMS for review, as specified in § 403.232(b) or § 403.239(a); and

(ii) Any additional information, that the insuring organization submits to CMS.

(3) Within 15 days after the administrative review is completed, CMS will inform the insuring organization in writing of the final decision, with an explanation of the final decision.

(4) If the final decision is that a policy loses its certification, the loss of certification will go into effect 15 days after the date of CMS's notice informing the insuring organization of the final decision.

## PART 405—FEDERAL HEALTH INSURANCE FOR THE AGED AND DISABLED

### Subpart G—Reconsiderations and Appeals under Medicare Part A

**NOTE: Section G applies only to appeals filed prior to January 1, 2006. Appeals filed subsequent to January 1, 2006 are subject to the Part I regulations.**

**Authority:** Secs. 1102, 1155, 1869(b), 1871, 1872, and 1879 of the Social Security Act (42 U.S.C. 1302, 1320c-4, 1395ff(b), 1395hh, 1395ii, and 1395pp).

**Source:** 37 FR 5814, Mar. 22, 1972, unless otherwise noted. Redesignated at 42 FR 52826, Sept. 30, 1977.

**§ 405.701 Basis, purpose and definitions.**

(a) This subpart implements section 1869 of the Social Security Act. Section 1869(a) provides that the Secretary will make determinations about the following matters, and section 1869(b) provides for a hearing for an individual who is dissatisfied with the Secretary's determination as to:

(1) Whether the individual is entitled to hospital insurance (Part A) or supplementary medical insurance (Part B) under title XVIII of the Act; or

(2) The amount payable under hospital insurance.

(b) This subpart establishes the procedures governing initial determinations, reconsidered determinations, hearings, and final agency review, and the reopening of determinations and decisions that are applicable to matters arising under paragraph (a) of this section.

(c) Subparts J and R of 20 CFR part 404 (dealing with determinations, the administrative review process and representation of parties) are also applicable to matters arising under paragraph (a) of this section, except to the extent that specific provisions are contained in this subpart.

(d) *Definitions.* As used in subpart G of this part, the term—

*Appellant* designates the beneficiary, provider or other person or entity that has filed an appeal concerning a particular determination of benefits under Medicare Part A. Designation as an appellant does not in itself convey standing to appeal the determination in question.

*Common issues of law and fact,* with respect to the aggregation of claims by two or more appellants to meet the minimum amount in controversy needed for a hearing, occurs when the claims sought to be aggregated are denied or reduced for similar reasons and arise from a similar fact pattern material to the reason the claims are denied.

*Delivery of similar or related services,* with respect to the aggregation of claims by two or more provider appellants to meet the minimum amount in controversy needed for a hearing, means like or coordinated services or items provided to the same beneficiary by the appellants.
[55 FR 11020, Mar. 26, 1990, as amended at 59 FR 12181, Mar. 16, 1994]

**§ 405.702 Notice of initial determination.**
After a request for payment under Part A of title XVIII of the Act is filed with the intermediary by or on behalf of the individual who received inpatient hospital services, extended care services, or home health services, and the intermediary has ascertained whether the items and services furnished are covered under Part A of title XVIII, and where appropriate, ascertained and made payment of amounts due or has ascertained that no payments were due, the individual will be notified in writing of the initial determination in his case. In addition, if the items or services furnished such individual are not covered under Part A of title XVIII by reason of § 411.15(g) or § 411.15(k) and payment may not be made for such items or services under § 411.400 only because the requirements of § 411.400(a)(2) are not met, the provider of services which furnished such items or services will be notified in writing of the initial determination in such individual's case. These notices shall be mailed to the individual and the provider of services at their last known addresses and shall state in detail the basis for the determination. Such written notices shall also inform the individual and the provider of services of their right to reconsideration of the determination if they are dissatisfied with the determination.
[55 FR 11020, Mar. 26, 1990]

**§ 405.704 Actions which are initial determinations.**

(a) *Applications and entitlement of individuals.* An initial determination with respect to an individual includes the following—

(1) A determination with respect to entitlement to hospital insurance or supplementary medical insurance;

(2) A disallowance of an individual's application for entitlement to hospital or supplementary medical insurance, if the individual fails to submit evidence requested by SSA to support the application. (SSA will specify in the initial determination the conditions of entitlement that the applicant failed to establish by not submitting the requested evidence);

(3) A denial of a request for withdrawal of an application for hospital or supplementary medical insurance;

(4) A denial of a request for cancellation of a "request for withdrawal"; and

(5) A determination as to whether an individual, previously determined to be entitled to hospital or supplementary medical insurance, is no longer entitled to such benefits, including a determination based on nonpayment of premiums.

(b) *Requests for payment by or on behalf of individuals.* An initial determination with respect to an individual includes any determination made on the basis of a request for payment by or on behalf of the individual under Part A of Medicare, including a determination with respect to:

(1) The coverage of items and services furnished;

(2) The amount of an applicable deductible;

(3) The application of the coinsurance feature;

(4) The number of days of inpatient hospital benefits utilized during a spell of illness or for purposes of the inpatient psychiatric hospital 190-day lifetime maximum;

(5) The number of days of the 60-day lifetime reserve utilized for inpatient hospital coverage;

(6) The number of days of posthospital extended care benefits utilized;

(7) The number of home health visits utilized;

(8) The physician certification requirement;

(9) The request for payment requirement;

(10) The beginning and ending of a spell of illness, including a determination made under the presumptions established under § 409.60(c)(2) of this chapter, as specified in § 409.60(c)(4) of this chapter.

(11) The medical necessity of services (See parts 466 and 473 of this chapter for provisions pertaining to initial and reconsidered determinations made by a QIO);

(12) When services are excluded from coverage as custodial care (§ 411.15(g)) or as not reasonable and necessary (§ 411.15(k)), whether the individual or the provider of services who furnished the services, or both, knew or could reasonably have been expected to know that the services were excluded from coverage (see § 411.402);

(13) Any other issues having a present or potential effect on the amount of benefits to be paid under Part A of Medicare, including a determination as to whether there has been an overpayment or underpayment of benefits paid under Part A, and if so, the amount thereof; and

(14) Whether a waiver of adjustment or recovery under sections 1870(b) and (c) of the Act is appropriate when an overpayment of hospital insurance benefits or supplementary medical insurance benefits (including a payment under section 1814(e) of the Act) has been made with respect to an individual.

(c) *Initial determination with respect to a provider of services.* An initial determination with respect to a provider of services shall be a determination made on the basis of a request for payment filed by the provider under Part A of Medicare on behalf of an individual who was furnished items or services by the provider, but only if the determination involves the following:

(1) A finding by the intermediary that such items or services are not covered by reason of § 411.15(g) or § 411.15(k); and

(2) A finding by the intermediary that either such individual or such provider of services, or both, knew or could reasonably have been expected to know that such items or services were excluded from coverage under the program.

[55 FR 11020, Mar. 26, 1990]

**§ 405.705 Actions which are not initial determinations.**

An initial determination under Part A of Medicare does not include determinations relating to:

(a) The reasonable cost of items or services furnished under Part A of Medicare;

(b) Whether an institution or agency meets the conditions for participation in the program;

(c) Whether an individual is qualified for use of the expedited appeals process as provided in § 405.718;

(d) An action regarding compromise of a claim arising under the Medicare program, or termination or suspension of collection action on such a claim under the Federal Claims Collection Act of 1966 (31 U.S.C. 3711). See 20 CFR 404.515 for overpayment claims against an individual, § 405.376 for overpayment claims against a provider, physician or other supplier, and § 408.110 for claims concerning unpaid Medicare premiums;

(e) The transfer or discharge of residents of skilled nursing facilities in accordance with § 483.12 of this chapter; or

(f) The preadmission screening and annual resident review processes required by part 483 subparts C and E of this chapter.

[45 FR 73932, Nov. 7, 1980; 46 FR 24565, May 1, 1981, as amended at 52 FR 22454, June 12, 1987; 52 FR 48123, Dec. 18, 1987; 57 FR 56504, Nov. 30, 1992; 61 FR 63749, Dec. 2, 1996]

**§ 405.706 Decisions of utilization review committees.**

(a) *General rule.* A decision of a utilization review committee is a medical determination by a staff committee of the provider or a group similarly composed and does not constitute a determination by the Secretary within the meaning of section 1869 of the Act. The decision of a utilization review committee may be considered by CMS along with other pertinent medical evidence in determining whether or not an individual has the right to have payment made under Part A of title XVIII.

(b) *Applicability under the prospective payment system.* CMS may consider utilization review committee decisions related to inpatient hospital services paid for under the prospective payment system (see part 412 of this chapter) only as those decisions concern:

(1) The appropriateness of admissions resulting in payments under subparts D, E and G of part 412 of this chapter.

(2) The covered days of care involved in determinations of outlier payments under § 412.80(a)(1)(i) of this chapter; and

(3) The necessity of professional services furnished in high cost outliers under § 412.80(a)(1)(ii) of this chapter.

[48 FR 39831, Sept. 1, 1983]

**§ 405.708 Effect of initial determination.**

(a) The initial determination under § 405.704(a) or (b) shall be binding upon the individual on whose behalf payment under Part A has been requested or, if such individual is deceased, upon the representative of such individual's estate, unless it is reconsidered in accordance with §§ 405.710 through 405.717 or revised in accordance with § 405.750. Such individual (or the representative of such individual's estate if the individual is deceased) shall be the party to such initial determination.

(b) The initial determination under § 405.704(c) shall be binding upon the provider of services unless it is reconsidered in accordance with §§ 405.710 through 405.717 or revised in accordance with § 405.750. Such provider of services shall be the party to such initial determination.

[55 FR 11021, Mar. 26, 1990, as amended at 62 FR 25855, May 12, 1997]

**§ 405.710 Right to reconsideration.**

(a) An individual who is a party to an initial determination, as specified in § 405.704(a) and (b), (or if such individual is deceased, the representative of such individual's estate) and who is dissatisfied with the initial determination may request a reconsideration of such determination in accordance with § 405.711 regardless of the amount in controversy.

(b) A provider of services who is a party to an initial determination (as specified in § 405.704(c)) and who is dissatisfied with such initial determination may request a reconsideration of such determination in accordance with § 405.711, regardless of the amount in controversy, but only if the individual on whose behalf the request for payment was made has indicated in writing that he does not intend to request reconsideration of the intermediary's initial determination on such request for payment, or if the intermediary has made a finding (see § 405.704(c)) that such individual did not know or could not reasonably have been expected to know that the expenses incurred for the items or services for which such request for payment was made were not reimbursable by reason of § 411.15(g) or § 411.15(k).

[55 FR 11021, Mar. 26, 1990]

**§ 405.711 Time and place of filing request for reconsideration.**

The request for reconsideration shall be made in writing and filed at an office of the SSA or the CMS or, in the case of a qualified railroad retirement beneficiary (see 20 CFR 404.368) filed at an office of the Railroad Retirement Board, within 60 days after the date of receipt of notice of initial determination, unless such time is extended as provided in § 405.712. A request for reconsideration which is filed with the intermediary which received the request for payment submitted on behalf of the individual is considered to have been filed with the CMS as of the date it is filed with the intermediary. For purposes of this section, the date of receipt of notice of the initial determination shall be presumed to be 5 days after the date of such notice, unless there is a reasonable showing to the contrary.

[41 FR 47917, Nov. 1, 1976. Redesignated at 42 FR 52826, Sept. 30, 1977, as amended at 62 FR 25855, May 12, 1997]

**§ 405.712 Extension of time to request reconsideration.**

If a party to an initial determination desires to file a request for reconsideration after the time for filing such request in accordance with § 405.711 has passed,

such party may file a petition with the SSA or the CMS or, in the case of a qualified railroad retirement beneficiary, with the Railroad Retirement Board, for an extension of time for the filing of such request. Such petition shall be in writing and shall state the reasons why the request for reconsideration was not filed within the required time. For good cause shown, the CMS may extend the time for filing the request for reconsideration.
[37 FR 5814, Mar. 22, 1972. Redesignated at 42 FR 52826, Sept. 30, 1977, as amended at 62 FR 25855, May 12, 1997]

**§ 405.714 Withdrawal of request for reconsideration.**
A request for reconsideration may be withdrawn by the party to the initial determination who filed the request or by his representative provided that the withdrawal is made in writing and filed at an office of the SSA or the CMS or, in the case of a qualified railroad retirement beneficiary, with the Railroad Retirement Board prior to the date of the mailing of the notice of reconsidered determination. A withdrawal filed with the intermediary which received the request for payment submitted on behalf of the individual is considered to have been filed with the CMS as of the date it is filed with the intermediary.
[40 FR 1025, Jan. 6, 1975. Redesignated at 42 FR 52826, Sept. 30, 1977, as amended at 62 FR 25855, May 12, 1997]

**§ 405.715 Reconsidered determination.**
(a) In reconsidering an initial determination, the CMS shall review such initial determination, the evidence and findings upon which such determination was based, and any additional evidence submitted to the SSA or the CMS or otherwise obtained by the intermediary or the CMS; and shall make a determination affirming or revising, in whole or in part, such initial determination.

(b) If the request for reconsideration is filed by an individual with respect to an initial determination specified in § 405.704(b)(12), the provider of services who furnished the items or services shall, prior to the making of the reconsidered determination, be made a party thereto. If pursuant to § 405.710(b) a request for reconsideration is filed by a provider of services with respect to an individual determination under § 405.704(c), the individual who was furnished the items or services shall, prior to the making of the reconsidered determination, be made a party thereto.
[55 FR 11021, Mar. 26, 1990, as amended at 62 FR 25855, May 12, 1997]

**§ 405.716 Notice of reconsidered determination.**
Written notice of the reconsidered determination shall be mailed by the CMS to the parties and their representatives at their last known addresses. Such notice shall state the specific reasons for the reconsidered determination and shall advise the parties of their right to a hearing if the amount in controversy is $100 or more, or, if appropriate, advise them of the requirements for use of the expedited appeals process (see § 405.718).
[40 FR 53387, Nov. 18, 1975. Redesignated at 42 FR 52826, Sept. 30, 1977, as amended at 62 FR 25855, May 12, 1997]

**§ 405.717 Effect of a reconsidered determination.**
The reconsidered determination is binding upon all parties unless–

(a) A request for a hearing is filed with SSA or CMS within 60 days after the date of receipt of notice of the reconsidered determination by the parties (for purposes of this section, the date of receipt of notice of the reconsidered determination is presumed to be 5 days after the date of the notice, unless it is shown that the notice was received earlier or later); or

(b) The reconsidered determination is revised in accordance with § 405.750; or

(c) The expedited appeals process is used in accordance with § 405.718.
[62 FR 25852, May 12, 1997]

**§ 405.718 Expedited appeals process.**

(a) *Conditions for use of expedited appeals process (EAP).* A party may use the EAP to request court review in place of an administrative law judge (ALJ) hearing or Departmental Appeals Board (DAB) review if the following conditions are met:

(1) CMS has made a reconsideration determination; an ALJ has made a hearing decision; or DAB review has been requested, but a final decision has not been issued.

(2) The filing entity is a party referred to in § 405.718(d).

(3) The party has filed a request for an ALJ hearing in accordance with § 405.722, or DAB review in accordance with 20 CFR 404.968.

(4) The amount remaining in controversy is $1,000 or more.

(5) If there is more than one party to the reconsideration determination or hearing decision, each party concurs, in writing, with the request for the EAP.

(b) *Content of the request for EAP.* The request for the EAP:

(1) Alleges that there are no material issues of fact in dispute; and

(2) Asserts that the only factor precluding a decision favorable to the party is a statutory provision that is unconstitutional or a regulation, national coverage decision under section 1862(a)(1) of the Act, or CMS Ruling that is invalid.

(c) *Place and time for requesting an EAP*–

(1) *Place for filing request.* The person must file a written request–

(i) At an office of SSA or CMS; or

(ii) If the person is in the Philippines, at the Veterans Administration Regional Office or with an ALJ; or

(iii) If the person is a qualified railroad retirement beneficiary, at an office of the Railroad Retirement Board.

(2) *Time of filing request.* The party may file a request for the EAP–

(i) If the party has requested a hearing, at any time prior to receipt of the notice of the ALJ's decision;

(ii) Within 60 days after the date of receipt of notice of the ALJ's decision or dismissal, unless the time is extended in accordance with the standards set out in 20 CFR 404.925(c). For purposes of this section, the date of receipt of the notice is presumed to be 5 days after the date on the notice, unless it is shown that the notice was received later; or

(iii) If the party has requested DAB review, at any time prior to receipt of notice of the Board's decision.

(d) *Parties to the EAP.* The parties to the EAP are the persons who were parties to the reconsideration determination and, if appropriate, to the hearing.

(e) *Determination on request for EAP.* (1) For EAP requests initiated at the ALJ level, an ALJ determines whether all conditions of paragraphs (a) and (b) of this section are met.

(2) If a hearing decision has been issued, the DAB determines whether all conditions of paragraphs (a) and (b) of this section are met.

(f) *ALJ or DAB certification for the EAP.* If the party meets the requirements for the EAP, the ALJ or the DAB, as appropriate, certifies the case in writing stating that:

(1) The facts involved in the claim are not in dispute;

(2) Except as indicated in paragraph (f)(3) of this section, CMS's interpretation of the law is not in dispute;

(3) The sole issue(s) in dispute is the constitutionality of a statutory provision or the validity of a regulation, CMS Ruling, or national coverage decision based on section 1862(a)(1) of the Act.

(4) Except for the provision challenged, the right(s) of the party is established; and

(5) The determination or decision made by the ALJ or DAB is final for purposes of seeking judicial review.

(g) *Effect of ALJ or DAB certification.* (1) Following the issuance of the certification described in paragraph (f) of this section, the party waives completion of the remaining steps of the administrative appeals process.

(2) The 60-day period for filing a civil suit in a Federal district court begins on the date of receipt of the ALJ or DAB certification.

(h) *Effect of a request for EAP that does not result in certification.* If a request for the EAP does not meet all the conditions for use of the process, the ALJ or DAB so advises the party and treats the request as a request for hearing or DAB review, as appropriate.
[62 FR 25852, May 12, 1997]

**§ 405.720 Hearing; right to hearing.**

A person has a right to a hearing regarding any initial determination made under § 405.704 if:

(a) Such initial determination has been reconsidered by the CMS;

(b) Such person was a party to the reconsidered determination;

(c) Such person or his representative has filed a written request for a hearing in accordance with the procedure described in § 405.722; and

(d) The amount in controversy is $100 or more.

[40 FR 1025, Jan. 6, 1975. Redesignated at 42 FR 52826, Sept. 30, 1977, as amended at 62 FR 25855, May 12, 1997]

**§ 405.722 Time and place of filing request for a hearing.**

The request for a hearing shall be made in writing and filed at an office of the SSA or the CMS or with a ALJ, or, in the case of a qualified railroad retirement

beneficiary, at an office of the Railroad Retirement Board. Such request must be filed within 60 days after the date of receipt of notice of the reconsidered determination by such individual, except where the time is extended as provided in 20 CFR 404.933(c). For purposes of this section, the date of receipt of notice of the reconsidered determination shall be presumed to be 5 days after the date of such notice, unless there is a reasonable showing to the contrary.
[45 FR 73933, Nov. 7, 1980, as amended at 62 FR 25855, May 12, 1997]

**§ 405.724 Departmental Appeals Board (DAB) review.**
Regulations beginning at 20 CFR 404.967 regarding SSA Appeals Council Review are also applicable to DAB review of matters addressed by this subpart.
[62 FR 25852, May 12, 1997]

**§ 405.730 Court review.**

(a) To the extent authorized by sections 1869, 1876(c)(5)(B), and 1879(d) of the Act, a party to a Departmental Appeals Board (DAB) decision or an ALJ decision if the DAB does not review the ALJ decision, may obtain a court review if the amount remaining in controversy is $1,000 or more. A party may obtain court review by filing a civil action in a district court of the United States in accordance with the provisions of section 205(g) of the Act. The filing procedure is set forth at 20 CFR 422.210.

(b) A party to a reconsidered determination or an ALJ hearing decision may obtain a court review if the amount in controversy is $1,000 or more, and he or she requests and meets the conditions for the expedited appeals process set forth in § 405.718.
[62 FR 25852, May 12, 1997]

**§ 405.732 Review of a national coverage determination (NCD).**

(a) *General rule.* (1) An NCD is a determination by the Secretary for whether or not a particular item or service is covered nationally under title XVIII of the Act.

(2) An NCD does not include a determination of what code, if any, is assigned to a particular item or service covered under title XVIII or a determination for the amount of payment made for a particular item or service.

(3) NCDs are made under section 1862(a)(1) of the Act or other applicable provisions of the Act.

(4) An NCD is binding on all Medicare carriers, fiscal intermediaries, QIOs, HMOs, CMPs, HCPPs, the Medicare Appeals Council, and ALJs.

(b) *Review by ALJ.* (1) An ALJ may not disregard, set aside, or otherwise review an NCD.

(2) An ALJ may review the facts of a particular case to determine whether an NCD applies to a specific claim for benefits and, if so, whether the NCD has been applied correctly to the claim.

(c) *Review by court.* For initial determinations and NCD challenges under section 1862(a)(1) of the Act, arising before October 1, 2002, a court's review of an NCD is limited to whether the record is incomplete or otherwise lacks adequate information to support the validity of the decision, unless the case has been remanded to

the Secretary to supplement the record regarding the NCD. In these cases, the court may not invalidate an NCD except upon review of the supplemental record.
[68 FR 63715, Nov. 7, 2003]

**§ 405.740 Principles for determining the amount in controversy.**

(a) *Individual appellants.* For the purpose of determining whether an individual appellant meets the minimum amount in controversy needed for a hearing ($100), the following rules apply:

(1) The amount in controversy is computed as the actual amount charged the individual for the items and services in question, less any amount for which payment has been made by the intermediary and less any deductible and coinsurance amounts applicable in the particular case.

(2) A single beneficiary may aggregate claims from two or more providers to meet the $100 hearing threshold and a single provider may aggregate claims for services provided to one or more beneficiaries to meet the $100 hearing threshold.

(3) In either of the circumstances specified in paragraph (a)(2) of this section, two or more claims may be aggregated by an individual appellant only if the claims have previously been reconsidered and a request for hearing has been made within 60 days after receipt of the reconsideration determination(s).

(4) When requesting a hearing, the appellant must specify in his or her appeal request the specific claims to be aggregated.

(b) *Two or more appellants.* As specified below, under section 1869(b)(2) of the Act, two or more appellants may aggregate their claims together to meet the minimum amount in controversy needed for a hearing ($100). The right to aggregate under this statutory provision applies to claims for items and services furnished on or after January 1, 1987.

(1) The aggregate amount in controversy is computed as the actual amount charged the individual(s) for the items and services in question, less any amount for which payment has been made by the intermediary and less any deductible and coinsurance amounts applicable in the particular case.

(2) In determining the amount in controversy, two or more appellants may aggregate their claims together under the following circumstances:

(i) Two or more beneficiaries may combine claims representing services from the same or different provider(s) if the claims involve common issues of law and fact;

(ii) Two or more providers may combine their claims if the claims involve the delivery of similar or related services to the same beneficiary; or

(iii) Two or more providers may combine their claims if the claims involve common issues of law and fact with respect to services furnished to two or more beneficiaries.

(iv) In any of the circumstances specified in paragraphs (b)(2)(i) through (b)(2)(iii) of this section, the claims may be aggregated only if the claims have previously been reconsidered and a request for hearing has been made within

60 days after receipt of the reconsideration determination(s). Moreover, in the request for hearing, the appellants must specify the claims that they seek to aggregate.

(c) The determination as to whether the amount in controversy is $100 or more is made by the administrative law judge (ALJ).

(d) In determining the amount in controversy under paragraph (b) of this section, the ALJ also makes the determination as to what constitutes "similar or related services" or "common issues of law and fact."

(e) When a civil action is filed by either an individual appellant or two or more appellants, the Secretary may assert that the aggregation principles contained in this subpart may be applied to determine the amount in controversy for judicial review ($1000).

(f) Notwithstanding the provisions of paragraphs (a)(1) and (b)(1) of this section, when payment is made for certain excluded services under § 411.400 of this chapter or the liability of the beneficiary for those services is limited under § 411.402 of this chapter, the amount in controversy is computed as the amount that would have been charged the beneficiary for the items or services in question, less any deductible and coinsurance amounts applicable in the particular case, had such expenses not been paid pursuant to § 411.400 of this chapter or had such liability not been limited pursuant to § 411.402 of this chapter.

(g) Under this subpart, an appellant may not combine Part A and Part B claims together to meet the requisite amount in controversy for a hearing. HMO, CMP and HCPP appellants under part 417 of this chapter may combine Part A and Part B claims together to meet the requisite amounts in controversy for a hearing.

[59 FR 12181, Mar. 16, 1994]

**§ 405.745 Amount in controversy ascertained after reconsideration.**

For the purpose of determining whether a party to a reconsidered determination is entitled to a hearing, the amount in controversy after the reconsideration action rather than the amount in controversy initially at issue shall be controlling.

[40 FR 1026, Jan. 6, 1975. Redesignated at 42 FR 52826, Sept. 30, 1977]

**§ 405.747 Dismissal of request for hearing; amount in controversy less than $100.**

The ALJ shall, without holding a hearing, dismiss the request for hearing if the request for hearing plainly shows that less than $100 is in controversy. If a hearing is held and the ALJ finds that the amount in controversy is less than $100, the ALJ shall dismiss the request for hearing and will not rule on the substantive issues involved in the appeal.

[37 FR 5814, Mar. 23, 1972. Redesignated at 42 FR 52826, Sept. 30, 1977, as amended at 62 FR 25855, May 12, 1997]

**§ 405.750 Time period for reopening initial, revised, or reconsidered determinations and decisions or revised decisions of an ALJ or the Departmental Appeals Board (DAB); binding effect of determination and decisions.**

(a) *Reopenings concerning applications and entitlement.* A determination, or decision, or revised determination or decision made by the SSA concerning any matter under § 405.704(a), may be reopened and revised under 20 CFR 404.988 (conditions for reopening).

(b) *Reopenings concerning a request for payment.* An initial, revised, or reconsidered determination of CMS, or a decision or revised decision of an ALJ or of the DAB, with respect to an individual's right concerning a request for payment under Medicare Part A, which is otherwise binding under 20 CFR 404.955 or 404.981 and §§ 405.708 or 405.717 of this subpart may be reopened:

(1) Within 12 months from the date of the notice of the initial or reconsidered determination to the party to such determination;

(2) After such 12-month period, but within 4 years after the date of the notice of the initial determination to the individual, upon establishment of good cause for reopening such determination or decision (see 20 CFR 404.988(b) and 404.989); or

(3) At any time, when:

(i) Such initial, revised, or reconsidered determination or such decision or revised decision is unfavorable, in whole or in part, to the party thereto, but only for the purpose of correcting clerical error or error on the face of the evidence on which such determination or decision was based; or

(ii) Such initial, revised, or reconsidered determination or such decision or revised decision was procured by fraud or similar fault of the beneficiary or some other person.

[45 FR 73933, Nov. 7, 1980, as amended at 61 FR 32348, June 24, 1996; 62 FR 25853, 25855, May 12, 1997]

**§ 405.753 Appeal of a categorization of a device.**

(a) CMS's acceptance of the FDA categorization of a device as an experimental/investigational (Category A) device under § 405.203 is a national coverage decision under section 1862(a)(1) of the Act.

(b) CMS's acceptance of the FDA categorization of a device as an experimental/investigational (Category A) device under § 405.203 is an aspect of an initial determination that, under section 1862 of the Act, payment may not be made.

(c) In accordance with section 1869(b)(3)(A) of the Act, CMS's acceptance of the FDA categorization of a device as an experimental/investigational (Category A) device under § 405.203 may not be reviewed by an administrative law judge.

[60 FR 48424, Sept. 19, 1995]

**Subpart H—Appeals under the Medicare Part B Program**

**NOTE: Section G applies only to appeals filed prior to January 1, 2006. Appeals filed subsequent to January 1, 2006 are subject to the Part I regulations.**

**Authority:** Secs. 1102, 1842(b)(3)(C), 1869(b), and 1871 of the Social Security Act (42 U.S.C. 1302, 1395u(b)(3)(C), 1395ff(b), and 1395hh).

**Source:** 32 FR 18028, Dec. 16, 1967, unless otherwise noted. Redesignated at 42 FR 52826, Sept. 30, 1977.

**§ 405.801 Part B appeals—general description.**

(a) The Medicare carrier makes an initial determination when a request for payment for Part B benefits is submitted. If an individual beneficiary is dissatisfied with the initial determination, he or she may request, and the carrier will perform, a review of the claim. Following the carrier's review determination, the beneficiary may obtain a carrier hearing if the amount remaining in controversy is at least $100. The beneficiary is also entitled to a carrier hearing without the benefit of a review determination when the initial request for payment is not being acted upon with reasonable promptness (as defined in § 405.802). Following the carrier hearing, the beneficiary may obtain a hearing before an ALJ if the amount remaining in controversy is at least $500. If the beneficiary is dissatisfied with the decision of the ALJ, he or she may request the Departmental Appeals Board (DAB) to review the case. Following the action of the DAB, the beneficiary may file suit in Federal district court if the amount remaining in controversy is at least $1,000.

(b) The rights of a beneficiary under paragraph (a) of this section to appeal the carrier's initial determination are granted also to—

(1) A physician or supplier that furnishes services to a beneficiary and that accepts an assignment from the beneficiary, or

(2) A physician who meets the conditions of section 1842(l)(1)(A) of the Act pertaining to refund requirements for nonparticipating physicians who have not taken assignment on the claim(s) at issue.

(c) Procedures governing the determinations by SSA as to whether an individual has met basic Part B entitlement requirements are covered in subpart G of this part and 20 CFR part 404, subpart J. Subparts J and R of 20 CFR part 404 are also applicable to ALJ, DAB, and judicial review conducted under subpart H, except to the extent that specific provisions are contained in this subpart.

[62 FR 25853, May 12, 1997]

**§ 405.802 Definitions.**

As used in subpart H of this part, the term—

*After receipt of the notice* means 5 days after the date on the notice, unless it is shown that the notice was received earlier or later.

*Appellant* designates the beneficiary, assignee or other person or entity that has filed an appeal concerning a particular determination of benefits under

Medicare Part B. Designation as an appellant does not in itself convey standing to appeal the determination in question.

*Assignee* means a physician or supplier who furnishes services to a beneficiary under Medicare Part B and who has accepted a valid assignment executed by the beneficiary.

*Assignment* means the transfer by the assignor of his or her claim for payment to the assignee in return for the latter's promise not to charge more for his or her services than the carrier finds to be the reasonable charge or other approved amount.

*Assignor* means a beneficiary under Medicare Part B whose physician or supplier has taken assignment of a claim.

*Carrier* means an organization which has entered into a contract with the Secretary pursuant to section 1842 of the Act and which is authorized to make determinations with respect to Part B of title XVIII of the Act. For purposes of this subpart, the term carrier also refers to an intermediary that has entered into a contract with the Secretary under section 1816 of the Act and is authorized to make determinations with respect to Part B provider services, as specified in § 421.5(c) of this chapter.

*Common issues of law and fact,* with respect to the aggregation of claims by two or more appellants to meet the minimum amount in controversy needed for an ALJ hearing, occurs when the claims sought to be aggregated are denied or reduced for similar reasons and arise from a similar fact pattern material to the reason the claims are denied.

*Delivery of similar or related services,* with respect to the aggregation of claims by two or more physician/supplier appellants to meet the minimum amount in controversy needed for an ALJ hearing, means like or coordinated services or items provided to the same beneficiary by the appellants.

*Representative* means an individual meeting the conditions described in §§ 405.870 through 405.871.

*With reasonable promptness* means within a period of 60 consecutive days after the receipt by the carrier of a request for payment.

[59 FR 12182, Mar. 16, 1994, as amended at 62 FR 25853, May 12, 1997]

**§ 405.803 Initial determination.**

(a) Carriers make initial determinations regarding claims for benefits under Medicare Part B.

(b) An initial determination for purposes of this subpart includes determinations such as the following:

(1) Whether services furnished are covered.

(2) Whether the deductible has been met.

(3) Whether the receipted bill or other evidence of payment is acceptable.

(4) Whether the charges for services furnished are reasonable.

(5) If the services furnished to a beneficiary by a physician or a supplier pursuant to an assignment under § 424.55 of this chapter are not covered because they are determined to be not reasonable and necessary under § 411.15(k) of this

chapter, whether the beneficiary, physician or supplier, or a physician who meets the requirements of § 411.408, knew or could reasonably have been expected to know at the time the services were furnished that the services were not covered.

(c) The following are not initial determinations for purposes of this subpart:

(1) Any issue or factor for which SSA or CMS has sole responsibility, for example, whether an independent laboratory meets the conditions for coverage of services; whether a Medicare overpayment claim should be compromised, or collection action terminated or suspended.

(2) Any issue or factor which relates to hospital insurance benefits under Medicare Part A.

[62 FR 25853, May 12, 1997]

**§ 405.804 Notice of initial determination.**

After a carrier has made an initial determination on a request for payment written notice of this determination shall be mailed to each party to the determination at his last known address. The notice of the determination shall inform each party to the determination of his right to have such determination reviewed.

**§ 405.805 Parties to the initial determination.**

The parties to the initial determination (see § 405.803) may be any party described in § 405.802.

[64 FR 52670, Sept. 30, 1999]

**§ 405.806 Effect of initial determination.**

The initial determination is binding upon all parties to the claim for benefits unless the determination is–

(a) Reviewed in accordance with §§ 405.810 through 405.812; or

(b) Revised as a result of a reopening in accordance with § 405.841.

[62 FR 25853, May 12, 1997]

**§ 405.807 Request for review of initial determination.**

(a) *General.* A party to an initial determination by a carrier, that is dissatisfied with the initial determination and wants to appeal the matter, may request that the carrier review the determination. The request for review by the party to an initial determination must clearly indicate that he or she is dissatisfied with the initial determination and wants to appeal the matter. The request for review does not constitute a waiver of the party's right to a hearing (under § 405.815) after the review.

(b) *Place and method of filing a request.* A request by a party for a carrier to review the initial determination may be made in one of the following ways:

(1) In writing and filed at an office of the carrier, SSA, or CMS.

(2) By telephone to the telephone number designated by the carrier as the appropriate number for the receipt of requests for review.

(c) *Time of filing request.* (1) The carrier must provide a period of 6 months after the date of the notice of the initial determination within which the party to the initial determination may request a review.

(2) The carrier may, upon request by the party, extend the period for requesting the review of the initial determination.
[64 FR 52670, Sept. 30, 1999]

**§ 405.808 Parties to the review.**
The parties to the review (as provided for in § 405.807(a)) shall be the persons who were parties to the carrier's initial determination as described in § 405.805, and any other party whose rights with respect to the particular claim being reviewed may be affected by such review.
[39 FR 12097, Apr. 3, 1974. Redesignated at 42 FR 52826, Sept. 30, 1977]

**§ 405.809 Opportunity to submit evidence.**
The parties to the review (as provided for in § 405.807(a)) shall have a reasonable opportunity to submit written evidence and contentions as to fact or law relative to the claim at issue.
[39 FR 12097, Apr. 3, 1974. Redesignated at 42 FR 52826, Sept. 30, 1977]

**§ 405.810 Review determination.**
Subject to the provisions of §§ 405.807 through 405.809, the carrier shall review the claim in dispute and, upon the basis of the evidence of record, shall make a separate determination affirming or revising in whole or in part the findings and determination in question.
[39 FR 12097, Apr. 3, 1974. Redesignated at 42 FR 52826, Sept. 30, 1977]

**§ 405.811 Notice of review determination.**
Written notice of the review determination is mailed to a party at his or her last known address. The review determination states the basis of the determination and advises the party of his or her right to a carrier hearing when the amount in controversy is $100 or more as determined in accordance with § 405.817. The notice states the place and manner of requesting a carrier hearing as well as the time limit under which a hearing must be requested (see § 405.821).
[59 FR 12182, Mar. 16, 1994]

**§ 405.812 Effect of review determination.**
The review determination is binding upon all parties to the review unless a carrier hearing decision is issued pursuant to a request for hearing made in accordance with § 405.821 or is revised as a result of reopening in accordance with § 405.841.
[59 FR 12182, Mar. 16, 1994, as amended at 62 FR 25855, May 12, 1997]

**§ 405.815 Amount in controversy for carrier hearing, ALJ hearing and judicial review.**
Any party designated in § 405.822 is entitled to a carrier hearing after a review determination has been made by the carrier if the amount remaining in controversy is $100 or more and the party meets the requirements of § 405.821 of this subpart. To be entitled to a hearing before an ALJ following the carrier hearing, the amount remaining in controversy must be $500 or more, and for judicial

review following the ALJ hearing and Departmental Appeals Board Review, the amount remaining in controversy must be $1,000 or more.
[59 FR 12182, Mar. 16, 1994, as amended at 61 FR 32348, June 24, 1996]

**§ 405.817 Principles for determining amount in controversy.**

(a) *Individual appellants.* For the purpose of determining whether an individual appellant meets the minimum amount in controversy needed for a carrier hearing ($100) or ALJ hearing ($500), the following rules apply:

(1) The amount in controversy is computed as the actual amount charged the individual for the items and services in question, less any amount for which payment has been made by the carrier and less any deductible and coinsurance amounts applicable in the particular case.

(2) A single beneficiary may aggregate claims from two or more physicians/suppliers to meet the $100 or $500 thresholds. A single physician/supplier may aggregate claims from two or more beneficiaries to meet the $100 or $500 threshold levels of appeal.

(3) In either of the circumstances specified in paragraph (a)(2) of this section, two or more claims may be aggregated by an individual appellant to meet the amount in controversy for a carrier hearing only if the claims have previously been reviewed and a request for hearing has been made within six months after the date of the review determination(s).

(4) In either of the circumstances specified in paragraph (a)(2) of this section, two or more claims may be aggregated by an individual appellant to meet the amount in controversy for an ALJ hearing only if the claims have previously been decided by a carrier hearing officer and a request for an ALJ hearing has been made within 60 days after receipt of the carrier hearing officer decision(s).

(5) When requesting a carrier hearing or an ALJ hearing, the appellant must specify in his or her appeal request the specific claims to be aggregated.

(b) *Two or more appellants.* As specified in this paragraph, under section 1869(b)(2) of the Act, two or more appellants may aggregate their claims together to meet the minimum amount in controversy needed for an ALJ hearing ($500). The right to aggregate under this statutory provision applies to claims for items and services furnished on or after January 1, 1987.

(1) The aggregate amount in controversy is computed as the actual amount charged the individual(s) for the items and services in question, less any amount for which payment has been made by the carrier and less any deductible and coinsurance amounts applicable in the particular case.

(2) In determining the amount in controversy, two or more appellants may aggregate their claims together under the following circumstances:

(i) Two or more beneficiaries may combine claims representing services from the same or different physician(s) or supplier(s) if the claims involve common issues of law and fact;

(ii) Two or more physicians/suppliers may combine their claims if the claims involve the delivery of similar or related services to the same beneficiary;

(iii) Two or more physicians/suppliers may combine their claims if the claims involve common issues of law and fact with respect to services furnished to two or more beneficiaries.

(iv) In any of the circumstances specified in paragraphs (b)(2)(i) through (b)(2)(iii) of this section, the claims may be aggregated only if the claims have previously been decided by a carrier hearing officer(s) and a request for ALJ hearing has been made within 60 days after receipt of the carrier hearing officer decision(s). Moreover, in a request for ALJ hearing, the appellants must specify the claims that they seek to aggregate.

(c) The determination as to whether the amount in controversy is $100 or more is made by the carrier hearing officer. The determination as to whether the amount in controversy is $500 or more is made by the ALJ.

(d) In determining the amount in controversy under paragraph (b) of this section, the ALJ will also make the determination as to what constitutes "similar or related services"or "common issues of law and fact."

(e) When a civil action is filed by either an individual appellant or two or more appellants, the Secretary may assert that the aggregation principles contained in this subpart may be applied to determine the amount in controversy for judicial review ($1000).

(f) Notwithstanding the provisions of paragraphs (a)(1) and (b)(1) of this section, when payment is made for certain excluded services under § 411.400 of this chapter or the liability of the beneficiary for those services is limited under § 411.402 of this chapter, the amount in controversy is computed as the amount that would have been charged the beneficiary for the items or services in question, less any deductible and coinsurance amounts applicable in the particular case, had such expenses not been paid under § 411.400 of this chapter or had such liability not been limited under § 411.402 of this chapter.

(g) Under this subpart, an appellant may not combine Part A and Part B claims together to meet the requisite amount in controversy for a carrier hearing or ALJ hearing. HMO, CMP and HCPP appellants under part 417 of this chapter may combine Part A and Part B claims together to meet the requisite amount in controversy for a hearing.

[59 FR 12182, Mar. 16, 1994]

**§ 405.821 Request for carrier hearing.**

(a) A request for a carrier hearing is any clear expression in writing by a claimant asking for a hearing to adjudicate a claim when not acted upon with reasonable promptness or by a party to a review determination who states, in effect, that he or she is dissatisfied with the carrier's review determination and wants further opportunity to appeal the matter to the carrier.

(b) The hearing request must be filed at an office of the carrier or at an office of SSA or CMS.

(c) Except when a carrier hearing is held because the carrier did not act upon a claim with reasonable promptness, a party to the review determination may request a carrier hearing within six months after the date of the notice of the

review determination. The carrier may, upon request by the party affected, extend the period for filing the request for hearing.
[59 FR 12183, Mar. 16, 1994, as amended at 62 FR 25855, May 12, 1997]

**§ 405.822 Parties to a carrier hearing.**
The parties to a hearing shall be the persons who were parties to the carrier's review determination (§ 405.808) which is in question. Any other person may be made a party if that person's rights with respect to supplementary medical insurance benefits may be prejudiced by the decision.
[39 FR 12097, Apr. 3, 1974. Redesignated at 42 FR 52826, Sept. 30, 1977, as amended at 59 FR 12183, Mar. 16, 1994]

**§ 405.823 Carrier hearing officer.**
Any hearing provided for in this subpart shall be conducted by a hearing officer designated by the appropriate official of the carrier.
[39 FR 12097, Apr. 3, 1974. Redesignated at 42 FR 52826, Sept. 30, 1977, and amended at 59 FR 12183, Mar. 16, 1994]

**§ 405.824 Disqualification of carrier hearing officer.**
A hearing officer shall not conduct a hearing in any case in which he is prejudiced or partial with respect to any party, or if he has any interest in the matter before him. Notice of any objection with respect to the hearing officer who will conduct the hearing shall be made by the objecting party at his earliest opportunity. The hearing officer shall consider such objection and shall, at his discretion, withdraw. If the hearing officer withdraws, the appropriate official of the carrier shall designate another hearing officer to conduct the hearing. If the hearing officer does not withdraw, the objecting party may present his objections to the carrier for consideration at any time prior to the issuance of a decision. The carrier shall review the request and take appropriate action. The fact that a hearing officer is an employee of the carrier may not serve as prima facie cause for disqualification.
[32 FR 18028, Dec. 16, 1967. Redesignated at 42 FR 52826, Sept. 30, 1977, as amended at 59 FR 12183, Mar. 16, 1994]

**§ 405.825 Location of carrier hearing.**
(a) *Time and place.* The hearing officer shall fix a time and place for the hearing reasonably convenient to the requesting party and not inconsistent with the public interest.
(b) *Adjournment or postponement.* The hearing officer may, for a good and sufficient reason, fix a new time and/or place for the hearing; he may change the time and place for the hearing or adjourn the hearing on his own motion upon reasonable notification to the parties.
[32 FR 18028, Dec. 16, 1967. Redesignated at 42 FR 52826, Sept. 30, 1977, as amended at 59 FR 12183, Mar. 16, 1994]

**§ 405.826 Notice of carrier hearing.**
The notice of hearing is to include notice of the time and place of the hearing; information as to the specific issues to be determined; and the matters on which

findings will be made and conclusions will be reached. The notice is to contain sufficient information about the hearing procedure (including the party's right to representation) for effective preparation for the hearing.
[32 FR 18028, Dec. 16, 1967. Redesignated at 42 FR 52826, Sept. 30, 1977, as amended at 59 FR 12183, Mar. 16, 1994]

**§ 405.830 Conduct of the carrier hearing.**

(a) *General.* Hearings shall be open to the parties and to such other persons as the hearing officer deems necessary and proper for the orderly and efficient conduct of the hearing. The hearing officer shall inquire fully into the matters at issue and shall receive in evidence the testimony of witnesses and any documents which are relevant and material to such matters. The parties shall be provided an opportunity to enter any objection to the inclusion of any document. The order in which evidence and allegations shall be presented and the procedure at the hearing, except as this subpart otherwise expressly provides, shall be at the discretion of the hearing officer and of such nature as to afford the parties a proper hearing.

(b) *Evidence.* Evidence may be received at the hearing even though inadmissible under rules of evidence applicable to court procedures.

(c) *Witnesses.* The hearing officer may examine the witnesses and shall allow the parties or their representatives to do so. If the hearing officer conducts the examination of a witness, he may allow the parties to suggest matters upon which they desire the witness to be questioned, and the hearing officer shall question the witness with respect to such matters if they are relevant and material to any issue pending for decision before him.

(d) *Oral argument and written allegations.* The parties, upon their request, shall be allowed a reasonable time for the presentation of oral argument or for the filing of briefs or other written statements or allegations of facts or law.

(e) *Consolidated issues.* When one or more new issues are raised at any time after a request for hearing has been made, but before the mailing of notice of the decision, the hearing officer may, at his discretion, consider the issues along with the other issues pending before him on the same request for hearing.
[32 FR 18028, Dec. 16, 1967. Redesignated at 42 FR 52826, Sept. 30, 1977, as amended at 59 FR 12183, Mar. 16, 1994]

**§ 405.831 Waiver of right to appear at carrier hearing and present evidence.**

If all parties waive their right to appear before the hearing officer and present evidence and contentions personally or by representative, it shall not be necessary for the hearing officer to give notice of or conduct a formal hearing as provided in §§ 405.825 through 405.830. A waiver of the right to appear is to be in writing and filed with the hearing officer or the carrier. Such waiver may be withdrawn by a party at any time prior to the mailing of notice of the decision in the case. Even though all of the parties have filed a waiver of the right to appear and present evidence and contentions at a hearing before the hearing officer, the hearing officer may, nevertheless, give notice of a time and place and conduct a hearing as provided in §§ 405.825 through 405.830, if he believes that the personal appearance and testimony of the party or parties would assist him to ascertain the facts at issue in the case. For purposes of this section, failure of the parties to appear shall not be cause for a finding of abandonment and the hearing officer shall make his decision on the basis of all evidence adduced.

[32 FR 18028, Dec. 16, 1967. Redesignated at 42 FR 52826, Sept. 30, 1977, as amended at 62 FR 25855, May 12, 1997]

**§ 405.832 Dismissal of request for carrier hearing.**

(a) *By application of party.* With the approval of the hearing officer, a request for a hearing may be withdrawn or dismissed at any time prior to the mailing of notice of the decision upon the application of the party or parties filing the request for such hearing. A party may request a dismissal by filing a written notice of such request with the carrier, the hearing officer or orally stating such request at the hearing. The dismissal of a request for hearing shall be binding unless vacated (see paragraph (d) of this section).

(b) *Dismissal by abandonment of party.* A hearing officer may dismiss a request for hearing upon abandonment by the party or parties who filed the request. A party shall be deemed to have abandoned a request for hearing, other than where personal appearance is waived in accordance with § 405.831, if neither the party nor his representative appears at the time and place fixed for the hearing and within 10 days after the mailing of a notice to him by the hearing officer to show cause, such party does not show good and sufficient cause for such failure to appear and failure to notify the hearing officer prior to the time fixed for hearing that he cannot appear.

(c) *Dismissal for cause.* The hearing officer may, on his own motion, dismiss a hearing request, either entirely or as to any stated issue, under either of the following circumstances:

(1) Where the party requesting a hearing is not a proper party under § 405.822 or does not otherwise have a right to a hearing under section 1842(b)(3)(C) of the Act; or

(2) Where the party who filed the hearing request dies and there is no information before the hearing officer showing that an individual who is not a party may be prejudiced by the carrier's determination.

(d) *Dismissal without prejudice.* The hearing officer may on his own motion dismiss without prejudice a hearing request where the amount in controversy is less than $100.

(e) *Vacation of dismissal.* A hearing officer may, on request of a party and for good and sufficient cause shown, vacate any dismissal of a request for hearing at any time within 6 months from the date of mailing notice of the dismissal to the party requesting the hearing at his last known address.

[32 FR 18028, Dec. 16, 1967, as amended at 39 FR 12098, Apr. 3, 1974. Redesignated at 42 FR 52826, Sept. 30, 1977, as amended at 59 FR 12183, Mar. 16, 1994; 62 FR 25855, May 12, 1997]

**§ 405.833 Record of carrier hearing.**
A complete record of the proceedings at the carrier hearing is made. The testimony is transcribed and copies of other documentary evidence are reproduced in any case when directed by the hearing officer, the carrier, or CMS. The record will also be transcribed and reproduced at the request of any party to the hearing provided the requesting party bears the cost.
[62 FR 25853, May 12, 1997]

**§ 405.834 Carrier hearing officer's decision.**
(a) As soon as practicable after the close of a carrier hearing, the carrier hearing officer issues a decision in the case based upon the evidence presented at the hearing or otherwise included in the hearing record. The decision is issued as a written notice to the parties and contains—

(1) Findings of fact,

(2) A statement of reasons, and

(3) Notification to the parties of their right to an ALJ hearing when the amount remaining in controversy is at least $500.

(b) A copy of the decision is mailed to the parties to the hearing at their last known addresses.
[62 FR 25854, May 12, 1997]

**§ 405.835 Effect of carrier hearing officer's decision.**
The carrier hearing officer's decision is binding upon all parties to the hearing unless—

(a) A request for an ALJ hearing is filed in accordance with § 405.855, or

(b) The decision is revised in accordance with § 405.841.
[62 FR 25854, May 12, 1997]

**§ 405.836 Authority of the carrier hearing officer.**
The carrier hearing officer, in adjudicating Medicare Part B claims, complies with all of the provisions of, and regulations issued under, title XVIII of the Act, as well as with CMS Rulings, national coverage decisions, and other policy statements, instructions, and guides issued by CMS.
[62 FR 25854, May 12, 1997]

**§ 405.841 Reopening initial or review determination of the carrier, and decision of a carrier hearing officer.**
An initial or review determination of a carrier or a decision of a hearing officer may be reopened by such carrier or hearing officer:

(a) Within 12 months from the date of the notice of such initial or review determination or decision to the party to such determination or decision; or

(b) After such 12-month period, but within 4 years from the date of the notice of the initial determination to the party to such determination, upon establishment of good cause for reopening such determination or decision (see 20 CFR 404.988(b) and 404.989); or

(c) At any time, when:

(1) Such initial or review determination or decision was procured by fraud or similar fault of the beneficiary or some other person, or

(2) Such initial or review determination or decision is unfavorable, in whole or in part, to the party thereto, but only for the purpose of correcting a clerical error or error on the face of the evidence on which such determination or decision was based.

[39 FR 12098, Apr. 3, 1974. Redesignated at 42 FR 52826, Sept. 30, 1977, as amended at 59 FR 12183, Mar. 16, 1994; 62 FR 25855, May 12, 1997]

**§ 405.842 Notice of reopening and revision.**

(a) *Notice.* When any determination or decision is reopened as provided in § 405.841, notice of such reopening shall be mailed to the parties to such determination or decision at their last known addresses. A notice of revision following a reopening of a decision, shall be mailed to the parties and shall state the basis for the revised determination or decision.

(b) *Effect of revised determination.* The revision of a determination (see § 405.841) shall be binding upon all parties thereto unless a party files a written request for a hearing with respect to a revised determination when the amount in controversy is $100 or more.

[32 FR 18028, Dec. 16, 1967, as amended at 39 FR 12098, Apr. 3, 1974. Redesignated at 42 FR 52826, Sept. 30, 1977; 62 FR 25855, May 12, 1997]

**§ 405.850 Change of ruling or legal precedent.**

Change of a legal interpretation or administrative ruling upon which a determination or decision was made shall not be considered as good and sufficient reason for reopening the determination or decision.

**§ 405.853 Expedited appeals process.**

(a) *Conditions for use of expedited appeals process (EAP).* A party may use the EAP set forth in § 405.718 of this chapter to request court review in place of the ALJ hearing or Departmental Appeals Board (DAB) review if the following conditions are met:

(1) The carrier hearing officer has made a decision; an ALJ has made a hearing decision; or DAB review has been requested, but a final decision has not been issued.

(2) The filing entity is a party referred to in § 405.718(d) of this chapter.

(3) The party has filed a request for an ALJ hearing in accordance with § 405.855, or DAB review in accordance with 20 CFR 404.968.

(4) The amount remaining in controversy is $1,000 or more.

(5) If there is more than one party to the hearing decision, each party concurs, in writing, with the request for an EAP.

(b) *Content of the request for EAP.* The request for an EAP:

(1) Alleges that there are no material issues of fact in dispute; and

(2) Asserts that the only factor precluding a decision favorable to the party is a statutory provision that is unconstitutional or a regulation, national coverage decision under section 1862(a)(1) of the Act, or CMS Ruling that is invalid.

[62 FR 25854, May 12, 1997]

**§ 405.855 ALJ hearing.**

(a) *Right to hearing.* A party to the carrier hearing has a right to a hearing before an ALJ if–

(1) The party files a written request for an ALJ hearing within 60 days after receipt of the notice of the carrier hearing decision; and

(2) The amount remaining in controversy is $500 or more.

(b) *Place of filing hearing request.* The request for an ALJ hearing must be made in writing and filed with the carrier that issued the decision, a Social Security office, or, in the case of a qualified railroad retirement beneficiary, an office of the Railroad Retirement Board.

(c) *Effect of ALJ hearing decision.* (1) An ALJ's decision is binding on all parties to the hearing unless–

(i) The DAB reviews the ALJ decision;

(ii) The DAB does not review the ALJ decision, and the party requests judicial review;

(iii) The decision is revised by the DAB or an ALJ in accordance with the provisions of § 405.750 of this chapter; or

(iv) The expedited appeals process is used.

[62 FR 25854, May 12, 1997]

**§ 405.856 Departmental Appeals Board (DAB) review.**

Regulations beginning at 20 CFR 404.967 regarding SSA Appeals Council Review are applicable to DAB review of matters addressed by this subpart.

[62 FR 25854, May 12, 1997]

**§ 405.857 Court review.**

(a) *General rule.* To the extent authorized by sections 1869, 1876(c)(5)(B), and 1879(d) of the Act, a party to a DAB decision, or an ALJ decision if the DAB does not review the ALJ's decision, may obtain a court review if the amount remaining in controversy is $1,000 or more. A party may obtain court review by filing a civil action in a district court of the United States in accordance with the provisions of section 205(g) of the Act. The filing procedure is set forth in 20 CFR 422.210.

(b) *Prohibition against court review of certain Part B regulations or instructions.* Under section 1869(b)(4) of the Act, a court may not review a regulation or instruction that relates to a method of payment under Part B if the regulation was promulgated, or the instruction issued, before January 1, 1981.

[62 FR 25854, May 12, 1997]

**§ 405.860 Review of a national coverage determination (NCD).**

(a) *General rule.* (1) An NCD is a determination by the Secretary for whether or not a particular item or service is covered nationally under title XVIII of the Act.

(2) An NCD does not include a determination of what code, if any, is assigned to a particular item or service covered under title XVIII or a determination for the amount of payment made for a particular item or service.

(3) NCDs are made under section 1862(a)(1) of the Act or other applicable provisions of the Act.

(4) An NCD is binding on all Medicare carriers, fiscal intermediaries, QIOs, HMOs, CMPs, HCPPs, the Medicare Appeals Council, and ALJs.

(b) *Review by ALJ.* (1) An ALJ may not disregard, set aside, or otherwise review an NCD.

(2) An ALJ may review the facts of a particular case to determine whether an NCD applies to a specific claim for benefits and, if so, whether the NCD is applied correctly to the claim.

(c) *Review by court.* For initial determinations and NCD challenges under section 1862(a)(1) of the Act, arising before October 1, 2002, a court's review of an NCD is limited to whether the record is incomplete or otherwise lacks adequate information to support the validity of the decision, unless the case is remanded to the Secretary to supplement the record regarding the NCD. In these cases, the court may not invalidate an NCD except upon review of the supplemental record.

[68 FR 63716, Nov. 7, 2003]

**§ 405.870 Appointment of representative.**

A party to an initial determination, informal review or hearing as provided in §§ 405.803 through 405.934, may appoint as his representative in any such proceeding any person qualified under § 405.871. Where the representative is an attorney, in the absence of information to the contrary, his representation that he has such authority shall be accepted as evidence of the attorney's authority to represent a party.

**§ 405.871 Qualifications of representatives.**

Any individual may be appointed to act as representative in accordance with § 405.870, unless he is disqualified or suspended from acting as a representative in proceedings before the SSA or the CMS or unless otherwise prohibited by law.

[39 FR 12098, Apr. 3, 1974. Redesignated at 42 FR 52826, Sept. 30, 1977, as amended at 62 FR 25855, May 12, 1997]

**§ 405.872 Authority of representatives.**

A representative, appointed and qualified as provided in §§ 405.870 and 405.871, may make or give, on behalf of the party he represents, any request or notice relative to any proceeding before the carrier including review and hearing. A representative shall be entitled to present evidence and allegations as to facts and law in any proceeding affecting the party he represents and to obtain information with respect to the claim of such party to the same extent as such party. Notice to any party or any action, determination, or decision, or request to any party for the production of evidence, shall be sent to the representative of such party.

**§ 405.874 Appeals of carrier decisions that supplier standards are not met.**

(a) An entity serving as a National Supplier Clearinghouse must act promptly to determine if any entity submitting a request for a billing number as a Medicare supplier of Part B items meets the standards set forth in part 424. Effective July 1,

1993, the National Supplier Clearinghouse must accept, reject or request additional information within 15 days of the receipt of an enrollment application.

(b) If the National Supplier Clearinghouse disallows an entity's request for a billing number or revokes, with the concurrence of CMS, an entity's billing number, the National Supplier Clearinghouse notifies the entity by certified mail. Revocation is effective 15 days after the National Supplier Clearinghouse mails notice of its determination. The carrier disallows payment for items furnished by the supplier beginning with that effective date. The notice must inform the entity of the reason for the rejection or revocation, its right to appeal, the date by which it must file that appeal (90 days after the postmark of the notice) and the address to which the appeal must be sent in writing.

(c) A fair hearing officer not involved in the original determination to disallow an entity's request for a billing number, or to revoke an entity's billing number, must schedule a hearing to be held within one week of receipt of an appeal, or later at the request of the entity. Both the entity and carrier may offer evidence. The hearing officer issues notice of his/her decision within 2 weeks of the hearing. The notice is sent by certified letter to CMS, the carrier, and the appealing entity. This notice must include information about the supplier's further right to appeal, the carrier's right to appeal, the date by which the appeal must be filed (90 days after the postmark of the notice) and the address to which the appeals must be sent in writing. Either the carrier or entity may appeal the hearings officer's decision to CMS.

(d) A CMS official, designated by the Administrator of CMS, must make an appeal decision based on the evidence presented to the fair hearing officer and his or her decision. The CMS official requests any additional information he or she deems necessary from either the carrier or the entity within two weeks of receipt by the CMS of the appeal. Notice of the CMS official's decision–

(1) Is issued within two weeks of when the last information is received by the CMS official, or four weeks of when the information is requested, whichever is shorter, unless the party appealing the fair hearing decision requests a delay;

(2) Is sent by the CMS official by certified mail to both the carrier and the entity; and

(3) Contains information on any further appeals the entity and carrier may have.

(e) A billing number is not issued, or remains revoked, and payment is not made, for items or services furnished by any entity which a carrier determines does not qualify for a billing number, until the carrier (upon reapplication of the entity), a fair hearing officer, or a CMS official designated to hear such appeals, determines that the entity qualifies for a billing number. Any claims for items or services furnished after revocation of the supplier's billing number and submitted by the entity during the appeals period are held and not processed, i.e., are neither approved, denied nor developed, until all administrative appeals have been exhausted. If an entity is determined not to have qualified for a billing number in one period but to have qualified in another, the carrier pays for claims for items sold or rented to beneficiaries during the period the entity qualified as a supplier. If there is evidence of an overpayment, see subpart C of part 405 of this chapter.

(f) A billing number may be reinstated after revocation when an entity completes a corrective action plan, to which CMS has agreed, and provided sufficient assurance of its intent to comply fully with the supplier standards.

[57 FR 27305, June 18, 1992]

**§ 405.877 Appeal of a categorization of a device.**

(a) CMS's acceptance of the FDA categorization of a device as an experimental/investigational (Category A) device under § 405.203 is a national coverage decision under section 1862(a)(1) of the Act.

(b) CMS's acceptance of the FDA categorization of a device as an experimental/investigational (Category A) device under § 405.203 is an aspect of an initial determination that, under section 1862 of the Act, payment may not be made.

(c) In accordance with section 1869(b)(3)(A) of the Act, CMS's acceptance of the FDA categorization of a device as an experimental/investigational (Category A) device under § 405.203 may not be reviewed by an administrative law judge.

[60 FR 48424, Sept. 19, 1995]

**Subpart I—Determinations, Redeterminations, Reconsiderations, and Appeals under Original Medicare (Part A and Part B)**

**Source:** 70 FR 11472, Mar. 8, 2005, unless otherwise noted.

**§ 405.900 Basis and scope.**

(a) *Statutory basis.* This subpart is based on the provisions of sections 1869 (a) through (e) and (g) of the Act.

(b) *Scope.* This subpart establishes the requirements for appeals of initial determinations for benefits under Part A or Part B of Medicare, including the following:

(1) The initial determination of whether an individual is entitled to benefits under Part A or Part B. (Regulations governing reconsiderations of these initial determinations are at 20 CFR, part 404, subpart J.)

(2) The initial determination of the amount of benefits available to an individual under Part A or Part B.

(3) Any other initial determination relating to a claim for benefits under Part A or Part B, including an initial determination made by a quality improvement organization under section 1154(a)(2) of the Act or by an entity under contract with the Secretary (other than a contract under section 1852 of the Act) to administer provisions of titles XVIII or XI of the Act.

**§ 405.902 Definitions.**

For the purposes of this subpart, the term—

*ALJ* means an Administrative Law Judge of the Department of Health and Human Services.

*Appellant* means the beneficiary, assignee or other person or entity that has filed and pursued an appeal concerning a particular initial determination. Designation as an appellant does not in itself convey standing to appeal the determination in question.

*Appointed representative* means an individual appointed by a party to represent the party in a Medicare claim or claim appeal.

*Assignee* means:

(1) A supplier that furnishes items or services to a beneficiary and has accepted a valid assignment of a claim or

(2) A provider or supplier that furnishes items or services to a beneficiary, who is not already a party, and has accepted a valid assignment of the right to appeal a claim executed by the beneficiary.

*Assignment of a claim* means the transfer by a beneficiary of his or her claim for payment to the supplier in return for the latter's promise not to charge more for his or her services than what the carrier finds to be the Medicare-approved amount, as provided in § 424.55 and § 424.56 of this chapter.

*Assignment of appeal rights* means the transfer by a beneficiary of his or her right to appeal under this subpart to a provider or supplier who is not already a party, as provided in section 1869(b)(1)(C) of the Act.

*Assignor* means a beneficiary whose provider of services or supplier has taken assignment of a claim or an appeal of a claim.

*Authorized representative* means an individual authorized under State or other applicable law to act on behalf of a beneficiary or other party involved in the appeal. The authorized representative will have all of the rights and responsibilities of a beneficiary or party, as applicable, throughout the appeals process.

*Beneficiary* means an individual who is enrolled to receive benefits under Medicare Part A or Part B.

*Carrier* means an organization that has entered into a contract with the Secretary in accordance to section 1842 of the Act and is authorized to make determinations for Part B of title XVIII of the Act.

*Clean claim* means a claim that has no defect or impropriety (including any lack of required substantiating documentation) or particular circumstance requiring special treatment that prevents timely payment from being made on the claim under title XVIII within the time periods specified in sections 1816(c) and 1842(c) of the Act.

*Family member* means for purposes of the QIC reconsideration panel under § 405.968 the following persons as they relate to the physician or healthcare provider.

(1) The spouse (other than a spouse who is legally separated from the physician or health care professional under a decree of divorce or separate maintenance);

(2) Children (including stepchildren and legally adopted children);

(3) Grandchildren;

(4) Parents; and

(5) Grandparents.

*Fiscal intermediary* means an organization that has entered into a contract with CMS in accordance with section 1816 of the Act and is authorized to make determinations and payments for Part A of title XVIII of the Act, and Part B provider services as specified in § 421.5(c) of this chapter.

*MAC* stands for the Medicare Appeals Council within the Departmental Appeals Board of the U.S. Department of Health and Human Services.

*Party* means an individual or entity listed in § 405.906 that has standing to appeal an initial determination and/or a subsequent administrative appeal determination.

*Provider* means a hospital, critical access hospital, skilled nursing facility, comprehensive outpatient rehabilitation facility, home health agency, or hospice that has in effect an agreement to participate in Medicare, or clinic, rehabilitation agency, or public health agency that has in effect a similar agreement, but only to furnish outpatient physical therapy or speech pathology services, or a community mental health center that has in effect a similar agreement but only to furnish partial hospitalization services.

*Qualified independent contractor (QIC)* means an entity which contracts with the Secretary in accordance with section 1869 of the Act to perform reconsiderations under § 405.960 through § 405.978.

*Quality improvement organization (QIO)* means an entity that contracts with the Secretary in accordance with sections 1152 and 1153 of the Act and 42 CFR subchapter F, to perform the functions described in section 1154 of the Act and 42 CFR subchapter F, including expedited determinations as described in § 405.1200 through § 405.1208.

*Reliable evidence* means evidence that is relevant, credible, and material.

*Remand* means to vacate a lower level appeal decision, or a portion of the decision, and return the case, or a portion of the case, to that level for a new decision.

*Similar fault* means to obtain, retain, convert, seek, or receive Medicare funds to which a person knows or should reasonably be expected to know that he or she or another for whose benefit Medicare funds are obtained, retained, converted, sought, or received is not legally entitled. This includes, but is not limited to, a failure to demonstrate that he or she filed a proper claim as defined in part 411 of this chapter.

*Supplier* means, unless the context otherwise requires, a physician or other practitioner, a facility, or other entity (other than a provider of services) that furnishes items or services under Medicare.

*Vacate* means to set aside a previous action.

### § 405.904 Medicare initial determinations, redeterminations and appeals: General description.

(a) *General overview*—(1) *Entitlement appeals.* The SSA makes an initial determination on an application for Medicare benefits and/or entitlement of an individual to receive Medicare benefits. A beneficiary who is dissatisfied with the initial determination may request, and SSA will perform, a reconsideration in accordance with 20 CFR part 404, subpart J if the requirements for obtaining a reconsideration are met. Following the reconsideration, the beneficiary may request a hearing before an Administrative Law Judge (ALJ) under this subpart (42 CFR part 405, subpart I). If the beneficiary obtains a hearing before an ALJ and is dissatisfied with the decision of the ALJ, he or she may request the Medicare Appeals Council (MAC) to review the case. Following the action of the MAC, the beneficiary may be entitled to file suit in Federal district court.

(2) *Claim appeals.* The Medicare contractor makes an initial determination when a claim for Medicare benefits under Part A or Part B is submitted. A beneficiary who is dissatisfied with the initial determination may request that the contractor perform a redetermination of the claim if the requirements for obtaining a redetermination are met. Following the contractor's redetermination, the beneficiary may request, and the qualified independent contractor (QIC) will perform, a reconsideration of the claim if the requirements for obtaining a reconsideration are met. Following the reconsideration, the beneficiary may request, and the ALJ will conduct a hearing if the amount remaining in controversy and other requirements for an ALJ hearing are met. If the beneficiary is dissatisfied with the decision of the ALJ, he or she may request the MAC to review the case. If the MAC reviews the case and issues a decision, and the beneficiary is dissatisfied with the decision, the beneficiary may file suit in Federal district court if the amount remaining in controversy and the other requirements for judicial review are met.

(b) *Non-beneficiary appellants.* In general, the procedures described in paragraph (a) of this section are also available to parties other than beneficiaries either directly or through a representative acting on a party's behalf, consistent with the requirements of this subpart I. A provider generally has the right to judicial review only as provided under section 1879(d) of the Act; that is, when a determination involves a finding that services are not covered because—

(1) They were custodial care (see § 411.15(g) of this chapter); they were not reasonable and necessary (see § 411.15(k) of this chapter); they did not qualify as covered home health services because the beneficiary was not confined to the home or did not need skilled nursing care on an intermittent basis (see § 409.42(a) and (c)(1) of this chapter); or they were hospice services provided to a non-terminally ill individual (see § 418.22 of this chapter); and

(2) Either the provider or the beneficiary, or both, knew or could reasonably be expected to know that those services were not covered under Medicare.

**§ 405.906 Parties to the initial determinations, redeterminations, reconsiderations, hearings and reviews.**

(a) *Parties to the initial determination.* The parties to the initial determination are the following individuals and entities:

(1) A beneficiary who files a claim for payment under Medicare Part A or Part B or has had a claim for payment filed on his or her behalf, or in the case of a deceased beneficiary, when there is no estate, any person obligated to make or entitled to receive payment in accordance with part 424, subpart E of this chapter. Payment by a third party payer does not entitle that entity to party status.

(2) A supplier who has accepted assignment for items or services furnished to a beneficiary that are at issue in the claim.

(3) A provider of services who files a claim for items or services furnished to a beneficiary.

(b) *Parties to the redetermination, reconsideration, hearing and MAC.* The parties to the redetermination, reconsideration, hearing and MAC review are—

(1) The parties to the initial determination in accordance with paragraph (a) of this section, except under paragraph (a)(1) of this section where a beneficiary has assigned appeal rights under § 405.912;

(2) A State agency in accordance with § 405.908;

(3) A provider or supplier that has accepted an assignment of appeal rights from the beneficiary according to § 405.912;

(4) A non-participating physician not billing on an assigned basis who, in accordance with section 1842(l) of the Act, may be liable to refund monies collected for services furnished to the beneficiary because those services were denied on the basis of section 1862(a)(1) of the Act; and

(5) A non-participating supplier not billing on an assigned basis who, in accordance with sections 1834(a)(18) and 1834(j)(4) of the Act, may be liable to refund monies collected for items furnished to the beneficiary.

(c) *Appeals by providers and suppliers when there is no other party available.* If a provider or supplier is not already a party to the proceeding in accordance with paragraphs (a) and (b) of this section, a provider of services or supplier may appeal an initial determination relating to services it rendered to a beneficiary who subsequently dies if there is no other party available to appeal the determination.

**§ 405.908 Medicaid State agencies.**

When a beneficiary is enrolled to receive benefits under both Medicare and Medicaid, the Medicaid State agency may file a request for an appeal with respect to a claim for items or services furnished to a dually eligible beneficiary only for services for which the Medicaid State agency has made payment, or for which it may be liable. A Medicaid State agency is considered a party only when it files a timely redetermination request with respect to a claim for items or services furnished to a beneficiary in accordance with 42 CFR parts 940 through 958. If a State agency files a request for redetermination, it may retain party status at the QIC, ALJ, MAC, and judicial review levels.

**§ 405.910 Appointed representatives.**

(a) *Scope of representation.* An appointed representative may act on behalf of an individual or entity in exercising his or her right to an initial determination or appeal. Appointed representatives do not have party status and may take action only on behalf of the individual or entity that they represent.

(b) *Persons not qualified.* A party may not name as an appointed representative, an individual who is disqualified, suspended, or otherwise prohibited by law from acting as a representative in any proceedings before DHHS, or in entitlement appeals, before SSA.

(c) *Completing a valid appointment.* For purposes of this subpart, an appointment of representation must:

(1) Be in writing and signed and dated by both the party and individual agreeing to be the representative;

(2) Provide a statement appointing the representative to act on behalf of the party, and in the case of a beneficiary, authorizing the adjudicator to release identifiable health information to the appointed representative.

(3) Include a written explanation of the purpose and scope of the representation;

(4) Contain both the party's and appointed representative's name, phone number, and address;

(5) Identify the beneficiary's Medicare health insurance claim number;

(6) Include the appointed representative's professional status or relationship to the party;

(7) Be filed with the entity processing the party's initial determination or appeal.

(d) *Curing a defective appointment of representative.* (1) If any one of the seven elements named in paragraph (c) of this section is missing from the appointment, the adjudicator should contact the party and provide a description of the missing documentation or information.

(2) Unless the defect is cured, the prospective appointed representative lacks the authority to act on behalf of the party, and is not entitled to obtain or receive any information related to the appeal, including the appeal decision.

(e) *Duration of appointment.* (1) Unless revoked, an appointment is considered valid for 1 year from the date that the Appointment of Representative (AOR) form or other conforming written instrument contains the signatures of both the party and the appointed representative.

(2) To initiate an appeal within the 1-year time frame, the representative must file a copy of the AOR form, or other conforming written instrument, with the appeal request. Unless revoked, the representation is valid for the duration of an individual's appeal of an initial determination.

(3) For an initial determination of a Medicare Secondary Payer recovery claim, an appointment signed in connection with the party's efforts to make a claim for third party payment is valid from the date that appointment is signed for the duration of any subsequent appeal, unless the appointment is specifically revoked.

(f) *Appointed representative fees*—(1) *General rule.* An appointed representative for a beneficiary who wishes to charge a fee for services rendered in connection with an appeal before the Secretary must obtain approval of the fee from the Secretary. Services rendered below the ALJ level are not considered proceedings before the Secretary.

(2) *No fees or costs against trust funds.* No award of attorney or any other representative's fees or any costs in connection with an appeal may be made against the Medicare trust funds.

(3) *Special rules for providers and suppliers.* A provider or supplier that furnished the items or services to a beneficiary that are the subject of the appeal may represent that beneficiary in an appeal under this subpart, but the provider or supplier may not charge the beneficiary any fee associated with the representation. If a provider or supplier furnishes services or items to a beneficiary, the provider or supplier may not represent the beneficiary on the issues described in section 1879(a)(2) of the Act, unless the provider or supplier waives the right to payment from the beneficiary for the services or items involved in the appeal.

(4) *Special rules for purposes of third party payment.* The Secretary does not review fee arrangements made by a beneficiary for purposes of making a claim for third party payment (as defined in 42 CFR 411.21) even though the representation may ultimately include representation for a Medicare Secondary Payer recovery claim.

(5) *Reasonableness of representative fees.* In determining the reasonableness of a representative's fee, the Secretary will not apply the test specified in sections 206(a)(2) and (a)(3) of the Act.

(g) *Responsibilities of an appointed representative.* (1) An appointed representative has an affirmative duty to–

(i) Inform the party of the scope and responsibilities of the representation;

(ii) Inform the party of the status of the appeal and the results of actions taken on behalf of the party, including, but not limited to, notification of appeal determinations, decisions, and further appeal rights;

(iii) Disclose to a beneficiary any financial risk and liability of a non-assigned claim that the beneficiary may have;

(iv) Not act contrary to the interest of the party; and

(v) Comply with all laws and CMS regulations, CMS Rulings, and instructions.

(2) An appeal request filed by a provider or supplier described in paragraph (f)(3) of this section must also include a statement signed by the provider or supplier stating that no financial liability is imposed on the beneficiary in connection with that representation. If applicable, the appeal request must also include a signed statement that the provider or supplier waives the right to payment from the beneficiary for services or items regarding issues described in section 1879(a)(2) of the Act.

(h) *Authority of an appointed representative.* An appointed representative may, on behalf of the party–

(1) Obtain appeals information about the claim to the same extent as the party;

(2) Submit evidence;

(3) Make statements about facts and law; and

(4) Make any request, or give, or receive, any notice about the appeal proceedings.

(i) *Notice or request to an appointed representative*—(1) *Initial determinations.* When a contractor takes an action or issues an initial determination, it sends the action or notice to the party.

(2) *Appeals.* When a contractor, QIC, ALJ, or the MAC takes an action or issues a redetermination, reconsideration, or appeal decision, in connection with an initial determination, it sends notice of the action to the appointed representative.

(3) The contractor, QIC, ALJ or MAC sends any requests for information or evidence regarding a claim that is appealed to the appointed representative. The contractor sends any requests for information or evidence regarding an initial determination to the party.

(4) For initial determinations and appeals involving Medicare Secondary Payer recovery claims, the adjudicator sends notices and requests to both the beneficiary and the appointed representative.

(j) *Effect of notice or request to an appointed representative.* A notice or request sent to the appointed representative has the same force and effect as if it was sent to the party.

(k) *Information available to the appointed representative.* An appointed representative may obtain any and all appeals information applicable to the claim at issue that is available to the party.

(l) *Delegation of appointment by appointed representative.* An appointed representative may not designate another individual to act as the appointed representative of the party unless—

(1) The appointed representative provides written notice to the party of the appointed representative's intent to delegate to another individual. The notice must include:

(i) The name of the designee; and

(ii) The designee's acceptance to be obligated and comply with the requirements of representation under this subpart.

(2) The party accepts the designation as evidenced by a written statement signed by the party. This signed statement is not required when the appointed representative and designee are attorneys in the same law firm or organization.

(m) *Revoking the appointment of representative.* (1) A party may revoke an appointment of representative without cause at any time.

(2) *Revocation.* Revocation is not effective until the adjudicator receives a signed, written statement from the party.

(3) *Death of the party.* (i) The death of a party terminates the authority of the appointed representative, except as specified in paragraph (m)(3)(ii) of this section.

(ii) A party's death does not terminate an appeal that is in progress if another individual or entity may be entitled to receive or obligated to make payment for the items or services that are the subject of the appeal. The appointment of representative remains in effect for the duration of the appeal except for MSP recovery claims.

**§ 405.912 Assignment of appeal rights.**

(a) *Who may be an assignee.* Only a provider, or supplier that–

(1) Is not a party to the initial determination as defined in § 405.906; and

(2) Furnished an item or service to the beneficiary may seek assignment of appeal rights from the beneficiary for that item or service.

(b) *Who may not be an assignee.* An individual or entity who is not a provider or supplier may not be an assignee. A provider or supplier that furnishes an item or service to a beneficiary may not seek assignment for that item or service when considered a party to the initial determination as defined in § 405.906.

(c) *Requirements for a valid assignment of appeal right.* The assignment of appeal rights must–

(1) Be executed using a CMS standard form;

(2) Be in writing and signed by both the beneficiary assigning his or her appeal rights and the assignee;

(3) Indicate the item or service for which the assignment of appeal rights is authorized;

(4) Contain a waiver of the assignee's right to collect payment from the assignor for the specific item or service that are the subject of the appeal except as set forth in paragraph (d)(2) of this section; and

(5) Be submitted at the same time the request for redetermination or other appeal is filed.

(d) *Waiver of right to collect payment.* (1) Except as specified in paragraph (d)(2) of this section, the assignee must waive the right to collect payment for the item or service for which the assignment of appeal rights is made. If the assignment is revoked under paragraph (g)(2) or (g)(3) of this section, the waiver of the right to collect payment nevertheless remains valid. A waiver of the right to collect payment remains in effect regardless of the outcome of the appeal decision.

(2) The assignee is not prohibited from recovering payment associated with coinsurance or deductibles or when an advance beneficiary notice is properly executed.

(e) *Duration of a valid assignment of appeal rights.* Unless revoked, the assignment of appeal rights is valid for all administrative and judicial review associated with the item or service as indicated on the standard CMS form, even in the event of the death of the assignor.

(f) *Rights of the assignee.* When a valid assignment of appeal rights is executed, the assignor transfers all appeal rights involving the particular item or service to the assignee. These include, but are not limited to–

(1) Obtaining information about the claim to the same extent as the assignor;

(2) Submitting evidence;

(3) Making statements about facts or law; and

(4) Making any request, or giving, or receiving any notice about appeal proceedings.

(g) *Revocation of assignment.* When an assignment of appeal rights is revoked, the rights to appeal revert to the assignor. An assignment of appeal rights may be revoked in any of the following ways:

(1) In writing by the assignor. The revocation of assignment must be delivered to the adjudicator and the assignee, and is effective on the date of receipt by the adjudicator.

(2) By abandonment if the assignee does not file an appeal of an unfavorable decision.

(3) By act or omission by the assignee that is determined by an adjudicator to be contrary to the financial interests of the assignor.

(h) *Responsibilities of the assignee.* Once the assignee files an appeal, the assignee becomes a party to the appeal. The assignee must meet all requirements for appeals that apply to any other party.

[70 FR 11472, Mar. 8, 2005, as amended at 70 FR 37702, June 30, 2005]

**§ 405.920 Initial determinations.**

After a claim is filed with the appropriate contractor in the manner and form described in subpart C of part 424 of this chapter, the contractor must—

(a) Determine if the items and services furnished are covered or otherwise reimbursable under title XVIII of the Act;

(b) Determine any amounts payable and make payment accordingly; and

(c) Notify the parties to the initial determination of the determination in accordance with § 405.921.

**§ 405.921 Notice of initial determination.**

(a) *Notice of initial determination sent to the beneficiary.* (1) The notice must be written in a manner calculated to be understood by the beneficiary, and sent to the last known address of the beneficiary;

(2) The notice of initial determination must contain—

(i) The reasons for the determination, including whether a local medical review policy, a local coverage determination, or national coverage determination was applied;

(ii) The procedures for obtaining additional information concerning the contractor's determination, such as a specific provision of the policy, manual, law or regulation used in making the determination;

(iii) Information on the right to a redetermination if the beneficiary is dissatisfied with the outcome of the initial determination and instructions on how to request a redetermination; and

(iv) Any other requirements specified by CMS.

(b) *Notice of initial determination sent to providers and suppliers.* (1) An electronic or paper remittance advice (RA) notice is the notice of initial determination sent to providers and suppliers that accept assignment. The electronic RA must comply with the format and content requirements of the standard adopted for national use by covered entities under the Health Insurance Portability and Accountability Act (HIPAA) and related CMS manual instructions. When a paper RA is mailed, it must comply with CMS manual instructions that parallel the HIPAA data content and coding requirements.

(2) The notice of initial determination must contain:

(i) The basis for any full or partial denial determination of services or items on the claim;

(ii) Information on the right to a redetermination if the provider or supplier is dissatisfied with the outcome of the initial determination;

(iii) All applicable claim adjustment reason and remark codes to explain the determination;

(iv) The source of the RA and who may be contacted if the provider or supplier requires further information;

(v) All content requirements of the standard adopted for national use by covered entities under HIPAA; and

(vi) Any other requirements specified by CMS.

**§ 405.922 Time frame for processing initial determinations.**
The contractor issues initial determinations on clean claims within 30 days of receipt if they are submitted by or on behalf of the beneficiary who received the items and/or services; otherwise, interest must be paid at the rate specified at 31 U.S.C. 3902(a) for the period beginning on the day after the required payment date and ending on the date payment is made.

**§ 405.924 Actions that are initial determinations.**

(a) *Applications and entitlement of individuals.* SSA makes initial determinations and processes reconsiderations with respect to an individual on the following:

(1) A determination with respect to entitlement to hospital insurance or supplementary medical insurance under Medicare.

(2) A disallowance of an individual's application for entitlement to hospital or supplementary medical insurance, if the individual fails to submit evidence requested by SSA to support the application. (SSA specifies in the initial determination the conditions of entitlement that the applicant failed to establish by not submitting the requested evidence).

(3) A denial of a request for withdrawal of an application for hospital or supplementary medical insurance, or a denial of a request for cancellation of a request for withdrawal.

(4) A determination as to whether an individual, previously determined as entitled to hospital or supplementary medical insurance, is no longer entitled to those benefits, including a determination based on nonpayment of premiums.

(b) *Claims made by or on behalf of beneficiaries.* The Medicare contractor makes initial determinations regarding claims for benefits under Medicare Part A and Part B. A finding that a request for payment or other submission does not meet the requirements for a Medicare claim as defined in § 424.32 of this chapter, is not considered an initial determination. An initial determination for purposes of this subpart includes, but is not limited to, determinations with respect to:

(1) If the items and/or services furnished are covered under title XVIII;

(2) In the case of determinations on the basis of section 1879(b) or (c) of the Act, if the beneficiary, or supplier who accepts assignment under § 424.55 of this chapter knew, or could reasonably have expected to know at the time the items or services were furnished, that the items or services were not covered;

(3) In the case of determinations on the basis of section 1842(l)(1) of the Act, if the beneficiary or physician knew, or could reasonably have expected to know at the time the services were furnished, that the services were not covered;

(4) Whether the deductible is met;

(5) The computation of the coinsurance amount;

(6) The number of days used for inpatient hospital, psychiatric hospital, or post-hospital extended care;

(7) The number of home health visits used;

(8) Periods of hospice care used;

(9) Requirements for certification and plan of treatment for physician services, durable medical equipment, therapies, inpatient hospitalization, skilled nursing care, home health, hospice, and partial hospitalization services;

(10) The beginning and ending of a spell of illness, including a determination made under the presumptions established under § 409.60(c)(2) of this chapter, and as specified in § 409.60(c)(4) of this chapter;

(11) The medical necessity of services, or the reasonableness or appropriateness of placement of an individual at an acute level of patient care made by the Quality Improvement Organization (QIO) on behalf of the contractor in accordance with § 476.86(c)(1) of this chapter;

(12) Any other issues having a present or potential effect on the amount of benefits to be paid under Part A or Part B of Medicare, including a determination as to whether there was an underpayment of benefits paid under Part A or Part B, and if so, the amount thereof;

(13) If a waiver of adjustment or recovery under sections 1870(b) and (c) of the Act is appropriate:

(i) When an overpayment of hospital insurance benefits or supplementary medical insurance benefits (including a payment under section 1814(e) of the Act) was made for an individual; or

(ii) For a Medicare Secondary Payer recovery claim against a beneficiary or against a provider or supplier.

(14) If a particular claim is not payable by Medicare based upon the application of the Medicare Secondary Payer provisions of section 1862(b) of the Act.

(15) Under the Medicare Secondary Payer provisions of sections 1862(b) of the Act that Medicare has a recovery claim against a provider, supplier, or beneficiary for services or items that were already paid by the Medicare program, except when the Medicare Secondary Payer recovery claim against the provider or supplier is based upon failure to file a proper claim as defined in part 411 of this chapter because this action is a reopening.

(c) *Determinations by QIOs.* An initial determination for purposes of this subpart also includes a determination made by a QIO that:

(1) A provider can terminate services provided to an individual when a physician certified that failure to continue the provision of those services is likely to place the individual's health at significant risk; or

(2) A provider can discharge an individual from the provider of services.

**§ 405.926 Actions that are not initial determinations.**

Actions that are not initial determinations and are not appealable under this subpart include, but are not limited to—

(a) Any determination for which CMS has sole responsibility, for example—

(1) If an entity meets the conditions for participation in the program;

(2) If an independent laboratory meets the conditions for coverage of services;

(b) The coinsurance amounts prescribed by regulation for outpatient services under the prospective payment system;

(c) Any issue regarding the computation of the payment amount of program reimbursement of general applicability for which CMS or a carrier has sole responsibility under Part B such as the establishment of a fee schedule set forth in part 414 of this chapter, or an inherent reasonableness adjustment pursuant to § 405.502(g), and any issue regarding the cost report settlement process under Part A;

(d) Whether an individual's appeal meets the qualifications for expedited access to judicial review provided in § 405.990;

(e) Any determination regarding whether a Medicare overpayment claim must be compromised, or collection action terminated or suspended under the Federal Claims Collection Act of 1966, as amended;

(f) Determinations regarding the transfer or discharge of residents of skilled nursing facilities in accordance with § 483.12 of this chapter;

(g) Determinations regarding the readmission screening and annual resident review processes required by subparts C and E of part 483 of this chapter;

(h) Determinations for a waiver of Medicare Secondary Payer recovery under section 1862(b) of the Act;

(i) Determinations for a waiver of interest;

(j) Determinations for a finding regarding the general applicability of the Medicare Secondary Payer provisions (as opposed to the application of these provisions to a particular claim or claims for Medicare payment for benefits);

(k) Determinations under the Medicare Secondary Payer provisions of section 1862(b) of the Act that Medicare has a recovery against an entity that was or is required or responsible (directly, as an insurer or self-insurer, as a third party administrator, as an employer that sponsors or contributes to a group health plan or a large group health plan, or otherwise) to make payment for services or items that were already reimbursed by the Medicare program;

(l) A contractor's, QIC's, ALJ's, or MAC's determination or decision to reopen or not to reopen an initial determination, redetermination, reconsideration, hearing decision, or review decision;

(m) Determinations that CMS or its contractors may participate in or act as parties in an ALJ hearing or MAC review;

(n) Determinations that a provider or supplier failed to submit a timely claim despite being requested to do so by the beneficiary or the beneficiary's subrogee;

(o) Determinations with respect to whether an entity qualifies for an exception to the electronic claims submission requirement under part 424 of this chapter;

(p) Determinations by the Secretary of sustained or high levels of payment errors in accordance with section 1893(f)(3)(A) of the Act;

(q) A contractor's prior determination related to coverage of physicians' services;

(r) Requests for anticipated payment under the home health prospective payment system under § 409.43(c)(ii)(2) of this chapter; and

(s) Claim submissions on forms or formats that are incomplete, invalid, or do not meet the requirements for a Medicare claim and returned or rejected to the provider or supplier.

[70 FR 11472, Mar. 8, 2005, as amended at 70 FR 37702, June 30, 2005]

**§ 405.927 Initial determinations subject to the reopenings process.**
Minor errors or omissions in an initial determination must be corrected only through the contractor's reopenings process under § 405.980(a)(3).

**§ 405.928 Effect of the initial determination.**

(a) An initial determination described in § 405.924(a) is binding unless it is revised or reconsidered in accordance with 20 CFR 404.907, or revised as a result of a reopening in accordance with 20 CFR 404.988.

(b) An initial determination described in § 405.924(b) is binding upon all parties to the initial determination unless—

(1) A redetermination is completed in accordance with § 405.940 through § 405.958; or

(2) The initial determination is revised as a result of a reopening in accordance with § 405.980.

(c) An initial determination listed in § 405.924(b) where a party submits a timely, valid request for redetermination under § 405.942 through § 405.944 must be processed as a redetermination under § 405.948 through § 405.958 unless the initial determination involves a clerical error or other minor error or omission.

**§ 405.940 Right to a redetermination.**
A person or entity that may be a party to a redetermination in accordance with § 405.906(b) and that is dissatisfied with an initial determination may request a redetermination by a contractor in accordance with § 405.940 through § 405.958, regardless of the amount in controversy.

**§ 405.942 Time frame for filing a request for a redetermination.**

(a) *Time frame for filing a request.* Except as provided in paragraph (b) of this section, any request for redetermination must be filed within 120 calendar days from the date a party receives the notice of the initial determination.

(1) For purposes of this section, the date of receipt of the initial determination will be presumed to be 5 days after the date of the notice of initial determination, unless there is evidence to the contrary.

(2) The request is considered as filed on the date it is received by the contractor.

(b) *Extending the time frame for filing a request—general rule.* If the 120-day period in which to file a request for a redetermination has expired and a party shows good cause, the contractor may extend the time frame for filing a request for redetermination.

(1) *How to request an extension.* A party may file a request for an extension of time for filing a request for a redetermination with the contractor. The party should include any evidence supporting the request for extension. The request for redetermination extension must—

(i) Be in writing;

(ii) State why the request for redetermination was not filed within the required time frame; and

(iii) Meet the requirements of § 405.944.

(2) *How the contractor determines if good cause exists.* In determining if a party has good cause for missing a deadline to request a redetermination, the contractor considers—

(i) The circumstances that kept the party from making the request on time;

(ii) If the contractor's action(s) misled the party; and

(iii) If the party had or has any physical, mental, educational, or linguistic limitations, including any lack of facility with the English language, that prevented the party from filing a timely request or from understanding or knowing about the need to file a timely request.

(3) *Examples of good cause.* Examples of circumstances when good cause may be found to exist include, but are not limited to, the following situations:

(i) The party was prevented by serious illness from contacting the contractor in person, in writing, or through a friend, relative, or other person; or

(ii) The party had a death or serious illness in his or her immediate family; or

(iii) Important records of the party were destroyed or damaged by fire or other accidental cause; or

(iv) The contractor gave the party incorrect or incomplete information about when and how to request a redetermination; or

(v) The party did not receive notice of the determination or decision; or

(vi) The party sent the request to a Government agency in good faith within the time limit, and the request did not reach the appropriate contractor until after the time period to file a request expired.

**§ 405.944 Place and method of filing a request for a redetermination.**

(a) *Filing location.* The request for redetermination must be filed with the contractor indicated on the notice of initial determination.

(b) *Content of redetermination request.* The request for redetermination must be in writing and should be made on a standard CMS form. A written request that is not made on a standard CMS form is accepted if it contains the same required elements as follows:

(1) The beneficiary's name;

(2) The Medicare health insurance claim number;

(3) Specific service(s) and/or item(s) for which the redetermination is being requested and the specific date(s) of the service;

(4) The name and signature of the party or the representative of the party.

(c) *Requests for redetermination by more than one party.* If more than one party timely files a request for redetermination on the same claim before a redetermination is made on the first timely filed request, the contractor must consolidate the separate requests into one proceeding and issue one redetermination.

**§ 405.946 Evidence to be submitted with the redetermination request.**

(a) *Evidence submitted with the request.* When filing the request for redetermination, a party must explain why it disagrees with the contractor's determination and should include any evidence that the party believes should be considered by the contractor in making its redetermination.

(b) *Evidence submitted after the request.* When a party submits additional evidence after filing the request for redetermination, the contractor's 60-day decision-making time frame is automatically extended for up to 14 calendar days for each submission.

[70 FR 11472, Mar. 8, 2005, as amended at 70 FR 37702, June 30, 2005]

**§ 405.948 Conduct of a redetermination.**

A redetermination consists of an independent review of an initial determination. In conducting a redetermination, the contractor reviews the evidence and findings upon which the initial determination was based, and any additional evidence the parties submit or the contractor obtains on its own. An individual who was not involved in making the initial determination must make a redetermination. The contractor may raise and develop new issues that are relevant to the claims in the particular case.

**§ 405.950 Time frame for making a redetermination.**

(a) *General rule.* The contractor mails, or otherwise transmits, written notice of the redetermination or dismissal to the parties to the redetermination at their last known addresses within 60 calendar days of the date the contractor receives a timely filed request for redetermination.

(b) *Exceptions.* (1) If a contractor grants an appellant's request for an extension of the 120-day filing deadline made in accordance with § 405.942(b), the 60-day decision-making time frame begins on the date the contractor receives the late-filed request for redetermination, or when the request for an extension is granted, whichever is later.

(2) If a contractor receives from multiple parties timely requests for redetermination of a claim determination, consistent with § 405.944(c), the contractor must issue a redetermination or dismissal within 60 days of the latest filed request.

(3) If a party submits additional evidence after the request for redetermination is filed, the contractor's 60-day decision-making time frame is extended for up to 14 calendar days for each submission, consistent with § 405.946(b).
[70 FR 11472, Mar. 8, 2005, as amended at 70 FR 37702, June 30, 2005]

**§ 405.952 Withdrawal or dismissal of a request for a redetermination.**

(a) *Withdrawing a request.* A party that files a request for redetermination may withdraw its request by filing a written and signed request for withdrawal. The request for withdrawal must contain a clear statement that the appellant is withdrawing the request for a redetermination and does not intend to proceed further with the appeal. The request must be received in the contractor's mailroom before a redetermination is issued. The appeal will proceed with respect to any other parties that have filed a timely request for redetermination.

(b) *Dismissing a request.* A contractor dismisses a redetermination request, either entirely or as to any stated issue, under any of the following circumstances:

(1) When the person or entity requesting a redetermination is not a proper party under § 405.906(b) or does not otherwise have a right to a redetermination under section 1869(a) of the Act;

(2) When the contractor determines the party failed to make out a valid request for redetermination that substantially complies with § 405.944;

(3) When the party fails to file the redetermination request within the proper filing time frame in accordance with § 405.942;

(4) When a beneficiary or the beneficiary's representative files a request for redetermination, but the beneficiary dies while the request is pending, and all of the following criteria apply:

(i) The beneficiary's surviving spouse or estate has no remaining financial interest in the case. In deciding this issue, the contractor considers if the surviving spouse or estate remains liable for the services for which payment was denied or a Medicare contractor held the beneficiary liable for subsequent similar services under the limitation of liability provisions based on the denial of payment for services at issue;

(ii) No other individual or entity with a financial interest in the case wishes to pursue the appeal; and

(iii) No other party filed a valid and timely redetermination request under § 405.942 and § 405.944,

(5) When a party filing the redetermination request submits a timely written request for withdrawal with the contractor; or

(6) When the contractor has not issued an initial determination on the claim or the matter for which a redetermination is sought.

(c) *Notice of dismissal.* A contractor mails or otherwise transmits a written notice of the dismissal of the redetermination request to the parties at their last known addresses. The notice states that there is a right to request that the contractor vacate the dismissal action.

(d) *Vacating a dismissal.* If good and sufficient cause is established, a contractor may vacate its dismissal of a request for redetermination within 6 months from the date of the notice of dismissal.

(e) *Effect of dismissal.* The dismissal of a request for redetermination is final and binding, unless it is modified or reversed by a QIC under § 405.974(b) or vacated under paragraph (d) of this section.

**§ 405.954 Redetermination.**

Upon the basis of the evidence of record, the contractor adjudicates the claim(s), and renders a redetermination affirming or reversing, in whole or in part, the initial determination in question.

**§ 405.956 Notice of a redetermination.**

(a) *Notification to parties*—(1) *General rule.* Written notice of a redetermination affirming, in whole or in part, the initial determination must be mailed or otherwise transmitted to all parties at their last known addresses in accordance with the time frames established in § 405.950. Written notice of a redetermination fully reversing the initial determination must be mailed or otherwise transmitted to the appellant in accordance with the time frames established in § 405.950. If the redetermination results in issuance of supplemental payment to a provider or supplier, the Medicare contractor must also issue an electronic or paper RA notice to the provider or supplier.

(2) *Overpayment cases involving multiple beneficiaries who have no liability.* In an overpayment case involving multiple beneficiaries who have no liability, the contractor may issue a written notice only to the appellant.

(b) *Content of the notice for affirmations, in whole or in part.* For decisions that are affirmations, in whole or in part, of the initial determination, the redetermination must be written in a manner calculated to be understood by a beneficiary, and contain—

(1) A clear statement indicating the extent to which the redetermination is favorable or unfavorable;

(2) A summary of the facts, including, as appropriate, a summary of the clinical or scientific evidence used in making the redetermination;

(3) An explanation of how pertinent laws, regulations, coverage rules, and CMS policies apply to the facts of the case;

(4) A summary of the rationale for the redetermination in clear, understandable language;

(5) Notification to the parties of their right to a reconsideration and a description of the procedures that a party must follow in order to request a reconsideration, including the time frame within which a reconsideration must be requested;

(6) A statement of any specific missing documentation that must be submitted with a request for a reconsideration, if applicable;

(7) A statement that all evidence the appellant wishes to introduce during the claim appeals process should be submitted with the request for a reconsideration;

(8) Notification that evidence not submitted to the QIC as indicated in paragraph (b)(6) of this section, is not considered at an ALJ hearing or further appeal, unless the appellant demonstrates good cause as to why that evidence was not provided previously; and

(9) The procedures for obtaining additional information concerning the redetermination, such as specific provisions of the policy, manual, or regulation used in making the redetermination.

(10) Any other requirements specified by CMS.

(c) *Content of the notice for a full reversal.* For decisions that are full reversals of the initial determination, the redetermination must be in writing and contain—

(1) A clear statement indicating that the redetermination is wholly favorable;

(2) Any other requirements specified by CMS.

(d) *Exception for beneficiary appeal requests.* (1) The notice must inform beneficiary appellants that the requirements of paragraph (b)(8) of this section are not applicable for purposes of beneficiary appeals.

(2) This exception does not apply for appeal requests from beneficiaries who are represented by providers or suppliers.

**§ 405.958 Effect of a redetermination.**

In accordance with section 1869 (a)(3)(D) of the Act, once a redetermination is issued, it becomes part of the initial determination. The redetermination is final and binding upon all parties unless—

(a) A reconsideration is completed in accordance with § 405.960 through § 405.978; or

(b) The redetermination is revised as a result of a reopening in accordance with § 405.980.

**§ 405.960 Right to a reconsideration.**

A person or entity that is a party to a redetermination made by a contractor as described under § 405.940 through § 405.958, and is dissatisfied with that determination, may request a reconsideration by a QIC in accordance with § 405.962 through § 405.966, regardless of the amount in controversy.

**§ 405.962 Time frame for filing a request for a reconsideration.**

(a) *Time frame for filing a request.* Except as provided in paragraph (b) of this section, any request for a reconsideration must be filed within 180 calendar days from the date the party receives the notice of the redetermination.

(1) For purposes of this section, the date of receipt of the redetermination will be presumed to be 5 days after the date of the notice of redetermination, unless there is evidence to the contrary.

(2) For purposes of meeting the 180-day filing deadline, the request is considered as filed on the date it is received by the QIC.

(b) *Extending the time for filing a request*—(1) *General rule.* A QIC may extend the 180-day time frame for filing a request for reconsideration for good cause.

(2) *How to request an extension.* A party to the redetermination must file its request for an extension of the time for filing the reconsideration request with its request for reconsideration. A party should include evidence to support the request for extension. The request for reconsideration and request for extension must—

(i) Be in writing;

(ii) State why the request for reconsideration was not filed within the required time frame; and

(iii) Meet the requirements of § 405.964.

(3) *How the QIC determines whether good cause exists.* In determining whether a party has good cause for missing a deadline to request reconsideration, the QIC applies the good cause provisions contained in § 405.942(b)(2) and (b)(3).

**§ 405.964 Place and method of filing a request for a reconsideration.**

(a) *Filing location.* The request for reconsideration must be filed with the QIC indicated on the notice of redetermination.

(b) *Content of reconsideration request.* The request for reconsideration must be in writing and should be made on a standard CMS form. A written request that is not made on a standard CMS form is accepted if it contains the same required elements, as follows:

(1) The beneficiary's name;

(2) Medicare health insurance claim number;

(3) Specific service(s) and item(s) for which the reconsideration is requested and the specific date(s) of service;

(4) The name and signature of the party or the representative of the party; and

(5) The name of the contractor that made the redetermination.

(c) *Requests for reconsideration by more than one party.* If more than one party timely files a request for reconsideration on the same claim before a reconsideration is made on the first timely filed request, the QIC must consolidate the separate requests into one proceeding and issue one reconsideration.

**§ 405.966 Evidence to be submitted with the reconsideration request.**

(a) *Evidence submitted with the request.* When filing a request for reconsideration, a party should present evidence and allegations of fact or law related to the issue in dispute and explain why it disagrees with the initial determination, including the redetermination.

(1) This evidence must include any missing documentation identified in the notice of redetermination, consistent with § 405.956(b)(6).

(2) Absent good cause, failure to submit all evidence, including documentation requested in the notice of redetermination prior to the issuance of the notice of reconsideration precludes subsequent consideration of that evidence.

(b) *Evidence submitted after the request.* Each time a party submits additional evidence after filing the request for reconsideration, the QIC's 60-day decision making time frame is automatically extended by up to 14 calendar days for each submission. This extension does not apply to timely submissions of documentation specifically requested by a QIC, unless the documentation was originally requested in the notice of redetermination.

(c) *Exception for beneficiaries and State Medicaid Agencies that file reconsideration requests.* (1) Beneficiaries and State Medicaid Agencies that file requests for reconsideration are not required to comply with the requirements of paragraph (a) of this section. However, the automatic 14-day extension described in paragraph (b) of this section applies to each evidence submission made after the request for reconsideration is filed.

(2) Beneficiaries who are represented by providers or suppliers must comply with the requirements of paragraph (a) of this section.

**§ 405.968 Conduct of a reconsideration.**

(a) *General rules.* (1) A reconsideration consists of an independent, on-the-record review of an initial determination, including the redetermination and all issues related to payment of the claim. In conducting a reconsideration, the QIC reviews the evidence and findings upon which the initial determination, including the redetermination, was based, and any additional evidence the parties submit or that the QIC obtains on its own. If the initial determination involves a finding on whether an item or service is reasonable and necessary for the diagnosis or treatment of illness or injury (under section 1862(a)(1)(A) of the Act), a QIC's reconsideration must involve consideration by a panel of physicians or other appropriate health care professionals, and be based on clinical experience, the patient's medical records, and medical, technical, and scientific evidence of record to the extent applicable.

(b) *Authority of the QIC.* (1) National coverage determinations (NCDs), CMS Rulings, and applicable laws and regulations are binding on the QIC.

(2) QICs are not bound by LCDs, LMRPs, or CMS program guidance, such as program memoranda and manual instructions, but give substantial deference to these policies if they are applicable to a particular case. A QIC may decline to follow a policy, if the QIC determines, either at a party's request or at its own discretion, that the policy does not apply to the facts of the particular case.

(3) If a QIC declines to follow a policy in a particular case, the QIC's reconsideration explains the reasons why the policy was not followed.

(4) A QIC's decision to decline to follow a policy under this section applies only to the specific claim being reconsidered and does not have precedential effect.

(5) A QIC may raise and develop new issues that are relevant to the claims in a particular case provided that the contractor rendered a redetermination with respect to the claims.

(c) *Qualifications of the QIC's panel members.* (1) Members of a QIC's panel who conduct reconsiderations must have sufficient medical, legal, and other expertise, including knowledge of the Medicare program.

(2) When a redetermination is made with respect to whether an item or service is reasonable and necessary (section 1862(a)(1)(A) of the Act), the QIC designates a panel of physicians or other appropriate health care professionals to consider the facts and circumstances of the redetermination.

(3) Where a claim pertains to the furnishing of treatment by a physician, or the provision of items or services by a physician, a reviewing professional must be a physician.

(d) *Disqualification of a QIC panel member.* No physician or health care professional employed by or otherwise working for a QIC may review determinations regarding–

(1) Health care services furnished to a patient if that physician or health care professional was directly responsible for furnishing those services; or

(2) Health care services provided in or by an institution, organization, or agency, if that physician or health care professional or any member of the physician's family or health care professional's family has, directly or indirectly, a significant financial interest in that institution, organization, or agency (see the term family member as defined in § 405.902).

**§ 405.970 Time frame for making a reconsideration.**

(a) *General rule.* Within 60 calendar days of the date the QIC receives a timely filed request for reconsideration or any additional time provided by paragraph (b) of this section, the QIC mails, or otherwise transmits to the parties at their last known addresses, written notice of–

(1) The reconsideration;

(2) Its inability to complete its review within 60 days in accordance with paragraphs (c) through (e) of this section; or

(3) Dismissal.

(b) *Exceptions.* (1) If a QIC grants an appellant's request for an extension of the 180-day filing deadline made in accordance with § 405.962(b), the QIC's 60-day decision-making time frame begins on the date the QIC receives the late filed request for reconsideration, or when the request for an extension that meets the requirements of § 405.962(b) is granted, whichever is later.

(2) If a QIC receives timely requests for reconsideration from multiple parties, consistent with § 405.964(c), the QIC must issue a reconsideration, notice that it cannot complete its review, or dismissal within 60 days for each submission of the latest filed request.

(3) Each time a party submits additional evidence after the request for reconsideration is filed, the QIC's 60-day decision making time frame is extended by up to 14 days for each submission, consistent with § 405.966(b).

(c) *Responsibilities of the QIC.* Within 60 days of receiving a request for a reconsideration, or any additional time provided for under paragraph (b) of this section, a QIC must take one of the following actions:

(1) Notify all parties of its reconsideration, consistent with § 405.976.

(2) Notify the parties that it cannot complete the reconsideration by the deadline specified in paragraph (b) of this section and offer the appellant the

opportunity to escalate the appeal to an ALJ. The QIC continues to process the reconsideration unless it receives a written request from the appellant to escalate the case to an ALJ after the adjudication period has expired.

(d) *Responsibilities of the appellant.* If an appellant wishes to exercise the option of escalating the case to an ALJ, the appellant must notify the QIC in writing.

(e) *Actions following appellant's notice.* (1) If the appellant fails to notify the QIC, or notifies the QIC that the appellant does not choose to escalate the case, the QIC completes its reconsideration and notifies the appellant of its action consistent with § 405.972 or § 405.976.

(2) If the appellant notifies the QIC that the appellant wishes to escalate the case, the QIC must take one of the following actions within 5 days of receipt of the notice or 5 days from the end of the applicable adjudication period under paragraph (a) or (b) of this section:

(i) Complete its reconsideration and notify all parties of its decision consistent with § 405.972 or § 405.976.

(ii) Acknowledge the escalation notice in writing and forward the case file to the ALJ hearing office.

[70 FR 11472, Mar. 8, 2005, as amended at 70 FR 37702, June 30, 2005]

**§ 405.972 Withdrawal or dismissal of a request for a reconsideration.**

(a) *Withdrawing a request.* An appellant that files a request for reconsideration may withdraw its request by filing a written and signed request for withdrawal. The request for withdrawal must–

(1) Contain a clear statement that the appellant is withdrawing the request for reconsideration and does not intend to proceed further with the appeal.

(2) Be received in the QIC's mailroom before the reconsideration is issued.

(b) *Dismissing a request.* A QIC dismisses a reconsideration request, either entirely or as to any stated issue, under any of the following circumstances:

(1) When the person or entity requesting reconsideration is not a proper party under § 405.906(b) or does not otherwise have a right to a reconsideration under section 1869(b) of the Act;

(2) When the QIC determines that the party failed to make out a valid request for reconsideration that substantially complies with § 405.964(a) and (b);

(3) When the party fails to file the reconsideration request in accordance with the time frames established in § 405.962;

(4) When a beneficiary or the beneficiary's representative files a request for reconsideration, but the beneficiary dies while the request is pending, and all of the following criteria apply:

(i) The beneficiary's surviving spouse or estate has no remaining financial interest in the case. In deciding this issue, the QIC considers if the surviving spouse or estate remains liable for the services for which payment was denied or a Medicare contractor held the beneficiary liable for subsequent similar services under the limitation of liability provisions based on the denial of payment for services at issue;

(ii) No other individual or entity with a financial interest in the case wishes to pursue the appeal; and

(iii) No other party to the redetermination filed a valid and timely request for reconsideration under § 405.962 and § 405.964.

(5) When a party filing for the reconsideration submits a written request of withdrawal to the QIC and satisfies the criteria set forth in paragraph (a) of this section before the reconsideration has been issued; or

(6) When the contractor has not issued a redetermination on the initial determination for which a reconsideration is sought.

(c) *Notice of dismissal.* A QIC mails or otherwise transmits written notice of the dismissal of the reconsideration request to the parties at their last known addresses. The notice states that there is a right to request that the contractor vacate the dismissal action. The appeal will proceed with respect to any other parties that have filed a timely request for reconsideration.

(d) *Vacating a dismissal.* If good and sufficient cause is established, a QIC may vacate its dismissal of a request for reconsideration within 6 months of the date of the notice of dismissal.

(e) *Effect of dismissal.* The dismissal of a request for reconsideration is final and binding, unless it is modified or reversed by an ALJ under § 405.1004 or vacated under paragraph (d) of this section.

**§ 405.974 Reconsideration.**

(a) *Reconsideration of a contractor determination.* Except as provided in § 405.972, upon the basis of the evidence of record, the QIC must issue a reconsideration affirming or reversing, in whole or in part, the initial determination, including the redetermination, in question.

(b) *Reconsideration of contractor's dismissal of a redetermination request.* (1) A party to a contractor's dismissal of a request for redetermination has a right to have the dismissal reviewed by a QIC, if the party files a written request for review of the dismissal with the QIC within 60 days after receipt of the contractor's notice of dismissal.

(i) For purposes of this section, the date of receipt of the contractor's notice of dismissal is presumed to be 5 days after the date of the notice of dismissal, unless there is evidence to the contrary.

(ii) For purposes of meeting the 60-day filing deadline, the request is considered as filed on the date it is received by the QIC indicated on the notice of dismissal.

(2) If the QIC determines that the contractor's dismissal was in error, it vacates the dismissal and remands the case to the contractor for a redetermination.

(3) A QIC's reconsideration of a contractor's dismissal of a redetermination request is final and not subject to any further review.

[70 FR 11472, Mar. 8, 2005, as amended at 70 FR 37703, June 30, 2005]

**§ 405.976 Notice of a reconsideration.**

(a) *Notification to parties—(1) General rules.* (i) Written notice of the reconsideration must be mailed or otherwise transmitted to all parties at their last known addresses, in accordance with the time frames established in § 405.970(a) or (b).

(ii) The notice must be written in a manner reasonably calculated to be understood by a beneficiary.

(iii) The QIC must promptly notify the entity responsible for payment of claims under Part A or Part B of its reconsideration. If the reconsideration results in issuance of supplemental payment to a provider or supplier, the Medicare contractor must also issue an electronic or paper RA notice to the provider or supplier.

(2) *Overpayment cases involving multiple beneficiaries who have no liability.* In an overpayment case involving multiple beneficiaries who have no liability, the QIC may issue a written notice only to the appellant.

(b) *Content of the notice.* The reconsideration must be in writing and contain—

(1) A clear statement indicating whether the reconsideration is favorable or unfavorable;

(2) A summary of the facts, including as appropriate, a summary of the clinical or scientific evidence used in making the reconsideration;

(3) An explanation of how pertinent laws, regulations, coverage rules, and CMS policies, apply to the facts of the case, including, where applicable, the rationale for declining to follow an LCD, LMRP, or CMS program guidance;

(4) In the case of a determination on whether an item or service is reasonable or necessary under section 1862(a)(1)(A) of the Act, an explanation of the medical and scientific rationale for the decision;

(5) A summary of the rationale for the reconsideration.

(i) If the notice of redetermination indicated that specific documentation should be submitted with the reconsideration request, and the documentation was not submitted with the request for reconsideration, the summary must indicate how the missing documentation affected the reconsideration; and

(ii) The summary must also specify that, consistent with § 405.956(b)(8) and § 405.966(b), all evidence, including evidence requested in the notice of redetermination, that is not submitted prior to the issuance of the reconsideration will not be considered at an ALJ level, or made part of the administrative record, unless the appellant demonstrates good cause as to why the evidence was not provided prior to the issuance of the QIC's reconsideration. This requirement does not apply to beneficiaries, unless the beneficiary is represented by a provider or supplier or to State Medicaid Agencies;

(6) Information concerning to the parties' right to an ALJ hearing, including the applicable amount in controversy requirement and aggregation provisions;

(7) A statement of whether the amount in controversy needed for an ALJ hearing is met when the reconsideration is partially or fully unfavorable;

(8) A description of the procedures that a party must follow in order to obtain an ALJ hearing of an expedited reconsideration, including the time frame under which a request for an ALJ hearing must be filed;

(9) If appropriate, advice as to the requirements for use of the expedited access to judicial review process set forth in § 405.990;

(10) The procedures for obtaining additional information concerning the reconsideration, such as specific provisions of the policy, manual, or regulation used in making the reconsideration; and

(11) Any other requirements specified by CMS.

**§ 405.978 Effect of a reconsideration.**

A reconsideration is final and binding on all parties, unless—

(a) An ALJ decision is issued in accordance to a request for an ALJ hearing made in accordance with § 405.1014;

(b) A review entity issues a decision in accordance to a request for expedited access to judicial review under § 405.990; or

(c) The reconsideration is revised as a result of a reopening in accordance with § 405.980.

**§ 405.980 Reopenings of initial determinations, redeterminations, and reconsiderations, hearings and reviews.**

(a) *General rules.* (1) A reopening is a remedial action taken to change a final determination or decision that resulted in either an overpayment or underpayment, even though the final determination or decision may have been correct at the time it was made based on the evidence of record. That action may be taken by—

(i) A contractor to revise the initial determination or redetermination;

(ii) A QIC to revise the reconsideration;

(iii) An ALJ to revise the hearing decision; or

(iv) The MAC to revise the hearing or review decision.

(2) If a contractor issues a denial of a claim because it did not receive requested documentation during medical review and the party subsequently requests a redetermination, the contractor must process the request as a reopening.

(3) Notwithstanding paragraph (a)(4) of this section, a contractor must process clerical errors (which includes minor errors and omissions) as reopenings, instead of as redeterminations as specified in § 405.940. If the contractor receives a request for reopening and disagrees that the issue is a clerical error, the contractor must dismiss the reopening request and advise the party of any appeal rights, provided the time frame to request an appeal on the original denial has not expired. For purposes of this section, clerical error includes human or mechanical errors on the part of the party or the contractor such as—

(i) Mathematical or computational mistakes;

(ii) Inaccurate data entry; or

(iii) Denials of claims as duplicates.

(4) When a party has filed a valid request for an appeal of an initial determination, redetermination, reconsideration, hearing, or MAC review, no adjudicator has jurisdiction to reopen an issue on a claim that is under appeal until all appeal rights for that issue are exhausted. Once the appeal rights for the issue have been exhausted, the contractor, QIC, ALJ, or MAC may reopen as set forth in this section.

(5) The contractor's, QIC's, ALJ's, or MAC's decision on whether to reopen is final and not subject to appeal.

(6) A determination under the Medicare secondary payer provisions of section 1862(b) of the Act that Medicare has an MSP recovery claim for services or items that were already reimbursed by the Medicare program is not a reopening, except where the recovery claim is based upon a provider's or supplier's failure to demonstrate that it filed a proper claim as defined in part 411 of this chapter.

(b) *Time frames and requirements for reopening initial determinations and redeterminations initiated by a contractor.* A contractor may reopen and revise its initial determination or redetermination on its own motion—

(1) Within 1 year from the date of the initial determination or redetermination for any reason.

(2) Within 4 years from the date of the initial determination or redetermination for good cause as defined in § 405.986.

(3) At any time if there exists reliable evidence as defined in § 405.902 that the initial determination was procured by fraud or similar fault as defined in § 405.902.

(4) At any time if the initial determination is unfavorable, in whole or in part, to the party thereto, but only for the purpose of correcting a clerical error on which that determination was based.

(5) At any time to effectuate a decision issued under the coverage appeals process.

(c) *Time frame and requirements for reopening initial determinations and redeterminations requested by a party.* (1) A party may request that a contractor reopen its initial determination or redetermination within 1 year from the date of the initial determination or redetermination for any reason.

(2) A party may request that a contractor reopen its initial determination or redetermination within 4 years from the date of the initial determination or redetermination for good cause in accordance with § 405.986.

(3) A party may request that a contractor reopen its initial determination at any time if the initial determination is unfavorable, in whole or in part, to the party thereto, but only for the purpose of correcting a clerical error on which that determination was based. Third party payer error does not constitute clerical error. *See* § 405.986(c).

(d) *Time frame and requirements for reopening reconsiderations, hearing decisions and reviews initiated by a QIC, ALJ, or the MAC.* (1) A QIC may reopen its reconsideration on its own motion within 180 days from the date of the reconsideration for good cause in accordance with § 405.986. If the QIC's reconsideration was procured by fraud or similar fault, then the QIC may reopen at any time.

(2) An ALJ or the MAC may reopen a hearing decision on its own motion within 180 days from the date of the decision for good cause in accordance with § 405.986. If the hearing decision was procured by fraud or similar fault, then the ALJ or the MAC may reopen at any time.

(3) The MAC may reopen its review decision on its own motion within 180 days from the date of the review decision for good cause in accordance with § 405.986. If the MAC's decision was procured by fraud or similar fault, then the MAC may reopen at any time.

(e) *Time frames and requirements for reopening reconsiderations, hearing decisions, and reviews requested by a party.* (1) A party to a reconsideration may request that a QIC reopen its reconsideration within 180 days from the date of the reconsideration for good cause in accordance with § 405.986.

(2) A party to a hearing may request that an ALJ or the MAC reopen a hearing decision within 180 days from the date of the hearing decision for good cause in accordance with § 405.986.

(3) A party to a review may request that the MAC reopen its decision within 180 days from the date of the review decision for good cause in accordance with § 405.986.

[70 FR 11472, Mar. 8, 2005, as amended at 70 FR 37703, June 30, 2005]

**§ 405.982 Notice of a revised determination or decision.**

(a) *When adjudicators initiate reopenings.* When any determination or decision is reopened and revised as provided in § 405.980, the contractor, QIC, ALJ, or the MAC must mail its revised determination or decision to the parties to that determination or decision at their last known address. In the case of a full or partial reversal resulting in issuance of a payment to a provider or supplier, a revised electronic or paper remittance advice notice must be issued by the Medicare contractor. An adverse revised determination or decision must state the rationale and basis for the reopening and revision and any right to appeal.

(b) *Reopenings initiated at the request of a party.* The contractor, QIC, ALJ, or the MAC must mail its revised determination or decision to the parties to that determination or decision at their last known address. In the case of a full or partial reversal resulting in issuance of a payment to a provider or supplier, a revised electronic or paper remittance advice notice must be issued by the Medicare contractor. An adverse revised determination or decision must state the rationale and basis for the reopening and revision and any right to appeal.

**§ 405.984 Effect of a revised determination or decision.**

(a) *Initial determinations.* The revision of an initial determination is binding upon all parties unless a party files a written request for a redetermination that is accepted and processed in accordance with § 405.940 through § 405.958.

(b) *Redeterminations.* The revision of a redetermination is binding upon all parties unless a party files a written request for a QIC reconsideration that is accepted and processed in accordance with § 405.960 through § 405.978.

(c) *Reconsiderations.* The revision of a reconsideration is binding upon all parties unless a party files a written request for an ALJ hearing that is accepted and processed in accordance with § 405.1000 through § 405.1064.

(d) *ALJ hearing decisions.* The revision of a hearing decision is binding upon all parties unless a party files a written request for a MAC review that is accepted and processed in accordance with § 405.1100 through § 405.1130.

(e) *MAC review.* The revision of a MAC review is binding upon all parties unless a party files a civil action in which a Federal district court accepts jurisdiction and issues a decision.

(f) *Appeal of only the portion of the determination or decision revised by the reopening.* Only the portion of the initial determination, redetermination, reconsideration, or hearing decision revised by the reopening may be subsequently appealed.

(g) *Effect of a revised determination or decision.* A revised determination or decision is binding unless it is appealed or otherwise reopened.

**§ 405.986 Good cause for reopening.**

(a) *Establishing good cause.* Good cause may be established when–

(1) There is new and material evidence that–

(i) Was not available or known at the time of the determination or decision; and

(ii) May result in a different conclusion; or

(2) The evidence that was considered in making the determination or decision clearly shows on its face that an obvious error was made at the time of the determination or decision.

(b) *Change in substantive law or interpretative policy.* A change of legal interpretation or policy by CMS in a regulation, CMS ruling, or CMS general instruction, or a change in legal interpretation or policy by SSA in a regulation, SSA ruling, or SSA general instruction in entitlement appeals, whether made in response to judicial precedent or otherwise, is not a basis for reopening a determination or hearing decision under this section. This provision does not preclude contractors from conducting reopenings to effectuate coverage decisions issued under the authority granted by section 1869(f) of the Act.

(c) *Third party payer error.* A request to reopen a claim based upon a third party payer's error in making a primary payment determination when Medicare processed the claim in accordance with the information in its system of records or on the claim form does not constitute good cause for reopening.

[70 FR 11472, Mar. 8, 2005, as amended at 70 FR 37703, June 30, 2005]

**§ 405.990 Expedited access to judicial review.**

(a) *Process for expedited access to judicial review.* (1) For purposes of this section, a "review entity" means an entity of up to three reviewers who are ALJs or members of the Departmental Appeals Board (DAB), as determined by the Secretary.

(2) In order to obtain expedited access to judicial review (EAJR), a review entity must certify that the Medicare Appeals Council (MAC) does not have the authority to decide the question of law or regulation relevant to the matters in dispute and that there is no material issue of fact in dispute.

(3) A party may make a request for EAJR only once with respect to a question of law or regulation for a specific matter in dispute in an appeal.

(b) *Conditions for making the expedited appeals request.* (1) A party may request EAJR in place of an ALJ hearing or MAC review if the following conditions are met:

(i) A QIC has made a reconsideration determination and the party has filed a request for–

(A) An ALJ hearing in accordance with § 405.1002 and a final decision of the ALJ has not been issued;

(B) MAC review in accordance with § 405.1102 and a final decision of the MAC has not been issued; or

(ii) The appeal has been escalated from the QIC to the ALJ level after the period described in § 405.970(a) and § 405.970(b) has expired, and the QIC does not issue a final action within the time frame described in § 405.970(e).

(2) The requestor is a party, as defined in paragraph (e) of this section.

(3) The amount remaining in controversy meets the requirements of § 405.1006(b) or (c).

(4) If there is more than one party to the reconsideration, hearing, or MAC review, each party concurs, in writing, with the request for the EAJR.

(5) There are no material issues of fact in dispute.

(c) Content of the request for EAJR. The request for EAJR must—

(1) Allege that there are no material issues of fact in dispute and identify the facts that the requestor considers material and that are not disputed; and

(2) Assert that the only factor precluding a decision favorable to the requestor is—

(i) A statutory provision that is unconstitutional, or a provision of a regulation or national coverage determination and specify the statutory provision that the requestor considers unconstitutional or the provision of a regulation or a national coverage determination that the requestor considers invalid, or

(ii) A CMS Ruling that the requester considers invalid;

(3) Include a copy of any QIC reconsideration and of any ALJ hearing decision that the requester has received;

(4) If any QIC reconsideration or ALJ hearing decision was based on facts that the requestor is disputing, state why the requestor considers those facts to be immaterial; and

(5) If any QIC reconsideration or ALJ hearing decision was based on a provision of a law, regulation, national coverage determination or CMS Ruling in addition to the one the requestor considers unconstitutional or invalid, a statement as to why further administrative review of how that provision applies to the facts is not necessary.

(d) *Place and time for an EAJR request*—(1) *Method and place for filing request.* The requestor may include an EAJR request in his or her request for an ALJ hearing or MAC review, or, if an appeal is already pending with an ALJ or the MAC, file a written EAJR request with the ALJ hearing office or MAC where the appeal is being considered. The ALJ hearing office or MAC forwards the request to the review entity within 5 calendar days of receipt.

(2) *Time of filing request.* The party may file a request for the EAJR—

(i) If the party has requested a hearing, at any time before receipt of the notice of the ALJ's decision; or

(ii) If the party has requested MAC review, at any time before receipt of notice of the MAC's decision.

(e) *Parties to the EAJR.* The parties to the EAJR are the persons or entities who were parties to the QIC's reconsideration determination and, if applicable, to the ALJ hearing.

(f) *Determination on EAJR request.* (1) The review entity described in paragraph (a) of this section will determine whether the request for EAJR meets all of the requirements of paragraphs (b), (c), and (d) of this section.

(2) Within 60 days after the date the review entity receives a request and accompanying documents and materials meeting the conditions in paragraphs (b), (c), and (d) of this section, the review entity will issue either a certification in accordance to paragraph (g) of this section or a denial of the request.

(3) A determination by the review entity either certifying that the requirements for EAJR are met pursuant to paragraph (g) of this section or denying the request is final and not subject to review by the Secretary.

(4) If the review entity fails to make a determination within the time frame specified in paragraph (f)(2) of this section, then the requestor may bring a civil action in Federal district court within 60 days of the end of the time frame.

(g) *Certification by the review entity.* If a party meets the requirements for the EAJR, the review entity certifies in writing that—

(1) The material facts involved in the claim are not in dispute;

(2) Except as indicated in paragraph (g)(3) of this section, the Secretary's interpretation of the law is not in dispute;

(3) The sole issue(s) in dispute is the constitutionality of a statutory provision, or the validity of a provision of a regulation, CMS Ruling, or national coverage determination;

(4) But for the provision challenged, the requestor would receive a favorable decision on the ultimate issue (such as whether a claim should be paid); and

(5) The certification by the review entity is the Secretary's final action for purposes of seeking expedited judicial review.

(h) *Effect of certification by the review entity.* If an EAJR request results in a certification described in paragraph (g) of this section—

(1) The party that requested the EAJR is considered to have waived any right to completion of the remaining steps of the administrative appeals process regarding the matter certified.

(2) The requestor has 60 days, beginning on the date of the review entity's certification within which to bring a civil action in Federal district court.

(3) The requestor must satisfy the requirements for venue under section 1869(b)(2)(C)(iii) of the Act, as well as the requirements for filing a civil action in a Federal district court under § 405.1136(a) and § 405.1136(c) through § 405.1136(f).

(i) *Rejection of EAJR.* (1) If a request for EAJR request does not meet all the conditions set out in paragraphs (b), (c) and (d) of this section, or if the review entity does not certify a request for EAJR, the review entity advises in writing all parties that the request has been denied, and returns the request to the ALJ hearing office or the MAC, which will treat it as a request for hearing or for MAC review, as appropriate.

(2) Whenever a review entity forwards a rejected EAJR request to an ALJ hearing office or the MAC, the appeal is considered timely filed and the 90-day decision making time frame begins on the day the request is received by the hearing office or the MAC.

(j) *Interest on any amounts in controversy.* (1) If a provider or supplier is granted judicial review in accordance with this section, the amount in controversy, if any, is subject to annual interest beginning on the first day of the first month beginning after the 60-day period as determined in accordance with paragraphs (f)(4) or (h)(2) of this section, as applicable.

(2) The interest is awarded by the reviewing court and payable to a prevailing party.

(3) The rate of interest is equal to the rate of interest applicable to obligations issued for purchase by the Federal Supplementary Medical Insurance Trust Fund for the month in which the civil action authorized under this subpart is commenced.

(4) No interest awarded in accordance with this paragraph shall be income or cost for purposes of determining reimbursement due to providers or suppliers under Medicare.

[70 FR 11472, Mar. 8, 2005, as amended at 70 FR 37703, June 30, 2005]

**§ 405.1000 Hearing before an ALJ: General rule.**

(a) If a party is dissatisfied with a QIC's reconsideration or if the adjudication period specified in § 405.970 for the QIC to complete its reconsideration has elapsed, the party may request a hearing.

(b) A hearing may be conducted in-person, by video-teleconference (VTC), or by telephone. At the hearing, the parties may submit evidence (subject to the restrictions in § 405.1018 and § 405.1028), examine the evidence used in making the determination under review, and present and/or question witnesses.

(c) In some circumstances, a representative of CMS or its contractor, including the QIC, QIO, fiscal intermediary or carrier, may participate in or join the hearing as a party. (*see* § 405.1010 and § 405.1012).

(d) The ALJ issues a decision based on the hearing record.

(e) If all parties to the hearing waive their right to appear at the hearing in person or by telephone or video-teleconference, the ALJ may make a decision based on the evidence that is in the file and any new evidence that is submitted for consideration.

(f) The ALJ may require the parties to participate in a hearing if it is necessary to decide the case. If the ALJ determines that it is necessary to obtain testimony from a non-party, he or she may hold a hearing to obtain that testimony, even if all of the parties have waived the right to appear. In that event, however, the ALJ will give the parties the opportunity to appear when the testimony is given, but may hold the hearing even if none of the parties decide to appear.

(g) An ALJ may also issue a decision on the record on his or her own initiative if the evidence in the hearing record supports a fully favorable finding.

**§ 405.1002 Right to an ALJ hearing.**

(a) A party to a QIC reconsideration may request a hearing before an ALJ if—

(1) The party files a written request for an ALJ hearing within 60 days after receipt of the notice of the QIC's reconsideration.

(2) The party meets the amount in controversy requirements of § 405.1006.

(3) For purposes of this section, the date of receipt of the reconsideration is presumed to be 5 days after the date of the reconsideration, unless there is evidence to the contrary.

(4) For purposes of meeting the 60-day filing deadline, the request is considered as filed on the date it is received by the entity specified in the QIC's reconsideration.

(b) A party who files a timely appeal before a QIC and whose appeal continues to be pending before a QIC at the end of the period described in § 405.970 has a right to a hearing before an ALJ if—

(1) The party files a written request with the QIC to escalate the appeal to the ALJ level after the period described in § 405.970(a) and (b) has expired and the party files the request in accordance with § 405.970(d);

(2) The QIC does not issue a final action within 5 days of receiving the request for escalation in accordance with § 405.970(e)(2); and

(3) The party has an amount remaining in controversy specified in § 405.1006.

[70 FR 11472, Mar. 8, 2005, as amended at 70 FR 37703, June 30, 2005]

**§ 405.1004 Right to ALJ review of QIC notice of dismissal.**

(a) A party to a QIC's dismissal of a request for reconsideration has a right to have the dismissal reviewed by an ALJ if—

(1) The party files a written request for an ALJ review within 60 days after receipt of the notice of the QIC's dismissal.

(2) The party meets the amount in controversy requirements of § 405.1006.

(3) For purposes of this section, the date of receipt of the QIC's dismissal is presumed to be 5 days after the date of the dismissal notice, unless there is evidence to the contrary.

(4) For purposes of meeting the 60-day filing deadline, the request is considered as filed on the date it is received by the entity specified in the QIC's dismissal.

(b) If the ALJ determines that the QIC's dismissal was in error, he or she vacates the dismissal and remands the case to the QIC for a reconsideration.

(c) An ALJ's decision regarding a QIC's dismissal of a reconsideration request is final and not subject to further review.

[70 FR 11472, Mar. 8, 2005, as amended at 70 FR 37703, June 30, 2005]

**§ 405.1006 Amount in controversy required to request an ALJ hearing and judicial review.**

(a) *Definitions.* For the purposes of aggregating claims to meet the amount in controversy requirement for an ALJ hearing or judicial review:

(1) "Common issues of law and fact" means the claims sought to be aggregated are denied, or payment is reduced, for similar reasons and arise from a similar fact pattern material to the reason the claims are denied or payment is reduced.

(2) "Delivery of similar or related services" means like or coordinated services or items provided to one or more beneficiaries.

(b) *ALJ review.* To be entitled to a hearing before an ALJ, the party must meet the amount in controversy requirements of this section.

(1) For ALJ hearing requests, the required amount remaining in controversy must be $100 increased by the percentage increase in the medical care component of the consumer price index for all urban consumers (U.S. city average) as measured from July 2003 to the July preceding the current year involved.

(2) If the figure in paragraph (b)(1) of this section is not a multiple of $10, then it is rounded to the nearest multiple of $10. The Secretary will publish changes to the amount in controversy requirement in the *Federal Register* when necessary.

(c) *Judicial review.* To be entitled to judicial review, a party must meet the amount in controversy requirements of this subpart at the time it requests judicial review.

(1) For review requests, the required amount remaining in controversy must be $1,000 or more, adjusted as specified in paragraphs (b)(1) and (b)(2) of this section.

**(2) [Reserved]**

(d) *Calculating the amount remaining in controversy.* (1) The amount remaining in controversy is computed as the actual amount charged the individual for the items and services in question, reduced by—

(i) Any Medicare payments already made or awarded for the items or services; and

(ii) Any deductible and coinsurance amounts applicable in the particular case.

(2) Notwithstanding paragraph (d)(1) of this section, when payment is made for items or services under section 1879 of the Act or § 411.400 of this chapter, or the liability of the beneficiary for those services is limited under § 411.402 of this chapter, the amount in controversy is computed as the amount that the beneficiary would have been charged for the items or services in question if those expenses were not paid under § 411.400 of this chapter or if that liability was not limited under § 411.402 of this chapter, reduced by any deductible and coinsurance amounts applicable in the particular case.

(e) *Aggregating claims to meet the amount in controversy—*

(1) *Appealing QIC reconsiderations to the ALJ level.* Either an individual appellant or multiple appellants may aggregate two or more claims to meet the amount in controversy for an ALJ hearing if–

(i) The claims were previously reconsidered by a QIC;

(ii) The request for ALJ hearing lists all of the claims to be aggregated and is filed within 60 days after receipt of all of the reconsiderations being appealed; and

(iii) The ALJ determines that the claims that a single appellant seeks to aggregate involve the delivery of similar or related services, or the claims that multiple appellants seek to aggregate involve common issues of law and fact. Part A and Part B claims may be combined to meet the amount in controversy requirements.

(2) *Aggregating claims that are escalated from the QIC level to the ALJ level.* Either an individual appellant or multiple appellants may aggregate two or more claims to meet the amount in controversy for an ALJ hearing if–

(i) The claims were pending before the QIC in conjunction with the same request for reconsideration;

(ii) The appellant(s) requests aggregation of the claims to the ALJ level in the same request for escalation; and

(iii) The ALJ determines that the claims that a single appellant seeks to aggregate involve the delivery of similar or related services, or the claims that multiple appellants seek to aggregate involve common issues of law and fact. Part A and Part B claims may be combined to meet the amount in controversy requirements.

(f) *Content of request for aggregation.* When an appellant(s) seeks to aggregate claims in a request for an ALJ hearing, the appellant(s) must–

(1) Specify all of the claims the appellant(s) seeks to aggregate; and

(2) State why the appellant(s) believes that the claims involve common issues of law and fact or delivery of similar or related services.

**§ 405.1008 Parties to an ALJ hearing.**

(a) *Who may request a hearing.* Any party to the QIC's reconsideration may request a hearing before an ALJ. However, only the appellant (that is, the party that filed and maintained the request for reconsideration by a QIC) may request that the appeal be escalated to the ALJ level if the QIC does not complete its action within the time frame described in § 405.970.

(b) *Who are parties to the ALJ hearing.* The party who filed the request for hearing and all other parties to the reconsideration are parties to the ALJ hearing. In addition, a representative of CMS or its contractor may be a party under the circumstances described in § 405.1012.

**§ 405.1010 When CMS or its contractors may participate in an ALJ hearing.**

(a) An ALJ may request, but may not require, CMS and/or one or more of its contractors, to participate in any proceedings before the ALJ, including the oral hearing, if any. CMS and/or one or more of its contractors, including a QIC, may also elect to participate in the hearing process.

(b) If CMS or one or more of its contractors elects to participate, it advises the ALJ, the appellant, and all other parties identified in the notice of hearing of its intent to participate no later than 10 days after receiving the notice of hearing.

(c) Participation may include filing position papers or providing testimony to clarify factual or policy issues in a case, but it does not include calling witnesses or cross-examining the witnesses of a party to the hearing.

(d) When CMS or its contractor participates in an ALJ hearing, the agency or its contractor may not be called as a witness during the hearing.

(e) CMS or its contractor must submit any position papers within the time frame designated by the ALJ.

(f) The ALJ cannot draw any adverse inferences if CMS or a contractor decides not to participate in any proceedings before an ALJ, including the hearing.

**§ 405.1012 When CMS or its contractors may be a party to a hearing.**

(a) CMS and/or one or more of its contractors, including a QIC, may be a party to an ALJ hearing unless the request for hearing is filed by an unrepresented beneficiary.

(b) CMS and/or the contractor(s) advises the ALJ, appellant, and all other parties identified in the notice of hearing that it intends to participate as a party no later than 10 days after receiving the notice of hearing.

(c) When CMS or one or more of its contractors participate in a hearing as a party, it may file position papers, provide testimony to clarify factual or policy issues, call witnesses or cross-examine the witnesses of other parties. CMS or its contractor(s) will submit any position papers within the time frame specified by the ALJ. CMS or its contractor(s), when acting as parties, may also submit additional evidence to the ALJ within the time frame designated by the ALJ.

(d) The ALJ may not require CMS or a contractor to enter a case as a party or draw any adverse inferences if CMS or a contractor decides not to enter as a party.

**§ 405.1014 Request for an ALJ hearing.**

(a) *Content of the request.* The request for an ALJ hearing must be made in writing. The request must include all of the following–

(1) The name, address, and Medicare health insurance claim number of the beneficiary whose claim is being appealed.

(2) The name and address of the appellant, when the appellant is not the beneficiary.

(3) The name and address of the designated representatives if any.

(4) The document control number assigned to the appeal by the QIC, if any.

(5) The dates of service.

(6) The reasons the appellant disagrees with the QIC's reconsideration or other determination being appealed.

(7) A statement of any additional evidence to be submitted and the date it will be submitted.

(b) *When and where to file.* The request for an ALJ hearing after a QIC reconsideration must be filed–

(1) Within 60 days from the date the party receives notice of the QIC's reconsideration;

(2) With the entity specified in the QIC's reconsideration. The appellant must also send a copy of the request for hearing to the other parties. Failure to do so will toll the ALJ's 90-day adjudication deadline until all parties to the QIC reconsideration receive notice of the requested ALJ hearing. If the request for hearing is timely filed with an entity other than the entity specified in the QIC's reconsideration, the deadline specified in § 405.1016 for deciding the appeal begins on the date the entity specified in the QIC's reconsideration receives the request for hearing. If the request for hearing is filed with an entity, other than the entity specified in the QIC's reconsideration, the ALJ hearing office must notify the appellant of the date of receipt of the request and the commencement of the 90-day adjudication time frame.

(c) *Extension of time to request a hearing.* (1) If the request for hearing is not filed within 60 calendar days of receipt of the QIC's reconsideration, an appellant may request an extension for good cause (*See* §§ 405.942(b)(2) and 405.942(b)(3)).

(2) Any request for an extension of time must be in writing, give the reasons why the request for a hearing was not filed within the stated time period, and must be filed with the entity specified in the notice of reconsideration.

(3) If the ALJ finds there is good cause for missing the deadline, the time period for filing the hearing request will be extended. To determine whether good cause for late filing exists, the ALJ uses the standards set forth in § 405.942(b)(2) and § 405.942(b)(3).

(4) If a request for hearing is not timely filed, the adjudication period in § 405.1016 begins the date the ALJ grants the request to extend the filing deadline.

[70 FR 11472, Mar. 8, 2005, as amended at 70 FR 37703, June 30, 2005]

**§ 405.1016 Time frames for deciding an appeal before an ALJ.**

(a) When a request for an ALJ hearing is filed after a QIC has issued a reconsideration, the ALJ must issue a decision, dismissal order, or remand to the QIC, as appropriate, no later than the end of the 90-day period beginning on the date the request for hearing is received by the entity specified in the QIC's notice of reconsideration, unless the 90-day period has been extended as provided in this subpart.

(b) The adjudication period specified in paragraph (a) of this section begins on the date that a timely filed request for hearing is received by the entity specified in the QIC's reconsideration, or, if it is not timely filed, the date that the ALJ grants any extension to the filing deadline.

(c) When an appeal is escalated to the ALJ level because the QIC has not issued a reconsideration determination within the period specified in § 405.970, the ALJ must issue a decision, dismissal order, or remand to the QIC, as appropriate, no later than the end of the 180-day period beginning on the date that the request for escalation is received by the ALJ hearing office, unless the 180-day period is extended as provided in this subpart.

(d) When CMS or its contractor is a party to an ALJ hearing and a party requests discovery under § 405.1037 against another party to the hearing, the adjudication periods discussed in paragraphs (a) and (c) of this section are tolled.

[70 FR 11472, Mar. 8, 2005, as amended at 70 FR 37703, June 30, 2005]

**§ 405.1018 Submitting evidence before the ALJ hearing.**

(a) Except as provided in this section, parties must submit all written evidence they wish to have considered at the hearing with the request for hearing (or within 10 days of receiving the notice of hearing).

(b) If a party submits written evidence later than 10 days after receiving the notice of hearing, the period between the time the evidence was required to have been submitted and the time it is received is not counted toward the adjudication deadline specified in § 405.1016.

(c) Any evidence submitted by a provider, supplier, or beneficiary represented by a provider or supplier that is not submitted prior to the issuance of the QIC's reconsideration determination must be accompanied by a statement explaining why the evidence was not previously submitted to the QIC, or a prior decision-maker (see § 405.1028).

(d) The requirements of this section do not apply to oral testimony given at a hearing, or to evidence submitted by an unrepresented beneficiary.

[70 FR 11472, Mar. 8, 2005, as amended at 70 FR 37704, June 30, 2005]

**§ 405.1020 Time and place for a hearing before an ALJ.**

(a) *General.* The ALJ sets the time and place for the hearing, and may change the time and place, if necessary.

(b) *Determining how appearances are made.* The ALJ will direct that the appearance of an individual be conducted by video teleconferencing (VTC) if the ALJ finds that VTC technology is available to conduct the appearance. The ALJ may also offer to conduct a hearing by telephone if the request for hearing or administrative record suggests that a telephone hearing may be more convenient for one or more of the parties. The ALJ, with the concurrence of the Managing Field Office ALJ, may determine that an in-person hearing should be conducted if–

(1) VTC technology is not available; or

(2) Special or extraordinary circumstances exist.

(c) *Notice of hearing.* (1) The ALJ sends a notice of hearing to all parties that filed an appeal or participated in the reconsideration, any party who was found liable for the services at issue subsequent to the initial determination, the contractor that issued the initial determination, and the QIC that issued the reconsideration, advising them of the proposed time and place of the hearing.

(2) The notice of hearing will require all parties to the ALJ hearing (and any potential participant from CMS or its contractor who wishes to attend the hearing) to reply to the notice by:

(i) Acknowledging whether they plan to attend the hearing at the time and place proposed in the notice of hearing; or

(ii) Objecting to the proposed time and/or place of the hearing.

(d) *A party's right to waive a hearing.* A party may also waive the right to a hearing and request that the ALJ issue a decision based on the written evidence in the record. As provided in § 405.1000, the ALJ may require the parties to attend a hearing if it is necessary to decide the case. If the ALJ determines that it is necessary to obtain testimony from a non-party, he or she may still hold a hearing to obtain that testimony, even if all of the parties have waived the right to appear. In those cases, the ALJ will give the parties the opportunity to appear when the testimony is given but may hold the hearing even if none of the parties decide to appear.

(e) *A party's objection to time and place of hearing.* (1) If a party objects to the time and place of the hearing, the party must notify the ALJ at the earliest possible opportunity before the time set for the hearing.

(2) The party must state the reason for the objection and state the time and place he or she wants the hearing to be held.

(3) The request must be in writing.

(4) The ALJ may change the time or place of the hearing if the party has good cause. (Section 405.1052(a) (2) provides the procedures the ALJ follows when a party does not respond to a notice of hearing and fails to appear at the time and place of the hearing.)

(f) *Good cause for changing the time or place.* The ALJ can find good cause for changing the time or place of the scheduled hearing and reschedule the hearing if the information available to the ALJ supports the party's contention that—

(1) The party or his or her representative is unable to attend or to travel to the scheduled hearing because of a serious physical or mental condition, incapacitating injury, or death in the family; or

(2) Severe weather conditions make it impossible to travel to the hearing; or

(3) Good cause exists as set forth in paragraph (g) of this section.

(g) *Good cause in other circumstances.* (1) In determining whether good cause exists in circumstances other than those set forth in paragraph (f) of this section, the ALJ considers the party's reason for requesting the change, the facts supporting the request, and the impact of the proposed change on the efficient administration of the hearing process.

(2) Factors evaluated to determine the impact of the change include, but are not limited to, the effect on processing other scheduled hearings, potential delays in rescheduling the hearing, and whether any prior changes were granted the party.

(3) Examples of other circumstances a party might give for requesting a change in the time or place of the hearing include, but are not limited to, the following:

(i) The party has attempted to obtain a representative but needs additional time.

(ii) The party's representative was appointed within 10 days of the scheduled hearing and needs additional time to prepare for the hearing.

(iii) The party's representative has a prior commitment to be in court or at another administrative hearing on the date scheduled for the hearing.

(iv) A witness who will testify to facts material to a party's case is unavailable to attend the scheduled hearing and the evidence cannot be otherwise obtained.

(v) Transportation is not readily available for a party to travel to the hearing.

(vi) The party is unrepresented, and is unable to respond to the notice of hearing because of any physical, mental, educational, or linguistic limitations (including any lack of facility with the English language) that he or she has.

(h) *Effect of rescheduling hearing.* If a hearing is postponed at the request of the appellant for any of the above reasons, the time between the originally scheduled hearing date and the new hearing date is not counted toward the adjudication deadline specified in § 405.1016.

(i) *A party's request for an in-person hearing.* (1) If a party objects to a VTC hearing or to the ALJ's offer to conduct a hearing by telephone, the party must notify the ALJ at the earliest possible opportunity before the time set for the hearing and request an in-person hearing.

(2) The party must state the reason for the objection and state the time or place he or she wants the hearing to be held.

(3) The request must be in writing.

(4) When a party's request for an in-person hearing is granted, the party is deemed to have waived the 90-day time frame specified in § 405.1016.

(5) The ALJ may grant the request, with the concurrence of the Managing Field Office ALJ, upon a finding of good cause and will reschedule the hearing for a time and place when the party may appear in person before the ALJ.
[70 FR 11472, Mar. 8, 2005, as amended at 70 FR 37704, June 30, 2005]

**§ 405.1022 Notice of a hearing before an ALJ.**

(a) *Issuing the notice.* After the ALJ sets the time and place of the hearing, notice of the hearing will be mailed to the parties and other potential participants, as provided in § 405.1020(c) at their last known addresses, or given by personal service, unless the parties have indicated in writing that they do not wish to receive this notice. The notice is mailed or served at least 20 days before the hearing.

(b) *Notice information.* (1) The notice of hearing contains a statement of the specific issues to be decided and will inform the parties that they may designate a person to represent them during the proceedings.

(2) The notice must include an explanation of the procedures for requesting a change in the time or place of the hearing, a reminder that, if the appellant fails to appear at the scheduled hearing without good cause, the ALJ may dismiss the hearing request, and other information about the scheduling and conduct of the hearing.

(3) The appellant will also be told if his or her appearance or that of any other party or witness is scheduled by VTC, telephone, or in person. If the ALJ has scheduled the appellant or other party to appear at the hearing by VTC, the notice of hearing will advise that the scheduled place for the hearing is a VTC site and explain what it means to appear at the hearing by VTC.

(4) The notice advises the appellant or other parties that if they object to appearing by VTC or telephone, and wish instead to have their hearing at a time and place where they may appear in person before the ALJ, they must follow the procedures set forth at § 405.1020(i) for notifying the ALJ of their objections and for requesting an in-person hearing.

(c) *Acknowledging the notice of hearing.* (1) If the appellant, any other party to the reconsideration, or their representative does not acknowledge receipt of the notice of hearing, the ALJ hearing office attempts to contact the party for an explanation.

(2) If the party states that he or she did not receive the notice of hearing, an amended notice is sent to him or her by certified mail or e-mail, if available. (See § 405.1052 for the procedures the ALJ follows in deciding if the time or place of a scheduled hearing will be changed if a party does not respond to the notice of hearing.)

**§ 405.1024 Objections to the issues.**

(a) If a party objects to the issues described in the notice of hearing, he or she must notify the ALJ in writing at the earliest possible opportunity before the time set for the hearing, and no later than 5 days before the hearing.

(b) The party must state the reasons for his or her objections and send a copy of the objections to all other parties to the appeal.

(c) The ALJ makes a decision on the objections either in writing or at the hearing.

**§ 405.1026 Disqualification of the ALJ.**

(a) An ALJ cannot conduct a hearing if he or she is prejudiced or partial to any party or has any interest in the matter pending for decision.

(b) If a party objects to the ALJ who will conduct the hearing, the party must notify the ALJ within 10 calendar days of the date of the notice of hearing. The ALJ considers the party's objections and decides whether to proceed with the hearing or withdraw.

(c) If the ALJ withdraws, another ALJ will be appointed to conduct the hearing. If the ALJ does not withdraw, the party may, after the ALJ has issued an action in the case, present his or her objections to the MAC in accordance with § 405.1100 *et seq.* The MAC will then consider whether the hearing decision should be revised or a new hearing held before another ALJ. If the case is escalated to the MAC after a hearing is held but before the ALJ issues a decision, the MAC considers the reasons the party objected to the ALJ during its review of the case and, if the MAC deems it necessary, may remand the case to another ALJ for a hearing and decision.

**§ 405.1028 Prehearing case review of evidence submitted to the ALJ.**

(a) *Examination of any new evidence.* After a hearing is requested but before it is held, the ALJ will examine any new evidence submitted with the request for hearing (or within 10 days of receiving the notice of hearing) as specified in § 405.1018, by a provider, supplier, or beneficiary represented by a provider or supplier to determine whether the provider, supplier, or beneficiary represented by a provider or supplier had good cause for submitting the evidence for the first time at the ALJ level.

(b) *Determining if good cause exists.* An ALJ finds good cause, for example, when the new evidence is material to an issue addressed in the QIC's reconsideration and that issue was not identified as a material issue prior to the QIC's reconsideration.

(c) *If good cause does not exist.* If the ALJ determines that there was not good cause for submitting the evidence for the first time at the ALJ level, the ALJ must exclude the evidence from the proceeding and may not consider it in reaching a decision.

(d) *Notification to all parties.* As soon as possible, but no later than the start of the hearing, the ALJ must notify all parties that the evidence is excluded from the hearing.

**§ 405.1030 ALJ hearing procedures.**

(a) *General rule.* A hearing is open to the parties and to other persons the ALJ considers necessary and proper.

(b) *At the hearing.* At the hearing, the ALJ fully examines the issues, questions the parties and other witnesses, and may accept documents that are material to the issues consistent with § 405.1018 and § 405.1028.

(c) *Missing evidence.* The ALJ may also stop the hearing temporarily and continue it at a later date if he or she believes that there is material evidence missing at the hearing. If the missing evidence is in the possession of the appellant, and the appellant is a provider, supplier, or a beneficiary represented by a provider or supplier, the ALJ must determine if the appellant had good cause for not producing the evidence earlier.

(d) *Good cause exists.* If good cause exists, the ALJ considers the evidence in deciding the case and the adjudication period specified in § 405.1016 is tolled from the date of the hearing to the date the evidence is submitted.

(e) *Good cause does not exist.* If the ALJ determines that there was not good cause for not submitting the evidence sooner, the evidence is excluded.

(f) *Reopen the hearing.* The ALJ may also reopen the hearing at any time before he or she mails a notice of the decision in order to receive new and material evidence pursuant to § 405.986. The ALJ may decide when the evidence is presented and when the issues are discussed.

**§ 405.1032 Issues before an ALJ.**

(a) *General rule.* The issues before the ALJ include all the issues brought out in the initial determination, redetermination, or reconsideration that were not decided entirely in a party's favor. (For purposes of this provision, the term "party"does not include a representative of CMS or one of its contractors that may be participating in the hearing.) However, if evidence presented before the hearing causes the ALJ to question a favorable portion of the determination, he or she notifies the parties before the hearing and may consider it an issue at the hearing.

(b) *New issues*—(1) *General.* The ALJ may consider a new issue at the hearing if he or she notifies all of the parties about the new issue any time before the start of the hearing. The new issue may include issues resulting from the participation of CMS at the ALJ level of adjudication and from any evidence and position papers submitted by CMS for the first time to the ALJ. The ALJ or any party may raise a new issue; however, the ALJ may only consider a new issue if its resolution—

(i) Could have a material impact on the claim or claims that are the subject of the request for hearing; and

(ii) Is permissible under the rules governing reopening of determinations and decisions (see § 405.980).

**(2) [Reserved]**

(c) *Adding claims to a pending appeal.* An ALJ cannot add any claim, including one that is related to an issue that is appropriately before an ALJ, to a pending appeal unless it has been adjudicated at the lower appeals levels and all parties are notified of the new issue(s) before the start of the hearing.

**§ 405.1034 When an ALJ may remand a case to the QIC.**

(a) *General.* If an ALJ believes that the written record is missing information that is essential to resolving the issues on appeal and that information can be provided only by CMS or its contractors, then the ALJ may either:

(1) Remand the case to the QIC that issued the reconsideration or

(2) Retain jurisdiction of the case and request that the contractor forward the missing information to the appropriate hearing office.

(b) *ALJ remands a case to a QIC.* Consistent with § 405.1004 (b), the ALJ will remand a case to the appropriate QIC if the ALJ determines that a QIC's dismissal of a request for reconsideration was in error.

(c) *Relationship to local and national coverage determination appeals process.* (1) The ALJ remands an appeal to the QIC that made the reconsideration if the appellant is entitled to relief pursuant to 42 CFR 426.460(b)(1), 426.488(b), or 426.560(b)(1).

(2) Unless the appellant is entitled to relief pursuant to 42 CFR 426.460(b)(1), 426.488(b), or 426.560(b)(1), the ALJ applies the LCD or NCD in place on the date the item or service was provided.

**§ 405.1036 Description of an ALJ hearing process.**

(a) *The right to appear and present evidence.* (1) Any party to a hearing has the right to appear before the ALJ to present evidence and to state his or her position. A party may appear by video-teleconferencing (VTC), telephone, or in person as determined under § 405.1020.

(2) A party may also make his or her appearance by means of a representative, who may make the appearance by VTC, telephone, or in person, as determined under § 405.1020.

(3) Witness testimony may be given and CMS participation may also be accomplished by VTC, telephone, or in person, as determined under § 405.1020.

(b) *Waiver of the right to appear.* (1) A party may send the ALJ a written statement indicating that he or she does not wish to appear at the hearing.

(2) The appellant may subsequently withdraw his or her waiver at any time before the notice of the hearing decision is issued; however, by withdrawing the waiver the appellant agrees to an extension of the adjudication period as specified in § 405.1016 that may be necessary to schedule and hold the hearing.

(3) Other parties may withdraw their waiver up to the date of the scheduled hearing, if any. Even if all of the parties waive their right to appear at a hearing, the ALJ may require them to attend an oral hearing if he or she believes that a personal appearance and testimony by the appellant or any other party is necessary to decide the case.

(c) *Presenting written statements and oral arguments.* A party or a person designated to act as a party's representative may appear before the ALJ to state the party's case, to present a written summary of the case, or to enter written statements about the facts and law material to the case in the record. A copy of any written statements must be provided to the other parties to a hearing, if any, at the same time they are submitted to the ALJ.

(d) *Waiver of adjudication period.* At any time during the hearing process, the appellant may waive the adjudication deadline specified in § 405.1016 for issuing a hearing decision. The waiver may be for a specific period of time agreed upon by the ALJ and the appellant.

(e) *What evidence is admissible at a hearing.* The ALJ may receive evidence at the hearing even though the evidence is not admissible in court under the rules of evidence used by the court.

(f) *Subpoenas.* (1) When it is reasonably necessary for the full presentation of a case, an ALJ may, on his or her own initiative or at the request of a party, issue subpoenas for the appearance and testimony of witnesses and for a party to make books, records, correspondence, papers, or other documents that are material to an issue at the hearing available for inspection and copying.

(2) A party's written request for a subpoena must—

(i) Give the names of the witnesses or documents to be produced;

(ii) Describe the address or location of the witnesses or documents with sufficient detail to find them;

(iii) State the important facts that the witness or document is expected to prove; and

(iv) Indicate why these facts cannot be proven without issuing a subpoena.

(3) Parties to a hearing who wish to subpoena documents or witnesses must file a written request for the issuance of a subpoena with the requirements

set out in paragraph (f)(2) of this section with the ALJ within 10 calendar days of receipt of the notice of hearing.

(4) Where a party has requested a subpoena, a subpoena will be issued only where a party—

(i) Has sought discovery;

(ii) Has filed a motion to compel;

(iii) Has had that motion granted by the ALJ; and

(iv) Nevertheless, has not received the requested discovery.

(5) Reviewability of subpoena rulings—

(i) *General rule.* An ALJ ruling on a subpoena request is not subject to immediate review by the MAC. The ruling may be reviewed solely during the course of the MAC's review specified in § 405.1102, § 405.1104, or § 405.1110, as applicable. *Exception.* To the extent a subpoena compels disclosure of a matter for which an objection based on privilege, or other protection from disclosure such as case preparation, confidentiality, or undue burden, was made before an ALJ, the MAC may review immediately the subpoena or that portion of the subpoena as applicable.

(ii) Where CMS objects to a discovery ruling, the MAC must take review and the discovery ruling at issue is automatically stayed pending the MAC's order.

(iii) Upon notice to the ALJ that a party or non-party, as applicable, intends to seek MAC review of the subpoena, the ALJ must stay all proceedings affected by the subpoena.

(iv) The ALJ determines the length of the stay under the circumstances of a given case, but in no event is the stay less than 15 days beginning after the day on which the ALJ received notice of the party or non-party's intent to seek MAC review.

(v) If the MAC grants a request for review of the subpoena, the subpoena or portion of the subpoena, as applicable, is stayed until the MAC issues a written decision that affirms, reverses, or modifies the ALJ's action on the subpoena.

(vi) If the MAC does not grant review or take own motion review within the time allotted for the stay, the stay is lifted and the ALJ's action stands.

(6) Enforcement. (i) If the ALJ determines, whether on his or her own motion or at the request of a party, that a party or non-party subject to a subpoena issued under this section has refused to comply with the subpoena, the ALJ may request the Secretary to seek enforcement of the subpoena in accordance with section 205(e) of the Act, 42 U.S.C. 405(e).

(ii) Any enforcement request by an ALJ must consist of a written notice to the Secretary describing in detail the ALJ's findings of noncompliance and his or her specific request for enforcement, and providing a copy of the subpoena and evidence of its receipt by certified mail by the party or nonparty subject to the subpoena.

(iii) The ALJ must promptly mail a copy of the notice and related documents to the party subject to the subpoena, and to any other party and affected non-party to the appeal.

(g) *Witnesses at a hearing.* Witnesses may appear at a hearing. They testify under oath or affirmation, unless the ALJ finds an important reason to excuse them from taking an oath or affirmation. The ALJ may ask the witnesses any questions relevant to the issues and allows the parties or their designated representatives to do so.

**§ 405.1037 Discovery.**

(a) *General rules.* (1) Discovery is permissible only when CMS or its contractor elects to participate in an ALJ hearing as a party.

(2) The ALJ may permit discovery of a matter that is relevant to the specific subject matter of the ALJ hearing, provided the matter is not privileged or otherwise protected from disclosure and the ALJ determines that the discovery request is not unreasonable, unduly burdensome or expensive, or otherwise inappropriate.

(3) Any discovery initiated by a party must comply with all requirements and limitations of this section, along with any further requirements or limitations ordered by the ALJ.

(b) *Limitations on discovery.* Any discovery before the ALJ is limited.

(1) A party may request of another party the reasonable production of documents for inspection and copying.

(2) A party may not take the deposition, upon oral or written examination, of another party unless the proposed deponent agrees to the deposition or the ALJ finds that the proposed deposition is necessary and appropriate in order to secure the deponent's testimony for an ALJ hearing.

(3) A party may not request admissions or send interrogatories or take any other form of discovery not permitted under this section.

(c) *Time limits.* (1) A party's discovery request is timely if the date of receipt of a request by another party is no later than the date specified by the ALJ.

(2) A party may not conduct discovery any later than the date specified by the ALJ.

(3) Before ruling on a request to extend the time for requesting discovery or for conducting discovery, the ALJ must give the other parties to the appeal a reasonable period to respond to the extension request.

(4) The ALJ may extend the time in which to request discovery or conduct discovery only if the requesting party establishes that it was not dilatory or otherwise at fault in not meeting the original discovery deadline.

(5) If the ALJ grants the extension request, it must impose a new discovery deadline and, if necessary, reschedule the hearing date so that all discoveries end no later than 45 days before the hearing.

(d) *Motions to compel or for protective order.* (1) Each party is required to make a good faith effort to resolve or narrow any discovery dispute.

(2) A party may submit to the ALJ a motion to compel discovery that is permitted under this section or any ALJ order, and a party may submit a motion for a protective order regarding any discovery request to the ALJ.

(3) Any motion to compel or for protective order must include a self-sworn declaration describing the movant's efforts to resolve or narrow the discovery dispute. The declaration must also be included with any response to a motion to compel or for protective order.

(4) The ALJ must decide any motion in accordance with this section and any prior discovery ruling in the appeal.

(5) The ALJ must issue and mail to each party a discovery ruling that grants or denies the motion to compel or for protective order in whole or in part; if applicable, the discovery ruling must specifically identify any part of the disputed discovery request upheld and any part rejected, and impose any limits on discovery the ALJ finds necessary and appropriate.

(e) *Reviewability of discovery and disclosure rulings—*

(1) *General rule.* An ALJ discovery ruling, or an ALJ disclosure ruling such as one issued at a hearing is not subject to immediate review by the MAC. The ruling may be reviewed solely during the course of the MAC's review specified in § 405.1100, § 405.1102, § 405.1104, or § 405.1110, as applicable.

(2) *Exception.* To the extent a ruling authorizes discovery or disclosure of a matter for which an objection based on privilege, or other protection from disclosure such as case preparation, confidentiality, or undue burden, was made before the ALJ, the MAC may review that portion of the discovery or disclosure ruling immediately.

(i) Where CMS objects to a discovery ruling, the MAC must take review and the discovery ruling at issue is automatically stayed pending the MAC's order.

(ii) Upon notice to the ALJ that a party intends to seek MAC review of the ruling, the ALJ must stay all proceedings affected by the ruling.

(iii) The ALJ determines the length of the stay under the circumstances of a given case, but in no event must the length of the stay be less than 15 days beginning after the day on which the ALJ received notice of the party or non-party's intent to seek MAC review.

(iv) Where CMS requests the MAC to take review of a discovery ruling or where the MAC grants a request, made by a party other than CMS, to review a discovery ruling, the ruling is stayed until the time the MAC issues a written decision that affirms, reverses, modifies, or remands the ALJ's ruling.

(v) With respect to a request from a party, other than CMS, for review of a discovery ruling, if the MAC does not grant review or take own motion review within the time allotted for the stay, the stay is lifted and the ruling stands.

(f) *Adjudication time frames.* If a party requests discovery from another party to the ALJ hearing, the ALJ adjudication time frame specified in § 405.1016 is tolled until the discovery dispute is resolved.

[70 FR 11472, Mar. 8, 2005, as amended at 70 FR 37704, June 30, 2005]

**§ 405.1038 Deciding a case without a hearing before an ALJ.**

(a) *Decision wholly favorable.* If the evidence in the hearing record supports a finding in favor of appellant(s) on every issue, the ALJ may issue a hearing decision without giving the parties prior notice and without holding a hearing. The notice of the decision informs the parties that they have the right to a hearing and a right to examine the evidence on which the decision is based.

(b) *Parties do not wish to appear.* (1) The ALJ may decide a case on the record and not conduct a hearing if—

(i) All the parties indicate in writing that they do not wish to appear before the ALJ at a hearing, including a hearing conducted by telephone or videoconferencing, if available; or

(ii) The appellant lives outside the United States and does not inform the ALJ that he or she wants to appear, and there are no other parties who wish to appear.

(2) When a hearing is not held, the decision of the ALJ must refer to the evidence in the record on which the decision was based.

**§ 405.1040 Prehearing and posthearing conferences.**

(a) The ALJ may decide on his or her own, or at the request of any party to the hearing, to hold a prehearing or posthearing conference to facilitate the hearing or the hearing decision.

(b) The ALJ informs the parties of the time, place, and purpose of the conference at least 7 calendar days before the conference date, unless a party indicates in writing that it does not wish to receive a written notice of the conference.

(c) At the conference, the ALJ may consider matters in addition to those stated in the notice of hearing, if the parties consent in writing. A record of the conference is made.

(d) The ALJ issues an order stating all agreements and actions resulting from the conference. If the parties do not object, the agreements and actions become part of the hearing record and are binding on all parties.

**§ 405.1042 The administrative record.**

(a) *Creating the record.* (1) The ALJ makes a complete record of the evidence, including the hearing proceedings, if any.

(2) The record will include marked as exhibits, the documents used in making the decision under review, including, but not limited to, claims, medical records, written statements, certificates, reports, affidavits, and any other evidence the ALJ admits. In the record, the ALJ must also discuss any evidence excluded under § 405.1028 and include a justification for excluding the evidence.

(3) A party may review the record at the hearing, or, if a hearing is not held, at any time before the ALJ's notice of decision is issued.

(4) If a request for review is filed or the case is escalated to the MAC, the complete record, including any recording of the hearing, is forwarded to the MAC.

(5) A typed transcription of the hearing is prepared if a party seeks judicial review of the case in a Federal district court within the stated time period and all other jurisdictional criteria are met, unless, upon the Secretary's motion prior to the filing of an answer, the court remands the case.

(b) *Requesting and receiving copies of the record.* (1) A party may request and receive a copy of all or part of the record, including the exhibits list, documentary evidence, and a copy of the tape of the oral proceedings. The party may be asked to pay the costs of providing these items.

(2) If a party requests all or part of the record from the ALJ and an opportunity to comment on the record, the time beginning with the ALJ's receipt of the request through the expiration of the time granted for the party's response does not count toward the 90-day adjudication deadline.

[70 FR 11472, Mar. 8, 2005, as amended at 70 FR 37704, June 30, 2005]

**§ 405.1044 Consolidated hearing before an ALJ.**

(a) A consolidated hearing may be held if one or more of the issues to be considered at the hearing are the same issues that are involved in another request for hearing or hearings pending before the same ALJ.

(b) It is within the discretion of the ALJ to grant or deny an appellant's request for consolidation. In considering an appellant's request, the ALJ may consider factors such as whether the claims at issue may be more efficiently decided if the requests for hearing are combined. In considering the appellant's request for consolidation, the ALJ must take into account the adjudication deadlines for each case and may require an appellant to waive the adjudication deadline associated with one or more cases if consolidation otherwise prevents the ALJ from deciding all of the appeals at issue within their respective deadlines.

(c) The ALJ may also propose on his or her own motion to consolidate two or more cases in one hearing for administrative efficiency, but may not require an appellant to waive the adjudication deadline for any of the consolidated cases.

(d) Before consolidating a hearing, the ALJ must notify CMS of his or her intention to do so, and CMS may then elect to participate in the consolidated hearing, as a party, by sending written notice to the ALJ within 10 days after receipt of the ALJ's notice of the consolidation.

(e) If the ALJ decides to hold a consolidated hearing, he or she may make either a consolidated decision and record or a separate decision and record on each claim. The ALJ ensures that any evidence that is common to all claims and material to the common issue to be decided is included in the consolidated record or each individual record, as applicable.

**§ 405.1046 Notice of an ALJ decision.**

(a) *General rule.* Unless the ALJ dismisses the hearing, the ALJ will issue a written decision that gives the findings of fact, conclusions of law, and the reasons for the decision. The decision must be based on evidence offered at the hearing or otherwise admitted into the record. The ALJ mails a copy of the decision to all the parties at their last known address, to the QIC that issued the reconsideration determination, and to the contractor that issued the initial determination. For overpayment cases involving multiple beneficiaries, where there is no beneficiary liability, the ALJ may choose to send written notice only to the appellant. In the event a payment will be made to a provider or supplier in conjunction with this ALJ decision, the contractor must also issue a revised electronic or paper remittance advice to that provider or supplier.

(b) *Content of the notice.* The decision must be written in a manner calculated to be understood by a beneficiary and must include—

(1) The specific reasons for the determination, including, to the extent appropriate, a summary of any clinical or scientific evidence used in making the determination;

(2) The procedures for obtaining additional information concerning the decision; and

(3) Notification of the right to appeal the decision to the MAC, including instructions on how to initiate an appeal under this section.

(c) *Limitation on decision.* When the amount of payment for an item or service is an issue before the ALJ, the ALJ may make a finding as to the amount of payment due. If the ALJ makes a finding concerning payment when the amount of payment was not an issue before the ALJ, the contractor may independently determine the payment amount. In either of the aforementioned situations, an ALJ's decision is not final for purposes of determining the amount of payment due. The amount of payment determined by the contractor in effectuating the ALJ's decision is a new initial determination under § 405.924.

(d) *Timing of decision.* The ALJ issues a decision by the end of the 90-day period beginning on the date when the request for hearing is received by the entity specified in the QIC's reconsideration, unless the 90-day period is extended as provided in § 405.1016.

(e) *Recommended decision.* An ALJ issues a recommended decision if he or she is directed to do so in the MAC's remand order. An ALJ may not issue a recommended decision on his or her own motion. The ALJ mails a copy of the recommended decision to all the parties at their last known address.

[70 FR 11472, Mar. 8, 2005, as amended at 70 FR 37704, June 30, 2005]

**§ 405.1048 The effect of an ALJ's decision.**

The decision of the ALJ is binding on all parties to the hearing unless—

(a) A party to the hearing requests a review of the decision by the MAC within the stated time period or the MAC reviews the decision issued by an ALJ under the procedures set forth in § 405.1110, and the MAC either issues a final action or the appeal is escalated to Federal district court under the provisions at § 405.1132 and the Federal district court issues a decision.

(b) The decision is reopened and revised by an ALJ or the MAC under the procedures explained in § 405.980;

(c) The expedited access to judicial review process at § 405.990 is used;

(d) The ALJ's decision is a recommended decision directed to the MAC and the MAC issues a decision; or

(e) In a case remanded by a Federal district court, the MAC assumes jurisdiction under the procedures in § 405.1138 and the MAC issues a decision.

**§ 405.1050 Removal of a hearing request from an ALJ to the MAC.**
If a request for hearing is pending before an ALJ, the MAC may assume responsibility for holding a hearing by requesting that the ALJ send the hearing request to it. If the MAC holds a hearing, it conducts the hearing according to the rules for hearings before an ALJ. Notice is mailed to all parties at their last known address informing them that the MAC has assumed responsibility for the case.

**§ 405.1052 Dismissal of a request for a hearing before an ALJ.**
Dismissal of a request for a hearing is in accordance with the following:

(a) An ALJ dismisses a request for a hearing under any of the following conditions:

(1) At any time before notice of the hearing decision is mailed, if only one party requested the hearing and that party asks to withdraw the request. This request may be submitted in writing to the ALJ or made orally at the hearing. The request for withdrawal must include a clear statement that the appellant is withdrawing the request for hearing and does not intend to further proceed with the appeal. If an attorney, or other legal professional on behalf of a beneficiary or other appellant files the request for withdrawal, the ALJ may presume that the representative has advised the appellant of the consequences of the withdrawal and dismissal.

(2) Neither the party that requested the hearing nor the party's representative appears at the time and place set for the hearing, if—

(i) The party was notified before the time set for the hearing that the request for hearing might be dismissed without further notice for failure to appear;

(ii) The party did not appear at the time and place of hearing and does not contact the ALJ hearing office within 10 days and provide good cause for not appearing; or

(iii) The ALJ sends a notice to the party asking why the party did not appear; and the party does not respond to the ALJ's notice within 10 days or does not provide good cause for the failure to appear.

(iv) In determining whether good cause exists under this paragraph (a)(2), the ALJ considers any physical, mental, educational, or linguistic limitations (including any lack of facility with the English language), that the party may have.

(3) The person or entity requesting a hearing has no right to it under § 405.1002.

(4) The party did not request a hearing within the stated time period and the ALJ has not found good cause for extending the deadline, as provided in § 405.1014(c).

(5) The beneficiary whose claim is being appealed died while the request for hearing is pending and all of the following criteria apply:

(i) The request for hearing was filed by the beneficiary or the beneficiary's representative, and the beneficiary's surviving spouse or estate has no remaining financial interest in the case. In deciding this issue, the ALJ considers if the surviving spouse or estate remains liable for the services that were denied or a Medicare contractor held the beneficiary liable for subsequent similar services under the limitation of liability provisions based on the denial of the services at issue.

(ii) No other individuals or entities that have a financial interest in the case wish to pursue an appeal under § 405.1002.

(iii) No other individual or entity filed a valid and timely request for an ALJ hearing in accordance to § 405.1014.

(6) The ALJ dismisses a hearing request entirely or refuses to consider any one or more of the issues because a QIC, an ALJ or the MAC has made a previous determination or decision under this subpart about the appellant's rights on the same facts and on the same issue(s) or claim(s), and this previous determination or decision has become final by either administrative or judicial action.

(7) The appellant abandons the request for hearing. An ALJ may conclude that an appellant has abandoned a request for hearing when the ALJ hearing office attempts to schedule a hearing and is unable to contact the appellant after making reasonable efforts to do so.

(b) *Notice of dismissal.* The ALJ mails a written notice of the dismissal of the hearing request to all parties at their last known address. The notice states that there is a right to request that the MAC vacate the dismissal action.
[70 FR 11472, Mar. 8, 2005, as amended at 70 FR 37704, June 30, 2005]

**§ 405.1054 Effect of dismissal of a request for a hearing before an ALJ.**
The dismissal of a request for a hearing is binding, unless it is vacated by the MAC under § 405.1108(b).

**Applicability of Medicare Coverage Policies**

**§ 405.1060 Applicability of national coverage determinations (NCDs).**

(a) *General rule.* (1) An NCD is a determination by the Secretary of whether a particular item or service is covered nationally under Medicare.

(2) An NCD does not include a determination of what code, if any, is assigned to a particular item or service covered under Medicare or a determination of the amount of payment made for a particular item or service.

(3) NCDs are made under section 1862(a)(1) of the Act as well as under other applicable provisions of the Act.

(4) An NCD is binding on fiscal intermediaries, carriers, QIOs, QICs, ALJs, and the MAC.

(b) *Review by an ALJ.* (1) An ALJ may not disregard, set aside, or otherwise review an NCD.

(2) An ALJ may review the facts of a particular case to determine whether an NCD applies to a specific claim for benefits and, if so, whether the NCD was applied correctly to the claim.

(c) *Review by the MAC.* (1) The MAC may not disregard, set aside, or otherwise review an NCD for purposes of a section 1869 claim appeal, except that the DAB may review NCDs as provided under part 426 of this title.

(2) The MAC may review the facts of a particular case to determine whether an NCD applies to a specific claim for benefits and, if so, whether the NCD was applied correctly to the claim.
[70 FR 11472, Mar. 8, 2005, as amended at 70 FR 37704, June 30, 2005]

**§ 405.1062 Applicability of local coverage determinations and other policies not binding on the ALJ and MAC.**

(a) ALJs and the MAC are not bound by LCDs, LMRPs, or CMS program guidance, such as program memoranda and manual instructions, but will give substantial deference to these policies if they are applicable to a particular case.

(b) If an ALJ or MAC declines to follow a policy in a particular case, the ALJ or MAC decision must explain the reasons why the policy was not followed. An ALJ or MAC decision to disregard such policy applies only to the specific claim being considered and does not have precedential effect.

(c) An ALJ or MAC may not set aside or review the validity of an LMRP or LCD for purposes of a claim appeal. An ALJ or the DAB may review or set aside an LCD (or any part of an LMRP that constitutes an LCD) in accordance with part 426 of this title.

**§ 405.1063 Applicability of CMS Rulings.**

CMS Rulings are published under the authority of the Administrator, CMS. Consistent with § 401.108 of this chapter, rulings are binding on all CMS components, on all HHS components that adjudicate matters under the jurisdiction of CMS, and on the Social Security Administration to the extent that components of the Social Security Administration adjudicate matters under the jurisdiction of CMS.

**§ 405.1064 ALJ decisions involving statistical samples.**

When an appeal from the QIC involves an overpayment issue and the QIC used a statistical sample in reaching its reconsideration, the ALJ must base his or her decision on a review of the entire statistical sample used by the QIC.

**Medicare Appeals Council Review**

**§ 405.1100 Medicare Appeals Council review: General.**

(a) The appellant or any other party to the hearing may request that the MAC review an ALJ's decision or dismissal.

(b) Under circumstances set forth in § 405.1104 and 405.1108, the appellant may request that a case be escalated to the MAC for a decision even if the ALJ has not issued a decision or dismissal in his or her case.

(c) When the MAC reviews an ALJ's decision, it undertakes a de novo review. The MAC issues a final action or remands a case to the ALJ within 90 days of receipt of the appellant's request for review, unless the 90-day period is extended as provided in this subpart.

(d) When deciding an appeal that was escalated from the ALJ level to the MAC, the MAC will issue a final action or remand the case to the ALJ within 180 days of receipt of the appellant's request for escalation, unless the 180-day period is extended as provided in this subpart.

**§ 405.1102 Request for MAC review when ALJ issues decision or dismissal.**

(a)(1) A party to the ALJ hearing may request a MAC review if the party files a written request for a MAC review within 60 days after receipt of the ALJ's decision or dismissal.

(2) For purposes of this section, the date of receipt of the ALJ's decision or dismissal is presumed to be 5 days after the date of the notice of the decision or dismissal, unless there is evidence to the contrary.

(3) The request is considered as filed on the date it is received by the entity specified in the notice of the ALJ's action.

(b) A party requesting a review may ask that the time for filing a request for MAC review be extended if–

(1) The request for an extension of time is in writing;

(2) It is filed with the MAC; and

(3) It explains why the request for review was not filed within the stated time period. If the MAC finds that there is good cause for missing the deadline, the time period will be extended. To determine whether good cause exists, the MAC uses the standards outlined at §§ 405.942(b)(2) and 405.942(b)(3).

(c) A party does not have the right to seek MAC review of an ALJ's remand to a QIC or an ALJ's affirmation of a QIC's dismissal of a request for reconsideration.

(d) For purposes of requesting MAC review (§ 405.1100 through § 405.1140), unless specifically excepted the term, "party," includes CMS where CMS has entered into a case as a party according to § 405.1012. The term, "appellant," does not include CMS, where CMS has entered into a case as a party according to § 405.1012.
[70 FR 11472, Mar. 8, 2005, as amended at 70 FR 37704, June 30, 2005]

**§ 405.1104 Request for MAC review when an ALJ does not issue a decision timely.**

(a) *Requesting escalation.* An appellant who files a timely request for hearing before an ALJ and whose appeal continues to be pending before the ALJ at the end of the applicable ALJ adjudication period under § 405.1016 may request MAC review if–

(1) The appellant files a written request with the ALJ to escalate the appeal to the MAC after the adjudication period has expired; and

(2) The ALJ does not issue a final action or remand the case to the QIC within the later of 5 days of receiving the request for escalation or 5 days from the end of the applicable adjudication period set forth in § 405.1016.

(b) *Escalation.* (1) If the ALJ is not able to issue a final action or remand within the time period set forth in paragraph (a)(2) of this section, he or she sends notice to the appellant.

(2) The notice acknowledges receipt of the request for escalation, and confirms that the ALJ is not able to issue a final action or remand order within the statutory time frame.

(3) If the ALJ does not act on a request for escalation within the time period set forth in paragraph (a)(2) of this section or does not send the required notice to the appellant, the QIC decision becomes a final administrative decision for purposes of MAC review.

(c) *No escalation.* If the ALJ's adjudication period set forth in § 405.1016 expires, the case remains with the ALJ until a final action is issued or the appellant requests escalation to the MAC.

[70 FR 11472, Mar. 8, 2005, as amended at 70 FR 37704, June 30, 2005]

**§ 405.1106 Where a request for review or escalation may be filed.**

(a) When a request for a MAC review is filed after an ALJ has issued a decision or dismissal, the request for review must be filed with the entity specified in the notice of the ALJ's action. The appellant must also send a copy of the request for review to the other parties to the ALJ decision or dismissal. Failure to copy the other parties tolls the MAC's adjudication deadline set forth in § 405.1100 until all parties to the hearing receive notice of the request for MAC review. If the request for review is timely filed with an entity other than the entity specified in the notice of the ALJ's action, the MAC's adjudication period to conduct a review begins on the date the request for review is received by the entity specified in the notice of the ALJ's action. Upon receipt of a request for review from an entity other than the entity specified in the notice of the ALJ's action, the MAC sends written notice to the appellant of the date of receipt of the request and commencement of the adjudication time frame.

(b) If an appellant files a request to escalate an appeal to the MAC level because the ALJ has not completed his or her action on the request for hearing within the adjudication deadline under § 405.1016, the request for escalation must be filed with both the ALJ and the MAC. The appellant must also send a copy of the request for escalation to the other parties. Failure to copy the other parties tolls the MAC's adjudication deadline set forth in § 405.1100 until all parties to the hearing receive notice of the request for MAC review. In a case that has been escalated from the ALJ, the MAC's 180-day period to issue a final action or remand the case to the ALJ begins on the date the request for escalation is received by the MAC.

[70 FR 11472, Mar. 8, 2005, as amended at 70 FR 37704, June 30, 2005]

**§ 405.1108 MAC actions when request for review or escalation is filed.**

(a) Except as specified in paragraphs (c) and (d) of this section, when a party requests that the MAC review an ALJ's decision, the MAC will review the ALJ's decision *de novo.* The party requesting review does not have a right to a hearing before the MAC. The MAC will consider all of the evidence in the administrative record. Upon completion of its review, the MAC may adopt, modify, or reverse the ALJ's decision or remand the case to an ALJ for further proceedings.

(b) When a party requests that the MAC review an ALJ's dismissal, the MAC may deny review or vacate the dismissal and remand the case to the ALJ for further proceedings.

(c) The MAC will dismiss a request for review when the party requesting review does not have a right to a review by the MAC, or will dismiss the request for a hearing for any reason that the ALJ could have dismissed the request for hearing.

(d) When an appellant requests escalation of a case from the ALJ level to the MAC, the MAC may take any of the following actions:

(1) Issue a decision based on the record constructed at the QIC and any additional evidence, including oral testimony, entered in the record by the ALJ before the case was escalated.

(2) Conduct any additional proceedings, including a hearing, that the MAC determines are necessary to issue a decision.

(3) Remand the case to an ALJ for further proceedings, including a hearing.

(4) Dismiss the request for MAC review because the appellant does not have the right to escalate the appeal.

(5) Dismiss the request for a hearing for any reason that the ALJ could have dismissed the request.

**§ 405.1110 MAC reviews on its own motion.**

(a) *General rule.* The MAC may decide on its own motion to review a decision or dismissal issued by an ALJ. CMS or any of its contractors may refer a case to the MAC for it to consider reviewing under this authority any time within 60 days after the date of an ALJ's decision or dismissal.

(b) *Referral of cases.* (1) CMS or any of its contractors may refer a case to the MAC if, in their view, the decision or dismissal contains an error of law material to the outcome of the claim or presents a broad policy or procedural issue that may affect the public interest. CMS may also request that the MAC take own motion review of a case if–

(i) CMS or its contractor participated in the appeal at the ALJ level; and

(ii) In CMS' view, the ALJ's decision or dismissal is not supported by the preponderance of evidence in the record or the ALJ abused his or her discretion.

(2) CMS's referral to the MAC is made in writing and must be filed with the MAC no later than 60 days after the ALJ's decision or dismissal is issued. The written referral will state the reasons why CMS believes that the MAC must review the case on its own motion. CMS will send a copy of its referral to all parties to the ALJ's action and to the ALJ. Parties to the ALJ's action may file exceptions to the referral by submitting written comments to the MAC within 20 days of the referral notice. A party submitting comments to the MAC must send such comments to CMS and all other parties to the ALJ's decision.

(c) *Standard of review.* (1) Referral by CMS after participation at the ALJ level. If CMS or its contractor participated in an appeal at the ALJ level, the MAC exercises its own motion authority if there is an error of law material to the outcome of the case, an abuse of discretion by the ALJ, the decision is not consistent with the preponderance of the evidence of record, or there is a broad policy or procedural issue that may affect the general public interest. In deciding whether to accept review under this standard, the MAC will limit its consideration of the ALJ's action to those exceptions raised by CMS.

(2) *Referral by CMS when CMS did not participate in the ALJ proceedings or appear as a party.* The MAC will accept review if the decision or dismissal contains an error of law material to the outcome of the case or presents a broad policy or procedural issue that may affect the general public interest. In deciding whether to accept review, the MAC will limit its consideration of the ALJ's action to those exceptions raised by CMS.

(d) *MAC's action.* If the MAC decides to review a decision or dismissal on its own motion, it will mail the results of its action to all the parties to the hearing and to CMS if it is not already a party to the hearing. The MAC may adopt, modify, or reverse the decision or dismissal, may remand the case to an ALJ for further proceedings or may dismiss a hearing request. The MAC must issue its action no later than 90 days after receipt of the CMS referral, unless the 90-day period has been extended as provided in this subpart. The MAC may not, however, issue its action before the 20-day comment period has expired, unless it determines that the agency's referral does not provide a basis for reviewing the case. If the MAC does not act within the applicable adjudication deadline, the ALJ's decision or dismissal remains the final action in the case.

**§ 405.1112 Content of request for review.**

(a) The request for MAC review must be filed with the MAC or appropriate ALJ hearing office. The request for review must be in writing and may be made on a standard form. A written request that is not made on a standard form is accepted if it contains the beneficiary's name; Medicare health insurance claim number; the specific service(s) or item(s) for which the review is requested; the specific date(s) of service; the date of the ALJ's final action, if any, if the party is requesting escalation from the ALJ to the MAC, the hearing office in which the appellant's request for hearing is pending; and the name and signature of the party or the representative of the party; and any other information CMS may decide.

(b) The request for review must identify the parts of the ALJ action with which the party requesting review disagrees and explain why he or she disagrees with the ALJ's decision, dismissal, or other determination being appealed. For example, if the party requesting review believes that the ALJ's action is inconsistent with a statute, regulation, CMS Ruling, or other authority, the request for review should explain why the appellant believes the action is inconsistent with that authority.

(c) The MAC will limit its review of an ALJ's actions to those exceptions raised by the party in the request for review, unless the appellant is an unrepresented beneficiary. For purposes of this section only, we define a representative as anyone who has accepted an appointment as the beneficiary's representative, except a member of the beneficiary's family, a legal guardian, or an individual who routinely acts on behalf of the beneficiary, such as a family member or friend who has a power of attorney.

[70 FR 11472, Mar. 8, 2005, as amended at 70 FR 37704, June 30, 2005]

**§ 405.1114 Dismissal of request for review.**

The MAC dismisses a request for review if the party requesting review did not file the request within the stated period of time and the time for filing has not been extended. The MAC also dismisses the request for review if–

(a) The party asks to withdraw the request for review;

(b) The party does not have a right to request MAC review; or

(c) The beneficiary whose claim is being appealed died while the request for review is pending and all of the following criteria apply:

(1) The request for review was filed by the beneficiary or the beneficiary's representative, and the beneficiary's surviving spouse or estate has no remaining financial interest in the case. In deciding this issue, the MAC considers whether the surviving spouse or estate remains liable for the services that were denied or a Medicare contractor held the beneficiary liable for subsequent similar services under the limitation of liability provisions based on the denial of the services at issue;

(2) No other individual or entity with a financial interest in the case wishes to pursue an appeal under § 405.1102;

(3) No other party to the ALJ hearing filed a valid and timely review request under § 405.1102 and § 405.1112.

**§ 405.1116 Effect of dismissal of request for MAC review or request for hearing.**

The dismissal of a request for MAC review or denial of a request for review of a dismissal issued by an ALJ is binding and not subject to further review unless reopened and vacated by the MAC. The MAC's dismissal of a request for hearing is also binding and not subject to judicial review.

**§ 405.1118 Obtaining evidence from the MAC.**

A party may request and receive a copy of all or part of the record of the ALJ hearing, including the exhibits list, documentary evidence, and a copy of the tape of the oral proceedings. However, the party may be asked to pay the costs of providing these items. If a party requests evidence from the MAC and an opportunity to comment on that evidence, the time beginning with the MAC's receipt of the request for evidence through the expiration of the time granted for the party's response will not be counted toward the 90-day adjudication deadline.

**§ 405.1120 Filing briefs with the MAC.**

Upon request, the MAC will give the party requesting review, as well as all other parties, a reasonable opportunity to file briefs or other written statements about the facts and law relevant to the case. Any party who submits a brief or statement must send a copy to all of the other parties. Unless the party requesting review files the brief or other statement with the request for review, the time beginning with the date of receipt of the request to submit the brief and ending with the date the brief is received by the MAC will not be counted toward the adjudication time frame set forth in § 405.1100. The MAC may also request, but not require, CMS or its contractor to file a brief or position paper if the MAC determines that it is necessary to resolve the issues in the case. The MAC will not draw any adverse inference if CMS or a contractor either participates, or decides not to participate in MAC review.

**§ 405.1122 What evidence may be submitted to the MAC.**

(a) *Appeal before the MAC on request for review of ALJ's decision.* (1) If the MAC is reviewing an ALJ's decision, the MAC limits its review of the evidence to the evidence contained in the record of the proceedings before the ALJ. However, if the hearing decision decides a new issue that the parties were not afforded an opportunity to address at the ALJ level, the MAC considers any evidence related to that issue that is submitted with the request for review.

(2) If the MAC determines that additional evidence is needed to resolve the issues in the case and the hearing record indicates that the previous decision-makers have not attempted to obtain the evidence, the MAC may remand the case to an ALJ to obtain the evidence and issue a new decision.

(b) *Appeal before MAC as a result of appellant's request for escalation.* (1) If the MAC is reviewing a case that is escalated from the ALJ level to the MAC, the MAC will decide the case based on the record constructed at the QIC and any additional evidence, including oral testimony, entered in the record by the ALJ before the case was escalated.

(2) If the MAC receives additional evidence with the request for escalation that is material to the question to be decided, or determines that additional evidence is needed to resolve the issues in the case, and the record provided to the MAC indicates that the previous decision-makers did not attempt to obtain the evidence before escalation, the MAC may remand the case to an ALJ to consider or obtain the evidence and issue a new decision.

(c) *Evidence related to issues previously considered by the QIC.* (1) If new evidence related to issues previously considered by the QIC is submitted to the MAC by a provider, supplier, or a beneficiary represented by a provider or supplier, the MAC must determine if the provider, supplier, or the beneficiary represented by a provider or supplier had good cause for submitting it for the first time at the MAC level.

(2) If the MAC determines that good cause does not exist, the MAC must exclude the evidence from the proceeding, may not consider it in reaching a decision, and may not remand the issue to an ALJ.

(3) The MAC must notify all parties if it excludes the evidence. The MAC may remand to an ALJ if–

(i) The ALJ did not consider the new evidence submitted by the provider, supplier, or beneficiary represented by a provider or supplier because good cause did not exist; and

(ii) The MAC finds that good cause existed under § 405.1028 and the ALJ should have reviewed the evidence.

(iii) The new evidence is submitted by a party that is not a provider, supplier, or a beneficiary represented by a provider or supplier.

(d) *Subpoenas.* (1) When it is reasonably necessary for the full presentation of a case, the MAC may, on its own initiative or at the request of a party, issue subpoenas requiring a party to make books, records, correspondence, papers, or other documents that are material to an issue at the hearing available for inspection and copying.

(2) A party's request for a subpoena must—

(i) Give a sufficient description of the documents to be produced;

(ii) State the important facts that the documents are expected to prove; and

(iii) Indicate why these facts could not be proven without issuing a subpoena.

(3) A party to the MAC review on escalation that wishes to subpoena documents must file a written request that complies with the requirements set out in paragraph (d)(2) of this section within 10 calendar days of the request for escalation.

(4) A subpoena will issue only where a party—

(i) Has sought discovery;

(ii) Has filed a motion to compel;

(iii) Has had that motion granted; and

(iv) Nevertheless, has still not received the requested discovery.

(e) Reviewability of subpoena rulings—

(1) *General rule.* A MAC ruling on a subpoena request is not subject to immediate review by the Secretary.

(2) *Exception.* (i) To the extent a subpoena compels disclosure of a matter for which an objection based on privilege, or other protection from disclosure such as case preparation, confidentiality, or undue burden, was made before the MAC, the Secretary may review immediately that subpoena or portion of the subpoena.

(ii) Upon notice to the MAC that a party or non-party, as applicable, intends to seek Secretary review of the subpoena, the MAC must stay all proceedings affected by the subpoena.

(iii) The MAC determines the length of the stay under the circumstances of a given case, but in no event is less than 15 days after the day on which the MAC received notice of the party or non-party's intent to seek Secretary review.

(iv) If the Secretary grants a request for review, the subpoena or portion of the subpoena, as applicable, is stayed until the Secretary issues a written decision that affirms, reverses, modifies, or remands the MAC's action for the subpoena.

(v) If the Secretary does not grant review or take own motion review within the time allotted for the stay, the stay is lifted and the MAC's action stands.

(f) *Enforcement.* (1) If the MAC determines, whether on its own motion or at the request of a party, that a party or non-party subject to a subpoena issued under this section has refused to comply with the subpoena, the MAC may request the Secretary to seek enforcement of the subpoena in accordance with section 205(c) of the Act, 42 U.S.C. 405(c).

(2) Any enforcement request by the MAC must consist of a written notice to the Secretary describing in detail the MAC's findings of noncompliance and its specific request for enforcement, and providing a copy of the subpoena and evidence of its receipt by certified mail by the party or nonparty subject to the subpoena.

(3) The MAC must promptly mail a copy of the notice and related documents to the party or non-party subject to the subpoena, and to any other party and affected non-party to the appeal.

(4) If the Secretary does not grant review or take own motion review within the time allotted for the stay, the stay is lifted and the subpoena stands.

**§ 405.1124 Oral argument.**

A party may request to appear before the MAC to present oral argument.

(a) The MAC grants a request for oral argument if it decides that the case raises an important question of law, policy, or fact that cannot be readily decided based on written submissions alone.

(b) The MAC may decide on its own that oral argument is necessary to decide the issues in the case. If the MAC decides to hear oral argument, it tells the parties of the time and place of the oral argument at least 10 days before the scheduled date.

(c) In case of a previously unrepresented beneficiary, a newly hired representative may request an extension of time for preparation of the oral argument and the MAC must consider whether the extension is reasonable.

(d) The MAC may also request, but not require, CMS or its contractor to appear before it if the MAC determines that it may be helpful in resolving the issues in the case.

(e) The MAC will not draw any inference if CMS or a contractor decides not to participate in the oral argument.

**§ 405.1126 Case remanded by the MAC.**

(a) *When the MAC may remand a case.* Except as specified in § 405.1122(c), the MAC may remand a case in which additional evidence is needed or additional action by the ALJ is required. The MAC will designate in its remand order whether the ALJ will issue a final decision or a recommended decision on remand.

(b) *Action by ALJ on remand.* The ALJ will take any action that is ordered by the MAC and may take any additional action that is not inconsistent with the MAC's remand order.

(c) *Notice when case is returned with a recommended decision.* When the ALJ sends a case to the MAC with a recommended decision, a notice is mailed to the parties at their last known address. The notice tells them that the case was sent to the

MAC, explains the rules for filing briefs or other written statements with the MAC, and includes a copy of the recommended decision.

(d) *Filing briefs with the MAC when ALJ issues recommended decision.* (1) Any party to the recommended decision may file with the MAC briefs or other written statements about the facts and law relevant to the case within 20 days of the date on the recommended decision. Any party may ask the MAC for additional time to file briefs or statements. The MAC will extend this period, as appropriate, if the party shows that it has good cause for requesting the extension.

(2) All other rules for filing briefs with and obtaining evidence from the MAC follow the procedures explained in this subpart.

(e) *Procedures before the MAC.* (1) The MAC, after receiving a recommended decision, will conduct proceedings and issue its decision or dismissal according to the procedures explained in this subpart.

(2) If the MAC determines that more evidence is required, it may again remand the case to an ALJ for further inquiry into the issues, rehearing, receipt of evidence, and another decision or recommended decision. However, if the MAC decides that it can get the additional evidence more quickly, it will take appropriate action.

**§ 405.1128 Action of the MAC.**

(a) After it has reviewed all the evidence in the administrative record and any additional evidence received, subject to the limitations on MAC consideration of additional evidence in § 405.1122, the MAC will make a decision or remand the case to an ALJ.

(b) The MAC may adopt, modify, or reverse the ALJ hearing decision or recommended decision.

(c) The MAC mails a copy of its decision to all the parties at their last known addresses. For overpayment cases involving multiple beneficiaries where there is no beneficiary liability, the MAC may choose to send written notice only to the appellant. In the event the decision will result in a payment to a provider or supplier, the Medicare contractor must issue any electronic or paper remittance advice notice to that provider or supplier.

**§ 405.1130 Effect of the MAC's decision.**

The MAC's decision is binding on all parties unless a Federal district court issues a decision modifying the MAC's decision or the decision is revised as the result of a reopening in accordance with § 405.980. A party may file an action in a Federal district court within 60 days after the date it receives notice of the MAC's decision.

**§ 405.1132 Request for escalation to Federal court.**

(a) If the MAC does not issue a decision or dismissal or remand the case to an ALJ within the adjudication period specified in § 405.1100, or as extended as provided in this subpart, the appellant may request that the appeal, other than an appeal of an ALJ dismissal, be escalated to Federal district court. Upon receipt of a request for escalation, the MAC may—

(1) Issue a decision or dismissal or remand the case to an ALJ, if that action is issued within the latter of 5 calendar days of receipt of the request for escalation or 5 calendar days from the end of the applicable adjudication time period set forth in § 405.1100; or

(2) If the MAC is not able to issue a decision or dismissal or remand as set forth in paragraph (a)(1) of this section, it will send a notice to the appellant acknowledging receipt of the request for escalation and confirming that it is not able to issue a decision, dismissal or remand order within the statutory time frame.

(b) A party may file an action in a Federal district court within 60 days after the date it receives the MAC's notice that the MAC is not able to issue a final action or remand unless the party is appealing an ALJ dismissal.

**§ 405.1134 Extension of time to file action in Federal district court.**

(a) Any party to the MAC's decision or to a request for EAJR that has been certified by the review entity other than CMS may request that the time for filing an action in a Federal district court be extended.

(b) The request must–

(1) Be in writing.

(2) Give the reasons why the action was not filed within the stated time period.

(3) Be filed with the MAC.

(c) If the party shows that he or she had good cause for missing the deadline, the time period will be extended. To determine whether good cause exists, the MAC uses the standards specified in § 405.942(b)(2) or (b)(3).

**§ 405.1136 Judicial review.**

(a) *General rules.* (1) To the extent authorized by sections 1869, 1876(c)(5)(B), and 1879(d) of the Act, a party to a MAC decision, or an appellant who requests escalation to Federal district court if the MAC does not complete its review of the ALJ's decision within the applicable adjudication period, may obtain a court review if the amount remaining in controversy satisfies the requirements of § 405.1006(c).

(2) If the MAC's adjudication period set forth in § 405.1100 expires and the appellant does not request escalation to Federal district court, the case remains with the MAC until a final action is issued.

(b) *Court in which to file civil action.* (1) Any civil action described in paragraph (a) of this section must be filed in the District Court of the United States for the judicial district in which the party resides or where such individual, institution, or agency has its principal place of business.

(2) If the party does not reside within any judicial district, or if the individual, institution, or agency does not have its principal place of business within any such judicial district, the civil action must be filed in the District Court of the United States for the District of Columbia.

(c) *Time for filing civil action.* (1) Any civil action described in paragraph (a) of this section must be filed within the time periods specified in § 405.1130, § 405.1132, or § 405.1134, as applicable.

(2) For purposes of this section, the date of receipt of the notice of the MAC's decision or the MAC's notice that it is not able to issue a decision within the statutory time frame shall be presumed to be 5 calendar days after the date of the notice, unless there is a reasonable showing to the contrary.

(3) Where a case is certified for judicial review in accordance with the expedited access to judicial review process in § 405.990, the civil action must be filed within 60 days after receipt of the review entity's certification, except where the time is extended by the ALJ or MAC, as applicable, upon a showing of good cause.

(d) *Proper defendant.* (1) In any civil action described in paragraph (a) of this section, the Secretary of HHS, in his or her official capacity, is the proper defendant. Any civil action properly filed shall survive notwithstanding any change of the person holding the Office of the Secretary of HHS or any vacancy in such office.

(2) If the complaint is erroneously filed against the United States or against any agency, officer, or employee of the United States other than the Secretary, the plaintiff will be notified that he or she has named an incorrect defendant and is granted 60 days from the date of receipt of the notice in which to commence the action against the correct defendant, the Secretary.

(e) *Prohibition against judicial review of certain Part B regulations or instructions.* Under section 1869(e)(1) of the Act, a court may not review a regulation or instruction that relates to a method of payment under Medicare Part B if the regulation was published, or the instructions issued, before January 1, 1991.

(f) *Standard of review.* (1) Under section 205(g) of the Act, the findings of the Secretary of HHS as to any fact, if supported by substantial evidence, are conclusive.

(2) When the Secretary's decision is adverse to a party due to a party's failure to submit proof in conformity with a regulation prescribed under section 205(a) of the Act pertaining to the type of proof a party must offer to establish entitlement to payment, the court will review only whether the proof conforms with the regulation and the validity of the regulation.

[70 FR 11472, Mar. 8, 2005, as amended at 70 FR 37705, June 30, 2005]

**§ 405.1138 Case remanded by a Federal district court.**

When a Federal district court remands a case to the Secretary for further consideration, unless the court order specifies otherwise, the MAC, acting on behalf of the Secretary, may make a decision, or it may remand the case to an ALJ with instructions to take action and either issue a decision, take other action, or return the case to the MAC with a recommended decision. If the MAC remands a case, the procedures specified in § 405.1140 will be followed.

**§ 405.1140 MAC review of ALJ decision in a case remanded by a Federal district court.**

(a) *General rules.* (1) In accordance with § 405.1138, when a case is remanded by a Federal district court for further consideration and the MAC remands the case to an ALJ, a decision subsequently issued by the ALJ becomes the final decision of the Secretary unless the MAC assumes jurisdiction.

(2) The MAC may assume jurisdiction based on written exceptions to the decision of the ALJ that a party files with the MAC or based on its authority under paragraph (c) of this section.

(3) The MAC either makes a new, independent decision based on the entire record that will be the final decision of the Secretary after remand, or remands the case to an ALJ for further proceedings.

(b) *A party files exceptions disagreeing with the decision of the ALJ.* (1) If a party disagrees with an ALJ decision described in paragraph (a) of this section, in whole or in part, he or she may file exceptions to the decision with the MAC. Exceptions may be filed by submitting a written statement to the MAC setting forth the reasons for disagreeing with the decision of the ALJ. The party must file exceptions within 30 days of the date the party receives the decision of the ALJ or submit a written request for an extension within the 30-day period. The MAC will grant a timely request for a 30-day extension. A request for an extension of more than 30 days must include a statement of reasons as to why the party needs the additional time and may be granted if the MAC finds good cause under the standard established in § 405.942(b)(2) or (b)(3).

(2) If written exceptions are timely filed, the MAC considers the party's reasons for disagreeing with the decision of the ALJ. If the MAC concludes that there is no reason to change the decision of the ALJ, it will issue a notice addressing the exceptions and explaining why no change in the decision of the ALJ is warranted. In this instance, the decision of the ALJ is the final decision of the Secretary after remand.

(3) When a party files written exceptions to the decision of the ALJ, the MAC may assume jurisdiction at any time. If the MAC assumes jurisdiction, it makes a new, independent decision based on its consideration of the entire record adopting, modifying, or reversing the decision of the ALJ or remanding the case to an ALJ for further proceedings, including a new decision. The new decision of the MAC is the final decision of the Secretary after remand.

(c) *MAC assumes jurisdiction without exceptions being filed.* (1) Any time within 60 days after the date of the decision of the ALJ, the MAC may decide to assume jurisdiction of the case even though no written exceptions have been filed.

(2) Notice of this action is mailed to all parties at their last known address.

(3) The parties will be provided with the opportunity to file briefs or other written statements with the MAC about the facts and law relevant to the case.

(4) After the briefs or other written statements are received or the time allowed (usually 30 days) for submitting them has expired, the MAC will either issue a final decision of the Secretary affirming, modifying, or reversing the decision of the ALJ, or remand the case to an ALJ for further proceedings, including a new decision.

(d) *Exceptions are not filed and the MAC does not otherwise assume jurisdiction.* If no exceptions are filed and the MAC does not assume jurisdiction of the cases within

60 days after the date of the ALJ's decision, the decision of the ALJ becomes the final decision of the Secretary after remand.

**Subpart J—Expedited Determinations and Reconsiderations of Provider Service Terminations, and Procedures for Inpatient Hospital Discharges**

**Source:** 69 FR 69624, Nov. 26, 2004, unless otherwise noted.

**§ 405.1200 Notifying beneficiaries of provider service terminations.**

(a) *Applicability and scope.* (1) For purposes of §§ 405.1200 through 405.1204, the term, provider, is defined as a home health agency (HHA), skilled nursing facility (SNF), comprehensive outpatient rehabilitation facility (CORF), or hospice.

(2) For purposes of §§ 405.1200 through 405.1204, a termination of Medicare-covered service is a discharge of a beneficiary from a residential provider of services, or a complete cessation of coverage at the end of a course of treatment prescribed in a discrete increment, regardless of whether the beneficiary agrees that the services should end. A termination does not include a reduction in services. A termination also does not include the termination of one type of service by the provider if the beneficiary continues to receive other Medicare-covered services from the provider.

(b) *Advance written notice of service terminations.* Before any termination of services, the provider of the service must deliver valid written notice to the beneficiary of the provider's decision to terminate services. The provider must use a standardized notice, as specified by CMS, in accordance with the following procedures:

(1) *Timing of notice.* A provider must notify the beneficiary of the decision to terminate covered services no later than 2 days before the proposed end of the services. If the beneficiary's services are expected to be fewer than 2 days in duration, the provider must notify the beneficiary at the time of admission to the provider. If, in a non-residential setting, the span of time between services exceeds 2 days, the notice must be given no later than the next to last time services are furnished.

(2) *Content of the notice.* The standardized termination notice must include the following information:

(i) The date that coverage of services ends;

(ii) The date that the beneficiary's financial liability for continued services begins;

(iii) A description of the beneficiary's right to an expedited determination under § 405.1202, including information about how to request an expedited determination and about a beneficiary's right to submit evidence showing that services must continue;

(iv) A beneficiary's right to receive the detailed information specified under § 405.1202(f); and

(v) Any other information required by CMS.

(3) *When delivery of the notice is valid.* Delivery of the termination notice is valid if–

(i) The beneficiary (or the beneficiary's authorized representative) has signed and dated the notice to indicate that he or she has received the notice and can comprehend its contents; and

(ii) The notice is delivered in accordance with paragraph (b)(1) of this section and contains all the elements described in paragraph (b)(2) of this section.

(4) *If a beneficiary refuses to sign the notice.* The provider may annotate its notice to indicate the refusal, and the date of refusal is considered the date of receipt of the notice.

(5) *Financial liability for failure to deliver valid notice.* A provider is financially liable for continued services until 2 days after the beneficiary receives valid notice as specified under paragraph (b)(3) of this section, or until the service termination date specified on the notice, whichever is later. A beneficiary may waive continuation of services if he or she agrees with being discharged sooner than the planned service termination date.

**§ 405.1202 Expedited determination procedures.**

(a) *Beneficiary's right to an expedited determination by the QIO.* A beneficiary has a right to an expedited determination by a QIO under the following circumstances:

(1) For services furnished by a non-residential provider, the beneficiary disagrees with the provider of those services that services should be terminated, and a physician certifies that failure to continue the provision of the service(s) may place the beneficiary's health at significant risk.

(2) For services furnished by a residential provider or a hospice, the beneficiary disagrees with the provider's decision to discharge the beneficiary.

(b) *Requesting an expedited determination.* (1) A beneficiary who wishes to exercise the right to an expedited determination must submit a request for a determination to the QIO in the State in which the beneficiary is receiving those provider services, in writing or by telephone, by no later than noon of the calendar day following receipt of the provider's notice of termination. If the QIO is unable to accept the beneficiary's request, the beneficiary must submit the request by noon of the next day the QIO is available to accept a request.

(2) The beneficiary, or his or her representative, must be available to answer questions or to supply information that the QIO may request to conduct its review.

(3) The beneficiary may, but is not required to, submit evidence to be considered by a QIO in making its decision.

(4) If a beneficiary makes an untimely request for an expedited determination by a QIO, the QIO will accept the request and make a determination as soon as possible, but the 72-hour time frame under paragraph (e)(6) and the financial liability protection under paragraph (g) of this section do not apply.

(c) *Coverage of provider services.* Coverage of provider services continues until the date and time designated on the termination notice, unless the QIO reverses the provider's service termination decision. If the QIO's decision is delayed because the provider did not timely supply necessary information or records, the provider may be liable for the costs of any additional coverage, as determined by the QIO in accordance with paragraph (e)(7) of this section. If the QIO finds that the beneficiary did not receive valid notice, coverage of provider services continues until at least 2 days after valid notice has been received. Continuation of coverage is not required if the QIO determines that coverage could pose a threat to the beneficiary's health or safety.

(d) *Burden of proof.* When a beneficiary requests an expedited determination by a QIO, the burden of proof rests with the provider to demonstrate that termination of coverage is the correct decision, either on the basis of medical necessity, or based on other Medicare coverage policies.

(1) In order for the QIO to determine whether the provider has met the burden of proof, the provider should supply any and all information that a QIO requires to sustain the provider's termination decision, consistent with paragraph (f) of this section.

(2) The beneficiary may submit evidence to be considered by a QIO in making its decision.

(e) *Procedures the QIO must follow.* (1) On the day the QIO receives the request for an expedited determination under paragraph (b) of this section, it must immediately notify the provider of those services that a request for an expedited determination has been made.

(2) The QIO determines whether the provider delivered valid notice of the termination decision consistent with § 405.1200(b) and paragraph (f) of this section.

(3) The QIO examines the medical and other records that pertain to the services in dispute. If applicable, the QIO determines whether a physician has certified that failure to continue the provision of services may place the beneficiary's health at significant risk.

(4) The QIO must solicit the views of the beneficiary who requested the expedited determination.

(5) The QIO must provide an opportunity for the provider/practitioner to explain why the termination or discharge is appropriate.

(6) No later than 72 hours after receipt of the request for an expedited determination, the QIO must notify the beneficiary, beneficiary's physician, and the provider of services of its determination whether termination of Medicare coverage is the correct decision, either on the basis of medical necessity or based on other Medicare coverage policies.

(7) If the QIO does not receive the information needed to sustain a provider's decision to terminate services, it may make its determination based on the evidence at hand, or it may defer a decision until it receives the necessary information. If this delay results in extended Medicare coverage of an individual's

provider services, the provider may be held financially liable for these services, as determined by the QIO.

(8) The QIO's initial notification may be by telephone, followed by a written notice including the following information:

(i) The rationale for the determination;

(ii) An explanation of the Medicare payment consequences of the determination and the date a beneficiary becomes fully liable for the services; and

(iii) Information about the beneficiary's right to a reconsideration of the QIO's determination, including how to request a reconsideration and the time period for doing so.

(f) *Responsibilities of providers.* (1) When a QIO notifies a provider that a beneficiary has requested an expedited determination, the provider must send a detailed notice to the beneficiary by close of business of the day of the QIO's notification. The detailed termination notice must include the following information:

(i) A specific and detailed explanation why services are either no longer reasonable and necessary or are no longer covered;

(ii) A description of any applicable Medicare coverage rule, instruction, or other Medicare policy, including citations to the applicable Medicare policy rules or information about how the beneficiary may obtain a copy of the Medicare policy;

(iii) Facts specific to the beneficiary and relevant to the coverage determination that are sufficient to advise the beneficiary of the applicability of the coverage rule or policy to the beneficiary's case; and

(iv) Any other information required by CMS.

(2) Upon notification by the QIO of the request for an expedited determination, the provider must supply all information that the QIO needs to make its expedited determination, including a copy of the notices required under § 405.1200(b) and under paragraph (f)(1) of this section. The provider must furnish this information as soon as possible, but no later than by close of business of the day the QIO notifies the provider of the request for an expedited determination. At the discretion of the QIO, the provider may make the information available by phone or in writing (with a written record of any information not transmitted initially in writing).

(3) At a beneficiary's request, the provider must furnish the beneficiary with a copy of, or access to, any documentation that it sends to the QIO including records of any information provided by telephone. The provider may charge the beneficiary a reasonable amount to cover the costs of duplicating the documentation and/or delivering it to the beneficiary. The provider must accommodate such a request by no later than close of business of the first day after the material is requested.

(g) *Coverage during QIO review.* When a beneficiary requests an expedited determination in accordance with the procedures required by this section, the provider may not bill the beneficiary for any disputed services until the expedited determination process (and reconsideration process, if applicable) has been completed.

**§ 405.1204 Expedited reconsiderations.**

(a) *Beneficiary's right to an expedited reconsideration.* A beneficiary who is dissatisfied with a QIO's expedited determination may request an expedited reconsideration by the appropriate QIC.

(b) *Requesting an expedited reconsideration.* (1) A beneficiary who wishes to obtain an expedited reconsideration must submit a request for the reconsideration to the appropriate QIC, in writing or by telephone, by no later than noon of the calendar day following initial notification (whether by telephone or in writing) of receipt of the QIO's determination. If the QIC is unable to accept the beneficiary's request, the beneficiary must submit the request by noon of the next day the QIC is available to accept a request.

(2) The beneficiary, or his or her representative, must be available to answer questions or supply information that the QIC may request to conduct its reconsideration.

(3) The beneficiary may, but is not required to, submit evidence to be considered by a QIC in making its decision.

(4) A beneficiary who does not file a timely request for an expedited QIC reconsideration subsequently may request a reconsideration under the standard claims appeal process, but the coverage protections described in paragraph (f) of this section would not extend through this reconsideration, nor would the time frames or the escalation process described in paragraphs (c)(3) and (c)(5) of this section, respectively.

(c) *Procedures the QIC must follow.* (1) On the day the QIC receives the request for an expedited determination under paragraph (b) of this section, the QIC must immediately notify the QIO that made the expedited determination and the provider of services of the request for an expedited reconsideration.

(2) The QIC must offer the beneficiary and the provider an opportunity to provide further information.

(3) Unless the beneficiary requests an extension in accordance with paragraph (c)(6) of this section, no later than 72 hours after receipt of the request for an expedited reconsideration, and any medical or other records needed for such reconsideration, the QIC must notify the QIO, the beneficiary, the beneficiary's physician, and the provider of services, of its decision on the reconsideration request.

(4) The QIC's initial notification may be done by telephone, followed by a written notice including:

(i) The rationale for the reconsideration decision;

(ii) An explanation of the Medicare payment consequences of the determination and the beneficiary's date of liability; and

(iii) Information about the beneficiary's right to appeal the QIC's reconsideration decision to an ALJ, including how to request an appeal and the time period for doing so.

(5) Unless the beneficiary requests an extension in accordance with paragraph (c)(6) of this section, if the QIC does not issue a decision within 72

hours of receipt of the request, the QIC must notify the beneficiary of his or her right to have the case escalated to the ALJ hearing level if the amount remaining in controversy after the QIO determination is $100 or more.

(6) A beneficiary requesting an expedited reconsideration under this section may request (either in writing or orally) that the QIC grant such additional time as the beneficiary specifies (not to exceed 14 days) for the reconsideration. If an extension is granted, the deadlines in paragraph (c)(3) of this section do not apply.

(d) *Responsibilities of the QIO.* (1) When a QIC notifies a QIO that a beneficiary has requested an expedited reconsideration, the QIO must supply all information that the QIC needs to make its expedited reconsideration as soon as possible, but no later than by close of business of the day that the QIC notifies the QIO of the request for an expedited reconsideration.

(2) At a beneficiary's request, the QIO must furnish the beneficiary with a copy of, or access to, any documentation that it sends to the QIC. The QIO may charge the beneficiary a reasonable amount to cover the costs of duplicating the documentation and/or delivering it to the beneficiary. The QIO must accommodate the request by no later than close of business of the first day after the material is requested.

(e) *Responsibilities of the provider.* A provider may, but is not required to, submit evidence to be considered by a QIC in making its decision. If a provider fails to comply with a QIC's request for additional information beyond that furnished to the QIO for purposes of the expedited determination, the QIC makes its reconsideration decision based on the information available.

(f) *Coverage during QIC reconsideration process.* When a beneficiary requests an expedited reconsideration in accordance with the deadline specified in (b)(1) of this section, the provider may not bill the beneficiary for any disputed services until the QIC makes its determination.

**§ 405.1206 Expedited determinations for inpatient hospital discharges.**

(a) *Beneficiary's right to an expedited determination for an inpatient hospital discharge.* A beneficiary who has received a notice of noncoverage under section 1154(e)(1) of the Act and 42 CFR 412.42(c)(3) may request an expedited determination by the QIO when a hospital (acting directly or through its utilization review committee), with physician concurrence, determines that inpatient care is no longer necessary. A beneficiary who timely requests an expedited QIO review in accordance with paragraph (d)(1) of this section and who meets the conditions of section 1879(a)(2) of the Social Security Act (that is, the individual did not know, and could not reasonably have been expected to know, that payment would not be made for such items or services under Part A or Part B) may remain in the hospital with no additional financial liability until the QIO makes its determination.

(b) *When delivery of the notice is valid.* (1) Except as provided in paragraph (b)(2) of this section, valid delivery of the notice of non-coverage requires that the beneficiary (or the beneficiary's authorized representative) has signed and dated the notice to indicate that he or she has received the notice and can comprehend its contents.

(2) If a beneficiary refuses to sign the notice, the provider may annotate its notice to indicate the refusal, and the date of refusal is considered the date of receipt of the notice.

(c) *Beneficiary's right to other review.* (1) A beneficiary who fails to request an expedited determination in accordance with paragraph (d)(1) of this section, and remains in the hospital, may request an expedited review at any time during the course of his or her inpatient hospital stay. The QIO will issue a decision in accordance with paragraph (e)(5)(ii) of this section. The escalation procedures described in § 405.1204(c)(5) and the financial liability rules of paragraph (f)(2) of this section do not apply.

(2) A beneficiary who fails to request an expedited determination in accordance with paragraph (d)(1) of this section, and who is no longer an inpatient in the hospital, may request QIO review within 30 calendar days after receipt of the notice of noncoverage as provided under section 1154(e)(1) or at any time for good cause. The QIO will issue a decision in accordance with paragraph (e)(5)(iii) of this section. The escalation procedures described in § 405.1204(c)(5) and the financial liability rules of paragraph (f)(2) of this section do not apply.

(d) *Procedures the beneficiary must follow.* For the expedited appeal process, the following rules apply:

(1) The beneficiary must submit the request for an expedited determination–

(i) To the QIO that has an agreement with the hospital under part 475 of this chapter;

(ii) In writing or by telephone; and

(iii) By noon of the first working day after he or she receives written notice that the hospital has determined that the hospital stay is no longer necessary.

(2) The beneficiary (or his or her authorized representative), upon request by the QIO, must be prepared to discuss the case with the QIO.

(e) *Procedures the QIO must follow.* On the date that the QIO receives the beneficiary's request:

(1) The QIO must notify the hospital that the beneficiary has filed a request for immediate review.

(2) The hospital must supply any information, including medical records, that the QIO requires to conduct its review and must make it available, by phone or in writing, by the close of business of the first full working day after the day the beneficiary receives notice of the planned discharge.

(3) The QIO must examine the pertinent records pertaining to the services.

(4) The QIO must solicit the views of the beneficiary (or the beneficiary's authorized representative) who requested the expedited determination.

(5)(i) When the beneficiary requests an expedited determination in accordance with paragraph (d)(1) of this section, the QIO must make a determination and notify the beneficiary, the hospital, and physician of its determination by close of business of the first working day after it receives all requested pertinent information.

(ii) When the beneficiary does not request an expedited determination in accordance with paragraph (d)(1) of this section, and remains an inpatient in the hospital, the QIO will make a determination and notify the beneficiary, the hospital, and physician of its determination within 2 working days following receipt of the request and pertinent information.

(iii) When the beneficiary does not request an expedited initial determination in accordance with paragraph (d)(1) of this section, and is no longer an inpatient in the hospital, the QIO will make a determination and notify the beneficiary, the hospital, and physician of its determination within 30 calendar days after receipt of the request and pertinent information.

(f) *Coverage during QIO expedited review.* (1) In general, if the beneficiary remains in the hospital after receiving the hospital issued notice of non-coverage, and the hospital, the physician who concurred in the hospital's determination on which the advanced written notice of termination was based, or the QIO subsequently finds that the beneficiary requires an acute level of inpatient hospital care, the beneficiary is not financially responsible for continued care until the hospital once again determines that the beneficiary no longer requires inpatient care, secures concurrence from the physician responsible for the beneficiary's care or the QIO and notifies the beneficiary.

(2) *Timely filing and limitation on liability.* If a beneficiary both files a request for an expedited determination by the QIO in accordance with paragraph (d)(1) of this section, and meets the conditions of section 1879(a)(2) of the Social Security Act (that is, the individual did not know, and could not reasonably have been expected to know, that payment would not be made for such items or services under Part A or Part B), the beneficiary is not financially responsible for inpatient hospital services furnished before noon of the calendar day after the date the beneficiary (or his or her representative) receives notification (either orally or in writing) of the expedited determination by the QIO.

(3) *Untimely filing.* When a beneficiary does not file a request for an expedited determination by the QIO in accordance with paragraph (d)(1) of this section, that beneficiary may be responsible for charges that extend beyond the date specified on the hospital's advance written notice of termination or as otherwise stated by the QIO.

(4) *Hospital requests expedited review.* When the hospital requests review in accordance with § 405.1208, and the QIO concurs with the hospital's decision, a hospital may not charge a beneficiary until the date specified by the QIO.

(g) *Notice of an expedited determination.* (1) When a QIO issues an expedited determination in accordance with paragraph (e)(5) of this section, the QIO must notify the beneficiary, physician, and hospital of its decision, by telephone and subsequently in writing.

(2) A written notice of the expedited determination must contain the following:

(i) The basis for the determination;

(ii) A detailed rationale for the determination;.

(iii) A statement explaining the Medicare payment consequences of the expedited determination and date of liability, if any; and

(iv) A statement informing the beneficiary of his or her subsequent appeal rights, and the time frame for requesting a reconsideration by the QIC.

(h) *Effect of an expedited QIO determination.* The QIO determination is binding upon the beneficiary, physician, and hospital, except in the following circumstances:

(1) *When beneficiary remains in the hospital.* If the beneficiary is still an inpatient in the hospital and is dissatisfied with the determination, he or she may request a reconsideration according to the procedures described in § 405.1204. If the beneficiary does not make a request in accordance with paragraph (d)(1) of this section, the time frames described in § 405.1204(c)(3), the escalation procedures described in § 405.1204(c)(5), and the coverage rule described in § 405.1204(f) will not apply.

(2) *When beneficiary is no longer an inpatient in the hospital.* If the beneficiary is no longer an inpatient in the hospital and is dissatisfied with this determination, the determination is subject to the general claims appeal process.

**§ 405.1208 Hospital requests expedited QIO review.**

(a) *General rule.* If the hospital (acting directly or through its utilization review committee) believes that the beneficiary does not require further inpatient hospital care but is unable to obtain the agreement of the physician, it may request an expedited determination by the QIO.

(b) *Procedures hospital must follow.* (1) The hospital must (acting directly or through its utilization review committee) notify the beneficiary (or his or her representative) that it has requested that review.

(2) The hospital must supply any pertinent information the QIO requires to conduct its review and must make it available by phone or in writing, by close of business of the first full working day immediately following the day the hospital submits the request for review.

(c) *Procedures the QIO must follow.* (1) The QIO must notify the hospital that it has received the request for review and must notify the hospital if it has not received all pertinent records.

(2) The QIO must examine the pertinent records pertaining to the services.

(3) The QIO must solicit the views of the beneficiary in question.

(4) The QIO must make a determination and notify the beneficiary, the hospital, and physician within 2 working days of the hospital's request and receipt of any pertinent information submitted by the hospital.

(d) *Notice of an expedited determination.* (1) When a QIO issues an expedited determination as stated in paragraph (c)(4) of this section, it must notify the beneficiary, physician, and hospital of its decision, by telephone and subsequently in writing.

(2) A written notice of the expedited initial determination must contain the following:

(i) The basis for the determination;.

(ii) A detailed rationale for the determination;

(iii) A statement explaining the Medicare payment consequences of the expedited determination and date of liability, if any; and

(iv) A statement informing the beneficiary of his or her appeal rights and the time frame for requesting an appeal.

(e) *Effect of an expedited determination.* The expedited determination under this section is binding upon the beneficiary, physician, and hospital, except in the following circumstances:

(1) *When a beneficiary remains in the hospital.* If the beneficiary is still an inpatient in the hospital and is dissatisfied with this determination, he or she may request a reconsideration according to the procedures described in § 405.1204. The procedures described in § 405.1204 will apply to reconsiderations requested under this section. If the beneficiary does not make a request in accordance with paragraph (d)(1) of this section, the time frames described in § 405.1204(c)(3), the escalation procedures described in § 405.1204(c)(5), and the coverage rule described in § 405.1204(f) will not apply.

(2) *When a beneficiary is no longer an inpatient in the hospital.* If the beneficiary is no longer an inpatient in the hospital and is dissatisfied with this determination, this determination is subject to the general claims appeal process.

## Subpart R—Provider Reimbursement Determinations and Appeals

**Authority:** Secs. 205, 1102, 1814(b), 1815(a), 1833, 1861(v), 1871, 1872, 1878, and 1886 of the Social Security Act (42 U.S.C. 405, 1302, 1395f(b), 1395g(a), 1395l, 1395x(v), 1395hh, 1395ii, 1395oo, and 1395ww).

**Source:** 39 FR 34515, Sept. 26, 1974, unless otherwise noted. Redesignated at 42 FR 52826, Sept. 30, 1977.

### § 405.1801 Introduction.

(a) *Definitions.* As used in this subpart:

*Administrator* means the Administrator or Deputy Administrator of CMS.

*Administrator's review* means that review provided for in section 1878(f) of the Act (42 U.S.C. § 1395oo(f)) and § 405.1875.

*Board* means the Provider Reimbursement Review Board established in accordance with section 1878 of the Act (42 U.S.C. § 1395oo) and § 405.1845.

*Board hearing* means that hearing provided for in section 1878(a) of the Act (42 U.S.C. § 1395oo(a)), and § 405.1835.

*Date of filing* and *date of submission of materials* mean the day of the mailing (as evidenced by the postmark) or hand-delivery of materials, unless otherwise defined in this subpart.

*Date of receipt* means the date on the return receipt of "return receipt requested" mail, unless otherwise defined in this subpart.

*Intermediary determination* means the following:

(1) With respect to a provider of services that has filed a cost report under §§ 413.20 and 413.24(f) of this chapter, the term means a determination of the amount of total reimbursement due the provider, pursuant to § 405.1803 following the close of the provider's cost reporting period, for items and services furnished to beneficiaries for which reimbursement may be made on a reasonable cost basis under Medicare for the period covered by the cost report.

(2) With respect to a hospital that receives payments for inpatient hospital services under the prospective payment system (part 412 of this chapter), the term means a determination of the total amount of payment due the hospital, pursuant to § 405.1803 following the close of the hospital's cost reporting period, under that system for the period covered by the determination.

(3) For purposes of appeal to the Provider Reimbursement Review Board, the term is synonymous with the phrases "intermediary's final determination" and "final determination of the Secretary", as those phrases are used in section 1878(a) of the Act.

(4) For purposes of § 405.376 concerning claims collection activities, the term does not include an action by CMS with respect to a compromise of a Medicare overpayment claim, or termination or suspension of collection action on an overpayment claim, against a provider or physician or other supplier.

*Intermediary hearing* means that hearing provided for in § 405.1809.

(b) *General rule*–(1) *Providers.* The principles of reimbursement for determining reasonable cost and prospective payment are contained in parts 413 and 412, respectively, of this chapter. In order to be reimbursed for covered services furnished to Medicare beneficiaries, providers of services are obliged to file cost reports with their intermediaries as specified in § 413.24(f) of this chapter. Where the term "provider"appears in this subpart, it includes hospitals paid under the prospective payment system for purposes of applying the appeal procedures described in this subpart to those hospitals.

(2) *Other entities participating in Medicare Part A.* In addition to providers of services whose status as such is indicated in the Act, there are entities (such as health maintenance organizations) that do not meet the statutory test for providers of services, which may also participate in Medicare. These entities are required to file periodic cost reports and are reimbursed on the basis of information furnished in the reports. Although the entities do not qualify for Board review, the rules as set forth in this subpart with respect to intermediary hearings are applicable to the entities to the maximum extent possible, for cost-reporting periods ending on or after December 31, 1971, where the amount of program reimbursement in controversy is at least $1,000.

(c) *Effective dates.* (1) Except as provided in paragraphs (c)(2) and (c)(3) of this section or in § 405.1885(e), this subpart applies to all cost reporting periods ending on or after December 31, 1971, for which reimbursement may be made on a reasonable cost basis.

(2) Sections 405.1835 to 405.1877 apply only to cost reporting periods ending on or after June 30, 1973, for which reimbursement may be made on a reasonable cost basis.

(3) With respect to hospitals under the prospective payment system (see part 412 of this chapter), the appeals procedures in §§ 405.1811 to 405.1877 that apply become applicable with the hospital's first cost reporting period beginning on or after October 1, 1983.

[39 FR 34515, Sept. 26, 1974. Redesignated at 42 FR 52826, Sept. 30, 1977, as amended at 48 FR 39834, Sept. 1, 1983; 48 FR 45773, Oct. 7, 1983; 49 FR 322, Jan. 3, 1984; 49 FR 23013, June 1, 1984; 51 FR 34793, Sept. 30, 1986; 61 FR 63749, Dec. 2, 1996]

**§ 405.1803 Intermediary determination and notice of amount of program reimbursement.**

(a) *General requirement.* Upon receipt of a provider's cost report, or amended cost report where permitted or required, the intermediary must within a reasonable period of time (see § 405.1835(b)), furnish the provider and other parties as appropriate (see § 405.1805) a written notice reflecting the intermediary's determination of the total amount of reimbursement due the provider. The intermediary must include the following information in the notice, as appropriate:

(1) *Reasonable cost.* The notice must—

(i) Explain the intermediary's determination of total program reimbursement due the provider on the basis of reasonable cost for the reporting period covered by the cost report or amended cost report; and

(ii) Relate this determination to the provider's claimed total program reimbursement due the provider for this period.

(2) *Prospective payment.* With respect to a hospital that receives payments for inpatient hospital services under the prospective payment system (see part 412 of this chapter), the intermediary must include in the notice its determination of the total amount of the payments due the hospital under that system for the cost reporting period covered by the notice. The notice must explain (with appropriate use of the applicable money amounts) any difference in the amount determined to be due, and the amounts received by the hospital during the cost reporting period covered by the notice.

(b) *Requirements for intermediary notices.* The intermediary must include in each notice appropriate references to law, regulations, CMS Rulings, or program instructions to explain why the intermediary's determination of the amount of program reimbursement for the period differs from the amount the provider claimed. The notice must also inform the provider of its right to an intermediary or Board hearing (see §§ 405.1809, 405.1811, 405.1815, 405.1835, and 405.1843) and that the provider must request the hearing within 180 days after the date of the notice.

(c) *Use of notice as basis for recoupment of overpayments.* The intermediary's determination contained in its notice is the basis for making the retroactive adjustment (required by § 413.64(f) of this chapter) to any program payments made to the provider during the period to which the determination applies, including recoupment under § 405.373 from ongoing payments to the provider of any overpayments to the provider identified in the determination. Recoupment is made notwithstanding any request for hearing on the determination the provider may make under § 405.1811 or § 405.1835.

[48 FR 39834, Sept. 1, 1983, as amended at 49 FR 322, Jan. 3, 1984; 51 FR 34793, Sept. 30, 1986; 61 FR 63748, Dec. 2, 1996]

**§ 405.1804 Matters not subject to administrative and judicial review under prospective payment.**

Neither administrative nor judicial review is available for controversies about the following matters:

(a) The determination of the requirement, or the proportional amount, of any budget neutrality adjustment in the prospective payment rates.

(b) The establishment of–

(1) Diagnosis related groups (DRGs);

(2) The methodology for the classification of inpatient discharges within the DRGs; or

(3) Appropriate weighting factors that reflect the relative hospital resources used with respect to discharge within each DRG.

[49 FR 322, Jan. 1, 1984]

**§ 405.1805 Parties to intermediary determination.**

The parties to the intermediary's determination are the provider and any other entity found by the intermediary to be a related organization of the provider under § 413.17 of this chapter.

[48 FR 39835, Sept. 1, 1983, as amended at 51 FR 34793, Sept. 30, 1986]

**§ 405.1807 Effect of intermediary determination.**

The determination shall be final and binding on the party or parties to such determination unless:

(a) An intermediary hearing is requested in accordance with § 405.1811 and an intermediary hearing decision rendered in accordance with § 405.1831; or

(b) The intermediary determination is revised in accordance with § 405.1885; or

(c) A Board hearing is requested in accordance with § 405.1835 and a hearing decision rendered pursuant thereto.

**§ 405.1809 Intermediary hearing procedures.**

(a) *Hearings.* Each intermediary must establish and maintain written procedures for intermediary hearings, in accordance with the regulations in this subpart, for resolving issues that may arise between the intermediary and a provider concerning the amount of reasonable cost reimbursement, or prospective payment due the provider (except as provided in § 405.1804) under the Medicare program. The procedures must provide for a hearing on the intermediary determination contained in the notice of program reimbursement (§ 405.1803), if the provider files a timely request for a hearing.

(b) *Amount in controversy.* In order for an intermediary to grant a hearing, the following dates and amounts in controversy apply:

(1) For cost reporting periods ending prior to June 30, 1973, the amount of program reimbursement in controversy must be at least $1,000.

(2) For cost reporting periods ending on or after June 30, 1973, the amount of program reimbursement in controversy must be at least $1,000 but less than $10,000.

[48 FR 39835, Sept. 1, 1983, as amended at 49 FR 323, Jan. 1, 1984]

**§ 405.1811 Right to intermediary hearing; time, place, form, and content of request for intermediary hearing.**

(a) A provider that has been furnished a notice of amount of program reimbursement may request an intermediary hearing if it is dissatisfied with the intermediary's determination contained in the notice and the amount in controversy requirement described in § 405.1809 is met. The request must be in writing and be filed with the intermediary within 180 calendar days after the date of the notice (see § 405.1835(c)). No other individual, entity, or party has the right to an intermediary hearing.

(b) The request must (1) identify the aspect(s) of the determination with which the provider is dissatisfied, and (2) explain why the provider believes the determination on these matters is incorrect, and (3) be submitted with any documentary evidence the provider considers necessary to support its position.

(c) Following the timely filing of the request for hearing, the provider may identify in writing, prior to the onset of the hearing proceedings, additional aspects of the determination with which it is dissatisfied and furnish any documentary evidence in support thereof. If such additional aspects are submitted, the hearing officer may postpone the hearing to allow for his examination of such additional aspects.

[39 FR 34515, Sept. 26, 1974. Redesignated at 42 FR 52826, Sept. 30, 1977, as amended at 48 FR 39835, Sept. 1, 1983]

**§ 405.1813 Failure to timely request an intermediary hearing.**

If a provider requests an intermediary hearing on an intermediary's determination after the time limit prescribed in § 405.1811, the designated intermediary hearing officer or panel of hearing officers will dismiss the request and furnish the provider a written notice that explains the time limitation, except that for good cause shown, the time limit prescribed in § 405.1811 may be extended. However, an extension may not be granted if the extension request is filed more than 3 years after the date of the original notice of the intermediary determination.

[48 FR 39835, Sept. 1, 1983]

**§ 405.1815 Parties to the intermediary hearing.**

The parties to the intermediary hearing shall be the parties to the intermediary determination and any other entity determined by the intermediary to be a related organization of such provider. Said parties shall be given reasonable notice of the time, date, and place of such hearing. Neither the intermediary nor the Centers for Medicare & Medicaid Services are parties (see § 405.1819).

**§ 405.1817 Hearing officer or panel of hearing officers authorized to conduct intermediary hearing; disqualification of officers.**

The intermediary hearing provided for in § 405.1809 shall be conducted by a hearing officer or panel of hearing officers designated by the intermediary. Such hearing officer or officers shall be persons knowledgeable in the field of health care reimbursement. The hearing officer or officers shall not have had any direct responsibility for the program reimbursement determination with respect to which a request for hearing is filed; no hearing officer (or officers) shall conduct a hearing in a case in which he is prejudiced or partial with respect to any party, or where he has any interest in the matter pending for determination before him. Notice of any objection which a party may have with respect to a hearing officer shall be presented in writing to such officer by the objecting party at the party's earliest opportunity. The hearing officer shall consider the objection and shall, at his discretion, either proceed in the conduct of the hearing or withdraw. If the hearing officer does not withdraw, the objecting party may, after the hearing, present his objections to an executive official of the intermediary, who shall rule promptly on the objection.

**§ 405.1819 Conduct of intermediary hearing.**

The hearing shall be open to all parties thereto (see § 405.1815) and to representatives of the intermediary and of the Centers for Medicare & Medicaid Services (see § 405.1815). The hearing officer(s) shall inquire fully into all of the matters at issue and shall receive into evidence the testimony and any documents which are relevant and material to such matters. If the hearing officer(s) believes that there is relevant and material evidence available which has not been presented at the hearing, he (they) may, at any time prior to the mailing of notice of the decision, reopen the hearing record for the receipt of such evidence. The order in which the evidence and the allegations shall be presented and the conduct of the hearing shall be at the discretion of the hearing officer(s).

**§ 405.1821 Prehearing discovery and other proceedings prior to the intermediary hearing.**

(a) Prehearing discovery shall be permitted upon timely request of any party. To be timely, a request for discovery and inspection shall be made before the beginning of the hearing. A reasonable time for inspection and reproduction of documents shall be provided by order of the hearing officer(s).

(b) If, in the discretion of the hearing officer(s), the purpose of defining the issues more clearly would be served, the hearing officer(s) may schedule a prehearing conference. For this purpose, a single member of a panel of hearing officers, when such is the case, may be appointed to act for the panel with respect to prehearing activities.

**§ 405.1823 Evidence at intermediary hearing.**
Evidence may be received at the intermediary hearing even though inadmissible under the rules of evidence applicable to court procedure. The hearing officer(s) shall give the parties opportunity for submission and consideration of facts and arguments, and during the course of the hearing, should in ruling upon admissibility of evidence, exclude irrelevant, immaterial, or unduly repetitious evidence. The hearing officer(s) shall render a final ruling on the admissibility of evidence.

**§ 405.1825 Witnesses at intermediary hearing.**
The hearing officer(s) may examine the witnesses and shall allow the parties and their representatives to do so. Parties to the proceedings may also cross-examine witnesses.

**§ 405.1827 Record of intermediary hearing.**
A complete recordation of the proceedings at the intermediary hearing shall be made and transcribed in all cases. It shall be made available to any party upon request. The record will not be closed until a decision (see § 405.1831) has been issued.

**§ 405.1829 Authority of hearing officer(s) at intermediary hearing.**
(a) The hearing officer(s) in exercising his authority must comply with all the provisions of title XVIII of the Act and regulations issued thereunder, as well as with CMS Rulings issued under the authority of the Administrator of the Centers for Medicare & Medicaid Services (see 42 CFR 401.108), and with the general instructions issued by the Centers for Medicare & Medicaid Services in accordance with the Secretary's agreement with the intermediary.

(b) The determination of a fiscal intermediary that no payment may be made under title XVIII of the Act for any expense incurred for items and services furnished to an individual because such items and services are excluded from coverage pursuant to section 1862 of the Act, 42 U.S.C. 1395y (see subpart C of this part), shall not be reviewed by the hearing officer(s). Such determination shall be reviewed only in accordance with the applicable provisions of subparts G and H of this part.

**§ 405.1831 Intermediary hearing decision and notice.**
The hearing officer(s) shall, on a timely basis, render a decision in writing based on the evidence in the record; such decision shall constitute the final determination of the intermediary. In such decision, he will cite applicable law, regulations, CMS Rulings, and general instructions of the Centers for Medicare & Medicaid Services, as well as findings on all the matters in issue at the hearing. A copy of the decision will be mailed to all parties to the hearing at their last known addresses.

**§ 405.1833 Effect of intermediary hearing decision.**
The intermediary hearing decision provided for in § 405.1831 shall be final and binding upon all parties to the hearing unless such intermediary determination is revised in accordance with § 405.1885.

**§ 405.1835 Right to Board hearing.**

(a) *Criteria.* The provider (but no other individual, entity, or party) has a right to a hearing before the Board about any matter designated in § 405.1801(a)(1), if:

(1) An intermediary determination has been made with respect to the provider; and

(2) The provider has filed a written request for a hearing before the Board under the provisions described in § 405.1841(a)(1); and

(3) The amount in controversy (as determined in § 405.1839(a)) is $10,000 or more.

(b) *Prospective payment exceptions.* Except with respect to matters for which administrative or judicial review is not permitted as specified in § 405.1804, hospitals that are paid under the prospective payment system are entitled to hearings before the Board under this section if they otherwise meet the criteria described in paragraph (a) of this section.

(c) *Right to hearing based on late intermediary determination about reasonable cost.* Notwithstanding the provisions of paragraph (a)(1) of this section, the provider also has a right to a hearing before the Board if an intermediary's determination concerning the amount of reasonable cost reimbursement due a provider is not rendered within 12 months after receipt by the intermediary of a provider's perfected cost report or amended cost report (as permitted or as required to furnish sufficient data for purposes of making such determination—see § 405.1803(a)) provided such delay was not occasioned by the fault of the provider.

[48 FR 39835, Sept. 1, 1983]

**§ 405.1837 Group appeal.**

(a) *Criteria for group appeals.* Subject to paragraph (b) of this section, a group of providers may bring an appeal before the Board but only if—

(1) Each provider in the group is identified as one which would, upon the filing of a request for a hearing before the Board, but without regard to the $10,000 amount in controversy requirement, be entitled to a hearing under § 405.1835;

(2) The matters at issue involve a common question of fact or of interpretation of law, regulations or CMS Rulings; and

(3) The amount in controversy is, in the aggregate, $50,000 or more.

(b) *Providers under common ownership or control.* Effective April 20, 1983, any appeal filed by providers that are under common ownership or control must be brought by the providers as a group appeal in accordance with the provisions of paragraph (a) of this section with respect to any matters involving an issue common to the providers and for which the amount in controversy is, in the aggregate, $50,000 or more (see § 405.1841(a)(2)). A single provider involved in a group appeal that also wishes to appeal issues that are not common to the other providers in the group must file a separate hearing request (see § 405.1841(a)(1)) and must separately meet the requirements in § 405.1811 or § 405.1835, as applicable.

[48 FR 39836, Sept. 1, 1983]

**§ 405.1839 Amount in controversy.**

(a) *Single appeals.* The $1,000 amount in controversy required under § 405.1809 for an intermediary hearing and the $10,000 amount in controversy required under § 405.1835 for a Board hearing is, as applicable to the matters for which the provider has requested a hearing, the combined total of the amounts computed as follows:

(1) *Providers under prospective payment.* For providers that are paid under the prospective payment system, by deducting–

(i) The total of the payment due the provider on other than a reasonable cost basis under the prospective payment system from the total amount that would be payable after a recomputation that takes into account any exclusion, exception, adjustment, or additional payment denied the provider under part 412 of this chapter, as applicable;

(ii) The total of the payment due the provider on a reasonable cost basis under the prospective payment system from the total reimbursable costs claimed by the provider; and

(iii) The adjusted total reimbursable costs due the provider on a reasonable cost basis under other than the prospective payment system from the total reimbursable costs claimed by the provider.

(2) *Providers not under prospective payment.* For providers that are not paid under the prospective payment system, by deducting the adjusted total reimbursable program costs due the provider on a reasonable cost basis from the total reimbursable costs claimed by the provider.

(b) *Group appeals.* The $50,000 amount in controversy required under § 405.1837 for group appeals to the Board is, as applicable to the common matters for which the group of providers have requested a hearing, the combined total of the amounts computed as follows:

(1) *Providers under prospective payment.* For providers that are paid under the prospective payment system, by deducting–

(i) The total of the payment due the providers (in the aggregate) on other than a reasonable cost basis under the prospective payment system from the total amount that would be payable to the providers (in the aggregate) after a recomputation that takes into account any applicable exception, exclusion, adjustment, or additional payment denied the providers under part 412 of this chapter.

(ii) The total of the payment due the providers (in the aggregate) on a reasonable cost basis under the prospective payment system from the total reimbursable costs claimed in the aggregate by the providers; and

(iii) The adjusted total reimbursable costs due the providers (in the aggregate) on a reasonable cost basis under other than the prospective payment system from the total reimbursable costs claimed in the aggregate by the providers.

(2) *Providers not under prospective payment.* For providers that are not paid under the prospective payment system, by deducting the adjusted total

reimbursable program costs due the providers (in the aggregate) on a reasonable cost basis from the total reimbursable costs claimed in the aggregate by the providers.
[49 FR 323, Jan. 3, 1984]

**§ 405.1841 Time, place, form, and content of request for Board hearing.**

(a) *General requirements.* (1) The request for a Board hearing must be filed in writing with the Board within 180 days of the date the notice of the intermediary's determination was mailed to the provider or, where notice of the determination was not timely rendered, within 180 days after the expiration of the period specified in § 405.1835(c). Such request for Board hearing must identify the aspects of the determination with which the provider is dissatisfied, explain why the provider believes the determination is incorrect in such particulars, and be accompanied by any documenting evidence the provider considers necessary to support its position. Prior to the commencement of the hearing proceedings, the provider may identify in writing additional aspects of the intermediary's determination with which it is dissatisfied and furnish any documentary evidence in support thereof.

(2) Effective April 20, 1983, any request for a Board hearing by providers that are under common ownership or control (see § 413.17 of this chapter) must be brought by the providers as a group appeal (see § 405.1837(b)) with respect to any matters at issue involving a question of fact or of interpretation of law, regulations, or CMS Rulings common to the providers and for which the amount in controversy is $50,000 or more in the aggregate. If a group appeal is filed, the provider seeking the appeal must be separately identified in the request for hearing, which must be prepared and filed consistently with the requirements of paragraph (a)(1) of this section.

(b) *Extension of time limit for good cause.* A request for a Board hearing filed after the time limit prescribed in paragraph (a) of this section shall be dismissed by the Board, except that for good cause shown, the time limit may be extended. However, no such extension shall be granted by the Board if such request is filed more than 3 years after the date the notice of the intermediary's determination is mailed to the provider.
[48 FR 39836, Sept. 1, 1983, as amended at 51 FR 34793, Sept. 30, 1986]

**§ 405.1842 Expediting Board proceedings.**

(a) *Basis and purpose.* This section implements section 1878(f)(1) of the Social Security Act, as amended by section 955 of Public Law 96-499 (42 U.S.C. 1395oo(f)(1)). The amendment provides an opportunity for providers to obtain expedited administrative review when the Board determines that it does not have the authority to decide a question of law, regulation, or CMS Ruling relevant to the case (see § 405.1867).

(b) *Basic rule.* (1) Except as provided in paragraph (b)(4) of this section, a provider may submit a written request to the Board, with supporting documentation, to determine whether the Board has the authority to decide a question of law, regulations, or CMS Rulings relevant to and controlling upon an issue to be reviewed by the Board. The Board is required to make an expedited review determination in writing, either denying or granting the request, within 30 days after the date of receipt of the request, as defined in paragraph (1) of this section. The Board may also issue a determination on its own motion that it lacks authority to decide a question of law, regulations, or CMS Rulings.

(2) The Board must determine that the provider (including each provider in a group appeal) is entitled to a hearing under section 1878(a) of the Act before making the determination described in paragraph (b)(1) of this section. Thus, the provider must file (or have already filed) a written request for a Board hearing that meets the requirements in § 405.1841. The information and documentation required with respect to the filing of a request for a hearing are used by the Board to determine jurisdiction under section 1878(a) of the Act.

(3) A provider's request for an expedited review determination cannot be considered to be filed with the Board, nor can the 30-day time period during which the Board is required to make an expedited review determination begin, until such time as the Board accepts jurisdiction of the case.

(4) Proceedings conducted by the Board under an authority other than section 1878(a) of the Act and §§ 405.1835 through 405.1873 of this subpart are not hearings for purposes of this section and are not subject to the expedited Board proceedings set forth in this section. For example, proceedings concerning reimbursement for capital expenditures conducted under section 1122(f) of the Act and § 405.1890 of this subpart are not hearings for purposes of this section. (Section 1122(f) specifically bars any administrative or judicial review.)

(c) *"Own motion" review.* If the Board is considering issuing a determination on its own motion that it lacks the authority to decide a question of law, regulations, or CMS Rulings, it will notify the provider and intermediary of its proposed determination and allow them a reasonable period of time to file evidence or arguments either to support or oppose the proposed determination.

(d) *Provider requests.* (1) If a provider seeks an expedited Board proceeding, it must–

(i) File its appropriately documented request in writing with the Board; and

(ii) Send a copy of the request and documentation simultaneously to the intermediary.

(2) The request to the Board for an expedited review determination must–

(i) Identify the issues and the controlling law, regulation, or CMS Ruling for which the Board is to make a determination;

(ii) Allege and demonstrate that there are no factual issues in dispute;

(iii) Contain an explanation of why the provider believes the Board cannot decide the legal issue or issues that are in dispute; and

(iv) Include all other information or details that support the request.

(3) If the information in the provider request is insufficient for the Board to determine whether it has the authority to decide an issue, the Board will request more information from the provider. Such a request will affect the 30-day

time limit as provided in paragraph (i) of this section. If the provider does not send more information or sends inadequate information, the Board will determine that it has the authority to decide the issue and will begin the regular procedure for a hearing.

(e) *Intermediary participation.* (1) After receiving a copy of the provider's request for an expedited review determination, the intermediary may send comments to the Board on the provider's request and supporting documentation. The intermediary will send a copy of its comments to the provider simultaneously.

(2) If the intermediary's comments raise questions about the provider's request for expedited review, the Board may request additional information from the provider as provided in paragraph (d)(3) of this section.

(f) *Criteria for a Board determination.* The Board will review all documentation forwarded by the provider and the intermediary relevant to the request for a Board determination concerning the Board's authority to decide an issue. In its review, the Board will consider–

(1) The controlling facts in the case;

(2) The applicability of law, regulations, or CMS rulings;

(3) Whether there are factual issues for the Board to resolve; and

(4) Whether there are legal issues within the authority of the Board to decide.

(g) *Board determination.* (1) Within 30 days after the date of receipt (as defined in paragraph (i) of this section) of a provider's request and all necessary documentation, the Board will issue a determination concerning its authority to decide the question of law, regulations, or CMS Rulings relevant to the issues identified by the provider in its request.

(2) If there are factual or legal issues in dispute on an issue within the authority of the Board to decide, the Board will not make an expedited review determination on the particular issue but will proceed with a hearing. The Board has the authority to decide when two or more issues are sufficiently related to preclude separation for purposes of an expedited review determination on one or more of them and a hearing on the other or others.

(3) The Board will promptly notify the provider in writing of its determination and will send a copy of the determination to the intermediary.

(4) The Board's determination concerning its authority or its lack of a determination is not subject to the Secretary's review under § 405.1875.

(h) *Effect of a Board decision.* (1) The Board's determination, issued on its own motion or at the request of a provider, that it lacks authority to decide a question of law, regulations, or CMS Rulings is a final decision permitting a provider to seek judicial review with respect to the matter or matters in controversy contained in the determination, within 60 days of the date of the Board's determination.

(2) After the Board has determined that it does not have the authority to decide an issue, the provider will not be granted a hearing on the same issue.

(3) If the Board fails to issue an expedited review determination within 30 days of the date of receipt of a complete request (as determined under paragraph

(i) of this section), the provider may, within 60 days from the end of that period, seek judicial review of the matters for which it requested the Board's determination.

(4) If the Board fails to make an expedited review determination within the required 30 days, it will begin regular hearing procedures as though it has the authority to decide the issue.

(5) If the provider seeks judicial review because the Board fails to make a determination as provided in paragraph (g)(1) of this section, it should notify the Board at the time it files for judicial review. The Board will not hold a hearing, even if one has been scheduled, on the matter or matters for which the provider is seeking judicial review.

(6) The Board's determination does not affect the right of the provider to a Board hearing for issues for which the provider did not request expedited review, or for which the Board determines it does have the authority to decide, or for which the Board did not make a determination and the provider did not request judicial review.

(i) *Date of receipt.* For purposes of this section, the date of receipt of the provider's request is the later of—

(1) The actual date of receipt by the Board of the information required under paragraph (d)(2) of this section, or of additional information requested by the Board under paragraph (d)(3) of this section, whichever the Board receives later; or

(2) The date indicated on the Board's written notification to the provider that the Board has accepted jurisdiction of the case.

(j) *Examples.* Below are examples showing when a provider may expect to receive an expedited review determination, in relation to various circumstances affecting its request for the determination.

(1) The provider requests a hearing and expedited review at or about the same time. If all information is complete, the Board could send notification that it has accepted jurisdiction of the case and the expedited review determination simultaneously.

(2) The provider requests both a hearing and an expedited review determination, and supplies complete information. The Board accepts jurisdiction but, for example, because of the complexity of the case, the Board makes its expedited review determination within 30 days after it has accepted jurisdiction.

(3) The provider requests both a hearing and an expedited review determination, but the request for a hearing does not contain enough information for the Board to determine jurisdiction. The Board would request more information to determine jurisdiction and would make its expedited review determination within 30 days after it has accepted jurisdiction.

(4) The provider requests both a hearing and an expedited review determination, but does not send enough information for the Board to make an expedited review determination. Assuming the Board accepts jurisdiction, the Board would request more information about the request for expedited review

and make its determination within 30 days after it receives the additional information.

(5) The provider requests an expedited review determination after the Board has accepted jurisdiction. The Board would make its determination within 30 days after receipt of an appropriately documented request for an expedited review determination.

[47 FR 31690, July 22, 1982, as amended at 48 FR 22925, May 23, 1983]

**§ 405.1843 Parties to Board hearing.**

(a) The parties to the Board hearing shall be the provider, the intermediary (including the Centers for Medicare & Medicaid Services when acting directly as intermediary) that rendered the determination being appealed (see § 405.1833), and any other entity found by the intermediary to be a related organization of such provider.

(b) Except as provided in paragraph (a), neither the Secretary nor the Centers for Medicare & Medicaid Services may be made a party to the hearing. However, the Board may call as a witness any employee or officer of the Department of Health and Human Services having personal knowledge of the facts and the issues in controversy in a hearing pending before the Board and may call as a consultant to the Board in connection with any such hearing any individual designated by the Secretary for such purpose. (See § 405.1863.)

**§ 405.1845 Composition of Board.**

(a) The Board will consist of five members appointed by the Secretary. All shall be knowledgeable in the field of cost reimbursement. At least one shall be a certified public accountant. Two Board members shall be representative of providers of services.

(b) The term of office for Board members shall be 3 years, except that initial appointments may be for such shorter terms as the Secretary may designate to permit staggered terms of office. No member shall serve more than two consecutive 3-year terms of office. The Secretary shall have the authority to terminate a Board member's term of office for good cause.

(c) One member of the Board shall be designated by the Secretary as Chairman thereof, and shall coordinate and direct the administrative activities of the Board, and shall have such other authority which may be granted to him by the Board.

(d) A quorum shall be required for the rendering of Board decisions. Three members, at least one of whom is representative of providers of services, shall be required to constitute a quorum. The Chairman of the Board, with approval of the provider, may designate one or more Board members to conduct any hearing and to prepare a recommended decision (where less than a quorum conducts the hearing). (See § 405.1869.)

[39 FR 34515, Sept. 26, 1974, as amended at 41 FR 52051, Nov. 26, 1976. Redesignated at 42 FR 52826, Sept. 30, 1977]

**§ 405.1847 Disqualification of Board members.**
No Board member shall join in the conduct of a hearing in a case in which he is prejudiced or partial with respect to any party or in which he has any interest in the matter pending for decision before him. Notice of any objection which a party may have with respect to a Board member shall be presented in writing to such Board member by the objecting party at its earliest opportunity. The Board member shall consider the objection and shall, in his discretion, either proceed to join in the conduct of the hearing or withdraw. If he does not withdraw, the objecting party may petition the Board, presenting its objection and reasons therefore, and be entitled to a ruling thereon before the hearing can proceed.

**§ 405.1849 Establishment of time and place of hearing by the Board.**
The Board shall fix the time and place for the hearing and shall mail written notice thereof to the parties at their last known addresses, not less than 30 days prior to the scheduled time. Either on its own motion or for good cause shown by a party, the Board may, as appropriate, reschedule, adjourn, postpone, or reopen the hearing, provided that reasonable written notice is given to the parties.

**§ 405.1851 Conduct of Board hearing.**
The Board hearing shall be open to the parties, to representatives of the Centers for Medicare & Medicaid Services, and to such other persons as the Board deems necessary and proper. The Board shall inquire fully into all of the matters at issue and shall receive into evidence the testimony of witnesses and any documents which are relevant and material to such matters. If the Board believes that there is relevant and material evidence available which has not been presented at the hearing, it may at any time prior to the mailing of notice of the decision, reconvene the hearing for the receipt of such evidence. The order in which the evidence and the allegations shall be presented and the conduct of the hearing shall be at the discretion of the Board.

**§ 405.1853 Prehearing discovery and other proceedings prior to the Board hearing.**

(a) Upon notification that a request for Board hearing has been filed, the intermediary shall forthwith review the materials submitted by the provider in accordance with § 405.1841. Simultaneously, the intermediary shall review the information which formed the basis for its determination of the amount of program reimbursement. Based on the findings of such review, the intermediary shall expeditiously attempt to join with the provider in written stipulations setting forth the issues that said review has resolved and designating the issues that remain for Board resolution. Having obtained such stipulations and being satisfied that no further agreements can be negotiated, the intermediary shall ensure that all available documentary evidence in support of each party's position is part of the record. Such evidence will ordinarily include a position paper from the provider, a position paper from the intermediary, and any documents which support the issues addressed in the stipulations. These materials, in addition to all relevant documents which formed the basis for its determination of the amount of program reimbursement, shall be forwarded to the Board within 60 days after the date of the provider's request for Board review.

(b) Prehearing discovery shall be permitted upon timely request of a party. To be timely, a request for discovery and inspection shall be made before the beginning of the hearing. A reasonable time for inspection and reproduction of documents shall be provided by order of the Board. The Board's order on all discovery matters shall be final.

(c) If, in the discretion of the Board, the purpose of defining the issues more clearly would be served, the Board may schedule a prehearing conference. For this purpose, a single member of the Board may be appointed to act for the Board with respect to prehearing activities.

**§ 405.1855 Evidence at Board hearing.**
Evidence may be received at the Board hearing even though inadmissible under the rules of evidence applicable to court procedure. The Board shall give the parties opportunity for submission and consideration of facts and arguments and during the course of the hearing should, in ruling upon admissibility of evidence, exclude irrelevant, immaterial, or unduly repetitious evidence. The Board shall render a final ruling on the admissibility of evidence.

**§ 405.1857 Subpoenas.**
When reasonably necessary for the full presentation of a case, the Board may, either upon its own motion or upon the request of a party, issue subpoenas for the attendance and testimony of witnesses and for the production of books, records, correspondence, papers, or other documents which are relevant and material to any matter in issue at the hearing. Parties who desire the issuance of a subpoena shall, not less than 10 days prior to the time fixed for the hearing, file with the Board a written request therefore, designating the witnesses or documents to be produced, and describing the address, or location thereof with sufficient particularity to permit such witnesses or documents to be found. The request for a subpoena shall state the pertinent facts which the party expects to establish by such witnesses or documents and whether such facts could be established by other evidence without the use of a subpoena. Subpoenas, as provided for above, shall be issued in the name of the Board, and the Centers for Medicare & Medicaid Services shall assume the cost of the issuance and the fees and mileage of any witness so subpoenaed, as provided in section 205(d) of the Act, 42 U.S.C. 405(d).

**§ 405.1859 Witnesses.**
Witnesses at the hearing shall testify under oath or affirmation, unless excused by the Board for cause. The Board may examine the witnesses and shall allow the parties or their representatives to do so. Parties to the proceeding may also cross-examine witnesses.

**§ 405.1861 Oral argument and written allegations.**
The parties, upon their request, shall be allowed a reasonable time for the presentation of oral argument or for the filing of briefs or other written statements of allegations as to facts or law. Copies of any brief or other written statement shall be filed in sufficient number that they may be made available to all parties and to the Centers for Medicare & Medicaid Services.

**§ 405.1863 Administrative policy at issue.**
Where a party to the Board hearing puts into issue an administrative policy which is interpretative of the law or regulations, the Board will promptly notify to the Centers for Medicare & Medicaid Services.

**§ 405.1865 Record of Board hearing.**
A complete record of the proceedings at the hearing shall be made and transcribed in all cases. It shall be made available to the parties upon request. The record will not be closed until a decision has been issued.

**§ 405.1867 Sources of Board's authority.**
In exercising its authority to conduct the hearings described herein, the Board must comply with all the provisions of title XVIII of the Act and regulations issued thereunder, as well as CMS Rulings issued under the authority of the Administrator of the Centers for Medicare & Medicaid Services (see § 401.108 of this subchapter). The Board shall afford great weight to interpretive rules, general statements of policy, and rules of agency organization, procedure, or practice established by CMS.
[48 FR 22925, May 23, 1983]

**§ 405.1869 Scope of Board's decision-making authority.**
The Board shall have the power to affirm, modify, or reverse a determination of an intermediary with respect to a cost report and to make any other modifications on matters covered by such cost report (including modifications adverse to the provider or other parties) even though such matters were not considered in the intermediary's determination. The opinion of the majority of those Board members deciding the case will constitute the Board's decision.

**§ 405.1871 Board hearing decision and notice.**

(a) The Board shall, as soon as practicable after the conclusion of its hearing, render a written decision based upon the record made at such hearing, the record established in support of the determination of the intermediary (see § 405.1803), and such other evidence as may be obtained or received by the Board. Such Board decision shall be supported by substantial evidence when the record of the Board hearing is viewed as a whole and shall cite applicable law, regulations, and CMS Rulings. A copy of the decision shall be mailed to all parties to the hearing at their last known addresses and, at the same time, to the Administrator and CMS.

(b) The decision of the Board provided for in paragraph (a) of this section shall be final and binding upon all parties to the hearing before the Board unless it is reviewed by the Secretary in accordance with § 405.1875, or revised in accordance with § 405.1885.

[39 FR 34515, Sept. 26, 1974, as amended at 41 FR 52051, Nov. 26, 1976. Redesignated at 42 FR 52826, Sept. 30, 1977, as amended at 48 FR 45773, Oct. 7, 1983]

**§ 405.1873 Board's jurisdiction.**

(a) *Board decides jurisdiction.* The Board decides questions relating to its jurisdiction to grant a hearing, including (1) the timeliness of an intermediary determination (see § 405.1835(c)), and (2) the right of a provider to a hearing before the Board when the amount in controversy is in issue (see §§ 405.1835(a)(3) and 405.1837).

(b) *Matters not subject to board review.* (1) The determination of a fiscal intermediary that no payment may be made under title XVIII of the Act for any expenses incurred for items and services furnished to an individual because such items and services are excluded from coverage pursuant to section 1862 of the Act, 42 U.S.C. 1395y (see subpart C of this part), may not be reviewed by the Board. (Such determination shall be reviewed only in accordance with the applicable provisions of subpart G or H of this part.)

(2) The Board may not review certain matters affecting payments to hospitals under the prospective payment system as provided in § 405.1804.

[48 FR 39836, Sept. 1, 1983]

**§ 405.1875 Administrator's review.**

(a) *General rule.* (1) Except for a Board determination under § 405.1842 that it lacks the authority to decide an issue, the Administrator, at his or her discretion, may review any final decision of the Board, including a decision under § 405.1873 about the Board's jurisdiction to grant a hearing. The Administrator may exercise this discretion on his or her own motion, in response to a request from a party to a Board hearing or in response to a request from CMS.

(2) The Office of the Attorney Advisory will examine the Board's decisions, the requests made by a party or CMS and any submission made in accordance with the provisions of this section in order to assist the Administrator in deciding whether to exercise this review authority.

(b) *Request for review.* A party or CMS requesting the Administrator to review a Board decision must file a written request with the Administrator within 15 days of the receipt of the Board decision.

(c) *Criteria for deciding whether to review.* In deciding whether to review a Board decision, either on his or her own motion or in response to a request from a party to the hearing or CMS, the Administrator will normally consider whether it appears that:

(1) The Board made an erroneous interpretation of law, regulation, or CMS Ruling;

(2) The Board's decision is not supported by substantial evidence; or

(3) The case presents a significant policy issue having a basis in law and regulations, and review is likely to lead to the issuance of a CMS Ruling or other directive needed to clarify a statutory or regulatory provision;

(4) The Board has incorrectly assumed or denied jurisdiction or extended its authority to a degree not provided for by statute, regulation, or CMS Ruling; and

(5) The decision of the Board requires clarification, amplification, or an alternative legal basis for the decision.

(d) *Decision to review.* (1) Whether or not a party or CMS has requested review, the Administrator will promptly notify the parties and CMS whether he or she has decided to review a decision of the Board and, if so, will indicate the particular issues he or she will consider.

(2) The Administrator may decline to review a case or any issue in a case even if a party has filed a written request for review under paragraph (b) of this section.

(e) *Written submissions.* (1) Within 15 days of receipt of a notice that the Administrator has decided to review a Board decision, a party or CMS may submit to the Administrator, in writing:

(i) Proposed findings and conclusions;

(ii) Supporting views or exceptions to the Board decision;

(iii) Supporting reasons for the exceptions and proposed findings; and

(iv) A rebuttal of the other party's request for review or other submissions already filed with the Administrator.

(2) These submissions shall be limited to issues the Administrator has decided to review and confined to the record of the Board hearing.

(3) A party or CMS, within 15 days of receipt of a notice that the Administrator has decided to review a decision, may also request that the decision be remanded and state reasons for doing so. Reasons for a request to remand may include new, substantial evidence concerning—

(i) Issues presented to the Board; and

(ii) New issues that have arisen since the case was presented to the Board.

(4) A copy of any written submission made under this paragraph shall be sent simultaneously to each other party to the Board hearing and to CMS, if CMS has previously—

(i) Requested that the Administrator review a Board decision or filed a written submission in response to a party's request for review.

(ii) Responded to a party's request for review; or

(iii) Submitted material after the Administrator has announced that he or she will review a Board decision.

(f) *Ex parte communications prohibited.* All communications from any of the parties or CMS about a Board decision being reviewed by the Administrator must be in writing and must contain a certification that copies have been served on the parties and CMS, as appropriate. The Administrator will not consider any communication that does not meet these requirements or is not submitted within the required time limits.

(g) *Administrator's decision.* (1) If the Administrator has notified the parties and CMS that he or she has decided to review a Board decision, the Administrator will affirm, reverse, modify, or remand the case.

(2) The Administrator will make this decision within 60 days after the provider received notification of the Board decision and will promptly mail a copy of the decision to each party and to CMS.

(3) Any decision other than to remand will be confined to—

(i) The record of the Board, as forwarded by the Board;

(ii) Any materials submitted under paragraphs (b) or (e) of this section; and

(iii) Generally known facts that are not subject to reasonable dispute.

(4) The Administrator may rely on prior decisions of the Board, the Administrator and the courts, and other applicable law, whether or not cited by the parties and CMS.

(h) *Remand.* (1) A remand to the Board by the Administrator vacates the Board's decision.

(2) The Administrator may direct the Board to take further action with respect to the development of additional facts or new issues, or to consider the applicability of laws or regulations other than those considered by the Board. The following are not acceptable bases for remand—

(i) Presentation of evidence existing at the time of the Board hearing that was known or reasonably could have been known;

(ii) Introduction of a favorable court case that was either not available in print at the time of the Board hearing or was decided after the Board hearing;

(iii) Change of a party's representation before the Board;

(iv) Presentation of an alternative legal basis concerning an issue in dispute; or

(v) Attempted retraction of a waiver of a right made before or at the Board hearing.

(3) After remand, the Board will take the action requested in the remand action and issue a new decision.

(4) The new decision will be final unless the Administrator reverses, affirms, modifies, or again remands the decision in accordance with the provisions of the section.

[48 FR 45773, Oct. 7, 1983]

**§ 405.1877 Judicial review.**

(a) *General rule.* Section 1878(f) of the Act permits a provider to obtain judicial review of a final decision of the Board, or of a reversal, affirmation, or modification by the Administrator of a Board decision, by filing a civil action pursuant to the Federal Rules of Civil Procedure within 60 days of the date on which the provider received notice of—

(1) A final decision by the Board; or

(2) Any reversal, affirmance, or modification by the Administrator.

The Board's decision is not final if the Administrator reverses, affirms, or modifies the decision within 60 days of the date on which the provider received notice of the decision.

(b) *Administrator declines to review a Board decision.* If the Administrator declines to review a Board decision, the provider must file its appeal within 60 days of receipt of the decision of the Board.

(c) *Administrator does not act after reviewing a Board decision.* If the Administrator notifies the parties that he or she has decided to review a Board decision and then does not make a decision within the 60 days allotted for his or her review, this subsequent inaction constitutes an affirmance allowing a provider an additional 60 days in which to file for judicial review, beginning with the date the Administrator's time expires for taking action under § 405.1875(g)(2).

(d) *Matters not subject to judicial review.* Certain matters affecting payments to hospital under the prospective payment system are not subject to judicial review, as provided in section 1886(d)(7) of the Act and § 405.1804.

(e) *Group appeals.* Any action under this section by providers that are under common ownership or control (see § 413.17 of this chapter) must be brought by the providers as a group with respect to any matter involving an issue common to the providers.

(f) *Venue for appeals.* An action for judicial review must be brought in the District Court of the United States for the judicial district in which the provider is located (or, effective April 20, 1983, in an action brought jointly by several providers, the judicial district in which the greatest number of such providers are located) or in the District Court for the District of Columbia. Effective April 20, 1983, any action for judicial review by providers under common ownership or control (§ 413.17 of this chapter), must be brought by such providers as a group with respect to any matter involving an issue common to the providers.

(g) *Service of process.* Process must be served as described under 45 CFR part 4. [48 FR 39836, Sept. 1, 1983, as amended at 48 FR 45774, Oct. 7, 1983; 51 FR 34793, Sept. 30, 1986]

**§ 405.1881 Appointment of representative.**

A provider or other party may be represented by legal counsel or any other person it appoints to act as its representative at the proceedings, conducted in accordance with §§ 405.1819 and 405.1851.

**§ 405.1883 Authority of representative.**

A representative appointed by a provider or other party may accept or give on behalf of the provider or other party any request or notice relative to any proceeding before a hearing officer or the Board. A representative shall be entitled to present evidence and allegations as to facts and law in any proceeding affecting the party he represents and to obtain information with respect to a request for an intermediary hearing or a Board hearing made in accordance with §§ 405.1811, 405.1835, or 405.1837 to the same extent as the party he represents. Notice to a provider or other party of any action, determination, or decision, or a request for the production of evidence by a hearing officer or the Board sent to the representative of the provider or other party shall have the same force and effect as if it had been sent to the provider or other party.

**§ 405.1885 Reopening a determination or decision.**

(a) A determination of an intermediary, a decision by a hearing officer or panel of hearing officers, a decision by the Board, or a decision of the Secretary may be reopened with respect to findings on matters at issue in such determination or decision, by such intermediary officer or panel of hearing officers, Board, or Secretary, as the case may be, either on motion of such intermediary officer or panel of hearing officers, Board, or Secretary, or on the motion of the provider affected by such determination or decision to revise any matter in issue at any such proceedings. Any such request to reopen must be made within 3 years of the date of the notice of the intermediary or Board hearing decision, or where there has been no such decision, any such request to reopen must be made within 3 years of the date of notice of the intermediary determination. No such determination or decision may be reopened after such 3-year period except as provided in paragraphs (d) and (e) of this section.

(b)(1) An intermediary determination or an intermediary hearing decision must be reopened and revised by the intermediary if, within the 3-year period specified in paragraph (a) of this section, CMS—

(i) Provides notice to the intermediary that the intermediary determination or the intermediary hearing decision is inconsistent with the applicable law, regulations, CMS ruling, or CMS general instructions in effect, and as CMS understood those legal provisions, at the time the determination or decision was rendered by the intermediary; and

(ii) Explicitly directs the intermediary to reopen and revise the intermediary determination or the intermediary hearing decision.

(2) A change of legal interpretation or policy by CMS in a regulation, CMS ruling, or CMS general instruction, whether made in response to judicial precedent or otherwise, is not a basis for reopening an intermediary determination or an intermediary hearing decision under this section.

(3) Notwithstanding paragraph (b)(1)(i) of this section, CMS may direct the intermediary to reopen a particular intermediary determination or intermediary hearing decision in order to implement, for the same intermediary determination or intermediary decision—

(i) A final agency decision under §§ 405.1833, 405.1871(b), 405.1875, or 405.1877(a) of this part;

(ii) A final nonappealable court judgment; or

(iii) An agreement to settle an administrative appeal or a lawsuit.

(c) Jurisdiction for reopening a determination or decision rests exclusively with that administrative body that rendered the last determination or decision.

(d) Notwithstanding the provisions of paragraph (a) of this section, an intermediary determination or hearing decision, a decision of the Board, or a decision of the Secretary shall be reopened and revised at any time if it is established that such determination or decision was procured by fraud or similar fault of any party to the determination or decision.

(e) Notwithstanding an intermediary's discretion to reopen or not reopen an intermediary determination or an intermediary hearing decision under paragraphs (a) and (c) of this section, CMS may direct an intermediary to reopen, or not to reopen, an intermediary determination or an intermediary hearing decision in accordance with paragraphs (a) and (c) of this section.

(f) Paragraphs (a) and (b) of this section apply to determinations on cost reporting periods ending on or after December 31, 1971. (See § 405.1801(c).) However, the 3-year period described shall also apply to determinations with respect to cost reporting periods ending prior to December 31, 1971, but only if the reopening action was undertaken after May 27, 1972 (the effective date of regulations which, prior to the publication of this subpart R, governed the reopening of such determinations).

[39 FR 34515, Sept. 26, 1974. Redesignated at 42 FR 52826, Sept. 30, 1977, and amended at 50110, Aug. 1, 2002]

**§ 405.1887 Notice of reopening.**

(a) All parties to any reopening described above shall be given written notice of the reopening. When such reopening results in any revision in the prior decision notice of said revision or revisions will be mailed to the parties with a complete explanation of the basis for the revision or revisions. Notices of reopenings by the Board shall also be sent to the Secretary.

(b) In any such reopening, the parties to the prior decision shall be allowed a reasonable period of time in which to present any additional evidence or argument in support of their position.

**§ 405.1889 Effect of a revision.**

Where a revision is made in a determination or decision on the amount of program reimbursement after such determination or decision has been reopened as provided in § 405.1885, such revision shall be considered a separate and distinct determination or decision to which the provisions of §§ 405.1811, 405.1835, 405.1875, and 405.1877 are applicable. (See § 405.1801(c) for applicable effective dates.)

## PART 408—PREMIUMS FOR SUPPLEMENTARY MEDICAL INSURANCE

### Subpart F—Termination and Reinstatement of Coverage

**§ 408.100 Termination of coverage for nonpayment of premiums.**

(a) *Effective date of termination.* Termination is effective on the last day of the grace period. The determination is not made until 15 days after that day to allow for processing of remittances mailed late in the grace period, as provided in § 408.68.

(b) *Notice of termination.* (1) SSA sends the enrollee notice of termination between 15 and 30 days after the end of the grace period and includes information regarding the enrollee's right of appeal.

(2) CMS notifies any intermediary or carrier that had previously been informed that the enrollee had met the SMI deductible for the year in which the termination is effective.

**§ 408.102 Reconsideration of termination.**

(a) *Basic rules.* Coverage may be reinstated without interruption of benefits if the following conditions are met:

(1) The enrollee appeals the termination by the end of the month following the month in which SSA sent the notice of termination.

(2) The enrollee alleges and it is found that the enrollee did not receive timely and adequate notice that the premiums were overdue.

(3) The enrollee pays, within 30 days after SSA's subsequent request for payment, all premiums due through the month in which he or she appealed the termination.

(b) *Basis for reinstating coverage.* Coverage may be reinstated if the evidence establishes one of the following:

(1) The enrollee acted diligently to pay the premiums or to request relief upon receiving a premium notice very late in the grace period or shortly after its end, and the delayed notice was not the enrollee's fault. (For example, if the billing notice was misaddressed or lost in the mail, it would not be the enrollee's fault; if the enrollee had moved and not notified SSA of the new address, he or she would be responsible for the delay.)

(2) On the basis of information given by SSA, the enrollee could reasonably have believed that the premiums were being paid by deduction from benefits or by some other means. (An example would be a notice indicating that premiums would be paid by a State Medicaid agency or a group payer or would be deducted from the spouse's civil service annuity.)

(c) *No basis for reinstating coverage.* Coverage may not be reinstated if the enrollee–

(1) Received timely and adequate notice but failed to pay within the grace period, for example because of insufficient income or resources; or

(2) Appealed the termination more than 1 month after the month in which SSA sent the termination notice.

**§ 408.104 Reinstatement procedures.**

(a) *Request for payment.* If the conditions of § 408.102(a)(1) and (2) are met, SSA sends written notice requesting the enrollee to pay, within 30 days, all premiums due through the month in which the enrollee appealed the termination.

(b) *Reinstatement of coverage.* If SSA receives the requested payment within 30 days, it sets aside the termination and reinstates the enrollee's coverage without interruption.

## PART 411—EXCLUSIONS FROM MEDICARE AND LIMITATIONS ON MEDICARE PAYMENT

### Subpart E—Limitations on Payment for Services Covered under Group Health Plans: General Provisions

**Source:** 60 FR 45362, Aug. 31, 1995, unless otherwise noted.

**§ 411.100 Basis and scope.**

(a) *Statutory basis.* (1) Section 1862(b) of the Act provides in part that Medicare is secondary payer, under specified conditions, for services covered under any of the following:

(i) Group health plans of employers that employ at least 20 employees and that cover Medicare beneficiaries age 65 or older who are covered under the plan by virtue of the individual's current employment status with an employer or the current employment status of a spouse of any age. (Section 1862(b)(1)(A))

(ii) Group health plans (without regard to the number of individuals employed and irrespective of current employment status) that cover individuals who have ESRD. Except as provided in § 411.163, group health plans are always primary payers throughout the first 18 months of ESRD-based Medicare eligibility or entitlement. (Section 1862(b)(1)(C))

(iii) Large group health plans (that is, plans of employers that employ at least 100 employees) and that cover Medicare beneficiaries who are under age 65, entitled to Medicare on the basis of disability, and covered under the plan by virtue of the individual's or a family member's current employment status with an employer. (Section 1862(b)(1)(B))

(2) Sections 1862(b)(1)(A), (B), and (C) of the Act provide that group health plans and large group health plans may not take into account that the individuals described in paragraph (a)(1) of this section are entitled to Medicare on the basis of age or disability, or eligible for, or entitled to Medicare on the basis of ESRD.

(3) Section 1862(b)(1)(A)(i)(II) of the Act provides that group health plans of employers of 20 or more employees must provide to any employee or spouse age 65 or older the same benefits, under the same conditions, that it provides to employees and spouses under 65. The requirement applies regardless of whether the individual or spouse 65 or older is entitled to Medicare.

(4) Section 1862(b)(1)(C)(ii) of the Act provides that group health plans may not differentiate in the benefits they provide between individuals who have ESRD and other individuals covered under the plan on the basis of the existence of ESRD, the need for renal dialysis, or in any other manner. Actions that constitute "differentiating"are listed in § 411.161(b).

(b) *Scope.* This subpart sets forth general rules pertinent to—

(1) Medicare payment for services that are covered under a group health plan and are furnished to certain beneficiaries who are entitled on the basis of ESRD, age, or disability.

(2) The prohibition against taking into account Medicare entitlement based on age or disability, or Medicare eligibility or entitlement based on ESRD.

(3) The prohibition against differentiation in benefits between individuals who have ESRD and other individuals covered under the plan.

(4) The requirement to provide to those 65 or over the same benefits under the same conditions as are provided to those under 65.

(5) The appeals procedures for group health plans that CMS determines are nonconforming plans.

**§ 411.120 Appeals.**

(a) *Parties to the determination.* The parties to the determination are CMS, the GHP or LGHP for which CMS determined nonconformance, and any employers or employee organizations that contributed to the plan during the calendar year for which CMS determined nonconformance.

(b) *Request for hearing.* (1) A party's request for hearing must be in writing (not in facsimile or other electronic medium) and in the manner stipulated in the notice of nonconformance; it must be filed within 65 days from the date on the notice.

(2) The request may include rationale showing why the parties believe that CMS's determination is incorrect and supporting documentation.

(3) A request is considered filed on the date it is received by the appropriate office, as shown by the receipt date stamped on the request.

**§ 411.121 Hearing procedures.**

(a) *Nature of hearing.* (1) If any of the parties requests a hearing within 65 days from the date on the notice of the determination of nonconformance, the CMS Administrator appoints a hearing officer.

(2) If no party files a request within the 65-day period, the initial determination of nonconformance is binding upon all parties unless it is reopened in accordance with § 411.126.

(3) If more than one party requests a hearing, the hearing officer conducts a single hearing in which all parties may participate.

(4) *On the record review.* Ordinarily, the hearing officer makes a decision based upon review of the data and documents on which CMS based its determination of nonconformance and any other documentation submitted by any of the parties within 65 days from the date on the notice.

(5) *Oral hearing.* The hearing officer may provide for an oral hearing either on his or her own motion or in response to a party's request if the party demonstrates to the hearing officer's satisfaction that an oral hearing is necessary. Within 30 days of receipt of the request, the hearing officer gives all known parties written notice of the request and whether the request for oral hearing is granted.

(b) *Notice of time and place of oral hearing.* If the hearing officer provides an oral hearing, he or she gives all known parties written notice of the time and place of the hearing at least 30 days before the scheduled date.

(c) *Prehearing discovery.* (1) The hearing officer may permit prehearing discovery if it is requested by a party at least 10 days before the scheduled date of the hearing.

(2) If the hearing officer approves the request, he or she—

(i) Provides a reasonable time for inspection and reproduction of documents; and

(ii) In ruling on discovery matters, is guided by the Federal Rules of Civil Procedure. (28 U.S.C.A. Rules 26-37)

(3) The hearing officer's orders on all discovery matters are final.

(d) *Conduct of hearing.* The hearing officer determines the conduct of the hearing, including the order in which the evidence and the allegations are presented.

(e) *Evidence at hearing.* (1) The hearing officer inquires into the matters at issue and may receive from all parties documentary and other evidence that is pertinent and material, including the testimony of witnesses, and evidence that would be inadmissible in a court of law.

(2) Evidence may be received at any time before the conclusion of the hearing.

(3) The hearing officer gives the parties opportunity for submission and consideration of evidence and arguments and, in ruling on the admissibility of evidence, excludes irrelevant, immaterial, or unduly repetitious evidence.

(4) The hearing officer's ruling on admissibility of evidence is final and not subject to further review.

(f) *Subpoenas.* (1) The hearing officer may, either on his or her own motion or upon the request of any party, issue subpoenas for either or both of the following if they are reasonably necessary for full presentation of the case:

(i) The attendance and testimony of witnesses.

(ii) The production of books, records, correspondence, papers, or other documents that are relevant and material to any matter at issue.

(2) A party that wishes the issuance of a subpoena must, at least 10 days before the date fixed for the hearing, file with the hearing officer a written request that identifies the witnesses or documents to be produced and describes the address or location in sufficient detail to permit the witnesses or documents to be found.

(3) The request for a subpoena must state the pertinent facts that the party expects to establish by the witnesses or documents and whether those facts could be established by other evidence without the use of a subpoena.

(4) The hearing officer issues the subpoenas at his or her discretion, and CMS assumes the cost of the issuance and the fees and mileage of any subpoenaed witness, in accordance with section 205(d) of the Act (42 U.S.C. 405(d)).

(g) *Witnesses.* Witnesses at the hearing testify under oath or affirmation, unless excused by the hearing officer for cause. The hearing officer may examine the witnesses and shall allow the parties to examine and cross-examine witnesses.

(h) *Record of hearing.* A complete record of the proceedings at the hearing is made and transcribed in all cases. It is made available to the parties upon request. The record is not closed until a decision has been issued.

(i) *Sources of hearing officer's authority.* In the conduct of the hearing, the hearing officer complies with all the provisions of title XVIII of the Act and implementing regulations, as well as with CMS Rulings issued under § 401.108 of this chapter. The hearing officer gives great weight to interpretive rules, general statements of policy, and rules of agency organization, procedure, or practice established by CMS.

**§ 411.122 Hearing officer's decision.**

(a) *Timing.* (1) If the decision is based on a review of the record, the hearing officer mails the decision to all known parties within 120 days from the date of receipt of the request for hearing.

(2) If the decision is based on an oral hearing, the hearing officer mails the decision to all known parties within 120 days from the conclusion of the hearing.

(b) *Basis, content, and distribution of hearing decision.* (1) The written decision is based on substantial evidence and contains findings of fact, a statement of reasons, and conclusions of law.

(2) The hearing officer mails a copy of the decision to each of the parties, by certified mail, return receipt requested, and includes a notice that the administrator may review the hearing decision at the request of a party or on his or her own motion.

(c) *Effect of hearing decision.* The hearing officer's decision is the final Departmental decision and is binding upon all parties unless the Administrator chooses to review that decision in accordance with § 411.124 or it is reopened by the hearing officer in accordance with § 411.126.

**§ 411.124 Administrator's review of hearing decision.**

(a) *Request for review.* A party's request for review of a hearing officer's decision must be in writing (not in facsimile or other electronic medium) and must be received by the Administrator within 25 days from the date on the decision.

(b) *Office of the Attorney Advisor responsibility.* The Office of the Attorney Advisor examines the hearing officer's decision, the requests made by any of the parties or CMS, and any submission made in accordance with the provisions of this section in order to assist the Administrator in deciding whether to review the decision.

(c) *Administrator's discretion.* The Administrator may–

(1) Review or decline to review the hearing officer's decision;

(2) Exercise this discretion on his or her own motion or in response to a request from any of the parties; and

(3) Delegate review responsibility to the Deputy Administrator. (As used in this section, the term "Administrator" includes "Deputy Administrator" if review responsibility has been delegated.)

(d) *Basis for decision to review.* In deciding whether to review a hearing officer's decision, the Administrator considers–

(1) Whether the decision–

(i) Is based on a correct interpretation of law, regulation, or CMS Ruling;

(ii) Is supported by substantial evidence;

(iii) Presents a significant policy issue having a basis in law and regulations;

(iv) Requires clarification, amplification, or an alternative legal basis for the decision; and

(v) Is within the authority provided by statute, regulation, or CMS Ruling; and

(2) Whether review may lead to the issuance of a CMS Ruling or other directive needed to clarify a statute or regulation.

(e) *Notice of decision to review or not to review.* (1) The Administrator gives all parties prompt written notice of his or her decision to review or not to review.

(2) The notice of a decision to review identifies the specific issues the Administrator will consider.

(f) *Response to notice of decision to review.* (1) Within 20 days from the date on a notice of the Administrator's decision to review a hearing officer's decision, any of the parties may file with the Administrator any or all of the following:

(i) Proposed findings and conclusions.

(ii) Supporting views or exceptions to the hearing officer's decision.

(iii) Supporting reasons for the proposed findings and exceptions.

(iv) A rebuttal to another party's request for review or to other submissions already filed with the Administrator.

(2) The submissions must be limited to the issues the Administrator has decided to review and confined to the record established by the hearing officer.

(3) All communications from the parties concerning a hearing officer's decision being reviewed by the Administrator must be in writing (not in facsimile or other electronic medium) and must include a certification that copies have been sent to all other parties.

(4) The Administrator does not consider any communication that does not meet the requirements of this paragraph.

(g) *Administrator's review decision.* (1) The Administrator bases his or her decision on the following:

(i) The entire record developed by the hearing officer.

(ii) Any materials submitted in connection with the hearing or under paragraph (f) of this section.

(iii) Generally known facts not subject to reasonable dispute.

(2) The Administrator mails copies of the review decision to all parties within 120 days from the date of the hearing officer's decision.

(3) The Administrator's review decision may affirm, reverse, or modify the hearing decision or may remand the case to the hearing officer.

(h) *Basis and effect of remand*—(1) *Basis.* The bases for remand do not include the following:

(i) Evidence that existed at the time of the hearing and that was known or could reasonably have been expected to be known.

(ii) A court case that was either not available at the time of the hearing or was decided after the hearing.

(iii) Change of the parties' representation.

(iv) An alternative legal basis for an issue in dispute.

(2) *Effect of remand.* (i) The Administrator may instruct the hearing officer to take further action with respect to the development of additional facts or new issues or to consider the applicability of laws or regulations other than those considered during the hearing.

(ii) The hearing officer takes the action in accordance with the Administrator's instructions in the remand notice and again issues a decision.

(iii) The Administrator may review or decline to review the hearing officer's remand decision in accordance with the procedures set forth in this section.

(i) *Finality of decision.* The Administrator's review decision, or the hearing officer's decision following remand, is the final Departmental decision and is binding on all parties unless the Administrator chooses to review the decision in accordance with this section, or the decision is reopened in accordance with § 411.126.

**§ 411.126 Reopening of determinations and decisions.**

(a) A determination that a GHP or LGHP is a nonconforming GHP or the decision or revised decision of a hearing officer or of the CMS Administrator may be reopened within 12 months from the date on the notice of determination or decision or revised decision, for any reason by the entity that issued the determination or decision.

(b) The decision to reopen or not to reopen is not appealable.

**§ 411.130 Referral to Internal Revenue Service (IRS).**

(a) *CMS responsibility.* After CMS determines that a plan has been a nonconforming GHP in a particular year, it refers its determination to the IRS, but only after the parties have exhausted all CMS appeal rights with respect to the determination.

(b) *IRS responsibility.* The IRS administers section 5000 of the Internal Revenue Code (IRC), which imposes a tax on employers (other than governmental entities) and employee organizations that contribute to a nonconforming GHP. The tax is equal to 25 percent of the employer's or employee organization's expenses, incurred during the calendar year in which the plan is a nonconforming GHP, for each GHP, both conforming and nonconforming, to which the employer or employee organization contributes.

**Subpart L—The Medicare Geographic Classification Review Board**

**Source:** 55 FR 36766, Sept. 6, 1990, unless otherwise noted.

**Criteria and Conditions for Redesignation**

**§ 412.230 Criteria for an individual hospital seeking redesignation to another rural area or an urban area.**

(a) *General*—(1) *Purposes.* Except as specified in paragraph (a) (5)—

(i) For fiscal years prior to fiscal year 2005, an individual hospital may be redesignated from a rural area to an urban area, from a rural area to another rural area, or from an urban area to another urban area for the purposes of using the other area's standardized amount for inpatient operating costs, the wage index value, or both.

(ii) Effective for fiscal year 2005 and subsequent fiscal years, an individual hospital may be redesignated from an urban area to another urban area, from a rural area to another rural area, or from a rural area to another urban area for the purposes of using the other area's wage index value.

(2) *Proximity.* Except as provided in paragraph (a)(3) of this section, to be redesignated to another rural area or an urban area, a hospital must demonstrate a close proximity to the area to which it seeks redesignation by meeting the criteria in paragraph (b) of this section, and submitting data requested under paragraph (c) of this section.

(3) *Special rules for sole community hospitals and rural referral centers.* To be redesignated under the special rules in this paragraph, a hospital must be a sole community hospital or a rural referral center as of the date of the MGCRB's review.

(i) A hospital that is a rural referral center, a sole community hospital, or both does not have to demonstrate a close proximity to the area to which it seeks redesignation.

(ii) If a hospital that is a rural referral center, a sole community hospital, or both qualifies for urban redesignation, it is redesignated to the urban area that is closest to the hospital. If the hospital is closer to another rural area than to any urban area, it may seek redesignation to either the closest rural or the closest urban area.

(iii) If a sole community hospital or rural referral center loses its special status as a result of redesignation, the hospital is considered to retain its special status for the purpose of applicability of the special rules in paragraph (a)(3) of this section.

(iv) A hospital that is redesignated under paragraph (a)(3) of this section may not be redesignated in the same fiscal year under paragraph (a)(2) of this section.

(4) *Application of criteria.* In applying the numeric criteria contained in paragraphs (b)(1), (b)(2), (d)(1)(iii), (d)(1)(iv)(A), and (d)(1)(iv)(B) of this section, rounding of numbers to meet the mileage or qualifying percentage standards is not permitted.

(5) *Limitations on redesignation.* The following limitations apply to redesignation:

(i) An individual hospital may not be redesignated to another area for purposes of the wage index if the pre-reclassified average hourly wage for that area is lower than the pre-reclassified average hourly wage for the area in which the hospital is located.

(ii) A hospital may not be redesignated to more than one area.

(iii) An urban hospital that has been granted redesignation as rural under § 412.103 cannot receive an additional reclassification by the MGCRB based on this acquired rural status for a year in which such redesignation is in effect.

(iv) Beginning with wage index reclassification applications for FY 2003, if a hospital is already reclassified to a given geographic area for wage index purposes for a 3-year period, and submits an application for reclassification to the same area for either the second or third year of the 3-year period, that application will not be approved.

(b) *Proximity criteria.* A hospital demonstrates a close proximity with the area to which it seeks redesignation if one of the following conditions applies:

(1) The distance from the hospital to the area is no more than 15 miles for an urban hospital and no more than 35 miles for a rural hospital.

(2) At least 50 percent of the hospital's employees reside in the area.

(c) *Appropriate proximity data.* For redesignation to an area, the hospital must submit appropriate data relating to its proximity to that area.

(1) To demonstrate proximity to the area, the hospital must submit evidence of the shortest route over improved roads to the area and the distance of that route.

(2) For employee address data, the hospital must submit current payroll records that include information that establishes the home addresses by zip code of its employees.

(d) *Use of urban or other rural area's wage index*—(1) *Criteria for use of area's wage index.* Except as provided in paragraphs (d)(3) and (d)(4) of this section, to use an area's wage index, a hospital must demonstrate the following:

(i) The hospital's incurred wage costs are comparable to hospital wage costs in an urban or other rural area;

(ii) The hospital has the necessary geographic relationship as specified in paragraphs (a) and (b) of this section;

(iii) One of the following conditions apply:

(A) With respect to redesignations for Federal fiscal years 1994 through 2001, the hospital's average hourly wage is at least 108 percent of the average hourly wage of hospitals in the area in which the hospital is located;

(B) With respect to redesignations for Federal fiscal years 2002 through 2005, the hospital's average hourly wage is, in the case of a hospital located in a rural area, at least 106 percent and in the case of a hospital located in an urban area, at least 108 percent of the average hourly wage of hospitals in the area in which the hospital is located; or

(C) With respect to redesignations for Federal fiscal year 2006 and subsequent years, the hospital's average hourly wage is, in the case of a hospital located in a rural area, at least 106 percent and in the case of a hospital located in an urban area, at least 108 percent of the average hourly wage of all other hospitals in the area in which the hospital is located;

(iv) One of the following conditions apply:

(A) For redesignations effective before fiscal year 1999, the hospital's average hourly wage weighted for occupational categories is at least 90 percent of the average hourly wages of hospitals in the area to which it seeks redesignation.

(B) With respect to redesignations for fiscal year 1994 through 2001, the hospital's average hourly wage is equal to at least 84 percent of the average hourly wage of hospitals in the area to which it seeks redesignation.

(C) With respect to redesignations for fiscal year 2002 and later years, the hospital's average hourly wage is equal to, in the case of a hospital located in a rural area, at least 82 percent, and in the case of a hospital located in an urban area, at least 84 percent of the average hourly wage of hospitals in the area to which it seeks redesignation.

(2) *Appropriate wage data.* For a wage index change, the hospital must submit appropriate wage data as follows:

(i) For redesignations effective through FY 2002:

(A) For hospital-specific data, the hospital must provide data from the CMS hospital wage survey used to construct the wage index in effect for prospective payment purposes during the fiscal year prior to the fiscal year for which the hospital requests reclassification.

(B) For data for other hospitals, the hospital must provide data concerning the average hourly wage in the area in which the hospital is located and the average hourly wage in the area to which the hospital seeks reclassification. The wage data are taken from the CMS hospital wage survey used to construct the wage index in effect for prospective payment purposes during the fiscal year prior to the fiscal year for which the hospital requests reclassification.

(ii) For redesignations effective beginning FY 2003:

(A) For hospital-specific data, the hospital must provide a weighted 3-year average of its average hourly wages using data from the CMS hospital wage survey used to construct the wage index in effect for prospective payment purposes. However, for the limited purpose of qualifying for geographic reclassification based on wage data from cost reporting periods beginning prior to FY 2000, a hospital may request that its wage data be revised if the hospital is in an urban area that was subject to the rural floor for the period during which the wage data the hospital wishes to revise were used to calculate its wage index.

(B) For data for other hospitals, the hospital must provide a weighted 3-year average of the average hourly wage in the area in which the hospital is located and a weighted 3-year average of the average hourly wage in the area to which the hospital seeks reclassification. The wage data are taken from the CMS hospital wage survey used to construct the wage index in effect for prospective payment purposes.

(iii) For applications submitted for reclassifications effective in FYs 2006 through 2008, a campus of a multicampus hospital may seek reclassification only to a CBSA in which another campus(es) is located. If the campus is seeking reclassification to a CBSA in which another campus(es) is located, as part of its reclassification request, the requesting entity must submit the composite wage data for the entire multicampus hospital as its hospital-specific data.

(iv) For purposes of this paragraph (d)(2), if a new owner does not accept assignment of the existing hospital's provider agreement in accordance with § 489.18 of this chapter, the hospital will be treated as a new provider with a new provider number. In this case, the wage data associated with the previous hospital's provider number cannot be used in calculating the new hospital's 3-year average hourly wage. Once a new hospital has accumulated at least 1 year of wage data, it is eligible to apply for reclassification on the basis of those data.

(3) *Rural referral center exceptions.* (i) If a hospital was ever a rural referral center, it does not have to demonstrate that it meets the average hourly wage criterion set forth in paragraph (d)(1)(iii) of this section.

(ii) If a hospital was ever a rural referral center, it is required to meet only the criterion that applies to rural hospitals under paragraph (d)(1)(iv) of this section, regardless of its actual location in an urban or rural area.

(4) *Special dominating hospital exception.* The requirements of paragraph (d)(1)(i) and (d)(1)(iii) of this section do not apply if a hospital meets the following criteria:

(i) Its average hourly wage is at least 108 percent of the average hourly wage of all other hospitals in the area in which the hospital is located.

(ii) It pays at least 40 percent of the adjusted uninflated wages in the MSA.

(iii) It was approved for redesignation under this paragraph (d) for each year from fiscal year 1992 through fiscal year 1997.

[55 FR 36766, Sept. 6, 1990, as amended at 56 FR 25488, June 4, 1991; 57 FR 39825, Sept. 1, 1992; 59 FR 45399, Sept. 1, 1994; 60 FR 45848, Sept. 1, 1995; 62 FR 46031, Aug. 29, 1997; 63 FR 26357, May 12, 1998; 65 FR 47108, Aug. 1, 2000; 66 FR 39934, Aug. 1, 2001; 68 FR 45470, Aug. 1, 2003; 68 FR 45470, Aug. 1, 2003; 69 FR 49249, Aug. 11, 2004; 69 FR 60252, Oct. 7, 2004; 69 FR 78529, Dec. 30, 2004; 70 FR 47484, Aug. 12, 2005; 70 FR 57162, Sept. 30, 2005; 70 FR 57786, Oct. 4, 2005]

**§ 412.232 Criteria for all hospitals in a rural county seeking urban redesignation.**

(a) *Criteria.* For all hospitals in a rural county to be redesignated to an urban area, the following conditions must be met:

(1) The county in which the hospitals are located–

(i) For fiscal years prior to fiscal year 2006, must be adjacent to the MSA or NECMA to which they seek redesignation.

(ii) For fiscal years beginning with fiscal year 2006, must be adjacent to the MSA to which they seek redesignation.

(2) All hospitals in a rural county must apply for redesignation as a group.

(3) The hospitals must demonstrate that the rural county in which they are located currently meets the criteria for metropolitan character under paragraph (b) of this section and the wage criteria under paragraph (c) of this section.

(4) The hospital may be redesignated only if one of the following conditions is met:

(i) The prereclassified average hourly wage for the area to which they seek redesignation is higher than the prereclassified average hourly wage for the area in which they are currently located.

(ii) For fiscal years prior to fiscal year 2006, the standardized amount for the area to which they seek redesignation is higher than the standardized amount for the area in which they are located.

(b) *Metropolitan character.* (1) For fiscal years prior to FY 2005, the group of hospitals must demonstrate that the county in which the hospitals are located meets the standards for redesignation to an MSA or an NECMA as an outlying county that were published in the *Federal Register* on March 30, 1990 (55 FR 12154) using Bureau of the Census data or Bureau of Census estimates made after 1990.

(2) For fiscal years beginning with FY 2005, the group of hospitals must demonstrate that the county in which the hospitals are located meets the standards for redesignation to an MSA as an outlying county that were published in the *Federal Register* on December 27, 2000 (65 FR 82228) using Census Bureau data or Census Bureau estimates made after 2000.

(c) *Wage criteria.* In applying the following numeric criteria, rounding of numbers to meet the qualifying percentages is not permitted.

(1) *Aggregate hourly wage.* The aggregate average hourly wage for all hospitals in the rural county must be equal to at least 85 percent of the average hourly wage in the adjacent urban area; or

(2) *Aggregate hourly wage weighted for occupational mix.* For redesignations effective before fiscal year 1999, the aggregate hourly wage for all hospitals in the rural county, weighted for occupational categories, is at least 90 percent of the average hourly wage in the adjacent urban area.

(d) *Appropriate data*—(1) *Metropolitan character.* (i) To meet the criteria in paragraph (b) of this section, the hospitals may submit data, estimates, or projections, made by the Bureau of the Census concerning population density or growth, or changes in designation of urban areas.

(ii) The MGCRB only considers data developed by the Bureau of the Census.

(2) *Appropriate wage data.* The hospitals must submit appropriate data as follows:

(i) For redesignations effective through FY 2002:

(A) For hospital-specific data, the hospitals must provide data from the CMS wage survey used to construct the wage index in effect for prospective payment purposes during the fiscal year prior to the fiscal year for which the hospitals request reclassification.

(B) For data for other hospitals, the hospitals must provide the following:

(*1*) The average hourly wage in the adjacent area, which is taken from the CMS hospital wage survey used to construct the wage index in effect for prospective payment purposes during the fiscal year prior to the fiscal year for which the hospitals request reclassification.

(*2*) Occupational-mix data to demonstrate the average occupational mix for each employment category in the adjacent area. Occupational-mix data can be obtained from surveys conducted by the American Hospital Association.

(ii) For redesignations effective beginning FY 2003:

(A) For hospital-specific data, the hospital must provide a weighted 3-year average of its average hourly wages using data from the CMS hospital wage survey used to construct the wage index in effect for prospective payment purposes.

(B) For data for other hospitals, the hospital must provide a weighted 3-year average of the average hourly wage in the area in which the hospital is located and a weighted 3-year average of the average hourly wage in the area to which the hospital seeks reclassification. The wage data are taken from the CMS hospital wage survey used to construct the wage index in effect for prospective payment purposes.

[55 FR 36766, Sept. 6, 1990, as amended at 57 FR 39826, Sept. 1, 1992; 58 FR 46339, Sept. 1, 1993; 59 FR 45399, Sept. 1, 1994; 60 FR 45849, Sept. 1, 1995; 62 FR 46031, Aug. 29, 1997; 66 FR 39934, Aug. 1, 2001; 69 FR 49249, Aug. 11, 2004; 69 FR 60252, Oct. 7, 2004]

**§ 412.234 Criteria for all hospitals in an urban county seeking redesignation to another urban area.**

(a) *General criteria.* For all prospective payment hospitals in an urban county to be redesignated to another urban area, the following conditions must be met:

(1) All hospitals in an urban county must apply for redesignation as a group.

(2) The county in which the hospitals are located must be adjacent to the urban area to which they seek redesignation.

(3) (i) For Federal fiscal years before fiscal year 2006, the counties in which the hospitals are located must be part of the Consolidated Metropolitan Statistical Area (CMSA) that includes the urban area to which they seek redesignation.

(ii) For fiscal year 2006, hospitals located in counties that are in the same Combined Statistical Area (CSA) (under the MSA definitions announced by the OMB on June 6, 2003) as the urban area to which they seek redesignation; or in the same Consolidated Metropolitan Statistical Area (CMSA) (under the standards published by the OMB on March 30, 1990) as the urban area to which they seek designation qualify as meeting the proximity requirements for reclassification to the urban area to which they seek redesignation.

(iii) For Federal fiscal year 2007, hospitals located in counties that are in the same Combined Statistical Area (CSA) (under the MSA definitions announced by the OMB on June 6, 2003) as the urban area to which they seek redesignation qualify as meeting the proximity requirement for reclassification to the urban area to which they seek redesignation.

(iv) For Federal fiscal year 2008 and thereafter, hospitals located in counties that are in the same Combined Statistical Area (CSA) or Core-Based Statistical Area (CBSA) (under the MSA definitions announced by the OMB on June 6, 2003) as the urban area to which they seek redesignation qualify as meeting the proximity requirements for reclassification to the urban area to which they seek redesignation.

(4) The hospital may be redesignated only if one of the following conditions is met:

(i) The prereclassified average hourly wage for the area to which they seek redesignation is higher than the prereclassified average hourly wage for the area in which they are currently located.

(ii) For fiscal years prior to fiscal year 2005, the standardized amount for the area to which they seek redesignation is higher than the standardized amount for the area in which they are located.

(b) *Wage criteria.* In applying the following numeric criteria, rounding of numbers to meet the qualifying percentages is not permitted.

(1) *Aggregate hourly wage.* The aggregate average hourly wage of all hospitals in the urban county must be at least 85 percent of the average hospital hourly wage in the MSA to which the hospitals in the county seek reclassification; or

(2) *Aggregate hourly wage weighted for occupational mix.* For redesignations effective before fiscal year 1999, the aggregate average hourly wage for all hospitals in the county, weighted for occupational categories, is at least 90 percent of the average hourly wage in the adjacent urban area.

(c) *Appropriate wage data.* The hospitals must submit appropriate wage data as provided for in § 412.230(d)(2).

[56 FR 25488, June 4, 1991, as amended at 57 FR 39826, Sept. 1, 1992; 58 FR 46339, Sept. 1, 1993; 60 FR 45849, Sept. 1, 1995; 62 FR 46031, Aug. 29, 1997; 69 FR 49249, Aug. 11, 2004; 70 FR 47487, Aug. 12, 2005, 71 FR 48140, Aug. 18, 2006]

**§ 412.235 Criteria for all hospitals in a State seeking a statewide wage index redesignation.**

(a) *General criteria.* For all prospective payment system hospitals in a State to be redesignated to a statewide wage index, the following conditions must be met:

(1) All prospective payment system hospitals in the State must apply as a group for reclassification to a statewide wage index through a signed single application.

(2) All prospective payment system hospitals in the State must agree to the reclassification to a statewide wage index through a signed affidavit on the application.

(3) All prospective payment system hospitals in the State must agree, through an affidavit, to withdrawal of an application or to termination of an approved statewide wage index reclassification.

(4) All hospitals in the State must waive their rights to any wage index classification that they would otherwise receive absent the statewide wage index

classification, including a wage index that any of the hospitals might have received through individual geographic reclassification.

(5) New hospitals that open within the State prior to the deadline for submitting an application for a statewide wage index reclassification (September 1), regardless of whether a group application has already been filed, must agree to the use of the statewide wage index as part of the group application. New hospitals that open within the State after the deadline for submitting a statewide wage index reclassification application or during the approved reclassification period will be considered a party to the statewide wage index application and reclassification.

(b) *Effect on payments.* (1) An individual hospital within the State may receive a wage index that could be higher or lower under the statewide wage index reclassification in comparison to its otherwise redesignated wage index.

(2) Any new prospective payment system hospital that opens in the State during the effective period of an approved statewide wage index reclassification will be designated to receive the statewide wage index for the duration of that period.

(c) *Terms of the decision.* (1) A decision by the MGCRB on an application for a statewide wage index reclassification will be effective for 3 years beginning with discharges occurring on the first day (October 1) of the second Federal fiscal year following the Federal fiscal year in which the hospitals filed a complete application.

(2) The procedures and time frames specified in § 412.273 apply to withdrawals of applications for redesignation to a statewide wage index and terminations of approved statewide wage index reclassifications, including the requirement that, to withdraw an application or terminate an approved reclassification, the request must be made in writing by all hospitals that are party to the application, except hospitals reclassified into the State for purposes of receiving the statewide wage index.

[66 FR 39935, Aug. 1, 2001]

**Composition and Procedures**

**§ 412.246 MGCRB members.**

(a) *Composition.* The Medicare Geographical Classification Review Board (MGCRB) consists of five members, including a Chairman, all of whom are appointed by the Secretary. The members include two members who are representative of prospective payment system hospitals located in rural areas, and at least one individual who is knowledgeable in analyzing the costs of inpatient hospital services.

(b) *Term of office.* The term of office for an MGCRB member may not exceed 3 years. A member may serve more than one term. The Secretary may terminate a member's tenure prior to its full term.

[55 FR 36766, Sept. 6, 1990, as amended at 61 FR 46224, Aug. 30, 1996; 61 FR 51217, Oct. 1, 1996]

**§ 412.248 Number of members needed for a decision or a hearing.**

(a) *A quorum.* A quorum, consisting of at least a majority of the MGCRB members, one of whom is representative of rural hospitals if possible, is required for making MGCRB decisions.

(b) *Number of members for a hearing.* If less than a quorum is present for an oral hearing, the chairman with the consent of the hospital may allow those members present to conduct the hearing and to prepare a recommended decision, which is then submitted to a quorum.

**§ 412.250 Sources of MGCRB's authority.**

(a) *Compliance.* The MGCRB, in issuing decisions under section 1886(d)(10)(C) of the Act, complies with all the provisions of title XVIII and related provisions of the Act and implementing regulations, including the criteria and conditions located at § 412.230 through § 412.236, issued by the Secretary under the authority of section 1886(d)(10)(D) of the Act; and CMS Rulings issued under the authority of the Administrator.

(b) *Affords great weight.* The MGCRB affords great weight to other interpretive rules, general statements of policy and rules of agency organization, procedure, and practice established by CMS.

[55 FR 36766, Sept. 6, 1990, as amended at 56 FR 25488, June 4, 1991]

**§ 412.252 Applications.**

(a) *By one hospital.* An individual prospective payment system hospital seeking redesignation to a different rural or urban area has the right to submit an application to the MGCRB.

(b) *By a group of hospitals.* A group of hospitals has the right to submit an application to the MGCRB requesting redesignation of all prospective payment hospitals in a county if all prospective payment hospitals located in a county agree to the request.

[55 FR 36766, Sept. 6, 1990, as amended at 69 FR 49250, Aug. 11, 2004]

**§ 412.254 Proceedings before MGCRB.**

(a) *On-the-record decision.* The MGCRB will ordinarily issue an on-the-record decision without conducting an oral hearing. The MGCRB will issue a decision based upon all documents, data, and other written evidence and comments submitted timely to the MGCRB by the parties.

(b) *Oral hearing.* The MGCRB may hold an oral hearing on its own motion or if a party demonstrates to the MGCRB's satisfaction that an oral hearing is necessary.

**§ 412.256 Application requirements.**

(a) *Written application.* A request for reclassification must be in writing and must constitute a complete application in accordance with paragraph (b) of this section.

(1) An application must be mailed or delivered to the MGCRB, with a copy to CMS, and may not be submitted through the facsimile (FAX) process or by other electronic means.

(2) A complete application must be received not later than the first day of the 13-month period preceding the Federal fiscal year for which reclassification is requested.

(3) The filing date of an application is the date the application is received by the MGCRB.

(b) *Criteria for a complete application.* An application is complete if the application from an individual hospital or from all hospitals in a county includes the following information:

(1) The Federal fiscal year for which the hospital is applying for redesignation.

(2) Which criteria constitute the basis of the request for reclassification.

(3) An explanation of how the hospital or hospitals meet the relevant criteria in §§ 412.230 through 412.236, including any necessary data to support the application.

(c) *Opportunity to complete a submitted application.* (1) The MGCRB will review an application within 15 days of receipt to determine if the application is complete. If the MGCRB determines that an application is incomplete, the MGCRB will notify the hospital, with a copy to CMS, within the 15-day period, that it has determined that the application is incomplete and may dismiss the application if a complete application is not filed by September 1.

(2) At the request of the hospital, the MGCRB may, for good cause, grant a hospital that has submitted an application by September 1, an extension beyond September 1 to complete its application.

(d) *Appeal of MGCRB dismissal.* (1) The hospital may appeal the MGCRB dismissal to the Administrator within 15 days of the date of the notice of dismissal.

(2) Within 20 days of receipt of the hospital's request for appeal, the Administrator will affirm the dismissal or reverse the dismissal and remand the case to the MGCRB to determine whether reclassification is appropriate.

(e) *Notification of complete application.* When the MGCRB determines that the hospital's application contains all the necessary elements for a complete application, it notifies the hospital in writing, with a copy to CMS, that the application is complete and that the case may proceed to an MGCRB decision.

[55 FR 36766, Sept. 6, 1990, as amended at 56 FR 25488, June 4, 1991; 62 FR 46031, Aug. 29, 1997; 63 FR 26357, May 12, 1998; 64 FR 41541, July 30, 1999]

**§ 412.258 Parties to MGCRB proceeding.**

(a) The party or parties to an MGCRB proceeding are the hospital or group of hospitals requesting a change in geographic designation.

(b) CMS has 30 days from the date of receipt of notice of a complete application to submit written comments and recommendations (with a copy to the hospital) for consideration by the MGCRB.

(c) The hospital has 15 days from the date of receipt of CMS's comments to submit written comments to the MGCRB, with a copy to CMS, for the purpose of responding to CMS's comments.

**§ 412.260 Time and place of the oral hearing.**
If the MGCRB decides that an oral hearing is necessary, it sets the time and place for the hearing and notifies the parties in writing, with a copy to CMS, not less than 10 days before the time scheduled for the hearing. The MGCRB may reschedule, adjourn, postpone, or reconvene the hearing provided that reasonable written notice is given to the parties, with a copy to CMS.

**§ 412.262 Disqualification of an MGCRB member.**
(a) *Grounds for disqualification.* An MGCRB member may not participate in any decision in a case in which he or she may be prejudiced or partial with respect to a party or has any other interest in the case.

(b) *Request for disqualification.* If a party believes that an MGCRB member should not participate in a decision, the party submits the objection in writing to the MGCRB at its earliest opportunity, explaining the grounds for the request. CMS may also submit such a suggestion to the MGCRB.

(c) *Consideration by the MGCRB member.* The MGCRB member will consider the objection and, at his or her discretion, either will proceed or withdraw.

(d) *Consideration by the MGCRB.* If the member does not withdraw, a party may petition the MGCRB for withdrawal and the MGCRB will consider the objection and rule on whether the member may participate in the decision before it decides the case.

**§ 412.264 Evidence and comments in MGCRB proceeding.**
(a) *Submission by the parties.* Before a decision is issued and during an oral hearing, the parties may present evidence or comments to the MGCRB regarding the matters at issue in the case.

(b) *Content of evidence and comments.* The MGCRB may receive evidence and comments without regard for the rules of evidence applicable to court procedures.

(c) *Ex parte communications.* (1) The members of the MGCRB and its staff may not consult or be consulted by an individual representing the interests of an applicant hospital or by any other individual on any matter in issue before the MGCRB without notice to the hospital or CMS. If such communication occurs, the MGCRB will disclose it to the hospital or CMS, as appropriate, and make it part of the record after the hospital or CMS has had an opportunity to comment. MGCRB members and staff may not consider any information outside the record about matters concerning a hospital's application for reclassification.

(2) The provisions in paragraph (c)(1) of this section do not apply to the following:

(i) Communications among MGCRB members and staff.

(ii) Communications concerning the MGCRB's administrative functions or procedures.

(iii) Requests from the MGCRB to a party or CMS for a document.

(iv) Material that the MGCRB includes in the record after notice and an opportunity to comment.

(d) *MGCRB rulings on evidence and comments.* The MGCRB rules upon the admissibility of evidence and comments and excludes irrelevant, immaterial, or unduly repetitious evidence and comments.

**§ 412.266 Availability of wage data.**
A hospital may obtain the average hourly wage data necessary to prepare its application to the MGCRB from *Federal Register* documents published in accordance with the provisions of § 412.8(b).
[60 FR 45849, Sept. 1, 1995]

**§ 412.268 Subpoenas.**

(a) *In general.* When reasonably necessary for the full presentation of a case, and only after a pre-decision request for information or data has failed to produce the necessary evidence, either upon its own motion or upon the request of a party, the MGCRB may issue subpoenas for the attendance and testimony of witnesses, for an oral hearing or the production of books, records, correspondence, papers, or other documents that are relevant and material to any matter at issue.

(b) *Content of request.* The request must designate which witnesses or documents are to be produced, and describe addresses or locations with sufficient particularity to permit these witnesses or documents to be found. The request for a subpoena must state the pertinent facts that the party expects to establish by the requested witnesses or documents and whether these facts could be established by other evidence without the use of a subpoena.

(c) *Issuance.* Subpoenas are issued as provided in section 205(d) of the Act.

(d) *Payment for subpoena cost.* CMS pays for the cost of issuing subpoenas and the fees and mileage of any witness who is subpoenaed, as provided in section 205(d) of the Act.

**§ 412.270 Witnesses.**
Witnesses at an oral hearing testify under oath or affirmation, unless excused by the MGCRB for cause. The MGCRB may examine the witnesses and may allow the parties or their representatives to also examine any witnesses called.

**§ 412.272 Record of proceedings before the MGCRB.**
A complete record of the proceedings before the MGCRB is made in all cases. The record will not be closed until a decision has been issued by the MGCRB. A transcription of an oral hearing will be made at a party's request, at the expense of the requesting party.

**§ 412.273 Withdrawing an application, terminating an approved 3-year reclassification, or canceling a previous withdrawal or termination.**

(a) *Timing of a withdrawal.* The MGCRB allows a hospital, or group of hospitals, to withdraw its application if the request for withdrawal is submitted to the MGCRB during the following time periods:

(1) At any time before the MGCRB issues a decision on the application; or

(2) After the MGCRB issues a decision, provided that the request for withdrawal is received by the MGCRB within 45 days of publication of CMS's annual notice of proposed rulemaking concerning changes to the inpatient hospital prospective payment system and proposed payment rates for the fiscal year for which the application has been filed.

(b) *Request for termination of approved 3-year wage index reclassifications.*

(1) A hospital, or a group of hospitals, that has been issued a decision on its application for a 3-year reclassification for wage index purposes only or for redesignation to a statewide wage index and has not withdrawn that application under the procedures specified in paragraph (a) of this section may request termination of its approved 3-year wage index reclassification under the following conditions:

(i) The request to terminate must be received by the MGCRB within 45 days of the publication of the annual notice of proposed rulemaking concerning changes to the inpatient hospital prospective payment system and proposed payment rates for the fiscal year for which the termination is to apply.

(ii) A request to terminate a 3-year reclassification will be effective only for the full fiscal year(s) remaining in the 3-year period at the time the request is received. Requests for terminations for part of a fiscal year will not be considered.

(2) *Reapplication within the approved 3-year period.* (i) If a hospital elects to withdraw its wage index application after the MGCRB has issued its decision, it may cancel its withdrawal in a subsequent year and request the MGCRB to reinstate its wage index reclassification for the remaining fiscal year(s) of the 3-year period.

(ii) A hospital may apply for reclassification for purposes of the wage index to a different area (that is, an area different from the one to which it was originally reclassified for the 3-year period). If the application is approved, the reclassification will be effective for 3 years. Once a 3-year reclassification becomes effective, a hospital may no longer cancel a withdrawal or termination of another 3-year reclassification, regardless of whether the withdrawal or termination request is made within 3 years from the date of the withdrawal or termination.

(iii) In a case in which a hospital with an existing 3-year wage index reclassification applies to be reclassified to another area, its existing 3-year reclassification will be terminated when a second 3-year wage index reclassification goes into effect for payments for discharges on or after the following October 1.

(c) *Written request only.* A request to withdraw an application or terminate an approved reclassification must be made in writing to the MGCRB by all hospitals that are party to the application or reclassification.

(d) *Process for canceling a previous withdrawal or termination.* A hospital may cancel a previous withdrawal or termination by submitting written notice of its intent to the MGCRB no later than the deadline for submitting reclassification applications for the following fiscal year, as specified in § 412.256(a)(2).

(e) *Appeal of the MGCRB's denial of a hospital's request for withdrawal.* (1) A hospital may file an appeal of the MGCRB's denial of its request for withdrawal of an application to the Administrator. The appeal must be received within 15 days of the date of the notice of the denial.

(2) Within 20 days of receipt of the hospital's request for appeal, the Administrator affirms or reverses the denial.

[56 FR 25489, June 4, 1991, as amended at 56 FR 43241, Aug. 30, 1991; 57 FR 39826, Sept. 1, 1992; 66 FR 39935, Aug. 1, 2001; 67 FR 50113, Aug. 1, 2002]

**§ 412.274 Scope and effect of an MGCRB decision.**

(a) *Scope of decision.* The MGCRB may affirm or change a hospital's geographic designation. The MGCRB's decision is based upon the evidence of record, including the hospital's application and other evidence obtained or received by the MGCRB.

(b) *Effective date and term of the decision.* (1) For reclassifications prior to fiscal year 2005, a standardized amount classification change is effective for 1 year beginning with discharges occurring on the first day (October 1) of the second Federal fiscal year following the Federal fiscal year in which the complete application is filed and ending effective at the end of that Federal fiscal year (the end of the next September 30).

(2) A wage index classification change is effective for 3 years beginning with discharges occurring on the first day (October 1) of the second Federal fiscal year in which the complete application is filed.

[55 FR 36766, Sept. 6, 1990, as amended at 62 FR 46031, Aug. 29, 1997; 66 FR 39935, Aug. 1, 2001; 69 FR 49250, Aug. 11, 2004]

**§ 412.276 Timing of MGCRB decision and its appeal.**

(a) *Timing.* The MGCRB notifies the parties in writing, with a copy to CMS, and issues a decision within 180 days after the first day of the 13-month period preceding the Federal fiscal year for which a hospital has filed a complete application. The hospital has 15 days from the date of the decision to request Administrator review.

(b) *Appeal.* The decision of the MGCRB is final and binding upon the parties unless it is reviewed by the Administrator and the decision is changed by the Administrator in accordance with § 412.278.

[55 FR 36766, Sept. 6, 1990, as amended at 64 FR 41541, July 30, 1999]

**§ 412.278 Administrator's review.**

(a) *Hospitals requests for review.* A hospital or group of hospitals dissatisfied with the MGCRB's decision regarding its geographic designation may request the Administrator to review the MGCRB decision. (A hospital or group of hospitals may also request that the Administrator review the MGCRB's dismissal of an application as untimely filed or incomplete, as provided in § 412.256(d).)

(b) *Procedures for hospital's request for review.* (1) The hospital's request for review must be in writing and sent to the Administrator, in care of the Office of the Attorney Advisor. The request must be received by the Administrator within

15 days after the date the MGCRB issues its decision. A request for Administrator review filed by facsimile (FAX) or other electronic means will not be accepted. The hospital must also mail a copy of its request for review to CMS's Hospital and Ambulatory Policy Group.

(2) The request for review may contain proposed findings of fact and conclusions of law, exceptions to the MGCRB's decision, and supporting reasons therefore.

(3) Within 15 days of receipt of the hospital's request for review, CMS may submit to the Administrator, in writing, with a copy to the party, comments and recommendations concerning the hospital's submission.

(4) Within 10 days of receipt of CMS's submission, the hospital may submit in writing, with a copy to CMS, a response to the Administrator.

(c) *Discretionary review by the Administrator.* (1) The Administrator may, at his or her discretion, review any final decision of the MGCRB.

(2) The Administrator promptly notifies the hospital that he or she has decided to review a decision of the MGCRB. The notice of review indicates the particular issues to be considered and includes copies of any comments submitted to the Administrator by CMS staff concerning the MGCRB decision.

(3) Within 15 days of the receipt of the Administrator's notice of review, the hospital may submit a response in writing to the Administrator, with a copy of CMS.

(d) *Criteria for discretionary review.* In deciding whether to review an MGCRB decision, the Administrator normally considers whether it appears that any of the following situations apply:

(1) The MGCRB made an erroneous interpretation of law, regulation, or CMS Ruling.

(2) The MGCRB's decision is not supported by substantial evidence.

(3) The case presents a significant policy issue having a basis in law and regulations, and review is likely to lead to issuance of a CMS Ruling or other directive needed to clarify a provision in the law or regulations.

(4) The decision of the MGCRB requires clarification, amplification, or an alternative legal basis.

(5) The MGCRB has incorrectly extended its authority to a degree not provided for by law, regulation, or CMS Ruling.

(e) *Communication procedures.* All communications between CMS staff and the Administrator concerning the Administrator's review of an MGCRB decision must be in writing. As specified in paragraphs (b) and (c) of this section, copies of comments by CMS staff are sent to applicant hospitals within 15 days of receipt of a hospital's request for review, or, in cases in which the Administrator decides to review a case at his or her discretion, are included with the Administrator's notice of review. In the event there are additional communications between CMS staff and the Administrator concerning MGCRB decisions reviewed by the Administrator under paragraphs (b) or (c) of this section, CMS furnishes copies of the communications to the hospital or group of hospitals.

(f) *Administrator's decision.* (1) The Administrator may not receive or consider any new evidence and must issue a decision based only upon the record as it appeared before the MGCRB and comments submitted under paragraphs (b)(2), (b)(3), (b)(4), (c)(2), and (c)(3) of this section.

(2) The Administrator issues a decision in writing to the party with a copy to CMS—

(i) Not later than 90 days following receipt of the party's request for review, except the Administrator may, at his or her discretion, for good cause shown, toll such 90 days; or

(ii) Not later than 105 days following issuance of the MGCRB decision in the case of review at the discretion of the Administrator.

(3) The Administrator's decision issued under § 412.278(a) or (c) is the final Departmental decision, unless it is amended under § 412.278(g). The final Departmental decision is not subject to judicial review.

(4) The Administrator's decision is not subject to judicial review.

(g) *Amendment of Administrator decision*—(1) *Hospital's request for amendment.* The hospital may request the Administrator to amend the decision for the limited purpose of correcting mathematical or computational errors, or to correct the decision if the evidence that was considered in making the decision clearly shows on its face that an error was made. The following procedure is followed:

(i) The hospital's request for amendment must be received by the Administrator within 10 days after the date the Administrator issues a decision. The request for amendment must be in writing, with a copy to CMS.

(ii) The Administrator promptly reviews the hospital's request and amends the decision, if necessary, within 5 days following receipt of the hospital's request for amendment.

(2) *Discretionary review by the Administrator.* Within 15 days following the issuance of the Administrator's decision, the Administrator, at his or her discretion, may amend the decision to correct mathematical or computational errors, or to correct the decision if the evidence that was considered in making the decision clearly shows on its face that an error was made. The Administrator's amended decision is final and is not subject to judicial review.

[55 FR 36766, Sept. 6, 1990, as amended at 56 FR 25489, June 4, 1991; 57 FR 39826, Sept. 1, 1992; 68 FR 45471, Aug. 1, 2003; 70 FR 47487, Aug. 12, 2005]

**§ 412.280 Representation.**

(a) *General.* A party may be represented by legal counsel or by any other person appointed to act as its representative at any proceeding before the MGCRB or the Administrator.

(b) *Rights of a representative.* A representative appointed by a party may accept or give on behalf of the party any request or notice connected with any proceeding before the MGCRB or the Administrator. A representative is entitled to present evidence and argument as to facts and law in any MGCRB proceeding affecting the party represented and to obtain information to the same extent as the party represented. Notice of any action or decision sent to the representative of a party has the same effect as if it had been sent to the party itself.

## PART 414—PAYMENT FOR PART B MEDICAL AND OTHER HEALTH SERVICES

### Subpart K—Payment for Drugs and Biologicals under Part B

**Source:** 69 FR 66424, Nov. 15, 2004, unless otherwise noted.

**§ 414.900 Basis and scope.**

(a) This subpart implements sections 1842(o), 1847A, and 1847B of the Act and outlines two payment methodologies applicable to drugs and biologicals covered under Medicare Part B that are not paid on a cost or prospective payment system basis.

(b) Examples of drugs that are subject to the requirements specified in this subpart are:

(1) Drugs furnished incident to a physician's service; durable medical equipment (DME) drugs.

(2) Separately billable drugs at independent dialysis facilities not under the ESRD composite rate.

(3) Statutorily covered drugs, for example—

(i) Influenza.

(ii) Pneumococcal and hepatitis B vaccines.

(iii) Antigens.

(iv) Hemophilia blood clotting factor.

(v) Immunosuppressive drugs.

(vi) Certain oral anti-cancer drugs.

[69 FR 66424, Nov. 15, 2004, as amended at 70 FR 39093, July 6, 2005]

**§ 414.902 Definitions.**

As used in this subpart, unless the context indicates otherwise—

*Approved CAP vendor* means an entity that has been awarded a contract by CMS to participate in the competitive acquisition program under 1847B of the Act.

*Bid* means an offer to furnish a CAP drug within a category of CAP drugs in a competitive acquisition area for a particular price and time period.

*CAP drug* means a physician-administered drug or biological furnished on or after January 1, 2006 described in section 1842(o)(1)(C) of the Act and supplied by an approved CAP vendor under the CAP as provided in this subpart.

*Competitive acquisition area* means a geographic area established by the Secretary for purposes of implementing the CAP required by section 1847B of the Act.

*Competitive acquisition program* (CAP) means a program as defined under section 1847B of the Act.

*Designated carrier* means an entity assigned by CMS to process and pay claims for drugs and biologicals under the CAP.

*Drug* means both drugs and biologicals.

*Emergency delivery* means delivery of a CAP drug within one business day in appropriate shipping and packaging, in all areas of the United States and its territories, with the exception of the Pacific Territories. In the Pacific Territories, emergency delivery means delivery of a CAP drug within 5 business days in appropriate shipping and packaging. In each case, this time frame shall be reduced if product stability requires it, meaning that the manufacturer's labeling instructions, drug compendia, or specialized drug stability references indicate that a shorter delivery time frame is necessary to avoid adversely affecting the product's integrity, safety, or efficacy.

*Emergency situation* means, for the purposes of the CAP, an unforeseen occurrence or situation determined by the participating CAP physician, in his or her clinical judgment, to require prompt action or attention for purposes of permitting the participating CAP physician to use a drug from his or her own stock, if the other requirements of § 414.906(e) are met.

*Local carrier* means an entity assigned by CMS to process and pay claims for administration of drugs and biologicals under the CAP.

*Manufacturer's average sales price* means the price calculated and reported by a manufacturer under part 414, subpart J of this chapter.

*Multiple source drug* means a drug described by section 1847A(c)(6)(C) of the Act.

*Pacific Territories* means, for purposes of the CAP, American Samoa, Guam, or the Northern Mariana Islands.

*Participating CAP physician* means a physician electing to participate in the CAP, as described in this subpart. The participating CAP physician must complete and sign the participating CAP physician election agreement. Physicians who do not participate in Medicare but who elect to participate in the CAP must agree to accept assignment for CAP drug administration claims.

*Participating CAP physician election agreement* means the agreement that the physician signs to notify CMS of the physician's election to participate in the CAP and to agree to the terms and conditions of CAP participation as set forth in this subpart.

*Prescription order* means a written order submitted by the participating CAP physician to the approved CAP vendor that meets the requirements of this subpart.

*Routine delivery* means delivery of a drug within 2 business days in appropriate shipping and packaging in all areas of the United States and its territories, with the exception of the Pacific Territories. In the Pacific Territories, routine delivery of drug means delivery of a CAP drug within 7 business days in appropriate shipping and packaging. In each case, this time frame will be reduced if product stability requires it, meaning that the manufacturer's labeling instructions, drug compendia, or specialized drug stability references indicate that a shorter delivery time frame is necessary to avoid adversely affecting the product's integrity, safety, or efficacy.

*Single source drug* means a drug described by section 1847A(c)(6)(D) of the Act.

*Timely delivery* means delivery of a CAP drug within the defined routine and emergency delivery time frames. Compliance with timely delivery standards is also a factor for evaluation of potential and approved CAP vendors.

*Unit* is defined as in part 414, subpart J of this chapter.

*Wholesale acquisition cost (WAC)* means the price described by section 1847A(c)(6)(B) of the Act.

[69 FR 66424, Nov. 15, 2004, as amended at 70 FR 39093, July 6, 2005]

**§ 414.916 Dispute resolution for vendors and beneficiaries.**

(a) *General rule.* Cases of an approved CAP vendor's dissatisfaction with denied drug claims are resolved through a voluntary alternative dispute resolution process delivered by the designated carrier, and a reconsideration process provided by CMS.

(b) *Dispute resolution.* (1) When an approved CAP vendor is not paid on claims submitted to the designated carrier, the vendor may appeal to the designated carrier to counsel the responsible participating CAP physician on his or her agreement to file a clean claim and pursue an administrative appeal in accordance with subpart H of part 405 of this chapter. If problems persist, the approved CAP vendor may ask the designated carrier to—

(i) Review the participating CAP physician's performance; and

(ii) Potentially recommend to CMS that CMS suspend the participating CAP physician's CAP election agreement.

(2) The designated carrier—

(i) Gathers information from the local carrier, the participating CAP physician, the beneficiary, and the approved CAP vendor; and

(ii) Makes a recommendation to CMS on whether the participating CAP physician has been filing his or her CAP drug administration claims in accordance with the requirements for physician participation in the CAP as set forth in § 414.908(a)(3). The recommendation will include numbered findings of fact.

(3) CMS will review the recommendation of the designated carrier and gather relevant additional information from the participating CAP physician before deciding whether to suspend the participating CAP physician's CAP election agreement. A suspension commencing before October 1 will conclude on December 31 of the same year. A suspension commencing on or after October 1 will conclude on December 31 of the next year.

(4) The participating CAP physician may appeal that suspension by requesting a reconsideration of CMS's decision. The reconsideration will address whether the participating CAP physician's denied claims and appeals were the result of the participating CAP physician's failure to participate in accordance with the requirements of § 414.908(a)(3).

(c) *Reconsideration*—(1) *Right to reconsideration.* A participating CAP physician dissatisfied with a determination that his or her CAP election agreement has been suspended by CMS is entitled to a reconsideration as provided in this subpart.

(2) *Eligibility for reconsideration.* CMS reconsiders any determination to suspend a participating CAP physician's election agreement if the participating CAP physician files a written request for reconsideration in accordance with paragraphs (c)(3) and (c)(4) of this section.

(3) *Manner and timing of request for reconsideration.* A participating CAP physician who is dissatisfied with a CMS decision to suspend his or her CAP election agreement may request a reconsideration of the decision by filing a request with CMS. The request must be filed within 30 days of receipt of the CMS

decision letter notifying the participating CAP physician of CMS's decision to suspend his or her CAP election agreement. From the date of receipt of the decision letter until the day the reconsideration determination is final, the ASP payment methodology under section 1847A of the Act applies to the physician.

(4) *Content of request.* The request for reconsideration must specify—

(i) The findings or issues with which the participating CAP physician disagrees;

(ii) The reasons for the disagreement;

(iii) A recital of the facts and law supporting the participating CAP physician's position;

(iv) Any supporting documentation; and

(v) Any supporting statements from approved CAP vendors, local carriers, or beneficiaries.

(5) *Withdrawal of request for reconsideration.* A participating CAP physician may withdraw his or her request for reconsideration at any time before the issuance of a reconsideration determination.

(6) *Discretionary informal hearing.* In response to a request for reconsideration, CMS may, at its discretion, provide the participating CAP physician the opportunity for an informal hearing that—

(i) Is conducted by a hearing officer appointed by the director of the CMS Center for Medicare Management or his or her designee; and

(ii) Provides the participating CAP physician the opportunity to present, by telephone or in person, evidence to rebut CMS's decision to suspend or terminate a participating CAP physician's CAP election agreement.

(7) *Informal hearing procedures.* (i) CMS provides written notice of the time and place of the informal hearing at least 10 days before the scheduled date.

(ii) The informal reconsideration hearing will be conducted in accordance with the following procedures:

(A) The hearing is open to CMS and the participating CAP physician requesting the reconsideration, including—

(*1*) Authorized representatives;

(*2*) Technical advisors (individuals with knowledge of the facts of the case or presenting interpretation of the facts);

(*3*) Representatives from the local carrier;

(*4*) Representatives from the approved CAP vendor; and

(*5*) Legal counsel.

(B) The hearing is conducted by the hearing officer who receives relevant testimony;

(C) Testimony and other evidence may be accepted by the hearing officer even though it would be inadmissible under the rules of evidence applied in Federal courts;

(D) Either party may call witnesses from among those individuals specified in paragraph (c)(7)(ii)(A) of this section; and

(E) The hearing officer does not have the authority to compel by subpoena the production of witnesses, papers, or other evidence.

(8) *Hearing officer's findings.* (i) Within 30 days of the hearing officer's receipt of the hearing request, the hearing officer presents the findings and recommendations to the participating CAP physician who requested the reconsideration. If the hearing officer decides to conduct an in-person or telephone hearing, the hearing officer will send a hearing notice to the participating CAP physician within 10 days of receipt of the hearing request, and the findings and recommendations are due to the participating CAP physician within 30 days of the hearing's conclusion.

(ii) The written report of the hearing officer includes separate numbered findings of fact and the legal conclusions of the hearing officer.

(9) *Final reconsideration determination.* (i) The hearing officer's decision is final unless the director of the CMS Center for Medicare Management or his or her designee chooses to review that decision within 30 days. If the decision is favorable to the participating CAP physician, then the participating CAP physician may resume his or her participation in CAP. The hearing officer and the CMS official may review decisions that are favorable or unfavorable to the participating CAP physician.

(ii) The CMS official may accept, reject, or modify the hearing officer's findings.

(iii) If the CMS official reviews the hearing officer's decision, the CMS official issues a final reconsideration determination to the participating CAP physician on the basis of the hearing officer's findings and recommendations and other relevant information.

(iv) The reconsideration determination of the CMS official is final. If the final decision is unfavorable to the participating CAP physician, then the participating CAP physician's CAP election agreement is terminated.

(d) The approved CAP vendor may not charge the beneficiary for the full drug coinsurance amount if the designated contractor did not pay the approved CAP vendor in full, unless a properly executed advance beneficiary notice is in place. When a beneficiary receives an inappropriate coinsurance bill, the beneficiary may participate in the approved CAP vendor's grievance process to request correction of the approved CAP vendor's file. If the beneficiary is dissatisfied with the result of the approved CAP vendor's grievance process, the beneficiary may request intervention from the designated carrier. This is in addition to, rather than in place of, any other beneficiary appeal rights. The designated carrier will first investigate the facts and then facilitate correction to the appropriate claim record and beneficiary file.

[70 FR 39097, July 6, 2005]

**§ 414.917 Dispute resolution and process for suspension or termination of approved CAP contract.**

(a) *General rule.* If a participating CAP physician finds an approved CAP vendor's service, or the quality of a CAP drug supplied by the approved CAP vendor to be unsatisfactory, then the physician may address the issue first through the approved CAP vendor's grievance process, and second through an alternative dispute resolution process administered by the designated carrier and CMS. If

CMS suspends an approved CAP vendor's CAP contract for noncompliance or terminates the CAP contract in accordance with § 414.914(a), the approved CAP vendor may request a reconsideration in accordance with paragraph (c) of this section.

(b) *Dispute resolution.* (1) When a participating CAP physician is dissatisfied with an approved CAP vendor's service or the quality of a CAP drug supplied by the approved CAP vendor, then the participating CAP physician may use the approved CAP vendor's grievance process. If the service or quality issues are not resolved through the grievance process to the physician's satisfaction, then the participating CAP physician may ask the designated carrier to—

(i) Review the approved CAP vendor's performance; and

(ii) Potentially recommend termination of the approved CAP vendor's CAP contract.

(2) *Responsibility of the designated carrier.* The designated carrier—

(i) Gathers information from the local carrier, the participating CAP physician, the beneficiary, and the approved CAP vendor; and

(ii) Makes a recommendation to CMS on whether the approved CAP vendor has been meeting the service and quality obligations of its CAP contract. This recommendation will include numbered findings of fact.

(3) CMS will review the recommendation of the designated carrier and gather relevant additional information from the approved CAP vendor, the participating CAP physician, the local carrier, and the beneficiary before deciding whether to terminate the approved CAP vendor's CAP contract.

(4) The approved CAP vendor may appeal that termination by requesting a reconsideration. A determination must be made as to whether the approved CAP vendor has been meeting the service and quality obligations of its CAP contract.

(c) *Reconsideration*—(1) *Right to reconsideration.* An approved CAP vendor dissatisfied with a determination that its CAP contract has been suspended or terminated by CMS is entitled to a reconsideration as provided in this subpart.

(2) *Eligibility for reconsideration.* CMS will reconsider any determination to suspend or terminate an approved CAP vendor's contract if the approved CAP vendor files a written request for reconsideration in accordance with paragraphs (c)(3) and (c)(4) of this section.

(3) *Manner and timing of request for reconsideration.* An approved CAP vendor that is dissatisfied with a CMS decision to suspend or terminate its CAP contract may request a reconsideration of the decision by filing a request with CMS. The request must be filed within 30 days of receipt of the CMS decision letter notifying the approved CAP vendor of the suspension or termination of its CAP contract.

(4) *Content of request.* The request for reconsideration must specify—

(i) The findings or issues with which the approved CAP vendor disagrees;

(ii) The reasons for the disagreement;

(iii) A recital of the facts and law supporting the approved CAP vendor's position;

(iv) Any supporting documentation; and

(v) Any supporting statements from participating CAP physicians, the local carrier, or beneficiaries.

(5) *Withdrawal of request for reconsideration.* An approved CAP vendor may withdraw its request for reconsideration at any time before the issuance of a reconsideration determination.

(6) *Discretionary informal hearing.* In response to a request for reconsideration, CMS may, at its discretion, provide the approved CAP vendor the opportunity for an informal hearing that—

(i) Is conducted by a hearing officer appointed by the Director of the CMS Center for Medicare Management or his or her designee; and

(ii) Provides the approved CAP vendor the opportunity to present, by telephone or in person, evidence to rebut CMS' decision to suspend or terminate the approved CAP vendor's CAP contract.

(7) *Informal hearing procedures.* (i) CMS will provide written notice of the time and place of the informal hearing at least 10 days before the scheduled date.

(ii) The informal reconsideration hearing will be conducted in accordance with the following procedures:

(A) The hearing is open to CMS and the approved CAP vendor requesting the reconsideration, including—

(*1*) Authorized representatives;

(*2*) Technical advisors (individuals with knowledge of the facts of the case or presenting interpretation of the facts);

(*3*) Representatives from the local carriers and the designated carrier;

(*4*) The participating CAP physician who requested the suspension, if any; and

(*5*) Legal counsel.

(B) The hearing will be conducted by the hearing officer, who will receive relevant testimony;

(C) Testimony and other evidence may be accepted by the hearing officer even though it would be inadmissible under the rules of evidence applied in Federal courts;

(D) Either party may call witnesses from among those individuals specified in the paragraph (c)(7)(ii)(A) of this section; and

(E) The hearing officer does not have the authority to compel by subpoena the production of witnesses, papers, or other evidence.

(8) *Hearing officer's findings.* (i) Within 30 days of the hearing officer's receipt of the hearing request, the hearing officer will present the findings and recommendations to the approved CAP vendor that requested the reconsideration. If the hearing officer conducts a hearing in person or by phone, the hearing

officer will send a hearing notice to the approved CAP vendor within 10 days of receipt of the hearing request, and the findings and recommendations are due to the approved CAP vendor within 30 days from of the hearing's conclusion.

(ii) The written report of the hearing officer will include separate numbered findings of fact and the legal conclusions of the hearing officer.

(9) *Final reconsideration determination.* (i) The hearing officer's decision is final unless the Director of the CMS Center for Medicare Management or his or her designee (CMS official) chooses to review that decision within 30 days. If the decision is favorable to the approved CAP vendor, then the approved CAP vendor may resume participation in CAP. The hearing officer and the CMS official may review decisions that are favorable or unfavorable to the approved CAP vendor.

(ii) The CMS official may accept, reject, or modify the hearing officer's findings.

(iii) If the CMS official reviews the hearing officer's decision, the CMS official will issue a final reconsideration determination to the approved CAP vendor on the basis of the hearing officer's findings and recommendations and other relevant information.

(iv) The reconsideration determination of the CMS official is final.

[70 FR 39098, July 6, 2005]

**§ 414.918 Assignment.**

Payment for a CAP drug may be made only on an assignment-related basis.

[70 FR 39099, July 6, 2005]

**§ 414.920 Judicial review.**

The following areas under the CAP are not subject to administrative or judicial review:

(a) The establishment of payment amounts.

(b) The awarding of vendor contracts.

(c) The establishment of competitive acquisition areas.

(d) The selection of CAP drugs.

(e) The bidding structure.

(f) The number of vendors selected.

[70 FR 39099, July 6, 2005]

## PART 416—AMBULATORY SURGICAL SERVICES

### Subpart E—Payment for Facility Services

**§ 416.150 Beneficiary appeals.**

A beneficiary (or ASC as his or her assignee) may request a hearing by a carrier (subject to the limitations and conditions set forth in part 405, subpart H of this chapter) if the beneficiary or the ASC—

(a) Is dissatisfied with a carrier's denial of a request for payment made on his or her behalf by an ASC;

(b) Is dissatisfied with the amount of payment; or

(c) Believes the request for payment is not being acted upon with reasonable promptness.

## PART 417—HEALTH MAINTENANCE ORGANIZATIONS, COMPETITIVE MEDICAL PLANS, AND HEALTH CARE PREPAYMENT PLANS

### Subpart R—Medicare Contract Appeals

**Source:** 50 FR 1346, Jan. 10, 1985, unless otherwise noted.

**§ 417.640 Determinations subject to appeal.**
This subpart establishes the procedures for making and reviewing the following initial determinations:

(a) A determination that an HMO or CMP is not qualified to enter into a contract with CMS under section 1876 of the Act.

(b) A determination that an HMO or CMP is qualified only for a reasonable cost contract.

(c) A determination to terminate, or to refuse to renew, a contract with an HMO or CMP because—

(1) The HMO or CMP has failed substantially to carry out the terms of the contract;

(2) The HMO or CMP is carrying out the contract in a manner that is inconsistent with the efficient and effective administration of section 1876 of the Act;

(3) The HMO or CMP no longer meets the applicable conditions necessary to qualify as an HMO or CMP under section 1876 of the Act and this subpart; or

(4) The HMO or CMP has failed to comply with the composition of enrollment requirements specified in § 417.413(d).

[50 FR 1346, Jan. 10, 1985, as amended at 56 FR 46572, Sept. 13, 1991; 58 FR 38080, July 15, 1993]

**§ 417.642 Administrative actions that are not initial determinations.**
Administrative actions that are not initial determinations under this subpart include, but are not limited to, CMS's refusal to renew a contract with an HMO or CMP when the refusal is not based on the causes specified in § 417.640(c).

[50 FR 1346, Jan. 10, 1985, as amended at 58 FR 38080, July 15, 1993]

**§ 417.644 Notice of initial determination.**

(a) When CMS makes an initial determination, it gives the HMO or CMP written notice.

(b) The notice specifies—

(1) The reasons for the determination; and

(2) The HMO's or CMP's right to request reconsideration.

(c) CMS mails the notice to the HMO or CMP at least 90 days before the end of the contract period, or in the case of termination, at least 90 days before the effective date of the termination.

[50 FR 1346, Jan. 10, 1985, as amended at 58 FR 38083, July 15, 1993; 60 FR 46234, Sept. 6, 1995]

**§ 417.646 Effect of initial determination.**

The initial determination is final and binding on all parties unless—

(a) It is reconsidered in accordance with §§ 417.648 through 417.658;

(b) In the case of an initial determination described in § 417.640(c), a request for a hearing is filed; or

(c) It is revised as a result of a reopening under § 417.692.

**§ 417.648 Reconsideration: Applicability.**

(a) Reconsideration is the first step for appealing an organization determination specified in § 417.640(a) or (b).

(b) CMS reconsiders either of the specified determinations if the HMO or CMP files a written request in accordance with § 417.650.

[60 FR 46234, Sept. 6, 1995]

**§ 417.650 Request for reconsideration.**

(a) *Method and place for filing a request.* A request for reconsideration must be made in writing and filed with any CMS office.

(b) *Time for filing a request.* Except as provided in paragraph (c) of this section, the request for reconsideration must be filed within 60 days from the date of the notice of the initial determination.

(c) *Extension of time to file a request.* CMS may, in response to a party's written petition showing good cause, accept a request for reconsideration after the expiration of the 60-day period.

(d) *Proper party to file a request.* Only an authorized official of the entity that was a party to an initial determination may file the request for reconsideration.

(e) *Withdrawal of a request.* A request for reconsideration may be withdrawn by the party who filed the request at any time before the notice of the reconsidered determination is mailed. The request for withdrawal must be in writing and filed with CMS. If CMS approves, the request for reconsideration is withdrawn.

**§ 417.652 Opportunity to submit evidence.**

CMS provides the parties to the reconsideration reasonable opportunity to present as evidence any documents or written statements that are relevant and material to the matters at issue.

[50 FR 1346, Jan. 10, 1985, as amended at 60 FR 46234, Sept. 6, 1995]

**§ 417.654 Reconsidered determination.**

A reconsidered determination is a new determination that—

(a) Is based on a review of the initial determination, the evidence and findings upon which that was based, and any other written evidence submitted before notice of the reconsidered determination is mailed, including facts relating to the status of the entity subsequent to the initial determination; and

(b) Affirms, reverses, or modifies the initial determination.

**§ 417.656 Notice of reconsidered determination.**

(a) CMS gives the parties written notice of the reconsidered determination.

(b) The notice–

(1) Contains findings with respect to the HMO's or CMP's qualifications to enter into a contract with CMS under section 1876 of the Act;

(2) States the specific reasons for the reconsidered determination; and

(3) Informs the party of its right to a hearing if it is dissatisfied with the determination.

[60 FR 46234, Sept. 6, 1995]

**§ 417.658 Effect of reconsidered determination.**

A reconsidered determination is final and binding on all parties unless a request for a hearing is filed in accordance with § 417.662 or it is revised in accordance with § 417.692.

**§ 417.660 Right to a hearing.**

The following parties are entitled to a hearing:

(a) An entity that has been determined in a reconsidered determination to be unqualified to enter into a contract with CMS under section 1876 of the Act.

(b) An HMO or CMP that has been determined in a reconsidered determination to be qualified only for a reasonable cost contract.

(c) An HMO or CMP whose contract with CMS has been terminated or has not been renewed as a result of an initial determination as provided in § 417.640(c).

[50 FR 1346, Jan. 10, 1985, as amended at 58 FR 38083, July 15, 1993]

**§ 417.662 Request for hearing.**

(a) *Method and place for filing a request.* A request for a hearing must be made in writing and filed by an authorized official of the entity or HMO or CMP that was the party to the determination under appeal. The request for a hearing must be filed with any CMS office.

(b) *Time for filing a request.* Except as provided in paragraph (c) of this section, a request for a hearing must be filed within 60 days after the date of receipt of the notice of initial or reconsidered determination.

(c) *Extension of time to file a request.* If good cause is shown, the 60-day period to request a hearing may be extended by CMS.

(d) *Parties to a hearing.* The parties to a hearing must be–

(1) The parties described in § 417.660;

(2) At the discretion of the hearing officer, any interested parties who make a showing that their rights may be prejudiced by the decision to be rendered at the hearing; and

(3) CMS.

[50 FR 1346, Jan. 10, 1985, as amended at 58 FR 38083, July 15, 1993]

**§ 417.664 Postponement of effective date of initial determination.**
When a request for a hearing with respect to an initial determination is filed timely—

(a) The effective date of the initial determination to terminate a contract with an HMO or CMP will be postponed until a hearing decision is reached; and

(b) The current contract will be extended at the end of the contract period (in the case of a determination not to renew) only—

(1) If CMS finds that an extension of the contract will be consistent with the purpose of section 1876 of the Act; and

(2) For such period as CMS and the HMO or CMP agree.

[50 FR 1346, Jan. 10, 1985, as amended at 58 FR 38083, July 15, 1993]

**§ 417.666 Designation of hearing officer.**
CMS designates a hearing officer to conduct the hearing. The hearing officer need not be an ALJ.

[50 FR 1346, Jan. 10, 1985, as amended at 60 FR 46234, Sept. 6, 1995]

**§ 417.668 Disqualification of hearing officer.**

(a) A hearing officer may not conduct a hearing in a case in which he or she is prejudiced or partial to any party or has any interest in the matter pending for decision.

(b) A party to the hearing who objects to the designated hearing officer must notify that officer in writing at the earliest opportunity.

(c) The hearing officer must consider the objections, and may, at his or her discretion, either proceed with the hearing or withdraw.

(1) If the hearing officer withdraws, CMS designates another hearing officer to conduct the hearing.

(2) If the hearing officer does not withdraw, the objecting party may, after the hearing, present objections and request that the officer's decision be revised or a new hearing be held before another hearing officer. The objections must be submitted to CMS.

[50 FR 1346, Jan. 10, 1985, as amended at 60 FR 46234, Sept. 6, 1995]

**§ 417.670 Time and place of hearing.**

(a) The hearing officer fixes a time and place for the hearing and sends written notice to the parties. The notice also informs the parties of the general and specific issues to be resolved and information about the hearing procedure.

(b) The hearing officer may, on his or her own motion, or at the request of a party, change the time and place for the hearing. The hearing officer may adjourn or postpone the hearing.

(c) The hearing officer will give the parties reasonable notice of any change in the time or place of hearing, or of adjournment or postponement.

[50 FR 1346, Jan. 10, 1985, as amended at 58 FR 38081, July 15, 1993; 60 FR 46234, Sept. 6, 1995]

**§ 417.672 Appointment of representatives.**
A party may appoint as its representative at the hearing anyone not disqualified or suspended from acting as a representative before CMS or otherwise prohibited by law.

**§ 417.674 Authority of representatives.**

(a) A representative appointed and qualified in accordance with § 417.672 may, on behalf of the represented party—

(1) Give or accept any notice or request pertinent to the proceedings set forth in this subpart;

(2) Present evidence and allegations as to facts and law in any proceedings affecting that party; and

(3) Obtain information to the same extent as the party.

(b) A notice or request sent to the representative has the same force and effect as if it had been sent to the party.

**§ 417.676 Conduct of hearing.**

(a) The hearing is open to the parties and to the public.

(b) The hearing officer inquires fully into all the matters at issue and receives in evidence the testimony of witnesses and any documents that are relevant and material.

(c) The hearing officer provides the parties an opportunity to enter any objection to the inclusion of any document.

(d) The hearing officer decides the order in which the evidence and the arguments of the parties are presented and the conduct of the hearing.

[50 FR 1346, Jan. 10, 1985, as amended at 60 FR 46234, Sept. 6, 1995]

**§ 417.678 Evidence.**
The hearing officer rules on the admissibility of evidence and may admit evidence that would be inadmissible under rules applicable to court procedures.

[50 FR 1346, Jan. 10, 1985, as amended at 60 FR 46234, Sept. 6, 1995]

**§ 417.680 Witnesses.**

(a) The hearing officer may examine the witnesses.

(b) The parties or their representatives are permitted to examine their witnesses and cross-examine witnesses of other parties.

[50 FR 1346, Jan. 10, 1985, as amended at 60 FR 46234, Sept. 6, 1995]

**§ 417.682 Discovery.**

(a) Prehearing discovery is permitted upon timely request of a party.

(b) A request is timely if it is made before the beginning of the hearing.

(c) A reasonable time for inspection and reproduction of documents is provided by order of the hearing officer.

(d) The hearing officer's order on all discovery matters is final.

[50 FR 1346, Jan. 10, 1985, as amended at 60 FR 46234, Sept. 6, 1995]

**§ 417.684 Prehearing.**

The hearing officer may schedule a prehearing conference if he or she believes that a conference would more clearly define the issues.

**§ 417.686 Record of hearing.**

(a) A complete record of the proceedings at the hearing is made and transcribed and made available to all parties upon request.

(b) The record may not be closed until a hearing decision has been issued.

[50 FR 1346, Jan. 10, 1985, as amended at 60 FR 46234, Sept. 6, 1995]

**§ 417.688 Authority of hearing officer.**

In exercising his or her authority, the hearing officer must comply with the provisions of title XVIII and related provisions of the Act, the regulations issued by CMS, and general instructions issued by CMS in implementing that Act.

**§ 417.690 Notice and effect of hearing decision.**

(a) As soon as practical after the close of the hearing, the hearing officer issues a written decision that—

(1) Is based upon the evidence of record; and

(2) Contains separately numbered findings of fact and conclusions of law.

(b) The hearing officer provides a copy of the hearing decision to each party.

(c) The hearing decision is final and binding unless it is reopened and revised in accordance with § 417.692.

[50 FR 1346, Jan. 10, 1985, as amended at 60 FR 46234, Sept. 6, 1995]

**§ 417.692 Reopening of initial or reconsidered determination or decision of a hearing officer.**

(a) *Initial or reconsidered determination.* An initial or reconsidered determination may be reopened and revised by CMS upon its own motion within 1 year of the date of the notice of determination.

(b) *Decision of hearing officer.* A decision of a hearing officer that is unfavorable to any party and is otherwise final may be reopened and revised by the hearing officer upon the officer's own motion within 1 year of the notice of the hearing decision. It may be reopened and revised by another hearing officer designated by CMS if the hearing officer who issued the decision is unavailable.

(c) *Notices.* (1) The notice of reopening and of any revisions following the reopening is mailed to the parties.

(2) The notice of revision specifies the reasons for revisions.

[50 FR 1346, Jan. 10, 1985, as amended at 60 FR 46234, Sept. 6, 1995]

**§ 417.694 Effect of revised determination.**

The revision of an initial or reconsidered determination is binding unless a party files a written request for hearing of the revised determination in accordance with § 417.662.

[50 FR 1346, Jan. 10, 1985, as amended at 60 FR 46234, Sept. 6, 1995]

## PART 418—HOSPICE CARE

### Subpart G—Payment for Hospice Care

**§ 418.301 Basic rules.**

(a) Medicare payment for covered hospice care is made in accordance with the method set forth in § 418.302.

(b) Medicare reimbursement to a hospice in a cap period is limited to a cap amount specified in § 418.309.

(c) The hospice may not charge a patient for services for which the patient is entitled to have payment made under Medicare or for services for which the patient would be entitled to payment, as described in § 489.21 of this chapter.

[48 FR 56026, Dec. 16, 1983, as amended at 56 FR 26919, June 12, 1991; 70 FR 70547, Nov. 22, 2005]

**§ 418.311 Administrative appeals.**

A hospice that believes its payments have not been properly determined in accordance with these regulations may request a review from the intermediary or the Provider Reimbursement Review Board (PRRB) if the amount in controversy is at least $1,000 or $10,000, respectively. In such a case, the procedure in 42 CFR part 405, subpart R, will be followed to the extent that it is applicable. The PRRB, subject to review by the Secretary under § 405.1874 of this chapter, shall have the authority to determine the issues raised. The methods and standards for the calculation of the payment rates by CMS are not subject to appeal.

## PART 421—INTERMEDIARIES AND CARRIERS

**§ 421.100 Intermediary functions.**

An agreement between CMS and an intermediary specifies the functions to be performed by the intermediary, which must include, but are not necessarily limited to, the following:

(a) *Coverage.* (1) The intermediary ensures that it makes payments only for services that are:

(i) Furnished to Medicare beneficiaries;

(ii) Covered under Medicare; and

(iii) In accordance with QIO determinations when they are services for which the QIO has assumed review responsibility under its contract with CMS.

(2) The intermediary takes appropriate action to reject or adjust the claim if—

(i) The intermediary or the QIO determines that the services furnished or proposed to be furnished were not reasonable, not medically necessary, or not furnished in the most appropriate setting; or

(ii) The intermediary determines that the claim does not properly reflect the kind and amount of services furnished.

(b) *Fiscal management.* The intermediary must receive, disburse, and account for funds in making Medicare payments.

(c) *Provider audits.* The intermediary must audit the records of providers of services as necessary to assure proper payments.

(d) *Utilization patterns.* The intermediary must assist providers to—

(1) Develop procedures relating to utilization practices;

(2) Make studies of the effectiveness of those procedures and recommend methods to improve them;

(3) Evaluate the results of utilization review activity; and

(4) Assist in the application of safeguards against unnecessary utilization of services.

(e) *Resolution of cost report disputes.* The intermediary must establish and maintain procedures approved by CMS to consider and resolve any disputes that may result from provider dissatisfaction with an intermediary's determinations concerning provider cost reports.

(f) *Reconsideration of determinations.* The intermediary must establish and maintain procedures approved by CMS for the reconsideration of its determinations to deny payments to an individual or to the provider that furnished services to the individual. The QIO performs reconsideration of cases in which it made a determination subject to reconsideration.

(g) *Information and reports.* The intermediary must furnish to CMS any information and reports that CMS requests in order to carry out its responsibilities in the administration of the Medicare program.

(h) *Other terms and conditions.* The intermediary must comply with all applicable laws and regulations and with any other terms and conditions included in its agreement.

(i) *Dual intermediary responsibilities.* With respect to the responsibility for service to provider-based HHAs and provider-based hospices, where the HHA or hospice and its parent provider will be served by different intermediaries under § 421.117 of this part, the designated regional intermediary will process bills, make coverage determinations and make payments to the HHAs and hospices. The intermediary serving the parent provider will perform all fiscal functions, including audits and settlement of the Medicare cost reports and the HHA and hospice supplement worksheets.

[45 FR 42179, June 23, 1980, as amended at 48 FR 7178, Feb. 18, 1983; 49 FR 3659, Jan. 30, 1984; 51 FR 43198, Dec. 1, 1986; 53 FR 17944, May 19, 1988; 54 FR 4026, Jan. 27, 1989]

**§ 421.124 Intermediary's failure to perform efficiently and effectively.**

(a) Failure by an intermediary to meet, or to demonstrate the capacity to meet, the criteria or standards specified in §§ 421.120 and 421.122 may be grounds for adverse action by the Secretary or by CMS, such as reassignment of providers, offer of a short-term agreement, termination of a contract, or non-renewal of a contract. If an intermediary meets all criteria and standards in its overall performance, but does not meet them with respect to a specific provider or class of providers, CMS may reassign that provider or class of providers to another intermediary in accordance with § 421.114.

(b) In addition, notwithstanding whether an intermediary meets the criteria and standards, if the cost incurred by the intermediary to meet its contractual requirements exceeds the amount which CMS finds to be reasonable and adequate to meet the cost which must be incurred by an efficiently and economically operated intermediary, those high costs may also be grounds for adverse action.

[59 FR 682, Jan. 6, 1994]

**§ 421.126 Termination of agreements.**

(a) *Termination by intermediary.* An intermediary may terminate its agreement at any time by–

(1) Giving written notice of its intention to CMS and to the providers it services at least 180 days before its intended termination date; and

(2) Giving public notice of its intention by publishing a statement of the effective date of termination at least 60 days before that date. Publication must be in a newspaper of general circulation in each community served by the intermediary.

(b) *Termination by the Secretary, and right of appeal.* (1) The Secretary may terminate an agreement if–

(i) The intermediary fails to comply with the requirements of this subpart;

(ii) The intermediary fails to meet the criteria or standards specified in §§ 421.120 and 421.122; or

(iii) CMS has reassigned, under § 421.114 or § 421.116, all of the providers assigned to the intermediary.

(2) If the Secretary decides to terminate an agreement, he or she will offer the intermediary an opportunity for a hearing, in accordance with § 421.128.

(3) If the intermediary does not request a hearing, or if the hearing decision affirms the Secretary's decision, the Secretary will provide reasonable notice of the effective date of termination to–

(i) The intermediary;

(ii) The providers served by the intermediary; and

(iii) The general public.

(4) The providers served by the intermediary will be given the opportunity to nominate another intermediary, in accordance with § 421.104.

**§ 421.128 Intermediary's opportunity for hearing and right to judicial review.**

(a) *Basis for appeal.* An intermediary adversely affected by any of the following actions shall be granted an opportunity for a hearing:

(1) Assignment or reassignment of providers to another intermediary.

(2) Designation of a national or regional intermediary to serve a class of providers.

(3) Termination of the agreement.

(b) *Request for hearing.* The intermediary shall file the request with CMS within 20 days from the date on the notice of intended action.

(c) *Hearing procedures.* The hearing officer shall be a representative of the Secretary and not otherwise a party to the initial administrative decision. The intermediary may be represented by counsel and may present evidence and examine witnesses. A complete recording of the proceedings at the hearing will be made and transcribed.

(d) *Judicial review.* An adverse hearing decision concerning action under paragraph (a)(1) or (a)(2) of this section is subject to judicial review in accordance with 5 U.S.C. chapter 7.

(e) As specified in § 421.118, contracts awarded under the experimental authority of CMS are not subject to the provisions of this section.

(f) *Exception.* An intermediary adversely affected by the designation of a regional intermediary or an alternative regional intermediary for HHAs, or an intermediary for hospices, under § 421.117 of this subpart is not entitled to a hearing or judicial review concerning adverse effects caused by the designation of an intermediary.

[45 FR 42179, June 23, 1980, as amended at 47 FR 38540, Sept. 1, 1982; 49 FR 3660, Jan. 30, 1984; 53 FR 17945, May 19, 1988]

**§ 421.200 Carrier functions.**

A contract between CMS and a carrier, other than a regional DMEPOS carrier, specifies the functions to be performed by the carrier which must include, but are not necessarily limited to, the following:

(a) *Coverage.* (1) The carrier ensures that payment is made only for services that are:

(i) Furnished to Medicare beneficiaries;

(ii) Covered under Medicare; and

(iii) In accordance with QIO determinations when they are services for which the QIO has assumed review responsibility under its contract with CMS.

(2) The carrier takes appropriate action to reject or adjust the claim if—

(i) The carrier or the QIO determines that the services furnished or proposed to be furnished were not reasonable, not medically necessary, or not furnished in the most appropriate setting;

(ii) The carrier determines that the claim does not properly reflect the kind and amount of services furnished.

(b) *Payment on a cost basis.* If payment is on a cost basis, the carrier must assure that payments are based on reasonable costs, as determined under part 413 of this chapter.

(c) *Payment on a charge basis.* If payment is on a charge basis, under part 405, subpart E of this chapter, the carrier must ensure that—

(1) Charges are reasonable and not higher than the charge for a comparable service furnished under comparable circumstances to the carrier's policy holders and subscribers; and

(2) The payment is based on one of the following—

(i) An itemized bill.

(ii) An assignment under the terms of which the reasonable charge is the full charge for the service, as specified in § 424.55 of this chapter.

(iii) If the beneficiary has died, the procedures set forth in §§ 424.62 and 424.64 of this chapter.

(d) *Fiscal management.* The carrier must receive, disburse, and account for funds in making payments under Medicare.

(e) *Provider audits.* The carrier must audit the records of providers to whom it makes Medicare Part B payments to assure that payments are made properly.

(f) *Utilization patterns.* (1) The carrier must have methods and procedures for identifying utilization patterns that deviate from professionally established norms and bring the deviant patterns to the attention of appropriate professional groups.

(2) The carrier must assist providers and other persons who furnish Medicare Part B services to—

(i) Develop procedures relating to utilization practices;

(ii) Make studies of the effectiveness of those procedures and devise methods to improve them;

(iii) Apply safeguards against unnecessary utilization of services; and

(iv) Develop procedures for utilization review, and establish groups to perform such reviews of providers to whom it makes Medicare Part B payments.

(g) *Information and reports.* The carrier must furnish to CMS any information and reports that CMS requests in order to carry out CMS's responsibilities in the administration of the Medicare program. The carrier must be responsive to requests for information from the public.

(h) *Maintenance and availability of records.* The carrier must maintain and make available to CMS the records necessary for verification of payments and for other related purposes.

(i) *Hearings to Part B beneficiaries.* (1) The carrier must provide an opportunity for a fair hearing if it denies the beneficiary's request for payment, does not act upon the request with reasonable promptness, or pays less than the amount claimed.

(2) The hearing procedures must be in accordance with part 405, subpart H, of this chapter (Review and Hearing Under the Supplementary Medical Insurance Program).

(j) *Other terms and conditions.* The carrier must comply with any other terms and conditions included in its contract.

[45 FR 42183, June 23, 1980; 45 FR 64913, Oct. 1, 1980, as amended at 49 FR 3660, Jan. 30, 1984; 49 FR 9174, Mar. 12, 1984; 51 FR 34833, Sept. 30, 1986; 51 FR 41350, Nov. 14, 1986; 51 FR 43198, Dec. 1, 1986; 52 FR 4499, Feb. 12, 1987;

53 FR 6648, Mar. 2, 1988; 54 FR 4027, Jan. 27, 1989; 57 FR 27307, June 18, 1992]

**§ 421.203 Carrier's failure to perform efficiently and effectively.**

(a) Failure by a carrier to meet, or demonstrate the capacity to meet, the criteria and standards specified in § 421.201 may be grounds for adverse action by the Secretary, such as contract termination or non-renewal.

(b) Notwithstanding whether or not a carrier meets the criteria and standards specified in § 421.201, if the cost incurred by the carrier to meet its contractual requirements exceeds the amount that CMS finds to be reasonable and adequate to meet the cost which must be incurred by an efficiently and economically operated carrier, those high costs may also be grounds for adverse action.

[59 FR 682, Jan. 6, 1994]

**§ 421.205 Termination by the Secretary.**

(a) *Cause for termination.* The Secretary may terminate a contract with a carrier at any time if he or she determines that the carrier has failed substantially to carry out any material terms of the contract or has performed its function in a manner inconsistent with the effective and efficient administration of the Medicare Part B program.

(b) *Notice and opportunity for hearing.* Upon notification of the Secretary's intent to terminate the contract, the carrier may request a hearing within 20 days after the date on the notice of intent to terminate.

(c) *Hearing procedures.* The hearing procedures will be those specified in § 421.128(c).

## PART 422—MEDICARE ADVANTAGE PROGRAM

### Subpart M—Grievances, Organization Determinations and Appeals

**Source:** 63 FR 35107, June 26, 1998, unless otherwise noted.

**§ 422.560 Basis and scope.**

(a) *Statutory basis.* (1) Section 1852(f) of the Act provides that an MA organization must establish meaningful grievance procedures.

(2) Section 1852(g) of the Act establishes requirements that an MA organization must meet concerning organization determinations and appeals.

(3) Section 1869 of the Act specifies the amount in controversy needed to pursue a hearing and judicial review and authorizes representatives to act on behalf of individuals that seek appeals. These provisions are incorporated for MA appeals by section 1852(g)(5) of the Act and part 405 of this chapter.

(b) *Scope.* This subpart sets forth—

(1) Requirements for MA organizations with respect to grievance procedures, organization determinations, and appeal procedures.

(2) The rights of MA enrollees with respect to organization determinations, and grievance and appeal procedures.

(3) The rules concerning notice of noncoverage of inpatient hospital care.

(4) The rules that apply when an MA enrollee requests immediate QIO review of a determination that he or she no longer needs inpatient hospital care.

(c) *Relation to ERISA requirements.* Consistent with section 1857(i)(2) of the Act, provisions of this subpart may, to the extent applicable under regulations adopted by the Secretary of Labor, apply to claims for benefits under group health plans subject to the Employee Retirement Income Security Act (ERISA).
[63 FR 35107, June 26, 1998, as amended at 70 FR 4738, Jan. 28, 2005]

**§ 422.561 Definitions.**

As used in this subpart, unless the context indicates otherwise—

*Appeal* means any of the procedures that deal with the review of adverse organization determinations on the health care services the enrollee believes he or she is entitled to receive, including delay in providing, arranging for, or approving the health care services (such that a delay would adversely affect the health of the enrollee), or on any amounts the enrollee must pay for a service, as defined under § 422.566(b). These procedures include reconsiderations by the MA organization, and if necessary, an independent review entity, hearings before ALJs, review by the Medicare Appeals Council (MAC), and judicial review.

*Enrollee* means an MA eligible individual who has elected an MA plan offered by an MA organization.

*Grievance* means any complaint or dispute, other than one that constitutes an organization determination, expressing dissatisfaction with any aspect of an MA organization's or provider's operations, activities, or behavior, regardless of whether remedial action is requested.

*Physician* has the meaning given the term in section 1861(r) of the Act.

*Representative* means an individual appointed by an enrollee or other party, or authorized under State or other applicable law, to act on behalf of an enrollee or other party involved in the appeal. Unless otherwise stated in this subpart, the representative will have all of the rights and responsibilities of an enrollee or party in obtaining an organization determination or in dealing with any of the levels of the appeals process, subject to the applicable rules described in part 405 of this chapter.
[63 FR 35067, June 26, 1998, as amended at 65 FR 40328, June 29, 2000; 68 FR 16667, Apr. 4, 2003; 70 FR 4738, Jan. 28, 2005]

**§ 422.562 General provisions.**

(a) *Responsibilities of the MA organization.* (1) An MA organization, with respect to each MA plan that it offers, must establish and maintain—

(i) A grievance procedure as described in § 422.564 for addressing issues that do not involve organization determinations;

(ii) A procedure for making timely organization determinations;

(iii) Appeals procedures that meet the requirements of this subpart for issues that involve organization determinations; and

(2) An MA organization must ensure that all enrollees receive written information about the—

(i) Grievance and appeals procedures that are available to them through the MA organization; and

(ii) Complaint process available to the enrollee under the QIO process as set forth under section 1154(a)(14) of the Act.

(3) In accordance with subpart K of this part, if the MA organization delegates any of its responsibilities under this subpart to another entity or individual through which the organization provides health care services, the MA organization is ultimately responsible for ensuring that the entity or individual satisfies the relevant requirements of this subpart.

(b) *Rights of MA enrollees.* In accordance with the provisions of this subpart, enrollees have the following rights:

(1) The right to have grievances between the enrollee and the MA organization heard and resolved, as described in § 422.564.

(2) The right to a timely organization determination, as provided under § 422.566.

(3) The right to request an expedited organization determination, as provided under § 422.570.

(4) If dissatisfied with any part of an organization determination, the following appeal rights:

(i) The right to a reconsideration of the adverse organization determination by the MA organization, as provided under § 422.578.

(ii) The right to request an expedited reconsideration, as provided under § 422.584.

(iii) If, as a result of a reconsideration, an MA organization affirms, in whole or in part, its adverse organization determination, the right to an automatic reconsidered determination made by an independent, outside entity contracted by CMS, as provided in § 422.592.

(iv) The right to an ALJ hearing if the amount in controversy is met, as provided in § 422.600.

(v) The right to request MAC review of the ALJ hearing decision, as provided in § 422.608.

(vi) The right to judicial review of the hearing decision if the amount in controversy is met, as provided in § 422.612.

(c) *Limits on when this subpart applies.* (1) If an enrollee receives immediate QIO review (as provided in § 422.622) of a determination of noncoverage of inpatient hospital care—

(i) The enrollee is not entitled to review of that issue by the MA organization; and

(ii) The QIO review decision is subject only to the appeal procedures set forth in parts 476 and 478 of this chapter.

(2) If an enrollee has no further liability to pay for services that were furnished by an MA organization, a determination regarding these services is not subject to appeal.

(d) *When other regulations apply.* Unless this subpart provides otherwise, the regulations in part 405 of this chapter (concerning the administrative review and hearing processes and representation of parties under titles II and XVIII of the Act), apply under this subpart to the extent they are appropriate.
[63 FR 35067, June 26, 1998, as amended at 65 FR 40329, June 29, 2000; 70 FR 4738, Jan. 28, 2005; 70 FR 52027, Sept. 1, 2005]

**§ 422.564 Grievance procedures.**

(a) *General rule.* Each MA organization must provide meaningful procedures for timely hearing and resolving grievances between enrollees and the organization or any other entity or individual through which the organization provides health care services under any MA plan it offers.

(b) *Distinguished from appeals.* Grievance procedures are separate and distinct from appeals procedures, which address organization determinations as defined in § 422.566(b). Upon receiving a complaint, an MA organization must promptly determine and inform the enrollee whether the complaint is subject to its grievance procedures or its appeals procedures.

(c) *Distinguished from the quality improvement organization (QIO) complaint process.* Under section 1154(a)(14) of the Act, the QIO must review beneficiaries' written complaints about the quality of services they have received under the Medicare program. This process is separate and distinct from the grievance procedures of the MA organization. For quality of care issues, an enrollee may file a grievance with the MA organization; file a written complaint with the QIO, or both. For any complaint submitted to a QIO, the MA organization must cooperate with the QIO in resolving the complaint.

(d) *Method for filing a grievance.* (1) An enrollee may file a grievance with the MA organization either orally or in writing.

(2) An enrollee must file a grievance no later than 60 days after the event or incident that precipitates the grievance.

(e) *Grievance disposition and notification.* (1) The MA organization must notify the enrollee of its decision as expeditiously as the case requires, based on the enrollee's health status, but no later than 30 days after the date the organization receives the oral or written grievance.

(2) The MA organization may extend the 30-day time frame by up to 14 days if the enrollee requests the extension or if the organization justifies a need for additional information and documents how the delay is in the interest of the enrollee. When the MA organization extends the deadline, it must immediately notify the enrollee in writing of the reasons for the delay.

(3) The MA organization must inform the enrollee of the disposition of the grievance in accordance with the following procedures:

(i) All grievances submitted in writing must be responded to in writing.

(ii) Grievances submitted orally may be responded to either orally or in writing, unless the enrollee requests a written response.

(iii) All grievances related to quality of care, regardless of how the grievance is filed, must be responded to in writing. The response must include a description of the enrollee's right to file a written complaint with the QIO. For any complaint submitted to a QIO, the MA organization must cooperate with the QIO in resolving the complaint.

(f) *Expedited grievances.* An MA organization must respond to an enrollee's grievance within 24 hours if:

(1) The complaint involves an MA organization's decision to invoke an extension relating to an organization determination or reconsideration.

(2) The complaint involves an MA organization's refusal to grant an enrollee's request for an expedited organization determination under § 422.570 or reconsideration under § 422.584.

(g) *Recordkeeping.* The MA organization must have an established process to track and maintain records on all grievances received both orally and in writing, including, at a minimum, the date of receipt, final disposition of the grievance, and the date that the MA organization notified the enrollee of the disposition.
[68 FR 16667, Apr. 4, 2003, as amended at 70 FR 4738, Jan. 28, 2005]

**§ 422.566 Organization determinations.**

(a) *Responsibilities of the MA organization.* Each MA organization must have a procedure for making timely organization determinations (in accordance with the requirements of this subpart) regarding the benefits an enrollee is entitled to receive under an MA plan, including basic benefits as described under § 422.100(c)(1) and mandatory and optional supplemental benefits as described under § 422.102, and the amount, if any, that the enrollee is required to pay for a health service. The MA organization must have a standard procedure for making determinations, in accordance with § 422.568, and an expedited procedure for situations in which applying the standard procedure could seriously jeopardize the enrollee's life, health, or ability to regain maximum function, in accordance with §§ 422.570 and 422.572.

(b) *Actions that are organization determinations.* An organization determination is any determination made by an MA organization with respect to any of the following:

(1) Payment for temporarily out of the area renal dialysis services, emergency services, post-stabilization care, or urgently needed services.

(2) Payment for any other health services furnished by a provider other than the MA organization that the enrollee believes—

(i) Are covered under Medicare; or

(ii) If not covered under Medicare, should have been furnished, arranged for, or reimbursed by the MA organization.

(3) The MA organization's refusal to provide or pay for services, in whole or in part, including the type or level of services, that the enrollee believes should be furnished or arranged for by the MA organization.

(4) Discontinuation or reduction of a service if the enrollee believes that continuation of the services is medically necessary.

(5) Failure of the MA organization to approve, furnish, arrange for, or provide payment for health care services in a timely manner, or to provide the

enrollee with timely notice of an adverse determination, such that a delay would adversely affect the health of the enrollee.

(c) *Who can request an organization determination.* (1) Those individuals or entities who can request an organization determination are–

(i) The enrollee (including his or her authorized representative);

(ii) Any provider that furnishes, or intends to furnish, services to the enrollee; or

(iii) The legal representative of a deceased enrollee's estate.

(2) Those who can request an expedited determination are–

(i) An enrollee (including his or her authorized representative); or

(ii) A physician (regardless of whether the physician is affiliated with the MA organization).

[63 FR 35067, June 26, 1998, as amended at 65 FR 40329, June 29, 2000; 68 FR 50858, Aug. 22, 2003; 70 FR 4739, Jan. 28, 2005]

**§ 422.568 Standard time frames and notice requirements for organization determinations.**

(a) *Time frame for requests for service.* When a party has made a request for a service, the MA organization must notify the enrollee of its determination as expeditiously as the enrollee's health condition requires, but no later than 14 calendar days after the date the organization receives the request for a standard organization determination. The MA organization may extend the time frame by up to 14 calendar days if the enrollee requests the extension or if the organization justifies a need for additional information and how the delay is in the interest of the enrollee (for example, the receipt of additional medical evidence from noncontract providers may change an MA organization's decision to deny). When the MA organization extends the time frame, it must notify the enrollee in writing of the reasons for the delay, and inform the enrollee of the right to file an expedited grievance if he or she disagrees with the MA organization's decision to grant an extension.

(b) *Time frame for requests for payment.* The MA organization must process requests for payment according to the "prompt payment"provisions set forth in § 422.520.

(c) *Written notice for MA organization denials.* If an MA organization decides to deny service or payment in whole or in part, or if an enrollee disagrees with an MA organization's decision to discontinue or reduce the level of care for an ongoing course of treatment, the organization must give the enrollee written notice of the determination.

(d) *Written notice for MA organization denials.* If an enrollee requests an MA organization to provide an explanation of a practitioner's denial of an item or service, in whole or in part, the MA organization must give the enrollee a written notice.

(e) *Form and content of the MA organization notice.* The notice of any denial under paragraph (d) of this section must–

(1) Use approved notice language in a readable and understandable form;

(2) State the specific reasons for the denial;

(3) Inform the enrollee of his or her right to a reconsideration;

(4)(i) For service denials, describe both the standard and expedited reconsideration processes, including the enrollee's right to, and conditions for, obtaining an expedited reconsideration and the rest of the appeals process; and

(ii) For payment denials, describe the standard reconsideration process and the rest of the appeals process; and

(5) Comply with any other notice requirements specified by CMS.

(f) *Effect of failure to provide timely notice.* If the MA organization fails to provide the enrollee with timely notice of an organization determination as specified in this section, this failure itself constitutes an adverse organization determination and may be appealed.

[65 FR 40329, June 29, 2000, as amended at 70 FR 4739, Jan. 28, 2005; 70 FR 52027, Sept. 1, 2005]

**§ 422.570 Expediting certain organization determinations.**

(a) *Request for expedited determination.* An enrollee or a physician (regardless of whether the physician is affiliated with the MA organization) may request that an MA organization expedite an organization determination involving the issues described in § 422.566(b)(3) and (b)(4). (This does not include requests for payment of services already furnished.)

(b) *How to make a request.* (1) To ask for an expedited determination, an enrollee or a physician must submit an oral or written request directly to the MA organization or, if applicable, to the entity responsible for making the determination, as directed by the MA organization.

(2) A physician may provide oral or written support for a request for an expedited determination.

(c) *How the MA organization must process requests.* The MA organization must establish and maintain the following procedures for processing requests for expedited determinations:

(1) Establish an efficient and convenient means for individuals to submit oral or written requests. The MA organization must document all oral requests in writing and maintain the documentation in the case file.

(2) Promptly decide whether to expedite a determination, based on the following requirements:

(i) For a request made by an enrollee the MA organization must provide an expedited determination if it determines that applying the standard time frame for making a determination could seriously jeopardize the life or health of the enrollee or the enrollee's ability to regain maximum function.

(ii) For a request made or supported by a physician, the MA organization must provide an expedited determination if the physician indicates that applying the standard time frame for making a determination could seriously jeopardize the life or health of the enrollee or the enrollee's ability to regain maximum function.

(d) *Actions following denial.* If an MA organization denies a request for expedited determination, it must take the following actions:

(1) Automatically transfer a request to the standard time frame and make the determination within the 14-day time frame established in § 422.568 for a standard determination. The 14-day period begins with the day the MA organization receives the request for expedited determination.

(2) Give the enrollee prompt oral notice of the denial and subsequently deliver, within 3 calendar days, a written letter that–

(i) Explains that the MA organization will process the request using the 14-day time frame for standard determinations;

(ii) Informs the enrollee of the right to file an expedited grievance if he or she disagrees with the MA organization's decision not to expedite; and

(iii) Informs the enrollee of the right to resubmit a request for an expedited determination with any physician's support; and

(iv) Provides instructions about the grievance process and its time frames.

(e) *Action on accepted request for expedited determination.* If an MA organization grants a request for expedited determination, it must make the determination and give notice in accordance with § 422.572.

(f) *Prohibition of punitive action.* An MA organization may not take or threaten to take any punitive action against a physician acting on behalf or in support of an enrollee in requesting an expedited determination.

[63 FR 35107, June 26, 1998, as amended at 65 FR 40329, June 29, 2000; 70 FR 4739, Jan. 28, 2005]

**§ 422.572 Time frames and notice requirements for expedited organization determinations.**

(a) *Time frame.* Except as provided in paragraph (b) of this section, an MA organization that approves a request for expedited determination must make its determination and notify the enrollee (and the physician involved, as appropriate) of its decision, whether adverse or favorable, as expeditiously as the enrollee's health condition requires, but no later than 72 hours after receiving the request.

(b) *Extensions.* The MA organization may extend the 72-hour deadline by up to 14 calendar days if the enrollee requests the extension or if the organization justifies a need for additional information and how the delay is in the interest of the enrollee (for example, the receipt of additional medical evidence from noncontract providers may change an MA organization's decision to deny). When the MA organization extends the deadline, it must notify the enrollee in writing of the reasons for the delay and inform the enrollee of the right to file an expedited grievance if he or she disagrees with the MA organization's decision to grant an extension. The MA organization must notify the enrollee of its determination as expeditiously as the enrollee's health condition requires, but no later than upon expiration of the extension.

(c) *Confirmation of oral notice.* If the MA organization first notifies an enrollee of an adverse expedited determination orally, it must mail written confirmation to the enrollee within 3 calendar days of the oral notification.

(d) *How the MA organization must request information from noncontract providers.* If the MA organization must receive medical information from noncontract providers, the MA organization must request the necessary information from the noncontract provider within 24 hours of the initial request for an expedited organization determination. Noncontract providers must make reasonable and diligent efforts to expeditiously gather and forward all necessary information to assist the MA organization in meeting the required time frame. Regardless of whether the MA organization must request information from noncontract providers, the MA organization is responsible for meeting the time frame and notice requirements of this section.

(e) *Content of the notice of expedited determination.* (1) The notice of any expedited determination must state the specific reasons for the determination in understandable language.

(2) If the determination is not completely favorable to the enrollee, the notice must—

(i) Inform the enrollee of his or her right to a reconsideration;

(ii) Describe both the standard and expedited reconsideration processes, including the enrollee's right to request, and conditions for obtaining, an expedited reconsideration, and the rest of the appeal process; and

(iii) Comply with any other requirements specified by CMS.

(f) *Effect of failure to provide a timely notice.* If the MA organization fails to provide the enrollee with timely notice of an expedited organization determination as specified in this section, this failure itself constitutes an adverse organization determination and may be appealed.

[63 FR 35107, June 26, 1998, as amended at 65 FR 40329, June 29, 2000; 70 FR 4739, Jan. 28, 2005]

**§ 422.574 Parties to the organization determination.**

The parties to the organization determination are—

(a) The enrollee (including his or her authorized representative);

(b) An assignee of the enrollee (that is, a physician or other provider who has furnished a service to the enrollee and formally agrees to waive any right to payment from the enrollee for that service);

(c) The legal representative of a deceased enrollee's estate; or

(d) Any other provider or entity (other than the MA organization) determined to have an appealable interest in the proceeding.

**§ 422.576 Effect of an organization determination.**

The organization determination is binding on all parties unless it is reconsidered under §§ 422.578 through 422.596 or is reopened and revised under § 422.616.

**§ 422.578 Right to a reconsideration.**
Any party to an organization determination (including one that has been reopened and revised as described in § 422.616) may request that the determination be reconsidered under the procedures described in § 422.582, which address requests for a standard reconsideration. An enrollee or physician (acting on behalf of an enrollee) may request an expedited reconsideration as described in § 422.584.

**§ 422.580 Reconsideration defined.**
A reconsideration consists of a review of an adverse organization determination, the evidence and findings upon which it was based, and any other evidence the parties submit or the MA organization or CMS obtains.

**§ 422.582 Request for a standard reconsideration.**

(a) *Method and place for filing a request.* A party to an organization determination must ask for a reconsideration of the determination by making a written request to the MA organization that made the organization determination. The MA organization may adopt a policy for accepting oral requests.

(b) *Time frame for filing a request.* Except as provided in paragraph (c) of this section, a party must file a request for reconsideration within 60 calendar days from the date of the notice of the organization determination.

(c) *Extending the time for filing a request*—(1) *General rule.* If a party shows good cause, the MA organization may extend the time frame for filing a request for reconsideration.

(2) *How to request an extension of time frame.* If the 60-day period in which to file a request for reconsideration has expired, a party to the organization determination may file a request for reconsideration with the MA organization. The request for reconsideration and to extend the time frame must—

(i) Be in writing; and

(ii) State why the request for reconsideration was not filed on time.

(d) *Parties to the reconsideration.* The parties to the reconsideration are the parties to the organization determination, as described in § 422.574, and any other provider or entity (other than the MA organization) whose rights with respect to the organization determination may be affected by the reconsideration, as determined by the entity that conducts the reconsideration.

(e) *Withdrawing a request.* The party who files a request for reconsideration may withdraw it by filing a written request for withdrawal at one of the places listed in paragraph (a) of this section.

[63 FR 35107, June 26, 1998, as amended at 70 FR 4739, Jan. 28, 2005]

**§ 422.584 Expediting certain reconsiderations.**

(a) *Who may request an expedited reconsideration.* An enrollee or a physician (regardless of whether he or she is affiliated with the MA organization) may request that an MA organization expedite a reconsideration of a determination that involves the issues described in § 422.566(b)(3) and (b)(4). (This does not include requests for payment of services already furnished.)

(b) *How to make a request.* (1) To ask for an expedited reconsideration, an enrollee or a physician acting on behalf of an enrollee must submit an oral or written request directly to the MA organization or, if applicable, to the entity responsible for making the reconsideration, as directed by the MA organization.

(2) A physician may provide oral or written support for a request for an expedited reconsideration.

(c) *How the MA organization must process requests.* The MA organization must establish and maintain the following procedures for processing requests for expedited reconsiderations:

(1) *Handling of requests.* The MA organization must establish an efficient and convenient means for individuals to submit oral or written requests, document all oral requests in writing, and maintain the documentation in the case file.

(2) *Prompt decision.* Promptly decide on whether to expedite the reconsideration or follow the time frame for standard reconsideration based on the following requirements:

(i) For a request made by an enrollee, the MA organization must provide an expedited reconsideration if it determines that applying the standard time frame for reconsidering a determination could seriously jeopardize the life or health of the enrollee or the enrollee's ability to regain maximum function.

(ii) For a request made or supported by a physician, the MA organization must provide an expedited reconsideration if the physician indicates that applying the standard time frame for conducting a reconsideration could seriously jeopardize the life or health of the enrollee or the enrollee's ability to regain maximum function.

(d) *Actions following denial.* If an MA organization denies a request for expedited reconsideration, it must take the following actions:

(1) Automatically transfer a request to the standard time frame and make the determination within the 30-day time frame established in § 422.590(a). The 30-day period begins the day the MA organization receives the request for expedited reconsideration.

(2) Give the enrollee prompt oral notice, and subsequently deliver, within 3 calendar days, a written letter that—

(i) Explains that the MA organization will process the enrollee's request using the 30-day time frame for standard reconsiderations;

(ii) Informs the enrollee of the right to file a grievance if he or she disagrees with the organization's decision not to expedite;

(iii) Informs the enrollee of the right to resubmit a request for an expedited reconsideration with any physician's support; and

(iv) Provides instructions about the grievance process and its time frames.

(e) *Action following acceptance of a request.* If an MA organization grants a request for expedited reconsideration, it must conduct the reconsideration and give notice in accordance with § 422.590.

(f) *Prohibition of punitive action.* An MA organization may not take or threaten to take any punitive action against a physician acting on behalf or in support of an enrollee in requesting an expedited reconsideration.

[63 FR 35107, June 26, 1998, as amended at 65 FR 40330, June 29, 2000; 70 FR 4739, Jan. 28, 2005]

**§ 422.586 Opportunity to submit evidence.**

The MA organization must provide the parties to the reconsideration with a reasonable opportunity to present evidence and allegations of fact or law, related to the issue in dispute, in person as well as in writing. In the case of an expedited reconsideration, the opportunity to present evidence is limited by the short time frame for making a decision. Therefore, the MA organization must inform the parties of the conditions for submitting the evidence.

**§ 422.590 Time frames and responsibility for reconsiderations.**

(a) *Standard reconsideration: Request for services.* (1) If the MA organization makes a reconsidered determination that is completely favorable to the enrollee, the MA organization must issue the determination (and effectuate it in accordance with § 422.618(a)) as expeditiously as the enrollee's health condition requires, but no later than 30 calendar days from the date it receives the request for a standard reconsideration. The MA organization may extend the time frame by up to 14 calendar days if the enrollee requests the extension or if the organization justifies a need for additional information and how the delay is in the interest of the enrollee (for example, the receipt of additional medical evidence from noncontract providers may change an MA organization's decision to deny). When the MA organization extends the time frame, it must notify the enrollee in writing of the reasons for the delay, and inform the enrollee of the right to file an expedited grievance if he or she disagrees with the MA organization's decision to grant an extension. For extensions, the MA organization must issue and effectuate its determination as expeditiously as the enrollee's health condition requires, but no later than upon expiration of the extension.

(2) If the MA organization makes a reconsidered determination that affirms, in whole or in part, its adverse organization determination, it must prepare a written explanation and send the case file to the independent entity contracted by CMS as expeditiously as the enrollee's health condition requires, but no later than 30 calendar days from the date it receives the request for a standard reconsideration (or no later than the expiration of an extension described in paragraph (a)(1) of this section). The organization must make reasonable and diligent efforts to assist in gathering and forwarding information to the independent entity.

(b) *Standard reconsideration: Request for payment.* (1) If the MA organization makes a reconsidered determination that is completely favorable to the enrollee, the MA organization must issue its reconsidered determination to the enrollee (and effectuate it in accordance with § 422.618(a)) no later than 60 calendar days from the date it receives the request for a standard reconsideration.

(2) If the MA organization affirms, in whole or in part, its adverse organization determination, it must prepare a written explanation and send the case file to the independent entity contracted by CMS no later than 60 calendar days from the date it receives the request for a standard reconsideration. The organization must make reasonable and diligent efforts to assist in gathering and forwarding information to the independent entity.

(c) *Effect of failure to meet time frame for standard reconsideration.* If the MA organization fails to provide the enrollee with a reconsidered determination within the time frames specified in paragraph (a) or paragraph (b) of this section, this failure constitutes an affirmation of its adverse organization determination, and the MA organization must submit the file to the independent entity in the same manner as described under paragraphs (a)(2) and (b)(2) of this section.

(d) *Expedited reconsideration*—(1) *Time frame.* Except as provided in paragraph (d)(2) of this section, an MA organization that approves a request for expedited reconsideration must complete its reconsideration and give the enrollee (and the physician involved, as appropriate) notice of its decision as expeditiously as the enrollee's health condition requires but no later than 72 hours after receiving the request.

(2) *Extensions.* The MA organization may extend the 72-hour deadline by up to 14 calendar days if the enrollee requests the extension or if the organization justifies a need for additional information and how the delay is in the interest of the enrollee (for example, the receipt of additional medical evidence from noncontract providers may change an MA organization's decision to deny). When the MA organization extends the time frame, it must notify the enrollee in writing of the reasons for the delay, and inform the enrollee of the right to file an expedited grievance if he or she disagrees with the MA organization's decision to grant an extension. The MA organization must notify the enrollee of its determination as expeditiously as the enrollee's health condition requires but no later than upon expiration of the extension.

(3) *Confirmation of oral notice.* If the MA organization first notifies an enrollee of a completely favorable expedited reconsideration, it must mail written confirmation to the enrollee within 3 calendar days.

(4) *How the MA organization must request information from noncontract providers.* If the MA organization must receive medical information from noncontract providers, the MA organization must request the necessary information from the noncontract provider within 24 hours of the initial request for an expedited reconsideration. Noncontract providers must make reasonable and diligent efforts to expeditiously gather and forward all necessary information to assist the MA organization in meeting the required time frame. Regardless of whether the MA organization must request information from noncontract providers, the MA organization is responsible for meeting the time frame and notice requirements.

(5) *Affirmation of an adverse expedited organization determination.* If, as a result of its reconsideration, the MA organization affirms, in whole or in part, its adverse expedited organization determination, the MA organization must submit a written explanation and the case file to the independent entity contracted by CMS as expeditiously as the enrollee's health condition requires, but not later than within 24 hours of its affirmation. The organization must make reasonable and diligent efforts to assist in gathering and forwarding information to the independent entity.

(e) *Notification of enrollee.* If the MA organization refers the matter to the independent entity as described under this section, it must concurrently notify the enrollee of that action.

(f) *Failure to meet time frame for expedited reconsideration.* If the MA organization fails to provide the enrollee with the results of its reconsideration within the time frame described in paragraph (d) of this section, this failure constitutes an adverse reconsidered determination, and the MA organization must submit the file to the independent entity within 24 hours of expiration of the time frame set forth in paragraph (d) of this section.

(g) *Who must reconsider an adverse organization determination.* (1) A person or persons who were not involved in making the organization determination must conduct the reconsideration.

(2) When the issue is the MA organization's denial of coverage based on a lack of medical necessity (or any substantively equivalent term used to describe the concept of medical necessity), the reconsidered determination must be made by a physician with expertise in the field of medicine that is appropriate for the services at issue. The physician making the reconsidered determination need not, in all cases, be of the same specialty or subspecialty as the treating physician.

[63 FR 35107, June 26, 1998, as amended at 65 FR 40330, June 29, 2000; 70 FR 4739, Jan. 28, 2005]

**§ 422.592 Reconsideration by an independent entity.**

(a) When the MA organization affirms, in whole or in part, its adverse organization determination, the issues that remain in dispute must be reviewed and resolved by an independent, outside entity that contracts with CMS.

(b) The independent outside entity must conduct the review as expeditiously as the enrollee's health condition requires but must not exceed the deadlines specified in the contract.

(c) When the independent entity conducts a reconsideration, the parties to the reconsideration are the same parties listed in § 422.582(d) who qualified during the MA organization's reconsideration, with the addition of the MA organization.

**§ 422.594 Notice of reconsidered determination by the independent entity.**

(a) *Responsibility for the notice.* When the independent entity makes the reconsidered determination, it is responsible for mailing a notice of its reconsidered determination to the parties and for sending a copy to CMS.

(b) *Content of the notice.* The notice must—

(1) State the specific reasons for the entity's decisions in understandable language;

(2) If the reconsidered determination is adverse (that is, does not completely reverse the MA organization's adverse organization determination), inform the parties of their right to an ALJ hearing if the amount in controversy is $100 or more;

(3) Describe the procedures that a party must follow to obtain an ALJ hearing; and

(4) Comply with any other requirements specified by CMS.

[63 FR 35107, June 26, 1998, as amended at 65 FR 40330, June 29, 2000]

**§ 422.596 Effect of a reconsidered determination.**

A reconsidered determination is final and binding on all parties unless a party other than the MA organization files a request for a hearing under the provisions of § 422.602, or unless the reconsidered determination is revised under § 422.616.

[65 FR 40331, June 29, 2000]

**§ 422.600 Right to a hearing.**

(a) If the amount remaining in controversy after reconsideration meets the threshold requirement established annually by the Secretary, any party to the reconsideration (except the MA organization) who is dissatisfied with the reconsidered determination has a right to a hearing before an ALJ.

(b) The amount remaining in controversy, which can include any combination of Part A and Part B services, is computed in accordance with part 405 of this chapter.

(c) If the basis for the appeal is the MA organization's refusal to provide services, CMS uses the projected value of those services to compute the amount remaining in controversy.

[63 FR 35107, June 26, 1998, as amended at 70 FR 4740, Jan. 28, 2005]

**§ 422.602 Request for an ALJ hearing.**

(a) *How and where to file a request.* A party must file a written request for a hearing with the entity specified in the IRE's reconsideration notice.

(b) *When to file a request.* Except when an ALJ extends the time frame as provided in part 405 of this chapter, a party must file a request for a hearing within 60 days of the date of the notice of a reconsidered determination. The time and place for a hearing before an ALJ will be set in accordance with § 405.1020.

(c) *Parties to a hearing.* The parties to a hearing are the parties to the reconsideration, the MA organization, and any other person or entity whose rights with respect to the reconsideration may be affected by the hearing, as determined by the ALJ.

(d) *Insufficient amount in controversy.* (1) If a request for a hearing clearly shows that the amount in controversy is less than that required under § 422.600, the ALJ dismisses the request.

(2) If, after a hearing is initiated, the ALJ finds that the amount in controversy is less than the amount required under § 422.600, the ALJ discontinues the hearing and does not rule on the substantive issues raised in the appeal.

[63 FR 35107, June 26, 1998, as amended at 70 FR 4740, Jan. 28, 2005]

**§ 422.608 Medicare Appeals Council (MAC) review.**

Any party to the hearing, including the MA organization, who is dissatisfied with the ALJ hearing decision, may request that the MAC review the ALJ's decision or dismissal. The regulations under part 405 of this chapter regarding MAC review apply to matters addressed by this subpart to the extent that they are appropriate.

[70 FR 4740, Jan. 28, 2005]

**§ 422.612 Judicial review.**

(a) *Review of ALJ's decision.* Any party, including the MA organization, may request judicial review (upon notifying the other parties) of an ALJ's decision if—

(1) The Board denied the party's request for review; and

(2) The amount in controversy meets the threshold requirement established annually by the Secretary.

(b) *Review of MAC decision.* Any party, including the MA organization, may request judicial review (upon notifying the other parties) of the MAC decision if it is the final decision of CMS and the amount in controversy meets the threshold established in paragraph (a)(2) of this section.

(c) *How to request judicial review.* In order to request judicial review, a party must file a civil action in a district court of the United States in accordance with section 205(g) of the Act. See part 405 of this chapter for a description of the procedures to follow in requesting judicial review.

[63 FR 35107, June 26, 1998; 63 FR 52614, Oct. 1, 1998, as amended at 65 FR 40331, June 29, 2000; 70 FR 4740, Jan. 28, 2005]

**§ 422.616 Reopening and revising determinations and decisions.**

(a) An organization or reconsidered determination made by an MA organization, a reconsidered determination made by the independent entity described in § 422.592, or the decision of an ALJ or the MAC that is otherwise final and binding may be reopened and revised by the entity that made the determination or decision, under the rules in part 405 of this chapter.

(b) Reopening may be at the instigation of any party.

(c) The filing of a request for reopening does not relieve the MA organization of its obligation to make payment or provide services as specified in § 422.618.

(d) Once an entity issues a revised determination or decision, any party may file an appeal.

[63 FR 35107, June 26, 1998; 63 FR 52614, Oct. 1, 1998, as amended at 70 FR 4740, Jan. 28, 2005]

**§ 422.618 How an MA organization must effectuate standard reconsidered determinations or decisions.**

(a) *Reversals by the MA organization*—(1) *Requests for service.* If, on reconsideration of a request for service, the MA organization completely reverses its organization determination, the organization must authorize or provide the service under dispute as expeditiously as the enrollee's health condition requires, but no later than 30 calendar days after the date the MA organization receives the request for reconsideration (or no later than upon expiration of an extension described in § 422.590(a)(1)).

(2) *Requests for payment.* If, on reconsideration of a request for payment, the MA organization completely reverses its organization determination, the organization must pay for the service no later than 60 calendar days after the date the MA organization receives the request for reconsideration.

(b) *Reversals by the independent outside entity*—(1) *Requests for service.* If, on reconsideration of a request for service, the MA organization's determination is reversed in whole or in part by the independent outside entity, the MA organization must authorize the service under dispute within 72 hours from the date it receives notice reversing the determination, or provide the service under dispute as expeditiously as the enrollee's health condition requires, but no later than 14 calendar days from that date. The MA organization must inform the independent outside entity that the organization has effectuated the decision.

(2) *Requests for payment.* If, on reconsideration of a request for payment, the MA organization's determination is reversed in whole or in part by the independent outside entity, the MA organization must pay for the service no later than 30 calendar days from the date it receives notice reversing the organization determination. The MA organization must inform the independent outside entity that the organization has effectuated the decision.

(c) *Reversals other than by the MA organization or the independent outside entity.*—(1) *General rule.* If the independent outside entity's determination is reversed in whole or in part by the ALJ, or at a higher level of appeal, the MA organization must pay for, authorize, or provide the service under dispute as expeditiously as the enrollee's health condition requires, but no later than 60 calendar days from the date it receives notice reversing the determination. The MA organization must inform the independent outside entity that the organization has effectuated the decision or that it has appealed the decision.

(2) *Effectuation exception when the MA organization files an appeal with the Medicare Appeals Council.* If the MA organization requests Medicare Appeals Council (the Board) review consistent with § 422.608, the MA organization may await the outcome of the review before it pays for, authorizes, or provides the service under dispute. A MA organization that files an appeal with the Board must concurrently send a copy of its appeal request and any accompanying documents to the enrollee and must notify the independent outside entity that it has requested an appeal.

[63 FR 35107, June 26, 1998, as amended at 65 FR 40331, June 29, 2000; 68 FR 50858, Aug. 22, 2003]

**§ 422.619 How an MA organization must effectuate expedited reconsidered determinations.**

(a) *Reversals by the MA organization.* If on reconsideration of an expedited request for service, the MA organization completely reverses its organization determination, the MA organization must authorize or provide the service under dispute as expeditiously as the enrollee's health condition requires, but no later than 72 hours after the date the MA organization receives the request for reconsideration (or no later than upon expiration of an extension described in § 422.590(d)(2)).

(b) *Reversals by the independent outside entity.* If the MA organization's determination is reversed in whole or in part by the independent outside entity, the MA organization must authorize or provide the service under dispute as expeditiously as the enrollee's health condition requires but no later than 72 hours from the date it receives notice reversing the determination. The MA organization must inform the independent outside entity that the organization has effectuated the decision.

(c) *Reversals other than by the MA organization or the independent outside entity*—(1) *General rule.* If the independent outside entity's expedited determination is reversed in whole or in part by the ALJ, or at a higher level of appeal, the MA organization must authorize or provide the service under dispute as expeditiously as the enrollee's health condition requires, but no later than 60 days from the date it receives notice reversing the determination. The MA organization must inform the independent outside entity that the organization has effectuated the decision.

(2) *Effectuation exception when the MA organization files an appeal with the Medicare Appeals Council.* If the MA organization requests Medicare Appeals Council (the Board) review consistent with § 422.608, the MA organization may await the outcome of the review before it authorizes or provides the service under dispute. A MA organization that files an appeal with the Board must concurrently send a copy of its appeal request and any accompanying documents to the enrollee and must notify the independent outside entity that it has requested an appeal.

[65 FR 40331, June 29, 2000, as amended at 68 FR 50859, Aug. 22, 2003]

**§ 422.620 How enrollees of MA organizations must be notified of noncovered inpatient hospital care.**

(a) *Enrollee's entitlement.* (1) Where an MA organization has authorized coverage of the inpatient admission of an enrollee, either directly or by delegation (or the admission constitutes emergency or urgently needed care, as described in §§ 422.2 and 422.113), the MA organization (or hospital that has been delegated the authority to make the discharge decision) must provide a written notice of noncoverage when—

(i) The beneficiary disagrees with the discharge decision; or

(ii) The MA organization (or the hospital that has been delegated the authority to make the discharge decision) is not discharging the individual but no longer intends to continue coverage of the inpatient stay.

(2) An enrollee is entitled to coverage until at least noon of the day after such notice is provided. If QIO review is requested under § 422.622, coverage is extended as provided in that section.

(b) *Physician concurrence required.* Before discharging an individual or changing the level of care in an inpatient hospital setting, the MA organization must obtain the concurrence of the physician who is responsible for the enrollee's inpatient care.

(c) *Notice to the enrollee.* When applicable, the written notice of non-coverage must be issued no later than the day before hospital coverage ends. The written notice must include the following elements:

(1) The reason why inpatient hospital care is no longer needed or covered;

(2) The effective date and time of the enrollee's liability for continued inpatient care;

(3) The enrollee's appeal rights;

(4) If applicable, the new lower level of care being covered in the hospital setting; and

(5) Any additional information specified by CMS.

[68 FR 16667, Apr. 4, 2003, as amended at 70 FR 4740, Jan. 28, 2005]

**Effective Date Note:** At 68 FR 20349, Apr. 4, 2003, § 422.620 was revised. This section contains information collection and recordkeeping requirements and will not become effective until approval has been given by the Office of Management and Budget

**§ 422.622 Requesting immediate QIO review of noncoverage of inpatient hospital care.**

(a) *Enrollee's right to review or reconsideration.* (1) An enrollee who wishes to appeal a determination by an MA organization or hospital that inpatient care is no longer necessary must request immediate QIO review of the determination in accordance with paragraph (b) of this section. An enrollee who requests immediate QIO review may remain in the hospital with no additional financial liability as specified in paragraph (c) of this section.

(2) An enrollee who fails to request immediate QIO review in accordance with the procedures in paragraph (b) of this section may request expedited reconsideration by the MA organization as described in § 422.584, but the financial liability rules of paragraph (c) of this section do not apply.

(b) *Procedures enrollee must follow.* For the immediate QIO review process, the following rules apply:

(1) The enrollee must submit the request for immediate review—

(i) To the QIO that has an agreement with the hospital under parts 476 and 478 of this chapter.

(ii) In writing or by telephone; and

(iii) By noon of the first working day after he or she receives written notice that the MA organization or hospital has determined that the hospital stay is no longer necessary.

(2) On the date it receives the enrollee's request, the QIO must notify the MA organization that the enrollee has filed a request for immediate review.

(3) The MA organization must supply any information that the QIO requires to conduct its review and must make it available, by phone or in writing, by the close of business of the first full working day immediately following the day the enrollee submits the request for review.

(4) In response to a request from the MA organization, the hospital must submit medical records and other pertinent information to the QIO by close of business of the first full working day immediately following the day the organization makes its request.

(5) The QIO must solicit the views of the enrollee who requested the immediate QIO review.

(6) The QIO must make a determination and notify the enrollee, the hospital, and the MA organization by close of business of the first working day after it receives all necessary information from the hospital, or the organization, or both.

(c) *Liability for hospital costs*—(1) *When the MA organization determines that hospital services are not, or are no longer, covered.* (i) Except as provided in paragraph (c)(1)(ii) of this section, if the MA organization authorized coverage of the inpatient admission directly or by delegation (or the admission constitutes emergency or urgently needed care, as described in §§ 422.2 and 422.112(c)), the organization continues to be financially responsible for the costs of the hospital stay when a timely appeal is filed under paragraph (a)(1) of this section until noon of the calendar day following the day the QIO notifies the enrollee of its review determination. If coverage of the hospital admission was never approved by the MA organization (or the admission does not constitute emergency or urgently needed care, as described in §§ 422.2 and 422.112(c)), the MA organization is liable for the hospital costs only if it is determined on appeal that the hospital stay should have been covered under the MA plan.

(ii) The hospital may not charge the MA organization (or the enrollee) if—

(A) It was the hospital (acting on behalf of the enrollee) that filed the request for immediate QIO review; and

(B) The QIO upholds the noncoverage determination made by the MA organization.

(2) *When the hospital determines that hospital services are no longer required.* If the hospital determines that inpatient hospital services are no longer necessary, and the enrollee could not reasonably be expected to know that the services would not be covered, the hospital may not charge the enrollee for inpatient services received before noon of the calendar day following the day the QIO notifies the enrollee of its review determination.

[63 FR 35107, June 26, 1998; 63 FR 52614, Oct. 1, 1998, as amended at 70 FR 4740, Jan. 28, 2005; 70 FR 52027, Sept. 1, 2005]

**§ 422.624 Notifying enrollees of termination of provider services.**

(a) *Applicability.* (1) For purposes of §§ 422.624 and 422.626, the term provider includes home health agencies (HHAs), skilled nursing facilities (SNFs), and comprehensive outpatient rehabilitation facilities (CORFs).

(2) *Termination of service defined.* For purposes of this section and § 422.626, a termination of service is the discharge of an enrollee from covered provider services, or discontinuation of covered provider services, when the enrollee has been authorized by the MA organization, either directly or by delegation, to receive an ongoing course of treatment from that provider. Termination includes cessation of coverage at the end of a course of treatment preauthorized in a discrete increment, regardless of whether the enrollee agrees that such services should end.

(b) *Advance written notification of termination.* Prior to any termination of service, the provider of the service must deliver valid written notice to the enrollee of the MA organization's decision to terminate services. The provider must use a standardized notice, required by the Secretary, in accordance with the following procedures—

(1) *Timing of notice.* The provider must notify the enrollee of the MA organization's decision to terminate covered services no later than 2 days before the proposed end of the services. If the enrollee's services are expected to be fewer than 2 days in duration, the provider should notify the enrollee at the time of admission to the provider. If, in a non-institutional setting, the span of time between services exceeds 2 days, the notice should be given no later than the next to last time services are furnished.

(2) *Content of the notice.* The standardized termination notice must include the following information:

(i) The date that coverage of services ends.

(ii) The date that the enrollee's financial liability for continued services begins.

(iii) A description of the enrollee's right to a fast-track appeal under § 422.626, including information about how to contact an independent review entity (IRE), an enrollee's right (but not obligation) to submit evidence showing that services should continue, and the availability of other MA appeal procedures if the enrollee fails to meet the deadline for a fast-track IRE appeal.

(iv) The enrollee's right to receive detailed information in accordance with § 422.626(e)(1) and (2).

(v) Any other information required by the Secretary.

(c) *When delivery of notice is valid.* Delivery of the termination notice is not valid unless—

(1) The enrollee (or the enrollee's authorized representative) has signed and dated the notice to indicate that he or she has received the notice and can comprehend its contents; and

(2) The notice is delivered in accordance with paragraph (b)(1) of this section and contains all the elements described in paragraph (b)(2) of this section.

(d) *Financial liability for failure to deliver valid notice.* An MA organization is financially liable for continued services until 2 days after the enrollee receives valid notice as specified under paragraph (c) of this section. An enrollee may waive continuation of services if he or she agrees with being discharged sooner than 2 days after receiving the notice.

**Effective Date Note:** At 68 FR 20349, Apr. 4, 2003, § 422.624 was added. This section contains information collection and recordkeeping requirements and will not become effective until approval has been given by the Office of Management and Budget

### § 422.626 Fast-track appeals of service terminations to independent review entities (IREs).

(a) *Enrollee's right to a fast-track appeal of an MA organization's termination decision.* An enrollee of an MA organization has a right to a fast-track appeal of an MA organization's decision to terminate provider services.

(1) An enrollee who desires a fast-track appeal must submit a request for an appeal to an IRE under contract with CMS, in writing or by telephone, by noon of the first day after the day of delivery of the termination notice. If, due to an emergency, the IRE is closed and unable to accept the enrollee's request for a fast-track appeal, the enrollee must file a request by noon of the next day that the IRE is open for business.

(2) When an enrollee fails to make a timely request to an IRE, he or she may request an expedited reconsideration by the MA organization as described in § 422.584.

(3) If, after delivery of the termination notice, an enrollee chooses to leave a provider or discontinue receipt of covered services on or before the proposed termination date, the enrollee may not later assert fast-track IRE appeal rights under this section relative to the services or expect the services to resume, even if the enrollee requests an appeal before the discontinuation date in the termination notice.

(b) *Coverage of provider services.* Coverage of provider services continues until the date and time designated on the termination notice, unless the enrollee appeals and the IRE reverses the MA organization's decision. If the IRE's decision is delayed because the MA organization did not timely supply necessary information or records, the MA organization is liable for the costs of any additional coverage required by the delayed IRE decision. If the IRE finds that the enrollee did not receive valid notice, coverage of provider services by the MA organization continues until at least 2 days after valid notice has been received. Continuation of coverage is not required if the IRE determines that coverage could pose a threat to the enrollee's health or safety.

(c) *Burden of proof.* When an enrollee appeals an MA organization's decision to terminate services to an IRE, the burden of proof rests with the MA organization to demonstrate that termination of coverage is the correct decision, either on the basis of medical necessity, or based on other Medicare coverage policies.

(1) To meet this burden, the MA organization must supply any and all information that an IRE requires to sustain the MA organization's termination decision, consistent with paragraph (e) of this section.

(2) The enrollee may submit evidence to be considered by an IRE in making its decision.

(3) The MA organization or an IRE may require an enrollee to authorize release to the IRE of his or her medical records, to the extent that the records are necessary for the MA organization to demonstrate the correctness of its decision or for an IRE to determine the appeal.

(d) *Procedures an IRE must follow.* (1) On the date an IRE receives the enrollee's request for an appeal, the IRE must immediately notify the MA organization and the provider that the enrollee has filed a request for a fast-track appeal, and of the MA organization's responsibility to submit documentation consistent with paragraph (e)(3) of this section.

(2) When an enrollee requests a fast-track appeal, the IRE must determine whether the provider delivered a valid notice of the termination decision, and whether a detailed notice has been provided, consistent with paragraph (e)(1) of this section.

(3) The IRE must notify CMS about each case in which it determines that improper notification occurs.

(4) Before making its decision, the IRE must solicit the enrollee's views regarding the reason(s) for termination of services as specified in the detailed written notice provided by the MA organization, or regarding any other reason that the IRE uses as the basis of its review determination.

(5) An IRE must make a decision on an appeal and notify the enrollee, the MA organization, and the provider of services, by close of business of the day after it receives the information necessary to make the decision. If the IRE does not receive the information needed to sustain an MA organization's decision to terminate services, it may make a decision on the case based on the information at hand, or it may defer its decision until it receives the necessary information. If the IRE defers its decision, coverage of the services by the MA organization would continue until the decision is made, consistent with paragraph (b) of this section, but no additional termination notice would be required.

(e) *Responsibilities of the MA organization.* (1) When an IRE notifies an MA organization that an enrollee has requested a fast-track appeal, the MA organization must send a detailed notice to the enrollee by close of business of the day of the IRE's notification. The detailed termination notice must include the following information:

(i) A specific and detailed explanation why services are either no longer reasonable and necessary or are no longer covered.

(ii) A description of any applicable Medicare coverage rule, instruction or other Medicare policy including citations, to the applicable Medicare policy rules, or the information about how the enrollee may obtain a copy of the Medicare policy from the MA organization.

(iii) Any applicable MA organization policy, contract provision, or rationale upon which the termination decision was based.

(iv) Facts specific to the enrollee and relevant to the coverage determination that are sufficient to advise the enrollee of the applicability of the coverage rule or policy to the enrollee's case.

(v) Any other information required by CMS.

(2) Upon an enrollee's request, the MA organization must provide the enrollee a copy of, or access to, any documentation sent to the IRE by the MA organization, including records of any information provided by telephone. The MA organization may charge the enrollee a reasonable amount to cover the costs of duplicating the information for the enrollee and/or delivering the documentation to the enrollee. The MA organization must accommodate such a request by no later than close of business of the first day after the day the material is requested.

(3) Upon notification by the IRE of a fast-track appeal, the MA organization must supply any and all information, including a copy of the notice sent to the enrollee, that the IRE needs to decide on the appeal. The MA organization must supply this information as soon as possible, but no later than by close of business of the day that the IRE notifies the MA organization that an appeal has been received from the enrollee. The MA organization must make the information available by phone (with a written record made of what is transmitted in this manner) and/or in writing, as determined by the IRE.

(4) An MA organization is financially responsible for coverage of services as provided in paragraph (b) of this section, regardless of whether it has delegated responsibility for authorizing coverage or termination decisions to its providers.

(5) If an IRE reverses an MA organization's termination decision, the MA organization must provide the enrollee with a new notice consistent with § 422.624(b).

(f) *Reconsiderations of IRE decisions.* (1) If the IRE upholds an MA organization's termination decision in whole or in part, the enrollee may request, no later than 60 days after notification that the IRE has upheld the decision that the IRE reconsider its original decision.

(2) The IRE must issue its reconsidered determination as expeditiously as the enrollee's health condition requires but no later than within 14 days of receipt of the enrollee's request for a reconsideration.

(3) If the IRE reaffirms its decision, in whole or in part, the enrollee may to appeal the IRE's reconsidered determination to an ALJ, the MAC, or a Federal court, as provided for under this subpart.

(4) If on reconsideration the IRE determines that coverage of provider services should terminate on a given date, the enrollee is liable for the costs of continued services after that date unless the IRE's decision is reversed on appeal. If the IRE's decision is reversed on appeal, the MA organization must reimburse the enrollee, consistent with the appealed decision, for the costs of any covered services for which the enrollee has already paid the MA organization or provider.

**Effective Date Note:** At 68 FR 20349, Apr. 4, 2003, § 422.626 was added. This section contains information collection and recordkeeping requirements and will not become effective until approval has been given by the Office of Management and Budget

## PART 422—MEDICARE ADVANTAGE PROGRAM

### Subpart N—Medicare Contract Determinations and Appeals

**Source:** 63 FR 35113, June 26, 1998, unless otherwise noted.

**§ 422.641 Contract determinations.**

This subpart establishes the procedures for making and reviewing the following contract determinations:

(a) A determination that an entity is not qualified to enter into a contract with CMS under Part C of title XVIII of the Act.

(b) A determination to terminate a contract with an MA organization in accordance with § 422.510(a).

(c) A determination not to authorize a renewal of a contract with an MA organization in accordance with § 422.506(b).

**§ 422.644 Notice of contract determination.**

(a) When CMS makes a contract determination, it gives the MA organization written notice.

(b) The notice specifies—

(1) The reasons for the determination; and

(2) The MA organization's right to request reconsideration.

(c) For CMS-initiated terminations, CMS mails notice 90 days before the anticipated effective date of the termination. For terminations based on initial determinations described at § 422.510(a)(5), CMS immediately notifies the MA organization of its decision to terminate the organization's MA contract.

(d) When CMS determines that it will not authorize a contract renewal, CMS mails the notice to the MA organization by May 1 of the current contract year.

**§ 422.646 Effect of contract determination.**

The contract determination is final and binding unless—

(a) The determination is reconsidered in accordance with §§ 422.648 through 422.658;

(b) A timely request for a hearing is filed under § 422.662; or

(c) The reconsideration decision is revised as a result of a reopening under § 422.696.

**§ 422.648 Reconsideration: Applicability.**

(a) Reconsideration is the first step for appealing a contract determination specified in § 422.641.

(b) CMS reconsiders the specified determinations if the contract applicant or the MA organization files a written request in accordance with § 422.650.

(c) Notice of any redetermination favorable to the MA organization applicant, including those resulting from a hearing or Administrator review conducted under this subpart, must be issued by July 15 for the contract in question to be effective on January 1 of the following year.

[63 FR 35113, June 26, 1998, as amended at 65 FR 40331, June 29, 2000; 70 FR 4741, Jan. 28, 2005]

**§ 422.650 Request for reconsideration.**

(a) *Method and place for filing a request.* A request for reconsideration must be made in writing and filed with any CMS office.

(b) *Time for filing a request.* The request for reconsideration must be filed within 15 days from the date of the notice of the initial determination.

(c) *Proper party to file a request.* Only an authorized official of the contract applicant or MA organization that was the subject of a contract determination may file the request for reconsideration.

(d) *Withdrawal of a request.* The MA organization or contract applicant who filed the request for a reconsideration may withdraw it at any time before the notice of the reconsidered determination is mailed. The request for withdrawal must be in writing and filed with CMS.

[63 FR 35113, June 26, 1998, as amended at 65 FR 40331, June 29, 2000]

**§ 422.652 Opportunity to submit evidence.**

CMS provides the MA organization or contract applicant and the CMS official or officials who made the contract determination reasonable opportunity, not to exceed the time frame in which an MA organization could choose to request a hearing as described at § 422.662, to present as evidence any documents or written statements that are relevant and material to the matters at issue.

[65 FR 40332, June 29, 2000]

**§ 422.654 Reconsidered determination.**

A reconsidered determination is a new determination that—

(a) Is based on a review of the contract determination, the evidence and findings upon which that was based, and any other written evidence submitted before notice of the reconsidered determination is mailed, including facts relating to the status of the MA organization subsequent to the contract determination; and

(b) Affirms, reverses, or modifies the initial determination.

**§ 422.656 Notice of reconsidered determination.**

(a) CMS gives the MA organization or contract applicant written notice of the reconsidered determination.

(b) The notice—

(1) Contains findings with respect to the contract applicant's qualifications to enter into, or the MA organization's qualifications to remain under, a contract with CMS under Part C of title XVIII of the Act;

(2) States the specific reasons for the reconsidered determination; and

(3) Informs the MA organization or contract applicant of its right to a hearing if it is dissatisfied with the determination.

[63 FR 35113, June 26, 1998, as amended at 65 FR 40332, June 29, 2000]

**§ 422.658 Effect of reconsidered determination.**

A reconsidered determination is final and binding unless a request for a hearing is filed in accordance with § 422.662 or it is revised in accordance with § 422.696.

**§ 422.660 Right to a hearing.**

The following parties are entitled to a hearing:

(a) A contract applicant that has been determined in a reconsidered determination to be unqualified to enter into a contract with CMS under Part C of title XVIII of the Act.

(b) An MA organization whose contract with CMS has been terminated or has not been renewed as a result of a contract determination as provided in § 422.641.

[63 FR 35113, June 26, 1998, as amended at 65 FR 40332, June 29, 2000]

**§ 422.662 Request for hearing.**

(a) *Method and place for filing a request.* A request for a hearing must be made in writing and filed by an authorized official of the contract applicant or MA organization that was the party to the determination under appeal. The request for a hearing must be filed with any CMS office.

(b) *Time for filing a request.* A request for a hearing must be filed within 15 days after the date of the reconsidered determination.

(c) *Parties to a hearing.* The parties to a hearing must be—

(1) The parties described in § 422.660;

(2) At the discretion of the hearing officer, any interested parties who make a showing that their rights may be prejudiced by the decision to be rendered at the hearing; and

(3) CMS.

[63 FR 35113, June 26, 1998, as amended at 65 FR 40332, June 29, 2000]

**§ 422.664 Postponement of effective date of a contract determination when a request for a hearing with respect to a contract determination is filed timely.**

(a) CMS postpones the proposed effective date of the contract determination to terminate a contract with an MA organization until a hearing decision is reached and affirmed by the Administrator following review under § 422.692 in instances where an MA organization requests review by the Administrator; and

(b) CMS extends the current contract at the end of the contract period (in the case of a determination not to renew) only—

(1) If CMS finds that an extension of the contract will be consistent with the purpose of this part; and

(2) For such period as CMS and the MA organization agree.

(c) Exception: A contract terminated in accordance with § 422.510(a)(5) will be immediately terminated and will not be postponed if a hearing is requested.

**§ 422.666 Designation of hearing officer.**

CMS designates a hearing officer to conduct the hearing. The hearing officer need not be an ALJ.

**§ 422.668 Disqualification of hearing officer.**

(a) A hearing officer may not conduct a hearing in a case in which he or she is prejudiced or partial to any party or has any interest in the matter pending for decision.

(b) A party to the hearing who objects to the designated hearing officer must notify that officer in writing at the earliest opportunity.

(c) The hearing officer must consider the objections, and may, at his or her discretion, either proceed with the hearing or withdraw.

(1) If the hearing officer withdraws, CMS designates another hearing officer to conduct the hearing.

(2) If the hearing officer does not withdraw, the objecting party may, after the hearing, present objections and request that the officer's decision be revised or a new hearing be held before another hearing officer. The objections must be submitted in writing to CMS.

**§ 422.670 Time and place of hearing.**

(a) The hearing officer fixes a time and place for the hearing, which is not to exceed 30 days from the receipt of the request for the hearing, and sends written notice to the parties. The notice also informs the parties of the general and specific issues to be resolved and information about the hearing procedure.

(b) The hearing officer may, on his or her own motion, or at the request of a party, change the time and place for the hearing. The hearing officer may adjourn or postpone the hearing.

(c) The hearing officer will give the parties reasonable notice of any change in time or place of hearing, or of adjournment or postponement.

**§ 422.672 Appointment of representatives.**

A party may appoint as its representative at the hearing anyone not disqualified or suspended from acting as a representative before the Secretary or otherwise prohibited by law.

**§ 422.674 Authority of representatives.**

(a) A representative appointed and qualified in accordance with § 422.672 may, on behalf of the represented party—

(1) Gives or accepts any notice or request pertinent to the proceedings set forth in this subpart;

(2) Presents evidence and allegations as to facts and law in any proceedings affecting that party; and

(3) Obtains information to the same extent as the party.

(b) A notice or request sent to the representative has the same force and effect as if it had been sent to the party.

**§ 422.676 Conduct of hearing.**

(a) The hearing is open to the parties and to the public.

(b) The hearing officer inquires fully into all the matters at issue and receives in evidence the testimony of witnesses and any documents that are relevant and material.

(c) The hearing officer provides the parties an opportunity to enter any objection to the inclusion of any document.

(d) The hearing officer decides the order in which the evidence and the arguments of the parties are presented and the conduct of the hearing.

**§ 422.678 Evidence.**

The hearing officer rules on the admissibility of evidence and may admit evidence that would be inadmissible under rules applicable to court procedures.

**§ 422.680 Witnesses.**

(a) The hearing officer may examine the witnesses.

(b) The parties or their representatives are permitted to examine their witnesses and cross-examine witnesses of other parties.

**§ 422.682 Discovery.**

(a) Prehearing discovery is permitted upon timely request of a party.

(b) A request is timely if it is made before the beginning of the hearing.

(c) A reasonable time for inspection and reproduction of documents is provided by order of the hearing officer.

(d) The hearing officer's order on all discovery matters is final.

**§ 422.684 Prehearing.**

The hearing officer may schedule a prehearing conference if he or she believes that a conference would more clearly define the issues.

**§ 422.686 Record of hearing.**

(a) A complete record of the proceedings at the hearing is made and transcribed and made available to all parties upon request.

(b) The record may not be closed until a hearing decision has been issued.

**§ 422.688 Authority of hearing officer.**

In exercising his or her authority, the hearing officer must comply with the provisions of title XVIII and related provisions of the Act, the regulations issued by the Secretary, and general instructions issued by CMS in implementing the Act.

**§ 422.690 Notice and effect of hearing decision.**

(a) As soon as practical after the close of the hearing, the hearing officer issues a written decision that—

(1) Is based upon the evidence of record; and

(2) Contains separately numbered findings of fact and conclusions of law.

(b) The hearing officer provides a copy of the hearing decision to each party.

(c) The hearing decision is final and binding unless it is reversed or modified by the Administrator following review under § 422.692, or reopened and revised in accordance with § 422.696.

**§ 422.692 Review by the Administrator.**

(a) *Request for review by Administrator.* An MA organization that has received a hearing decision upholding a contract termination determination may request review by the Administrator within 15 days of receiving the hearing decision as provided under § 422.690(b).

(b) *Review by the Administrator.* The Administrator shall review the hearing officer's decision, and determine, based upon this decision, the hearing record, and any written arguments submitted by the MA organization, whether the termination decision should be upheld, reversed, or modified.

(c) *Decision by the Administrator.* The Administrator issues a written decision, and furnishes the decision to the MA organization requesting review.

**§ 422.694 Effect of Administrator's decision.**

A decision by the Administrator under section 422.692 is final and binding unless it is reopened and revised in accordance with § 422.696.

**§ 422.696 Reopening of contract or reconsidered determination or decision of a hearing officer or the Administrator.**

(a) *Initial or reconsidered determination.* CMS may reopen and revise an initial or reconsidered determination upon its own motion within 1 year of the date of the notice of determination.

(b) *Decision of hearing officer.* A decision of a hearing officer that is unfavorable to any party and is otherwise final may be reopened and revised by the hearing officer upon the officer's own motion within 1 year of the notice of the hearing decision. Another hearing officer designated by CMS may reopen and revise the decision if the hearing officer who issued the decision is unavailable.

(c) *Decision of Administrator.* A decision by the Administrator that is otherwise final may be reopened and revised by the Administrator upon the Administrator's own motion within 1 year of the notice of the Administrator's decision.

(d) *Notices.* (1) The notice of reopening and of any revisions following the reopening is mailed to the parties.

(2) The notice of revision specifies the reasons for revisions.

**§ 422.698 Effect of revised determination.**

The revision of a contract or reconsidered determination is binding unless a party files a written request for hearing of the revised determination in accordance with § 422.662.

**Subpart O—Intermediate Sanctions**

**Source:** 63 FR 35115, June 26, 1998, unless otherwise noted.

**§ 422.750 Kinds of sanctions.**

(a) The following intermediate sanctions and civil money penalties may be imposed:

(1) Civil money penalties ranging from $10,000 to $100,000 depending upon the violation.

(2) Suspension of enrollment of Medicare beneficiaries.

(3) Suspension of payment to the MA organization for Medicare beneficiaries who enroll.

(4) Require the MA organization to suspend all marketing activities to Medicare beneficiaries for the MA plan subject to the intermediate sanctions.

(b) The enrollment, payment, and marketing sanctions continue in effect until CMS is satisfied that the deficiency on which the determination was based has been corrected and is not likely to recur.

**§ 422.752 Basis for imposing sanctions.**

(a) *All intermediate sanctions.* For the violations listed in this paragraph (a), we may impose one, or more, of the sanctions specified in § 422.750(a)(2), (a)(3), or (a)(4) on any MA organization that has a contract in effect. The MA organization may also be subject to other applicable remedies available under law.

(1) Fails substantially to provide, to an MA enrollee, medically necessary services that the organization is required to provide (under law or under the contract) to an MA enrollee, and that failure adversely affects (or is substantially likely to adversely affect) the enrollee.

(2) Imposes on MA enrollees premiums in excess of the monthly basic and supplemental beneficiary premiums permitted under section 1854 of the Act and subpart F of this part.

(3) Expels or refuses to reenroll a beneficiary in violation of the provisions of this part.

(4) Engages in any practice that could reasonably be expected to have the effect of denying or discouraging enrollment of individuals whose medical condition or history indicates a need for substantial future medical services.

(5) Misrepresents or falsifies information that it furnishes—

(i) To CMS; or

(ii) To an individual or to any other entity.

(6) Fails to comply with the requirements of § 422.206, which prohibits interference with practitioners' advice to enrollees.

(7) Fails to comply with § 422.216, which requires the organization to enforce the limit on balance billing under a private fee-for service plan.

(8) Employs or contracts with an individual or entity who is excluded from participation in Medicare under section 1128 or 1128A of the Act (or with an entity that employs or contracts with such an excluded individual or entity) for the provision of any of the following:

(i) Health care.
(ii) Utilization review.
(iii) Medical social work.
(iv) Administrative services.

(b) *Suspension of enrollment and marketing.* If CMS makes a determination under § 422.510(a), CMS may impose the intermediate sanctions in § 422.750(a)(2) and (a)(4).

[63 FR 35115, June 26, 1998; 63 FR 52614, Oct. 1, 1998, as amended at 69 FR 78338, Dec. 30, 2004; 70 FR 4741, Jan. 28, 2005; 70 FR 52027, Sept. 1, 2005]

**§ 422.756 Procedures for imposing sanctions.**

(a) *Notice of sanction and opportunity to respond*—(1) *Notice of sanction.* Before imposing the intermediate sanctions specified in paragraph (c) of this section CMS—

(i) Sends a written notice to the MA organization stating the nature and basis of the proposed sanction; and

(ii) Sends the OIG a copy of the notice.

(2) *Opportunity to respond.* CMS allows the MA organization 15 days from receipt of the notice to provide evidence that it has not committed an act or failed to comply with the requirements described in § 422.752, as applicable. CMS may allow a 15-day addition to the original 15 days upon receipt of a written request from the MA organization. To be approved, the request must provide a credible explanation of why additional time is necessary and be received by CMS before the end of the 15-day period following the date of receipt of the sanction notice. CMS does not grant an extension if it determines that the MA organization's conduct poses a threat to an enrollee's health and safety.

(b) *Informal reconsideration.* If, consistent with paragraph (a)(2) of this section the MA organization submits a timely response to CMS's notice of sanction, CMS conducts an informal reconsideration that:

(1) Consists of a review of the evidence by an CMS official who did not participate in the initial decision to impose a sanction; and

(2) Gives the MA organization a concise written decision setting forth the factual and legal basis for the decision that affirms or rescinds the original determination.

(c) *Specific sanctions.* If CMS determines that an MA organization has acted or failed to act as specified in § 422.752 and affirms this determination in accordance with paragraph (b) of this section, CMS may—

(1) Require the MA organization to suspend acceptance of applications made by Medicare beneficiaries for enrollment in the sanctioned MA plan during the sanction period;

(2) In the case of a violation under § 422.752(a), suspend payments to the MA organization for Medicare beneficiaries enrolled in the sanctioned MA plan during the sanction period; and

(3) Require the MA organization to suspend all marketing activities for the sanctioned MA plan to Medicare enrollees.

(d) *Effective date and duration of sanctions*—(1) *Effective date.* Except as provided in paragraph (d)(2) of this section, a sanction is effective 15 days after the date that the organization is notified of the decision to impose the sanction or, if the MA organization timely seeks reconsideration under paragraph (b) of this section, on the date specified in the notice of CMS's reconsidered determination.

(2) *Exception.* If CMS determines that the MA organization's conduct poses a serious threat to an enrollee's health and safety, CMS may make the sanction effective on a date before issuance of CMS's reconsidered determination.

(3) *Duration of sanction.* The sanction remains in effect until CMS notifies the MA organization that CMS is satisfied that the basis for imposing the sanction has been corrected and is not likely to recur.

(e) *Termination by CMS.* In addition to or as an alternative to the sanctions described in paragraph (c) of this section, CMS may decline to authorize the renewal of an organization's contract in accordance with § 422.506(b)(2) and (b)(3), or terminate the contract in accordance with § 422.510.

(f) *Civil money penalties.* (1) If CMS determines that an MA organization has committed an act or failed to comply with a requirement described in § 422.752, CMS notifies the OIG of this determination, and also notifies OIG when CMS reverses or terminates a sanction imposed under this part.

(2) In the case of a violation described in paragraph (a) of § 422.752, or a determination under paragraph (b) of § 422.752 based upon a violation under § 422.510(a)(4) (involving fraudulent or abusive activities), in accordance with the provisions of part 1003 of this chapter, the OIG may impose civil money penalties on the MA organization in accordance with part 1003 of this chapter in addition to, or in place of, the sanctions that CMS may impose under paragraph (c) of this section.

(3) In the case of a determination under § 422.752(b) other than a determination based upon a violation under § 422.510(a)(4), CMS may impose civil money penalties on the MA organization in the amounts specified in § 422.758 in addition to, or in place of, the sanctions that CMS may impose under paragraph (c) of this section.

[63 FR 35113, June 26, 1998, as amended at 68 FR 50859, Aug. 22, 2003; 70 FR 4741, Jan. 28, 2005]

**§ 422.758 Maximum amount of civil money penalties imposed by CMS.**

If CMS makes a determination under § 422.510(a), as described in § 422.752(b) excepting those determinations under § 422.510(a)(4), CMS may impose civil money penalties in addition to, or in place of, the sanctions that CMS may impose under § 422.756(c) in the following amounts:

(a) If the deficiency on which the determination is based has directly adversely affected (or has the substantial likelihood of adversely affecting) one or more Medicare Advantage enrollees—up to $25,000 for each determination.

(b) For each week that a deficiency remains uncorrected after the week in which the Medicare Advantage organization receives CMS' notice of the determination—up to $10,000.

(c) If CMS makes a determination that a MA organization has terminated its contract other than in a manner described under § 422.512 and that the MA organization has therefore failed to substantially carry out the terms of the contract—$250 per Medicare enrollee from the terminated MA plan or plans at the time the MA organization terminated its contract, or $100, 000, whichever is greater.
[69 FR 78338, Dec. 30, 2004, as amended at 70 FR 4741, Jan. 28, 2005]

**§ 422.760 Other applicable provisions.**
The provisions of section 1128A of the Act (except subsections (a) and (b)) apply to civil money penalties under this subpart to the same extent that they apply to a civil money penalty or procedure under section 1128A of the Act.

## PART 423—VOLUNTARY MEDICARE PRESCRIPTION DRUG BENEFIT

### Subpart M—Grievances, Coverage Determinations, and Appeals

**§ 423.560 Definitions.**
As used in this subpart, unless the context indicates otherwise—

*Appeal* means any of the procedures that deal with the review of adverse coverage determinations made by the Part D plan sponsor on the benefits under a Part D plan the enrollee believes he or she is entitled to receive, including delay in providing or approving the drug coverage (when a delay would adversely affect the health of the enrollee), or on any amounts the enrollee must pay for the drug coverage, as defined in § 423.566(b). These procedures include redeterminations by the Part D plan sponsor, reconsiderations by the independent review entity, ALJ hearings, reviews by the Medicare Appeals Council (MAC), and judicial reviews.

*Appointed representative* means an individual either appointed by an enrollee or authorized under State or other applicable law to act on behalf of the enrollee in obtaining a coverage determination or in dealing with any of the levels of the appeals process. Unless otherwise stated in this subpart, the appointed representative has all of the rights and responsibilities of an enrollee in obtaining a coverage determination or in dealing with any of the levels of the appeals process, subject to the rules described in part 422, subpart M of this chapter.

*Drug use* means an enrollee is receiving the drug in the course of treatment, including time off if it is part of the treatment.

*Enrollee* means a Part D eligible individual who has elected or has been enrolled in a Part D plan.

*Grievance* means any complaint or dispute, other than one that involves a coverage determination, expressing dissatisfaction with any aspect of the operations, activities, or behavior of a Part D plan sponsor, regardless of whether remedial action is requested.

*Physician* has the meaning given the term in section 1861(r) of the Act.

*Projected value* means the charges incurred by the enrollee and future charges that are incurred within 12 months from the date the request for coverage determination or exception is received by the plan. Projected value includes enrollee co-payments, all expenditures incurred after an enrollee's expenditures exceed the initial coverage limit, and expenditures paid by other entities.

*Reconsideration* means a review of an adverse coverage determination by an independent review entity (IRE), the evidence and findings upon which it was based, and any other evidence the enrollee submits or the IRE obtains.

*Redetermination* means a review of an adverse coverage determination by a Part D plan sponsor, the evidence and findings upon which it is based, and any other evidence the enrollee submits or the Part D plan sponsor obtains.

**§ 423.562 General provisions.**

(a) *Responsibilities of the Part D plan sponsor.* A Part D plan sponsor must meet all of the following requirements.

(1) A Part D plan sponsor, for each Part D plan that it offers, must establish and maintain—

(i) A grievance procedure as described in § 423.564 for addressing issues that do not involve coverage determinations;

(ii) A procedure for making timely coverage determinations, including determinations on requests for exceptions to a tiered cost-sharing structure or to a formulary; and

(iii) Appeals procedures that meet the requirements of this subpart for issues that involve coverage determinations.

(2) A Part D plan sponsor must ensure that all enrollees receive written information about the—

(i) Grievance and appeals procedures that are available to them through the Part D plan sponsor; and

(ii) Complaint process available to the enrollee under the QIO process as set forth under section 1154(a)(14) of the Act.

(3) A Part D plan sponsor must arrange with its network pharmacies to post or distribute notices instructing enrollees to contact their plans to obtain a coverage determination or request an exception if they disagree with the information provided by the pharmacist.

(4) In accordance with subpart K of this part, if the Part D plan sponsor delegates any of its responsibilities under this subpart to another entity or individual through which the Part D plan sponsor provides covered benefits, the Part D plan sponsor is ultimately responsible for ensuring that the entity or individual satisfies the relevant requirements of this subpart.

(b) *Rights of enrollees.* In accordance with the provisions of this subpart, enrollees have all of the following rights under Part D plans:

(1) The right to have grievances between the enrollee and the Part D plan sponsor heard and resolved by the plan sponsor, as described in § 423.564.

(2) The right to a timely coverage determination by the Part D plan sponsor, as specified in § 423.566 and § 423.568, including the right to request from the Part D plan sponsor an exception to its tiered cost-sharing structure or formulary, as specified in § 423.578.

(3) The right to request from the Part D plan sponsor an expedited coverage determination, as specified in § 423.570.

(4) If dissatisfied with any part of a coverage determination, all of the following appeal rights:

(i) The right to a redetermination of the adverse coverage determination by the Part D plan sponsor, as specified in § 423.580.

(ii) The right to request an expedited redetermination, as provided under § 423.584.

(iii) If, as a result of a redetermination, a Part D plan sponsor affirms, in whole or in part, its adverse coverage determination, the right to a reconsideration or expedited reconsideration by an independent review entity (IRE) contracted by CMS, as specified in § 423.600.

(iv) If the IRE affirms the plan's adverse coverage determination, in whole or in part, the right to an ALJ hearing if the amount in controversy meets the requirements in § 423.610.

(v) If the ALJ affirms the IRE's adverse coverage determination, in whole or in part, the right to request MAC review of the ALJ hearing decision, as specified in § 423.620.

(vi) If the MAC affirms the ALJ's adverse coverage determination, in whole or in part, the right to judicial review of the hearing decision if the amount in controversy meets the requirements in § 423.630.

(c) *When other regulations apply.* Unless this subpart provides otherwise, the regulations in part 422, subpart M of this chapter (concerning the administrative review and hearing processes under titles II and XVIII, and representation of parties under title XVIII of the Act) and any interpretive rules or CMS rulings issued under these regulations, apply under this subpart to the extent they are appropriate.

(d) *Relation to ERISA requirements.* Consistent with section 1860D-22(b) of the Act, provisions of this subpart may, to the extent applicable under the regulations adopted by the Secretary of Labor, apply to claims for benefits under group health plans subject to the Employee Retirement Income Security Act.

**§ 423.564 Grievance procedures.**

(a) *General rule.* Each Part D plan sponsor must provide meaningful procedures for timely hearing and resolving grievances between enrollees and the Part D plan sponsor or any other entity or individual through whom the Part D plan sponsor provides covered benefits under any Part D plan it offers.

(b) *Distinguished from appeals.* Grievance procedures are separate and distinct from appeal procedures, which address coverage determinations as defined in § 423.566(b). Upon receiving a complaint, a Part D plan sponsor must promptly determine and inform the enrollee whether the complaint is subject to its grievance procedures or its appeal procedures.

(c) *Distinguished from the quality improvement organization complaint process.* Under section 1154(a)(14) of the Act, the quality improvement organization (QIO) must review enrollees' written complaints about the quality of services they have received under the Medicare program. This process is separate and distinct from the grievance procedures of the Part D plan sponsor. For quality of care issues, an enrollee may file a grievance with the Part D plan sponsor, file a written complaint with the QIO, or both. For any complaint submitted to a QIO, the Part D plan sponsor must cooperate with the QIO in resolving the complaint.

(d) *Method for filing a grievance.* (1) An enrollee may file a grievance with the Part D plan sponsor either orally or in writing.

(2) An enrollee must file a grievance no later than 60 days after the event or incident that precipitates the grievance.

(e) *Grievance disposition and notification.* (1) The Part D plan sponsor must notify the enrollee of its decision as expeditiously as the case requires, based on the enrollee's health status, but no later than 30 days after the date the Part D plan sponsor receives the oral or written grievance.

(2) The Part D plan sponsor may extend the 30-day time frame by up to 14 days if the enrollee requests the extension or if the Part D plan sponsor justifies a need for additional information and documents how the delay is in the interest of the enrollee. When the Part D plan sponsor extends the deadline, it must immediately notify the enrollee in writing of the reason(s) for the delay.

(3) The Part D plan sponsor must inform the enrollee of the disposition of the grievance in accordance with the following procedures:

(i) All grievances submitted in writing must be responded to in writing.

(ii) Grievances submitted orally may be responded to either orally or in writing, unless the enrollee requests a written response.

(iii) All grievances related to quality of care, regardless of how the grievance is filed, must be responded to in writing. The response must include a description of the enrollee's right to file a written complaint with the QIO. For any complaint submitted to a QIO, the Part D plan sponsor must cooperate with the QIO in resolving the complaint.

(f) *Expedited grievances.* A Part D plan sponsor must respond to an enrollee's grievance within 24 hours if the complaint involves a refusal by the Part D plan sponsor to grant an enrollee's request for an expedited coverage determination under § 423.570 or an expedited redetermination under § 423.584, and the enrollee has not yet purchased or received the drug that is in dispute.

(g) *Record keeping.* The Part D plan sponsor must have an established process to track and maintain records on all grievances received both orally and in writing, including, at a minimum, the date of receipt, final disposition of the grievance, and the date that the enrollee was notified of the disposition.

**§ 423.566 Coverage determinations.**

(a) Responsibilities of the Part D plan sponsor. Each Part D plan sponsor must have a procedure for making timely coverage determinations in accordance with the requirements of this subpart regarding the prescription drug benefits an enrollee is entitled to receive under the plan, including basic prescription drug coverage as specified in § 423.100 and supplemental benefits as specified in

§ 423.104(f)(1)(ii), and the amount, including cost sharing, if any, that the enrollee is required to pay for a drug. The Part D plan sponsor must have a standard procedure for making determinations, in accordance with § 423.568, and an expedited procedure for situations in which applying the standard procedure may seriously jeopardize the enrollee's life, health, or ability to regain maximum function, in accordance with § 423.570.

(b) Actions that are coverage determinations. The following actions by a Part D plan sponsor are coverage determinations:

(1) A decision not to provide or pay for a Part D drug (including a decision not to pay because the drug is not on the plan's formulary, because the drug is determined not to be medically necessary, because the drug is furnished by an out-of-network pharmacy, or because the Part D plan sponsor determines that the drug is otherwise excludable under section 1862(a) of the Act if applied to Medicare Part D) that the enrollee believes may be covered by the plan;

(2) Failure to provide a coverage determination in a timely manner, when a delay would adversely affect the health of the enrollee;

(3) A decision concerning an exceptions request under § 423.578(a);

(4) A decision concerning an exceptions request under § 423.578(b); or

(5) A decision on the amount of cost sharing for a drug.

(c) Who can request a coverage determination. Individuals who can request a standard or expedited coverage determination are–

(1) The enrollee;

(2) The enrollee's appointed representative, on behalf of the enrollee; or

(3) The prescribing physician, on behalf of the enrollee.

**§ 423.568 Standard time frame and notice requirements for coverage determinations.**

(a) *Time frame for requests for drug benefits.* When a party makes a request for a drug benefit, the Part D plan sponsor must notify the enrollee (and the prescribing physician involved, as appropriate) of its determination as expeditiously as the enrollee's health condition requires, but no later than 72 hours after receipt of the request, or, for an exceptions request, the physician's supporting statement.

(b) *Time frame for requests for payment.* When a party makes a request for payment, the Part D plan sponsor must notify the enrollee of its determination no later than 72 hours after receipt of the request.

(c) *Written notice for denials by a Part D plan sponsor.* If a Part D plan sponsor decides to deny a drug benefit, in whole or in part, it must give the enrollee written notice of the determination.

(d) *Form and content of the denial notice.* The notice of any denial under paragraph (c) of this section must–

Use approved notice language in a readable and understandable form;

State the specific reasons for the denial;

Inform the enrollee of his or her right to a redetermination;

(i) For drug coverage denials, describe both the standard and expedited redetermination processes, including the enrollee's right to, and conditions for, obtaining an expedited redetermination and the rest of the appeals process;

(ii) For payment denials, describe the standard redetermination process and the rest of the appeals process; and

(iii) Comply with any other notice requirements specified by CMS.

(e) *Effect of failure to meet the adjudicatory time frames.* If the Part D plan sponsor fails to notify the enrollee of its determination in the appropriate time frame under paragraphs (a) or (b) of this section, the failure constitutes an adverse coverage determination, and the plan sponsor must forward the enrollee's request to the IRE within 24 hours of the expiration of the adjudication time frame.

**§ 423.570 Expediting certain coverage determinations.**

(a) *Request for expedited determination.* An enrollee or an enrollee's prescribing physician may request that a Part D plan sponsor expedite a coverage determination involving issues described in § 423.566(b). This does not include requests for payment of Part D drugs already furnished.

(b) *How to make a request.* (1) To ask for an expedited determination, an enrollee or an enrollee's prescribing physician on behalf of the enrollee must submit an oral or written request directly to the Part D plan sponsor, or if applicable, to the entity responsible for making the determination, as directed by the Part D plan sponsor.

(2) A prescribing physician may provide oral or written support for an enrollee's request for an expedited determination.

(c) *How the Part D plan sponsor must process requests.* The Part D plan sponsor must establish and maintain the following procedures for processing requests for expedited determinations:

(1) An efficient and convenient means for accepting oral or written requests submitted by enrollees or prescribing physicians.

(2) A method for documenting all oral requests and maintaining the documentation in the case file; and

(3) A means for issuing prompt decisions on expediting a determination, based on the following requirements:

(i) For a request made by an enrollee, provide an expedited determination if it determines that applying the standard time frame for making a determination may seriously jeopardize the life or health of the enrollee or the enrollee's ability to regain maximum function.

(ii) For a request made or supported by an enrollee's prescribing physician, provide an expedited determination if the physician indicates that applying the standard time frame for making a determination may seriously jeopardize the life or health of the enrollee or the enrollee's ability to regain maximum function.

(d) *Actions following denial.* If a Part D plan sponsor denies a request for expedited determination, it must take the following actions:

(1) Make the determination within the 72-hour time frame established in § 423.568(a) for a standard determination. The 72-hour period begins on the day

the Part D plan sponsor receives the request for expedited determination, or, for an exceptions request, the physician's supporting statement.

(2) Give the enrollee and prescribing physician prompt oral notice of the denial that—

(i) Explains that the Part D plan sponsor must process the request using the 72-hour time frame for standard determinations;

(ii) Informs the enrollee of the right to file an expedited grievance if he or she disagrees with the decision by the Part D plan sponsor not to expedite;

(iii) Informs the enrollee of the right to resubmit a request for an expedited determination with the prescribing physician's support; and

(iv) Provides instructions about the plan's grievance process and its time frames.

(3) Subsequently deliver, within 3 calendar days, equivalent written notice.

(e) *Actions on accepted requests for expedited determination.* If a Part D plan sponsor grants a request for expedited determination, it must make the determination and give notice in accordance with § 423.572.

**§ 423.572 Time frames and notice requirements for expedited coverage determinations.**

(a) *Time frame for determinations and notification.* Except as provided in paragraph (b) of this section, a Part D plan sponsor that approves a request for expedited determination must make its determination and notify the enrollee (and the prescribing physician involved, as appropriate) of its decision, whether adverse or favorable, as expeditiously as the enrollee's health condition requires, but no later than 24 hours after receiving the request, or, for an exceptions request, the physician's supporting statement.

(b) *Confirmation of oral notice.* If the Part D plan sponsor first notifies an enrollee of an adverse expedited determination orally, it must mail written confirmation to the enrollee within 3 calendar days of the oral notification.

(c) Content of the notice of expedited determination.

(1) The notice of any expedited determination must state the specific reasons for the determination in understandable language.

(2) If the determination is not completely favorable to the enrollee, the notice must—

(i) Inform the enrollee of his or her right to a redetermination;

(ii) Describe both the standard and expedited redetermination processes, including the enrollee's right to request, and conditions for obtaining, an expedited redetermination, and the rest of the appeal process; and

(iii) Comply with any other requirements specified by CMS.

(d) *Effect of failure to meet the adjudicatory time frames.* If the Part D plan sponsor fails to notify the enrollee of its determination in the time frame specified in paragraph (a) of this section, the failure constitutes an adverse coverage determination, and the Part D plan sponsor must forward the enrollee's request to the IRE within 24 hours of the expiration of the adjudication time frame.

**§ 423.576 Effect of a coverage determination.**

The coverage determination is binding on the Part D plan sponsor and the enrollee unless it is reviewed and revised under § 423.580 through § 423.630 or is reopened and revised under § 423.634.

**§ 423.578 Exceptions process.**

(a) *Requests for exceptions to a plan's tiered cost-sharing structure.* Each Part D plan sponsor that provides prescription drug benefits for Part D drugs and manages this benefit through the use of a tiered formulary must establish and maintain reasonable and complete exceptions procedures subject to CMS's approval for this type of coverage determination. The Part D plan sponsor grants an exception whenever it determines that the non-preferred drug for treatment of the enrollee's condition is medically necessary, consistent with the physician's statement under paragraph (a)(4) of this section.

(1) The exceptions procedures must address situations where a formulary's tiering structure changes during the year and an enrollee is using a drug affected by the change.

(2) The exceptions criteria of a Part D plan sponsor must include, but are not limited to—

(i) A description of the criteria a Part D plan sponsor uses to evaluate a determination made by the enrollee's prescribing physician under paragraph (a)(4) of this section.

(ii) Consideration of whether the requested Part D drug that is the subject of the exceptions request is the therapeutic equivalent, as defined in § 423.100, of any other drug on the plan's formulary.

(iii) Consideration of the number of drugs on the plan's formulary that are in the same class and category as the requested prescription drug that is the subject of the exceptions request.

(3) An enrollee or the enrollee's prescribing physician may file a request for an exception.

(4) A prescribing physician must provide an oral or written supporting statement that the preferred drug for the treatment of the enrollee's condition—

(i) Would not be as effective for the enrollee as the requested drug;

(ii) Would have adverse effects for the enrollee; or

(iii) Both paragraphs (a)(4)(i) and (a)(4)(ii) of this section apply.

(5) If the physician provides an oral supporting statement, the Part D plan sponsor may require the physician to subsequently provide a written supporting statement to demonstrate the medical necessity of the drug. The Part D plan sponsor may require the prescribing physician to provide additional supporting medical documentation as part of the written follow-up.

(6) In no case is a Part D plan sponsor required to cover a non-preferred drug at the generic drug cost-sharing level if the plan maintains a separate tier dedicated to generic drugs.

(7) If a Part D plan sponsor maintains a formulary tier in which it places very high cost and unique items, such as genomic and biotech products, the

sponsor may design its exception process so that very high cost or unique drugs are not eligible for a tiering exception.

(b) *Request for exceptions involving a non-formulary Part D drug.* Each Part D plan sponsor that provides prescription drug benefits for Part D drugs and manages this benefit through the use of a formulary must establish and maintain exceptions procedures subject to CMS' approval for receipt of an off-formulary drug. The Part D plan sponsor must grant an exception whenever it determines that the drug is medically necessary, consistent with the physician's statement under paragraph (b)(5) of this section, and that the drug would be covered but for the fact that it is an off-formulary drug. Formulary use includes the application of cost utilization tools, such as a dose restriction, including the dosage form, that causes a particular Part D drug not to be covered for the number of doses prescribed or a step therapy requirement that causes a particular Part D drug not to be covered until the requirements of the plan's coverage policy are met, or a therapeutic substitution requirement.

(1) The plan's formulary exceptions process must address each of the following circumstances:

(i) Situations where a formulary changes during the year, and situations where an enrollee is already using a given drug.

(ii) Continued coverage of a particular Part D prescription drug that the Part D plan sponsor is discontinuing coverage on the formulary for reasons other than safety or because the Part D prescription drug cannot be supplied by or was withdrawn from the market by the drug's manufacturer.

(iii) An exception to a plan's coverage policy that causes a Part D prescription drug not to be covered because of cost utilization tools, such as a requirement for step therapy, dosage limitations, or therapeutic substitution.

(2) The exception criteria of a Part D plan sponsor must include, but are not limited to—

(i) A description of the criteria a Part D plan sponsor uses to evaluate a prescribing physician's determination made under paragraph (b)(5) of this section;

(ii) A process for gathering and comparing applicable medical and scientific evidence on the safety and effectiveness of the requested non-formulary drug with the formulary drug for the enrollee, including safety information generated by an authoritative government body; and

(iii) A description of the cost-sharing scheme that will be applied when coverage is provided for a non-formulary drug.

(3) If the Part D plan sponsor covers a non-formulary drug, the cost(s) incurred by the enrollee for that drug are treated as being included for purposes of calculating and meeting the annual out-of-pocket threshold.

(4) An enrollee, the enrollee's appointed representative, or the prescribing physician (on behalf of the enrollee) may file a request for an exception.

(5) A prescribing physician must provide an oral or written supporting statement that the requested prescription drug is medically necessary to treat the enrollee's disease or medical condition because—

(i) All of the covered Part D drugs on any tier of a plan's formulary for treatment for the same condition would not be as effective for the enrollee as the non-formulary drug, would have adverse effects for the enrollee, or both;

(ii) The prescription drug alternative(s) listed on the formulary or required to be used in accordance with step therapy requirements—

(A) Has been ineffective in the treatment of the enrollee's disease or medical condition or, based on both sound clinical evidence and medical and scientific evidence and the known relevant physical or mental characteristics of the enrollee and known characteristics of the drug regimen, is likely to be ineffective or adversely affect the drug's effectiveness or patient compliance; or

(B) Has caused or based on sound clinical evidence and medical and scientific evidence, is likely to cause an adverse reaction or other harm to the enrollee; or

(iii) The number of doses that is available under a dose restriction for the prescription drug has been ineffective in the treatment of the enrollee's disease or medical condition or, based on both sound clinical evidence and medical and scientific evidence and the known relevant physical or mental characteristics of the enrollee and known characteristics of the drug regimen, is likely to be ineffective or adversely affect the drug's effectiveness or patient compliance.

(6) If the physician provides an oral supporting statement, the Part D plan sponsor may require the physician to subsequently provide a written supporting statement. The Part D plan sponsor may require the prescribing physician to provide additional supporting medical documentation as part of the written follow-up.

(c) *Requirements for exceptions*—(1) *General rule.* A decision by a Part D plan sponsor concerning an exceptions request under this section constitutes a coverage determination as specified at § 423.566.

(2) When a Part D plan sponsor does not make a timely decision. If the Part D plan sponsor fails to make a decision on an exceptions request and provide notice of the decision within the time frame required under § 423.568(a) or § 423.572(a), as applicable, the failure constitutes an adverse coverage determination, and the Part D plan sponsor must forward the enrollee's request to the IRE within 24 hours of the expiration of the adjudication time frame.

(3) *When a tiering exceptions request is approved.* Whenever an exceptions request made under § 423.578(a) is approved, the Part D plan sponsor must provide coverage for the approved prescription drug at the cost-sharing level that applies for preferred drugs, and may not require the enrollee to request approval for a refill, or a new prescription to continue using the Part D prescription drug after the refills for the initial prescription are exhausted, as long as—

(i) The enrollee's prescribing physician continues to prescribe the drug;

(ii) The drug continues to be considered safe for treating the enrollee's disease or medical condition; and

(iii) The enrollment period has not expired. If an enrollee renews his or her membership after the plan year, the plan may choose to continue coverage into the subsequent plan year.

(4) *When a non-formulary exceptions request is approved.* Whenever an exceptions request made under § 423.578(b) is approved—

(i) The Part D plan sponsor may not require the enrollee to request approval for a refill, or a new prescription to continue using the Part D prescription drug after the refills for the initial prescription are exhausted, as long as—

(A) The enrollee's prescribing physician continues to prescribe the drug;

(B) The drug continues to be considered safe for treating the enrollee's disease or medical condition; and

(C) The enrollment period has not expired. If an enrollee renews his or her membership after the plan year, the plan may choose to continue coverage into the subsequent plan year.

(ii) The Part D plan sponsor must not establish a special formulary tier or co-payment or other cost-sharing requirement that is applicable only to prescription drugs approved for coverage under this section.

(iii) An enrollee may not request a tiering exception for a non-formulary prescription drug approved under § 423.578(b).

(d) *Notice regarding formulary changes.* Whenever a Part D plan sponsor removes a covered part D drug from its formulary or makes any changes in the preferred or tiered cost-sharing status of such a drug, the Part D plan sponsor must provide notice in accordance with § 423.120(b)(5).

(e) *Limitation of the exceptions procedures to Part D drugs.* Nothing in this section may be construed to allow an enrollee to use the exceptions processes set out in this section to request or be granted coverage for a prescription drug that does not meet the definition of a Part D drug.

(f) *Implication of the physician's supporting statement.* Nothing in this section should be construed to mean that the physician's supporting statement required for an exceptions request will result in an automatic favorable determination.

**§ 423.580 Right to a redetermination.**

An enrollee who has received a coverage determination (including one that is reopened and revised as described in § 423.634) may request that it be redetermined under the procedures described in § 423.582, which address requests for a standard redetermination. An enrollee or an enrollee's prescribing physician (acting on behalf of an enrollee) may request an expedited redetermination specified in § 423.584.

**§ 423.582 Request for a standard redetermination.**

(a) *Method and place for filing a request.* An enrollee must ask for a redetermination by making a written request with the Part D plan sponsor that made the coverage determination. The Part D plan sponsor may adopt a policy for accepting oral requests.

(b) *Time frame for filing a request.* Except as provided in paragraph (c) of this section, an enrollee must file a request for a redetermination within 60 calendar days from the date of the notice of the coverage determination.

(c) *Extending the time for filing a request*—(1) *General rule.* If an enrollee shows good cause, the Part D plan sponsor may extend the time frame for filing a request for redetermination.

(2) *How to request an extension of time frame.* If the 60-day period in which to file a request for a redetermination has expired, an enrollee may file a request for redetermination and extension of time frame with the Part D plan sponsor. The request for redetermination and to extend the time frame must—

(i) Be in writing; and

(ii) State why the request for redetermination was not filed on time.

(d) *Withdrawing a request.* The person who files a request for redetermination may withdraw it by filing a written request with the Part D sponsor.

**§ 423.584 Expediting certain redeterminations.**

(a) *Who may request an expedited redetermination.* An enrollee or an enrollee's prescribing physician may request that a Part D plan sponsor expedite a redetermination that involves the issues specified in § 423.566(b). (This does not include requests for payment of drugs already furnished.)

(b) *How to make a request.* (1) To ask for an expedited redetermination, an enrollee or a prescribing physician acting on behalf of an enrollee must submit an oral or written request directly to the Part D plan sponsor or, if applicable, to the entity responsible for making the redetermination, as directed by the Part D plan sponsor.

(2) A prescribing physician may provide oral or written support for an enrollee's request for an expedited redetermination.

(c) *How the Part D plan sponsor must process requests.* The Part D plan sponsor must establish and maintain the following procedures for processing requests for expedited redetermination:

(1) *Handling of requests.* The Part D plan sponsor must establish an efficient and convenient means for individuals to submit oral or written requests, document all oral requests in writing, and maintain the documentation in the case file.

(2) *Prompt decision making.* The Part D plan sponsor must promptly decide whether to expedite the redetermination or follow the time frame for standard redetermination based on the following requirements:

(i) For a request made by an enrollee, the Part D plan sponsor must provide an expedited redetermination if it determines that applying the standard time frame for making a redetermination may seriously jeopardize the life or health of the enrollee or the enrollee's ability to regain maximum function.

(ii) For a request made or supported by a prescribing physician, the Part D plan sponsor must provide an expedited redetermination if the physician indicates that applying the standard time frame for conducting a redetermination may seriously jeopardize the life or health of the enrollee or the enrollee's ability to regain maximum function.

(d) *Actions following denial of a request.* If a Part D plan sponsor denies a request for expedited redetermination, it must take the following actions:

(1) Make the determination within the 7-day time frame established in § 423.590(a). The 7-day period begins the day the Part D plan sponsor receives the request for expedited redetermination.

(2) Give the enrollee prompt oral notice of the denial that–

(i) Explains that the Part D plan sponsor processes the enrollee's request using the 7-day time frame for standard redetermination;

(ii) Informs the enrollee of the right to file an expedited grievance if he or she disagrees with the decision by the Part D plan sponsor not to expedite;

(iii) Informs the enrollee of the right to resubmit a request for an expedited redetermination with the prescribing physician's support; and

(iv) Provides instructions about the expedited grievance process and its time frames.

(3) Subsequently deliver, within 3 calendar days, equivalent written notice.

(e) *Action following acceptance of a request.* If a Part D plan sponsor grants a request for expedited redetermination, it must conduct the redetermination and give notice in accordance with § 423.590(d).

**§ 423.586 Opportunity to submit evidence.**

The Part D plan sponsor must provide the enrollee or the prescribing physician, as appropriate, with a reasonable opportunity to present evidence and allegations of fact or law, related to the issue in dispute, in person as well as in writing. In the case of an expedited redetermination, the opportunity to present evidence is limited by the short time frame for making a decision. Therefore, the Part D plan sponsor must inform the enrollee or the prescribing physician of the conditions for submitting the evidence.

**§ 423.590 Time frames and responsibility for making redeterminations.**

(a) *Standard redetermination–request for covered drug benefits.* (1) If the Part D plan sponsor makes a redetermination that is completely favorable to the enrollee, the Part D plan sponsor must notify the enrollee in writing of its redetermination (and effectuate it in accordance with § 423.636(a)(1)) as expeditiously as the enrollee's health condition requires, but no later than 7 calendar days from the date it receives the request for a standard redetermination.

(2) If the Part D plan sponsor makes a redetermination that affirms, in whole or in part, its adverse coverage determination, it must notify the enrollee in writing of its redetermination as expeditiously as the enrollee's health condition requires, but no later than 7 calendar days from the date it receives the request for a standard redetermination.

(b) *Standard redetermination–request for payment.* (1) If the Part D plan sponsor makes a redetermination that is completely favorable to the enrollee, the Part D plan sponsor must issue its redetermination (and effectuate it in accordance with § 423.636(a)(2)) no later than 7 calendar days from the date it receives the request for redetermination.

(2) If the Part D plan sponsor affirms, in whole or in part, its adverse coverage determination, it must notify the enrollee in writing of its redetermination

no later than 7 calendar days from the date it receives the request for redetermination.

(c) *Effect of failure to meet time frame for standard redeterminations.* If the Part D plan sponsor fails to provide the enrollee with a redetermination within the time frames specified in paragraphs (a) or (b) of this section, the failure constitutes an adverse redetermination decision, and the Part D plan sponsor must forward the enrollee's request to the IRE within 24 hours of the expiration of the adjudication time frame.

(d) *Expedited redetermination*—(1) *Time frame.* A Part D plan sponsor that approves a request for expedited redetermination must complete its redetermination and give the enrollee (and the prescribing physician involved, as appropriate), notice of its decision as expeditiously as the enrollee's health condition requires but no later than 72 hours after receiving the request.

(2) How the Part D plan sponsor must request additional information. If the Part D plan sponsor must receive medical information, the Part D plan sponsor must request the necessary information within 24 hours of the initial request for an expedited redetermination. Regardless of whether the Part D plan sponsor requests additional information, the Part D plan sponsor is responsible for meeting the time frame and notice requirements.

(e) *Failure to meet time frame for expedited redetermination.* If the Part D plan sponsor fails to provide the enrollee or the prescribing physician, as appropriate, with the results of its expedited redetermination within the time frame described in paragraph (d) of this section, the failure constitutes an adverse redetermination decision, and the Part D plan sponsor must forward the enrollee's request to the IRE within 24 hours of the expiration of the adjudication time frame.

(f) *Who must conduct the review of an adverse coverage determination.* (1) A person or persons who were not involved in making the coverage determination must conduct the redetermination.

(2) When the issue is the denial of coverage based on a lack of medical necessity (or any substantively equivalent term used to describe the concept of medical necessity), the redetermination must be made by a physician with expertise in the field of medicine that is appropriate for the services at issue. The physician making the redetermination need not, in all cases, be of the same specialty or subspecialty as the prescribing physician.

(g) *Form and content of an adverse redetermination notice.* The notice of any adverse determination under paragraphs (a)(2) or (b)(2) of this section must—

(1) Use approved notice language in a readable and understandable form;

(2) State the specific reasons for the denial;

(3) Inform the enrollee of his or her right to a reconsideration;

(i) For adverse drug coverage redeterminations, describe both the standard and expedited reconsideration processes, including the enrollee's right to, and conditions for, obtaining an expedited reconsideration and the rest of the appeals process;

(ii) For adverse payment redeterminations, describe the standard reconsideration process and the rest of the appeals process; and

(4) Comply with any other notice requirements specified by CMS.

**§ 423.600 Reconsideration by an independent review entity (IRE).**

(a) An enrollee who is dissatisfied with the redetermination of a Part D plan sponsor has a right to a reconsideration by an independent review entity that contracts with CMS. An enrollee must file a written request for reconsideration with the IRE within 60 days of the date of the redetermination by the Part D plan sponsor.

(b) When an enrollee files an appeal, the IRE is required to solicit the views of the prescribing physician. The IRE may solicit the views of the prescribing physician orally or in writing. A written account of the prescribing physician's views (prepared by either the prescribing physician or IRE, as appropriate) must be contained in the IRE's record.

(c) In order for an enrollee to request an IRE reconsideration of a determination by a Part D plan sponsor not to provide for a Part D drug that is not on the formulary, the prescribing physician must determine that all covered Part D drugs on any tier of the formulary for treatment of the same condition would not be as effective for the individual as the non-formulary drug, would have adverse effects for the individual, or both.

(d) The independent review entity must conduct the reconsideration as expeditiously as the enrollee's health condition requires but must not exceed the deadlines applicable in § 423.590, including those deadlines that are applicable when a request for an expedited reconsideration is received and granted.

(e) When the issue is the denial of coverage based on a lack of medical necessity (or any substantively equivalent term used to describe the concept of medical necessity), the reconsideration must be made by a physician with expertise in the field of medicine that is appropriate for the services at issue. The physician making the reconsideration need not, in all cases, be of the same specialty or subspecialty as the prescribing physician.

**§ 423.602 Notice of reconsideration determination by the independent review entity.**

(a) *Responsibility for the notice.* When the IRE makes its reconsideration determination, it is responsible for mailing a notice of its determination to the enrollee and the Part D plan sponsor, and for sending a copy to CMS.

(b) *Content of the notice.* The notice must—

(1) State the specific reasons for the IRE's decision in understandable language;

(2) If the reconsideration determination is adverse (that is, does not completely reverse the adverse coverage determination by the Part D plan sponsor), inform the enrollee of his or her right to an ALJ hearing if the amount in controversy meets the threshold requirement under § 423.610;

(3) Describe the procedures that must be followed to obtain an ALJ hearing; and

(4) Comply with any other requirements specified by CMS.

**§ 423.604 Effect of a reconsideration determination.**
A reconsideration determination is final and binding on the enrollee and the Part D plan sponsor, unless the enrollee files a request for a hearing under the provisions of § 423.612.

**§ 423.610 Right to an ALJ hearing.**

(a) If the amount remaining in controversy after the IRE reconsideration meets the threshold requirement established annually by the Secretary, an enrollee who is dissatisfied with the IRE reconsideration determination has a right to a hearing before an ALJ.

(b) If the basis for the appeal is the refusal by the Part D plan sponsor to provide drug benefits, CMS uses the projected value of those benefits to compute the amount remaining in controversy. The projected value of a Part D drug or drugs shall include any costs the enrollee could incur based on the number of refills prescribed for the drug(s) in dispute during the plan year.

(c) *Aggregating appeals to meet the amount in controversy*—(1) *Enrollee.* Two or more appeals may be aggregated by an enrollee to meet the amount in controversy for an ALJ hearing if—

(i) The appeals have previously been reconsidered by an IRE;

(ii) The request for ALJ hearing lists all of the appeals to be aggregated and each aggregated appeal meets the filing requirement specified in § 423.612(b); and

(iii) The ALJ determines that the appeals the enrollee seeks to aggregate involve the delivery of prescription drugs to a single enrollee.

(2) *Multiple enrollees.* Two or more appeals may be aggregated by multiple enrollees to meet the amount in controversy for an ALJ hearing if—

The appeals have previously been reconsidered by an IRE;

The request for ALJ hearing lists all of the appeals to be aggregated and each aggregated appeal meets the filing requirement specified in § 423.612(b); and

The ALJ determines that the appeals the enrollees seek to aggregate involve the same prescription drug.

**§ 423.612 Request for an ALJ hearing.**

(a) *How and where to file a request.* The enrollee must file a written request for a hearing with the entity specified in the IRE's reconsideration notice.

(b) *When to file a request.* Except when an ALJ extends the time frame as provided in part 422, subpart M of this chapter, the enrollee must file a request for a hearing within 60 days of the date of the notice of an IRE reconsideration determination. The time and place for a hearing before an ALJ will be set in accordance with § 405.1020 of this chapter.

(c) *Insufficient amount in controversy.* (1) If a request for a hearing clearly shows that the amount in controversy is less than that required under § 423.610, the ALJ dismisses the request.

(2) If, after a hearing is initiated, the ALJ finds that the amount in controversy is less than the amount required under § 423.610, the ALJ discontinues the hearing and does not rule on the substantive issues raised in the appeal.

**§ 423.620 Medicare Appeals Council (MAC) review.**

An enrollee who is dissatisfied with an ALJ hearing decision may request that the MAC review the ALJ's decision or dismissal. The regulations under part 422, subpart M of this chapter regarding MAC review apply to matters addressed by this subpart, to the extent applicable.

**§ 423.630 Judicial review.**

(a) *Review of ALJ's decision.* The enrollee may request judicial review of an ALJ's decision if–

(1) The MAC denied the enrollee's request for review; and

(2) The amount in controversy meets the threshold requirement established annually by the Secretary.

(b) *Review of MAC decision.* The enrollee may request judicial review of the MAC decision if it is the final decision of CMS and the amount in controversy meets the threshold established in paragraph (a)(2) of this section.

(c) How to request judicial review. In order to request judicial review, an enrollee must file a civil action in a district court of the United States in accordance with section 205(g) of the Act. (See part 422, subpart M of this chapter, for a description of the procedures to follow in requesting judicial review.)

**§ 423.634 Reopening and revising determinations and decisions.**

(a) A coverage determination or redetermination made by a Part D plan sponsor, a reconsideration made by the independent review entity specified in § 423.600, or the decision of an ALJ or the MAC that is otherwise final and binding may be reopened and revised by the entity that made the determination or decision, under the rules in part 422, subpart M of this chapter.

(b) The filing of a request for reopening does not relieve the Part D plan sponsor of its obligation to make payment or provide benefits as specified in § 423.636 or § 423.638.

(c) Once an entity issues a revised determination or decision, the revisions made by the decision may be appealed.

(d) A decision not to reopen by the Part D plan sponsor or any other entity is not subject to review.

**§ 423.636 How a Part D plan sponsor must effectuate standard redeterminations, reconsiderations, or decisions.**

(a) *Reversals by the Part D plan sponsor*–(1) *Requests for benefits.* If, on redetermination of a request for benefit, the Part D plan sponsor reverses its coverage determination, the Part D plan sponsor must authorize or provide the benefit under dispute as expeditiously as the enrollee's health condition requires, but no later than 7 calendar days from the date it receives the request for redetermination.

(2) *Requests for payment.* If, on redetermination of a request for payment, the Part D plan sponsor reverses its coverage determination, the Part D plan sponsor must authorize payment for the benefit within 7 calendar days from the date it receives the request for redetermination, and make payment no later than 30 calendar days after the date the plan sponsor receives the request for redetermination.

(b) *Reversals other than by the Part D plan sponsor*—(1) *Requests for benefits.* If, on appeal of a request for benefit, the determination by the Part D plan sponsor is reversed in whole or in part by the independent review entity, or at a higher level of appeal, the Part D plan sponsor must authorize or provide the benefit under dispute within 72 hours from the date it receives notice reversing the determination. The Part D plan sponsor must inform the independent review entity that the Part D plan sponsor has effectuated the decision.

(2) *Requests for payment.* If, on appeal of a request for payment, the determination by the Part D plan sponsor is reversed in whole or in part by the independent review entity, or at a higher level of appeal, the Part D plan sponsor must authorize payment for the benefit within 72 hours, but make payment no later than 30 calendar days from the date it receives notice reversing the coverage determination. The Part D plan sponsor must inform the independent review entity that the Part D plan sponsor has effectuated the decision.

### § 423.638 How a Part D plan sponsor must effectuate expedited redeterminations or reconsiderations.

(a) *Reversals by the Part D plan sponsor.* If, on an expedited redetermination of a request for benefits, the Part D plan sponsor reverses its coverage determination, the Part D plan sponsor must authorize or provide the benefit under dispute as expeditiously as the enrollee's health condition requires, but no later than 72 hours after the date the Part D plan sponsor receives the request for redetermination.

(b) *Reversals other than by the Part D plan sponsor.* If the expedited determination or expedited redetermination for benefits by the Part D plan sponsor is reversed in whole or in part by the independent review entity, or at a higher level of appeal, the Part D plan sponsor must authorize or provide the benefit under dispute as expeditiously as the enrollee's health condition requires but no later than 24 hours from the date it receives notice reversing the determination. The Part D plan sponsor must inform the independent review entity that the Part D plan sponsor has effectuated the decision.

## Subpart N—Medicare Contract Determinations and Appeals

### § 423.641 Contract determinations.

This subpart establishes the procedures for reviewing the following contract determinations:

(a) A determination that an entity is not qualified to enter into a contract with CMS under Part D of title XVIII of the Act.

(b) A determination not to authorize a renewal of a contract with a PDP sponsor in accordance with § 423.507(b).

(c) A determination to terminate a contract with a PDP sponsor in accordance with § 423.509.

(d) Fallback entities are governed under subpart Q of this part, and are not subject to this subpart, except to the extent a fallback prescription drug plan contract is terminated by CMS.

**§ 423.642 Notice of contract determination.**

(a) When CMS makes a contract determination under § 423.641, it gives the PDP sponsor written notice.

(b) The notice specifies the–

(1) Reasons for the determination; and

(2) PDP sponsor's right to request reconsideration.

(c) For CMS-initiated terminations, CMS mails notice 90 days before the anticipated effective date of the termination. For terminations based on initial determinations described at § 423.509(a)(4) or (a)(5), CMS immediately notifies the PDP sponsor of its decision to terminate the organization's PDP contract.

(d) When CMS determines that it is not going to authorize a contract renewal, CMS mails the notice to the PDP sponsor by May 1 of the current contract year.

**§ 423.643 Effect of contract determination.**

The contract determination is final and binding unless–

(a) The determination is reconsidered in accordance with § 423.644 through § 423.649;

(b) A timely request for a hearing is filed under § 423.651; or

(c) The reconsideration decision is revised as a result of a reopening under § 423.668.

**§ 423.644 Reconsideration: Applicability.**

(a) Reconsideration is the first step for appealing a contract determination specified in § 423.641.

(b) CMS reconsiders the specified determinations if the contract applicant or the PDP sponsor files a written request in accordance with § 423.645.

**§ 423.645 Request for reconsideration.**

(a) *Method and place for filing a request.* A request for reconsideration must be made in writing and filed with any CMS office.

(b) *Time for filing a request.* The request for reconsideration must be filed within 15 days from the date of the notice of the initial determination.

(c) *Proper party to file a request.* Only an authorized official of the contract applicant or PDP sponsor that was the subject of a contract determination may file the request for reconsideration.

(d) *Withdrawal of a request.* The PDP sponsor or contract applicant who filed the request for a reconsideration may withdraw it at any time before the notice of the reconsidered determination is mailed. The request for withdrawal must be in writing and filed with CMS.

**§ 423.646 Opportunity to submit evidence.**

CMS provides the PDP sponsor or contract applicant and the CMS official or officials who made the contract determination reasonable opportunity, not to exceed the time frame in which a PDP sponsor chooses to request a hearing as described at § 423.651, to present as evidence any documents or written statements that are relevant and material to the matters at issue.

**§ 423.647 Reconsidered determination.**

A reconsidered determination is a new determination that—

(a) Is based on a review of the contract determination, the evidence and findings upon which that was based, and any other written evidence submitted before notice of the reconsidered determination is mailed, including facts relating to the status of the PDP sponsor subsequent to the contract determination; and

(b) Affirms, reverses, or modifies the initial determination.

(c) Any favorable redetermination, including those resulting from a hearing or Administrator review, must be made by July 15 for the contract in question to be effective on January of the following year.

**§ 423.648 Notice of reconsidered determination.**

(a) CMS gives the PDP sponsor or contract applicant written notice of the reconsidered determination.

(b) The notice—

(1) Contains findings for the contract applicant's qualifications to enter into, or the PDP sponsor's qualifications to remain under, a contract with CMS under Part D of the Act;

(2) States the specific reasons for the reconsidered determination; and

(3) Informs the PDP sponsor or contract applicant of its right to a hearing if it is dissatisfied with the determination.

**§ 423.649 Effect of reconsidered determination.**

A reconsidered determination is final and binding unless a request for a hearing is filed in accordance with § 423.651 or it is revised in accordance with § 423.668.

**§ 423.650 Right to a hearing.**

The following parties are entitled to a hearing:

(a) A contract applicant that is determined in a reconsidered determination to be unqualified to enter into a contract with CMS under Part D of title XVIII of the Act.

(b) A PDP sponsor whose contract with CMS is terminated or is not renewed as a result of a contract determination as provided in § 423.641.

**§ 423.651 Request for hearing.**

(a) *Method and place for filing a request.* A request for a hearing must be made in writing and filed by an authorized official of the contract applicant or PDP sponsor that was the party to the determination under appeal. The request for a hearing must be filed with any CMS office.

(b) *Time for filing a request.* A request for a hearing must be filed within 15 days after the date of the reconsidered determination.

(c) *Parties to a hearing.* The parties to a hearing must be—

(1) The parties described in § 423.650;

(2) At the discretion of the hearing officer, any interested parties who make a showing that their rights may be prejudiced by the decision to be rendered at the hearing; and

(3) CMS.

**§ 423.652 Postponement of effective date of a contract determination when a request for a hearing for a contract determination is filed timely.**

(a) CMS postpones the proposed effective date of the contract determination to terminate a contract with a PDP sponsor until a hearing decision is reached and affirmed by the Administrator following review under § 423.666 in instances where a PDP sponsor requests review by the Administrator; and

(b) CMS extends the current contract at the end of the contract period (in the case of a determination not to renew) only—

(1) If CMS finds that an extension of the contract is consistent with the purpose of this part; and

(2) For the period as CMS and the PDP sponsor agree.

(c) Exception: A contract terminated in accordance with § 423.509(a)(4) or (a)(5) is immediately terminated and is not postponed if a hearing is requested.

**§ 423.653 Designation of hearing officer.**

CMS designates a hearing officer to conduct the hearing. The hearing officer need not be an ALJ.

**§ 423.654 Disqualification of hearing officer.**

(a) A hearing officer may not conduct a hearing in a case in which he or she is prejudiced or partial to any party or has any interest in the matter pending for decision.

(b) A party to the hearing who objects to the designated hearing officer must notify that officer in writing at the earliest opportunity.

(c) The hearing officer must consider the objections, and may, at his or her discretion, either proceed with the hearing or withdraw.

(1) If the hearing officer withdraws, CMS designates another hearing officer to conduct the hearing.

(2) If the hearing officer does not withdraw, the objecting party may, after the hearing, present objections and request that the officer's decision be revised or a new hearing be held before another hearing officer. The objections must be submitted in writing to CMS.

**§ 423.655 Time and place of hearing.**

(a) The hearing officer fixes a time and place for the hearing, which is not to exceed 30 days from the receipt of the request for the hearing, and sends written notice to the parties. The notice also informs the parties of the general and specific issues to be resolved and information about the hearing procedure.

(b) The hearing officer may, on his or her own motion, or at the request of a party, change the time and place for the hearing. The hearing officer may adjourn or postpone the hearing.

(c) The hearing officer gives the parties reasonable notice of any change in time or place of hearing, or of adjournment or postponement.

**§ 423.656 Appointment of representatives.**
A party may appoint as its representative at the hearing anyone not disqualified or suspended from acting as a representative before the Secretary or otherwise prohibited by law.

**§ 423.657 Authority of representatives.**

(a) A representative appointed and qualified in accordance with § 423.656, on behalf of the represented party—

(1) Gives or accepts any notice or request pertinent to the proceedings set forth in this subpart;

(2) Presents evidence and allegations as to facts and law in any proceedings affecting that party; and

(3) Obtains information to the same extent as the party.

(b) A notice or request sent to the representative has the same force and effect as if it is sent to the party.

**§ 423.658 Conduct of hearing.**

(a) The hearing is open to the parties and to the public.

(b) The hearing officer inquires fully into all the matters at issue and receives in evidence the testimony of witnesses and any documents that are relevant and material.

(c) The hearing officer provides the parties an opportunity to enter any objection to the inclusion of any document.

(d) The hearing officer decides the order in which the evidence and the arguments of the parties are presented and the conduct of the hearing.

**§ 423.659 Evidence.**
The hearing officer rules on the admissibility of evidence and may admit evidence that is inadmissible under rules applicable to court procedures.

**§ 423.660 Witnesses.**

(a) The hearing officer may examine the witnesses.

(b) The parties or their representatives are permitted to examine their witnesses and cross-examine witnesses of other parties.

**§ 423.661 Discovery.**

(a) Prehearing discovery is permitted upon timely request of a party.

(b) A request is timely if it is made before the beginning of the hearing.

(c) A reasonable time for inspection and reproduction of documents is provided by order of the hearing officer.

(d) The hearing officer's order on all discovery matters is final.

**§ 423.662 Prehearing.**
The hearing officer may schedule a prehearing conference if he or she believes that a conference may more clearly define the issues.

**§ 423.663 Record of hearing.**

(a) A complete record of the proceedings at the hearing is made and transcribed and made available to all parties upon request.

(b) The record may not be closed until a hearing decision is issued.

**§ 423.664 Authority of hearing officer.**

In exercising his or her authority, the hearing officer must comply with the provisions of title XVIII and related provisions of the Act, the regulations issued by the Secretary, and general instructions issued by CMS in implementing the Act.

**§ 423.665 Notice and effect of hearing decision.**

(a) As soon as practical after the close of the hearing, the hearing officer issues a written decision that—

(1) Is based upon the evidence of record; and

(2) Contains separately numbered findings of fact and conclusions of law.

(b) The hearing officer provides a copy of the hearing decision to each party.

(c) The hearing decision is final and binding unless it is reversed or modified by the Administrator following review under § 423.666, or reopened and revised in accordance with § 423.668.

**§ 423.666 Review by the Administrator.**

(a) *Request for review by the Administrator.* A PDP sponsor that receives a hearing decision upholding a contract termination determination may request review by the Administrator within 15 days of receiving the hearing decision as provided under § 423.665(b).

(b) *Review by the Administrator.* The Administrator must review the hearing officer's decision, and determine, based upon this decision, the hearing record, and any written arguments submitted by the PDP sponsor, whether the termination decision must be upheld, reversed, or modified.

(c) *Decision by the Administrator.* The Administrator issues a written decision, and furnishes the decision to the PDP sponsor requesting review.

**§ 423.667 Effect of Administrator's decision.**

A decision by the Administrator under section § 423.666(c) is final and binding unless it is reopened and revised in accordance with § 423.668.

**§ 423.668 Reopening of contract or reconsidered determination or decision of a hearing officer or the Administrator.**

(a) *Initial or reconsidered determination.* CMS may reopen and revise an initial or reconsidered determination upon its own motion within 1 year of the date of the notice of determination.

(b) *Decision of hearing officer.* A decision of a hearing officer that is unfavorable to any party and is otherwise final may be reopened and revised by the hearing officer upon the officer's own motion within 1 year of the notice of the hearing decision. Another hearing officer designated by CMS may reopen and revise the decision if the hearing officer who issued the decision is unavailable.

(c) *Decision of Administrator.* A decision by the Administrator that is otherwise final may be reopened and revised by the Administrator upon the Administrator's own motion within 1 year of the notice of the Administrator's decision.

(d) *Notices.* (1) The notice of reopening and of any revisions following the reopening is mailed to the parties.

(2) The notice of revision specifies the reasons for revisions.

**§ 423.669 Effect of revised determination.**

The revision of a contract or reconsidered determination is binding unless a party files a written request for hearing of the revised determination in accordance with § 423.651.

**Subpart O—Intermediate Sanctions**

**§ 423.750 Kinds of sanctions.**

(a) The following intermediate sanctions and civil money penalties may be imposed:

(1) Civil money penalties ranging from $10,000 to $100,000 depending upon the violation.

(2) Suspension of enrollment of Medicare beneficiaries.

(3) Suspension of payment to the Part D sponsor for Medicare beneficiaries who enroll.

(4) Suspension of all Part D plan marketing activities to Medicare beneficiaries for the Part D plan subject to the intermediate sanctions.

(b) The enrollment, payment, and marketing sanctions continue in effect until CMS is satisfied that the deficiency on which the determination was based is corrected and is not likely to recur.

**§ 423.752 Basis for imposing sanctions.**

(a) *All intermediate sanctions.* For the violations listed below, we may impose one, or more, of the sanctions specified in § 423.750(a)(2), (a)(3) or (a)(4) on any Part D sponsor that has a contract in effect. The Part D sponsor may also be subject to other applicable remedies available under law.

(1) Fails substantially to provide, to a Part D plan enrollee, medically necessary services that the organization is required to provide (under law or under the contract) to a Part D plan enrollee, and that failure adversely affects (or is substantially likely to adversely affect) the enrollee.

(2) Imposes on Part D plan enrollees premiums in excess of the monthly basic and supplemental beneficiary premiums permitted under section 1860D-1 *et seq.* of the Act and subpart F of this part.

(3) Acts to expel or refuses to reenroll a beneficiary in violation of the provisions of this part.

(4) Engages in any practice that may reasonably be expected to have the effect of denying or discouraging enrollment of individuals whose medical condition or history indicates a need for substantial future medical services.

(5) Misrepresents or falsifies information that it furnishes—

(i) To CMS; or

(ii) To an individual or to any other entity under the Part D drug benefit program.

(6) Employs or contracts with an individual or entity who is excluded from participation in Medicare under section 1128 or 1128A of the Act (or with an entity that employs or contracts with an excluded individual or entity) for the provision of any of the following:

(i) Health care.

(ii) Utilization review.

(iii) Medical social work.

(iv) Administrative services.

(b) *Suspension of enrollment and marketing.* If CMS makes a determination that could lead to a contract termination under § 423.509(a), CMS may instead impose the intermediate sanctions in § 423.750(a)(2) and (a)(4).

**§ 423.756 Procedures for imposing sanctions.**

(a) *Notice of sanction and opportunity to respond*—(1) *Notice of sanction.* Before imposing the intermediate sanctions specified in paragraph (c) of this section, CMS—

(i) Sends a written notice to the Part D sponsor stating the nature and basis of the proposed sanction; and

(ii) Sends the Office of the Inspector General a copy of the notice.

(2) *Opportunity to respond.* CMS allows the Part D sponsor 15 days from receipt of the notice to provide evidence that it has not committed an act or failed to comply with the requirements described in § 423.752, as applicable. CMS may allow a 15-day addition to the original 15 days upon receipt of a written request from the Part D sponsor. To be approved, the request must provide a credible explanation of why additional time is necessary and be received by CMS before the end of the 15-day period following the date of receipt of the sanction notice. CMS does not grant an extension if it determines that the Part D sponsor's conduct poses a threat to an enrollee's health and safety.

(b) *Informal reconsideration.* If, consistent with paragraph (a)(2) of this section, the Part D sponsor submits a timely response to CMS' notice of sanction, CMS conducts an informal reconsideration that—

(1) Consists of a review of the evidence by an CMS official who did not participate in the initial decision to impose a sanction; and

(2) Gives the Part D sponsor a concise written decision setting forth the factual and legal basis for the decision that affirms or rescinds the original determination.

(c) *Specific sanctions.* If CMS determines that a Part D sponsor has acted or failed to act as specified in § 423.752 and affirms this determination in accordance with paragraph (b) of this section, CMS may—

(1) Require the Part D sponsor to suspend acceptance of applications made by Medicare beneficiaries for enrollment in the sanctioned plan during the sanction period;

(2) In the case of a violation under § 423.752(a), suspend payments to the Part D sponsor for Medicare beneficiaries enrolled in the sanctioned plan during the sanction period; and

(3) Require the Part D sponsor to suspend all marketing activities for the sanctioned plan to Medicare enrollees.

(d) *Effective date and duration of sanctions*—(1) *Effective date.* Except as provided in paragraph (d)(2) of this section, a sanction is effective 15 days after the date that the organization is notified of the decision to impose the sanction or, if the Part D sponsor seeks reconsideration in a timely manner under paragraph (b) of this section, on the date specified in the notice of CMS's reconsidered determination.

(2) *Exception.* If CMS determines that the Part D sponsor's conduct poses a serious threat to an enrollee's health and safety, CMS may make the sanction effective on a date before issuance of CMS' reconsidered determination.

(3) *Duration of sanction.* The sanction remains in effect until CMS notifies the Part D sponsor that CMS is satisfied that the basis for imposing the sanction is corrected and is not likely to recur.

(e) *Termination by CMS.* In addition to or as an alternative to the sanctions described in paragraph (c) of this section, CMS may decline to authorize the renewal of an organization's contract in accordance with § 423.507(b)(2) and (b)(3), or terminate the contract in accordance with § 423.509.

(f) *Civil money penalties.* (1) If CMS determines that a Part D sponsor has committed an act or failed to comply with a requirement described in § 423.752, CMS notifies the OIG of this determination, and also notifies OIG when CMS reverses or terminates a sanction imposed under this part.

(2) In the case of a violation described in § 423.752(a), or a determination under § 423.752(b) based upon a violation under § 423.509(a)(4) (involving fraudulent or abusive activities), in accordance with the provisions of part 1003 of this chapter, the OIG may impose civil money penalties on the Part D sponsor in accordance with part 1003 of this chapter in addition to, or in place of, the sanctions that CMS may impose under paragraph (c) of this section.

(3) In the case of a determination under § 423.752(b) other than a determination based upon a violation under § 423.509(a)(4), CMS may impose civil money penalties on the Part D sponsor in the amounts specified in § 423.758 in addition to, or in place of, the sanctions that CMS may impose under paragraph (c) of this section.

**§ 423.758 Maximum amount of civil money penalties imposed by CMS.**
If CMS makes a determination under § 423.509(a), as described in § 423.752(b), excepting those determinations under § 423.509(a)(4), CMS may impose civil money penalties, in addition to, or in place of, the sanctions that CMS may impose under § 423.756(c), in the following amounts:

(a) If the deficiency on which the determination is based has directly adversely affected (or has the substantial likelihood of adversely affecting) one or more Part D plan enrollees—up to $25,000 for each determination.

(b) For each week that a deficiency remains uncorrected after the week in which the Part D sponsor receives CMS' notice of the determination–up to $10,000 per week.

(c) If CMS makes a determination that a Part D sponsor has terminated its contract with CMS other than in a manner described in § 423.510 and that the sponsor has therefore failed to substantially carry of the terms of the contract, $250 per Medicare enrollee from the terminated Part D plan or plans at the time the Part D sponsor terminated its contract, or $100,000, whichever is greater.

**§ 423.760 Other applicable provisions.**

The provisions of section 1128A of the Act (except paragraphs (a) and (b)) apply to civil money penalties under this subpart to the same extent that they apply to a civil money penalty or procedure under section 1128A of the Act.

## Subpart R–Payments to Sponsors of Retiree Prescription Drug Plans

**§ 423.880 Basis and scope.**

(a) *Basis.* This subpart is based on section 1860D-22 of the Act, as amended by section 101 of the Medicare Prescription Drug, Improvement, and Modernization Act of 2003 (MMA).

(b) *Scope.* This section implements the statutory requirement that a subsidy payment be made to sponsors of qualified retiree prescription drug plans.

**§ 423.882 Definitions.**

For the purposes of this subpart, the following definitions apply:

Allowable retiree costs, in accordance with section 1860D-22(a)(3)(C)(i) of the Act, means gross covered retiree plan-related prescription drug costs that are actually paid (net any manufacturer or pharmacy discounts, chargebacks, rebates, and similar price concessions) by either the qualified retiree prescription drug plan or the qualifying covered retiree (or on the qualifying covered retiree's behalf).

*Benefit option* means a particular benefit design, category of benefits, or cost-sharing arrangement offered within a group health plan.

*Employment-based retiree health coverage* means coverage of health care costs under a group health plan based on an individual's status as a retired participant in the plan, or as the spouse or dependent of a retired participant. The term includes coverage provided by voluntary insurance coverage, or coverage as a result of a statutory or contractual obligation.

*Gross covered retiree plan-related prescription drug costs*, or *gross retiree costs means*, for a qualifying covered retiree who is enrolled in a qualified retiree prescription drug plan during a plan year, non-administrative costs incurred under the plan for Part D drugs during the year, whether paid for by the plan or the retiree, including costs directly related to the dispensing of Part D drugs.

*Group health* plans include plans as defined in section 607(1) of ERISA, 29 U.S.C. § 1167(1). They also include the following plans:

(1) A Federal or State governmental plan, which is a plan providing medical care that is established or maintained for its employees by the Government of

the United States, by the government of any State or political subdivision of a State (including a county or local government), or by any agency or instrumentality or any of the foregoing, including a health benefits plan offered under chapter 89 of title 5, United States Code (the Federal Employee Health Benefit Plan (FEHBP)).

(2) A collectively bargained plan, which is a plan providing medical care that is established or maintained under or by one or more collective bargaining agreements.

(3) A church plan, which is a plan providing medical care that is established and maintained for its employees or their beneficiaries by a church or by a convention or association of churches that is exempt from tax under section 501 of the Internal Revenue Code of 1986 (26 U.S.C. 501).

(4) An account-based medical plan such as a Health Reimbursement Arrangement (HRA) as defined in Internal Revenue Service Notice 2002-45, 2002-28 I.R.B. 93, a health Flexible Spending Arrangement (FSA) as defined in Internal Revenue Code (Code) section 106(c)(2), a health savings account (HSA) as defined in Code section 223, or an Archer MSA as defined in Code section 220, to the extent they are subject to ERISA as employee welfare benefit plans providing medical care (or would be subject to ERISA but for the exclusion in ERISA section 4(b), 29 U.S.C. § 1003(b), for governmental plans or church plans).

*Part D drug* is defined in § 423.100 of this part.

*Part D eligible individual* is defined in § 423.4 of this part.

*Qualified retiree prescription drug plan* means employment-based retiree health coverage that meets the requirements set forth in § 423.884 of this chapter for a Part D eligible individual who is a retired participant or the spouse or dependent of a retired participant under the coverage.

*Qualifying covered retiree* means a Part D eligible individual who is: a participant or the spouse or dependent of a participant; covered under employment-based retiree health coverage that qualifies as a qualified retiree prescription drug plan; and not enrolled in a Part D plan. For this purpose, the determination of whether an individual is covered under employment-based retiree health coverage is made by the sponsor in accordance with the rules of its plan. For purposes of this subpart, however, an individual is presumed not to be covered under employment-based retiree health coverage if, under the Medicare Secondary Payer rules in § 411.104 of this chapter and related CMS guidance, the person is considered to be receiving coverage by reason of current employment status. The presumption applies whether or not the Medicare Secondary Payer rules actually apply to the sponsor. For this purpose, a sponsor also may treat a person receiving coverage under its qualified retiree prescription drug plan as the dependent of a qualifying covered retiree in accordance with the rules of its plan, regardless of whether that person constitutes the qualifying covered retiree's dependent for Federal or State tax purposes.

*Retiree drug subsidy amount,* or *subsidy payment,* means the subsidy amount paid to sponsors of qualified retiree prescription drug coverage under § 423.886(a).

*Standard prescription drug coverage* is defined in § 423.100 of this part.

*Sponsor* is a plan sponsor as defined in section 3(16)(B) of the Employee Retirement Income Security Act of 1974 (ERISA), 29 U.S.C. 1002(16)(B), except that, in the case of a plan maintained jointly by one employer and an employee organization and for which the employer is the primary source of financing, the term means the employer.

*Sponsor agreement* means an agreement by the sponsor to comply with the provisions of this subpart.

**§ 423.890 Appeals.**

(a) *Informal written reconsideration*—(1) *Initial determinations.* A sponsor is entitled to an informal written reconsideration of an adverse initial determination. An initial determination is a determination regarding the following:

(i) The amount of the subsidy payment.

(ii) The actuarial equivalence of the sponsor's retiree prescription drug plan.

(iii) If an enrollee in a retiree prescription drug plan is a qualifying covered retiree; or

(iv) Any other similar determination (as determined by CMS) that affects eligibility for, or the amount of, a subsidy payment.

(2) *Effect of an initial determination regarding the retiree drug subsidy.* An initial determination is final and binding unless reconsidered in accordance with this paragraph (a) of this section.

(3) *Manner and timing for request.* A request for reconsideration must be made in writing and filed with CMS within 15 days of the date on the notice of adverse determination.

(4) *Content of request.* The request for reconsideration must specify the findings or issues with which the sponsor disagrees and the reasons for the disagreements. The request for reconsideration may include additional documentary evidence the sponsor wishes CMS to consider.

(5) *Conduct of informal written reconsideration.* In conducting the reconsideration, CMS reviews the subsidy determination, the evidence and findings upon which it was based, and any other written evidence submitted by the sponsor or by CMS before notice of the reconsidered determination is made.

(6) *Decision of the informal written reconsideration.* CMS informs the sponsor of the decision orally or through electronic mail. CMS sends a written decision to the sponsor on the sponsor's request.

(7) *Effect of CMS informal written reconsideration.* A reconsideration decision, whether delivered orally or in writing, is final and binding unless a request for hearing is filed in accordance with paragraph (b) of this section, or it is revised in accordance paragraph (d) of this section.

(b) *Right to informal hearing.* A sponsor dissatisfied with the CMS reconsideration decision is entitled to an informal hearing as provided in this section.

(1) *Manner and timing for request.* A request for a hearing must be made in writing and filed with CMS within 15 days of the date the sponsor receives the CMS reconsideration decision.

(2) *Content of request.* The request for informal hearing must include a copy of the CMS reconsideration decision (if any) and must specify the findings or issues in the decision with which the sponsor disagrees and the reasons for the disagreements.

(3) *Informal hearing procedures.* (i) CMS provides written notice of the time and place of the informal hearing at least 10 days before the scheduled date.

(ii) The hearing is conducted by a CMS hearing officer who neither receives testimony nor accepts any new evidence that was not presented with the reconsideration request. The CMS hearing officer is limited to the review of the record that was before CMS when CMS made both its initial and reconsideration determinations.

(iii) If CMS did not issue a written reconsideration decision, the hearing officer may request, but not require, a written statement from CMS or its contractors explaining CMS' determination, or CMS or its contractors may, on their own, submit the written statement to the hearing officer. Failure of CMS to submit a written statement does not result in any adverse findings against CMS and may not in any way be taken into account by the hearing officer in reaching a decision.

(4) *Decision of the CMS hearing officer.* The CMS hearing officer decides the case and sends a written decision to the sponsor, explaining the basis for the decision.

(5) *Effect of hearing officer decision.* The hearing officer decision is final and binding, unless the decision is reversed or modified by the Administrator in accordance with paragraph (c) of this section.

(c) *Review by the Administrator.* (1) A sponsor that has received a hearing officer decision upholding a CMS initial or reconsidered determination may request review by the Administrator within 15 days of receipt of the hearing officer's decision.

(2) The Administrator may review the hearing officer's decision, any written documents submitted to CMS or to the hearing officer, as well as any other information included in the record of the hearing officer's decision and determine whether to uphold, reverse or modify the hearing officer's decision.

(3) The Administrator's determination is final and binding.

(d) *Reopening*—(1) *Ability to reopen.* CMS may reopen and revise an initial or reconsidered determination upon its own motion or upon the request of a sponsor:

(i) Within 1 year of the date of the notice of determination for any reason.

(ii) Within 4 years for good cause.

(iii) At any time when the underlying decision was obtained through fraud or similar fault.

(2) *Notice of reopening.* (i) Notice of reopening and any revisions following the reopening are mailed to the sponsor.

(ii) Notice of reopening specifies the reasons for revision.

(3) *Effect of reopening.* The revision of an initial or reconsidered determination is final and binding unless-

(i) The sponsor requests reconsideration in accordance with paragraph (a) of this section;

(ii) A timely request for a hearing is filed under paragraph (b) of this section;

(iii) The determination is reviewed by the Administrator in accordance with paragraph (c) of this section; or

(iv) The determination is reopened and revised in accordance with paragraph (d) of this section.

(4) *Good cause.* For purposes of this section, CMS finds good cause if—

(i) New and material evidence exists that was not readily available at the time the initial determination was made;

(ii) A clerical error in the computation of payments was made; or

(iii) The evidence that was considered in making the determination clearly shows on its face that an error was made.

(5) For purposes of this section, CMS does not find good cause if the only reason for reopening is a change of legal interpretation or administrative ruling upon which the initial determination was made.

(6) A decision by CMS not to reopen an initial or reconsidered determination is final and binding and cannot be appealed.

## PART 426—REVIEW OF NATIONAL COVERAGE DETERMINATIONS AND LOCAL COVERAGE DETERMINATIONS

### Subpart C—General Provisions for the Review of LCDs and NCDs

#### § 426.300 Review of LCDs, NCDs, and deemed NCDs.

(a) Upon the receipt of an acceptable LCD complaint as described in § 426.400, an ALJ conducts a review of a challenged provision (or provisions) of an LCD using the reasonableness standard.

(b) Upon the receipt of an acceptable NCD complaint as described in § 426.500, the Board conducts an NCD review of a challenged provision (or provisions) of an NCD using the reasonableness standard.

(c) The procedures established in this part governing the review of NCDs also apply in cases in which a deemed NCD is challenged.

#### § 426.310 LCD and NCD reviews and individual claim appeals.

(a) LCD and NCD reviews are distinct from the claims appeal processes set forth in part 405, subparts G and H; part 417, subpart Q; and part 422, subpart M of this chapter.

(b) An aggrieved party must notify the ALJ or the Board, as appropriate, regarding the submission and disposition of any pending claim or appeal relating to the subject of the aggrieved party's LCD or NCD complaint. This reporting obligation continues through the entire LCD or NCD review process.

**§ 426.320 Who may challenge an LCD or NCD.**

(a) Only an aggrieved party may initiate a review of an LCD or NCD (including a deemed NCD), or provisions of an LCD or NCD by filing an acceptable complaint.

(b) Neither an ALJ nor the Board recognizes as valid any attempt to assign rights to request review under section 1869(f) of the Act.

**§ 426. 325 What may be challenged.**

(a) Only LCDs or NCDs (including deemed NCDs) that are currently effective may be challenged.

(b) Some items are not reviewable under this part, including the following:

(1) Pre-decisional materials, including–

(i) Draft LCDs;

(ii) Template LCDs or suggested LCDs; and

(iii) Draft NCDs, including national coverage decision memoranda.

(2) Retired LCDs or withdrawn NCDs.

(3) LCD or NCD provisions that are no longer in effect due to revisions or reconsiderations.

(4) Interpretive policies that are not an LCD or NCD.

(5) Contractor decisions that are not based on section 1862(a)(1)(A) of the Act.

(6) Contractor claims processing edits.

(7) Payment amounts or methodologies.

(8) Procedure coding issues, including determinations, methodologies, definitions, or provisions.

(9) Contractor bulletin articles, educational materials, or Web site frequently asked questions.

(10) Any M+C organization or managed care plan policy, rule, or procedure.

(11) An individual claim determination.

(12) Any other policy that is not an LCD or an NCD as set forth in § 400.202 of this chapter.

**§ 426.330 Burden of proof.**

During an LCD or NCD review, an aggrieved party bears the burden of proof and the burden of persuasion for the issue(s) raised in a complaint. The burden of persuasion is judged by a preponderance of the evidence.

**§ 426.340 Procedures for review of new evidence.**

(a) The process for review of new evidence is initiated once the ALJ/Board completes the taking of evidence.

(b) If an aggrieved party has submitted new evidence pertaining to the LCD/NCD provision(s) in question, and the ALJ or the Board finds that evidence admissible, the ALJ or the Board reviews the record as a whole and decides whether the new evidence has the potential to significantly affect the ALJ's or the Board's evaluation of the LCD/NCD provision(s) in question under the reasonableness standard.

(c) If the ALJ or the Board determines that the new evidence does not have the potential to significantly affect the ALJ's or the Board's evaluation of the LCD/NCD provision(s) in question under the reasonableness standard, this evidence is included in the review record, and the review goes forward to a decision on the merits.

(d) If the ALJ or the Board determines that the new evidence has the potential to significantly affect the ALJ's or the Board's evaluation of the LCD or NCD provision(s) in question under the reasonableness standard, then the ALJ or the Board—

(1) Stays the proceedings and ensures that the contractor or CMS, whichever is appropriate, has a copy of the new evidence for its examination; and

(2) Allows the contractor/CMS 10 days, generally, to examine the new evidence, and to decide whether the contractor or CMS initiates a reconsideration.

(e) If the contractor or CMS informs the ALJ or the Board by the end of the 10 days that a reconsideration is initiated, and then the ALJ or the Board—

(1) Continues the stay in proceedings; and

(2) Sets a reasonable time frame—

(i) For LCDs, of not more than 90 days, by which the contractor completes the reconsideration; or

(ii) For NCDs, in compliance with the time frames specified in section 1862(1) of the Act, by which CMS completes the reconsideration.

(f) The ALJ or Board lifts the stay in proceedings and continues the review on the challenged provision(s) of the original LCD or NCD, including the new evidence in the review record, if the contractor or CMS—

(1) Informs the ALJ or Board that a reconsideration is not initiated; or

(2) Does not meet—

(i) For LCDs, the 90-day reconsideration time frame; or

(ii) For NCDs, the reconsideration time frame specified by the Board, in compliance with section 1862(l) of the Act.

(g) If an LCD or NCD is reconsidered and revised within the time frame allotted by the ALJ or Board, then the revised LCD or NCD and any supplement to the LCD or NCD record is forwarded to the ALJ or the Board and all parties and the review proceeds on the LCD or NCD.

[68 FR 63716, Nov. 7, 2003, as amended at 70 FR 70335, Nov. 21, 2005; 71 FR 9461, Feb. 24, 2006]

### Subpart D—Review of an LCD

### § 426.400 Procedure for filing an acceptable complaint concerning a provision (or provisions) of an LCD.

(a) *The complaint.* An aggrieved party may initiate a review of an LCD by filing a written complaint with the office designated by CMS on the Medicare Web site, *http://www.medicare.gov/coverage/static/appeals.asp.*

(b) *Timeliness of a complaint.* An LCD complaint is not considered timely unless it is filed with the office designated by CMS within—

(1) 6 months of the issuance of a written statement from each aggrieved party's treating practitioner, in the case of aggrieved parties who choose to file an LCD challenge before receiving the service; or

(2) 120 days of the initial denial notice, in the case of aggrieved parties who choose to file an LCD challenge after receiving the service.

(c) *Components of a valid complaint.* A complaint must include the following:

(1) *Beneficiary-identifying information:*

(i) Name.

(ii) Mailing address.

(iii) State of residence, if different from mailing address.

(iv) Telephone number, if any.

(v) Health Insurance Claim number, if applicable.

(vi) E-mail address, if applicable.

(2) *If the beneficiary has a representative,* the representative-identifying information must include the following:

(i) Name.

(ii) Mailing address.

(iii) Telephone number.

(iv) E-mail address, if any.

(v) Copy of the written authorization to represent the beneficiary.

(3) *Treating physician written statement.* A copy of a written statement from the treating physician that the beneficiary needs the service that is the subject of the LCD. This statement may be in the form of a written order for the service or other documentation from the beneficiary's medical record (such as progress notes or discharge summary) indicating that the beneficiary needs the service.

(4) *LCD-identifying information:*

(i) Name of the contractor using the LCD.

(ii) Title of LCD being challenged.

(iii) The specific provision (or provisions) of the LCD adversely affecting the aggrieved party.

(5) *Aggrieved party statement.* A statement from the aggrieved party explaining what service is needed and why the aggrieved party thinks that the provision(s) of the LCD is (are) not valid under the reasonableness standard.

(6) *Clinical or scientific evidence.* (i) Copies of clinical or scientific evidence that support the complaint and an explanation for why the aggrieved party thinks that this evidence shows that the LCD is not reasonable.

(ii) Any documents or portions of documents that include proprietary data must be marked "proprietary data," and include a legal basis for that assertion.

(iii) Proprietary data submitted by a manufacturer concerning a drug or device for which the manufacturer has submitted information to the Food and Drug Administration, must be considered and given substantive weight only when supported by an affidavit certifying that the submission contains true and correct copies of all data submitted by the manufacturer to the Food and Drug Administration in relation to that drug or device.

(d) *Joint complaints*—(1) *Conditions for a joint complaint.* Two or more aggrieved parties may initiate the review of an LCD by filing a single written complaint with the ALJ if all of the following conditions are met:

(i) Each aggrieved party named in the joint complaint has a similar medical condition or there are other bases for combining the complaints.

(ii) Each aggrieved party named in the joint complaint is filing the complaint in regard to the same provision(s) of the same LCD.

(2) *Components of a valid joint complaint.* A joint complaint must contain the following information:

(i) The beneficiary-identifying information described in paragraph (c)(1) of this section for each aggrieved party named in the joint complaint.

(ii) The LCD-identifying information described in paragraph (c)(2) of this section.

(iii) The documentation described in paragraphs (c)(3) and (c)(4) of this section.

(3) *Timeliness of a joint complaint.* Aggrieved parties, who choose to seek review of an LCD—

(i) Before receiving the service, must file with the ALJ a joint complaint within 6 months of the written statement from each aggrieved party's treating physician.

(ii) After receiving the service, must file with the ALJ a complaint within 120 days of each aggrieved party's initial denial notice.

**§ 426.403 Submitting new evidence once an acceptable complaint is filed.**
Once an acceptable complaint is filed, the aggrieved party may submit additional new evidence without withdrawing the complaint until the ALJ closes the record.

**§ 426.405 Authority of the ALJ.**

(a) An ALJ conducts a fair and impartial hearing, avoids unnecessary delay, maintains order, and ensures that all proceedings are recorded.

(b) An ALJ defers only to reasonable findings of fact, reasonable interpretations of law, and reasonable applications of fact to law by the Secretary.

(c) The ALJ has the authority to do any of the following:

(1) Review complaints by an aggrieved party (or aggrieved parties).

(2) Dismiss complaints that fail to comply with § 426.400.

(3) Set and change the date, time, and place of a hearing upon reasonable notice to the parties.

(4) Continue or recess a hearing for a reasonable period of time.

(5) Hold conferences to identify or simplify the issues, or to consider other matters that may aid in the expeditious disposition of the proceeding.

(6) Consult with scientific and clinical experts on his or her own motion concerning clinical or scientific evidence.

(7) Set schedules for submission of exhibits and written reports of experts.

(8) Administer oaths and affirmations.

(9) Examine witnesses.

(10) Issue subpoenas requiring the attendance of witnesses at hearings as permitted by this part.

(11) Issue subpoenas requiring the production of existing documents before, and relating to, the hearing as permitted by this part.

(12) Rule on motions and other procedural matters.

(13) Stay the proceedings in accordance with § 426.340.

(14) Regulate the scope and timing of documentary discovery as permitted by this part.

(15) Regulate the course of a hearing and the conduct of representatives, parties, and witnesses.

(16) Receive, rule on, exclude, or limit evidence, as provided in § 426.340.

(17) Take official notice of facts, upon motion of a party.

(18) Decide cases, upon the motion of a party, by summary judgment when there is no disputed issue of material fact.

(19) Conduct any conference, argument, or hearing in person or, upon agreement of the parties, by telephone, picture-tel, or any other means.

(20) Issue decisions.

(21) Exclude a party from an LCD review for failure to comply with an ALJ order or procedural request without good cause shown.

(22) Stay the proceedings for a reasonable time when all parties voluntarily agree to mediation or negotiation, and provide mediation services upon request.

(d) The ALJ does not have authority to do any of the following under this part:

(1) Conduct an LCD review or conduct LCD hearings on his or her own motion or on the motion of a nonaggrieved party.

(2) Issue a decision based on any new evidence without following § 426.340, regarding procedures for review of new evidence.

(3) Review any decisions by contractors to develop a new or revised LCD.

(4) Conduct a review of any draft, retired, archived, template, or suggested LCDs.

(5) Conduct a review of any policy that is not an LCD, as defined in § 400.202 of this chapter.

(6) Conduct a review of any NCD according to section 1869(f)(1)(A)(i) of the Act.

(7) Conduct a review of the merits of an unacceptable LCD complaint as discussed in § 426.410.

(8) Allow participation by individuals or entities other than—

(i) The aggrieved party and/or his/her representative;

(ii) CMS and/or the contractor; and

(iii) Experts called by the parties or the ALJ.

(9) Compel the parties to participate in a mediation process or to engage in settlement negotiations.

(10) Deny a request for withdrawal of a complaint by an aggrieved party.

(11) Compel the contractor to conduct studies, surveys, or develop new information to support an LCD record.

(12) Deny a contractor the right to reconsider, revise or retire an LCD.

(13) Find invalid applicable Federal statutes, regulations, rulings, or NCDs.

(14) Enter a decision specifying terms to be included in an LCD.

**§ 426.406 Ex parte contacts.**
No party or person (except employees of the ALJ's office) communicates in any way with the ALJ on any substantive matter at issue in a case, unless on notice and opportunity for all parties to participate. This provision does not prohibit a person or party from inquiring about the status of a case or asking routine questions concerning administrative functions or procedures.

**§ 426.410 Docketing and evaluating the acceptability of LCD complaints.**

(a) *Docketing the complaint.* The office designated by CMS does the following upon receiving a complaint regarding an LCD:

(1) Dockets the complaint.

(2) Determines whether the complaint is–

(i) The first challenge to a particular LCD; or

(ii) Related to a pending LCD review.

(3) Forwards the complaint to the ALJ that conducts the review. In cases related to pending reviews, the complaint generally is forwarded to the ALJ who is conducting the review.

(b) *Evaluating the acceptability of the complaint.* The ALJ assigned to the LCD review determines if the complaint is acceptable by confirming all of the following:

(1) The complaint is being submitted by an aggrieved party or, in the case of a joint complaint, that each individual named in the joint complaint is an aggrieved party. (In determining if a complaint is acceptable, the ALJ assumes that the facts alleged by the treating physician's documentation regarding the aggrieved party's (or parties') clinical condition are true.)

(2) The complaint meets the requirements for a valid complaint in § 426.400 and does not challenge one of the documents in § 426.325(b).

(c) *Unacceptable complaint.* (1) If the ALJ determines that the complaint is unacceptable, the ALJ must provide the aggrieved party (or parties) one opportunity to amend the unacceptable complaint.

(2) If the aggrieved party (or parties) fail(s) to submit an acceptable amended complaint within a reasonable time frame as determined by the ALJ, the ALJ must issue a decision dismissing the unacceptable complaint.

(3) If a complaint is determined unacceptable after one amendment, the beneficiary is precluded from filing again for 6 months after being informed that it is unacceptable.

(d) *Acceptable complaint.* If the ALJ determines that the complaint (or amended complaint) is acceptable, the ALJ does the following:

(1) Sends a letter to the aggrieved party (or parties) acknowledging the complaint and informing the aggrieved party (or parties) of the docket number and the deadline for the contractor to produce the LCD record.

(2) Forwards a copy of the complaint, any evidence submitted in the complaint, and the letter described in paragraph (d)(1) of this section to the applicable contractor and CMS.

(3) Requires CMS or the contractor to send a copy of the LCD record to the ALJ and all parties to the LCD review within 30 days of receiving the ALJ's letter, the copy of the complaint, and any associated evidence, subject to extension for good cause shown.

(e) *Consolidation of complaints regarding an LCD*—(1) *Criteria for consolidation.* If a review is pending regarding a particular LCD provision(s) and no decision has been issued ending the review, and a new acceptable complaint is filed, the ALJ consolidates the complaints and conducts a consolidated LCD review if all of the following criteria are met:

(i) The complaints are in regard to the same provision(s) of the same LCD or there are other bases for consolidating the complaints.

(ii) The complaints contain common questions of law, common questions of fact, or both.

(iii) Consolidating the complaints does not unduly delay the ALJ's decision.

(2) *Decision to consolidate complaints.* If an ALJ decides to consolidate complaints, the ALJ does the following:

(i) Provides notification that the LCD review is consolidated and informs all parties of the docket number of the consolidated review.

(ii) Makes a single record of the proceeding.

(iii) Considers the relevant evidence introduced in each LCD complaint as introduced in the consolidated review.

(3) *Decision not to consolidate complaints.* If an ALJ decides not to consolidate complaints, the ALJ conducts separate LCD reviews for each complaint.

[68 FR 63716, Nov. 7, 2003; 68 FR 65346, Nov. 19, 2003]

**§ 426.415 CMS's role in the LCD review.**

CMS may provide to the ALJ, and all parties to the LCD review, information identifying the person who represents the contractor or CMS, if necessary, in the LCD review process.

**§ 426.416 Role of Medicare Managed Care Organizations (MCOs) and State agencies in the LCD review.**

Medicare MCOs and Medicaid State agencies have no role in the LCD review process. However, once the ALJ has issued its decision, the decision is made available to all Medicare MCOs and State agencies.

**§ 426.417 Contractor's statement regarding new evidence.**

(a) The contractor may review any new evidence that is submitted, regardless of whether the ALJ has stayed the proceedings, including but not limited to—

(1) New evidence submitted with the initial complaint;

(2) New evidence submitted with an amended complaint;

(3) New evidence produced during discovery;

(4) New evidence produced when the ALJ consults with scientific and clinical experts; and

(5) New evidence presented during any hearing.

(b) The contractor may submit a statement regarding whether the new evidence is significant under § 426.340, within such deadline as the ALJ may set.

**§ 426.418 LCD record furnished to aggrieved party.**

(a) *Elements of a contractor's LCD record furnished to the aggrieved party.* Except as provided in paragraph (b) of this section, the contractor's LCD record consists of any document or material that the contractor considered during the development of the LCD, including, but not limited to, the following:

(1) The LCD being challenged.

(2) Any medical evidence considered on or before the date the LCD was issued, including, but not limited to, the following:

(i) Scientific articles.

(ii) Technology assessments.

(iii) Clinical guidelines.

(iv) Statements from clinical experts, medical textbooks, claims data, or other indication of medical standard of practice.

(3) Comment and Response Document (a summary of comments received by the contractor concerning the draft LCD).

(4) An index of documents considered that are excluded under paragraph (b) of this section.

(b) *Elements of the LCD record not furnished to the aggrieved party.* The LCD record furnished to the aggrieved party does not include the following:

(1) Proprietary data or privileged information.

(2) Any new evidence.

**§ 426.419 LCD record furnished to the ALJ.**

The LCD record furnished to the ALJ includes the following:

(a) Documents included in § 426.418(a).

(b) Privileged information and proprietary data considered that must be filed with the ALJ under seal.

**§ 426.420 Retiring or revising an LCD under review.**

(a) A contractor may retire an LCD or LCD provision under review before the date the ALJ issues a decision regarding that LCD. Retiring an LCD or LCD provision under review has the same effect as a decision under § 426.460(b).

(b) A contractor may revise an LCD under review to remove or amend the LCD provision listed in the complaint through the reconsideration process before the date the ALJ issues a decision regarding that LCD. Revising an LCD under review to remove the LCD provision in question has the same effect as a decision under § 426.460(b).

(c) A contractor must notify the ALJ within 48 hours of—

(1) Retiring an LCD or LCD provision that is under review; or

(2) Issuing a revised version of the LCD that is under review.

(d) If the contractor issues a revised LCD, the contractor forwards a copy of the revised LCD to the ALJ.

(e) The ALJ must take the following actions upon receiving a notice that the contractor has retired or revised an LCD under review:

(1) If, before the ALJ issues a decision, the ALJ receives notice that the contractor has retired the LCD or revised the LCD to completely remove the provision in question, the ALJ must dismiss the complaint and inform the aggrieved party(ies) who sought the review that he or she or they receive individual claim review without the retired/withdrawn provision(s).

(2) If, before the ALJ issues a decision, the ALJ receives notice that the contractor has revised the LCD provision in question but has not removed it altogether, the ALJ must continue the review based on the revised LCD. In this case, the contractor must send a copy of the supplemental record to the ALJ and all parties. In that circumstance, the ALJ permits the aggrieved party to respond to the revised LCD and supplemental record.

**§ 426.423 Withdrawing a complaint regarding an LCD under review.**

(a) *Circumstance under which an aggrieved party may withdraw a complaint regarding an LCD.* An aggrieved party who filed a complaint regarding an LCD may withdraw the complaint before the ALJ issues a decision regarding that LCD. The aggrieved party may not file another complaint concerning the same coverage determination for 6 months.

(b) *Process for an aggrieved party withdrawing a complaint regarding an LCD.* To withdraw a complaint regarding an LCD, the aggrieved party who filed the complaint must send a written withdrawal notice to the ALJ (*see* § 426.400), CMS (if applicable), and the applicable contractor. Supplementing an acceptable complaint with new evidence does not constitute a withdrawal of a complaint, as described in § 426.403.

(c) *Actions the ALJ must take upon receiving a notice announcing the intent to withdraw a complaint regarding an LCD*—(1) *LCD reviews involving one aggrieved party.* If the ALJ receives a withdrawal notice regarding an LCD before the date the ALJ issued a decision regarding that LCD, the ALJ issues a decision dismissing the complaint under § 426.444 and informs the aggrieved party that he or she may not file another complaint to the same coverage determination for 6 months.

(2) *LCD reviews involving joint complaints.* If the ALJ receives a notice from an aggrieved party who is named in a joint complaint withdrawing a complaint regarding an LCD before the date the ALJ issued a decision regarding that LCD, the ALJ issues a decision dismissing only that aggrieved party from the complaint

under § 426.444. The ALJ continues the LCD review if there is one or more aggrieved party who does not withdraw from the joint complaint.

(3) *Consolidated LCD reviews.* If the ALJ receives a notice from an aggrieved party who is part of a consolidated LCD review withdrawing a complaint regarding an LCD before the date the ALJ issued a decision regarding that LCD, the ALJ removes that aggrieved party from the consolidated LCD review and issues a decision dismissing that aggrieved party's complaint under § 426.444. The ALJ continues the LCD review if there is one or more aggrieved party who does not withdraw from the joint complaint.

**§ 426.425 LCD review.**

(a) *Opportunity for the aggrieved party, after his or her review of the LCD record, to state why the LCD is not valid.* Upon receipt of the contractor's LCD record, the aggrieved party files a statement explaining why the contractor's LCD record is not complete, or not adequate to support the validity of the LCD under the reasonableness standard. This statement must be submitted to the ALJ and to the contractor, or CMS, as appropriate, within 30 days (or within the additional time as allowed by the ALJ for good cause shown) of the date the aggrieved party receives the contractor's LCD record.

(b) *Contractor response.* The contractor has 30 days after receiving the aggrieved party's statement to submit a response to the ALJ in order to defend the LCD.

(c) *ALJ evaluation.* (1) After the aggrieved party files a statement and the contractor responds, as described in § 426.425(a) and § 426.425(b), or the time for filing has expired, the ALJ applies the reasonableness standard to determine whether the LCD record is complete and adequate to support the validity of the LCD.

(2) Issuance of a decision finding the record complete and adequate to support the validity of the LCD ends the review process.

(3) If the ALJ determines that the LCD record is not complete and adequate to support the validity of the LCD, the ALJ permits discovery and the taking of evidence in accordance with § 426.432 and § 426.440 and evaluates the LCD in accordance with § 426.431.

(d) The process described in paragraphs (a), (b), and (c) of this section applies when an LCD record has been supplemented, except that discovery and the taking of evidence are not repeated. The period for the aggrieved party to file a statement begins when the aggrieved party receives the supplement.

**§ 426.431 ALJ's review of the LCD to apply the reasonableness standard.**

(a) *Required steps.* To review the provision(s) listed in the aggrieved party's complaint based on the reasonableness standard, an ALJ must:

(1) Confine the LCD review to the provision(s) of the LCD raised in the aggrieved party's complaint.

(2) Conduct a hearing, unless the matter can be decided on the written record.

(3) Close the LCD review record to the taking of evidence.

(4) Treat as precedential any previous Board decision under § 426.482 that involves the same LCD provision(s), same specific issue and facts in question, and the same clinical conditions.

(5) Issue a decision as described in § 426.447.

(b) *Optional steps.* The ALJ may do the following to apply the reasonableness standard to the provision(s) listed in the aggrieved party's complaint:

(1) Consult with appropriate scientific or clinical experts concerning evidence.

(2) Consider any previous ALJ decision made under § 426.447 regarding the same provision(s) of the LCD under review and for the same clinical conditions.

(c) *Authority for ALJs in LCD reviews when applying the reasonableness standard.* In applying the reasonableness standard to a provision (or provisions) of an LCD, the ALJ must follow all applicable laws, regulations, rulings, and NCDs.

**§ 426.432 Discovery.**

(a) *General rule.* If the ALJ orders discovery, the ALJ must establish a reasonable time frame for discovery.

(b) *Protective order*—(1) *Request for a protective order.* Any party receiving a discovery request may file a motion for a protective order before the date of production of the discovery.

(2) *The ALJ granting of a protective order.* The ALJ may grant a motion for a protective order if (s)he finds that the discovery sought—

(i) Is irrelevant or unduly repetitive;

(ii) Is unduly costly or burdensome; or

(iii) Unduly delays the proceeding.

(c) *Types of discovery available.* A party may obtain discovery via a request for the production of documents, and/or via the submission of up to 10 written interrogatory questions, relating to a specific LCD.

(d) *Types of documents.* For the purpose of this section, the term "documents" includes relevant information, reports, answers, records, accounts, papers, and other data and documentary evidence. Nothing contained in this section is interpreted to require the creation of a document.

(e) *Types of discovery not available.* Requests for admissions, depositions, or any other forms of discovery, other than those permitted under paragraph (c) of this section, are not authorized.

(f) *Privileged information and proprietary data.* The ALJ must not, under any circumstance, order the disclosure of privileged information or proprietary data filed under seal without the consent of the party who possesses the right to protection of the information.

(g) *Notification.* The ALJ notifies all parties in writing when the discovery period closes.

**§ 426.435 Subpoenas.**

(a) *Purpose of a subpoena.* A subpoena requires the attendance of an individual at a hearing and may also require a party to produce evidence authorized under § 426.440 at or before the hearing.

(b) *Filing a motion for a subpoena.* A party seeking a subpoena must file a written motion with the ALJ not less than 30 days before the date fixed for the hearing. The motion must do all of the following:

(1) Designate the witnesses.

(2) Specify any evidence to be produced.

(3) Describe the address and location with sufficient particularity to permit the witnesses to be found.

(4) State the pertinent facts that the party expects to establish by the witnesses or documents and whether other evidence may establish without the use of a subpoena.

(c) *Response to a motion for a subpoena.* Within 15 days after the written motion requesting issuance of a subpoena is served on all parties, any party may file an opposition to the motion or other response.

(d) *Extension for good cause shown.* The ALJ may modify the deadlines specified in paragraphs (b) and (c) of this section for good cause shown.

(e) *Motion for a subpoena granted.* If the ALJ grants a motion requesting issuance of a subpoena, the subpoena must do the following:

(1) Be issued in the name of the ALJ.

(2) Include the docket number and title of the LCD under review.

(3) Provide notice that the subpoena is issued according to sections 1872 and 205(d) and (e) of the Act.

(4) Specify the time and place at which the witness is to appear and any evidence the witness is to produce.

(f) *Delivery of the subpoena.* The party seeking the subpoena serves it by personal delivery to the individual named, or by certified mail return receipt requested, addressed to the individual at his or her last dwelling place or principal place of business.

(g) *Motion to quash a subpoena.* The individual to whom the subpoena is directed may file with the ALJ a motion to quash the subpoena within 10 days after service.

(h) *Refusal to obey a subpoena.* The exclusive remedy for contumacy by, or refusal to obey, a subpoena duly served upon any person is specified in section 205(e) of the Act (42 U.S.C. 405(e)) except that any reference to the "Commissioner of Social Security"shall be considered a reference to the "Secretary."

**§ 426.440 Evidence.**

(a) Except as provided in this part, the ALJ is not bound by the Federal Rules of Evidence. However, the ALJ may apply the Federal Rules of Evidence when appropriate, for example, to exclude unreliable evidence.

(b) The ALJ must exclude evidence that (s)he determines is clearly irrelevant, immaterial, or unduly repetitive.

(c) The ALJ may accept privileged information or proprietary data, but must maintain it under seal.

(d) The ALJ may permit the parties to introduce the testimony of expert witnesses on scientific and clinical issues, rebuttal witnesses, and other relevant evidence. The ALJ may require that the testimony of expert witnesses be submitted in the form of a written report, accompanied by the curriculum vitae of the expert preparing the report.

(e) Experts submitting reports must be available for cross-examination at an evidentiary hearing upon request of the ALJ or a party to the proceeding, or the reports will be excluded from the record.

(f) Except as set forth in paragraph (c) of this section or unless otherwise ordered by the ALJ for good cause shown, all documents and other evidence offered or taken for the record are open to examination by all parties.

**§ 426.444 Dismissals for cause.**

(a) The ALJ may, at the request of any party, or on his or her own motion, dismiss a complaint if the aggrieved party fails to do either of the following:

(1) Attend or participate in a prehearing conference (the pre-hearing may be conducted by telephone) or hearing without good cause shown.

(2) Comply with a lawful order of the ALJ without good cause shown.

(b) The ALJ must dismiss any complaint concerning LCD provision(s) if the following conditions exist:

(1) The ALJ does not have the authority to rule on that provision under § 426.405(d).

(2) The complaint is not timely. (*See* § 426.400(b).)

(3) The complaint is not filed by an aggrieved party.

(4) The complaint is filed by an individual who fails to provide an adequate statement of need for the service from the treating physician.

(5) The complaint challenges a provision or provisions of an NCD. (*See* § 426.405, regarding the authority of the ALJ.)

(6) The contractor notifies the ALJ that the LCD provision(s) is (are) no longer in effect.

(7) The aggrieved party withdraws the complaint. (*See* § 426.423 for requirements related to withdrawing a complaint regarding an LCD under review.)

**§ 426.445 Witness fees.**

(a) A witness testifying at a hearing before an ALJ receives the same fees and mileage as witnesses in Federal district courts of the United States. If the witness qualifies as an expert, he or she is entitled to an expert witness fee. Witness fees are paid by the party seeking to present the witness.

(b) If an ALJ requests expert testimony, the appropriate office overseeing the ALJ is responsible for paying all applicable fees and mileage, unless the expert waives payment.

**§ 426.446 Record of hearing.**
The ALJ must ensure that all hearings are open to the public and are electronically, mechanically or stenographically reported. Except for privileged information and proprietary data that are filed under seal, all evidence upon which the ALJ relies for decision must be admitted into the public record. All medical reports, exhibits, and any other pertinent document, either in whole or in material part, must be offered, marked for identification, and retained in the case record.

**§ 426.447 Issuance and notification of an ALJ's decision.**
An ALJ must issue to all parties to the LCD review, within 90 days of closing the LCD review record to the taking of evidence, one of the following:

(a) A written decision, including a description of appeal rights.

(b) A written notification stating that a decision is pending, and an approximate date of issuance for the decision.

**§ 426.450 Mandatory provisions of an ALJ's decision.**

(a) *Findings.* An ALJ's decision must include one of the following:

(1) A determination that the provision of the LCD is valid under the reasonableness standard.

(2) A determination that the provision of the LCD is not valid under the reasonableness standard.

(3) A statement dismissing the complaint regarding the LCD and a rationale for the dismissal.

(4) A determination that the LCD record is complete and adequate to support the validity of the LCD provisions under the reasonableness standard.

(b) *Other information.* An ALJ's decision must include all of the following:

(1) The date of issuance.

(2) The docket number of the LCD review.

(3) A statement as to whether the aggrieved party has filed a claim for the service(s) named in the complaint, the date(s)-of-service, and the disposition, if known.

(4) A basis for concluding that the LCD was or was not valid based on the application of the reasonableness standard to the record before the ALJ, including the contractor's:

(i) Findings of fact.

(ii) Interpretations of law.

(iii) Applications of fact to law.

(5) A summary of the evidence reviewed. If proprietary or privileged data were submitted under seal, the decision must state whether the data were material and what role they played in the determination, but without disclosing the substance or contents of the evidence under seal. A separate statement of the rationale for the ALJ's treatment of the sealed evidence must be prepared and kept under seal itself. If the ALJ decision is appealed to the Board, this statement must be provided to the Board under seal.

(6) A statement regarding appeal rights.

**§ 426.455 Prohibited provisions of an ALJ's decision.**
An ALJ's decision may not do any of the following:

(a) Order CMS or its contractors to add any language to a provision or provisions of an LCD.

(b) Order CMS or its contractors to pay a specific claim.

(c) Set a time limit for CMS or its contractors to establish a new or revised LCD.

(d) Review or evaluate an LCD other than the LCD under review.

(e) Include a requirement for CMS or its contractors that specifies payment, coding, or systems changes for an LCD, or deadlines for implementing these types of changes.

(f) Order or address how a contractor(s) must implement an LCD.

**§ 426.457 Optional provisions of an ALJ's decision.**
When appropriate, the ALJ may limit a decision holding invalid a specific provision(s) of an LCD to specific clinical indications and for similar conditions.

**§ 426.458 ALJ's LCD review record.**

(a) *Elements of the ALJ's LCD review record furnished to the public.* Except as provided in paragraph (b) of this section, the ALJ's LCD review record consists of any document or material that the ALJ compiled or considered during the LCD review, including, but not limited to, the following:

(1) The LCD complaint.

(2) The LCD and LCD record.

(3) The supplemental LCD record, if applicable.

(4) Transcripts of record.

(5) Any other relevant evidence gathered under § 426.440.

(6) The ALJ's decision.

(b) *Elements of the ALJ's LCD review record furnished to the Board under seal.* The ALJ's review record must include, under seal, any proprietary data or privileged information maintained under seal, and such data or information must not be included in the review record furnished to the public.

**§ 426.460 Effect of an ALJ's decision.**

(a) *Valid under the reasonableness standard.* If the ALJ finds that the provision or provisions of the LCD named in the complaint is (are) valid under the reasonableness standard, the aggrieved party or parties may appeal that (those) part(s) of the ALJ decision to the Board under § 426.465.

(b) *Not valid under the reasonableness standard.* If the ALJ finds that the provision or provisions of the LCD named in the complaint is (are) invalid under the reasonableness standard, and no appeal is filed by the contractor or CMS under § 426.465(b), the contractor, the M+C organization, or other Medicare managed care organization must provide the following—

(1) *Individual claim review.* (i) If neither the contractor nor CMS appeals the ALJ decision under § 426.425(b), and if the party's claim or appeal(s) was

previously denied, the contractor, an M+C organization or another Medicare managed care organization must reopen the claim of the party who challenged the LCD and adjudicate the claim without using the provision(s) of the LCD that the ALJ found invalid.

(ii) If a revised LCD is issued, the contractor, the M+C organization, and any other Medicare managed care organization within the contractor's jurisdiction uses the revised LCD in reviewing claim or appeal submissions or request for services delivered or services performed on or after the effective date of the revised LCD.

(iii) If the aggrieved party who sought the review has not yet submitted a claim, the contractor adjudicates the claim without using the provision(s) of the LCD that the ALJ found invalid.

(iv) In either case, the claim and any subsequent claims for the service provided under the same circumstances are adjudicated without using the LCD provision(s) found invalid.

(2) *Coverage determination relief.* If neither the contractor nor CMS appeals the ALJ decision under § 426.425(b), the contractor implements the ALJ decision within 30 days. Any change in policy applies prospectively to requests for service or claims filed with dates of service after the implementation of the ALJ decision.

**§ 426.462 Notice of an ALJ's decision.**

After the ALJ has made a decision regarding an LCD complaint, the ALJ sends a written notice of the decision to each party. The notice must–

(a) State the outcome of the review; and

(b) Inform each party to the determination of his or her rights to seek further review if he or she is dissatisfied with the determination, and the time limit under which an appeal must be requested.

**§ 426.463 Future new or revised LCDs.**

The contractor may not reinstate an LCD provision(s) found to be unreasonable unless the contractor has a different basis (such as additional evidence) than what the ALJ evaluated.

**§ 426.465 Appealing part or all of an ALJ's decision.**

(a) *Circumstances under which an aggrieved party may appeal part or all of an ALJ's decision.* An aggrieved party (including one or more aggrieved parties named in a joint complaint and an aggrieved party who is part of a consolidated LCD review) may appeal to the Board any part of an ALJ's decision that does the following:

(1) States that a provision of an LCD is valid under the reasonableness standard; or

(2) Dismisses a complaint regarding an LCD (except as prohibited in paragraph (b) of this section).

(b) *Circumstance under which a contractor or CMS may appeal part or all of an ALJ's decision.* A contractor or CMS may appeal to the Board any part of an ALJ's decision that states that a provision (or provisions) of an LCD is (are) unreasonable.

(c) *Stay of an implementation pending appeal.* (1) If an ALJ's decision finds a provision or provisions of an LCD unreasonable, an appeal by a contractor or CMS stays implementation as described under § 426.460(b) until the Board issues a final decision.

(2) The appeal request must be submitted to the Board in accordance with paragraph (e) of this section.

(d) *Circumstances under which an ALJ's decision may not be appealed.* An ALJ's decision dismissing a complaint is not subject to appeal in either of the following circumstances:

(1) The contractor has retired the LCD provision(s) under review.

(2) The aggrieved party who filed the complaint has withdrawn the complaint.

(e) *Receipt of the appeal by the Board.* Unless there is good cause shown, an appeal described in paragraphs (a) or (b) of this section must be filed with the Board within 30 days of the date the ALJ's decision was issued.

(f) *Filing an appeal.* (1) To file an appeal described in paragraph (a) of this section, an aggrieved party, who sought LCD review, a contractor, or CMS must send the following to the Board:

(i) The full names and addresses of the parties, including the name of the LCD.

(ii) The date of issuance of the ALJ's decision.

(iii) The docket number that appears on the ALJ's decision.

(iv) A statement identifying the part(s) of the ALJ's decision that are being appealed.

(2) If an appeal described in paragraph (a) of this section is filed with the Board later than the date described in paragraph (c) of this section, it must include a rationale stating why the Board must accept the late appeal.

(3) An appeal described in paragraph (a) of this section must include a statement explaining why the ALJ's decision should be reversed.

**§ 426.468 Decision to not appeal an ALJ's decision.**

(a) Failure to timely appeal without good cause shown waives the right to challenge any part(s) of the ALJ's decision under § 426.465.

(b) Unless the Board finds good cause shown for late filing, an untimely appeal is dismissed.

(c) If a party does not timely appeal any part(s) of the ALJ's decision on an LCD review to the Board, as provided in this subpart, then the ALJ's decision is final and not subject to further review.

**§ 426.470 Board's role in docketing and evaluating the acceptability of appeals of ALJ decisions.**

(a) *Docketing the appeal.* The Board does the following upon receiving an appeal of part or all of an ALJ's decision:

(1) Dockets the appeal either separately or with similar appeals.

(2) Assigns a docket number.

(b) *Evaluating the acceptability of the appeal.* The Board determines if the appeal is acceptable by confirming that the appeal meets all of the criteria in § 426.465.

(c) *Unacceptable appeal.* If the Board determines that an appeal is unacceptable, the Board must dismiss the appeal.

(d) *Acceptable appeal.* If the Board determines that an appeal is acceptable, the Board does the following:

(1) Sends a letter to the appellant to acknowledge that the appeal is acceptable, and informs them of the docket number.

(2) Forwards a copy of the appeal and the letter described in paragraph (d)(1) of this section to all parties involved in the appeal.

(3) Requires the ALJ to send a copy of the ALJ's LCD review record (maintaining any sealed documents) to the Board and a copy of the public record to all parties involved in the appeal.

(e) *No participation as amicus curiae.* The Board may not allow participation by amicus participants in the review of an LCD.

**§ 426.476 Board review of an ALJ's decision.**

(a) *Review steps.* If the Board determines that an appeal is acceptable, the Board—

(1) Permits the party that did not file the appeal an opportunity to respond to the appeal;

(2) Hears oral argument (which may be held by telephone) if the Board determines that oral argument would be helpful to the Board's review of the ALJ decision;

(3) Reviews the LCD review record and the parties' arguments; and

(4) Issues a written decision either upholding, modifying, or reversing the ALJ decision, or remanding the case to the ALJ for further proceedings.

(b) *Standard of review*—(1) *In general.* The Board determines whether the ALJ decision contains any material error, including any failure to properly apply the reasonableness standard.

(2) If the ALJ erred in determining that the contractor's record was complete and adequate to support the validity of the LCD, the Board remands the case to the ALJ for discovery and the taking of evidence.

(3) If a party alleges a prejudicial error of procedure, and the Board determines that such an error was made, the Board may remand the case to the ALJ for further proceedings consistent with the Board decision or may take other appropriate steps to correct the procedural error.

(4) Harmless error is not a basis for reversing an ALJ decision.

(c) *Scope of review.* In reaching its conclusions, the Board is bound by applicable laws, regulations, and NCDs.

(d) *Dismissal as moot.* The Board dismisses an appeal by an aggrieved party of an ALJ decision finding that an LCD was valid if the contractor notifies the Board that it has retired the LCD or revised the LCD to remove the LCD provision in question.

**§ 426.478 Retiring or revising an LCD during the Board's review of an ALJ's decision.**
A contractor may retire or revise an LCD during the Board's review of an ALJ's decision using the same process described in § 426.420. If an LCD is retired or revised to remove completely the challenged provision(s), the aggrieved party who sought the review is entitled to individual claim review provided at § 426.488(b).

**§ 426.480 Withdrawing an appeal of an ALJ's decision.**

(a) *Withdrawal of an appeal of an ALJ's decision.* A party who filed an appeal of an ALJ's decision may withdraw the appeal before the Board issues a decision regarding the ALJ's decision.

(b) *Process of withdrawing an appeal of an ALJ's decision.* To withdraw an appeal of an ALJ's decision, the party who filed the appeal must send a written notice announcing the intent to withdraw to the Board and to any other party.

(c) *Actions the Board must take upon receiving a notice announcing the intent to withdraw an appeal of an ALJ's decision*—(1) *Appeals involving one aggrieved party, or initiated by CMS or a contractor.* If the Board receives a notice withdrawing an appeal of an ALJ's decision before the Board has issued its decision, the Board must issue a decision dismissing the appeal.

(2) *Appeals involving joint complaints.* If the Board receives a notice withdrawing an appeal from an aggrieved party who is named in a joint appeal before the Board issues its decision, the Board must issue a decision dismissing only that aggrieved party from the appeal. The Board must continue its review of the ALJ's decision for the remaining aggrieved party or parties.

**§ 426.482 Issuance and notification of a Board decision.**
The Board must issue a written decision, including a description of appeal rights, to all parties to the review of the ALJ decision.

**§ 426.484 Mandatory provisions of a Board decision.**

(a) *Findings.* A Board decision must include at least one of the following:

(1) A statement upholding the part(s) of the ALJ decision named in the appeal.

(2) A statement reversing the part(s) of the ALJ decision named in the appeal.

(3) A statement modifying the part(s) of the ALJ decision named in the appeal.

(4) A statement dismissing the appeal of an ALJ decision and a rationale for the dismissal.

(b) *Other information.* A Board decision must include all of the following:

(1) The date of issuance.

(2) The docket number of the review of the ALJ decision.

(3) A summary of the ALJ's decision.

(4) A rationale for the basis of the Board's decision.

**§ 426.486 Prohibited provisions of a Board decision.**

A Board decision must not do any of the following:

(a) Order CMS or its contractors to add any language to a provision or provisions of an LCD.

(b) Order CMS or its contractors to pay a specific claim.

(c) Set a time limit to establish a new or revised LCD.

(d) Review or evaluate an LCD other than the LCD named in the ALJ's decision.

(e) Include a requirement for CMS or its contractors that specifies payment, coding, or system changes for an LCD or deadlines for implementing these changes.

(f) Order CMS or its contractors to implement an LCD in a particular manner.

**§ 426.487 Board's record on appeal of an ALJ's decision.**

(a) *Elements of the Board's LCD review record furnished to the public.* Except as provided in paragraph (b) of this section, the Board's LCD review record consists of any document or material that the Board compiled or considered during an LCD review, including, but not limited to, the following:

(1) The LCD complaint.

(2) The LCD and LCD record.

(3) The supplemental LCD record, if applicable.

(4) Transcripts of record.

(5) Any other relevant evidence gathered under § 426.440.

(6) The ALJ's decision.

(7) The Board's decision.

(b) *Elements of the Board's LCD appeal record furnished to the court under seal.* The Board's LCD review record must include, under seal, any proprietary data or privileged information submitted and reviewed in the LCD review process, and that data or information must not be included in the review record furnished to the public, but the information must be maintained, under seal, by the Board.

(c) *Protective order.* In any instance where proprietary data or privileged information is used in the LCD process and a court seeks to obtain or require disclosure of any proprietary data or privileged information contained in the LCD record, CMS or the Department will seek to have a protective order issued for that information, as appropriate.

**§ 426.488 Effect of a Board decision.**

(a) *The Board's decision upholds an ALJ decision that an LCD is valid or reverses an ALJ decision that an LCD is invalid.* If the Board's decision upholds the ALJ decision that an LCD is valid under the reasonableness standard or reverses an ALJ decision that an LCD is invalid, the contractor or CMS is not required to take any action.

(b) *The Board's decision upholds an ALJ determination that the LCD is invalid.* If the Board's decision upholds an ALJ determination that the LCD is invalid, then the contractor, the M+C organization, or other Medicare managed care organization implements the decision as described in § 426.460(b).

(c) *The Board's decision reverses a dismissal or an ALJ decision that the LCD is valid.* If the Board reverses an ALJ decision dismissing a complaint or holding that an LCD is valid without requiring discovery or the taking of evidence, the Board remands to the ALJ and the LCD review continues. If the Board reverses an ALJ decision holding that an LCD is valid that is reached after the ALJ has completed discovery and the taking of evidence, the Board may remand the case to the ALJ for further proceedings, or the Board may find that the provision(s) of the LCD named in the complaint is (are) invalid under the reasonableness standard, and the contractor, the M+C organization, or other Medicare managed care organization provides the relief in § 426.460(b).

**§ 426.489 Board remands.**

(a) *Notice when case is remanded to the ALJ.* If the Board remands a case to the ALJ, the Board—

(1) Notifies each aggrieved party who sought the LCD review, through his or her representative or at his or her last known address, the contractor, and CMS of the Board's remand decision; and

(2) Explains why the case is being remanded and the specific actions ordered by the Board.

(b) *Action by an ALJ on remand.* An ALJ takes any action that is ordered by the Board and may take any additional action that is not inconsistent with the Board's remand order.

**§ 426.490 Board decision.**

A decision by the Board (other than a remand) constitutes a final agency action and is subject to judicial review. Neither the contractor nor CMS may appeal a Board decision.

**Subpart E—Review of an NCD**

**§ 426.500 Procedure for filing an acceptable complaint concerning a provision (or provisions) of an NCD.**

(a) *The complaint.* An aggrieved party may initiate a review of an NCD by filing a written complaint with the Department of Health and Human Services Departmental Appeals Board.

(b) *Timeliness of a complaint.* An NCD complaint is not considered timely unless it is filed with the Board within—

(1) 6 months of the written statement from each aggrieved party's treating physician, in the case of aggrieved parties who choose to file an NCD challenge before receiving the service; or

(2) 120 days of the initial denial notice, in the case of aggrieved parties who choose to file an NCD challenge after receiving the service.

(c) *Components of a valid complaint.* A complaint must include the following:

(1) *Beneficiary-identifying information:*

(i) Name.

(ii) Mailing address.

(iii) State of residence, if different from mailing address.

(iv) Telephone number, if any.

(v) Health Insurance Claim number, if applicable.

(vi) E-mail address, if applicable.

(2) *If the beneficiary has a representative,* the representative's identifying information must include the following:

(i) Name.

(ii) Address.

(iii) Telephone number.

(iv) E-mail address (if any)

(v) Copy of the written authorization to represent the beneficiary.

(3) *Treating physician written statement.* A copy of a written statement from the treating physician that the beneficiary needs the service that is the subject of the NCD. This statement may be in the form of a written order for the service or other documentation from the beneficiary's medical record (such as progress notes or discharge summary) indicating that the beneficiary needs the service.

(4) *NCD-identifying information:*

(i) Title of NCD being challenged.

(ii) The specific provision or provisions of the NCD adversely affecting the aggrieved party.

(5) *Aggrieved party statement.* A statement from the aggrieved party explaining what service is needed and why the aggrieved party thinks that the provision(s) of the NCD is (are) not valid under the reasonableness standard.

(6) *Clinical or scientific evidence.* (i) Copies of clinical or scientific evidence that supports the complaint and an explanation for why the aggrieved party thinks that this evidence shows that the NCD is not reasonable.

(ii) Any documents or portions of documents that include proprietary data must be marked "proprietary data," and include a legal basis for that assertion.

(iii) Proprietary data submitted by a manufacturer concerning a drug or device for which the manufacturer has submitted information to the Food and Drug Administration, must be considered and given substantive weight only when supported by an affidavit certifying that the submission contains true and correct copies of all data submitted by the manufacturer to the Food and Drug Administration in relation to that drug or device.

(d) *Joint complaints*—(1) *Conditions for a joint complaint.* Two or more aggrieved parties may initiate the review of an NCD by filing a single written complaint with the Board if all of the following conditions are met:

(i) Each aggrieved party named in the joint complaint has a similar medical condition or there are other bases for combining the complaints.

(ii) Each aggrieved party named in the joint complaint is filing the complaint in regard to the same provision(s) of the same NCD.

(2) *Components of a valid joint complaint.* A joint complaint must contain the following information:

(i) The beneficiary-identifying information described in paragraph (c)(1) of this section for each aggrieved party named in the joint complaint.

(ii) The NCD-identifying information described in paragraph (c)(2) of this section.

(iii) The documentation described in paragraphs (c)(3) and (c)(4) of this section.

(3) *Timeliness of a joint complaint.* Aggrieved parties, who choose to seek review of an NCD—

(i) Before receiving the service, must file with the Board a joint complaint within 6 months of the written statement from each aggrieved party's treating physician; or

(ii) After receiving the service, must file with the Board a complaint within 120 days of each aggrieved party's initial denial notice.

**§ 426.503 Submitting new evidence once an acceptable complaint has been filed.**

Once an acceptable complaint has been filed, the aggrieved party may submit additional new evidence without withdrawing the complaint until the Board closes the record.

**§ 426.505 Authority of the Board.**

(a) The Board conducts a fair and impartial hearing, avoids unnecessary delay, maintains order, and ensures that all proceedings are recorded.

(b) The Board defers only to reasonable findings of fact, reasonable interpretations of law, and reasonable applications of fact to law by the Secretary.

(c) The Board has the authority to do any of the following:

(1) Review complaints by an aggrieved party (or aggrieved parties).

(2) Dismiss complaints that fail to comply with § 426.500.

(3) Set and change the date, time, and place of a hearing upon reasonable notice to the parties.

(4) Continue or recess a hearing for a reasonable period of time.

(5) Hold conferences to identify or simplify the issues, or to consider other matters that may aid in the expeditious disposition of the proceeding.

(6) Consult with scientific and clinical experts on its own motion, concerning clinical or scientific evidence.

(7) Set schedules for submission of exhibits and written reports of experts.

(8) Administer oaths and affirmations.

(9) Examine witnesses.

(10) Issue subpoenas requiring the attendance of witnesses at hearings as permitted by this part.

(11) Issue subpoenas requiring the production of existing documents before, and relating to, the hearing as permitted by this part.

(12) Rule on motions and other procedural matters.

(13) Stay the proceeding in accordance with § 426.340.

(14) Regulate the scope and timing of documentary discovery as permitted by this part.

(15) Regulate the course of a hearing and the conduct of representatives, parties, and witnesses.

(16) Receive, rule on, exclude, or limit evidence, as provided in this regulation.

(17) Take official notice of facts, upon motion of a party.

(18) Decide cases, upon the motion of a party, by summary judgment when there is no disputed issue of material fact.

(19) Conduct any conference, argument, or hearing in person or, upon agreement of the parties, by telephone, picture-tel, or any other means.

(20) Issue decisions.

(21) Exclude a party from an NCD review for failure to comply with a Board order or procedural request without good cause.

(22) Stay the proceedings for a reasonable time when all parties voluntarily agree to mediation or negotiation, and provide mediation services upon request.

(d) The Board does not have authority to do any of the following under this part:

(1) Conduct an LCD review or conduct LCD hearings, except as provided by § 426.465.

(2) Conduct an NCD review or conduct NCD hearings on its own motion or on the motion of a nonaggrieved party.

(3) Issue a decision based on any new evidence without following § 426.340, regarding procedures for review of new evidence.

(4) Review any decisions by CMS to develop a new or revised NCD.

(5) Conduct a review of any draft NCDs, coverage decision memoranda, or withdrawn NCDs.

(6) Conduct a review of the merits of an unacceptable NCD complaint as discussed in § 426.510.

(7) Conduct an NCD review of any policy that is not an NCD, as defined in § 400.202 of this chapter.

(8) Allow participation by individuals or entities other than—

(i) The aggrieved party and/or his or her representative;

(ii) CMS and/or the contractor;

(iii) Experts called by the parties or Board; or

(iv) Third parties with a clearly identifiable and substantial interest in the outcome of the dispute who have petitioned for and been granted permission by the Board to participate in the proceedings as *amicus curiae.*

(9) Compel the parties to participate in a mediation process or to engage in settlement negotiations.

(10) Deny a request for withdrawal of a complaint by an aggrieved party.

(11) Compel CMS to conduct studies, surveys, or develop new information to support an NCD record.

(12) Deny CMS the right to reconsider, revise, or withdraw an NCD.

(13) Subject to the timely filing requirements, deny an aggrieved party, CMS, or its contractor the right to appeal an ALJ decision.

(14) Find invalid applicable Federal statutes, regulations, or rulings.
(15) Enter a decision specifying terms to be included in an NCD.

**§ 426.506 Ex parte contacts.**
No party or person (except Board staff) communicates in any way with the Board on any substantive matter at issue in a case, unless on notice and opportunity for all parties to participate. This provision does not prohibit a person or party from inquiring about the status of a case or asking routine questions concerning administrative functions or procedures.

**§ 426.510 Docketing and evaluating the acceptability of NCD complaints.**

(a) *Docketing the complaint.* The Board does the following upon receiving a complaint regarding an NCD:

(1) Dockets the complaint.

(2) Determines whether the complaint is—

(i) The first challenge to a particular NCD; or

(ii) Related to a pending NCD review.

(3) Forwards the complaint to the Board member who conducts the review.

(b) *Evaluating the acceptability of the complaint.* The Board determines if the complaint is acceptable by confirming all of the following:

(1) The complaint is being submitted by an aggrieved party or, in the case of a joint complaint, that each individual named in the joint complaint is an aggrieved party. (In determining if a complaint is acceptable, the Board assumes that the facts alleged by the treating physician's documentation regarding the aggrieved party's (or parties') clinical condition are true.)

(2) The complaint meets the requirements for a valid complaint in § 426.500 and is not one of the documents in § 426.325(b).

(c) *Unacceptable complaint.* (1) If the Board determines that the complaint is unacceptable, the Board must provide the aggrieved party (or parties) one opportunity to amend the unacceptable complaint.

(2) If the aggrieved party (or parties) fail(s) to submit an acceptable amended complaint within a reasonable time frame as determined by the Board, the Board must issue a decision dismissing the unacceptable complaint.

(3) If a complaint is determined to be unacceptable after one amendment, the beneficiary is precluded from filing again for 6 months after being informed that it is unacceptable.

(d) *Acceptable complaint.* If the Board determines that the complaint (or amended complaint) is acceptable, the Board does the following:

(1) Sends a letter to the aggrieved party (or parties) acknowledging the complaint and informing the aggrieved party (or parties) of the docket number and the deadline for CMS to produce the NCD record.

(2) Forwards a copy of the complaint, any evidence submitted in the complaint, and the letter described in paragraph (d)(1) of this section to CMS.

(3) Requires CMS to send a copy of the NCD record to the Board and all parties to the NCD review within 30 days of receiving the Board's letter, a copy of the complaint, and any associated evidence, subject to extension for good cause shown.

(e) *Consolidation of complaints regarding an NCD*—(1) *Criteria for consideration.* If a review is pending regarding a particular NCD provision(s) and no decision has been issued ending the review, and a new acceptable complaint is filed, the Board consolidates the complaints and conducts a consolidated NCD review if all of the following criteria are met:

(i) The complaints are in regard to the same provision(s) of the same NCD, or there are other bases for consolidating the complaints.

(ii) The complaints contain common questions of law, common questions of fact, or both.

(iii) Consolidating the complaints does not unduly delay the Board's decision.

(2) *Decision to consolidate complaint.* If the Board decides to consolidate complaints, the Board does the following:

(i) Provides notification that the NCD review is consolidated and informs all parties of the docket number of the consolidated review.

(ii) Makes a single record of the proceeding.

(iii) Considers the relevant evidence introduced in each NCD complaint as introduced in the consolidated review.

(3) *Decision not to consolidate complaints.* If the Board decides not to consolidate complaints, the Board conducts separate NCD reviews for each complaint.

(f) *Public notice of complaint and opportunity for interested parties to participate.* (1) If an acceptable complaint is the first complaint the Board has received challenging the particular NCD or provision, then the Board posts notice on its Web site that it has received the complaint, specifying a time period for requests to participate in the review process.

(2) If an acceptable complaint challenges an NCD provision when review is pending and no decision has been issued ending the review, the Board may supplement the public notice on its Web site and extend the time for participation requests if indicated.

(3) The Board may allow participation, in the manner and by the deadlines established by the Board, when an NCD is being challenged and the Board decides that—

(i) The *amicus* participant has a clearly identifiable and substantial interest in the outcome of the dispute;

(ii) Participation would clarify the issues or otherwise be helpful in resolution of the dispute;

(iii) Participation does not result in substantial delay; and

(iv) The petition for participation meets the criteria in § 426.513.

### § 426.513 Participation as *amicus curiae*.

(a) *Petition for participation.* Any person or organization that wishes to participate as *amicus curiae* must timely file with the Board a petition that concisely states—

(1) The petitioner's interest in the hearing;

(2) Who will represent the petitioner; and

(3) The issues on which the petitioner intends to present argument.

(b) *The nature of the proposed* amicus *participation.* An *amicus curiae* is not a party to the hearing but may participate by–

(1) Submitting a written statement of position to the Board before the beginning of the hearing;

(2) Presenting a brief oral statement or other evidence at the hearing, at the point in the proceedings specified by the Board; and

(3) Submitting a brief or a written statement when the parties submit briefs.

(c) *Service by* amicus curiae. Serving copies of any briefs or written statements on all parties.

**§ 426.515 CMS's role in making the NCD record available.**

CMS will provide a copy of the NCD record (as described in § 426.518) to the Board and all parties to the NCD review within 30 days of the receipt of the Board's order.

**§ 426.516 Role of Medicare Managed Care Organizations (MCOs) and State agencies in the NCD review process.**

Medicare MCOs and Medicaid State agencies may participate in the NCD review process only if they meet the *amicus* participant criteria listed in § 426.510(f)(3) and § 426.513.

**§ 426.517 CMS's statement regarding new evidence.**

(a) CMS may review any new evidence that is submitted, regardless of whether the Board has stayed the proceedings, including but not limited to new evidence:

(1) Submitted with the initial complaint;

(2) Submitted with an amended complaint;

(3) Produced during discovery;

(4) Produced when the Board consults with scientific and clinical experts; and

(5) Presented during any hearing.

(b) CMS may submit a statement regarding whether the new evidence is significant under § 426.340, by a deadline set by the Board.

**§ 426.518 NCD record furnished to the aggrieved party.**

(a) *Elements of the NCD record furnished to the aggrieved party.* Except as provided in paragraph (b) of this section, the NCD record consists of any document or material that CMS considered during the development of the NCD, including, but not limited to, the following:

(1) The NCD being challenged.

(2) Any medical evidence considered on or before the date the NCD was issued, including, but not limited to, the following:

(i) Scientific articles.

(ii) Technology assessments.

(iii) Clinical guidelines.

(iv) Statements from clinical experts, medical textbooks, claims data, or other indication of medical standard of practice.

(v) MCAC transcripts.

(3) Public comments received during the notice and comment period.

(4) Coverage decision memoranda.

(5) An index of documents considered that are excluded under paragraph (b) of this section.

(b) *Elements of the NCD record not furnished to the aggrieved party.* The NCD record furnished to the aggrieved party does not include the following:

(1) Proprietary data or privileged information.

(2) Any new evidence.

**§ 426.519 NCD record furnished to the Board.**

The NCD record furnished to the Board includes—

(a) Documents included in § 426.518(a); and

(b) Privileged information and proprietary data considered that must be filed with the Board under seal.

**§ 426.520 Withdrawing an NCD under review or issuing a revised or reconsidered NCD.**

(a) CMS may withdraw an NCD or NCD provision under review before the date the Board issues a decision regarding that NCD. Withdrawing an NCD or NCD provision under review has the same effect as a decision under § 426.560(b).

(b) CMS may revise an NCD under review to remove or amend the NCD provision listed in the complaint through the reconsideration process before the date the Board issues a decision regarding that NCD. Revising an NCD under review to remove the NCD provision in question has the same effect as a decision under § 426.560(b).

(c) CMS must notify the Board within 48 hours of—

(1) Withdrawing an NCD or NCD provision that is under review; or

(2) Issuing a revised or reconsidered version of the NCD that is under review.

(d) If CMS issues a revised or reconsidered NCD, CMS forwards a copy of the revised/reconsidered NCD to the Board.

(e) The Board must take the following actions upon receiving a notice that CMS has withdrawn or revised/reconsidered an NCD under review:

(1) If, before the Board issues a decision, the Board receives notice that CMS has withdrawn the NCD or revised the NCD to completely remove the provision in question, the Board must dismiss the complaint and inform the aggrieved party (ies) who sought the review that he or she or they will receive individual claim review without the retired/withdrawn provisions.

(2) If, before the Board issues a decision, the Board receives notice that CMS has revised the NCD provision in question but has not removed it

altogether, the Board must continue the review based on the revised NCD. In this case, CMS must send a copy of the supplemental record to the Board and all parties. In that circumstance, the Board permits the aggrieved party to respond to the revised NCD and the supplemental record.

**§ 426.523 Withdrawing a complaint regarding an NCD under review.**

(a) *Circumstance under which an aggrieved party withdraws a complaint regarding an NCD.* An aggrieved party who filed a complaint regarding an NCD may withdraw the complaint before the Board issues a decision regarding that NCD. The aggrieved party may not file another complaint concerning the same coverage determination for 6 months.

(b) *Process for an aggrieved party withdrawing a complaint regarding an NCD.* To withdraw a complaint regarding an NCD, the aggrieved party who filed the complaint must send a written withdrawal notice to the Board (*see* § 426.500) and CMS. Supplementing an acceptable complaint with new evidence does not constitute a withdrawal of a complaint, as described in § 426.503.

(c) *Actions the Board must take upon receiving a notice announcing the intent to withdraw a complaint regarding an NCD*—(1) *NCD reviews involving one aggrieved party.* If the Board receives a withdrawal notice regarding an NCD before the date the Board issued a decision regarding that NCD, the Board issues a decision dismissing the complaint under § 426.544 and informs the aggrieved party that he or she may not file another complaint to the same coverage determination for 6 months.

(2) *NCD reviews involving joint complaints.* If the Board receives a notice from an aggrieved party who is named in a joint complaint withdrawing a complaint regarding an NCD before the date the Board issued a decision regarding that NCD, the Board issues a decision dismissing only that aggrieved party from the complaint under § 426.544. The Board continues the NCD review if there is one or more aggrieved party who does not withdraw from the joint complaint.

(3) *Consolidated NCD reviews.* If the Board receives a notice from an aggrieved party who is part of a consolidated NCD review withdrawing a complaint regarding an NCD before the date the Board issued a decision regarding that NCD, the Board removes that aggrieved party from the consolidated NCD review and issues a decision dismissing that aggrieved party's complaint under § 426.544. The Board continues the NCD review if there is one or more aggrieved party who does not withdraw from the joint complaint.

**§ 426.525 NCD review.**

(a) *Opportunity for the aggrieved party after his or her review of the NCD record to state why the NCD is not valid.* Upon receipt of the NCD record, the aggrieved party files a statement explaining why the NCD record is not complete, or not adequate to support the validity of the NCD under the reasonableness standard. This statement must be submitted to the Board and CMS, within 30 days (or within additional time as allowed by the Board for good cause shown) of the date the aggrieved party receives the NCD record.

(b) *CMS response.* CMS has 30 days, after receiving the aggrieved party's statement, to submit a response to the Board in order to defend the NCD.

(c) *Board evaluation.* (1) After the aggrieved party files a statement and CMS responds as described in § 426.525(a) and § 426.525(b), or the time for filing has expired, the Board applies the reasonableness standard to determine whether the NCD record is complete and adequate to support the validity of the NCD.

(2) Issuance of a decision finding the record complete and adequate to support the validity of the NCD ends the review process.

(3) If the Board determines that the NCD record is not complete and adequate to support the validity of the NCD, the Board permits discovery and the taking of evidence in accordance with § 426.532 and § 426.540, and evaluate the NCD in accordance with § 426.531.

(d) The process described in paragraphs (a), (b), and (c) of this section applies when an NCD record has been supplemented, except that discovery and the taking of evidence is not repeated. The period for the aggrieved party to file a statement begins when the aggrieved party receives the supplement.

**§ 426.531 Board's review of the NCD to apply the reasonableness standard.**

(a) *Required steps.* The Board must do the following to review the provision(s) listed in the aggrieved party's complaint based on the reasonableness standard:

(1) Confine the NCD review to the provision(s) of the NCD raised in the aggrieved party's complaint.

(2) Conduct a hearing unless the matter can be decided on the written record.

(3) Close the NCD review record to the taking of evidence.

(4) Treat as precedential any previous Board decision made under § 426.547 that involves the same NCD provision(s), same specific issue and facts in question, and the same clinical conditions.

(5) Issue a decision as described in § 426.547.

(b) *Optional steps.* The Board may consult with appropriate scientific or clinical experts concerning clinical and scientific evidence to apply the reasonableness standard to the provision(s) listed in the aggrieved party's complaint.

(c) *Authority for the Board in NCD reviews when applying the reasonableness standard.* In applying the reasonableness standard to a provision (or provisions) of an NCD, the Board must follow all applicable laws and regulations, as well as NCDs other than the one under review.

**§ 426.532 Discovery.**

(a) *General rule.* If the Board orders discovery, the Board must establish a reasonable time frame for discovery.

(b) *Protective order*—(1) *Request for a protective order.* Any party receiving a discovery request may file a motion for a protective order before the date of production of the discovery.

(2) *The Board granting of a protective order.* The Board may grant a motion for a protective order if it finds that the discovery sought—

(i) Is irrelevant or unduly repetitive;

(ii) Is unduly costly or burdensome; or

(iii) Will unduly delay the proceeding.

(c) *Types of discovery available.* A party may obtain discovery via a request for the production of documents, and/or via the submission of up to 10 written interrogatory questions, relating to a specific NCD.

(d) *Types of documents.* For the purpose of this section, the term documents includes relevant information, reports, answers, records, accounts, papers, and other data and documentary evidence. Nothing contained in this section will be interpreted to require the creation of a document.

(e) *Types of discovery not available.* Requests for admissions, depositions, or any other forms of discovery, other than those permitted under paragraph (c) of this section, are not authorized.

(f) *Privileged information or proprietary data.* The Board must not under any circumstances order the disclosure of privileged information or proprietary data filed under seal without the consent of the party who possesses the right to protection of the information.

(g) *Notification.* The Board notifies all parties in writing when the discovery period will be closed.

**§ 426.535 Subpoenas.**

(a) *Purpose of a subpoena.* A subpoena requires the attendance of an individual at a hearing and may also require a party to produce evidence authorized under § 426.540 at or before the hearing.

(b) *Filing a motion for a subpoena.* A party seeking a subpoena must file a written motion with the Board not less than 30 days before the date fixed for the hearing. The motion must do all of the following:

(1) Designate the witnesses.

(2) Specify any evidence to be produced.

(3) Describe the address and location with sufficient particularity to permit the witnesses to be found.

(4) State the pertinent facts that the party expects to establish by witnesses or documents and state whether those facts could be established by evidence other than by the use of a subpoena.

(c) *Response to a motion for a subpoena.* Within 15 days after the written motion requesting issuance of a subpoena is served on all parties, any party may file an opposition to the motion or other response.

(d) *Extension for good cause shown.* The Board may modify the deadlines specified in paragraphs (b) and (c) of this section for good cause shown.

(e) *Motion for a subpoena granted.* If the Board grants a motion requesting issuance of a subpoena, the subpoena must do the following:

(1) Be issued in the name of the presiding Board member.

(2) Include the docket number and title of the NCD under review.

(3) Provide notice that the subpoena is issued according to sections 1872 and 205(d) and (e) of the Act.

(4) Specify the time and place at which the witness is to appear and any evidence the witness is to produce.

(f) *Delivery of the subpoena.* The party seeking the subpoena serves it by personal delivery to the individual named, or by certified mail return receipt requested, addressed to the individual at his or her last dwelling place or principal place of business.

(g) *Motion to quash a subpoena.* The individual to whom the subpoena is directed may file with the Board a motion to quash the subpoena within 10 days after service.

(h) *Refusal to obey a subpoena.* The exclusive remedy for contumacy by, or refusal to obey, a subpoena duly served upon any person is specified in section 205(e) of the Act (42 U.S.C. 405(e)) except that any reference to the "Commissioner of Social Security"shall be considered a reference to the "Secretary."

**§ 426.540 Evidence.**

(a) Except as provided in this part, the Board is not bound by the Federal Rules of Evidence. However, the Board may apply the Federal Rules of Evidence when appropriate, for example, to exclude unreliable evidence.

(b) The Board must exclude evidence that it determines is clearly irrelevant or immaterial, or unduly repetitive.

(c) The Board may accept privileged information or proprietary data, but must maintain it under seal.

(d) The Board may permit the parties to introduce the testimony of expert witnesses on scientific and clinical issues, rebuttal witnesses, and other relevant evidence. The Board may require that the testimony of expert witnesses be submitted in the form of a written report, accompanied by the curriculum vitae of the expert preparing the report.

(e) Experts submitting reports must be available for cross-examination at an evidentiary hearing upon request of the Board or a party to the proceeding, or the report will be excluded from the record.

(f) Except as set forth in paragraph (c) of this section or unless otherwise ordered by the Board for good cause shown, all documents and other evidence offered or taken for the record are open to examination by all parties.

**§ 426.544 Dismissals for cause.**

(a) The Board may, at the request of any party, or on its own motion, dismiss a complaint if the aggrieved party fails to do either of the following:

(1) Attend or participate in a prehearing conference (the prehearing may be conducted by telephone) or hearing without good cause shown.

(2) Comply with a lawful order of the Board without cause shown.

(b) The Board must dismiss any complaint concerning NCD provision(s) if the following conditions exist:

(1) The Board does not have the authority to rule on that provision under § 426.505(d).

(2) The complaint is not timely. (*See* § 426.500(b)).

(3) The complaint is not filed by an aggrieved party.

(4) The complaint is filed by an individual who fails to provide an adequate statement of need for the service from the treating physician.

(5) The complaint challenges a provision or provisions of an LCD except as provided in § 426.476, regarding the Board's review of an ALJ decision. (*See* § 426.505, regarding the authority of the Board.)

(6) CMS notifies the Board that the NCD provision(s) is (are) no longer in effect.

(7) The aggrieved party withdraws the complaint. (*See* § 426.523, for requirements for withdrawing a complaint regarding an NCD under review.)

**§ 426.545 Witness fees.**

(a) A witness testifying at a hearing before the Board receives the same fees and mileage as witnesses in Federal district courts of the United States. If the witness qualifies as an expert, he or she is entitled to an expert witness fee. Witness fees are paid by the party seeking to present the witness.

(b) If the Board requests expert testimony, the Board is responsible for paying all applicable fees and mileage, unless the expert waives payment.

**§ 426.546 Record of hearing.**

The Board must ensure that all hearings are open to the public and are electronically, mechanically, or stenographically reported. Except for privileged information and proprietary data that are filed under seal, all evidence upon which the Board relies for decision must be admitted into the public record. All medical reports, exhibits, and any other pertinent document, either in whole or in material part, must be offered, marked for identification, and retained in the case record.

**§ 426.547 Issuance, notification, and posting of a Board's decision.**

The Board must do the following:

(a) Issue to all parties to the NCD review, within 90 days of closing the NCD review record to the taking of evidence, one of the following:

(1) A written decision, including a description of appeal rights.

(2) A written notification stating that a decision is pending, and an approximate date of issuance for the decision.

(b) Make the decision available at the HHS Medicare Internet site. The posted decision does not include any information that identifies any individual, provider of service, or supplier.

**§ 426.550 Mandatory provisions of the Board's decision.**

(a) *Findings.* The Board's decision must include one of the following:

(1) A determination that the provision of the NCD is valid under the reasonableness standard.

(2) A determination that the provision of the NCD is not valid under the reasonableness standard.

(3) A statement dismissing the complaint regarding the NCD, and a rationale for the dismissal.

(4) A determination that the LCD or NCD record is complete and adequate to support the validity of the LCD or NCD provisions under the reasonableness standard.

(b) *Other information.* The Board's decision must include all of the following:

(1) The date of issuance.

(2) The docket number of the NCD review.

(3) A statement as to whether the aggrieved party has filed a claim for the service(s) named in the complaint, the date(s)-of-service, and the disposition, if known.

(4) A basis for concluding that the NCD was or was not valid based on the application of the reasonableness standard to the record before the Board, including CMS':

(i) Findings of fact.

(ii) Interpretations of law.

(iii) Applications of fact to law.

(5) A summary of the evidence reviewed. Where proprietary or privileged data were submitted under seal, the decision must state whether the data were material and what role they played in the determination, but without disclosing the substance or contents of the evidence under seal. A separate statement of the rationale for the Board's treatment of the sealed evidence must be prepared and kept under seal itself. If the Board decision is appealed to the court, this statement must be provided to the court, under seal.

(6) A statement regarding the right to judicial review.

**§ 426.555 Prohibited provisions of the Board's decision.**

The Board's decision may not do any of the following:

(a) Order CMS to add any language to a provision or provisions of an NCD.

(b) Order CMS or its contractors to pay a specific claim.

(c) Set a time limit for CMS to establish a new or revised NCD.

(d) Review or evaluate an NCD other than the NCD under review.

(e) Include a requirement for CMS or its contractors that specifies payment, coding, or systems changes for an NCD, or deadlines for implementing these types of changes.

(f) Order or address how CMS implements an NCD.

**§ 426.557 Optional provisions of the Board's decision.**

When appropriate, the Board may limit a decision holding invalid a specific provision(s) of an NCD to specific clinical indications and for similar conditions.

**§ 426.560 Effect of the Board's decision.**

(a) *Valid under the reasonableness standard.* If the Board finds that the provision (or provisions) of an NCD named in the complaint is (are) valid under the reasonableness standard, the aggrieved party may challenge the final agency action in Federal court.

(b) *Not valid under the reasonableness standard.* If the Board finds that the provision (or provisions) of an NCD named in the complaint is (are) invalid under the reasonableness standard, then CMS instructs its contractor, M+C organization, or other Medicare managed care organization to provide the following—

(1) *Individual claim review.* (i) If the aggrieved party's claim/appeal(s) was previously denied, the contractor, an M+C organization, or another Medicare managed care organization must reopen the claim of the party who challenged the LCD and adjudicate the claim without using the provision(s) of the NCD that the Board found invalid.

(ii) If a revised NCD is issued, contractors, M+C organizations, and other Medicare managed care organizations must use the revised NCD in reviewing claim/appeal submissions or request for services delivered or services performed on or after the effective date of the revised NCD.

(iii) If the aggrieved party who sought review has not yet submitted a claim, the contractor must adjudicate the claim without using the provision(s) of the NCD that the Board found invalid.

(iv) In either case, the claim and any subsequent claims for the service provided under the same circumstances, must be adjudicated without using the NCD provision(s) found invalid.

(2) *Coverage determination relief.* Within 30 days, CMS implements the Board decision. Any change in policy is applied prospectively to requests for service or claims filed with dates of service after the implementation of the Board decision.

**§ 426.562 Notice of the Board's decision.**
After the Board has made a decision regarding an NCD complaint, the Board sends a written notice of the decision to each party. The notice must—

(a) State the outcome of the review; and

(b) Inform each party to the determination of his or her rights to seek further review if he or she is dissatisfied with the determination, and the time limit under which an appeal must be requested.

**§ 426.563 Future new or revised or reconsidered NCDs.**
CMS may not reinstate an NCD provision(s) found to be unreasonable unless CMS has a different basis (such as additional evidence) than what the Board evaluated.

**§ 426.565 Board's role in making an LCD or NCD review record available.**
Upon a request from a Federal Court, the Board must provide to the Federal Court a copy of the Board's LCD or NCD review record (as described in § 426.587).

**§ 426.566 Board decision.**
A decision by the Board constitutes a final agency action and is subject to judicial review. CMS may not appeal a Board decision.

### § 426.587 Record for appeal of a Board NCD decision.

(a) *Elements of the Board's NCD review record furnished to the public.* Except as provided in paragraph (b) of this section, the Board's NCD review record consists of any document or material that the Board compiled or considered during an NCD review, including, but not limited to, the following:

(1) The NCD complaint.

(2) The NCD and NCD record.

(3) The supplemental NCD record, if applicable.

(4) Transcripts of record.

(5) Any other evidence relevant gathered under § 426.540.

(6) The Board's decision.

(b) *Documents excluded from the NCD review record furnished to the court.* The NCD review record furnished to the court maintains the seal on privileged information or proprietary data that is maintained under seal by the Board. In the event a court seeks to obtain or requires disclosure of any documents excluded from the NCD record as privileged information or proprietary data, CMS or the Department seeks to have a protective order issued for those documents, as appropriate.

## PART 478—RECONSIDERATIONS AND APPEALS

### Subpart B—Utilization and Quality Control Quality Improvement Organization (QIO) Reconsiderations and Appeals

**Source:** 50 FR 15372, Apr. 17, 1985, unless otherwise noted. Redesignated at 64 FR 66279, Nov. 24, 1999.

### § 478.10 Scope.

This subpart establishes the requirements and procedures for—

(a) Reconsiderations conducted by a Utilization and Quality Control Quality Improvement Organization (QIO) or its subcontractor of initial denial determinations concerning services furnished or proposed to be furnished under Medicare;

(b) Hearings and judicial review of reconsidered determinations; and

(c) QIO review of a change in diagnostic and procedural coding information.

[50 FR 15372, Apr. 17, 1985; 50 FR 41887, Oct. 16, 1985. Redesignated at 64 FR 66279, Nov. 24, 1999]

### § 478.12 Statutory basis.

(a) Under section 1154 of the Act, a QIO may make an initial determination that services furnished or proposed to be furnished are not reasonable, necessary, or delivered in the most appropriate setting.

(b) Under section 1155 of the Act, the following rules apply:

(1) A Medicare beneficiary, a provider, or an attending practitioner who is dissatisfied with an initial denial determination under paragraph (a) of this section is entitled to a reconsideration by the QIO that made that determination.

(2) The beneficiary is also entitled to the following:

(i) A hearing by an administrative law judge if $200 or more is still in controversy after a reconsidered determination.

(ii) Judicial review if $2000 or more is still in controversy after a final determination by the Department.

(c) Under section 1866(a)(1)(F) of the Act, a hospital that is reimbursed by the Medicare program must maintain an agreement with a QIO under which the QIO reviews the validity of diagnostic information furnished by the hospital.

[50 FR 15372, Apr. 17, 1985, as amended at 60 FR 50442, Sept. 29, 1995. Redesignated at 64 FR 66279, Nov. 24, 1999]

**§ 478.14 Applicability.**

(a) *Basic provision.* This subpart applies to reconsiderations and hearings of a QIO initial denial determination involving the following issues:

(1) Reasonableness of services.

(2) Medical necessity of services.

(3) Appropriateness of the inpatient setting in which services were furnished or are proposed to be furnished.

(b) *Concurrent appeal.* A reconsideration or hearing provided under this subpart fulfills the requirements of any other review, hearing, or appeal under the Act to which a party may be entitled with respect to the same issues.

(c) *Nonapplicability of rules to related determinations.* (1) A QIO may not reconsider its decision whether to grant grace days.

(2) Limitation of liability determinations on excluded coverage of certain services are made under section 1879 of the Act. Initial determinations under section 1879 and further appeals are governed by the reconsideration and appeal procedures in part 405, subpart G of this chapter for determinations under Medicare Part A, and part 405, subpart H of this chapter for determinations under Medicare Part B. References in those subparts to initial and reconsidered determinations made by an intermediary, carrier or CMS should be read to mean initial and reconsidered determinations made by a QIO.

[50 FR 15372, Apr. 17, 1985; 50 FR 41887, Oct. 16, 1985. Redesignated at 64 FR 66279, Nov. 24, 1999]

**§ 478.15 QIO review of changes resulting from DRG validation.**

(a) *General rules.* (1) A provider or practitioner dissatisfied with a change to the diagnostic or procedural coding information made by a QIO as a result of DRG validation under section 1866(a)(1)(F) of the Act is entitled to a review of that change if–

(i) The change caused an assignment of a different DRG; and

(ii) Resulted in a lower payment.

(2) A beneficiary may obtain a review of a QIO DRG coding change only if that change results in noncoverage of a furnished service.

(3) The individual who reviews changes in DRG procedural or diagnostic information must be a physician, and the individual who reviews changes in DRG

coding must be qualified through training and experience with ICD-9-CM coding.

(b) *Procedures.* Procedures described in §§473.18 through 473.36, and 473.48 (a) and (c) for a QIO reconsideration or reopening also apply to QIO review of a DRG coding change.

(c) *Finality of review.* No additional review or appeal for matters governed by paragraph (a) of this section is available.

[50 FR 15372, Apr. 17, 1985; 50 FR 41887, Oct. 16, 1985. Redesignated at 64 FR 66279, Nov. 24, 1999]

**§ 478.16 Right to reconsideration.**

A beneficiary, provider or practitioner who is dissatisfied with a QIO initial denial determination on one of the issues specified in § 473.14(a) has a right to a reconsideration of that determination by the QIO that made the initial denial determination.

**§ 478.18 Location for submitting requests for reconsideration.**

(a) *Beneficiaries.* Except as provided in paragraph (c) of this section concerning requests for expedited reconsideration, a beneficiary who wishes to obtain a reconsideration must submit a written request to one of the following:

(1) The QIO or the QIO subcontractor that made the initial determination.

(2) An SSA District Office.

(3) A Railroad Retirement Board Office, if the beneficiary is a railroad retiree.

(b) *Others.* A provider, physician or other practitioner that wishes to obtain reconsideration must submit a written request to the QIO or QIO subcontractor that made the initial determination.

(c) *Expedited reconsideration.* A request for an expedited reconsideration of a preadmission denial determination must be submitted directly to the QIO.

**§ 478.20 Time limits for requesting reconsideration.**

(a) *Basic rules.* (1) Except for a request for expedited reconsideration as provided in paragraph (c) of this section, or a late request with good cause under § 473.22, a dissatisfied party must file a request for reconsideration within 60 days after receipt of the notice of an initial determination.

(2) The date of receipt of the notice of the initial determination is presumed to be five days after the date on the notice, unless there is a reasonable showing to the contrary.

(3) A request is considered filed on the date it is postmarked.

(b) *Late filing of request.* A QIO will accept a request filed after 60 days after receipt of the notice of the initial determination if the QIO finds under the criteria set forth in § 473.22 that there was good cause for the party's failure to file a timely request.

(c) *Request for expedited reconsideration.* A request for an expedited reconsideration under § 473.18(c) must be submitted within three days after receipt of the notice of the initial denial determination.

**§ 478.22 Good cause for late filing of a request for a reconsideration or hearing.**

(a) *General Rule.* In determining whether a party has good cause for not filing a request for reconsideration or hearing timely, the QIO or ALJ, respectively, must consider the following:

(1) What circumstances kept the party from making the request on time.

(2) Whether an action by the QIO misled the party.

(3) Whether the party understood the requirements of the Act as affected by amendments to the Act, other legislation, or court decisions.

(b) *Examples.* Examples of circumstances in which good cause may exist include, but are not limited to, the following:

(1) A party was seriously ill and was prevented from requesting a reconsideration in person, through another person, or in writing.

(2) There was a death or serious illness in a party's immediate family.

(3) Important records were accidentally destroyed or damaged by fire or other cause.

(4) A party made a diligent effort but could not find or obtain necessary relevent information within the appropriate time period.

(5) A party requested additional information to further explain the determination within the time limit, and requested reconsideration within 60 days of receiving the explanation (or within 30 days for a Departmental Appeals Board hearing).

(6) The QIO gave the party incorrect or incomplete information about when and how to request a reconsideration or hearing.

(7) A party sent the request to another Government agency in good faith within the time limit, but the request did not reach an office authorized to receive the request until after the time period had expired.

(8) Other unusual or unavoidable circumstances exist that–

(i) Show that a party could not have known of the need to file timely; or

(ii) Prevented a party from filing timely.

[50 FR 15372, Apr. 17, 1985, as amended at 61 FR 32349, June 24, 1996. Redesignated at 64 FR 66279, Nov. 24, 1999]

**§ 478.24 Opportunity for a party to obtain and submit information.**

(a) Subject to the rules concerning disclosure of QIO information in section 1160 of the Act, at the request of a provider, practitioner or beneficiary, the QIO must provide an opportunity for examination of the material upon which the initial denial determination was based. The QIO may not furnish a provider, practitioner or beneficiary with–

(1) A record of the QIO deliberation; or

(2) The identity of the QIO review coordinators, physician advisors, or consultants who assisted in the initial denial determination without their consent.

(b) The QIO may require the requester to pay a reasonable fee for the reproduction of the material requested.

(c) The QIO must provide a party with an opportunity to submit new evidence before the reconsidered determination is made.

**§ 478.26 Delegation of the reconsideration function.**
A QIO may delegate the authority to reconsider an initial determination to a nonfacility subcontractor, including the organization that made the initial determination as a QIO subcontractor.

**§ 478.28 Qualifications of a reconsideration reviewer.**
A reconsideration reviewer must be someone who is—

(a) Qualified under §466.98 of this chapter to make an initial determination.

(b) Not the individual who made the initial denial determination.

(c) A specialist in the type of services under review, except where meeting this requirement would compromise the effectiveness or efficiency of QIO review.

**§ 478.30 Evidence to be considered by the reconsideration reviewer.**
A reconsidered determination must be based on—

(a) The information that led to the initial determination;

(b) New information found in the medical records; or

(c) Additional evidence submitted by a party.

**§ 478.32 Time limits for issuance of the reconsidered determination.**

(a) *Beneficiaries.* If a beneficiary files a timely request for reconsideration of an initial denial determination, the QIO must complete its reconsidered determination and send written notice to the beneficiary within the following time limits—

(1) Within three working days after the QIO receives the request for reconsideration if—

(i) The beneficiary is still an inpatient in a hospital for the stay in question when the QIO receives the request for reconsideration; or

(ii) The initial determination relates to institutional services for which admission to the institution is sought, the initial determination was made before the patient was admitted to the institution; and a request was submitted timely for an expedited reconsideration.

(2) Within 10 working days after the QIO receives the request for reconsideration if the beneficiary is still an inpatient in a SNF for the stay in question when the QIO receives the request for reconsideration.

(3) Within 30 working days after the QIO receives the request for reconsideration if—

(i) The initial determination concerns ambulatory or noninstitutional services;

(ii) The beneficiary is no longer an inpatient in a hospital or SNF for the stay in question; or

(iii) The beneficiary does not submit a request for expedited reconsideration timely.

(b) *Providers or practitioners.* If the provider or practitioner files a request for reconsideration of an initial determination, the QIO must complete its reconsidered determination and send written notice to the provider or practitioner within 30 working days.

**§ 478.34 Notice of a reconsidered determination.**

(a) *Notice to parties.* A written notice of a QIO reconsidered determination must contain the following;

(1) The basis for the reconsidered determination.

(2) A detailed rationale for the reconsidered determination.

(3) A statement explaining the Medicare payment consequences of the reconsidered determination.

(4) A statement informing the parties of their appeal rights, including the information concerning what must be included in the request for hearing, the amount in controversy, locations for submitting a request for an administrative hearing and the time period for filing a request.

(b) *Notice to payers.* (1) A QIO must provide written notice of its reconsidered determination to the appropriate Medicare intermediary or carrier within 30-days if the initial determination is modified or reversed.

(2) This notice must contain adequate information to allow the intermediary or carrier to locate the claim file. This must include the name of the beneficiary, the Health Insurance Claim Number, the name of the provider, date of admission, and dates or services for which Medicare payment will not be made.

**§ 478.36 Record of reconsideration.**

(a) *QIO requirements.* A QIO must maintain the record of its reconsideration until the later of the following:

(1) Four years after the date on the notice of the QIO's reconsidered determination.

(2) Completion of litigation and the passage of the time period for filing all appeals.

(b) *Contents of the record.* The record of the reconsideration must include:

(1) The initial determination.

(2) The basis for the initial determination.

(3) Documentation of the date of the receipt of the request for reconsideration.

(4) The detailed basis for the reconsidered determination.

(5) Evidence submitted by the parties.

(6) A copy of the notice of the reconsidered determination that was provided to the parties.

(7) Documentation of the delivery or mailing and, if appropriate, the receipt of the notice of the reconsidered determination by the parties.

(c) *Confidentiality.* The record of a QIO reconsideration is subject to prohibitions against disclosure of information as specified in section 1160 of the Act.

**§ 478.38 Effect of a reconsidered determination.**

A QIO reconsidered determination is binding upon all parties to the reconsideration unless—

(a) A hearing is requested in accordance with § 473.40 and a final decision rendered; or

(b) The reconsidered determination is later reopened and revised in accordance with § 473.48.

[50 FR 15372, Apr. 17, 1985; 50 FR 41887, Oct. 16, 1985, as amended at 62 FR 25855, May 12, 1997; 62 FR 49938, Sept. 24, 1997. Redesignated at 64 FR 66279, Nov. 24, 1999]

**§ 478.40 Beneficiary's right to a hearing.**

(a) *Amount in controversy.* If the amount in controversy is at least $200, a beneficiary (but not a provider or practitioner) who is dissatisfied with a QIO reconsidered determination may obtain a hearing by an administrative law judge (ALJ) of the Office of Hearings and Appeals of the SSA.

(b) *Subject matter.* A beneficiary has a right to a hearing on the following issues:

(1) Reasonableness of the services.

(2) Medical necessity of the services.

(3) Appropriateness of the setting in which the services were furnished.

(c) *Governing provisions.* The provisions of subpart G, Reconsiderations and Appeals under the Hospital Insurance Program, of part 405 of this chapter apply to hearings and appeals under this subpart unless they are inconsistent with specific provisions in this subpart. References in subpart G to initial and reconsidered determinations made by an intermediary, carrier, or CMS should be read to mean initial and reconsidered determinations made by a QIO.

[50 FR 15372, Apr. 17, 1985; 50 FR 41887, Oct. 16, 1985. Redesignated at 64 FR 66279, Nov. 24, 1999]

**§ 478.42 Submitting a request for a hearing.**

(a) *Where to submit the written request.* A beneficiary who wants to obtain a hearing under § 473.40 must submit a written request to one of the following:

(1) The office of the QIO or QIO subcontractor that made the initial determination.

(2) A SSA District Office.

(3) An office of the Office of Hearings and Appeals of SSA.

(4) An office of the Railroad Retirement Board, in the case of a beneficiary who is a railroad retiree.

(b) *Time limit for submitting a request for a hearing.* (1) The request for a hearing must be filed within 60 days of receipt of the notice of the QIO reconsidered determination, unless the time is extended for good cause as provided in § 473.22.

(2) The date of receipt of the notice of the reconsidered determination is presumed to be five days after the date on the notice, unless there is a reasonable showing to the contrary.

(3) A request is considered filed on the date it is postmarked.

**§ 478.44 Determining the amount in controversy for a hearing.**

(a) After an individual appellant has submitted a request for a hearing, the ALJ determines the amount in controversy in accordance with § 405.740(a) of this chapter for Part A services or § 405.817(a) of this chapter for Part B services. When two or more appellants submit a request for hearing, the ALJ determines the amount in controversy in accordance with § 405.740(b) of this chapter for Part A services and § 405.817(b) of this chapter for Part B services.

(b) If the ALJ determines that the amount in controversy is less than $200, the ALJ, without holding a hearing, notifies the parties to the hearing that the parties have 15 calendar days to submit additional evidence to prove that the amount in controversy is at least $200.

(c) At the end of the 15-day period, if the ALJ determines that the amount in controversy is less than $200, the ALJ, without holding a hearing, dismisses the request for a hearing without ruling on the substantive issues involved in the appeal and notifies the parties to the hearing and the QIO that the QIO reconsidered determination is conclusive for Medicare payment purposes.

[50 FR 15372, Apr. 17, 1985, as amended at 59 FR 12184, Mar. 16, 1994. Redesignated at 64 FR 66279, Nov. 24, 1999]

**§ 478.46 Departmental Appeals Board and judicial review.**

(a) The circumstances under which the DAB will review an ALJ hearing decision or dismissal are the same as those set forth at 20 CFR 404.970, ("Cases the Appeals Council will review").

(b) If $2,000 or more is in controversy, a party may obtain judicial review of an Departmental Appeals Board decision, or an ALJ hearing decision if a request for review by the Departmental Appeals Board was denied, by filing a civil action under the Federal Rules of Civil Procedure within 60 days after the date the party received notice of the Departmental Appeals Board decision or denial.

[50 FR 15372, Apr. 17, 1985, as amended at 61 FR 32349, June 24, 1996; 62 FR 25855, May 12, 1997. Redesignated at 64 FR 66279, Nov. 24, 1999]

**§ 478.48 Reopening and revision of a reconsidered determination or a hearing decision.**

(a) *QIO reopenings*—(1) *General rule.* A QIO or QIO subcontractor that made a reconsidered determination, or conducted a review of a DRG change as described in § 473.15, that is otherwise binding, may reopen and revise the reconsidered determination or review, either on its own motion or at the request of a party, within one year from the date of the reconsidered determination or review.

(2) *Extension of time limit.* A QIO or QIO subcontractor may reopen and revise its reconsidered determination, or its review of a DRG change as described

in § 473.15, that is otherwise binding, after one year but within four years of the date of the determination or review if—

(i) The QIO receives new material evidence;

(ii) The QIO erred in interpretation or application of Medicare coverage policy;

(iii) There is an error apparent on the face of the evidence upon which the reconsidered determination was based; or

(iv) There is a clerical error in the statement of the reconsidered determination.

(b) *ALJ and Departmental Appeals Board Reopening—Applicable procedures.* The ALJ or the Departmental Appeals Board, whichever made the decision, may reopen and revise the decision in accordance with the procedures set forth in §405.750(b) of this chapter, which concerns reopenings and revisions under subpart G of part 405 of this chapter.

(c) *Fraud or similar abusive practice.* A reconsidered determination, a review of a DRG change, or a decision of an ALJ or the Departmental Appeals Board may be reopened and revised at any time, if the reconsidered determination, review, or decision was obtained through fraud or a similar abusive practice that does not support a formal finding of fraud.

[50 FR 15372, Apr. 17, 1985, as amended at 61 FR 32349, June 24, 1996; 62 FR 25855, May 12, 1997. Redesignated at 64 FR 66279, Nov. 24, 1999]

## PART 488—SURVEY, CERTIFICATION, AND ENFORCEMENT PROCEDURES

### Subpart E—Survey and Certification of Long-Term Care Facilities

#### § 488.335 Action on complaints of resident neglect and abuse, and misappropriation of resident property.

(a) *Investigation.* (1) The State must review all allegations of resident neglect and abuse, and misappropriation of resident property and follow procedures specified in § 488.332.

(2) If there is reason to believe, either through oral or written evidence that an individual used by a facility to provide services to residents could have abused or neglected a resident or misappropriated a resident's property, the State must investigate the allegation.

(3) The State must have written procedures for the timely review and investigation of allegations of resident abuse and neglect, and misappropriation of resident property.

(b) *Source of complaints.* The State must review all allegations regardless of the source.

(c) *Notification—(1) Individuals to be notified.* If the State makes a preliminary determination, based on oral or written evidence and its investigation, that the abuse, neglect or misappropriation of property occurred, it must notify in writing—

(i) The individuals implicated in the investigation; and

(ii) The current administrator of the facility in which the incident occurred.

(2) *Timing of the notice.* The State must notify the individuals specified in paragraph (c)(1) of this section in writing within 10 working days of the State's investigation.

(3) *Contents of the notice.* The notice must include the—

(i) Nature of the allegation(s);

(ii) Date and time of the occurrence;

(iii) Right to a hearing;

(iv) Intent to report the substantiated findings in writing, once the individual has had the opportunity for a hearing, to the nurse aide registry or appropriate licensure authority;

(v) Fact that the individual's failure to request a hearing in writing within 30 days from the date of the notice will result in reporting the substantiated findings to the nurse aide registry or appropriate licensure authority.

(vi) Consequences of waiving the right to a hearing;

(vii) Consequences of a finding through the hearing process that the alleged resident abuse or neglect, or misappropriation of resident property did occur; and

(viii) Fact that the individual has the right to be represented by an attorney at the individual's own expense.

(d) *Conduct of hearing.* (1) The State must complete the hearing and the hearing record within 120 days from the day it receives the request for a hearing.

(2) The State must hold the hearing at a reasonable place and time convenient for the individual.

(e) *Factors beyond the individual's control.* A State must not make a finding that an individual has neglected a resident if the individual demonstrates that such neglect was caused by factors beyond the control of the individual.

(f) *Report of findings.* If the finding is that the individual has neglected or abused a resident or misappropriated resident property or if the individual waives the right to a hearing, the State must report the findings in writing within 10 working days to—

(1) The individual;

(2) The current administrator of the facility in which the incident occurred; and

(3) The administrator of the facility that currently employs the individual, if different than the facility in which the incident occurred;

(4) The licensing authority for individuals used by the facility other than nurse aides, if applicable; and

(5) The nurse aide registry for nurse aides. Only the State survey agency may report the findings to the nurse aide registry, and this must be done within

10 working days of the findings, in accordance with § 483.156(c) of this chapter. The State survey agency may not delegate this responsibility.

(g) *Contents and retention of report of finding to the nurse aide registry.* (1) The report of finding must include information in accordance with § 483.156(c) of this chapter.

(2) The survey agency must retain the information as specified in paragraph (g)(1) of this section, in accordance with the procedures specified in § 483.156(c) of this chapter.

(h) *Survey agency responsibility.* (1) The survey agency must promptly review the results of all complaint investigations and determine whether or not a facility has violated any requirements in part 483, subPart B of this chapter.

(2) If a facility is not in substantial compliance with the requirements in part 483, subPart B of this chapter, the survey agency initiates appropriate actions, as specified in subpart F of this part.

[59 FR 56238, Nov. 10, 1994; 60 FR 50118, Sept. 28, 1995]

## PART 489—PROVIDER AGREEMENTS AND SUPPLIER APPROVAL

### Subpart E—Termination of Agreement and Reinstatement after Termination

#### § 489.52 Termination by the provider.

(a) *Notice to CMS.* (1) A provider that wishes to terminate its agreement must send CMS written notice of its intent.

(2) The notice may state the intended date of termination which must be the first day of a month.

(b) *Termination date.* (1) If the notice does not specify a date, or the date is not acceptable to CMS, CMS may set a date that will not be more than 6 months from the date on the provider's notice of intent.

(2) CMS may accept a termination date that is less than 6 months after the date on the provider's notice if it determines that to do so would not unduly disrupt services to the community or otherwise interfere with the effective and efficient administration of the Medicare program.

(3) A cessation of business is deemed to be a termination by the provider, effective with the date on which it stopped providing services to the community.

(c) *Public notice.* (1) The provider must give notice to the public at least 15 days before the effective date of termination.

(2) The notice must be published in one or more local newspapers and must—

(i) Specify the termination date; and

(ii) Explain to what extent services may continue after that date, in accordance with the exceptions set forth in § 489.55.

**§ 489.53 Termination by CMS.**

(a) *Basis for termination of agreement with any provider.* CMS may terminate the agreement with any provider if CMS finds that any of the following failings is attributable to that provider:

(1) It is not complying with the provisions of title XVIII and the applicable regulations of this chapter or with the provisions of the agreement.

(2) It places restrictions on the persons it will accept for treatment and it fails either to exempt Medicare beneficiaries from those restrictions or to apply them to Medicare beneficiaries the same as to all other persons seeking care.

(3) It no longer meets the appropriate conditions of participation or requirements (for SNFs and NFs) set forth elsewhere in this chapter. In the case of an RNHCI no longer meets the conditions for coverage, conditions of participation and requirements set forth elsewhere in this chapter.

(4) It fails to furnish information that CMS finds necessary for a determination as to whether payments are or were due under Medicare and the amounts due.

(5) It refuses to permit examination of its fiscal or other records by, or on behalf of CMS, as necessary for verification of information furnished as a basis for payment under Medicare.

(6) It failed to furnish information on business transactions as required in § 420.205 of this chapter.

(7) It failed at the time the agreement was entered into or renewed to disclose information on convicted individuals as required in § 420.204 of this chapter.

(8) It failed to furnish ownership information as required in § 420.206 of this chapter.

(9) It failed to comply with civil rights requirements set forth in 45 CFR parts 80, 84, and 90.

(10) In the case of a hospital or a critical access hospital as defined in section 1861(mm)(1) of the Act that has reason to believe it may have received an individual transferred by another hospital in violation of § 489.24(d), the hospital failed to report the incident to CMS or the State survey agency.

(11) In the case of a hospital requested to furnish inpatient services to CHAMPUS or CHAMPVA beneficiaries or to veterans, it failed to comply with § 489.25 or § 489.26, respectively.

(12) It failed to furnish the notice of discharge rights as required by § 489.27.

(13) It refuses to permit photocopying of any records or other information by, or on behalf of CMS, as necessary to determine or verify compliance with participation requirements.

(14) The hospital knowingly and willfully fails to accept, on a repeated basis, an amount that approximates the Medicare rate established under the inpatient hospital prospective payment system, minus any enrollee deductibles or copayments, as payment in full from a fee-for-service FEHB plan for inpatient hospital services provided to a retired Federal enrollee of a fee-for-service FEHB plan, age 65 or older, who does not have Medicare Part A benefits.

(15) It had its enrollment in the Medicare program revoked in accordance to § 424.535 of this chapter.

(b) *Termination of agreements with certain hospitals.* In the case of a hospital or critical access hospital that has an emergency department, as defined in § 489.24(b), CMS may terminate the provider agreement if—

(1) The hospital fails to comply with the requirements of § 489.24(a) through (e), which require the hospital to examine, treat, or transfer emergency medical condition cases appropriately, and require that hospitals with specialized capabilities or facilities accept an appropriate transfer; or

(2) The hospital fails to comply with § 489.20(m), (q), and (r), which require the hospital to report suspected violations of § 489.24(e), to post conspicuously in emergency departments or in a place or places likely to be noticed by all individuals entering the emergency departments, as well as those individuals waiting for examination and treatment in areas other than traditional emergency departments (that is, entrance, admitting area, waiting room, treatment area), signs specifying rights of individuals under this subpart, to post conspicuously information indicating whether or not the hospital participates in the Medicaid program, and to maintain medical and other records related to transferred individuals for a period of 5 years, a list of on-call physicians for individuals with emergency medical conditions, and a central log on each individual who comes to the emergency department seeking assistance.

(c) *Notice of termination*—(1) *Timing: Basic rule.* Except as provided in paragraph (c)(2) of this section, CMS gives the provider notice of termination at least 15 days before the effective date of termination of the provider agreement.

(2) *Timing exceptions: Immediate jeopardy situations*—(i) *Hospital with emergency department.* If CMS finds that a hospital with an emergency department is in violation of § 489.24, paragraphs (a) through (e), and CMS determines that the violation poses immediate jeopardy to the health or safety of individuals who present themselves to the hospital for emergency services, CMS—

(A) Gives the hospital a preliminary notice indicating that its provider agreement will be terminated in 23 days if it does not correct the identified deficiencies or refute the finding; and

(B) Gives a final notice of termination, and concurrent notice to the public, at least 2 , but not more than 4, days before the effective date of termination of the provider agreement.

(ii) *Skilled nursing facilities (SNFs).* For an SNF with deficiencies that pose immediate jeopardy to the health or safety of residents, CMS gives notice at least 2 days before the effective date of termination of the provider agreement.

(3) *Content of notice.* The notice states the reasons for, and the effective date of, the termination, and explains the extent to which services may continue after that date, in accordance with § 489.55.

(4) *Notice to public.* CMS concurrently gives notice of the termination to the public.

(d) *Appeal by the provider.* A provider may appeal the termination of its provider agreement by CMS in accordance with part 498 of this chapter.

[51 FR 24492, July 3, 1986, as amended at 52 FR 22454, June 12, 1987; 54 FR 5373, Feb. 2, 1989; 56 FR 48879, Sept. 26, 1991; 59 FR 32123, June 22, 1994; 59 FR 56251, Nov. 10, 1994; 60 FR 45851, Sept. 1, 1995; 60 FR 50119, Sept. 28, 1995; 62 FR 43937, Aug. 18, 1997; 62 FR 46037, Aug. 29, 1997; 62 FR 56111, Oct. 29, 1997; 68 FR 66720, Nov. 28, 2003; 69 FR 49272, Aug. 11, 2004; 71 FR 20781, Apr. 21, 2006]

**§ 489.54 Termination by the OIG.**

(a) *Basis for termination.* (1) The OIG may terminate the agreement of any provider if the OIG finds that any of the following failings can be attributed to that provider.

(i) It has knowingly and willfully made, or caused to be made, any false statement or representation of a material fact for use in an application or request for payment under Medicare.

(ii) It has submitted, or caused to be submitted, requests for Medicare payment of amounts that substantially exceed the costs it incurred in furnishing the services for which payment is requested.

(iii) It has furnished services that the OIG has determined to be substantially in excess of the needs of individuals or of a quality that fails to meet professionally recognized standards of health care. The OIG will not terminate a provider agreement under paragraph (a) if CMS has waived a disallowance with respect to the services in question on the grounds that the provider and the beneficiary could not reasonably be expected to know that payment would not be made. (The rules for determining such lack of knowledge are set forth in §§ 405.330 through 405.334 of this chapter.)

(b) *Notice of termination.* The OIG will give the provider notice of termination at least 15 days before the effective date of termination of the agreement, and will concurrently give notice of termination to the public.

(c) *Appeal by the provider.* A provider may appeal a termination of its agreement by the OIG in accordance with subpart O of part 405 of this chapter.

(d) *Other applicable rules.* The termination of a provider agreement by the OIG is subject to the additional procedures specified in §§ 1001.105 through 1001.109 of this title for notice and appeals.

[51 FR 24492, July 3, 1986, as amended at 51 FR 34788, Sept. 30, 1986]

**§ 489.55 Exceptions to effective date of termination.**

Payment is available for up to 30 days after the effective date of termination for—

(a) Inpatient hospital services (including inpatient psychiatric hospital services) and posthospital extended care services furnished to a beneficiary who was admitted before the effective date of termination; and

(b) Home health services and hospice care furnished under a plan established before the effective date of termination.[1]

---

[1]For termination before July 18, 1984, payment was available through the calendar year in which the termination was effective.

[50 FR 37376, Sept. 13, 1985]

**§ 489.57 Reinstatement after termination.**

When a provider agreement has been terminated by CMS under § 489.53, or by the OIG under § 489.54, a new agreement with that provider will not be accepted unless CMS or the OIG, as appropriate, finds—

(a) That the reason for termination of the previous agreement has been removed and there is reasonable assurance that it will not recur; and

(b) That the provider has fulfilled, or has made satisfactory arrangements to fulfill, all of the statutory and regulatory responsibilities of its previous agreement.

[51 FR 24493, July 3, 1986]

## PART 498—APPEALS PROCEDURES FOR DETERMINATIONS THAT AFFECT PARTICIPATION IN THE MEDICARE PROGRAM AND FOR DETERMINATIONS THAT AFFECT THE PARTICIPATION OF ICFs/MR AND CERTAIN NFs IN THE MEDICAID PROGRAM

### Subpart A—General Provisions

**§ 498.1 Statutory basis.**

(a) Section 1866(h) of the Act provides for a hearing and for judicial review of the hearing for any institution or agency dissatisfied with a determination that it is not a provider, or with any determination described in section 1866(b)(2) of the Act.

(b) Section 1866(b)(2) of the Act lists determinations that serve as a basis for termination of a provider agreement.

(c) Sections 1128(a) and (b) of the Act provide for exclusion of certain individuals or entities because of conviction of crimes related to their participation in Medicare and section 1128(f) provides for hearing and judicial review for exclusions.

(d) Section 1156 of the Act establishes certain obligations for practitioners and providers of health care services, and provides sanctions and penalties for those that fail to meet those obligations.

**(e)–(f) [Reserved]**

(g) Although § 1866(h) of the Act is silent regarding appeal rights for suppliers and practitioners, the rules in this part include procedures for review of determinations that affect those two groups.

(h) Section 1128A(c)(2) of the Act provides that the Secretary may not collect a civil money penalty until the affected entity has had notice and opportunity for a hearing.

(i) Section 1819(h) of the Act—

(1) Provides that, for SNFs found to be out of compliance with the requirements for participation, specified remedies may be imposed instead of, or in addition to, termination of the facility's Medicare provider agreement; and

(2) Makes certain provisions of section 1128A of the Act applicable to civil money penalties imposed on SNFs.

(j) Section 1891(e) of the Act provides that, for home health agencies (HHAs) found to be out of compliance with the conditions of participation, specified remedies may be imposed instead of, or in addition to, termination of the HHA's Medicare provider agreement.

(k) Section 1891(f) of the Act—

(1) Requires the Secretary to develop a range of such remedies; and

(2) Makes certain provisions of section 1128A of the Act applicable to civil money penalties imposed on HHAs.

[52 FR 22446, June 12, 1987, as amended at 59 FR 56251, Nov. 10, 1994; 61 FR 32349, June 24, 1996]

**§ 498.2 Definitions.**

As used in this part—

*Affected party* means a provider, prospective provider, supplier, prospective supplier, or practitioner that is affected by an initial determination or by any subsequent determination or decision issued under this part, and "party" means the affected party or CMS (or the OIG), as appropriate.

*ALJ* stands for Administrative Law Judge.

*Departmental Appeals Board* or *Board* means a Board established in the Office of the Secretary to provide impartial review of disputed decisions made by the operating components of the Department.

*OHA* stands for the Social Security Administration's Office of Hearings and Appeals.

*OIG* stands for the Department's Office of the Inspector General.

*Provider* means a hospital, critical access hospital (CAH), skilled nursing facility (SNF), comprehensive outpatient rehabilitation facility (CORF), home health agency (HHA), hospice, or religious nonmedical health care institution (RNHCI) that has in effect an agreement to participate in Medicare, that has in effect an agreement to participate in Medicaid, or a clinic, rehabilitation agency, or public health agency that has a similar agreement but only to furnish outpatient physical therapy or outpatient speech pathology services, and prospective provider means any of the listed entities that seeks to participate in Medicare as a provider or to have any facility or organization determined to be a department of the provider or provider-based entity under § 413.65 of this chapter.

*Supplier* means an independent laboratory, supplier of portable X-ray services, rural health clinic (RHC), Federally qualified health center (FQHC), ambulatory surgical center (ASC), an entity approved by CMS to furnish outpatient diabetes self-management training, or end-stage renal disease (ESRD) treatment facility that is approved by CMS as meeting the conditions for coverage of its services, and *prospective supplier* means any of the listed entities that seeks to be approved for coverage of its services under Medicare. (However, for purposes of the sanctions and penalties that may be imposed by the OIG, the term *supplier* has the meaning specified in § 1001.2 of this title.)

[52 FR 22446, June 12, 1987, as amended at 53 FR 6551, March 1, 1988; 57 FR 24984, June 12, 1992; 58 FR 30677, May 26, 1993; 59 FR 6579, Feb. 11, 1994; 59 FR 56251, Nov. 10, 1994; 61 FR 32350, June 24, 1996; 62 FR 46037, Aug. 29, 1997; 65 FR 18549, Apr. 7, 2000; 65 FR 83154, Dec. 29, 2000; 68 FR 66721, Nov. 28, 2003; 71 FR 31054, May 31, 2006]

**§ 498.3 Scope and applicability.**

(a) *Scope.* (1) This part sets forth procedures for reviewing initial determinations that CMS makes with respect to the matters specified in paragraph (b) of this section, and that the OIG makes with respect to the matters specified in paragraph (c) of this section. It also specifies, in paragraph (d) of this section, administrative actions that are not subject to appeal under this part.

(2) The determinations listed in this section affect participation in the Medicare program. Many of the procedures of this part also apply to other determinations that do not affect participation in Medicare. Some examples follow:

(i) CMS's determination to terminate an NF's Medicaid provider agreement.

(ii) CMS's determination to cancel the approval of an ICF/MR under section 1910(b) of the Act.

(iii) CMS's determination, under the Clinical Laboratory Improvement Act (CLIA), to impose alternative sanctions or to suspend, limit, or revoke the certificate of a laboratory even though it does not participate in Medicare.

(3) The following parts of this chapter specify the applicability of the provisions of this part 498 to sanctions or remedies imposed on the indicated entities:

(i) Part 431, subpart D—for nursing facilities (NFs).

(ii) Part 488, subpart E (§ 488.330(e))—for SNFs and NFs.

(iii) Part 493, subpart R (§ 493.1844)—for laboratories.

(b) *Initial determinations by CMS.* CMS makes initial determinations with respect to the following matters:

(1) Whether a prospective provider qualifies as a provider.

(2) Whether a prospective department of a provider, remote location of a hospital, satellite facility, or provider-based entity qualifies for provider-based status under § 413.65 of this chapter, or whether such a facility or entity currently treated as a department of a provider, remote location of a hospital, satellite facility, or a provider-based entity no longer qualifies for that status under § 413.65 of this chapter.

(3) Whether an institution is a hospital qualified to elect to claim payment for all emergency hospital services furnished in a calendar year.

(4) Whether an institution continues to remain in compliance with the qualifications for claiming reimbursement for all emergency services furnished in a calendar year.

(5) Whether a prospective supplier meets the conditions for coverage of its services as those conditions are set forth elsewhere in this chapter.

(6) Whether the services of a supplier continue to meet the conditions for coverage.

(7) Whether a physical therapist in independent practice or a chiropractor meets the requirements for coverage of his or her services as set forth in subpart D of part 486 of this chapter and § 410.22 of this chapter, respectively.

(8) The termination of a provider agreement in accordance with § 489.53 of this chapter, or the termination of a rural health clinic agreement in accordance with § 405.2404 of this chapter, or the termination of a Federally qualified health center agreement in accordance with § 405.2436 of this chapter.

(9) CMS's cancellation, under section 1910(b) of the Act, of an ICF/MR's approval to participate in Medicaid.

(10) Whether, for purposes of rate setting and reimbursement, an ESRD treatment facility is considered to be hospital-based or independent.

**(11) [Reserved]**

(12) Whether a hospital, skilled nursing facility, home health agency, or hospice program meets or continues to meet the advance directives requirements specified in subpart I of part 489 of this chapter.

(13) With respect to an SNF or NF, a finding of noncompliance that results in the imposition of a remedy specified in § 488.406 of this chapter, except the State monitoring remedy.

(14) The level of noncompliance found by CMS in a SNF or NF but only if a successful challenge on this issue would affect–

(i) The range of civil money penalty amounts that CMS could collect (The scope of review during a hearing on imposition of a civil money penalty is set forth in § 488.438(e) of this chapter.); or

(ii) A finding of substandard quality of care that results in the loss of approval for a SNF or NF of its nurse aide training program.

(15) The effective date of a Medicare provider agreement or supplier approval.

(16) The finding of substandard quality of care that leads to the loss by a SNF or NF of the approval of its nurse aide training program.

(17) Whether to deny or revoke a provider or supplier's Medicare enrollment in accordance with § 424.530 or § 424.535 of this chapter.

(c) *Initial determinations by the OIG.* The OIG makes initial determinations with respect to the following matters:

(1) The termination of a provider agreement in accordance with part 1001, subpart C of this title.

(2) The suspension, or exclusion from coverage and the denial of reimbursement for services furnished by a provider, practitioner, or supplier, because of fraud or abuse, or conviction of crimes related to participation in the program, in accordance with part 1001, subPart B of this title.

(3) The imposition of sanctions in accordance with part 1004 of this title.

(d) *Administrative actions that are not initial determinations.* Administrative actions that are not initial determination (and therefore not subject to appeal under this part) include but are not limited to the following:

(1) The finding that a provider or supplier determined to be in compliance with the conditions or requirements for participation or for coverage has deficiencies.

(2) The finding that a prospective provider does not meet the conditions of participation set forth elsewhere in this chapter, if the prospective provider is, nevertheless, approved for participation in Medicare on the basis of special access certification, as provided in subPart B of part 488 of this chapter.

(3) The refusal to enter into a provider agreement because the prospective provider is unable to give satisfactory assurance of compliance with the requirements of title XVIII of the Act.

(4) The finding that an entity that had its provider agreement terminated may not file another agreement because the reasons for terminating the previous agreement have not been removed or there is insufficient assurance that the reasons for the exclusion will not recur.

(5) The determination not to reinstate a suspended or excluded practitioner, provider, or supplier because the reason for the suspension or exclusion has not been removed, or there is insufficient assurance that the reason will not recur.

(6) The finding that the services of a laboratory are covered as hospital services or as physician's services, rather than as services of an independent laboratory, because the laboratory is not independent of the hospital or of the physician's office.

(7) The refusal to accept for filing an election to claim payment for all emergency hospital services furnished in a calendar year because the institution—

(i) Had previously charged an individual or other person for services furnished during that calendar year;

(ii) Submitted the election after the close of that calendar year; or

(iii) Had previously been notified of its failure to continue to comply.

(8) The finding that the reason for the revocation of a supplier's right to accept assignment has not been removed or there is insufficient assurance that the reason will not recur.

(9) The finding that a hospital accredited by the Joint Commission on Accreditation of Hospitals or the American Osteopathic Association is not in compliance with a condition of participation, and a finding that that hospital is no longer deemed to meet the conditions of participation.

(10) With respect to an SNF or NF-(i) The finding that the SNF's or NF's deficiencies pose immediate jeopardy to the health or safety of its residents;

(ii) Except as provided in paragraph (b)(13) of this section, a determination by CMS as to the facility's level of noncompliance; and

(iii) The imposition of State monitoring.

(11) The choice of alternative sanction or remedy to be imposed on a provider or supplier.

(12) The determination that the accreditation requirements of a national accreditation organization do not provide (or do not continue to provide) reasonable

assurance that the entities accredited by the accreditation organization meet the applicable long-term care requirements, conditions for coverage, conditions of certification, conditions of participation, or CLIA condition level requirements.

(13) The determination that requirements imposed on a State's laboratories under the laws of that State do not provide (or do not continue to provide) reasonable assurance that laboratories licensed or approved by the State meet applicable CLIA requirements.

(14) The choice of alternative sanction or remedy to be imposed on a provider or supplier.

(15) A decision by the State survey agency as to when to conduct an initial survey of a prospective provider or supplier.

(e) *Exclusion of civil rights issues.* The procedures in this subpart do not apply to the adjudication of issues relating to a provider's compliance with civil rights requirements that are set forth in part 489 of this chapter. Those issues are handled through the Department's Office of Civil Rights.

[52 FR 22446, June 12, 1987, as amended at 52 FR 27765, July 23, 1987; 53 FR 6551, March 1, 1988; 53 FR 6649, March 2, 1988; 54 FR 5373, Feb. 2, 1989; 56 FR 8854, Mar. 1, 1991; 56 FR 48879, Sept. 26, 1991; 57 FR 8204, Mar. 6, 1992; 57 FR 34021, July 31, 1992; 57 FR 43925, Sept. 23, 1992; 59 FR 56251, Nov. 10, 1994; 60 FR 2330, Jan. 9, 1995; 60 FR 50120, Sept. 28, 1995; 61 FR 32350, June 24, 1996; 62 FR 43937, Aug. 18, 1997; 64 FR 24957, May 10, 1999; 64 FR 39937, July 23, 1999; 64 FR 43295, Aug. 10, 1999; 65 FR 18549, Apr. 7, 2000; 65 FR 62646, Oct. 19, 2000; 71 FR 20781, Apr. 21, 2006; 71 FR 37505, June 30, 2006]

**§ 498.4 NFs subject to appeals process in part 498.**

An NF is considered a provider for purposes of this part when it has in effect an agreement to participate in Medicaid, including an agreement to participate in both Medicaid and Medicare and it is a—

(a) State-operated NF; or

(b) Non State-operated NF that is subject to compliance action as a result of—

(1) A validation survey by CMS; or

(2) CMS's review of the State's survey findings.

[59 FR 56252, Nov. 10, 1994]

**§ 498.5 Appeal rights.**

(a) *Appeal rights of prospective providers.* (1) Any prospective provider dissatisfied with an initial determination or revised initial determination that it does not qualify as a provider may request reconsideration in accordance with § 498.22(a).

(2) Any prospective provider dissatisfied with a reconsidered determination under paragraph (a)(1) of this section, or a revised reconsidered determination under § 498.30, is entitled to a hearing before an ALJ.

(b) *Appeal rights of providers.* Any provider dissatisfied with an initial determination to terminate its provider agreement is entitled to a hearing before an ALJ.

(c) *Appeal rights of providers and prospective providers.* Any provider or prospective provider dissatisfied with a hearing decision may request Departmental Appeals Board review, and has a right to seek judicial review of the Board's decision.

(d) *Appeal rights of prospective suppliers.* (1) Any prospective supplier dissatisfied with an initial determination or a revised initial determination that its services do not meet the conditions for coverage may request reconsideration in accordance with § 498.22(a).

(2) Any prospective supplier dissatisfied with a reconsidered determination under paragraph (d)(1) of this section, or a revised reconsidered determination under § 498.30, is entitled to a hearing before an ALJ.

(e) *Appeal rights of suppliers.* Any supplier dissatisfied with an initial determination that the services subject to the determination no longer meet the conditions for coverage, is entitled to a hearing before an ALJ.

(f) *Appeal rights of suppliers and prospective suppliers.* (1) Any supplier or prospective supplier dissatisfied with the hearing decision may request Departmental Appeals Board review of the ALJ's decision.

(2) Suppliers and prospective suppliers do not have a right to judicial review except as provided in paragraph (i) of this section.

(g) *Appeal rights for certain practitioners.* A physical therapist in independent practice or a chiropractor dissatisfied with a determination that he or she does not meet the requirements for coverage of his or her services has the same appeal rights as suppliers have under paragraphs (d), (e), and (f) of this section.

(h) *Appeal rights for nonparticipating hospitals that furnish emergency services.* A nonparticipating hospital dissatisfied with a determination or decision that it does not qualify to elect to claim payment for all emergency services furnished during a calendar year has the same appeal rights that providers have under paragraph (a), (b), and (c) of this section.

(i) *Appeal rights for suspended or excluded practitioners, providers, or suppliers.* (1) Any practitioner, provider, or supplier who has been suspended, or whose services have been excluded from coverage in accordance with § 498.3(c)(2), or has been sanctioned in accordance with § 498.3(c)(3), is entitled to a hearing before an ALJ.

(2) Any suspended or excluded practitioner, provider, or supplier dissatisfied with a hearing decision may request Departmental Appeals Board review and has a right to seek judicial review of the Board's decision by filing an action in Federal district court.

(j) *Appeal rights for Medicaid ICFs/MR terminated by CMS.* (1) Any Medicaid ICF/MR that has had its approval cancelled by CMS in accordance with § 498.3(b)(8) has a right to a hearing before an ALJ, to request Departmental Appeals Board review of the hearing decision, and to seek judicial review of the Board's decision.

(2) The Medicaid agreement remains in effect until the period for requesting a hearing has expired or, if the facility requests a hearing, until a hearing decision is issued, unless CMS—

(i) Makes a written determination that continuation of provider status for the SNF or ICF constitutes an immediate and serious threat to the health and safety of patients and specifies the reasons for that determination; and

(ii) Certifies that the facility has been notified of its deficiencies and has failed to correct them.

(k) *Appeal rights of NFs.* Under the circumstances specified in § 431.153(g) and (h) of this chapter, an NF has a right to a hearing before an ALJ, to request Board review of the hearing decision, and to seek judicial review of the Board's decision.
[52 FR 22446, June 12, 1987, as amended at 57 FR 43925, Sept. 23, 1992; 59 FR 56252, Nov. 10, 1994; 61 FR 32350, June 24, 1996]

**§ 498.10 Appointment of representatives.**

(a) An affected party may appoint as its representative anyone not disqualified or suspended from acting as a representative in proceedings before the Secretary or otherwise prohibited by law.

(b) If the representative appointed is not an attorney, the party must file written notice of the appointment with CMS, the ALJ, or the Departmental Appeals Board.

(c) If the representative appointed is an attorney, the attorney's statement that he or she has the authority to represent the party is sufficient.

**§ 498.11 Authority of representatives.**

(a) A representative appointed and qualified in accordance with § 498.10 may, on behalf of the represented party—

(1) Give and accept any notice or request pertinent to the proceedings set forth in this part;

(2) Present evidence and allegations as to facts and law in any proceedings affecting that party to the same extent as the party; and

(3) Obtain information to the same extent as the party.

(b) A notice or request may be sent to the affected party, to the party's representative, or to both. A notice or request sent to the representative has the same force and effect as if it had been sent to the party.

**§ 498.13 Fees for services of representatives.**

Fees for any services performed on behalf of an affected party by an attorney appointed and qualified in accordance with § 498.10 are not subject to the provisions of section 206 of Title II of the Act, which authorizes the Secretary to specify or limit those fees.

**§ 498.15 Charge for transcripts.**

A party that requests a transcript of prehearing or hearing proceedings or Board review must pay the actual or estimated cost of preparing the transcript unless, for good cause shown by that party, the payment is waived by the ALJ or the Departmental Appeals Board, as appropriate.
[52 FR 22446, June 12, 1987, as amended at 61 FR 51021, Sept. 30, 1996]

### § 498.17 Filing of briefs with the ALJ or Departmental Appeals Board, and opportunity for rebuttal.

(a) *Filing of briefs and related documents.* If a party files a brief or related document such as a written argument, contention, suggested finding of fact, conclusion of law, or any other written statement, it must submit an original and one copy to the ALJ or the Departmental Appeals Board, as appropriate. The material may be filed by mail or in person and must include a statement certifying that a copy has been furnished to the other party.

(b) *Opportunity for rebuttal.* (1) The other party will have 20 days from the date of mailing or personal service to submit any rebuttal statement or additional evidence. If a party submits a rebuttal statement or additional evidence, it must file an original and one copy with the ALJ or the Board and furnish a copy to the other party.

(2) The ALJ or the Board will grant an opportunity to reply to the rebuttal statement only if the party shows good cause.

## Subpart B—Initial, Reconsidered, and Revised Determinations

### § 498.20 Notice and effect of initial determinations.

(a) *Notice of initial determination*—(1) *General rule.* CMS or the OIG, as appropriate, mails notice of an initial determination to the affected party, setting forth the basis or reasons for the determination, the effect of the determination, and the party's right to reconsideration, if applicable, or to a hearing.

(2) *Special rules: Independent laboratories and suppliers of portable x-ray services.* If CMS determines that an independent laboratory or a supplier of portable x-ray services no longer meets the conditions for coverage of some or all of its services, the notice—

(i) Specifies an effective date of termination of coverage that is at least 15 days after the date of the notice;

(ii) Is also sent to physicians, hospitals, and other parties that might use the services of the laboratory or supplier; and

(iii) In the case of laboratories, specifies the categories of laboratory tests that are no longer covered.

(3) *Special rules: Nonparticipating hospitals that elect to claim payment for emergency services.* If CMS determines that a nonparticipating hospital no longer qualifies to elect to claim payment for all emergency services furnished in a calendar year, the notice—

(i) States the calendar year to which the determination applies;

(ii) Specifies an effective date that is at least 5 days after the date of the notice; and

(iii) Specifies that the determination applies to services furnished, in the specified calendar year, to patients accepted (as inpatients or outpatients) on or after the effective date of the determination.

(4) *Other special rules.* Additional rules pertaining, for example, to content and timing of notice, notice to the public and to other entities, and time allowed

for submittal of additional information, are set forth elsewhere in this chapter, as follows:

Part 405 Subpart X—for rural health clinics.

Part 416—for ambulatory surgical centers.

Part 489—for providers, when their provider agreements have been terminated.

Part 1001, Subpart B—for excluded or suspended providers, suppliers, physicians, or practitioners.

Part 1001, Subpart C—for providers, when their provider agreements are terminated by the OIG.

Part 1004—for sanctioned providers and practitioners.

(b) *Effect of initial determination.* An initial determination is binding unless it is—

(1) Reconsidered in accordance with § 498.24;

(2) Reversed or modified by a hearing decision in accordance with § 498.78; or

(3) Revised in accordance with § 498.32 or § 498.100.

**§ 498.22 Reconsideration.**

(a) *Right to reconsideration.* CMS reconsiders any initial determination that affects a prospective provider or supplier, or a hospital seeking to qualify to claim payment for all emergency hospital services furnished in a calendar year, if the affected party files a written request in accordance with paragraphs (b) and (c) of this section. (None of the determinations made by the OIG is subject to reconsideration.)

(b) *Request for reconsideration: Manner and timing.* The affected party specified in paragraph (a) of this section, if dissatisfied with the initial determination, may request reconsideration by filing the request—

(1) With CMS or with the State survey agency;

(2) Directly or through its legal representative or other authorized official; and

(3) Within 60 days from receipt of the notice of initial determination, unless the time is extended in accordance with paragraph (d) of this section. The date of receipt will be presumed to be 5 days after the date on the notice unless there is a showing that it was, in fact, received earlier or later.

(c) *Content of request.* The request for reconsideration must state the issues, or the findings of fact with which the affected party disagrees, and the reasons for disagreement.

(d) *Extension of time to file a request for reconsideration.* (1) If the affected party is unable to file the request within the 60 days specified in paragraph (b) of this section, it may file a written request with CMS, stating the reasons why the request was not filed timely.

(2) CMS will extend the time for filing a request for reconsideration if the affected party shows good cause for missing the deadline.

**§ 498.23 Withdrawal of request for reconsideration.**

A request for reconsideration is considered withdrawn if the requestor files a written withdrawal request before CMS mails the notice of reconsidered determination, and CMS approves the withdrawal request.

**§ 498.24 Reconsidered determination.**

When a request for reconsideration has been properly filed in accordance with § 498.22, CMS–

(a) Receives written evidence and statements that are relevant and material to the matters at issue and are submitted within a reasonable time after the request for reconsideration;

(b) Considers the initial determination, the findings on which the initial determination was based, the evidence considered in making the initial determination, and any other written evidence submitted under paragraph (a) of this section, taking into account facts relating to the status of the prospective provider or supplier subsequent to the initial determination; and

(c) Makes a reconsidered determination, affirming or modifying the initial determination and the findings on which it was based.

**§ 498.25 Notice and effect of reconsidered determination.**

(a) *Notice.* (1) CMS mails notice of a reconsidered determination to the affected party.

(2) The notice gives the reasons for the determination.

(3) If the determination is adverse, the notice specifies the conditions or requirements of law or regulations that the affected party fails to meet, and informs the party of its right to a hearing.

(b) *Effect.* A reconsidered determination is binding unless–

(1) CMS or the OIG, as appropriate, further revises the revised determination; or

(2) The revised determination is reversed or modified by a hearing decision.

**Subpart C–Reopening of Initial or Reconsidered Determinations**

**§ 498.30 Limitation on reopening.**

An initial or reconsidered determination that a prospective provider is a provider or that a hospital qualifies to elect to claim payment for all emergency services furnished in a calendar year may not be reopened. CMS or the OIG, as appropriate, may on its own initiative, reopen any other initial or reconsidered determination, within 12 months after the date of notice of the initial determination.

**§ 498.32 Notice and effect of reopening and revision.**

(a) *Notice.* (1) CMS or the OIG, as appropriate, gives the affected party notice of reopening and of any revision of the reopened determination.

(2) The notice of revised determination states the basis or reason for the revised determination.

(3) If the determination is that a supplier or prospective supplier does not meet the conditions for coverage of its services, the notice specifies the conditions with respect to which the affected party fails to meet the requirements of law and regulations, and informs the party of its right to a hearing.

(b) *Effect.* A revised determination is binding unless

(1) The affected party requests a hearing before an ALJ; or
(2) CMS or the OIG further revises the revised determination.

**Subpart D—Hearings**

**§ 498.40 Request for hearing.**

(a) *Manner and timing of request.* (1) An affected party entitled to a hearing under § 498.5 may file a request for a hearing with CMS or the OIG, as appropriate, or with OHA.

(2) The affected party or its legal representative or other authorized official must file the request in writing within 60 days from receipt of the notice of initial, reconsidered, or revised determination unless that period is extended in accordance with paragraph (c) of this section. (Presumed date of receipt is determined in accordance with § 498.22(b)(3).)

(b) *Content of request for hearing.* The request for hearing must—

(1) Identify the specific issues, and the findings of fact and conclusions of law with which the affected party disagrees; and

(2) Specify the basis for contending that the findings and conclusions are incorrect.

(c) *Extension of time for filing a request for hearing.* If the request was not filed within 60 days—

(1) The affected party or its legal representative or other authorized official may file with the ALJ a written request for extension of time stating the reasons why the request was not filed timely.

(2) For good cause shown, the ALJ may extend the time for filing the request for hearing.

**§ 498.42 Parties to the hearing.**

The parties to the hearing are the affected party and CMS or the OIG, as appropriate.

**§ 498.44 Designation of hearing official.**

(a) The Associate Commissioner for Hearings and Appeals, or his or her delegate designates an ALJ or a member or members of the Departmental Appeals Board to conduct the hearing.

(b) If appropriate, the Associate Commissioner or the delegate may substitute another ALJ or another member or other members of the Departmental Appeals Board to conduct the hearing.

(c) As used in this part, "ALJ"includes a member or members of the Departmental Appeals Board who are designated to conduct a hearing.

**§ 498.45 Disqualification of Administrative Law Judge.**

(a) An ALJ may not conduct a hearing in a case in which he or she is prejudiced or partial to the affected party or has any interest in the matter pending for decision.

(b) A party that objects to the ALJ designated to conduct the hearing must give notice of its objections at the earliest opportunity.

(c) The ALJ will consider the objections and decide whether to withdraw or proceed with the hearing.

(1) If the ALJ withdraws, another will be designated to conduct the hearing.

(2) If the ALJ does not withdraw, the objecting party may, after the hearing, present its objections to the Departmental Appeals Board as reasons for changing, modifying, or reversing the ALJ's decision or providing a new hearing before another ALJ.

**§ 498.47 Prehearing conference.**

(a) At any time before the hearing, the ALJ may call a prehearing conference for the purpose of delineating the issues in controversy, identifying the evidence and witnesses to be presented at the hearing, and obtaining stipulations accordingly.

(b) On the request of either party or on his or her own motion, the ALJ may adjourn the prehearing conference and reconvene at a later date.

**§ 498.48 Notice of prehearing conference.**

(a) *Timing of notice.* The ALJ will fix a time and place for the prehearing conference and mail written notice to the parties at least 10 days before the scheduled date.

(b) *Content of notice.* The notice will inform the parties of the purpose of the conference and specify what issues are sought to be resolved, agreed to, or excluded.

(c) *Additional issues.* Issues other than those set forth in the notice of determination or the request for hearing may be considered at the prehearing conference if—

(1) Either party gives timely notice to that effect to the ALJ and the other party; or

(2) The ALJ raises the issues in the notice of prehearing conference or at the conference.

**§ 498.49 Conduct of prehearing conference.**

(a) The prehearing conference is open to the affected party or its representative, to the CMS or OIG representatives and their technical advisors, and to any other persons whose presence the ALJ considers necessary or proper.

(b) The ALJ may accept the agreement of the parties as to the following:

(1) Facts that are not in controversy.

(2) Questions that have been resolved favorably to the affected party after the determination in dispute.

(3) Remaining issues to be resolved.

(c) The ALJ may request the parties to indicate the following:

(1) The witnesses that will be present to testify at the hearing.

(2) The qualifications of those witnesses.

(3) The nature of other evidence to be submitted.

**§ 498.50 Record, order, and effect of prehearing conference.**

(a) *Record of prehearing conference.* (1) A record is made of all agreements and stipulations entered into at the prehearing conference.

(2) The record may be transcribed at the request of either party or the ALJ.

(b) *Order and opportunity to object.* (1) The ALJ issues an order setting forth the results of the prehearing conference, including the agreements made by the parties as to facts not in controversy, the matters to be considered at the hearing, and the issues to be resolved.

(2) Copies of the order are sent to all parties and the parties have 10 days to file objections to the order.

(3) After the 10 days have elapsed, the ALJ settles the order.

(c) *Effect of prehearing conference.* The agreements and stipulations entered into at the prehearing conference are binding on all parties, unless a party presents facts that, in the opinion of the ALJ, would make an agreement unreasonable or inequitable.

**§ 498.52 Time and place of hearing.**

(a) The ALJ fixes a time and place for the hearing and gives the parties written notice at least 10 days before the scheduled date.

(b) The notice informs the parties of the general and specific issues to be resolved at the hearing.

**§ 498.53 Change in time and place of hearing.**

(a) The ALJ may change the time and place for the hearing either on his or her own initiative or at the request of a party for good cause shown, or may adjourn or postpone the hearing.

(b) The ALJ may reopen the hearing for receipt of new evidence at any time before mailing the notice of hearing decision.

(c) The ALJ gives the parties reasonable notice of any change in time or place or any adjournment or reopening of the hearing.

**§ 498.54 Joint hearings.**

When two or more affected parties have requested hearings and the same or substantially similar matters are at issue, the ALJ may, if all parties agree, fix a single time and place for the prehearing conference or hearing and conduct all proceedings jointly. If joint hearings are held, a single record of the preceedings is made and a separate decision issued with respect to each affected party.

**§ 498.56 Hearing on new issues.**

(a) *Basic rules.* (1) Within the time limits specified in paragraph (b) of this section, the ALJ may, at the request of either party, or on his or her own motion, provide a hearing on new issues that impinge on the rights of the affected party.

(2) The ALJ may consider new issues even if CMS or the OIG has not made initial or reconsidered determinations on them, and even if they arose after the request for hearing was filed or after a prehearing conference.

(3) The ALJ may give notice of hearing on new issues at any time after the hearing request is filed and before the hearing record is closed.

(b) *Time limits.* The ALJ will not consider any issue that arose on or after any of the following dates:

(1) The effective date of the termination of a provider agreement.

(2) The date on which it is determined that a supplier no longer meets the conditions for coverage of its services.

(3) The effective date of the notice to a hospital of its failure to remain in compliance with the qualifications for claiming reimbursement for all emergency services furnished to Medicare beneficiaries during the calendar year.

(4) The effective date of the suspension, or of the exclusion from coverage of services furnished by a suspended or excluded practitioner, provider, or supplier.

(5) With respect to Medicaid SNFs or ICFs surveyed under section 1910(c) of the Act–

(i) The completion date of the survey or resurvey that is the basis for a proposed cancellation of approval; or

(ii) If approval was cancelled before the hearings, because of immediate and serious threat to patient health and safety, the effective date of cancellation.

(c) *Notice and conduct of hearing on new issues.* (1) Unless the affected party waives its right to appear and present evidence, notice of the time and place of hearing on any new issue will be given to the parties in accordance with § 498.52.

(2) After giving notice, the ALJ will, except as provided in paragraph (d) of this section, proceed to hearing on new issues in the same manner as on an issue raised in the request for hearing.

(d) *Remand to CMS or the OIG.* At the request of either party, or on his or her own motion, in lieu of a hearing under paragraph (c) of this section, the ALJ may remand the case to CMS or the OIG for consideration of the new issue and, if appropriate, a determination. If necessary, the ALJ may direct CMS or the OIG to return the case to the ALJ for further proceedings.

[52 FR 22446, June 12, 1987, as amended at 53 FR 31335, Aug. 18, 1988]

**§ 498.58 Subpoenas.**

(a) *Basis for issuance.* The ALJ, upon his or her own motion or at the request of a party, may issue subpoenas if they are reasonably necessary for the full presentation of a case.

(b) *Timing of request by a party.* The party must file a written request for a subpoena with the ALJ at least 5 days before the date set for the hearing.

(c) *Content of request.* The request must:

(1) Identify the witnesses or documents to be produced;

(2) Describe their addresses or location with sufficient particularity to permit them to be found; and

(3) Specify the pertinent facts the party expects to establish by the witnesses or documents, and indicate why those facts could not be established without use of a subpoena.

(d) *Method of issuance.* Subpoenas are issued in the name of the Secretary, who pays the cost of issuance and the fees and mileage of any subpoenaed witnesses.

**§ 498.60 Conduct of hearing.**

(a) *Participants in the hearing.* The hearing is open to the parties and their representatives and technical advisors, and to any other persons whose presence the ALJ considers necessary or proper.

(b) *Hearing procedures.* (1) The ALJ inquires fully into all of the matters at issue, and receives in evidence the testimony of witnesses and any documents that are relevant and material.

(2) If the ALJ believes that there is relevant and material evidence available which has not been presented at the hearing, he may, at any time before mailing of notice of the decision, reopen the hearing to receive that evidence.

(3) The ALJ decides the order in which the evidence and the arguments of the parties are presented and the conduct of the hearing.

(c) *Scope of review: Civil money penalty.* In civil money penalty cases—

(1) The scope of review is as specified in § 488.438(e) of this chapter; and

(2) CMS's determination as to the level of noncompliance of an SNF or NF must be upheld unless it is clearly erroneous.

[52 FR 22446, June 12, 1987, as amended at 61 FR 32350, June 24, 1996]

**§ 498.61 Evidence.**

Evidence may be received at the hearing even though inadmissible under the rules of evidence applicable to court procedure. The ALJ rules on the admissibility of evidence.

[59 FR 56252, Nov. 10, 1994, as amended at 61 FR 32350, June 24, 1996]

**§ 498.62 Witnesses.**

Witnesses at the hearing testify under oath or affirmation. The representative of each party is permitted to examine his or her own witnesses subject to interrogation by the representative of the other party. The ALJ may ask any questions that he or she deems necessary. The ALJ rules upon any objection made by either party as to the propriety of any question.

**§ 498.63 Oral and written summation.**

The parties to a hearing are allowed a reasonable time to present oral summation and to file briefs or other written statements of proposed findings of fact and conclusions of law. Copies of any briefs or other written statements must be sent in accordance with § 498.17.

**§ 498.64 Record of hearing.**
A complete record of the proceedings at the hearing is made and transcribed in all cases.

**§ 498.66 Waiver of right to appear and present evidence.**

(a) *Waiver procedures.* (1) If an affected party wishes to waive its right to appear and present evidence at the hearing, it must file a written waiver with the ALJ.

(2) If the affected party wishes to withdraw a waiver, it may do so, for good cause, at any time before the ALJ mails notice of the hearing decision.

(b) *Effect of waiver.* If the affected party waives the right to appear and present evidence, the ALJ need not conduct an oral hearing except in one of the following circumstances:

(1) The ALJ believes that the testimony of the affected party or its representatives or other witnesses is necessary to clarify the facts at issue.

(2) CMS or the OIG shows good cause for requiring the presentation of oral evidence.

(c) *Dismissal for failure to appear.* If, despite the waiver, the ALJ sends notice of hearing and the affected party fails to appear, or to show good cause for the failure, the ALJ will dismiss the appeal in accordance with § 498.69.

(d) *Hearing without oral testimony.* When there is no oral testimony, the ALJ will—

(1) Make a record of the relevant written evidence that was considered in making the determination being appealed, and of any additional evidence submitted by the parties;

(2) Furnish to each party copies of the additional evidence submitted by the other party; and

(3) Give both parties a reasonable opportunity for rebuttal.

(e) *Handling of briefs and related statements.* If the parties submit briefs or other written statements of evidence or proposed findings of facts or conclusions of law, those documents will be handled in accordance with § 498.17.

**§ 498.68 Dismissal of request for hearing.**

(a) The ALJ may, at any time before mailing the notice of the decision, dismiss a hearing request if a party withdraws its request for a hearing or the affected party asks that its request be dismissed.

(b) An affected party may request a dismissal by filing a written notice with the ALJ.

**§ 498.69 Dismissal for abandonment.**

(a) The ALJ may dismiss a request for hearing if it is abandoned by the party that requested it.

(b) The ALJ may consider a request for hearing to be abandoned if the party or its representative—

(1) Fails to appear at the prehearing conference or hearing without having previously shown good cause for not appearing; and

(2) Fails to respond, within 10 days after the ALJ sends a "show cause" notice, with a showing of good cause.

**§ 498.70 Dismissal for cause.**

On his or her own motion, or on the motion of a party to the hearing, the ALJ may dismiss a hearing request either entirely or as to any stated issue, under any of the following circumstances:

(a) *Res judicata.* There has been a previous determination or decision with respect to the rights of the same affected party on the same facts and law pertinent to the same issue or issues which has become final either by judicial affirmance or, without judicial consideration, because the affected party did not timely request reconsideration, hearing, or review, or commence a civil action with respect to that determination or decision.

(b) *No right to hearing.* The party requesting a hearing is not a proper party or does not otherwise have a right to a hearing.

(c) *Hearing request not timely filed.* The affected party did not file a hearing request timely and the time for filing has not been extended.

**§ 498.71 Notice and effect of dismissal and right to request review.**

(a) Notice of the ALJ's dismissal action is mailed to the parties. The notice advises the affected party of its right to request that the dismissal be vacated as provided in § 498.72.

(b) The dismissal of a request for hearing is binding unless it is vacated by the ALJ or the Departmental Appeals Board.

**§ 498.72 Vacating a dismissal of request for hearing.**

An ALJ may vacate any dismissal of a request for hearing if a party files a request to that effect within 60 days from receipt of the notice of dismissal and shows good cause for vacating the dismissal. (Date of receipt is determined in accordance with § 498.22(b)(3).)

**§ 498.74 Administrative Law Judge's decision.**

(a) *Timing, basis, and content.* As soon as practical after the close of the hearing, the ALJ issues a written decision in the case. The decision is based on the evidence of record and contains separate numbered findings of fact and conclusions of law.

(b) *Notice and effect.* A copy of the decision is mailed to the parties and is binding on them unless—

(1) A party requests review by the Departmental Appeals Board within the time period specified in § 498.82, and the Board reviews the case;

(2) The Departmental Appeals Board denies the request for review and the party seeks judicial review by filing an action in a United States District Court or, in the case of a civil money penalty, in a United States Court of Appeals;

(3) The decision is revised by an ALJ or the Departmental Appeals Board; or

(4) The decision is a recommended decision directed to the Board.

[52 FR 22446, June 12, 1987, as amended at 61 FR 32351, June 24, 1996]

**§ 498.76 Removal of hearing to Departmental Appeals Board.**

(a) At any time before the ALJ receives oral testimony, the Board may remove to itself any pending request for a hearing.

(b) Notice of removal is mailed to each party.

(c) The Board conducts the hearing in accordance with the rules that apply to ALJ hearings under this subpart.

**§ 498.78 Remand by the Administrative Law Judge.**

(a) If CMS or the OIG requests remand, and the affected party concurs in writing or on the record, the ALJ may remand any case properly before him or her to CMS or the OIG for a determination satisfactory to the affected party.

(b) The ALJ may remand at any time before notice of hearing decision is mailed.

**Subpart E—Departmental Appeals Board Review**

**§ 498.80 Right to request Departmental Appeals Board review of Administrative Law Judge's decision or dismissal.**

Either of the parties has a right to request Departmental Appeals Board review of the ALJ's decision or dismissal order, and the parties are so informed in the notice of the ALJ's action.

**§ 498.82 Request for Departmental Appeals Board review.**

(a) *Manner and time of filing.* (1) Any party that is dissatisfied with an ALJ's decision or dismissal of a hearing request, may file a written request for review by the Departmental Appeals Board.

(2) The requesting party or its representative or other authorized official must file the request with the OHA within 60 days from receipt of the notice of decision or dismissal, unless the Board, for good cause shown by the requesting party, extends the time for filing. The rules set forth in § 498.40(c) apply to extension of time for requesting Departmental Appeals Board review. (The date of receipt of notice is determined in accordance with § 498.22(c)(3).)

(b) *Content of request for review.* A request for review of an ALJ decision or dismissal must specify the issues, the findings of fact or conclusions of law with which the party disagrees, and the basis for contending that the findings and conclusions are incorrect.

**§ 498.83 Departmental Appeals Board action on request for review.**

(a) *Request by CMS or the OIG.* The Departmental Appeals Board may dismiss, deny, or grant a request made by CMS or the OIG for review of an ALJ decision or dismissal.

(b) *Request by the affected party.* The Board will grant the affected party's request for review unless it dismisses the request for one of the following reasons:

(1) The affected party requests dismissal of its request for review.

(2) The affected party did not file timely or show good cause for late filing.

(3) The affected party does not have a right to review.

(4) A previous determination or decision, based on the same facts and law, and regarding the same issue, has become final through judicial affirmance or

because the affected party failed to timely request reconsideration, hearing, Board review, or judicial review, as appropriate.

(c) *Effect of dismissal.* The dismissal of a request for Departmental Appeals Board review is binding and not subject to further review.

(d) *Review panel.* If the Board grants a request for review of the ALJ's decision, the review will be conducted by a panel of at least two members of the Board, designated by the Chairperson or Deputy Chairperson, and one individual designated by the Secretary from the U.S. Public Health Service.

**§ 498.85 Procedures before the Departmental Appeals Board on review.**
The parties are given, upon request, a reasonable opportunity to file briefs or other written statements as to fact and law, and to appear before the Departmental Appeals Board to present evidence or oral arguments. Copies of any brief or other written statement must be sent in accordance with § 498.17.

**§ 498.86 Evidence admissible on review.**

(a) The Departmental Appeals Board may admit evidence into the record in addition to the evidence introduced at the ALJ hearing, (or the documents considered by the ALJ if the hearing was waived), if the Board considers that the additional evidence is relevant and material to an issue before it.

(b) If it appears to the Board that additional relevant evidence is available, the Board will require that it be produced.

(c) Before additional evidence is admitted into the record—

(1) Notice is mailed to the parties (unless they have waived notice) stating that evidence will be received regarding specified issues; and

(2) The parties are given a reasonable time to comment and to present other evidence pertinent to the specified issues.

(d) If additional evidence is presented orally to the Board, a transcript is prepared and made available to any party upon request.

**§ 498.88 Decision or remand by the Departmental Appeals Board.**

(a) When the Departmental Appeals Board reviews an ALJ's decision or order of dismissal, or receives a case remanded by a court, the Board may either issue a decision or remand the case to an ALJ for a hearing and decision or a recommended decision for final decision by the Board.

(b) In a remanded case, the ALJ initiates additional proceedings and takes other actions as directed by the Board in its order of remand, and may take other action not inconsistent with that order.

(c) Upon completion of all action called for by the remand order and any other consistent action, the ALJ promptly makes a decision or, as specified by the Board, certifies the case to the Board with a recommended decision.

(d) The parties have 20 days from the date of a notice of a recommended decision to submit to the Board any exception, objection, or comment on the findings of fact, conclusions of law, and recommended decision.

(e) After the 20-day period, the Board issues its decision adopting, modifying or rejecting the ALJ's recommended decision.

(f) If the Board does not remand the case to an ALJ, the following rules apply:

(1) The Board's decision–

(i) Is based upon the evidence in the hearing record and any further evidence that the Board receives during its review;

(ii) Is in writing and contains separate numbered findings of fact and conclusions of law; and

(iii) May modify, affirm, or reverse the ALJ's decision.

(2) A copy of the Board's decision is mailed to each party.

**§ 498.90 Effect of Departmental Appeals Board decision.**

(a) *General rule.* The Board's decision is binding unless–

(1) The affected party has a right to judicial review and timely files a civil action in a United States District Court or, in the case of a civil money penalty, in a United States Court of Appeals; or

(2) The Board reopens and revises its decision in accordance with § 498.102.

(b) *Right to judicial review.* Section 498.5 specifies the circumstances under which an affected party has a right to seek judicial review.

(c) *Special rules: Civil money penalty*–(1) *Finality of Board's decision.* When CMS imposes a civil money penalty, notice of the Board's decision (or denial of review) is the final administrative action that initiates the 60-day period for seeking judicial review.

(2) *Timing for collection of civil money penalty.* For SNFs and NFs, the rules that apply are those set forth in subpart F of part 488 of this chapter.

[61 FR 32351, June 24, 1996]

**§ 498.95 Extension of time for seeking judicial review.**

(a) Any affected party that is dissatisfied with an Departmental Appeals Board decision and is entitled to judicial review must commence civil action within 60 days from receipt of the notice of the Board's decision (as determined under § 498.22(c)(3)), unless the Board extends the time in accordance with paragraph (c) of this section.

(b) The request for extension must be filed in writing with the Board before the 60-day period ends.

(c) For good cause shown, the Board may extend the time for commencing civil action.

**Subpart F—Reopening of Decisions Made by Administrative Law Judges or the Departmental Appeals Board**

**§ 498.100 Basis, timing, and authority for reopening an ALJ or Board decision.**

(a) *Basis and timing for reopening.* An ALJ of Departmental Appeals Board decision may be reopened, within 60 days from the date of the notice of decision, upon the motion of the ALJ or the Board or upon the petition of either party to the hearing.

(b) *Authority to reopen.* (1) A decision of the Departmental Appeals Board may be reopened only by the Departmental Appeals Board.

(2) A decision of an ALJ may be reopened by that ALJ, by another ALJ if that one is not available, or by the Departmental Appeals Board. For purposes of this paragraph, an ALJ is considered to be unavailable if the ALJ has died, terminated employment, or been transferred to another duty station, is on leave of absence, or is unable to conduct a hearing because of illness.

**§ 498.102 Revision of reopened decision.**

(a) *Revision based on new evidence.* If a reopened decision is to be revised on the basis of new evidence that was not included in the record of that decision, the ALJ or the Departmental Appeals Board—

(1) Notifies the parties of the proposed revision; and

(2) Unless the parties waive their right to hearing or appearance—

(i) Grants a hearing in the case of an ALJ revision; and

(ii) Grants opportunity to appear in the case of a Board revision.

(b) *Basis for revised decision and right to review.* (1) If a revised decision is necessary, the ALJ or the Departmental Appeals Board, as appropriate, renders it on the basis of the entire record.

(2) If the decision is revised by an ALJ, the Departmental Appeals Board may review that revised decision at the request of either party or on its own motion.

**§ 498.103 Notice and effect of revised decision.**

(a) *Notice.* The notice mailed to the parties states the basis or reason for the revised decision and informs them of their right to Departmental Appeals Board review of an ALJ revised decision, or to judicial review of a Board reviewed decision.

(b) *Effect*—(1) *ALJ revised decision.* An ALJ revised decision is binding unless it is reviewed by the Departmental Appeals Board.

(2) *Departmental Appeals Board revised decision.* A Board revised decision is binding unless a party files a civil action in a district court of the United States within the time frames specified in § 498.95.

# Index

Abbreviations and acronyms, list of, 97-98
Abuse and neglect in long-term care facilities, 81-82, 375-377
Acronyms, list of, 97-98
Act. *see* Social Security Act
Administrative entities processing appeals, contact information, 99-100
Administrative Law Judge (ALJ)
  beneficiary appeals, 15-16
  contact information, 99
  disqualification of, 169, 392-393
  effect of decision, 178, 346, 398
  hearings, 15-16, 48-49, 160-180
  LCD appeals, 31-33, 335-350
  Medicare Advantage appeals, 282-283
  Part C appeals, 56
  Part D appeals, 72, 316-317
  provider termination review, 92
  QIC reconsiderations, 15-16, 161-180
  record, 176-177
  review of ALJ's decisions, 16-18, 111, 126, 317, 347-350
  text of regulations, 111, 160-180
Advocacy group contact information, 100
Aggrieved parties, 31, 34
ALJ. *see* Administrative Law Judge
Alternative dispute resolution
  provider appeals, 37
  *see also* Mediation
Ambulatory surgical center appeals, 28-29, 256-257
Amount in controversy
  for ALJ hearings, 162-163
  for carrier hearings, 118-120
  for judicial review, 162-163
  for Part A appeals, 112-113
  for provider reimbursement appeals, 211-212
  for QIO determinations, 374
Appeals
  ambulatory surgical center, 28-29, 256-257
  assignment of rights, 137-139
  beneficiary, 9-34, *see also* Beneficiary appeals
  claim, 11
  CMP contracts, 43-45
  contact information for administrative entities processing appeals, 99-100
  drugs and biologicals payment, 85-89
  entitlement, 11
  expedited. *see* Expedited procedures
  fee-for-service, 9-12, 95
  group health plan nonconformance, 83-85
  HMO contracts, 43-45
  LCD/NCD, 30-34, 331-367
  Medicare Advantage, 51-65, *see also* Medicare Advantage
  Medicare geographic classification, 39-43, *see also* Medicare geographic classification appeals
  Medicare Part A, 35-39, *see also* Medicare Part A appeals
  Medicare Part B coverage, 29-30, 115-129
  Medicare Part C, 51-65, *see also* Medicare Part C
  Medicare Part D, 67-79, *see also* Medicare Part D
  miscellaneous, 81-93
  original Medicare, text of regulations, 129-194
  processes, text of regulations, 101-402
  provider, 35-50, *see also* Provider appeals
  regulations, selected text, 101-402
  supplemental policy certification, 89-90

Area redesignation of hospitals, 39–43, 232–240
Assignment of appeal rights, 137–139

Balanced Budget Act of 1997, 1
Balanced Budget Refinement Act of 1999, 1
Beneficiary appeals, 9–34
  fee-for-service, 9–10, 17–18
  judicial review, 17
  LCD/NCDs, 30–34
  Medicare Part A, 19–28
  Medicare Part B coverage, 29–30
  process, 12–19
  of provider service terminations, 19–28
  of QIO determinations, 373–374
  who may appeal, 11–12
Biologicals payment, 85–89
  under Part B, text of regulations, 249–256
BIPA. *see* Medicare, Medicaid, and SCHIP Benefits and Improvement Act of 2000

CAP. *see* competitive acquisition program
Carriers, 6
  contract performance, 263–268
  contract terminations, 82–83, 268
  hearings, 118–129
  text of regulations, 118–129, 266–268
Center for Health Care Rights, 100
Center for Medicare Advocacy, Inc., 100
Centers for Medicare & Medicaid Services (CMS), 9, 36–49, 71–72
  Administrator, 38–42
  applicability of rulings, 181
  and CAP program, 85–89
  contact information, 99
  contract denial or termination, 62–64, 318–324, 377–381
  Medicare Advantage contracts, 62–64
  Office of Attorney Advisor, 38
  Part D drug plan sponsors, 73–76, 318–324
  program guidance as authority for reconsiderations, 14, 17
Certification
  loss of, 101–103
  of Medicare providers, 7
  of supplemental insurance policies, 89–90, 101–103
  text of regulations, 375–377
Claim appeals, 11
Claims processing, 82–83
CMPs. *see* Competitive Medical Plans
CMS. *see* Centers for Medicare & Medicaid Services
Comparison of former and current fee-for-service appeal processes, 95
Competitive acquisition program (CAP)
  for drugs, 85–89
  text of regulations, 249–256
Competitive Medical Plans (CMPs)
  contract appeals, 43–45
    text of regulations, 257–262
Comprehensive outpatient rehabilitation facilities (CORFs)
  as providers, 35
  termination of service by, 59–62, 288–292
Compromise Social Security Amendments of 1965, 1
Conditions of participation (CoPs), 7
Contact information for administrative entities processing appeals, 99–100
Contracts
  carriers, 82–83, 263–268
  determinations and appeals, 62–64, 257–263, 292–297, 318–324
  HMOs and CMPs, 43–45, 257–262
  intermediaries, 263–268
  Medicare Advantage, 62–64, 292–297
  Medicare carrier's, termination of, 83
  Part D plan sponsor termination, 73–77, 318–324
  physicians' CAP program suspension, 87
  provider termination appeals, 46–48, 90–93, 377–381
CoPs. *see* Conditions of participation
CORFs. *see* Comprehensive outpatient rehabilitation facilities
Cost report, 35–36

DAB. *see* Departmental Appeals Board
Deadlines, filing, 38–39, 42–43
Departmental Appeals Board (DAB), 48–49
  contact information, 99
  LCD/NCD review, 33–34
  provider termination review, 92, 399–402
  review, text of regulations, 111, 114, 126, 374
Determinations. *see* Initial determinations
Device categorization, 114, 129
Discharge from hospital, 23–28, 57–59, 199–203
Dismissal, 38, 41
DMEPOS. *see* Durable Medical Equipment, Prosthetics, Orthotics, and Supplies
DMERCs. *see* Durable Medical Equipment Regional Carriers
Drugs
  administered by physicians, 85–86
  payment appeals, 85–89
  payment for under Part B, text of regulations, 249–256
  payment for under Part D. *see* Medicare Part D
  plan sponsor contract determination appeals, 73–77, 318–324
  prescription drug plans, 4–6
  retirees' prescription drug plans, 327–331
  voluntary prescription coverage. *see* Medicare Part D
Durable Medical Equipment, Prosthetics, Orthotics, and Supplies (DMEPOS), 48–49
Durable Medical Equipment Regional Carriers (DMERCs), 82–83

End-stage renal disease (ESRD), 2, 36
Entitlement appeals, 11
Expedited procedures
  appeals process, 109–110
  carrier hearings, 125
  hospital discharge appeals, 23–26, 199–203
  judicial review for provider appeals, 37
  organization determinations, 54, 274–276
  Part C grievances, 52
  Part D determinations, 312–314
  Provider Reimbursement Review Board, 212–216
  reconsiderations, 26–28, 198–199
  service termination review, 20–23, 60–62, 194–203, 289–292
  text of regulations, 109–110, 157–160, 194–203, 212–216, 289–292

Families USA, 100
Federal court, request for escalation, 190–191
Fee-for-service appeals
  comparison of former and current appeals processes, 95
  generally, 10
  process, 12–19, 95
  reforms, 9
Fiscal Intermediaries (FI), 6, 35–37, 39, 82–83

Geographic designation of hospitals, 39–43, 232–240
Grievances
  Medicare Advantage, 268–292
  Medicare Part C, 51
  Medicare Part D, 67–68, 301–318
Group health plans (GHP)
  limits on Medicare payments, 227–232
  nonconformance appeals, 83–85

Health and Human Services Department (HHS), 6
  contact information, 99
  Office of Inspector General, 47, *see also* Office of Inspector General
  text of regulations, 101–402
Health Care Financing Administration (HCFA), 6
Health care prepayment plans, text of regulations, 257–262

Health care providers. *see* Providers
Health Maintenance Organizations (HMOs)
  contract appeals, 43-45, 257-262
    filing deadlines, 44-45
    text of regulations, 257-262
  contracts, 257-263
  who may appeal, 44, 48
HHAs. *see* Home health agencies
HHS. *see* Health and Human Services Department
HI Trust Fund. *see* Hospital Insurance Trust Fund
HMOs. *see* Health Maintenance Organizations
Home health agencies (HHAs)
  as providers, 35
  termination of provider status, 381-402
  termination of service by, 59-62, 288-292
Hospice care, 46, 263
Hospital Insurance Trust Fund, Medicare financing, 1
Hospitals
  discharge, 23-28, 57-59, 199-203
  emergency services, 91
  geographic redesignation, 39-43, 232-240
  noncoverage of inpatient care, 285-292
  Notice of Discharge and Medicare Appeals Rights, 57-58
  Part C appeals, 57-59
  as providers, 35
  termination of Medicare provider status, 90-93, 381-402

Independent review entity reconsiderations, 55-56, 289-292
  Medicare Advantage terminations, 289-292
  Part D determinations, 315
Initial determinations
  actions constituting, 104-106, 139-142
  fee-for service appeals, 10-11
  HMO and CMP contract appeals, 44-45, 257-258
  notice of, 12, 104, 389
  process, 12
  provider status determinations, 381-391
  text of regulations, 104-113, 116-118, 138-141, 257-258, 381-391
  under original Medicare, 131-133
  under Part B, 116-118
Inpatient prospective payment system, 39-40, 43, 205-206
Inpatients. *see* Hospitals
Insurance
  group health plans, 83-85, 227-232
  Hospital Insurance Trust Fund, 1
  supplemental. *see* Supplemental insurance policies
  Supplemental Medical Insurance Trust Fund, 2
Intermediaries
  contract termination, 82-83
  provider reimbursement determinations, 205-209
  text of regulations, 263-266
Intermediate sanctions, text of regulations, 298-301, 324-327
Internal Revenue Service, referral of nonconforming GHPs to, 232
Internal Review Service, 85
IPPS. *see* Inpatient prospective payment system
IRE. *see* Independent review entity
IRS. *see* Internal Review Service

Judicial review
  of ALJ decisions, 111, 317
  amount in controversy, 162-163
  of beneficiary appeals, 17, 111
  of DAB decisions, 34, 111, 126
  expedited access to, 157-160
  of MAC decisions, 191-194, 317
  of Medicare Advantage appeals, 283
  of Part C appeals, 56-57
  of Part D appeals, 73, 76, 317
  of prospective payment controversies, 206
  of provider appeals, 37-38, 93
  of Provider Reimbursement Review Board decisions, 222-225

of provider terminations, 93
Jurisdictional requirements, provider appeals, 36

LCDs. *see* Local Coverage Decisions
List of abbreviations and acronyms, 97–98
Local Coverage Decisions (LCDs)
appeals process, 31–34
as authority for reconsiderations, 14, 181
contact information, 99
text of regulations, 331–352
Local Medical Review Policies (LMRPs), as authority for reconsiderations, 14, 17
Long-term care facilities. *see* Skilled nursing facilities

M+C. *see* Medicare+Choice
MA. *see* Medicare Advantage
MAC. *see* Medicare Appeals Council
MACs. *see* Medicare Administrative Contractors
Mediation, 38–39
Medicaid
appeals by state agencies, 133
creation of program, 1
determinations affecting participation, 381–402
Medically necessary, defined, 2
Medicare
administration of program, 6–7
geographic classification. *see* Medicare geographic classification appeals
history of, 1
overview, 1–7
Parts. *see* Medicare Part A/B/C/D appeals
payments. *see* Reimbursement
as primary or secondary payor, 7, 83–84
supplemental policies. *see* Supplemental insurance policies
survey and certification, 7, 375–377
regulations, slected text, 101–402
Medicare+Choice, 3, *see also* Medicare Part C
Medicare Administrative Contractors (MACs), 83
Medicare Advantage (MA)
administrator's review, 64
appeals, 51–65
contract determinations and appeals, 62–65, 292–297
generally, 3–4
grievances, determinations, and appeals, text of regulations, 268–292
HMOs and CMPs, 43
intermediate sanctions, text of regulations, 298–301
licensing, 64
Medicare Appeals Council (MAC), 9
beneficiary appeals, 16–17
contact information, 99
effect of decision, 190
Medicare Advantage appeals, 283
Part C appeals, 56
Part D appeals, 72–73, 317
removal of hearing from ALJ, 179
reviews, 16–17, 56, 72, 181–194, 317
text of regulations, 181–194, 317
Medicare geographic classification appeals, 39–43
administrator's review, 42, 246–248
filing deadlines, 42–43
generally, 39–40
process, 40–42
who may appeal, 40
Medicare Geographic Classification Review Board (MGCRB), 39–43
contact information, 99
effect of decisions by, 246
text of regulations, 232–248
Medicare, Medicaid, and SCHIP Benefits and Improvement Act of 2000, 1
rule implementing, 9
Medicare Part A appeals, 35–39
administrator's review, 38
beneficiary appeals, 19–28
expedited judicial review, 37
filing deadlines, 38
generally, 1–2, 35
judicial review, 38
jurisdictional requirements, 36

Medicare Part A appeals (*continued*)
mediation, 38–39
process, 36–38
reconsiderations, 103–114
text of regulations, 103–114
under original Medicare, text of regulations, 129–194
who may appeal, 36
Medicare Part B appeals
coverage and eligibility, 2–3, 29–30
drugs and biologicals payments, 249–256
text of regulations, 115–129, 249–256
under original Medicare, text of regulations, 129–194
Medicare Part C appeals, 51–65
generally, 3–4
grievances, 51
hospital inpatients, 57–59
Medicare Advantage (MA). *see* Medicare Advantage
reconsideration, 55–56
who may appeal, 51, 63
Medicare Part D appeals, 67–79
and CAP, 86
contract determinations, 318–324
coverage, 5–6
coverage determinations, 68–73, 304–308
"doughnut hole" gap, 5–6
drug plan sponsor contract determination appeals, 73–79
eligibility, 4
exceptions process, 69–70, 308–311
generally, 4–6
grievances, 67–68, 301–318
intermediate sanctions, 324–327
judicial review, 73, 76, 317
network pharmacies, 5–6
plan sponsor contract termination, 73–77
premiums and deductibles, 5
retiree prescription drug plans, 77–79, 327–331
review by ALJ, 72, 316–317
review by Medicare appeals council, 72
text of regulations, 301–331
who may appeal, 67, 74, 77
Medicare Prescription Drug, Improvement, and Modernization Act of 2003 (MMA), 1
administrative reforms, 82–83
appeals process revisions, 10
HMOs and CMPs, 43
provider and supplier enrollment denial appeals, 48–49
rule implementing, 9
Medicare Rights Center, 100
MGCRB. *see* Medicare Geographic Classification Review Board
MMA. *see* Medicare Prescription Drug, Improvement, and Modernization Act of 2003

National Coverage Decisions (NCDs)
appeals process, 34
as authority for reconsiderations, 14, 17, 180–181
contact information, 99
review of, 111, 126, 352–367
text of regulations, 331–333, 352–367
National Health Law Program, 100
National Senior Citizens Law Center, 100
National Supplier Clearinghouse (NSC), 82–83
NCDs. *see* National Coverage Decisions
NFs, determination of provider status, 381–402
Nonconformance, group health plans, 83–85
Nonphysician practitioners, 3
Notice of Discharge and Medicare Appeals Rights (NODMAR), 57–58
Nursing homes. *see* Skilled nursing facilities

Office of Inspector General (OIG), termination of provider agreement, 47, 90–91, 380
Organization determinations, 52–54, 268–286

Part A–D. *see* Medicare Part A/B/C/D appeals
Payment. *see* Reimbursement

Pharmacies, Medicare Part D network, 5–6
Physicians
drugs administered by, 85–86
services defined, 2–3
Prescription drugs. *see* Drugs; Medicare Part D
Primary and secondary coverage, 7, 83–84
Provider appeals, 35–50
contract termination, 46–48, 377–381
determinations affecting participation in program, 381–402
enrollment denial, 48–49
expedited determinations of service terminations, 194–203
geographic classification, 39–43, *see also* Medicare geographic classification appeals
HMO & CMP contracts, 43–45
Medicare Part A, 35–39, *see also* Medicare Part A appeals
process, 36–37, 40–42, 44–47, 48
provider and supplier enrollment denial, 48–49
reimbursement review, 35–39, 203–225
termination and exclusion, 90–93, 377–402
Provider Reimbursement Review Board (PRRB), 35–39, 99, 203
hearings, 210–220
review of decisions of, 38, 220–225
Providers
appeals by. *see* Provider appeals
cost report, 35–36
defined, 35, 194
eligibility for Medicare participation, 7
termination of service by, 19–28, 59–62, 194–203, 288–292
termination of status as, 46–48, 90–93, 377–381
PRRB. *see* Provider Reimbursement Review Board

Qualified Independent Contractor (QIC), 9
reconsideration of claim by, 10, 13–15, 147–154
Quality improvement organization (QIO), 11
hospital discharge determinations, 23–28, 202–203
hospital noncoverage review, 58–59, 286–287
Part C grievances, 52
reconsiderations and appeals, 367–375
service termination review, 59–62

Reconsiderations
beneficiary appeals, 13–15
by independent review entity, 55–56
by Qualified Independent Contractor, 10, 13–15, 147–154
by quality improvement organization, 367–375
CMS/MA contract denials, 63
expedited, 26–28, 198–199
HMO and CMP contract appeals, 44, 44–46
Medicare Part A, text of regulations, 103–114
Medicare Part C, 55–56
Medicare Part D, text of regulations, 315–318
process, 13–15
of provider status determinations, 390–392
of provider termination, 91–92
of supplemental insurance termination, 226
text of regulations, 103–114, 147–154, 315–318
Redeterminations
fee-for service appeals, 10
process, 12–13
text of regulations, 142–147, 317–318
Regulations regarding appeals processes, selected text, 101–402
Reimbursement
appeals by providers, 35–50
determinations, text of regulations, 203–225
for drugs. *see* Drugs

Reimbursement (*continued*)
limitations under group health plans, 227–232
to providers, generally, 6–7
Representatives
for contract determination hearings, 322
for initial review hearings, 127, 133–136, 261
for MGCRB hearings, 248
for provider reimbursement hearings, 223–224
for provider status hearings, 388
Retirees, prescription drug plans, 327–331

Sanctions, text of regulations, 298–301, 324–327
Secondary coverage, 7, 83–84
Service termination. *see* Termination, of providers' service
Skilled nursing facilities (SNFs)
abuse, neglect, theft in, 81–82, 375–377
Part C appeals, 59–60
as providers, 35
termination of Medicare provider status, 90, 381–402
termination of service by, 59–62, 194–202, 288–292
SMI Trust Fund, 2
SNFs. *see* Skilled nursing facilities
Social Security Act, xvii
invalidation of provisions under, 37
payments to HMOs and CMPs, 43
Supplemental Health Insurance Panel, 89
Supplemental insurance policies
certification, 89–90, 101–103
premiums, text of regulations, 225–226
termination and reinstatement of coverage, text of regulations, 225–226
Supplemental Medical Insurance Trust Fund, 2
Suppliers. *see* Providers
Surgical centers, ambulatory, 28–29
Survey procedures, 7, 375–377

Tax Equity and Fiscal Responsibility Act of 1982 (TEFRA), 36
Termination
of CAP contracts, 87–89
of carriers' contracts, 82–83, 268
of intermediary contracts, 82–83
of MA organization contracts, 297
of Part D contracts, 73–77, 318–324
of provider status, 90–93, 381–402
of providers' contracts, 46–48, 377–381
of providers' service, 19–28, 59–62, 194–203, 288–292
of supplemental insurance policies, 225–226
Theft, in long-term care facilities, 81–82, 375–377

Video teleconference (VTC), 15
Voluntary Medicare prescription drug benefit. *see* Medicare Part D

Wage index reclassification, 39–41

# About the Authors

**Kathleen Scully-Hayes**

Kathleen Scully-Hayes is the Director of the Office of Hearings for the Centers for Medicare & Medicaid Services. The Office of Hearings provides administrative and legal support to the Provider Reimbursement Review Board, the Medicare Geographic Review Board, and the CMS Hearing Officer function. As Director, she oversees the Hearings and Decisions Division, the Jurisdiction and Case Management Division, and the mediation program. She also serves as a CMS Hearing Officer and is the Office of Hearings Attorney Advisor. Previously, she was a staff attorney for the Office of General Counsel, HCFA division, U.S. Department of Health and Human Services.

Ms. Scully-Hayes earned a J.D. degree from DePaul University, where she was a senior editor for the *DePaul Journal of Health Care Law*. She received her M.A. degree from Ball State University, and a B.A. degree from St. Mary-of-the-Woods College. She is a member of the Illinois bar.

**Daniel A. Cody**

Daniel Cody is a partner in Reed Smith LLP's Health Care Group in the firm's San Francisco, California, office. Mr. Cody's practice encompasses a wide variety of health law matters, including regulatory, fraud and abuse, privacy, and transactional practices. Mr. Cody has counseled and advised health care clients concerning complex Medicare and Medicaid reimbursement, coverage, and appeal issues. He has advised clients regarding compliance and investigations involving federal and state fraud and abuse laws, including the federal False Claims Act, federal and state anti-kickback statutes, federal and state referral prohibitions, and state corporate practice of medicine provisions. He has represented clients in regulatory and fraud and abuse matters in federal court, and before federal and state entities such as the Department of Justice, Centers for Medicare & Medicaid Services, Office of Inspector General, and state administrative agencies. Mr. Cody also has advised clients regarding health care privacy matters, and has prepared and negotiated general commercial agreements.

He received his B.A. in history from Swarthmore College in 1993, and his J.D. from the William and Mary School of Law in 1998. While at William and Mary, Mr. Cody was a staff member of the *William and Mary Law Review* and an Articles Editor for the *Environmental Law and Policy Review.*